EASIER
ENGLISH
BASIC
DICTIONARY

SECOND EDITION

Dictionary Titles in the Series

Visit our website for full details of all our books
http://www.bloomsbury.com/reference

EASIER ENGLISH

BASIC DICTIONARY

SECOND EDITION

General editor
P.H. Collin

BLOOMSBURY

A BLOOMSBURY REFERENCE BOOK

www.bloomsbury.com

Second edition published 2004
First published in Great Britain 2001

© Copyright P.H. Collin, F. Collin, S.M.H. Collin 2001
This edition © Copyright Bloomsbury Publishing 2004

Bloomsbury Publishing Plc
38 Soho Square
London W1D 3HB

British Library Cataloguing-in-Publication Data

A catalogue record for this book is available from the British Library

ISBN 0 7475 6644 5

Text processing and computer typesetting by Bloomsbury Publishing
Printed and bound in Great Britain by Clays Ltd, St Ives plc

All papers used by Bloomsbury Publishing are natural, recyclable
products made from wood grown in well-managed forests.
The manufacturing processes conform to the
environmental regulations of the country of origin.

GENERAL EDITOR
P. H. Collin

Editorial Contributors
Penelope Hands, Howard Sargeant

Text Production and Proofreading
Katy McAdam, Joel Adams,
Daisy Jackson, Sarah Lusznat

Preface

This dictionary contains the most frequently used words in English and provides the basic vocabulary needed for everyday communication by anyone starting to learn the language. It is especially useful for elementary and pre-intermediate students of all ages and would be suitable for those working towards an elementary level English examination such as KET or PET.

Each word is individually defined, and no words, not even adverbs, are given without a definition. Examples are included for many words to provide patterns for the user's own production of English sentences.

Each word, including compound words and phrasal verbs, has its own easy-to-find main entry in bold type. Each word has a pronunciation in the International Phonetic Alphabet. Common phrases and idioms associated with the main term are shown in bold type and separately defined within the entry.

The meanings of the main common senses of each word are given clearly and simply, using a limited and easily understood vocabulary. Meanings are grouped together by their part of speech.

Extra help is offered in Notes at the end of some entries. These include warnings about words which can confused with each other, unusual inflected forms and regularly collocating prepositions. The major differences in US and British spelling are noted.

A useful companion to this dictionary is *Easier English Basic Synonyms* which compares and contrasts words with similar meanings, showing the similarities and differences in usage.

Symbols

■	before a new part of speech
○	before examples
□	before a phrase or collocation
◇	before an idiom
◊	a definition of the word will be found at the place indicated
♦	extra information will be found at the place indicated

Pronunciation

The following symbols have been used to show the pronunciation of the main words in the dictionary.
Stress has been indicated by a main stress mark (') and a secondary stress mark (ˌ). Note that these are only guides, as the stress of the word changes according to its position in the sentence.

Vowels		Consonants	
æ	back	b	buck
ɑː	harm	d	dead
ɒ	stop	ð	other
aɪ	type	dʒ	jump
aʊ	how	f	fare
aɪə	hire	g	gold
aʊə	hour	h	head
ɔː	course	j	yellow
ɔɪ	annoy	k	cab
e	head	l	leave
eə	fair	m	mix
eɪ	make	n	nil
eʊ	go	ŋ	sing
ɜː	word	p	print
iː	keep	r	rest
i	happy	s	save
ə	about	ʃ	shop
ɪ	fit	t	take
ɪə	near	tʃ	change
u	annual	θ	theft
uː	pool	v	value
ʊ	book	w	work
ʊə	tour	x	loch
ʌ	shut	ʒ	measure
		z	zone

A

a¹ /eɪ/, **A** *noun* the first letter of the alphabet, followed by B ○ *Do you mean 'dependant' spelt with an 'a' or 'dependent' with an 'e'?* ◇ **from A to Z** completely, all the way through

a² /ə, eɪ/, **an** /ən, æn/ *article* **1.** one ○ *an enormous hole* ○ *a useful guidebook* ○ *She's bought a new car.* ○ *I want a cup of tea.* ○ *We had to wait an hour for the bus.* (NOTE: **an** is used before words beginning with **a, e, i, o, u** and with **h** if the **h** is not pronounced: *an apple* or *an hour*. **a** is used before words beginning with all other letters and also before **u** where **u** is pronounced /juː/ : *a useful guidebook*) **2.** for each or to each ○ *Apples cost £1.50 a kilo.* ○ *The car was travelling at 50 kilometres an hour.* ○ *He earns £100 a day.*

abandon /ə'bændən/ *verb* **1.** to leave someone or something in an unkind way ○ *The dog had been abandoned by its owner.* **2.** to give up or stop doing something ○ *The company has decided to abandon the project.* ○ *We abandoned the idea of setting up a London office.*

abbreviation /ə,briːvi'eɪʃ(ə)n/ *noun* a short form of a word

ability /ə'bɪlɪti/ *noun* **1.** a natural tendency to do something well ○ *I admire his ability to stay calm in difficult situations.* ○ *We can develop their natural abilities.* (NOTE: The plural is **abilities**.) □ **I'll do it to the best of my ability** I'll do it as well as I can **2.** the fact of being clever ○ *suitable for different levels of ability* (NOTE: no plural)

able /'eɪb(ə)l/ *adjective* **1.** □ **to be able to do something** to be capable of something or have the chance to do something ○ *They weren't able to find the house.* ○ *Will you be able to come to the meeting?* **2.** good at doing something, or good at doing many things ○ *She's a* very able manager. ○ *There are special activities for able children.*

about /ə'baʊt/ *preposition* **1.** referring to something ○ *He told me all about his operation.* ○ *What do you want to speak to the doctor about?* **2.** □ **to be about to do something** to be going to do something very soon ○ *We were about to go home when you arrived.* **3.** not exactly ○ *I've been waiting for about four hours.* ○ *She's only about fifteen years old.* ◇ **how about? 1.** what do you think about? ○ *We can't find a new chairperson for the club – What about Sarah?* **2.** would you like a cup of tea? ◇ **while you're about it** at the same time as the thing you are doing ○ *While you're about it, can you post this letter?*

above /ə'bʌv/ *preposition* **1.** higher than ○ *The plane was flying above the clouds.* ○ *The temperature in the street was above 30 degrees.* ○ *At prices above £20, nobody will buy it.* **2.** older than ○ *If you are above 18, you have to pay the full fare.* **3.** louder than ○ *I couldn't hear the telephone above the noise of the drills.*

abroad /ə'brɔːd/ *adverb* in or to another country ○ *They've gone abroad on holiday.* ○ *I lived abroad for three years.*

absence /'æbsəns/ *noun* the fact of being away from a place ○ *She did not explain her absence from the meeting.* ○ *The former president was sentenced in his absence.* □ **in the absence of** because someone or something is not there ○ *In the absence of the chairman, his deputy took over.* ○ *In the absence of any official support, we had to raise our own funds.*

absent /'æbsənt/ *adjective* not there ○ *Ten of the staff are absent with flu.*

absolute /'æbsəluːt/ *adjective* complete or total

absolutely *adverb* **1.** /'æbsəlu:tli/ completely ○ *I am absolutely sure I left the keys in my coat pocket.* **2.** /,æbsə'lu:tli/ yes, of course ○ *Did you build it yourself? – Absolutely!*

absorb /əb'zɔːb/ *verb* **1.** to take in something such as a liquid ○ *The water should be absorbed by the paper.* ○ *Salt absorbs moisture from the air.* **2.** to reduce a shock ○ *The car's springs are supposed to absorb any shock from the road surface.*

absurd /əb'sɜːd/ *adjective* completely unreasonable or impossible to believe ○ *It's absurd to expect you will win the lottery if you only buy one ticket.*

abuse[1] /ə'bjuːs/ *noun* **1.** rude words ○ *The people being arrested shouted abuse at the police.* **2.** very bad treatment ○ *the sexual abuse of children* ○ *She suffered physical abuse in prison.* (NOTE: [all senses] no plural)

abuse[2] /ə'bjuːz/ *verb* **1.** to treat someone very badly, usually physically or sexually ○ *She had been abused as a child.* **2.** to make the wrong use of something ○ *He abused his position as finance director.* **3.** to say rude things about someone ○ *The crowd noisily abused the group of politicians as they entered the building.*

academic /,ækə'demɪk/ *adjective* **1.** relating to study at a university ○ *Members of the academic staff received a letter from the principal.* **2.** only in theory, not in practice ○ *It is only of academic interest.* ■ *noun* a university teacher ○ *All her friends are academics.*

accelerate /ək'seləreɪt/ *verb* to go faster ○ *Don't accelerate when you get to traffic lights.*

accent /'æksənt/ *noun* **1.** a particular way of pronouncing something ○ *He speaks with an American accent.* **2.** the stronger or louder part of a word or sentence ○ *In the word 'letter' the accent is on the first syllable.* **3.** a mark over a letter showing a particular way of pronouncing it ○ *Café has an accent on the 'e'.*

accept /ək'sept/ *verb* **1.** to take and keep a present ○ *We hope you will accept this little gift.* **2.** to say 'yes' or to agree to something ○ *She accepted the offer of a job in Australia.* ○ *I invited her to come with us and she accepted.* (NOTE: Do not confuse with **except**.)

acceptable /ək'septəb(ə)l/ *adjective* good enough to be accepted, although not particularly good ○ *Fighting in the street is not acceptable behaviour.* ○ *Smoking is becoming less socially acceptable.* ○ *A small gift of flowers would be very acceptable.* ○ *The offer is not acceptable to the vendor.*

access /'ækses/ *noun* a way of reaching a place ○ *The concert hall has access for wheelchairs.* ○ *At present there is no access to the site.* □ **to have access to something** to be able to reach a place, meet a person, or obtain something ○ *I'll have access to the studio day and night.* ○ *The company has access to substantial funds.* ■ *verb* to get information from a computer ○ *She tried to access the address list.*

accident /'æksɪd(ə)nt/ *noun* **1.** an unpleasant thing which happens and causes damage or injury ○ *He lost his leg in an accident at work.* ○ *She was involved in a car accident and had to go to hospital.* **2.** something that happens unexpectedly ○ *Their third baby was an accident.* □ **by accident** without being planned or expected ○ *He found the missing papers by accident.*

accidental /,æksɪ'dent(ə)l/ *adjective* happening without being planned or expected ○ *an accidental meeting* ○ *accidental damage* ○ *His death was not accidental.*

accidentally /,æksɪ'dent(ə)li/ *adverb* without being planned or expected

accommodation /ə,kɒmə'deɪʃ(ə)n/ *noun* a place to live or somewhere to stay for a short time ○ *Are you still looking for accommodation?* ○ *Visitors have difficulty in finding hotel accommodation during the summer.* (NOTE: In British English, **accommodation** has no plural.)

accompany /ə'kʌmp(ə)ni/ *verb* **1.** to go with someone or something ○ *She accompanied me to the door.* **2.** to play a musical instrument while someone else plays another instrument or sings ○ *She sang and was accompanied on the piano by her father.* (NOTE: accompanied **by** someone *or* something)

accomplish /ə'kʌmplɪʃ/ *verb* to do something successfully ○ *You won't accomplish anything by arguing.*

according to /ə'kɔːdɪŋ tuː/ *preposition* **1.** as someone says or writes ○ *The washing machine was installed according to the manufacturer's instructions.* ○ *According to the police, the car was going too fast.* **2.** in agreement with rules or a system ○ *Everything went according to plan or schedule.* **3.** in relation to ○ *The teachers have separated the children into classes according to their ages.*

account /ə'kaʊnt/ *noun* **1.** same as **bank account 2.** □ **I was worried on her account** I was afraid something might happen to her ◇ **on account of** because of, due to ○ *The trains are late on account of the fog.* ○ *We don't use the car much on account of the price of petrol.* ◇ **take something into account** to consider something ○ *We have to take the weather into account.* ◇ **on no account** not at all

accurate /'ækjʊrət/ *adjective* correct in all details ○ *Are the figures accurate?* ○ *We asked them to make an accurate copy of the plan.*

accurately /'ækjʊrətli/ *adverb* correctly ○ *The weather forecast accurately predicted the storm.*

accuse /ə'kjuːz/ *verb* to say that someone has done something wrong ○ *The police accused her of stealing the money.* (NOTE: You accuse someone **of** a crime or **of** doing something.)

achieve /ə'tʃiːv/ *verb* to succeed in doing something after trying very hard ○ *Have you achieved all your aims?* ○ *The company has achieved great success in the USA.*

achievement /ə'tʃiːvmənt/ *noun* something which has been done successfully ○ *She is very modest about her achievements.* ○ *Coming sixth was a great achievement, since he had never entered the competition before.*

acid /'æsɪd/ *noun* a chemical substance that is able to dissolve metals

acknowledge /ək'nɒlɪdʒ/ *verb* **1.** to say that something has been received ○ *She didn't acknowledge receiving my letter.* **2.** to accept that something is true ○ *She acknowledged that she had seen me there.*

acknowledgement /ək'nɒlɪdʒmənt/ *noun* a letter or note sent to say that something has been received

acorn /'eɪkɔːn/ *noun* the fruit of an oak tree

acquaintance /ə'kweɪntəns/ *noun* a person you know slightly ○ *She has many acquaintances in the travel industry but no real friends.*

acquire /ə'kwaɪə/ *verb* to become the owner of something ○ *She has acquired a large collection of old books.*

across /ə'krɒs/ *preposition* **1.** from one side to the other ○ *Don't run across the road without looking to see if there is any traffic coming.* **2.** on the other side of ○ *He saw her across the street.* ■ *adverb* from one side to the other ○ *The river is only twenty feet across.* ○ *The stream is very narrow – you can easily jump across.*

act /ækt/ *noun* **1.** something which is done ○ *He thanked her for the many acts of kindness she had shown him over the years.* **2.** a part of a play or show ○ *Act 2 of the play takes place in the garden.* **3.** a short performance ○ *The show includes acts by several young singers.* **4.** a law passed by Parliament ○ *an act to ban the sale of weapons* ■ *verb* **1.** to do something ○ *You will have to act quickly if you want to stop the fire.* ○ *She acted in a very responsible way.* □ **to act as someone** or **something** to do the work of someone or something ○ *The thick curtain acts as a screen to cut out noise from the street.* **2.** to behave in a particular way ○ *She's been acting very strangely.* ◇ **to get your act together** to organise yourself properly ○ *If they don't get their act together, they'll miss their train.*

action /'ækʃən/ *noun* **1.** the fact of doing something ○ *We recommend swift ac-*

tion to prevent the problem spreading. ○ *What action are you going to take to prevent accidents?* □ **out of action** not working ○ *The car has been out of action for a week.* **2.** something that is done ○ *They've shown their commitment by their actions.* **3.** a movement ○ *Avoid sudden actions that could alarm the animals.* **4.** the things that happen in a performance such as a play or film ○ *The action of the play takes place in a flat in London.* **5.** a case in a law court where someone tries to get money from someone else ○ *to bring an action for damages against someone*

active /'æktɪv/ *adjective* **1.** involved in an activity or activities, especially in an energetic way ○ *He didn't play an active part in the attack on the police station.* ○ *My grandmother is still very active at the age of 88.* **2.** (*of a volcano*) exploding or likely to explode ○ *Scientists think the volcano is no longer active.* **3.** the form of a verb which shows that the subject is doing something (NOTE: If you say 'the car hit him' the verb is active, but in 'he was hit by the car' it is passive.)

activity /æk'tɪvɪti/ *noun* **1.** the act or fact of being active **2.** something that someone does to pass time pleasantly ○ *Children are offered various holiday activities – sailing, windsurfing and water-skiing.* (NOTE: The plural in this sense is **activities**.)

actor /'æktə/ *noun* a person who acts in the theatre, in films or on TV

actress /'æktrəs/ *noun* a woman who acts in the theatre, in films or on TV (NOTE: Many women prefer to call themselves actors rather than actresses.)

actual /'æktʃuəl/ *adjective* real ○ *It looks quite small but the actual height is 5 metres.* ○ *Her actual words were much stronger.*

actually /'æktʃuəli/ *adverb* really ○ *It looks quite small, but actually it is over 5 metres high.* ○ *He said he was ill, but actually he wanted to go to the football match.*

ad /æd/ *noun* an advertisement (*informal*) ○ *If you want to sell your car quickly, put an ad in the paper.*

adapt /ə'dæpt/ *verb* **1.** to change something to be suitable for a new situation ○ *She adapted the story for TV.* ○ *The car has been adapted for disabled drivers.* **2.** to change your behaviour to fit into a new situation ○ *We'll all have to learn to adapt to the new system.*

adaptable /ə'dæptəb(ə)l/ *adjective* able to change or be changed easily to deal with new situations or uses

add /æd/ *verb* **1.** to make a total of numbers ○ *If you add all these numbers together it should make fifty.* (NOTE: **Adding** is usually shown by the sign + : **10 + 4 = 14**.) **2.** to join one thing to another ○ *Interest is added to the account monthly.* ○ *Add two cupfuls of sugar.* ○ *Put a teabag into the pot and add boiling water.* ○ *By building the annexe, they have added thirty rooms to the hotel.* **3.** to say or to write something more ○ *I have nothing to add to what I put in my letter.* ○ *She added that we still owed her some money for work she did last month.*

add up *phrasal verb* to make a total □ **the figures do not add up** the total is not correct

addition /ə'dɪʃ(ə)n/ *noun* **1.** someone or something added to something else ○ *the latest addition to the family* ○ *He showed us the additions to his collection of paintings.* **2.** the act of adding figures to make a total ○ *You don't need a calculator to do a simple addition.* □ **in addition to** as well as ○ *There are twelve registered letters to be sent in addition to this parcel.* ◇ **in addition** as well ◇ **in addition to** as well as ○ *There are twelve registered letters to be sent in addition to this parcel.*

additional /ə'dɪʃ(ə)nəl/ *adjective* included as well as what there is already

address /ə'dres/ *noun* **1.** a set of details of the number of a house, the name of a street and the town where someone lives or works ○ *What is the doctor's address?* ○ *Our address is: 1 Cambridge Road, Teddington, Middlesex.* **2.** the set of letters, symbols and numbers that identify someone's email account ■ *verb* **1.** to write details such as someone's name, street and town on a letter or parcel ○ *That letter is addressed to me – don't open it!* **2.** to speak or write to someone ○ *Please address your questions to the information office.* ○ *Teachers are not normally addressed as 'Sir' here.* **3.** to make a formal speech to a group ○ *The chairman addressed the meeting.*

address book /ə'dres bʊk/ *noun* a notebook or computer file in which you can record people's names, home addresses, telephone numbers and email addresses

adequate /'ædɪkwət/ *adjective* **1.** enough for a purpose ○ *We don't have adequate supplies for the whole journey.* ○ *His salary alone is barely adequate.* **2.** only just satisfactory

adhesive /əd'hiːsɪv/ *adjective* able to stick to things ■ *noun* a substance which sticks things together

adjacent /ə'dʒeɪs(ə)nt/ *adjective* very close to or almost touching something ○ *My office is in an adjacent building.*

adjective /'ædʒɪktɪv/ *noun* a word which describes a noun ○ *In the phrase 'a big black cloud', 'big' and 'black' are both adjectives.*

adjust /ə'dʒʌst/ *verb* to make a slight change to something ○ *I need to adjust this belt a bit.* □ **to adjust to something** to become used to something ○ *How are you adjusting to being a parent?*

admiration /ˌædmə'reɪʃ(ə)n/ *noun* respect for someone or something

admire /əd'maɪə/ *verb* to consider someone or something with approval ○ *He was admired for his skill as a violinist.* ○ *We admired the view from the balcony.*

admission /əd'mɪʃ(ə)n/ *noun* **1.** the act or fact of being allowed to go in to a place ○ *Admission to the exhibition is free on Sundays.* ○ *My friend was refused admission to the restaurant because he was not wearing a tie.* □ **no admission** no one can enter **2.** a statement saying that something bad is true ○ *Her*

admission that she had taken the money led to her arrest.

admission fee /əd'mɪʃ(ə)n fiː/ *noun* an amount of money paid to go into a place such as a museum

admit /əd'mɪt/ *verb* to allow someone to go in to a place ○ *Children are admitted free, but adults have to pay.* ○ *This ticket admits three people.* (NOTE: **admits – admitting – admitted**) □ **to admit (to) doing something** to say that you have done something wrong ○ *They admitted stealing the car.*

adopt /ə'dɒpt/ *verb* **1.** to take someone legally as a son or daughter ○ *They have adopted a little boy.* **2.** to decide to start using something ○ *The book has been adopted for use in all English classes.* ○ *We need to adopt a more flexible approach.*

adore /ə'dɔː/ *verb* to like someone or something very much

adult /'ædʌlt/ *noun* a fully-grown person ■ *adjective* **1.** fully grown ○ *an adult tiger* **2.** relating to a mature person or people ○ *adult fiction*

advance /əd'vɑːns/ *verb* to move forward ○ *The police slowly advanced across the square.* ■ *noun* **1.** a movement forwards ○ *The police have made some advances in their fight against crime.* ○ *The team made an advance into their opponents' half.* **2.** money paid as a loan or as a part of a payment to be made later ■ *adjective* done before something happens ○ *She made an advance payment of £3000.* ◊ **in advance** earlier than the time something happens ○ *You must phone in advance to make an appointment.* ○ *They asked us to pay £200 in advance.*

advanced /əd'vɑːnst/ *adjective* which is studied at a higher level ○ *He's studying advanced mathematics.* ○ *She's studying for an advanced degree.*

advantage /əd'vɑːntɪdʒ/ *noun* something which will help you to be successful ○ *Being able to drive a car is an advantage.* ○ *Knowledge of two foreign languages is an advantage in this job.* ○ *She has several advantages over the other job candidates.* ◊ **to take advan-**

tage of something to profit from something ○ *They took advantage of the cheap fares on offer.* ◇ **to take advantage of someone** to get something unfairly from someone ◇ **to (good *or* best) advantage** in a way that helps someone or something appear especially good ○ *She used her knowledge of Italian to good advantage.*

adventure /əd'ventʃə/ *noun* a new, exciting and dangerous experience ○ *I must tell you about our adventures in the desert.*

adverb /'ædvɜːb/ *noun* a word which applies to a verb, an adjective, another adverb or a whole sentence ○ *In the sentence 'He walked slowly, because the snow was very thick.' both 'slowly' and 'very' are adverbs.*

adverse /'ædvɜːs/ *adjective* (*of conditions*) unpleasant and unwanted ○ *an adverse reaction* ○ *adverse effects*

advert /'ædvɜːt/ *noun* same as **advertisement**

advertise /'ædvətaɪz/ *verb* to make sure that people know that something is for sale, or that something is going to happen ○ *The company is advertising for secretaries.* ○ *Did you see that the restaurant is advertising cheap meals on Sundays?* ○ *I saw this watch advertised in the paper.*

advertisement /əd'vɜːtɪsmənt/ *noun* an announcement which tries to make sure that people know that something is for sale, or that something is going to happen

advertising /'ædvətaɪzɪŋ/ *noun* the act of making sure that people know that something is for sale, or that something is going to happen ○ *The company has increased the amount of money it spends on advertising.* ○ *They spent millions on the advertising campaign.*

advice /əd'vaɪs/ *noun* an opinion that someone gives you about what you should do ○ *He went to the bank manager for advice on how to pay his debts.* ○ *They would not listen to the doctor's advice.* ○ *My grandfather gave me a very useful piece of advice.* ○ *His mother's advice was to stay in bed.* (NOTE: no plu-

ral: use *some advice* or, for one item, *a piece of advice*)

advise /əd'vaɪz/ *verb* **1.** to suggest to someone what they should do ○ *He advised her to save some of the money.* **2.** to tell someone officially that something has happened (*formal*) ○ *They advised us that the sale of the house had been completed.*

adviser /əd'vaɪzə/, **advisor** *noun* someone who helps people to make decisions about what to do

aerial /'eəriəl/ *noun* a piece of equipment for receiving radio or TV signals

aeroplane /'eərəpleɪn/ *noun* a vehicle which flies in the air, carrying passengers or goods

affair /ə'feə/ *noun* **1.** something which is relevant to one person or group of people only ○ *That's his affair – it's nothing to do with me.* ○ *It's an affair for the police.* ○ *His business affairs were very complicated.* **2.** a sexual relationship with someone who is not your husband or wife ○ *He's having an affair with his boss's wife.* **3.** an event ○ *The party is just a family affair.* **4.** an event or situation that shocks people ○ *The whole sorry affair was on the front page of the newspapers for days.* ■ *plural noun* **affairs** situations or activities relating to public or private life

affect /ə'fekt/ *verb* to have an influence on someone or something ○ *The new regulations have affected our business.* ○ *Train services have been seriously affected by the strike.*

affection /ə'fekʃən/ *noun* a feeling of liking someone, especially a friend ○ *She always spoke of him with great affection.*

afford /ə'fɔːd/ *verb* to have enough money to pay for something ○ *How will you afford such an expensive holiday?* □ **be unable to afford, can't afford** to be unable to accept something because it might cause you a problem ○ *I can't afford a delay of more than three weeks.*

afraid /ə'freɪd/ *adjective* **1.** frightened of something or someone ○ *I am afraid of snakes.* ○ *He is too afraid to climb the ladder.* **2.** □ **to be afraid (that)** to be sorry to say ○ *I'm afraid that all the cakes have been sold.* ○ *You can't see the boss – I'm afraid he's ill.* ○ *Have you got a pocket calculator? – No, I'm afraid not.*

after /'ɑːftə/ *preposition* **1.** following or next in order to ○ *If today is Tuesday, the day after tomorrow is Thursday.* ○ *They spoke one after the other.* ○ *What's the letter after Q in the alphabet?* □ **after you** you go first **2.** later than ○ *We arrived after six o'clock.* ○ *We don't let the children go out alone after dark.* ■ *conjunction* later than a time ○ *After the snow fell, the motorways were blocked.* ○ *Phone me after you get home.* (NOTE: **after** is used with many phrasal verbs: **to look after, to take after,** etc.) ◇ **after all 1.** in spite of everything ○ *Everything was all right after all.* **2.** the fact is ○ *He should be OK; after all, he is eighteen now.*

afternoon /ˌɑːftə'nuːn/ *noun* the time between midday and the evening ○ *He always has a little sleep in the afternoon.* ○ *There is an afternoon flight to Paris.* ○ *Can we meet tomorrow afternoon?*

afterwards /'ɑːftəwədz/ *adverb* later ○ *We'll have lunch first and go shopping afterwards.*

again /ə'gen/ *adverb* **1.** another time ○ *He had to take his driving test again.* □ **again and again** several times, usually in a firm or determined way ○ *The police officer asked the same question again and again.* **2.** back as you were before ○ *Although I like going on holiday, I'm always glad to be home again.*

against /ə'genst/ *preposition* **1.** so as to touch ○ *He was leaning against the wall.* ○ *She hit her head against the low doorway.* **2.** in opposition to ○ *England is playing against South Africa tomorrow.* ○ *It's hard cycling uphill against the wind.* ○ *They went against his advice.*

age /eɪdʒ/ *noun* the number of years which you have lived ○ *She is thirty years of age.* ○ *He looks younger than his age.* ■ *plural noun* **ages** a very long time (*informal*) ○ *I've been waiting here for ages.* ○ *It took us ages to get served.*

aged¹ /eɪdʒd/ *adjective* with the age of ○ *a girl aged nine* ○ *She died last year, aged 83.*

aged² /'eɪdʒɪd/ *adjective* very old ○ *an aged man*

agency /'eɪdʒənsi/ *noun* an office which represents another firm ○ *an advertising agency*

agenda /ə'dʒendə/ *noun* a list of points for discussion □ **what's on the agenda?** what are we going to discuss? ■ a set of things that someone plans to do □ **top of your agenda** what someone wants most ○ *A holiday is top of my agenda at present.*

agent /'eɪdʒənt/ *noun* a person who works for or represents someone else ○ *Our head office is in London but we have an agent in Paris.*

aggression /ə'greʃ(ə)n/ *noun* a feeling of anger against someone that is expressed, especially in physical force □ **an act of aggression** an attack on someone

aggressive /ə'gresɪv/ *adjective* ready to attack someone

aggressively /ə'gresɪvli/ *adverb* as if wanting to attack someone

ago /ə'gəʊ/ *adverb* in the past ○ *He phoned a few minutes ago.* ○ *This all happened a long time ago.* (NOTE: **ago** always follows a word referring to time.)

agree /ə'griː/ *verb* **1.** to say yes or give permission ○ *After some discussion he agreed to our plan.* (NOTE: You agree **to** or **on** a plan.) **2.** to say or show that you have the same opinion as someone else ○ *Most of the group agreed with her suggestion.*

agreement /ə'griːmənt/ *noun* **1.** the act or fact of thinking the same ○ *to reach an agreement* or *to come to an agreement on salaries* ○ *Agreement between the two sides is still a long way off.* □ **they are in agreement with our plan** they agree with our plan ○ *We discussed the plan with them and they are in agreement.* **2.** a contract ○ *to draw up* or *to draft an agreement* ○ *We signed an agreement with the Italian company.*

ahead /ə'hed/ *adverb* **1.** in front ○ *Our team was losing, but now we are ahead again.* ○ *Run on ahead and find some seats for us.* ○ *You need to go straight ahead, and then turn left.* **2.** in future ○ *My diary is filled with appointments for six weeks ahead.* **3.** before ○ *We try to fill the vacancies at least three weeks ahead.* ◇ **ahead of** /ə'hed 'ɒv/ **1.** in front of ○ *Ahead of us was a steep hill.* ○ *They ran on ahead of the others.* **2.** in a future time ○ *You have a mass of work ahead of you.* **3.** before (*informal*) ○ *They drafted in extra police ahead of the international match.*

aid /eɪd/ *noun* **1.** help, especially money, food or other gifts given to people living in difficult conditions ○ *aid to the earthquake zone* ○ *an aid worker* (NOTE: This meaning of **aid** has no plural.) □ **in aid of** in order to help ○ *We give money in aid of the Red Cross.* ○ *They are collecting money in aid of refugees.* **2.** something which helps you to do something ○ *kitchen aids* ■ *verb* **1.** to help something to happen **2.** to help someone

aim /eɪm/ *noun* what you are trying to do ○ *His aim is to do well at school and then go to university.* ○ *One of our aims is to increase the speed of service.* ■ *verb* **1.** to plan to do something ○ *We aim to go on holiday in June.* **2.** to point a gun at someone or something ○ *He was aiming or aiming a gun at the policeman.*

air /eə/ *noun* **1.** a mixture of gases which cannot be seen, but which is all around us and which every animal breathes ○ *His breath was like steam in the cold air.* **2. the air** the space around things and above the ground ○ *He threw the ball up into the air.* (NOTE: These meanings of **air** have no plural.) ■ *adjective* referring to a method of travelling or sending goods using aircraft ○ *new air routes* □ **by air** in an aircraft ○ *I don't enjoy travelling by air.* ○ *It's quicker to send the letter by air.* ■ *verb* to make a room or clothes fresh by giving them more air ○ *Let's open the windows to air the room.*

aircraft /'eəkrɑːft/ *noun* a vehicle which flies in the air ○ *The passengers got into or boarded the aircraft.* ○ *The airline has a fleet of ten aircraft.* (NOTE: The plural is **aircraft**: *one aircraft, six aircraft*.)

airfare /'eəfeə/ *noun* the amount of money a passenger has to pay to travel on an aircraft

air force /'eə fɔːs/ *noun* a country's military air organisation

airline /'eəlaɪn/ *noun* a company which takes people or goods to places in aircraft ○ *The airline has been voted the most popular with business travellers.* ○ *He's an airline pilot.*

airplane /'eəpleɪn/ *noun US* an aircraft

airport /'eəpɔːt/ *noun* a place where aircraft land and take off ○ *You can take the underground to the airport.* ○ *We are due to arrive at Heathrow Airport at midday.*

alarm /ə'lɑːm/ *noun* **1.** a loud warning sound ○ *An alarm will sound if someone touches the wire.* □ **to raise the alarm** to warn everyone of danger **2.** same as **alarm clock** ■ *verb* to frighten someone ○ *I don't want to alarm you, but there's a police car parked outside your house.*

alarm clock /ə'lɑːm klɒk/ *noun* a clock which rings a bell to wake you up

album /'ælbəm/ *noun* **1.** a large book **2.** a collection of songs on a CD, cassette or record

alcohol /'ælkəhɒl/ *noun* a substance in drinks such as beer or wine that can make people drunk ○ *They will not serve alcohol to anyone under the age of 18.*

alcoholic /ˌælkə'hɒlɪk/ *adjective* relating to alcohol

alert /ə'lɜːt/ *adjective* watching or listening carefully, ready to notice something

alike /ə'laɪk/ *adjective* very similar ■ *adverb* in a similar way ○ *My sister and I just don't think alike.* ○ *The change will affect rich and poor alike.*

alive /ə'laɪv/ *adjective* **1.** living ○ *He was still alive when he was rescued from the burning building.* ○ *When my grandfather was alive, there were no supermarkets.* (NOTE: not used in front of a noun: *the fish is alive* but *a live fish*.) **2.** lively

○ *The holiday village really comes alive at night.* □ **to come alive** to become busy and active

all /ɔ:l/ *adjective, pronoun* everything or everyone ○ *They all* or *All of them like coffee.* ○ *All trains stop at Clapham Junction.* ○ *Did you pick all (of) the tomatoes?* ○ *Where are all the children?* ■ *adverb* **1.** completely ○ *The ground was all white after the snow had fallen.* ○ *I forgot all about her birthday.* **2.** □ **all by yourself** all alone ○ *You can't do it all by yourself.* ○ *I'm all by myself this evening – my girlfriend's gone out.* ◇ **all along** right from the beginning ◇ **all at once** suddenly ◇ **all in 1.** tired out **2.** including everything ◇ **all of a sudden** suddenly ◇ **all over 1.** everywhere over something **2.** finished ◇ **all right** well ○ *She was ill yesterday but she's all right now.* ◇ **all the same** in spite of this ○ *I'm not really keen on horror films, but I'll go with you all the same.*

allergic /ə'lɜːdʒɪk/ *adjective* suffering from or referring to an allergy □ **to be allergic to** to react badly to a substance ○ *Many people are allergic to grass pollen.* ○ *She is allergic to cats.*

allergy /'ælədʒi/ *noun* a bad reaction to a substance which makes you sneeze, or makes your skin itch, e.g. ○ *She has an allergy to household dust.* ○ *The baby has a wheat allergy.*

allow /ə'laʊ/ *verb* to let someone do something ○ *She allowed me to borrow her book.* ○ *Smoking is not allowed in the restaurant.* ○ *You are allowed to take two pieces of hand luggage onto the plane.*

allowance /ə'laʊəns/ *noun* **1.** an amount of money paid to someone regularly ○ *a weekly allowance* **2.** an amount of money which you are allowed to earn without paying tax on it **3.** □ **to make allowances for** to take something into account ○ *You must make allowances for his age.*

ally[1] /'ælaɪ/ *noun* **1.** a country which works together with another, especially in a war (NOTE: The plural is **allies**.) **2.** someone who is willing to support you in something you want to achieve ○

Jack has been my closest ally in the campaign.

ally[2] /ə'laɪ/ *verb* □ **to ally yourself with** *or* **to ally yourself to someone** to join forces with someone ○ *The unions have allied themselves with the opposition.* (NOTE: **allies – allying – allied**)

almost /'ɔːlməʊst/ *adverb* nearly ○ *London is almost as far from here as Paris.* ○ *She's almost as tall as I am.* *She'll eat almost anything.* ○ *Hurry up, it's almost time for the train to leave.*

alone /ə'ləʊn/ *adjective* **1.** with no one else ○ *She lives alone with her cats.* ○ *He was all alone in the shop.* **2.** only ○ *She alone knew the importance of the message.* ■ *adverb* without other people ○ *We don't let the children go out alone after dark.* ○ *I don't like travelling alone.* ◇ **leave alone 1.** not to disturb someone ○ *Leave your sister alone, she's trying to read.* **2.** to stop touching or playing with something ○ *Leave the cat alone, it doesn't like being stroked.* ○ *Leave those keys alone, the noise is annoying me.* ◇ **to go it alone** to do something, especially a business activity, without help from anyone

along /ə'lɒŋ/ *preposition* **1.** by the side of ○ *He has planted fruit trees along both sides of the garden path.* ○ *The river runs along one side of the castle.* **2.** in a straight forward direction ○ *She ran along the pavement.* ○ *Walk along the street until you come to the post office.* ○ *I was just driving along when I caught sight of my brother.* **3.** to a place ○ *John came along after about five minutes.* ○ *Is it ok if I bring a friend along?*

aloud /ə'laʊd/ *adverb* in a voice which can be easily heard

alphabet /'ælfəbet/ *noun* a series of letters in a specific order, e.g. A, B, C, etc ○ *G comes before H in the alphabet.* ○ *If you're going to Greece on holiday, you ought to learn the Greek alphabet.*

alphabetical /ˌælfə'betɪk(ə)l/ *adjective* relating to the alphabet □ **in alphabetical order** in order of the first letter of each word ○ *The words in the dictionary are in alphabetical order.* ○ *Sort out the address cards into alphabetical order of the people's names.*

already /ɔːlˈredi/ *adverb* before now or before the time mentioned ○ *I've already done my shopping.* ○ *It was already past ten o'clock when he arrived.*

also /ˈɔːlsəʊ/ *adverb* in addition to something or someone else that has been mentioned ○ *He's a keen cyclist and his sister also likes to cycle when she can.* ○ *She sings well and can also play the violin.* (NOTE: **also** is usually placed before the main verb or after a modal or auxiliary verb.)

alter /ˈɔːltə/ *verb* to become different, or make something different, especially in small ways or in parts only ○ *They wanted to alter the terms of the contract after they had signed it.* ○ *The shape of his face had altered slightly.*

alteration /ˌɔːltəˈreɪʃ(ə)n/ *noun* **1.** the act of becoming different or of making something different **2.** something that has been, or needs, changing ○ *She made some alterations in the design.*

alternate¹ /ɔːlˈtɜːnət/ *adjective* every other one ○ *We see each other on alternate Sundays.*

alternate² /ˈɔːltəneɪt/ *verb* to keep changing from one particular position or state to another

alternative /ɔːlˈtɜːnətɪv/ *adjective* **1.** in place of something else ○ *If the plane is full, we will put you on an alternative flight.* ○ *Do you have an alternative solution?* **2.** following a different way from usual ■ *noun* something which you do instead of something else ○ *Now that she's ill, do we have any alternative to calling the holiday off?*

although /ɔːlˈðəʊ/ *conjunction* in spite of the fact that ○ *Although it was freezing, she didn't put a coat on.* ○ *I've never been into that shop although I've often walked past it.*

altogether /ˌɔːltəˈgeðə/ *adverb* taking everything together ○ *The food was £10 and the drinks £5, so that makes £15 altogether.* ○ *The staff of the three shops come to 200 altogether.*

always /ˈɔːlweɪz/ *adverb* **1.** every time ○ *She is always late for work.* ○ *Why does it always rain when we want to go for a walk?* **2.** all the time ○ *It's always*

hot in tropical countries. **3.** frequently, especially when someone finds it annoying ○ *She's always asking me to lend her money.*

am /əm, æm/ 1st person present singular of **be**

a.m. /ˌeɪ ˈem/ *adverb* before midday ○ *I have to catch the 7 a.m. train to work every day.* ○ *Telephone calls made before 6 a.m. are charged at the cheap rate.* (NOTE: **a.m.** is usually used to show the exact hour and the word **o'clock** is left out)

amazement /əˈmeɪzmənt/ *noun* great surprise ○ *To his amazement he won first prize.*

amazing /əˈmeɪzɪŋ/ *adjective* **1.** very surprising ○ *It was amazing that she never suspected anything.* **2.** extremely interesting and unusual ○ *It was an amazing experience, sailing so far from land at night.*

ambition /æmˈbɪʃ(ə)n/ *noun* a wish to do something special ○ *His great ambition is to ride on an elephant.*

ambulance /ˈæmbjʊləns/ *noun* a van which carries sick or injured people to hospital ○ *When she fell down the stairs, her husband called an ambulance.*

American /əˈmerɪkən/ *adjective* relating to America or to the United States

among /əˈmʌŋ/, **amongst** /əˈmʌŋst/ *preposition* **1.** surrounded by or in the middle of ○ *He was standing among a crowd of tourists.* **2.** between a number of people in a group ○ *Let's share the cake among us.* **3.** in addition to other people or things ○ *Jack was there, among others.*

amount /əˈmaʊnt/ *noun* a quantity of something such as money ○ *The amount in my bank account has reached £1000.* ○ *We spent a large amount of time just waiting.* □ **a certain amount** some but not a lot ○ *Painting the house will take a certain amount of time.*

amount to *phrasal verb* **1.** to make a total of ○ *My year's savings amount to less than £1000.* **2.** to be similar or equal to something ○ *I think what he said amounts to a refusal to take part.* **3.** □ **to amount to the same thing** to mean the same, to be the same ○ *Whether he took cash or free holidays, it all amounts to the same thing.* ○ *The remaining problems don't amount to much.*

amuse /ə'mjuːz/ *verb* **1.** to make someone laugh ○ *This story will amuse you.* □ **to amuse yourself** to play or get pleasure from what you are doing ○ *The children amused themselves quietly while their parents talked.* **2.** to make the time pass pleasantly for someone ○ *How can we amuse the children on the journey?*

amusement /ə'mjuːzmənt/ *noun* **1.** a feeling of pleasure caused by something that is funny **2.** □ **to someone's amusement** making someone feel pleasure in a funny situation ○ *Much to her amusement, the band played 'Happy Birthday to you!'.* **3.** a way of passing the time pleasantly ○ *They had planned several visits for the guest's amusement.*

amusing /ə'mjuːzɪŋ/ *adjective* funny

an /ən, æn/ ♦ **a**

analysis /ə'næləsɪs/ *noun* a close examination of the parts or elements of something ○ *job analysis* ○ *to make an analysis of the sales* or *a sales analysis* ○ *to carry out an analysis of the market potential* (NOTE: The plural is **analyses** /ə'næləsiːz/.)

ancient /'eɪnʃənt/ *adjective* very old, or belonging to a time long ago ○ *He was riding an ancient bicycle.*

and /ən, ənd, ænd/ *conjunction* used to join two words or phrases ○ *All my uncles and aunts live in the country.* ○ *The children were running about and singing.* ○ *Come and sit down next to me.* (NOTE: **and** is used to say numbers after 100: 'seven hundred and two (702)') ◇ **and so on, and so forth, and so on and so forth** with other similar things ○ *He talked about plants, flowers, vegetables, and so on.*

anger /'æŋgə/ *noun* a feeling of being very annoyed ○ *He managed to control his anger.* ○ *She couldn't hide the anger she felt.*

angle /'æŋgəl/ *noun* a corner where two lines meet ○ *She planted the tree in the angle of the two walls.* ◇ **at an angle**

not straight ○ *The shop front is at an angle to the road.*

angrily /'æŋgrɪli/ *adverb* in an angry way ○ *He shouted angrily when the children climbed over the fence.*

angry /'æŋgri/ *adjective* upset and annoyed, and sometimes wanting to harm someone ○ *The shopkeeper is angry with the children because they broke his window.* ○ *He gets angry if the post is late.* ○ *I am angry that the government is doing nothing to prevent crime.* ○ *When the cashier still hadn't arrived at midday the boss got even angrier.* (NOTE: **angrier – angriest**)

animal /'ænɪm(ə)l/ *noun* a living thing that moves independently ○ *I love having animals as pets.* (NOTE: **animal** may include humans in scientific contexts.)

ankle /'æŋkəl/ *noun* the part of the body where your leg joins your foot

anniversary /ˌænɪ'vɜːs(ə)ri/ *noun* the same date as an important event that happened in the past

announce /ə'naʊns/ *verb* to say something officially or in public ○ *He announced his resignation.* ○ *She announced that she would be standing for parliament.*

announcement /ə'naʊnsmənt/ *noun* a statement made in public ○ *The managing director made an announcement to the staff.* ○ *There were several announcements concerning flight changes.*

annoy /ə'nɔɪ/ *verb* to make someone feel slightly angry or impatient ○ *Their rude behaviour really annoyed us.*

annoyance /ə'nɔɪəns/ *noun* a feeling of being slightly annoyed ○ *There was a tone of annoyance in her voice.*

annoyed /ə'nɔɪd/ *adjective* slightly angry or impatient ○ *He was annoyed with his neighbour who had cut down one of his trees.* ○ *I was annoyed to find someone had stolen my mobile phone.*

annoying /ə'nɔɪɪŋ/ *adjective* making you angry or impatient ○ *I find it very annoying that the post doesn't come before 10 o'clock.* ○ *How annoying! I forgot to buy the milk.* ○ *The baby has an annoying cough which won't go away.*

annual /'ænjuəl/ *adjective* happening once a year ○ *The village fair is an annual event.* ○ *I get annual interest of 6% on my savings account.*

another /ə'nʌðə/ *adjective, pronoun* **1.** one more ○ *I'd like another cake, please.* ○ *Would you like another?* **2.** a different one ○ *He's bought another car.* ○ *She tried on one dress after another, but couldn't find anything she liked.* ◊ **each other**

answer /'ɑːnsə/ *noun* **1.** something that you say or write when someone has asked you a question ○ *The answer to your question is yes.* ○ *I knocked on the door but there was no answer.* □ **in answer to** as a reply to ○ *I am writing in answer to your letter of October 6th.* **2.** the act of picking up a telephone that is ringing ○ *I phoned his office but there was no answer.* ■ *verb* **1.** to speak or write words to someone who has spoken to you or asked you a question ○ *He never answers my letters.* ○ *When he asked us if we had enjoyed the meal we all answered 'yes'.* **2.** □ **to answer the phone** to speak and listen to a telephone caller ○ *His mother usually answers the phone.* □ **to answer the door** to open the door to someone who knocks or rings the bell ○ *No-one answered the door though I knocked twice.*

ant /ænt/ *noun* a small insect that lives in large groups

antibiotic /ˌæntibaɪ'ɒtɪk/ *noun* a substance which kills harmful organisms such as bacteria

antique /æn'tiːk/ *noun* an old and valuable object ○ *He collects antiques.* ■ *adjective* old and valuable ○ *an antique Chinese vase*

antiseptic /ˌæntɪ'septɪk/ *noun* a substance which prevents infection ■ *adjective* preventing infection ○ *an antiseptic dressing*

antonym /'æntənɪm/ *noun* a word which means the opposite of another word

anxiety /æŋ'zaɪəti/ *noun* **1.** nervous worry about something ○ *Her anxiety about her job prospects began to affect her health.* **2.** the state of being keen to do something ○ *In his anxiety to get away quickly, he forgot to lock the door.*

anxious /'æŋkʃəs/ *adjective* **1.** nervous and very worried about something ○ *She's anxious about the baby.* **2.** keen to do something ○ *The shopkeeper is always anxious to please his customers.*

anxiously /'æŋkʃəsli/ *adverb* in a nervous, worried way ○ *They are waiting anxiously for the results of the exam.*

any /'eni/ *adjective, pronoun* **1.** it doesn't matter which ○ *I'm free any day next week except Tuesday.* **2.** (*usually in questions or negatives*) a small quantity ○ *Have you got any money left?* ○ *Is there any food for me?* ○ *Would you like any more to eat?* ○ *Will any of your friends be there?* **3.** □ **not…any** none ○ *I don't like any of the paintings in the exhibition.* ○ *There isn't any food left – they've eaten it all.* ○ *Can you lend me some money? – sorry, I haven't got any.*

anybody /'enibɒdi/ *pronoun* same as **anyone**

anymore /ˌeni'mɔː/, **any more** *adverb* □ **not … anymore** no longer ○ *We don't go there anymore.*

anyone /'eniwʌn/ *pronoun* any person at all ○ *Anyone can learn to ride a bike.* □ **anyone else** any other person ○ *Is there anyone else who can't see the screen?*

anything /'eniθɪŋ/ *pronoun* **1.** it doesn't matter what ○ *You can eat anything you want.* ○ *Our dog will bite anything that moves.* **2.** (*in questions or negatives*) something ○ *Did you do anything interesting at the weekend?* ○ *Did you hear anything make a noise during the night?* ○ *Has anything happened to their plans for a long holiday?* ○ *Do you want anything more to drink?*

anyway /'eniweɪ/ *adverb* despite something else ○ *I'm not supposed to drink during the daytime, but I'll have a beer anyway.* ○ *I think it's time to leave – anyway, the last bus is at 11.40.*

anywhere /'eniweə/ *adverb* **1.** it does not matter where ○ *Put the chair anywhere.* **2.** (*in questions or negatives*) somewhere ○ *I can't see your wallet anywhere.* ○ *Did you go anywhere at the* *weekend?* ○ *Is there anywhere where I can sit down?*

apart /ə'pɑːt/ *adverb* **1.** separated ○ *The two villages are about six miles apart.* **2.** in separate pieces ○ *He took the watch apart.* ◇ **apart from** except for ○ *Do you have any special interests apart from your work?* ○ *I'm feeling fine, apart from a slight cold.*

apartment /ə'pɑːtmənt/ *noun* a separate set of rooms for living in ○ *She shares an apartment with a friend.*

ape /eɪp/ *noun* a large monkey

apologise /ə'pɒlədʒaɪz/, **apologize** *verb* to say you are sorry ○ *He shouted at her and then apologised.* ○ *She apologised for being late.*

apology /ə'pɒlədʒi/ *noun* an act of indicating that you are sorry (NOTE: The plural is **apologies**.) ■ *plural noun* **apologies** a statement indicating that you are sorry, especially if you cannot attend a meeting ○ *My apologies for being so late.* ○ *Please give the chairman my apologies.*

apostrophe /ə'pɒstrəfi/ *noun* a printing sign ('), either showing that a letter has been left out, e.g. weren't, or after a noun to show possession, e.g. Ben's coat or the girls' coats

apparatus /ˌæpə'reɪtəs/ *noun* scientific or medical equipment

apparent /ə'pærənt/ *adjective* **1.** easy to see or accept as true ○ *It was apparent to everyone that she was annoyed.* **2.** possibly different from what something seems to be ○ *There is an apparent mistake in the accounts.*

apparently /ə'pærəntli/ *adverb* according to what you have seen or heard ○ *Apparently she took the last train home and then disappeared.* ○ *He didn't come to work today – apparently he's got a cold.*

appeal /ə'piːl/ *noun* **1.** an act of asking for help ○ *The police have made an appeal for witnesses.* ○ *The hospital is launching an appeal to raise £50,000.* **2.** an attractive quality ○ *the strong appeal of Greece as a holiday destination* ■ *verb* **1.** □ **to appeal for something** to ask for something ○ *They appealed for*

money to continue their work. **2.** □ **to appeal against a verdict** to make a legal request for a court to look again at a decision ○ *He has appealed against the sentence.* **3.** □ **to appeal to someone** to attract someone ○ *These CDs appeal to the teenage market.* ○ *The idea of working in Australia for six months appealed to her.*

appealing /ə'piːlɪŋ/ *adjective* **1.** attractive ○ *The design has proved appealing to our older customers.* **2.** wanting help or support ○ *The child gave her an appealing look as she got up to leave.* (NOTE: only used before a noun)

appear /ə'pɪə/ *verb* **1.** to start to be seen ○ *A ship appeared through the fog.* **2.** to seem ○ *There appears to be a mistake.* ○ *He appears to have forgotten the time.* ○ *She appeared rather cross.* **3.** to play a part in a film or play or take part in a TV programme ○ *She appears regularly on TV.* **4.** to come to a law court ○ *He appeared in court, charged with murder.*

appearance /ə'pɪərəns/ *noun* **1.** the way that someone or something looks ○ *You could tell from his appearance that he had been sleeping rough.* **2.** the fact of being present somewhere, especially unexpectedly ○ *The appearance of a teacher caused them to fall silent.* □ **to put in an appearance** to go somewhere where other people are for a short time **3.** the beginning of something new ○ *the rapid appearance of mobile phone shops all over the country* ○ *They were worried by the sudden appearance of a red rash.* **4.** an occasion when someone is performing in a film or play or on TV ○ *This is her second appearance in a film.*

appetite /'æpɪtaɪt/ *noun* a need or wish to eat ○ *Going for a long walk has given me an appetite.* ○ *He's not feeling well and has lost his appetite.*

applause /ə'plɔːz/ *noun* the act of clapping your hands together several times to show that you liked a performance

apple /'æp(ə)l/ *noun* a common fruit that is hard, round and sweet, and grows on a tree ○ *Don't eat apples that are not ripe – they'll make you ill.*

appliance /ə'plaɪəns/ *noun* a machine such as a washing machine or cooker used in the home

applicant /'æplɪkənt/ *noun* a person who applies for something ○ *job applicants* ○ *Applicants for licences must fill in this form.*

application /ˌæplɪ'keɪʃ(ə)n/ *noun* **1.** the process of putting something on something else ○ *Several applications of the cream will be necessary.* **2.** the process or act of applying for a job ○ *He wrote a letter of application.* ○ *We've received dozens of applications for the job of barman.*

application form /æplɪ'keɪʃ(ə)n fɔːm/ *noun* a form which has to be filled in to apply for something

apply /ə'plaɪ/ *verb* **1.** □ **to apply for a job** to ask for a job ○ *She applied for a job in the supermarket.* ○ *He's applying for a job as a teacher.* **2.** to put something on ○ *Wait until the first coat of paint is dry before you apply the second.* **3.** □ **to apply to** to affect or to be relevant to ○ *This rule only applies to people coming from outside the EU.* (NOTE: **applies – applying – applied**)

appoint /ə'pɔɪnt/ *verb* to give someone a job ○ *He was appointed (as) manager* or *to the post of manager.* ○ *We want to appoint someone to manage our sales department.* (NOTE: You appoint a person **to** a job.)

appointment /ə'pɔɪntmənt/ *noun* **1.** an agreed time for a meeting ○ *I want to make an appointment to see the doctor.* ○ *She was late for her appointment.* □ **on her appointment as manager** when she was made a manager **2.** the process of being given a job **3.** a job ○ *We are going to make three new appointments.*

appreciate /ə'priːʃiˌeɪt/ *verb* to recognise the value of something ○ *Shoppers always appreciate a bargain.* ○ *Customers don't appreciate having to wait to be served.*

apprentice /ə'prentɪs/ *noun* a young person who works as an assistant to a skilled person in order to learn from them ○ *He's started work as a plumber's apprentice.*

approach /ə'prəʊtʃ/ *noun* **1.** the fact of coming nearer ○ *With the approach of winter we need to get the central heating checked.* **2.** a way which leads to something ○ *The approaches to the city were crowded with coaches.* **3.** a way of dealing with a situation ○ *His approach to the question was different from hers.* ■ *verb* to come near ○ *The plane was approaching the airport when the lights went out.*

appropriate /ə'prəʊpriət/ *adjective* suitable for a particular situation ○ *That skirt is not really appropriate for gardening.* ○ *We leave it to you to take appropriate action.*

approval /ə'pruːv(ə)l/ *noun* the act of agreeing ○ *The committee gave their approval to the scheme.* ○ *Does the choice of colour have your approval* or *meet with your approval?*

approve /ə'pruːv/ *verb* **1.** to agree to something officially ○ *The committee approved the scheme.* **2.** □ **to approve of something** to think something is good ○ *He doesn't approve of loud music.*

approximately /ə'prɒksɪmətli/ *adverb* not exactly ○ *It takes approximately 35 minutes to get to the city centre from here.*

April /'eɪprəl/ *noun* the fourth month of the year, the month after March and before May ○ *Her birthday is in April.* ○ *We went on holiday last April.* (NOTE: **April 5th** or **April 5:** say 'the fifth of April' or 'April the fifth' or in US English 'April fifth'.)

aptitude /'æptɪˌtjuːd/ *noun* a natural ability that can be developed further

arch /ɑːtʃ/ *noun* a round structure forming a roof or entrance ■ *verb* to make something round like an arch ○ *The cat arched her back and started spitting.*

architect /'ɑːkɪtekt/ *noun* a person who designs buildings

architecture /'ɑːkɪtektʃə/ *noun* the design of buildings

are /ə, ɑː/ 1st person plural present of **be**. 2nd person singular present of **be**. 2nd person plural present of **be**. 3rd person plural present of **be**

area /'eəriə/ *noun* **1.** a space ○ *The whole area round the town hall is going to be rebuilt.* ○ *We always sit in the 'no smoking' area.* **2.** a measurement of the space taken up by something, calculated by multiplying the length by the width ○ *The area of the room is four square metres.* ○ *We are looking for a shop with a sales area of about 100 square metres.* **3.** a part of a town or country ○ *Our house is near the commercial area of the town.* ○ *The factory is in a very good area for getting to the motorways and airports.* □ **the London area** the part of England around London ○ *Houses in the London area are more expensive than elsewhere in the country.*

argue /'ɑːgjuː/ *verb* to discuss without agreeing, often in a noisy or angry way ○ *They argued over the prices.* ○ *She argued with the waiter about the bill.* ○ *I could hear them arguing in the next room.* (NOTE: You argue **with** someone **about** *or* **over** something.)

argument /'ɑːgjʊmənt/ *noun* a situation in which people discuss something without agreeing ○ *Nobody would back her up in her argument with the boss.* □ **to get into an argument with someone** to start to argue with someone ○ *He got into an argument with the taxi driver.*

arise /ə'raɪz/ *verb* to start to appear ○ *The problem arose in the planning department.* (NOTE: **arises – arising – arose** /ə'rəʊz/ **– arisen** /ə'rɪzən/)

arithmetic /ə'rɪθmətɪk/ *noun* calculations with numbers, especially as a subject studied at school

arm /ɑːm/ *noun* **1.** the part of the body which goes from the shoulder to the hand ○ *He held the parcel under his arm.* ○ *She tripped over the pavement and broke her arm.* **2.** the part of a chair which you can rest your arms on ○ *He put his coffee cup on the arm of his chair.* ■ *verb* to give weapons to ○ *The police were armed with guns.* ◇ **arm in arm** with arms linked together ○ *They walked down the street arm in arm.*

armchair /'ɑːmtʃeə/ *noun* a chair with arms

armed /ɑːmd/ *adjective* **1.** provided with weapons ○ *Most British policemen are* not armed. ○ *Armed guards surrounded the house.* **2.** involving weapons ○ *the armed struggle between the two groups* **3.** ready for use as a weapon ○ *The device is already armed.* ◇ **armed with** provided with ○ *Armed with picnic baskets, towels and cameras, we set off for the beach.*

armed forces /ˌɑːmd 'fɔːsɪz/, **armed services** /ˌɑːmd 'sɜːvɪsɪz/ *plural noun* the army, navy and air force of a country

army /'ɑːmi/ *noun* all the soldiers of a country, trained for fighting on land ○ *He left school at 16 and joined the army.* ○ *An army spokesman held a news conference.* (NOTE: The plural is **armies**.)

aroma /ə'rəʊmə/ *noun* a pleasant smell of something you can eat or drink ○ *the aroma of freshly baked bread*

arose /ə'rəʊz/ past tense of **arise**

around /ə'raʊnd/ *preposition* **1.** going all round something ○ *She had a gold chain around her neck.* ○ *The flood water was all around the village.* **2.** close to or in a place or area ○ *Is there a bus stop around here?* **3.** in various places ○ *We have lots of computers around the office.* **4.** not exactly ○ *It will cost around £200.* ○ *Around sixty people came to the meeting.* ■ *adverb* **1.** in various places ○ *Papers were lying around all over the floor.* ○ *The restaurants were all full, so we walked around for some time.* **2.** in a position that is fairly near ○ *We try not to talk about it when she's around.* ○ *It's the only swimming pool for miles around.* **3.** in existence ○ *She's one of the best eye surgeons around.* ○ *The new coins have been around for some weeks now.*

arrange /ə'reɪndʒ/ *verb* **1.** to put in order ○ *The chairs are arranged in rows.* ○ *The books are arranged in alphabetical order.* ○ *The ground floor is arranged as an open-plan area with a little kitchen at the side.* **2.** to make a plan for something ○ *Let's arrange to meet somewhere before we go to the theatre.* ○ *The tour has been arranged by the travel agent.* ○ *She arranged for a taxi to meet him at the airport.* ○ *I've arranged with my mother that she will feed the cat while we're away.* (NOTE:

You arrange **for** someone to do something; you arrange **for** something to be done; or you arrange **to** do something. Note also **arranges – arranging – arranged**.)

arrangement /əˈreɪndʒmənt/ noun **1.** the process of putting things in order ○ *the arrangement of the pictures in a book* **2.** the process of making plans for an event ○ *All the arrangements for the wedding were left to the bride's mother.*

arrest /əˈrest/ verb (of the police) to catch and hold someone who has broken the law ○ *The police arrested two men and took them to the police station.* ○ *He ended up getting arrested as he tried to leave the country.* ○ *She was arrested for stealing.* ■ noun the act of holding someone for breaking the law ○ *The police made several arrests at the demonstration.* □ **under arrest** held by the police ○ *After the fight, three people were under arrest.*

arrival /əˈraɪv(ə)l/ noun **1.** the act of reaching a place ○ *We announce the arrival of flight AB 987 from Tangiers.* ○ *We apologise for the late arrival of the 14.25 express from Edinburgh.* ○ *The time of arrival is 5 p.m.* □ **on arrival** when you arrive ○ *On arrival at the hotel, members of the party will be allocated rooms.* **2.** a person who has arrived ○ *He's a new arrival on our staff.* ■ plural noun **arrivals** the part of an airport that deals with passengers who are arriving

arrive /əˈraɪv/ verb to reach a place ○ *They arrived at the hotel tired out.* ○ *The train from Paris arrives in London at 5 p.m.* (NOTE: You arrive **in** a town or **in** a country but **at** a place. Note also: **arrives – arriving – arrived**.)

arrogant /ˈærəgənt/ adjective very proud in an unpleasant way ○ *He's such an arrogant young man.* ○ *What an arrogant way to treat customers!*

arrow /ˈærəʊ/ noun **1.** a weapon made of a piece of wood with a sharp point **2.** a printed sign ➙ which points to something

art /ɑːt/ noun **1.** the practice of creating objects, e.g. by painting, drawing or sculpture ○ *She is taking art lessons.* ○ *When you're in Washington, don't miss*

the Museum of Modern Art. **2.** the objects that are created in this way

artery /ˈɑːtəri/ noun a tube carrying blood from the heart around the body. Compare **vein** (NOTE: The plural is **arteries**.)

article /ˈɑːtɪk(ə)l/ noun **1.** a report in a newspaper ○ *Did you read the article on skiing in yesterday's paper?* **2.** an object or thing ○ *Several articles of clothing were found near the road.* **3.** a word used before a noun to show whether you are referring to a particular or general example of something. The definite article is 'the' and the indefinite article is 'a' or 'an'.

artificial /ˌɑːtɪˈfɪʃ(ə)l/ adjective not natural ○ *She was wearing artificial pearls.*

artificially /ˌɑːtɪˈfɪʃ(ə)li/ adverb in a way that is not natural

artist /ˈɑːtɪst/ noun a person who is skilled in making works of art such as paintings ○ *She collects paintings by 19th-century artists.*

as /əz, æz/ conjunction **1.** because ○ *As you can't drive, you'll have to go by bus.* ○ *As it's cold, you should wear an overcoat.* **2.** at the same time that something else happens ○ *As he was getting into the bath, the telephone rang.* ○ *The little girl ran into the road as the car was turning the corner.* **3.** in the same way ○ *Leave everything as it is.* ■ preposition **1.** in a particular job ○ *She had a job as a bus driver.* **2.** because of being a particular type of person ○ *As a doctor, he has to know the symptoms of all the common diseases.* **3.** in a particular way ○ *She was dressed as a nurse.* ○ *They treated him as a friend of the family.* ◇ **as from** from a particular time ○ *as from next Friday* ◇ **as if, as though** in the same way as ◇ **as...as** used in comparisons ○ *She is nearly as tall as I am.* ○ *I can't run as fast as you.* ◇ **as well** in addition to something or someone else that has been mentioned ○ *She came to have tea and brought her sister as well.* ○ *We visited the castle and swam in the pool as well.* ◇ **as well as** in addition to or together with ○ *He has a cottage in the country as well as a flat in town.* ○

As well as being a maths teacher, he is a part-time policeman.

ascend /ə'send/ *verb* to go up ○ *The balloon rapidly ascended to 3000m.*

ash /æʃ/ *noun* **1.** a grey dust left after something has burnt (NOTE: no plural in this sense) **2.** a type of tree that grows in the northern part of Europe

ashamed /ə'ʃeɪmd/ *adjective* embarrassed and sorry for something that you have done or not done

aside /ə'saɪd/ *adverb* to one side ○ *He took me aside and whispered in my ear.* ◇ **aside from** except for ○ *Aside from a minor infection, his health had been remarkably good.* ○ *I've got to read these three articles, and that's aside from all my regular work.*

ask /ɑːsk/ *verb* **1.** to put a question to get information ○ *She asked a policeman the way to the hospital.* ○ *Joe went to the station to ask about cheap tickets.* ○ *Ask the assistant how much the shoes cost.* **2.** to put a question to get someone to do something ○ *Ask your father to teach you how to drive.* ○ *Can I ask you not to make so much noise?* **3.** to invite someone to an event or to do something ○ *We asked them to our party.* ○ *She asked me to go skiing with her.*

ask for *phrasal verb* to say that you want something ○ *Someone came into the shop and asked for the manager.*

ask out *phrasal verb* to ask someone to go out with you, e.g. to a restaurant or to the cinema ○ *Bill wants to ask my sister out.*

asleep /ə'sliːp/ *adjective* sleeping ○ *He was asleep and didn't hear the fire alarm.* ○ *They were lying asleep on the ground.* □ **to fall asleep** to begin to sleep

aspect /'æspekt/ *noun* **1.** a way of considering something such as a situation or a problem ○ *There are several aspects of the problem to be considered before I can decide.* **2.** the direction in which a building or piece of ground faces

aspirin /'æsprɪn/ *noun* **1.** a common drug, used in the treatment of minor illnesses to reduce pain **2.** a pill that contains aspirin

assassinate /ə'sæsɪneɪt/ *verb* to kill a famous person, especially for political reasons ○ *Do you remember the day when the President was assassinated?*

assemble /ə'semb(ə)l/ *verb* **1.** (especially of people) to come together in a place, or to be brought together by someone ○ *We'll assemble outside the hotel by the coach at 9 a.m.* ○ *They assembled a panel of experts to renew the project.* **2.** (especially of people) to come together in a place, or to be brought together by someone, especially formally or in an ordered way ○ *We'll assemble outside the hotel at 9 a.m.* ○ *They assembled a panel of experts to renew the project.*

assembly /ə'semblɪ/ *noun* **1.** a meeting **2.** the process of putting the pieces of something together to make it complete

assess /ə'ses/ *verb* **1.** to consider something or someone in order to make a judgment or decision about it ○ *It's hard to assess how difficult it will be to make the necessary changes.* **2.** to consider someone's achievement or progress in order to decide if it is satisfactory ○ *Students are regularly assessed by their teachers and feedback.* **3.** to calculate an amount to be paid ○ *The cost of the new building is assessed at £1 million.*

assignment /ə'saɪnmənt/ *noun* a piece of work that has to be done in a specific time ○ *My literature assignment has to be finished by Wednesday.* ○ *He was given the assignment of reporting on the war.*

assist /ə'sɪst/ *verb* to help someone ○ *He assists me with my income tax forms.* ○ *I will be assisted in my work by Jackie Smith.* (NOTE: You assist someone **in** doing something or **with** something.)

assistance /ə'sɪst(ə)ns/ *noun* help ○ *He asked if he could be of any assistance.* ○ *She will need assistance with her luggage.* ○ *He was trying to change the wheel when a truck driver offered his assistance.*

assistant /ə'sɪst(ə)nt/ *noun* a person who helps someone as part of their job ○ *His assistant makes all his appointments.*

associate[1] /əˈsəʊsieɪt/ *verb* to connect different people or things in your mind ○ *I always associate that book with the wonderful holiday when I first read it.* □ **to be associated with** to be connected with or involved in something

associate[2] /əˈsəʊsiət/ *noun* a person who works in the same business as someone else

association /ə,səʊsiˈeɪʃ(ə)n/ *noun* **1.** an official group of people or a group of companies in the same trade ○ *an association offering support to victims of street violence* ○ *the Association of British Travel Agents* **2.** a connection formed in the mind between things ○ *For some people, a black cat has an association with luck.* ○ *Manchester has strong family associations for him.* **3.** □ **in association with** together with ○ *The guidebook is published in association with the local tourist board.* ○ *This programme is brought to you in association with British Airways.* ◇ **in association with** together with ○ *The guidebook is published in association with the local tourist board.* ○ *This programme is brought to you in association with British Airways.*

assume /əˈsjuːm/ *verb* **1.** to imagine or believe that something is true ○ *Let's assume that he is innocent.* ○ *I assume you have enough money to pay for the meal?* **2.** to take on something such as a job or responsibility ○ *When she was twenty-one, she assumed complete control of the family business.* ○ *He has assumed responsibility for fire safety.*

asthma /ˈæsmə/ *noun* a medical condition in which someone suffers breathing difficulties, often because a particular substance has a bad effect on his or her body

astonish /əˈstɒnɪʃ/ *verb* to surprise someone very much ○ *His success in maths astonished his teacher – he never came to any of her classes.*

astonished /əˈstɒnɪʃt/ *adjective* very surprised ○ *We were astonished to learn that the head teacher had left.*

astonishing /əˈstɒnɪʃɪŋ/ *adjective* very surprising ○ *They spent an aston-* ishing amount of money buying Christmas presents.

at /ət, æt/ *preposition* **1.** used for showing time ○ *We'll meet at eleven o'clock.* ○ *You must put your lights on when you drive at night.* ○ *At the weekend, we went to see my mother.* ○ *We went to Paris at Easter.* **2.** used for showing place ○ *Meet us at the post office.* ○ *She's got a job at the supermarket.* ○ *He's not at home, he's at work.* **3.** used for showing speed ○ *The train was travelling at 200 kilometres an hour.* **4.** showing direction ○ *She threw her slipper at the TV.* **5.** showing cause ○ *She laughed at my old coat.* (NOTE: **at** is often used after verbs, e.g. **to look at**, **to point at**.)

ate /et, eɪt/ past tense of **eat**

athlete /ˈæθliːt/ *noun* a person who takes part in sports especially those such as running

athletic /æθˈletɪk/ *adjective* referring to athletics

athletics /æθˈletɪks/ *noun* organised sports such as running which are competitions between individuals (NOTE: no plural)

atlas /ˈætləs/ *noun* a book of maps (NOTE: The plural is **atlases**.)

atmosphere /ˈætməsfɪə/ *noun* the air around the Earth ○ *The atmosphere surrounds the Earth to a height of several hundred kilometres.* ■ the air in a particular place ○ *The room had a hot stuffy atmosphere.* ■ *noun* a general feeling ○ *The atmosphere in the office was tense.* ○ *I like the friendly atmosphere at our college.*

atom /ˈætəm/ *noun* the smallest part of a chemical element that can exist independently

atomic /əˈtɒmɪk/ *adjective* relating to the energy produced if an atom is split apart

attach /əˈtætʃ/ *verb* to fasten something to something else ○ *The gate is attached to the post.* ○ *I am attaching a copy of my previous letter.*

attached /əˈtætʃt/ *adjective* having a strong liking for someone or something ○ *She's very attached to her old dog.*

attack /ə'tæk/ *noun* **1.** the act of trying to hurt someone or something ○ *They made an attack on the town.* □ **under attack** in the situation of being attacked ○ *The town is under attack from rebel guerrillas.* **2.** a criticism ○ *He launched an attack on the government.* **3.** a sudden return of a particular illness ○ *She had an attack of malaria.* ■ *verb* to try to hurt someone or to hit someone ○ *Three men attacked her as she walked home.* ○ *The old lady was attacked by muggers.*

attacker /ə'tækə/ *noun* a person who attacks someone or something ○ *Can you describe your attacker?*

attempt /ə'tempt/ *noun* to try to do something, especially something difficult ○ *She attempted to lift the box onto the table.* □ **an attempt on someone's life** the action of trying to kill someone ■ *verb* to try to do something, especially something difficult ○ *I'll attempt another trip to collect the books when my car has been repaired.* ○ *She attempted to lift the box onto the table.*

attend /ə'tend/ *verb* **1.** to be present at an event ○ *Twenty-five people attended the wedding.* ○ *They organised a meeting, but only one or two people attended.* **2.** to listen carefully ○ *Students should attend carefully to the teacher's instructions.*

attendant /ə'tendənt/ *noun* a person on duty in a public place such as a museum

attention /ə'tenʃən/ *noun* **1.** the act of concentrating on what you are doing ○ *Don't distract the driver's attention.* ○ *Please give the talk on safety procedures your full attention.* □ **to pay attention to** to concentrate on something and think about it carefully ○ *Pay attention to the instructions in the leaflet.* □ **Don't pay any attention to something** you can ignore something ○ *Don't pay any attention to what she says – she's making it up.* **2.** special care, help or extra work ○ *The garden is large and needs a lot of attention.* ○ *The children were quiet and shy but responded well to the special attention they were given.* □ **medical attention** treatment by doctors and nurses ○ *That cut needs urgent med-*

ical attention. **3.** the position of a soldier, standing straight, with heels together and looking straight ahead ○ *The guards stood to attention at the entrance of the palace.* ◇ **for the attention of** words written on a letter to show that it is intended for a particular person to deal with it ◇ **to attract (someone's) attention** to make someone notice someone or something ○ *The new play has attracted a lot of press attention* or *attention in the press.*

attitude /'ætɪtjuːd/ *noun* **1.** a way of thinking ○ *What is the government's attitude to the problem?* **2.** the position of your body, e.g. standing or sitting ○ *His portrait shows him in a thoughtful attitude.*

attract /ə'trækt/ *verb* to make someone want to come to a place or want to become involved in something such as a business ○ *The shops are lowering their prices to attract more customers.* ○ *The exhibition attracted hundreds of visitors.* ○ *We must see if we can attract more candidates for the job.*

attraction /ə'trækʃən/ *noun* **1.** a reason for liking someone or something ○ *The flat's main attraction is its closeness to the centre of town.* **2.** something which attracts people ○ *The Tower of London is a great tourist attraction.*

attractive /ə'træktɪv/ *adjective* **1.** pleasant to look at ○ *They found the mountain scenery very attractive.* ○ *She's an attractive woman.* **2.** having features which people like ○ *There are some attractive bargains in the sale.* ○ *The rival firm made him a very attractive offer.*

audience /'ɔːdiəns/ *noun* the people watching a performance, e.g. at a theatre or cinema or on television, or listening to a radio programme ○ *Members of the audience cheered.* (NOTE: Takes a singular or plural verb.)

August /'ɔːgəst/ *noun* the eighth month of the year, the month after July and before September ○ *My birthday is in August.* ○ *I left my job last August.* ○ *The letter is dated 15 August.* (NOTE: **August 15th** or **August 15**: say 'August

the fifteenth' or 'the fifteenth of August'
or in US English 'August fifteenth'.)

aunt /ɑːnt/ *noun* the sister of your mother
or father, or the wife of an uncle ○ *She
lives next door to my aunt.* ○ *Say goodbye to Aunt Anne.*

author /ˈɔːθə/ *noun* a writer ○ *She is the
author of a popular series of children's
books.*

authority /ɔːˈθɒrɪti/ *noun* **1.** power to
do something ○ *He has no authority to
act on our behalf.* (NOTE: no plural) **2.**
an organisation that has control over
something ○ *The education authority
pays teachers' salaries.* (NOTE: The plural is **authorities.**)

automatic /ˌɔːtəˈmætɪk/ *adjective* **1.**
working by itself ○ *There is an automatic device which cuts off the electric current.* **2.** done without thinking about it
very much ○ *She gave the receptionist
an automatic smile as she passed.* **3.**
based on an agreement or existing situation ○ *an automatic fine for parking*

automatically /ˌɔːtəˈmætɪkli/ *adverb*
1. by a machine, without people having
to do anything **2.** without thinking about
it very much ○ *I signed the bill automatically.* ■ as a result of an agreement or
existing situation ○ *The company automatically retires people at 60.*

automobile /ˈɔːtəməbiːl/ *noun especially US* a car

autumn /ˈɔːtəm/ *noun* the season of the
year between summer and winter ○ *In
autumn, the leaves turn brown.* ○ *We
went on a walking holiday last autumn.*
○ *I'll be starting my new job in the autumn term.*

auxiliary /ɔːɡˈzɪliəri/ *noun* a person
who helps other workers (NOTE: The
plural is **auxiliaries.**)

available /əˈveɪləb(ə)l/ *adjective* able to
be obtained ○ *The tablets are available
from most chemists.*

avenue /ˈævənjuː/ *noun* a wide street in
a town, often with trees along the side

average /ˈæv(ə)rɪdʒ/ *noun* **1.** the standard that is usual or typical ○ *The journey
time today was much slower than the
bus company's average.* **2.** a total calculated by adding several quantities together and dividing by the number of
different quantities added ○ *the average
for the last three months* or *the last three
months' average* ○ *The temperature has
been above the average for the time of
year.* ■ *adjective* **1.** ordinary or typical
○ *It was an average working day at the
office.* ○ *Their daughter is of above average intelligence.* □ **above** *or* **below
average** more or less than is usual or
typical **2.** not very good ○ *Their results
were only average.* **3.** calculated by dividing the total by the number of quantities ○ *His average speed was 30 miles
per hour.* ■ *verb* to be as an average ○
*Price increases have averaged 10% per
annum.*

avoid /əˈvɔɪd/ *verb* **1.** to keep away from
someone or something ○ *Travel early to
avoid the traffic jams.* ○ *Aircraft fly high
to avoid storms.* **2.** to try not to do something ○ *He's always trying to avoid taking a decision.* (NOTE: You avoid something or avoid **doing** something.) **3.** to
try to prevent something from happening ○ *I want to avoid discussing details
at this stage.* ○ *How can we avoid a
row?*

awake /əˈweɪk/ *adjective* not asleep ○
It's 2 o'clock and I'm still awake. ■ *verb*
1. to wake someone up ○ *He was awok-
en by the sound of the telephone.* (NOTE:
awake in this meaning only occurs in
the passive.) **2.** to wake up ○ *He awoke
when he heard them knocking on the
door.* ○ *They awoke to find a fox in their
tent.* (NOTE: **awakes – awaking –
awoke** /əˈwəʊk/ **– has awoken**)

award /əˈwɔːd/ *noun* something such as
a prize or a gift of money that is given to
someone ○ *a design award* ○ *He received an award of £1000.* ○ *The school
has been nominated for a technology
award.* ■ *verb* to give someone something such as a prize, a degree or diploma, money or a contract to do work ○
He was awarded first prize. ○ *She was
awarded £10,000 in damages.*

aware /əˈweə/ *adjective* knowing something ○ *I'm not aware of any problem.* ○
*Is he aware that we have to decide
quickly?* □ **not that I am aware of** not
as far as I know ○ *Has there ever been*

an accident here before? – Not that I am aware of.

away /ə'weɪ/ *adverb* **1.** at a particular distance or time ○ *The nearest shop is three kilometres away.* **2.** not here, somewhere else ○ *The managing director is away on business.* ○ *My assistant is away today.* **3.** (*in sports*) at your opponents' sports ground ○ *Our team is playing away next Saturday.* **4.** (*as emphasis, after verbs*) without stopping ○ *The birds were singing away in the garden.*

awful /'ɔːf(ə)l/ *adjective* very bad or unpleasant ○ *She felt awful about missing the party.* ○ *He's got an awful cold.* ○ *Turn off the television – that programme's awful!*

awfully /'ɔːf(ə)li/ *adverb* very (*informal*) ○ *It's awfully difficult to contact her.*

awkward /'ɔːkwəd/ *adjective* **1.** embarrassing or difficult to deal with ○ *awkward questions* **2.** difficult to use or deal with because of shape, size or position ○ *The handle's a very awkward shape.* **3.** not convenient ○ *Next Thursday is awkward for me – what about Friday?*

awoke /ə'wəʊk/ past tense of **awake**

awoken /ə'wəʊkən/ past participle of **awake**

axe /æks/ *noun* a tool with a heavy sharp metal head, used for cutting through something ■ *verb* to get rid of something or someone

B

b /biː/, **B** *noun* the second letter of the alphabet, between A and C

baby /'beɪbi/ *noun* **1.** a very young child ○ *Most babies start to walk when they are about a year old.* ○ *I've known him since he was a baby.* **2.** a very young animal ○ *a baby rabbit* (NOTE: The plural is **babies**. If you do not know if a baby is a boy or a girl, you can refer to it as **it**: *The baby was sucking its thumb.*)

back /bæk/ *noun* **1.** the part of the body which is behind you, between the neck and top of the legs ○ *She went to sleep lying on her back.* ○ *He carried his son on his back.* ○ *Don't lift that heavy box, you may hurt your back.* **2.** the opposite part to the front of something ○ *He wrote his address on the back of the envelope.* ○ *She sat in the back of the bus and went to sleep.* ○ *The dining room is at the back of the house.* ■ *adjective* **1.** on the opposite side to the front ○ *He knocked at the back door of the house.* ○ *The back tyre of my bicycle is flat.* **2.** (of money) owed from an earlier date ○ *back pay* ■ *adverb* **1.** towards the back of something ○ *She looked back and waved at me as she left.* **2.** in the past ○ *back in the 1950s* **3.** in the state that something was previously ○ *Put the telephone back on the table.* ○ *She watched him drive away and then went back into the house.* ○ *She gave me back the money she had borrowed.* ○ *I'll phone you when I am back in the office.* (NOTE: **Back** is often used after verbs: **to give back, to go back, to pay back,** etc.) ■ *verb* **1.** to go backwards, or make something go backwards ○ *He backed* or *backed his car out of the garage.* **2.** to encourage and support a person, organisation, opinion or activity, sometimes by giving money ○ *Her colleagues were willing to back the proposal.* ◊ **to put someone's back up** to annoy someone

back up *phrasal verb* **1.** to help or support someone ○ *Nobody would back her up when she complained about the service.* ○ *Will you back me up in the vote?* **2.** to make a car go backwards ○ *Can you back up, please – I want to get out of the parking space.*

background /'bækgraʊnd/ *noun* **1.** the part of a picture or view which is behind all the other things that can be seen ○ *The photograph is of a house with mountains in the background.* ○ *His white shirt stands out against the dark background.* Compare **foreground** □ **in the background** while other more obvious or important things are happening **2.** the experiences, including education and family life, which someone has had ○ *He comes from a working class background.* ○ *Her background is in the restaurant business.* **3.** information about a situation ○ *What is the background to the complaint?*

backward /'bækwəd/ *adverb* US same as **backwards**

backwards /'bækwədz/ *adverb* from the front towards the back ○ *Don't step backwards.* ○ *'Tab' is 'bat' spelt backwards.* □ **backwards and forwards** in one direction, then in the opposite direction ○ *The policeman was walking backwards and forwards in front of the bank.*

bacon /'beɪkən/ *noun* meat from a pig which has been treated with salt or smoke, usually cut into thin pieces

bacteria /bæk'tɪəriə/ *plural noun* very small living things, some of which can cause disease (NOTE: The singular is **bacterium**.)

bacterial /bæk'tɪəriəl/ *adjective* caused by bacteria ○ *a bacterial infection*

bad /bæd/ *adjective* **1.** causing problems, or likely to cause problems ○ *Eating too much fat is bad for your health.* ○ *We* *were shocked at their bad behaviour.* **2.** of poor quality or skill ○ *He's a bad driver.* ○ *She's good at singing but bad at playing the piano.* **3.** unpleasant ○ *He's got a bad cold.* ○ *She's in a bad temper.* ○ *I've got some bad news for you.* ○ *The weather was bad when we were on holiday in August.* **4.** serious ○ *He had a bad accident on the motorway.* (NOTE: **worse** /wɜːs/ – **worst** /wɜːst/)

badge /bædʒ/ *noun* a small sign attached to someone's clothes to show something such as who someone is or what company they belong to

badly /'bædli/ *adverb* **1.** not well or successfully ○ *She did badly in her driving test.* **2.** seriously ○ *He was badly injured in the motorway accident.* **3.** very much ○ *His hair badly needs cutting.* (NOTE: **badly – worse** /wɜːs/ – **worst** /wɜːst/)

bag /bæg/ *noun* **1.** a soft container made of plastic, cloth or paper and used for carrying things ○ *a bag of sweets* ○ *He put the apples in a paper bag.* **2.** same as **handbag** ○ *My keys are in my bag.* **3.** a suitcase or other container used for clothes and other possessions when travelling ○ *Have you packed your bags yet?*

baggage /'bægɪdʒ/ *noun* cases and bags which you take with you when travelling

bake /beɪk/ *verb* to cook food such as bread or cakes in an oven ○ *Mum's baking a cake for my birthday.* ○ *Bake the pizza for 35 minutes.*

baker /'beɪkə/ *noun* a person whose job is to make bread and cakes □ **the baker's** a shop that sells bread and cakes ○ *Can you go to the baker's and get a loaf of brown bread?*

balance /'bæləns/ *noun* **1.** the quality of staying steady ○ *The cat needs a good sense of balance to walk along the top of a fence.* □ **to keep your balance** not to fall over □ **to lose your balance** to fall down ○ *As he was crossing the river on the tightrope he lost his balance and fell.* **2.** an amount of money remaining in an account ○ *I have a balance of £25 in my bank account.* **3.** an amount of money still to be paid from a larger sum owed ○ *You can pay £100 now and the*

balance in three instalments. ○ *The balance outstanding is now £5000.* ■ *verb* **1.** to stay or stand in position without falling ○ *The cat balanced on the top of the fence.* **2.** to make something stay in position without falling ○ *The waiter balanced a pile of dirty plates on his arm.*

balcony /'bælkəni/ *noun* **1.** a small flat area that sticks out from an upper level of a building protected by a low wall or by posts ○ *The flat has a balcony overlooking the harbour.* ○ *Breakfast is served on the balcony.* **2.** the upper rows of seats in a theatre or cinema ○ *We booked seats at the front of the balcony.* (NOTE: The plural is **balconies**.)

bald /bɔːld/ *adjective* having no hair where there used to be hair, especially on the head ○ *His grandfather is quite bald.* ○ *He is beginning to go bald.*

ball /bɔːl/ *noun* **1.** a round object used in playing games, for throwing, kicking or hitting ○ *They played in the garden with an old tennis ball.* ○ *He kicked the ball into the goal.* **2.** any round object ○ *a ball of wool* ○ *He crumpled the paper up into a ball.* **3.** a formal dance ○ *We've got tickets for the summer ball.* ◇ **to start the ball rolling** to start something happening ○ *I'll start the ball rolling by introducing the visitors, then you can introduce yourselves.* ◇ **to play ball** to work well with someone to achieve something ○ *I asked them for a little more time but they won't play ball.* ◇ **to have a ball** to enjoy yourself a lot ○ *You can see from the photos we were having a ball.*

ballet /'bæleɪ/ *noun* **1.** a type of dance, given as a public entertainment, where dancers perform a story to music **2.** a performance of this type of dance ○ *We went to the ballet last night.*

balloon /bə'luːn/ *noun* **1.** a large ball which is blown up with air or gas **2.** a very large balloon which rises as the air inside it is heated, sometimes with a container attached for people to travel in ■ *verb* to increase quickly in size or amount

ban /bæn/ *noun* an official statement which says that people must not do something ○ *There is a ban on smoking in cinemas.* ■ *verb* to say officially that people must not do something ○ *She was banned from driving for three years.* (NOTE: **bans – banning – banned**)

banana /bə'nɑːnə/ *noun* a long yellow, slightly curved fruit which grows in hot countries

band /bænd/ *noun* **1.** a group of people who play music together ○ *The soldiers marched down the street, following the band.* ○ *My brother's in a rock band.* **2.** a group of people who do something together ○ *Bands of drunken football fans were wandering around the streets.* **3.** a narrow piece of something ○ *Her hair was tied back with a red band.* **4.** a long thin mark of a particular colour ○ *a black tee-shirt with a broad band of yellow across the front* **5.** a range of things taken together ○ *He's in the top salary band.* ○ *We're looking for something in the £10 – £15 price band.*

bandage /'bændɪdʒ/ *noun* a cloth for putting around an injured part of the body ○ *The nurse put a bandage round his knee.* ○ *His head was covered in bandages.*

bang /bæŋ/ *noun* a sudden noise like that made by a gun ○ *The car started with a series of loud bangs.* ○ *There was a bang and the tyre went flat.* ■ *verb* to hit something hard, so as to make a loud noise ○ *He banged (on) the table with his hand.* ○ *Can't you stop the door banging?*

bank /bæŋk/ *noun* **1.** a business which holds money for people, and lends them money ○ *I must go to the bank to get some money.* ○ *She took all her money out of the bank to buy a car.* ○ *How much money do you have in the bank?* **2.** land along the side of a river ○ *He sat on the river bank all day, trying to catch fish.* ○ *There is a path along the bank of the canal.* **3.** a long pile of earth, sand, snow or other substance ○ *The road was blocked by banks of snow blown by the wind.* ■ *verb* to store money in a bank ○ *I banked the cheque as soon as it arrived.* ○ *Have you banked the money yet?*

bank account /'bæŋk ə,kaʊnt/ *noun* an arrangement which you make with a bank to keep your money safely until you want it □ **to open a bank account** to start keeping money in a bank ○ *He opened a bank account when he started his first job.*

bank holiday /,bæŋk 'hɒlɪdeɪ/ *noun* a public holiday when most people do not go to work and the banks are closed

bar /bɑː/ *noun* a long piece of something hard ○ *The yard was full of planks and metal bars.* ■ a solid piece of a substance such as chocolate or soap ■ *noun* a place where you can buy and drink alcohol ○ *Let's meet in the bar before dinner.* ■ *preposition* except ○ *All of the suppliers replied bar one.* ○ *All bar two of the players in the team are British.* ■ *verb* **1.** to block something ○ *The road was barred by the police.* ○ *The path is barred to cyclists.* **2.** □ **to bar someone from doing something** to prevent someone officially from doing something ○ *He was barred from playing football for three months.* (NOTE: **bars – barring – barred**)

barbecue /'bɑːbɪkjuː/ *noun* **1.** a metal grill for cooking food on out of doors ○ *Light the barbecue at least half an hour before you start cooking.* **2.** food cooked on a barbecue ○ *Here is a recipe for chicken barbecue.* **3.** a meal or party where food is cooked out of doors ○ *We had a barbecue for twenty guests.* ○ *They were invited to a barbecue.* ■ *verb* to cook something on a barbecue ○ *Barbecued spare ribs are on the menu.* ○ *She was barbecuing sausages for lunch when it started to rain.*

bare /beə/ *adjective* **1.** not covered by clothes or shoes ○ *He walked on the beach in his bare feet.* ○ *I can't sit in the sun with my arms bare.* **2.** without any kind of cover ○ *They slept on the bare floorboards.* ○ *They saw the bare bones of dead animals in the desert.* **3.** without leaves ○ *bare branches* **4.** with just what is really needed and nothing extra ○ *We only took the bare essentials when we went travelling.* ○ *She thought £100 was the bare minimum she would accept.* (NOTE: Do not confuse with **bear.**)

barely /ˈbeəli/ *adverb* almost not ○ *She barely had enough money to pay for her ticket.* ○ *He barely had time to get dressed before the police arrived.* ○ *The noise is barely tolerable.*

bargain /ˈbɑːgɪn/ *noun* **1.** something bought more cheaply than usual ○ *The car was a real bargain at £500.* **2.** an agreement between two people or groups of people □ **into the bargain** as well as other things ○ *The plane was late and they lost my suitcase into the bargain.* ■ *verb* to discuss the terms of an agreement or sale ◇ **more than** *or* **not what you bargained for** different, usually worse, than you had expected

bargain on *phrasal verb* to expect something ○ *I hadn't bargained on it being so wet.* ○ *She's bargaining on someone dropping out so that she can take their place.*

bark /bɑːk/ *noun* **1.** the hard outer layer of a tree **2.** the loud sound a dog makes ○ *The dog gave a bark as we came into the house.*

barn /bɑːn/ *noun* a large farm building for storing produce or for keeping animals or machinery

barrel /ˈbærəl/ *noun* **1.** a container with curved sides for storing liquid ○ *a barrel of beer* ○ *a wine barrel* **2.** the tube of a gun out of which a bullet is fired

barrier /ˈbæriə/ *noun* **1.** a bar or fence which blocks a passage ○ *He lifted the barrier and we drove across the border.* **2.** an action or problem that makes it difficult for something to happen

base /beɪs/ *noun* **1.** the bottom part of something ○ *The table lamp has a flat base.* **2.** a place where you work from ○ *He lives in London but uses Paris as his base when travelling in France.* **3.** something from which something else develops or is produced ○ *The report will provide a good base from which to develop ideas.* ■ *verb* to use something or somewhere as a base ○ *The company is based in Paris.* ○ *The theory is based on research done in Russia.* □ **to be based at** *or* **in** to have a particular place as your main home or place of work ○ *She's based at head office or in Edinburgh.* □ **to base something on some-**thing else to use something as a model for something else ○ *The book is based on her mother's life.* ○ *His theory was based on years of observations.*

baseball /ˈbeɪsbɔːl/ *noun* **1.** an American game for two teams of nine players, in which a player hits a ball with a long, narrow bat and players from the other team try to catch it **2.** the hard ball used in playing baseball

-based /beɪst/ *suffix* **1.** produced or developed from ○ *a milk-based dessert* **2.** living or working at a particular place ○ *a London-based company*

basement /ˈbeɪsmənt/ *noun* a floor in a building below ground level

basic /ˈbeɪsɪk/ *adjective* very simple, or at the first level ○ *Being able to swim is a basic requirement if you are going canoeing.* ○ *Knowledge of basic Spanish will be enough for the job.*

basically /ˈbeɪsɪkli/ *adverb* considering only the most important information and not the details ○ *Basically, he's fed up with his job.*

basin /ˈbeɪs(ə)n/ *noun* **1.** same as **washbasin 2.** a large or small bowl, especially one for holding or mixing food items

basis /ˈbeɪsɪs/ *noun* **1.** the general facts on which something is based ○ *What is the basis for these proposals?* □ **on the basis of** based on ○ *The calculations are done on the basis of an exchange rate of 1.6 dollars to the pound.* **2.** the general terms of an agreement ○ *She is working for us on a temporary basis.* ○ *Many of the helpers at the hospice work on a voluntary basis.* (NOTE: The plural is **bases** /ˈbeɪsiːz/.)

basket /ˈbɑːskɪt/ *noun* a container made of thin pieces of wood, wire or fibre woven together

basketball /ˈbɑːskɪtbɔːl/ *noun* a game played by two teams of five players who try to throw the ball through an open net hung high up at each end of the playing area

bass /beɪs/ *noun* **1.** a male singer with a low-pitched voice **2.** a guitar with a low-pitched sound ■ *adjective* relating to a low-pitched voice or music ○ *He has a pleasant bass voice.* Compare **tenor**

bat /bæt/ *noun* **1.** a piece of wood used for hitting a ball ○ *a baseball bat* ○ *a cricket bat* **2.** a small animal with skin flaps like wings that flies at night and hangs upside down when resting

bath /bɑːθ/ *noun* **1.** a large container in which you can sit and wash your whole body ○ *There's a washbasin and a bath in the bathroom.* (NOTE: The plural is **baths** /bɑːθs/) **2.** □ **to have a bath** to wash your whole body in a bath ■ *verb* to wash yourself or someone else in a bath ○ *She's bathing the baby.* ○ *Do you prefer to bath or shower?* (NOTE: Do not confuse with **bathe**. Note also: **baths** – **bathing** /ˈbɑːθɪŋ/ – **bathed** /bɑːθt/.)

bathe /beɪð/ *verb* **1.** to go into water to swim or wash ○ *Thousands of people come to bathe in the Ganges.* **2.** to wash a cut or damaged part of the body carefully ○ *A nurse bathed the wound on his arm.* **3.** *US* to have a bath ○ *I just have enough time to bathe before my dinner guests arrive.* (NOTE: Do not confuse with **bath**. Note also: **bathes** /beɪðz/ – **bathing** /ˈbeɪðɪŋ/ – **bathed** /beɪðd/.)

bathroom /ˈbɑːθruːm/ *noun* **1.** a room in a house with a bath, a washbasin and usually a toilet ○ *The house has two bathrooms.* **2.** *US* a room containing a toilet ○ *Where's the bathroom?* ○ *Can I use your bathroom, please?*

battery /ˈbæt(ə)ri/ *noun* an object that fits into a piece of electrical equipment to provide it with electric energy ○ *My calculator needs a new battery.* ○ *The battery has given out so I can't use my radio.* ○ *My mobile phone has a rechargeable battery.*

battle /ˈbæt(ə)l/ *noun* **1.** an occasion when large groups of soldiers fight each other using powerful weapons ○ *Many soldiers died in the first battle of the war.* ○ *Wellington won the Battle of Waterloo.* **2.** an attempt to prevent something unpleasant and difficult to deal with ○ *the government's constant battle against crime* ○ *He lost his battle against cancer.* ■ *verb* □ **to battle against** to try to prevent something unpleasant and difficult to deal with ○ *She had to battle against the other members of the board to get the project approved.*

○ *His last years were spent battling against cancer.*

bay /beɪ/ *noun* **1.** an area along a coast where the land curves inwards ○ *a sheltered bay* **2.** a marked or enclosed area used for a particular purpose ○ *a bay marked 'Reserved Parking'*

be /bɪ, biː/ *verb* **1.** used for describing a person or thing ○ *Our house is older than yours.* ○ *She is bigger than her brother.* ○ *Lemons are yellow.* ○ *The soup is hot.* ○ *Put on your coat – it is cold outside.* ○ *I'm cold after standing waiting for the bus.* ○ *Are you tired after your long walk?* **2.** used for showing age or time ○ *He's twenty years old.* ○ *She will be two next month.* ○ *It is nearly ten o'clock.* ○ *It is time to get up.* ○ *September is the beginning of autumn.* **3.** used for showing price ○ *Onions are 80p a kilo.* ○ *The cakes are 50p each.* ○ *My car was worth £10,000 when it was new.* **4.** used for showing someone's job ○ *His father is a bus driver.* ○ *She wants to be a teacher.* **5.** used for showing things such as size, weight, height, ○ *He's 1.70m tall.* ○ *The room is three metres square.* ○ *Our house is ten miles from the nearest station.* **6.** to add up to ○ *Two and two are four.* **7.** used for showing that someone or something exists or is in a particular place ○ *There was a crowd of people waiting for the shop to open.* ○ *There were only two people left on the bus.* ○ *Where are we?* ○ *There's your hat!* (NOTE: **I am**; **you are**; **he/she/it is**; **we/you/they are**; **being**; **I/he/she/it was**; **we/you/they were**; **has been**; negative: **is not** usually **isn't**; **are not** usually **aren't**; **was not** usually **wasn't**; **were not** usually **weren't**.)

beach /biːtʃ/ *noun* an area of sand or small stones by the edge of the sea

beak /biːk/ *noun* the hard part of a bird's mouth

beam /biːm/ *noun* **1.** a long block of wood or metal which supports a structure, especially a roof ○ *You can see the old beams in the ceiling.* **2.** a ray of light ○ *The beam from the car's headlights shone into the barn.* ○ *Beams of sunlight came through the coloured glass.*

■ *verb* to give a big happy smile ○ *The little girl beamed at him.*

bean /biːn/ *noun* a seed or the long thin pod of various different plants, that is cooked and eaten

bear /beə/ *noun* a large wild animal covered with fur ■ *verb* **1.** to carry or support something ○ *The letter bore a London postmark.* ○ *Will this branch bear my weight?* **2.** to accept something bad or unpleasant in a calm way ○ *She bore the bad news bravely.* (NOTE: **bears – bearing – bore** /bɔː/ **– has borne** /bɔːn/) □ **be unable to bear someone** *or* **something** to strongly dislike someone or something ○ *I can't bear the smell of cooking fish.*

beard /bɪəd/ *noun* the hair growing on a man's chin and cheeks ○ *a long white beard*

beat /biːt/ *noun* a regular pattern of sound ○ *The patient's heart has a regular beat.* ○ *They danced to the beat of the drums.* ■ *verb* **1.** to make a regular sound ○ *His heart was still beating when the ambulance arrived.* ○ *Her heart beat faster as she went into the interview.* **2.** to hit something or someone hard ○ *He was beaten by a gang of youths.* **3.** to win a game against another player or team ○ *They beat their rivals into second place.* ○ *Our football team beat France 2 – 0.* ○ *They beat us by 10 goals to 2.* ○ *We beat the Australians at cricket last year.* (NOTE: **beats – beating – beat – has beaten**)

beautiful /ˈbjuːtɪf(ə)l/ *adjective* **1.** physically very attractive ○ *We have three beautiful daughters.* **2.** pleasant or enjoyable ○ *What beautiful weather for a walk.*

beautifully /ˈbjuːtɪf(ə)li/ *adverb* in a very pleasing way

beauty /ˈbjuːti/ *noun* **1.** the quality of being beautiful ○ *an object of great beauty* ○ *the beauty of the tall trees against the background of the blue lake* **2.** a beautiful woman or a beautiful thing ○ *At 18 she was a real beauty.* ○ *Look at these apples, they're real beauties.*

became /bɪˈkeɪm/ past tense of **become**

because /bɪˈkɒz/ *conjunction* for the reason that follows ○ *I was late because I missed the train.* ○ *The dog's wet because he's been in the river.* □ **because of** as a result of ○ *The plane was delayed because of bad weather.*

become /bɪˈkʌm/ *verb* **1.** to change to something different ○ *The sky became dark and the wind became stronger.* ○ *They became good friends.* ○ *As she got older she became rather deaf.* ○ *It soon became obvious that he didn't understand a word of what I was saying.* **2.** to start to work as ○ *He wants to become a doctor.* (NOTE: **becomes – becoming – became – has become**)

bed /bed/ *noun* **1.** a piece of furniture for sleeping on ○ *Lie down on my bed if you're tired.* **2.** a piece of ground for particular plants to grow in ○ *a strawberry bed* ○ *a rose bed* **3.** the ground at the bottom of water ○ *a river bed*

bedroom /ˈbedruːm/ *noun* a room where you sleep ○ *My bedroom is on the first floor.* ○ *The hotel has twenty-five bedrooms.* ○ *Shut your bedroom door if you want to be quiet.*

bee /biː/ *noun* an insect which makes honey, and can sting you

beef /biːf/ *noun* meat from a cow ○ *roast beef* ○ *beef stew*

been /biːn/ past participle of **be**

beer /bɪə/ *noun* **1.** an alcoholic drink made from grain and water ○ *Can I have a glass of beer?* (NOTE: no plural) **2.** a glass or bottle of beer ○ *Three beers, please.*

beetle /ˈbiːt(ə)l/ *noun* an insect with hard covers that protects its folded wings

before /bɪˈfɔː/ *preposition* earlier than ○ *They should have arrived before now.* ○ *You must be home before 9 o'clock.* ○ *G comes before H in the alphabet.* ■ *conjunction* earlier than ○ *The police got there before I did.* ○ *Think carefully before you start to answer the exam questions.* ○ *Wash your hands before you have your dinner.* ○ *Before you sit down, can you switch on the light?* ■ *adverb* earlier ○ *I didn't see him last week, but I had met him before.* ○ *Why didn't you tell me before?*

beg /beg/ *verb* **1.** to ask for things like money or food ○ *She sat begging on the steps of the station.* ○ *Children were begging for food.* **2.** to ask someone in an emotional way to do something or give something ○ *His mother begged him not to go.* ○ *He begged for more time to find the money.* (NOTE: **begs – begging – begged**)

begin /bɪˈgɪn/ *verb* to start doing something ○ *The children began to cry.* ○ *She has begun to knit a red pullover for her father.* ○ *The house is beginning to warm up.* ○ *His surname begins with an S.* ○ *The meeting is due to begin at ten o'clock sharp.* (NOTE: **begins – beginning – began – has begun**) □ **to begin again** to start a second time ○ *She played a wrong note and had to begin again.*

beginner /bɪˈgɪnə/ *noun* a person who is starting to learn something or do something ○ *The course is for absolute beginners.* ○ *I can't paint very well – I'm just a beginner.*

beginning /bɪˈgɪnɪŋ/ *noun* the first part ○ *The beginning of the film is rather boring.*

begun /bɪˈgʌn/ past participle of **begin**

behalf /bɪˈhɑːf/ *noun* □ **on behalf of someone, on someone's behalf** acting for someone ○ *She is speaking on behalf of the trade association.* ○ *He was chosen to speak on the workers' behalf.*

behave /bɪˈheɪv/ *verb* to act in a certain way with someone ○ *He behaved very pleasantly towards his staff.* ○ *She was behaving in a funny way.*

behaviour /bɪˈheɪvjə/ *noun* a way of doing things ○ *His behaviour was quite natural.* ○ *Local people complained about the behaviour of the football fans.*

behind /bɪˈhaɪnd/ *preposition* **1.** at the back of ○ *They hid behind the door.* ○ *I dropped my pen behind the sofa.* ○ *He was second, only three metres behind the winner.* **2.** responsible for ○ *The police believe they know who is behind the bombing campaign.* **3.** supporting ○ *All his colleagues were behind his decision.* ○ *We're behind you!* ■ *adverb* **1.** at the back ○ *He was first, and the rest of the runners were a long way behind.* **2.** later than you should be ○ *I am behind with my correspondence.* ○ *The company has fallen behind schedule with its deliveries.*

being /ˈbiːɪŋ/ *noun* **1.** a person **2.** a living thing, especially one that is not easily recognised **3.** a spiritual or magical force ○ *He dreamt he was being supported by supernatural beings.* **4.** a state of existing □ **to come into being** to start to exist ○ *The association came into being in 1946.*

belief /bɪˈliːf/ *noun* a strong feeling that something is true ○ *his firm belief in the power of law* ○ *her strong belief in God*

believe /bɪˈliːv/ *verb* **1.** to be sure that something is true, although you can't prove it ○ *People used to believe that the earth was flat.* ○ *Don't believe anything he tells you.* **2.** used when you are not absolutely sure of something ○ *I don't believe we've met.* ○ *I believe I have been here before.*

bell /bel/ *noun* **1.** a metal object shaped like a cup which makes a ringing noise when hit by a piece of metal inside it ○ *They rang the church bells at the wedding.* **2.** any object designed to make a ringing noise, especially one that uses electricity ○ *The alarm bell rings if you touch the door.* ○ *The postman rang the door bell.* ○ *You ought to have a bell on your bicycle.* ◇ **to ring a bell** *or* **any bells** to sound familiar or remind you of something ○ *Does the name Forsyth ring a bell?*

belly /ˈbeli/ *noun* the stomach and intestines (*informal*) (NOTE: The plural is **bellies**.)

belong /bɪˈlɒŋ/ *verb* **1.** to be kept in the usual or expected place ○ *That book belongs on the top shelf.* **2.** to be happy to be somewhere or with a group of people ○ *Within a week in my new job I felt I belonged.* **3.** □ **to belong to someone** to be the property of someone ○ *Does the car really belong to you?* **4.** □ **to belong to an organisation** to be a member of an organisation ○ *They still belong to the* *tennis club.* **5.** □ **to belong with** to be a part of or connected to something else ○ *These knives belong with the set in the kitchen.*

below /bɪˈləʊ/ *adverb* lower down ○ *Standing on the bridge we looked at the river below.* ○ *These toys are for children of two years and below.* ■ *preposition* lower down than ○ *The temperature was below freezing.* ○ *In Singapore, the temperature never goes below 25°C.* ○ *Do not write anything below this line.* ○ *These tablets should not be given to children below the age of twelve.* ○ *Can you see below the surface of the water?*

belt /belt/ *noun* a strap which goes round your waist to hold up a skirt or trousers ○ *She wore a skirt with a bright red belt.*

bench /bentʃ/ *noun* a long seat for several people ○ *We sat down on one of the park benches.*

bend /bend/ *noun* a curve in something such as a road or a pipe ○ *Don't drive too fast, there's a sudden bend in the road.* ○ *The pipe under the sink has an awkward bend in it.* ■ *verb* **1.** to move your shoulders and head into a lower position ○ *He bent to pick up the little girl.* ○ *You can reach it if you bend to the left.* **2.** to have the shape of a curve ○ *The road bends suddenly after the bridge.* (NOTE: **bends – bending – bent** /bent/)

bend down *phrasal verb* to move to a lower position, so that your head is lower than your waist ○ *He bent down to pick up the little girl.*

bend over *phrasal verb* to move to a different or a lower position ○ *You can read it if you bend over to the left.* ○ *Bend over till you can touch your toes.* ◇ **to bend over backwards for someone *or* to do something** to do everything you can to help someone ○ *Their friends bent over backwards for* or *to support the family after the accident.*

beneath /bɪˈniːθ/ *preposition* under ○ *There are dangerous rocks beneath the surface of the lake.* ○ *The river flows very fast beneath the bridge.* ■ *adverb* underneath (*formal*) ○ *They stood on the bridge and watched the river flowing beneath.*

beneficial /ˌbenɪˈfɪʃ(ə)l/ *adjective* having a helpful effect

benefit /ˈbenɪfɪt/ *noun* an advantage ○ *What benefit would I get from joining the club?* ■ *verb* **1.** to be useful to someone ○ *The book will benefit anyone who is planning to do some house repairs.* **2.** □ **to benefit from *or* by something** to get an advantage from something ○ *Tourists will benefit from improved transport links.* ○ *Older people can benefit from free bus passes.* (NOTE: **benefits – benefitting – benefitted**)

bent /bent/ *adjective* curved or twisted ○ *These nails are so bent we can't use them.*

berry /ˈberi/ *noun* a small round fruit with several small seeds inside (NOTE: The plural is **berries**. Do not confuse with **bury**.)

beside /bɪˈsaɪd/ *preposition* at the side of someone or something ○ *Come and sit down beside me.* ○ *The office is just beside the railway station.* ◇ **it's beside the point** it's got nothing to do with the main subject ○ *Whether or not the coat matches your hat is beside the point – it's simply too big for you.*

besides /bɪˈsaɪdz/ *preposition* as well as ○ *They have two other cars besides the big Ford.* ○ *Besides managing the shop, he also teaches in the evening.* □ **besides being *or* doing something** in addition to being or doing something ■ *adverb* used for adding another stronger reason for something ○ *I don't want to go for a picnic – besides, it's starting to rain.*

best /best/ *adjective* better than anything else ○ *She's my best friend.* ○ *He put on his best suit to go to the interview.* ○ *What is the best way of getting to London from here?* ■ *noun* the thing which is better than anything else ○ *The picture shows her at her best.* ■ *adverb* in the most effective or successful way ○ *The engine works best when it's warm.* ○ *Oranges grow best in hot countries.* ○ *Which of you knows London best?* ◇ **all the best** best wishes for the future ◇ **as best you can** in the best way you can, even though this may not be perfect ◇ **to do your best** to do as well as you can ◇ **to make the best of something** to take any advantage you can from something ◇ **to make the best of a bad job** to accept a bad situation cheerfully ◇ **to the best of someone's ability** as well as possible ○ *I'll help you to the best of my ability.* ◇ **to the best of my knowledge** as far as I know ◇ **best regards, best wishes** a greeting sent to someone ○ *Give my best wishes to your father.*

bet /bet/ *noun* a sum of money which is risked by trying to say which horse will come first in a race or which side will win a competition ○ *He placed a bet on his friend's horse but lost when the horse came last.* ○ *I've got a bet on Brazil to win the next World Cup.* ■ *verb* to risk money by saying which horse you think will come first in a race or which team will win a competition ○ *He bet me £10 the Prime Minister would lose the election.* ○ *She bet £30 on the horses.* (NOTE: **bets – betting – bet**) ◇ **I bet (you) (that)** *or* **I'll bet (you) (that)** I'm sure that ○ *I bet you she's going to be late*

better /'betə/ *adjective* **1.** good when compared to something else ○ *The weather is better today than it was yesterday.* ○ *His latest book is better than the first one he wrote.* ○ *She's better at maths than English.* ○ *Brown bread is better for you than white.* ○ *We will shop around to see if we can get a better price.* **2.** healthy again ○ *I had a cold last week but I'm better now.* ○ *I hope your sister will be better soon.* ■ *adverb* more successfully than something else ○ *She sings better than her sister.* ○ *My old knife cuts better than the new one.* □ **to think better of something** to decide that something is not a good idea ○ *He was going to drive to London, but thought better of it when he heard the traffic report on the news.* ◇ **for the better** in a way which makes a situation less unpleasant or difficult ○ *Her attitude has changed for the better since we reviewed her responsibilities.* ◇ **had better** *or* **would be better** it would be sensible to ○ *She'd better go to bed if*

she's got flu. ○ *It would be better if you phoned your father now.*

between /bɪ'twiːn/ *preposition* **1.** with people or things on both sides ○ *There's only a thin wall between his office and mine, so I hear everything he says.* ○ *Don't sit between him and his girlfriend.* **2.** connecting two places ○ *The bus goes between Oxford and London.* **3.** in the period after one time and before another ○ *I'm in a meeting between 10 o'clock and 12.* ○ *Can you come to see me between now and next Monday?* **4.** within a range between two amounts or numbers ○ *The parcel weighs between four and five kilos.* ○ *Cherries cost between £2 and £3 per kilo.* **5.** used for comparing two or more things ○ *Sometimes it's not easy to see a difference between blue and green.* ○ *She could choose between courses in German, Chinese or Russian.* **6.** among ◇ **between you and me** speaking privately ◇ **in between** with things on both sides ○ *There's only a thin wall between his bedroom and mine, so I hear everything he says on the phone.*

beware /bɪ'weə/ *verb* to be careful about something that might be dangerous or cause a problem ○ *Beware of cheap imitations.* ○ *You need to beware of being persuaded to spend more than you can afford.*

beyond /bɪ'jɒnd/ *preposition* **1.** further away than ○ *The post office is beyond the bank.* **2.** outside the usual range of something ○ *The delivery date is beyond our control.* ○ *I can't accept new orders beyond the end of next year.* □ **beyond someone's means** too expensive for someone to buy ○ *I'd love to buy a sports car, but I think it would be beyond my means.* **3.** later than ○ *The party went on beyond midnight.*

Bible /'baɪb(ə)l/ *noun* **1.** the holy book of the Christian religion **2.** an important and useful reference book ○ *She keeps an old French recipe book in the kitchen – it's her bible.*

bicycle /'baɪsɪk(ə)l/ *noun* a vehicle with two wheels which you ride by pushing on the pedals ○ *He goes to school by bicycle every day.* ○ *She's going to do the* *shopping on her bicycle.* ○ *He's learning to ride a bicycle.*

bid /bɪd/ *noun* **1.** an offer to buy something at a particular price ○ *His bid for the painting was too low.* **2.** an attempt to do something □ **she made a bid for power** she tried to seize power ■ *verb* to make an offer to buy something at an auction ○ *He bid £500 for the car.* (NOTE: **bids – bidding – bid**)

big /bɪg/ *adjective* of a large size ○ *I don't want a small car – I want a big one.* ○ *His father has the biggest restaurant in town.* ○ *I'm not afraid of him – I'm bigger than he is.* ○ *We had a big order from Germany.* (NOTE: **big – bigger – biggest**)

bike /baɪk/ *noun* a bicycle (*informal*) ○ *He goes to school by bike.* ○ *If the weather's good, we could go for a bike ride.*

bill /bɪl/ *noun* **1.** a piece of paper showing the amount of money you have to pay for something ○ *The total bill came to more than £200.* ○ *Ask the waiter for the bill.* ○ *Don't forget to pay your gas bill.* **2.** same as **beak** ○ *The bird was picking up food with its bill.* **3.** a proposal which, if passed by parliament, becomes law ○ *Parliament will consider the education bill this week.* ○ *He has drafted a bill to ban the sale of guns.* **4.** *US* a piece of paper money ○ *a 10-dollar bill*

billion /ˈbɪljən/ *noun* **1.** one thousand million ○ *The government raises billions in taxes each year.* **2.** one million million (*dated*) **3.** a great many ○ *Billions of Christmas cards are sent every year.* (NOTE: In American English billion has always meant one thousand million, but in British English it formerly meant one million million, and it is still sometimes used with this meaning. With figures it is usually written **bn**: *$5bn* say 'five billion dollars'.)

bin /bɪn/ *noun* **1.** a container for putting rubbish in ○ *Don't throw your litter on the floor – pick it up and put it in the bin.* **2.** a container for keeping things in ○ *a bread bin* ■ *verb* to throw something away into a rubbish bin ○ *He just binned*

the demand for payment. (NOTE: **bins – binning – binned**)

bind /baɪnd/ *verb* **1.** to tie someone's hands or feet so they cannot move ○ *They bound her arms with a rope.* **2.** to tie something or someone to something else ○ *Bind the sticks together with strings.* ○ *They bound him to the chair with strips of plastic.* **3.** to force someone to do something ○ *The contract binds him to make regular payments.* **4.** to put a cover on a book ○ *The book is bound in blue leather.* (NOTE: **binds – binding – bound – has bound**)

biologist /baɪˈɒlədʒɪst/ *noun* a scientist who does research in biology

biology /baɪˈɒlədʒi/ *noun* the study of living things

bird /bɜːd/ *noun* **1.** an animal with wings and feathers, most of which can fly **2.** a young woman (*informal; usually used by men and sometimes regarded as offensive by women*)

birth /bɜːθ/ *noun* the occasion of being born ○ *He was a big baby at birth.* □ **by birth** according to the country someone's parents come from ○ *He is French by birth.* □ **to give birth to a baby** to have a baby ○ *She gave birth to a boy last week.*

birthday /ˈbɜːθdeɪ/ *noun* the date on which someone was born ○ *April 23rd is Shakespeare's birthday.* ○ *My birthday is on 25th June.* ○ *What do you want for your birthday?*

biscuit /ˈbɪskɪt/ *noun* a small flat, usually sweet, hard cake (NOTE: The US term for a sweet biscuit is **cookie**)

bit /bɪt/ *noun* **1.** a little piece ○ *He tied the bundle of sticks together with a bit of string.* ○ *Would you like another bit of cake?* **2.** the smallest unit of information that a computer system can handle ■ *verb* ♦ **bite** ◇ **to bits 1.** into little pieces **2.** very much ○ *thrilled to bits* ◇ **to come *or* fall to bits** to fall apart ○ *The chair has come to bits.* ◇ **to take something to bits** to take something apart in order to repair it ○ *He's taking my old clock to bits.* ◇ **a bit** a little ○ *The painting is a bit too dark.* ○ *She always plays that tune a bit too fast.* ○ *Let him sleep* *a little bit longer.* ○ *Can you wait a bit? I'm not ready yet.* ○ *Have you got a piece of wood a bit bigger than this one?* ◇ **for a bit** for a short period of time ○ *Can you stop for a bit? I'm getting tired.*

bite /baɪt/ *verb* **1.** to cut someone or something with your teeth ○ *The dog tried to bite the postman.* ○ *She bit a piece out of the pie.* **2.** (*of an insect*) to make a small hole in your skin which turns red and itchy ○ *She's been bitten by a mosquito.* (NOTE: **bites – biting – bit** /bɪt/ **– has bitten** /'bɪt(ə)n/) ■ *noun* **1.** a small amount of food that you cut with your teeth in order to eat it ○ *She took a big bite out of the sandwich.* □ **a bite** *or* **a bite to eat** a small meal **2.** a place on someone's body where it has been bitten

bitter /'bɪtə/ *adjective* **1.** not sweet ○ *This black coffee is too bitter.* **2.** angry because something is not fair ○ *She was very bitter about the way the company treated her.* **3.** causing great disappointment or unhappiness ○ *a bitter winter night* ○ *a bitter wind coming from the Arctic* ○ *Losing her job was a bitter blow.*

bitterly /'bɪtəli/ *adverb* strongly ○ *He bitterly regrets what he said.*

bitterness /'bɪtənəs/ *noun* **1.** a bitter taste **2.** angry feelings ○ *His bitterness at being left out of the England team was very obvious.*

black /blæk/ *adjective* **1.** having a very dark colour, the opposite to white ○ *a black and white photograph* ○ *He has black hair.* **2.** belonging to a race of people with dark skin, whose families are African in origin

blackboard /'blækbɔːd/ *noun* a dark board which you can write on with chalk, especially on the wall of a classroom (NOTE: now often called a 'chalkboard')

blade /bleɪd/ *noun* **1.** a sharp cutting part ○ *the blades of a pair of scissors* ○ *Be careful – that knife has a very sharp blade.* **2.** a thin leaf of grass **3.** one of the long flat parts that spin round on some aircraft engines or to keep a helicopter in the air

blame /bleɪm/ *noun* criticism for having done something wrong ○ *I'm not going to take the blame for something I didn't do.* □ **to get the blame for something** to be accused of something ○ *Who got the blame for breaking the window? – Me, of course!* □ **to take the blame for something** to accept that you were responsible for something bad ■ *verb* □ **to blame someone for something, to blame something on someone** to say that someone is responsible for something ○ *Blame my sister for the awful food, not me.* ○ *He blamed the accident on the bad weather.* □ **I don't blame you** I think you're right to do that ○ *I don't blame you for being annoyed, when everyone else got a present and you didn't.* □ **you have only yourself to blame** no one else is responsible for what happened ○ *You have only yourself to blame if you missed the chance of a free ticket.* □ **to be to blame for** to be responsible for something ○ *The manager is to blame for the bad service.*

blank /blæŋk/ *adjective* not containing any information, sound or writing, e.g. ○ *She took a blank piece of paper and drew a map.* ○ *Have we got any blank videos left?* ■ *noun* an empty space, especially on a printed form, for something to be written in ○ *Just fill in the blanks on the second page – age, occupation, etc.* ◇ **to go blank** to be unable to remember something ○ *I went blank when they asked what I was doing last Tuesday.* ○ *When he asked for my work phone number, my mind just went blank.*

blank out *phrasal verb* **1.** to cross out or cover a piece of writing ○ *The surname had been blanked out.* **2.** to try to forget something deliberately ○ *She blanked out the days* or *the memory of the days immediately after the car crash.*

blanket /'blæŋkɪt/ *noun* **1.** a thick cover which you put over you to keep warm ○ *He woke up when the blankets fell off the bed.* ○ *She wrapped the children up in blankets to keep them warm.* **2.** a thick layer ○ *a blanket of leaves* ○ *A blanket of snow covered the fields.* ○ *The motorway was covered in a blanket* *of fog.* **3.** a barrier to protect something ○ *a blanket of secrecy* ■ *adjective* affecting everything or everyone ○ *a blanket ban on smoking*

blankly /'blæŋkli/ *adverb* not showing any reaction or emotion ○ *When the teacher asked him about his homework he just stared at her blankly.*

blast /blɑːst/ *noun* **1.** an explosion ○ *Several windows were shattered by the blast.* **2.** a strong current of wind ○ *an icy blast from the north* **3.** a sharp loud sound from a signal or whistle ○ *Three blasts of the alarm means that passengers should go on deck.* ■ *verb* to destroy with a bomb or bullets ○ *The burglars blasted their way into the safe.* ○ *They blasted their way out of the police trap.*

blaze /bleɪz/ *verb* to burn or shine strongly ○ *The fire was blazing.* ○ *The sun blazed through the clouds.* ■ *noun* a large bright fire ○ *The house was burned down in the blaze.*

bleed /bliːd/ *verb* to lose blood ○ *His chin bled after he cut himself shaving.* ○ *He was bleeding heavily from his wound.* (NOTE: **bleeds – bleeding – bled** /bled/)

blend /blend/ *noun* something, especially a substance, made by mixing different things together ○ *different blends of coffee* ■ *verb* **1.** to mix things together ○ *Blend the eggs, milk and flour together.* **2.** (*of colours*) to go well together ○ *The grey curtains blend with the pale wallpaper.*

bless /bles/ *verb* to make something holy by prayers ○ *The church was blessed by the bishop.* (NOTE: **blesses – blessing – blessed** /blest/) ◇ **to be blessed with** to experience happiness or good things ○ *They were blessed with two healthy children.* ◇ **bless you** said when someone sneezes

blew /bluː/ past tense of **blow**

blind /blaɪnd/ *adjective* not able to see ○ *He went blind in his early forties.* (NOTE: Some people avoid this word as it can cause offence and prefer terms such as **visually impaired** or **partially sighted**.) ■ *verb* to make someone un-

able to see, especially for a short time ○ *She was blinded by the bright lights of the oncoming cars.*

blindness /'blaɪndnəs/ *noun* the state of not being able to see ○ *The disease can cause blindness.* (NOTE: Some people avoid this term as it can cause offence and prefer **visual impairment**.)

blink /blɪŋk/ *noun* to close your eyes and open them again very quickly ○ *The sudden flash of light made him blink.* ■ *verb* (*of lights*) to go on and off ○ *The alarm light is blinking.*

block /blɒk/ *noun* **1.** a large building ○ *They live in a block of flats.* **2.** a large piece ○ *Blocks of ice were floating in the river.* **3.** something that prevents something happening ○ *a block on making payments* □ **to put a block on something** to stop something happening **4.** same as **blockage 1 5.** *US* a section of buildings surrounded by streets ○ *He lives two blocks away.* ■ *verb* to prevent something from passing along something ○ *The pipe is blocked with dead leaves.* ○ *The crash blocked the road for hours.*

blockage /'blɒkɪdʒ/ *noun* **1.** something which prevents movement ○ *There's a blockage further down the drain.* **2.** the state of being blocked

blood /blʌd/ *noun* the red liquid that flows around the body

blossom /'blɒs(ə)m/ *noun* **1.** the mass of flowers that appears on trees in the spring ○ *The hedges are covered with hawthorn blossom.* ○ *The trees are in full blossom.* **2.** a single flower ■ *verb* to produces flowers ○ *The roses were blossoming round the cottage door.*

blouse /blaʊz/ *noun* a woman's shirt

blow /bləʊ/ *verb* **1.** (*of air or wind*) to move ○ *The wind had been blowing hard all day.* **2.** to push air out from your mouth ○ *Blow on your soup if it's too hot.* (NOTE: **blows – blowing – blew – has blown**) □ **to blow your nose** to blow air through your nose into a handkerchief, especially if you have a cold ○ *She has a cold and keeps having to blow her nose.* ■ *noun* **1.** a knock or hit with the hand ○ *He received a blow to the* *head in the fight.* **2.** a shock, which comes from bad news ○ *The election result was a blow to the government.*

blow away *phrasal verb* **1.** to go away by blowing ○ *His hat blew away.* **2.** to make something go away by blowing ○ *The wind will blow the fog away.*

blow down *phrasal verb* **1.** to make something fall down by blowing ○ *Six trees were blown down in the storm.* **2.** to fall down by blowing ○ *The school fence has blown down.*

blow off *phrasal verb* to make something go away by blowing ○ *The wind blew his hat off.*

blow out *phrasal verb* to make something go out by blowing ○ *She blew out the candles on her birthday cake.*

blow over *phrasal verb* **1.** (*of a storm or a difficult situation*) to end ○ *We hope the argument will soon blow over.* **2.** to knock something down by blowing ○ *The strong winds blew over several trees.*

blow up *phrasal verb* **1.** to make something get bigger by blowing into it ○ *He blew up balloons for the party.* ○ *Your front tyre needs blowing up.* **2.** to destroy something by making it explode ○ *The soldiers blew up the railway bridge.* **3.** to make a photograph bigger ○ *The article was illustrated with a blown-up picture of the little girl and her stepfather.*

blue /bluː/ *adjective* of the colour of the sky ○ *He wore a pale blue shirt.* ○ *They live in the house with the dark blue door.* ■ *noun* the colour of the sky ○ *Is there a darker blue than this available?* ◇ **out of the blue** suddenly ○ *Out of the blue came an offer of a job in Australia.*

blues /bluːz/ *plural noun* sad songs from the southern US ○ *Bessie Smith, the great blues singer.*

blunder /ˈblʌndə/ *noun* a big mistake, often one that causes a lot of embarrassment ○ *A dreadful blunder by the goalkeeper allowed their opponents to score.*

blunt /blʌnt/ *adjective* **1.** not sharp ○ *He tried to cut the meat with a blunt knife.*

2. almost rude ○ *His blunt manner often upset people.*

bluntly /ˈblʌntli/ *adverb* in a direct way that may upset people

blurred /blɜːd/ *adjective* not clearly seen ○ *The paper printed a blurred photograph of the suspect.*

blush /blʌʃ/ *verb* to go red in the face because you are ashamed or embarrassed ○ *She blushed when he spoke to her.*

board /bɔːd/ *noun* **1.** a long flat piece of something such as wood ○ *The floor of the bedroom was just bare boards.* **2.** a blackboard or chalkboard ○ *The teacher wrote on the board.*

boast /bəʊst/ *verb* **1.** to have something good ○ *The house boasts a large garden and pond.* ○ *The town boasts an 18-hole golf course.* **2.** to say how good or successful you are ■ *noun* the act of talking about things that you are proud of ○ *Their proudest boast is that they never surrendered.*

boat /bəʊt/ *noun* a small vehicle that people use for moving on water ○ *They sailed their boat across the lake.* ○ *They went to Spain by boat.* ○ *When is the next boat to Calais?* ◇ **in the same boat** in the same difficult situation ○ *Don't expect special treatment – we're all in the same boat.*

body /ˈbɒdi/ *noun* **1.** the whole of a person or of an animal ○ *He had pains all over his body.* (NOTE: The plural is **bodies.**) **2.** the main part of an animal or person, but not the head and arms and legs ○ *She had scars on the arms and upper part of her body.* (NOTE: The plural is **bodies.**) **3.** the body of a dead person or animal ○ *The dead man's body was found in the river.* ○ *Bodies of infected cows were burnt in the fields.* **4.** the main structure of a vehicle ○ *The factory used to make car bodies.* **5.** the main part of something ○ *You'll find the details in the body of the report.* (NOTE: The plural is **bodies.**) **6.** the thickness of hair ○ *The shampoo will give your hair body.* (NOTE: no plural)

bodyguard /ˈbɒdiɡɑːd/ *noun* **1.** a person who guards someone ○ *The man was stopped by the president's body-*

guards. **2.** a group of people who guard someone ○ *He has a bodyguard of six people* or *a six-man bodyguard.*

boil /bɔɪl/ *verb* **1.** (*of water or other liquid*) to form bubbles and change into steam or gas because of being heated ○ *Put the egg in when you see that the water's boiling.* ○ *Don't let the milk boil.* **2.** to heat a liquid until it changes into steam ○ *Can you boil some water so we can make tea?* **3.** to cook food such as vegetables or eggs in boiling water ○ *Boil the potatoes in a large pan.* ■ *noun* an infected swelling ○ *He has a boil on the back of his neck.*

boiling /'bɔɪlɪŋ/ *adjective* **1.** which has started to boil (i.e. for water, at 100°C) ○ *Put the potatoes in a pan of boiling water.* **2.** also **boiling hot** very hot ○ *It is boiling in this room.*

bolt /bəʊlt/ *noun* **1.** a long piece of metal with a screw, fastened with a round piece of metal called a nut ○ *The legs of the table are secured to the top with bolts.* **2.** a long piece of metal which you slide into a hole to lock a door ○ *She pulled back the bolts.* **3.** □ **to make a bolt for it** to run away ○ *When the guards weren't looking two prisoners tried to make a bolt for it.* ■ *verb* **1.** to run fast suddenly ○ *The horse bolted.* **2.** to run away from someone or something ○ *When the boys saw him coming, they bolted.* **3.** to fasten something with a bolt ○ *He bolted the door when he went to bed.* ○ *The tables are bolted to the floor.* ◇ **to make a bolt for something** to rush towards something ○ *At the end of the show everyone made a bolt for the door.* ◇ **to make a bolt for it** to run away from someone or something ○ *When the guards weren't looking two prisoners tried to make a bolt for it.*

bomb /bɒm/ *noun* a weapon which explodes, and can be dropped from an aircraft or placed somewhere by hand ○ *The bomb was left in a suitcase in the middle of the station.* ○ *They phoned to say that a bomb had been planted in the main street.* ○ *Enemy aircraft dropped bombs on the army base.* ■ *verb* to drop bombs on something ○ *Enemy aircraft bombed the power station.*

bombing /'bɒmɪŋ/ *noun* an occasion when someone attacks a place with a bomb or bombs ○ *bombings in centre of major cities* ○ *a bombing raid by enemy aircraft*

bone /bəʊn/ *noun* one of the solid pieces in the body, which make up the skeleton ○ *He fell over and broke a bone in his leg.* ○ *Be careful when you're eating fish – they have lots of little bones.*

bonfire /'bɒnfaɪə/ *noun* a fire made outdoors

bonnet /'bɒnɪt/ *noun* **1.** the metal cover over the front part of a car, covering the engine ○ *He lifted up the bonnet and looked at the steam pouring out of the engine.* **2.** a hat with strings that tie under the chin

bonus /'bəʊnəs/ *noun* **1.** extra money ○ *Sales staff earn a bonus if they sell more than their target.* **2.** an advantage ○ *It was a bonus that the plane arrived early, as we were able to catch an earlier bus home.* (NOTE: The plural is **bonuses.**) □ **added bonus** an additional advantage ○ *I prefer this job and it's an added bonus that I can walk to work.*

bony /'bəʊni/ *adjective* **1.** thin, so that the bones can be seen easily ○ *She was riding a bony horse.* ○ *He grabbed her arm with his bony hand.* **2.** (*of fish*) with many bones ○ *I don't like kippers, they're usually too bony.* (NOTE: **bonier – boniest**)

book /bʊk/ *noun* **1.** sheets of printed paper attached together, usually with a stiff cover ○ *I'm reading a book on the history of London.* ○ *He wrote a book about butterflies.* **2.** sheets of paper to write or draw on, attached together in a cover. ◊ **exercise book, notebook, sketchbook** ■ *verb* to reserve a place, a seat, a table in a restaurant or a room in a hotel ○ *We have booked a table for tomorrow evening.* □ **to book someone on** or **onto a flight** to order a plane ticket for someone else ○ *I've booked you on the 10 o'clock flight to New York.*

booking /'bʊkɪŋ/ *noun* an arrangement to have something such as a seat, hotel room or a table in a restaurant kept for you

boom /buːm/ *noun* **1.** a sudden increase in the amount of money being earned in a country or region, or by a business ○ *The economy is improving and everyone is forecasting a boom for next year.* **2.** a loud deep noise, like the sound of an explosion ○ *There was such a loud boom that everyone jumped.* ■ *verb* **1.** to increase ○ *The economy is booming.* ○ *Sales to Europe are booming.* **2.** to make a loud deep noise ○ *His voice boomed across the square.*

boot /buːt/ *noun* a strong shoe which covers your foot and your ankle or the lower part of your leg ○ *long black riding boots* ○ *walking boots* ○ *ankle boots*

boot up *phrasal verb* **1.** to make a computer start **2.** (*of a computer*) to be started up and made ready for use

border /ˈbɔːdə/ *noun* **1.** an imaginary line between countries or regions ○ *They crossed the border into Switzerland.* ○ *The enemy shelled several border towns.* ○ *He was questioned by the border guards.* **2.** a pattern around the edge of something ○ *I don't like the pink border on the scarf.* **3.** a patch of soil at the side of a path or an area of grass where flowers or bushes are planted ■ *verb* to be along the edge of something ○ *The path is bordered with rose bushes.* ○ *The new houses border the west side of the park.*

border on *phrasal verb* same as **border** *verb*

bore /bɔː/ *noun* a dull person who is not very interesting ○ *I don't want to sit next to him, he's such a bore.* ■ *verb* to make a hole in something ○ *Bore three holes close together.*

bored /bɔːd/ *adjective* not interested in what is happening ○ *You get very bored having to do the same work every day.* ○ *I'm bored – let's go out to the club.*

boredom /ˈbɔːdəm/ *noun* the state of being bored

boring /ˈbɔːrɪŋ/ *adjective* not interesting ○ *I don't want to watch that TV programme – it's boring.*

born /bɔːn/ *verb* to come out of your mother's body and begin to live ○ *He*

was born in Scotland. ○ *She was born in 1989.* ○ *The baby was born last week.*

borne /bɔːn/ past participle of **bear**

borrow /ˈbɒrəʊ/ *verb* **1.** to take something for a short time, usually with the permission of the owner ○ *She borrowed three books from the school library.* ○ *He wants to borrow one of my CDs.* **2.** to take money for a time, usually from a bank ○ *Companies borrow from banks to finance their business.* ○ *She borrowed £100,000 from the bank to buy a flat.* Compare **lend**

boss /bɒs/ *noun* the person in charge, especially the owner of a business ○ *If you want a day off, ask the boss.* ○ *I left because I didn't get on with my boss.* (NOTE: The plural is **bosses**.)

both /bəʊθ/ *adjective, pronoun* two people or things together ○ *Hold onto the handle with both hands.* ○ *Both my shoes have holes in them.* ○ *Both her brothers are very tall.* ○ *She has two brothers, both of them in Canada.* ○ *She and her brother both go to the same school.* ○ *I'm talking to both of you.*

bother /ˈbɒðə/ *noun* trouble or worry ○ *We found the shop without any bother.* ○ *It was such a bother getting packed that we nearly didn't go on holiday.* ■ *verb* **1.** to make someone feel slightly angry, especially by disturbing them ○ *It bothers me that everyone is so lazy.* ○ *Stop bothering me – I'm trying to read.* **2.** □ **to bother to do something** to take the time or trouble to do something ○ *Don't bother to come with me to the station – I can find my way easily.*

bottle /ˈbɒt(ə)l/ *noun* **1.** a tall plastic or glass container for liquids, usually with a narrow part at the top ○ *He opened two bottles of red wine.* ○ *She drank the water straight out of the bottle.* ○ *He bought his wife a bottle of perfume on the plane.* **2.** confidence (*informal*) ○ *He hasn't got the bottle to do it.* ■ *verb* to put in bottles ○ *The wine is bottled in Germany.* ○ *Only bottled water is safe to drink.*

bottled /ˈbɒt(ə)ld/ *adjective* sold in bottles

bottom /'bɒtəm/ *noun* **1.** the lowest point ○ *The ship sank to the bottom of the sea.* ○ *Turn left at the bottom of the hill.* ○ *Is there any honey left in the bottom of the jar?* **2.** the far end ○ *Go down to the bottom of the street and you will see the station on your left.* ○ *The shed is at the bottom of the garden.* **3.** the part of the body on which you sit ○ *Does my bottom look big in these trousers?* ■ *plural noun* **bottoms** the lower part of a set of clothes ○ *He was wearing just his track suit bottoms.* ■ *adjective* lowest ○ *The jam is on the bottom shelf.* ○ *He was standing on the bottom rung of the ladder.*

bought /bɔːt/ past tense and past participle of **buy**

bounce /baʊns/ *noun* **1.** a movement of something such as a ball when it hits a surface and moves away again ○ *He hit the ball on the second bounce.* **2.** energy ○ *She's always full of bounce.* ■ *verb* to spring up and down or off a surface ○ *The ball bounced down the stairs.* ○ *He kicked the ball but it bounced off the post.* ○ *In this game you bounce the ball against the wall.*

bound /baʊnd/ *noun* a big jump ■ *adjective* **1.** very likely ○ *They are bound to be late.* **2.** obliged ○ *He felt bound to help her.* ○ *He is bound by the contract he signed last year.* **3.** tied up ○ *a bundle of old letters bound with pink ribbon* ○ *The burglars left him bound hand and foot.* ■ *verb* to make a big jump, or move fast suddenly ○ *She bounded into the room.* ○ *He bounded out of his chair.* ○ *The dog bounded into the bushes.* ◇ **bound for** on the way to ○ *a ship bound for the Gulf*

boundary /'baʊnd(ə)ri/ *noun* an imaginary line or physical barrier separating two things ○ *Their behaviour crossed the boundary between unkindness and cruelty.* ○ *The white fence marks the boundary between the two gardens.*

bow /baʊ/ *noun* **1.** the act of bending your body forwards as a greeting or sign of respect ○ *He made a deep bow to the audience.* □ **to take a bow** to stand on a stage and bend forwards to thank the audience ○ *The actors took their bows one after the other.* **2.** the front part of a ship ■ *verb* **1.** to bend your body forward as a greeting or sign of respect ○ *He bowed to the queen.* **2.** to bend your head forwards ○ *She bowed her head over her books.*

bowl /bəʊl/ *noun* **1.** a wide, round container for something such as food or water ○ *Put the egg whites in a bowl and beat them.* **2.** the food or liquid contained in a bowl ○ *He was eating a bowl of rice.* ○ *A bowl of hot thick soup is just what you need in this cold weather.* ■ *verb* **1.** (*especially in cricket*) to throw a ball to a batsman □ **to bowl someone (out)** to throw the ball to someone and hit his or her wicket **2.** (*in a game of bowls*) to roll a bowl along the ground to try to get close to the target

box /bɒks/ *noun* **1.** a container made of wood, plastic, cardboard or metal, with a lid ○ *The cakes came in a cardboard box.* **2.** a container and its contents ○ *He took a box of matches from his pocket.* ○ *He gave her a box of chocolates for her birthday.* ■ *verb* to fight by punching, especially when wearing special thick gloves ○ *He learnt to box at a gym in the East End.*

boxing /'bɒksɪŋ/ *noun* a sport in which two opponents fight each other in a square area wearing special thick gloves

boy /bɔɪ/ *noun* **1.** a male child ○ *A boy from our school won the tennis match.* ○ *I knew him when he was a boy.* **2.** a son ○ *Her three boys are all at university.* **3.** □ **the boys** men who are friends, or who play sport together (*informal*)

boyfriend /'bɔɪfrend/ *noun* a young or older man that someone is having a romantic relationship with ○ *She's got a new boyfriend.* ○ *She brought her boyfriend to the party.*

bra /brɑː/ *noun* a piece of women's underwear worn to support the breasts

bracelet /'breɪslət/ *noun* a piece of jewellery worn around your wrist or arm

brain /breɪn/ *noun* **1.** the nerve centre in the head, which controls all the body **2.** intelligence □ **to use your brain** to think sensibly □ **she's got brains**, **she's got a good brain** she's intelligent

brainy /'breɪni/ *adjective* very intelligent (*informal*) (NOTE: **brainier – brainiest**)

brake /breɪk/ *noun* a part of a vehicle used for stopping or making it go more slowly ○ *Put the brake on when you go down a hill.* ○ *The brakes aren't working!* ■ *verb* to slow down by pressing a vehicle's brakes ○ *The driver of the little white van braked, but too late to avoid the dog.*

branch /brɑːntʃ/ *noun* **1.** a thick part of a tree, growing out of the main part ○ *He hit his head against a low branch.* **2.** a local office of an organisation ○ *He's the manager of our local branch of Lloyds Bank.* ○ *The store has branches in most towns in the south of the country.* **3.** one part of something larger ○ *Genetics is a branch of biology.* ○ *I'm not in contact with the Irish branch of my family.* **4.** a section of a road, railway line or river that leads to or from the main part ■ *verb* to divide into two or more parts

brand /brænd/ *noun* a product with a name, made by a particular company ○ *a well-known brand of soap* ■ *verb* to describe someone or something publicly as bad ○ *He was branded as a thief.* ○ *The minister was publicly branded a liar in the newspaper.*

brand name /'brænd neɪm/ *noun* the official name of a product

brand-new /ˌbrænd 'njuː/ *adjective* completely new

brass /brɑːs/ *noun* **1.** a shiny yellow metal used for making things such as some musical instruments and door handles ○ *The doctor has a brass name plate on his door.* **2.** musical instruments made of brass, such as trumpets or trombones ○ *the brass section of the orchestra* ○ *He has composed several pieces of music for brass.*

brave /breɪv/ *adjective* not afraid of doing unpleasant or dangerous things ○ *It was very brave of him to dive into the river to rescue the little girl.* (NOTE: **braver – bravest**) ■ *verb* to accept unpleasant or dangerous conditions in order to achieve something ○ *We braved the Saturday crowds in the supermarket because we needed bread and milk.*

bravely /'breɪvli/ *adverb* in a brave way

bravery /'breɪvəri/ *noun* the ability to do dangerous or unpleasant things without being afraid ○ *We admired her bravery in coping with the illness.* ○ *He won an award for bravery.*

bread /bred/ *noun* food made from flour and water baked in an oven ○ *Can you get a loaf of bread from the baker's?* ○ *She cut thin slices of bread for sandwiches.*

breadth /bredθ/ *noun* **1.** a measurement of how wide something is ○ *The breadth of the piece of land is over 300m.* **2.** the fact of being full or complete ○ *His answers show the breadth of his knowledge of the subject.* ◇ **the length and breadth of something** everywhere in a place ○ *We walked the length and breadth of the field but found no mushrooms.*

break /breɪk/ *verb* **1.** to make something divide into pieces accidentally or deliberately ○ *He dropped the plate on the floor and broke it.* ○ *She broke her leg when she was skiing.* ○ *Break the chocolate into four pieces.* **2.** to divide into pieces accidentally ○ *The clock fell on the floor and broke.* **3.** to fail to carry out the terms of a contract or a rule ○ *The company has broken its agreement.* □ **to break a promise** not to do what you had promised to do ○ *He broke his promise and wrote to her again.* **4.** □ **to break it** or **to break the news to someone** to tell someone bad news ○ *We will have to break it to her as gently as possible.* (NOTE: Do not confuse with **brake**. Note also **breaks – breaking – broke** /brəʊk/ **– has broken** /'brəʊkən/.) ■ *noun* **1.** a short pause or rest ○ *There will be a 15-minute break in the middle of the meeting.* □ **without a break** without stopping ○ *They worked without a break.* □ **to take a break** to have a short rest ○ *We'll take a break now, and start again in fifteen minutes.* **2.** a short holiday ○ *a winter break* ◇ **to break your journey** to stop travelling for a while before going on ○ *We'll break our journey in Edinburgh.*

break down *phrasal verb* **1.** (*of a machine*) to stop working ○ *The lift has* *broken down again.* ○ *The car broke down and we had to push it.* **2.** to show all the items that are included in a total separately ○ *Can you break down this invoice into travel costs and extras?* **3.** to become upset and start crying ○ *When she got her results she just broke down.* **4.** to separate a substance into small parts, or to become separated ○ *Enzymes break down the food.* **5.** to fail ○ *Their relationship quickly broke down when he lost his job.* ○ *The discussions seem likely to break down over the amount of money being offered.*

break in *phrasal verb* **1.** □ **to break in, to break into a building** to use force to get into a building ○ *Burglars broke into the office during the night.* **2.** to interrupt something that is happening ○ *I'm sorry to break in, but I need to speak to Mr McGregor urgently.*

break into *phrasal verb* to start doing something ○ *When they saw the photos, they broke into laughter.*

break off *phrasal verb* **1.** to make something come off by breaking ○ *He broke a piece off his pie and gave it to the dog.* **2.** to come off by breaking ○ *The handle broke off the cup in the dishwasher.* ○ *Several branches broke off in the wind.* **3.** to stop something suddenly ○ *He broke off in the middle of his story.* ○ *They broke off the discussions.* □ **to break it off** to end a relationship ○ *They were going to get married, but she broke it off.*

break out *phrasal verb* **1.** to start ○ *War broke out between the countries in the area.* **2.** to escape ○ *Three prisoners broke out of jail.*

break up *phrasal verb* **1.** to divide into pieces ○ *The oil tanker was breaking up on the rocks.* **2.** (*of a meeting*) to end ○ *The meeting broke up at 3 p.m.*

breakable /ˈbreɪkəb(ə)l/ *adjective* that can break easily

breakdown /ˈbreɪkdaʊn/ *noun* **1.** a situation in which someone cannot continue to live normally any more because they are mentally ill or very tired **2.** a situation in which a machine or vehicle stops working ○ *We had a breakdown*

on the motorway. ○ *A breakdown truck came to tow us to the garage.*

breakfast /ˈbrekfəst/ *noun* the first meal of the day ○ *I had a boiled egg for breakfast.* ○ *She didn't have any breakfast because she was in a hurry.* ○ *The hotel serves breakfast from 7.30 to 9.30 every day.*

breast /brest/ *noun* **1.** one of two parts on a woman's chest which produce milk **2.** meat from the chest part of a bird ○ *We bought some chicken breasts to make a stir-fry.*

breath /breθ/ *noun* air which goes into and out of the body through the nose or mouth ○ *We could see our breath in the cold air.* □ **out of breath, gasping for breath** having difficulty in breathing ○ *He was out of breath after running all the way to the station.* □ **to hold your breath** to keep air in your lungs, e.g. in order to go under water ○ *She held her breath under water for a minute.* □ **to take a deep breath** to breathe in as much air as you can ◇ **to take someone's breath away** to surprise someone very much ○ *The beautiful view just took our breath away.* ◇ **under your breath** quietly ○ *He swore under his breath.* ◇ **don't hold your breath** don't expect it to happen ○ *He said he'll pay us next month, but don't hold your breath!*

breathe /briːð/ *verb* to take air into the lungs or let it out ○ *Relax and breathe in and then out slowly.* □ **to breathe deeply** to take a lot of air into the lungs □ **breathing down someone's neck** always watching and judging what someone is doing

breathless /ˈbreθləs/ *adjective* finding it difficult to breathe

breed /briːd/ *noun* a group of animals or plants specially developed with features that make it different from others of the same type ■ *verb* **1.** to produce young animals ○ *Rabbits breed very rapidly.* **2.** to keep animals which produce young ones ○ *They breed sheep for the meat and the wool.* (NOTE: **breeds – breeding – bred** /bred/)

breeze /briːz/ *noun* a slight wind ○ *A cool breeze is welcome on a hot day like* *this.* ■ *verb* to walk around looking very pleased with yourself ○ *He breezed into the meeting carrying a cup of coffee.*

breeze through *phrasal verb* to do something without any difficulty ○ *She breezed through the tests in an hour.*

brick /brɪk/ *noun* a hard block of baked clay used for building

bride /braɪd/ *noun* a woman who is getting married or has just married

bridge /brɪdʒ/ *noun* **1.** a road or path built over a road or river so that you can walk or drive from one side to the other **2.** a connection or helpful link between two things ○ *A shared interest can be a bridge between old and young.*

brief /briːf/ *adjective* short ○ *He wrote a brief note of thanks.* ○ *The meeting was very brief.* ◇ **in brief** in a few words, or without giving details ○ *We have food for only a few days; in brief, the situation is very serious.*

briefcase /ˈbriːfkeɪs/ *noun* a case for carrying papers or documents

briefly /ˈbriːfli/ *adverb* **1.** for a short time **2.** in a few words, or without giving details

bright /braɪt/ *adjective* **1.** full of light or sunlight ○ *a bright day* ○ *a bright room* □ **bright sunshine** *or* **sunlight** strong clear light from the sun **2.** (*of a colour*) very strong ○ *They have painted their front door bright orange.* **3.** a young person who is bright is intelligent ○ *Both children are very bright.* ○ *She's the brightest student we've had for many years.* **4.** clear and sunny ○ *There will be bright periods during the afternoon.* **5.** happy and pleasant ○ *She gave me a bright smile.*

brightly /ˈbraɪtli/ *adverb* **1.** in a strong clear light or colour ○ *A children's book with brightly painted pictures.* ○ *The streets were brightly lit for Christmas.* **2.** cheerfully ○ *She smiled brightly as she went into the hospital.*

brightness /ˈbraɪtnəs/ *noun* **1.** strong clear light **2.** strong colour

brilliant /ˈbrɪljənt/ *adjective* **1.** extremely clever ○ *He's the most brilliant student of his year.* ○ *She had a brilliant idea.* **2.** (*of light*) strong and clear ○ *She*

stepped out into the brilliant sunshine. **3.** very good (*informal*) ○ *The way the information is displayed on this website is brilliant.*

bring /brɪŋ/ *verb* to come with someone or something to this place ○ *She brought the books to school with her.* ○ *He brought his girlfriend home for tea.* ○ *Are you bringing any friends to the party?* (NOTE: **brings – bringing – brought** /brɔːt/)

bring up *phrasal verb* **1.** to look after and educate a child ○ *He was born in the USA but brought up in England.* ○ *He was brought up by his uncle in Scotland.* **2.** to mention a problem ○ *He brought up the question of the noise.*

brink /brɪŋk/ *noun* **the brink** the time when something is about to happen □ **on the brink of (doing) something** about to achieve something ○ *The company is on the brink of collapse.* ○ *She was on the brink of a nervous breakdown.*

British /ˈbrɪtɪʃ/ *adjective* relating to the United Kingdom ○ *a British citizen* ○ *the British army* ○ *The British press reported their death in a plane crash in Africa.* ○ *The ship was flying a British flag.*

broad /brɔːd/ *adjective* very wide ○ *a broad river* ◊ **breadth**

broadcast /ˈbrɔːdkɑːst/ *noun* a radio or TV programme ○ *The broadcast came live from the award ceremony.*

broke /brəʊk/ *adjective* with no money (*informal*) ■ past tense of **break**

broken /ˈbrəʊkən/ *adjective* **1.** in pieces ○ *She tried to mend the broken vase.* **2.** not working ○ *We can't use the lift because it's broken.*

brooch /brəʊtʃ/ *noun* a piece of jewellery fixed onto clothes with a pin (NOTE: The plural is **brooches.**)

brother /ˈbrʌðə/ *noun* a boy or man who has the same mother and father as someone else ○ *My brother John is three years older than me.* ○ *She came with her three brothers.*

brought /brɔːt/ past tense and past participle of **bring**

brown /braʊn/ *adjective* **1.** with a colour like earth or wood ○ *She has brown hair* *and blue eyes.* ○ *It's autumn and the leaves are turning brown.* **2.** with skin made dark by the sun ○ *He's very brown – he must have been sitting in the sun.*

bruise /bruːz/ *noun* a dark painful area on the skin, where you have been hit ○ *She had bruises all over her arms.* ■ *verb* to make a bruise on the skin by being hit or by knocking yourself on something ○ *She bruised her knee on the corner of the table.*

brush /brʌʃ/ *noun* **1.** a tool made of a handle and hairs or wire, used for doing things such as cleaning or painting ○ *You need a stiff brush to get the mud off your shoes.* ○ *She used a very fine brush to paint the details.* ○ *He was painting the front of the house with a large brush.* (NOTE: The plural is **brushes**.) **2.** the act of cleaning with a brush ○ *She gave the coat a good brush.* **3.** a short argument or fight with someone ○ *He's had several brushes with the police recently.* ■ *verb* **1.** to clean with a brush ○ *He brushed his shoes before going to the office.* ○ *Always remember to brush your teeth before you go to bed.* **2.** to go past something touching it gently ○ *She brushed against me as she came into the café.*

brush off *phrasal verb* **1.** to clean something off with a brush ○ *He brushed the mud off his boots.* **2.** to ignore something because it is not very important ○ *So far he has managed to brush off all the complaints about his work.*

brush up *phrasal verb* to learn more about something ○ *You'll need to brush up your English if you want to get a job as a guide.*

bubble /ˈbʌb(ə)l/ *noun* a ball of air or gas contained in a liquid or other substance ○ *Bubbles of gas rose to the surface of the lake.* ○ *He blew bubbles in his drink.* ■ *verb* to make bubbles, or have bubbles inside ○ *The porridge was bubbling in the pan.*

bucket /ˈbʌkɪt/ *noun* **1.** an open container with a handle, used mainly for carrying liquids ○ *Throw the water down the drain and pass the empty bucket back to me.* ○ *He filled a bucket from the tap.* **2.**

the contents of a bucket ○ *They threw buckets of water on the fire.* ■ *verb* to pour with rain (*informal*) ○ *It's bucketing down outside.*

bud /bʌd/ *noun* a place where a new shoot or flower will grow from on a plant ○ *It was spring and the buds on the trees were beginning to open.*

budget /ˈbʌdʒɪt/ *noun* an amount of money that can be spent on something ○ *There isn't enough money in the household budget to pay for a new carpet.* ■ *verb* to plan how you will spend money in the future ○ *It would be helpful if you learnt to budget.* ○ *They are having to budget carefully before going on holiday.*

bug /bʌg/ *verb* to make someone feel slightly angry, especially for a long time (*informal*) ○ *I can't remember his name, and it's really bugging me!* (NOTE: **bugging – bugged**)

build /bɪld/ *verb* **1.** to make something by putting its parts together ○ *The house was only built last year.* ○ *They are planning to build a motorway across the field.* **2.** to develop something ○ *He built his business from scratch.* ○ *We need to build a good team relationship.* (NOTE: **builds – building – built** /bɪlt/)

builder /ˈbɪldə/ *noun* a person who builds buildings

building /ˈbɪldɪŋ/ *noun* **1.** something such as a house, railway station or factory which has been built ○ *The flood washed away several buildings.* ○ *His office is on the top floor of the building.* **2.** the action of constructing something ○ *The building of the tunnel has taken many years.*

built /bɪlt/ past tense and past participle of **build**

bulb /bʌlb/ *noun* **1.** a round part of some plants, which stays under the ground, and from which leaves and flowers grow ○ *She planted spring bulbs all round the house.* **2.** a glass ball which gives electric light ○ *I need to change the bulb in the table lamp.*

bull /bʊl/ *noun* a male animal of the cow family

bullet /'bʊlɪt/ *noun* a piece of metal that you shoot from a gun ○ *He loaded his gun with bullets.* ○ *Two bullets had been fired.*

bullet point /'bʊlɪt pɔɪnt/ *noun* a printed symbol like a circle before an item in a list

bully /'bʊli/ *noun* a person who often hurts or is unkind to other people ○ *He's a bully, he's always trying to frighten smaller children.* (NOTE: The plural is **bullies**.) ■ *verb* to be unkind to someone often ○ *She was bullied by the other children in school.* (NOTE: **bullies – bullying – bullied**)

bump /bʌmp/ *noun* **1.** a slight knock ○ *The boat hit the landing stage with a bump.* **2.** a raised area ○ *Drive slowly, the road is full of bumps.* **3.** a raised area on your body, where something has hit it ○ *He has a bump on the back of his head.* ■ *verb* to hit something or a part of the body ○ *He's crying because he bumped his head on the door.*

bun /bʌn/ *noun* a small round piece of bread or a cake ○ *The burgers are served in a bun.* ○ *These buns are too sweet and sticky.*

bunch /bʌntʃ/ *noun* **1.** a group of things taken together ○ *He carries a bunch of keys attached to his belt.* ○ *He brought her a bunch of flowers.* **2.** a group of people ○ *I work with a nice bunch.* ○ *My friends are a mixed bunch.* (NOTE: The plural is **bunches**.) **3.** several fruits attached to the same stem ○ *a bunch of grapes* ○ *a bunch of bananas*

bundle /'bʌnd(ə)l/ *noun* **1.** a parcel of things wrapped up or tied up together ○ *A bundle of clothes was all she owned.* ○ *He produced a bundle of papers tied up with green string.* ○ *She left her clothes in a bundle on the floor.* **2.** a set of things sold or presented together ○ *a bundle of software* ■ *verb* **1.** to put things somewhere quickly without being careful ○ *He bundled the papers into a drawer.* ○ *She bundled the children off to school.* ○ *The police bundled him into the back of their van.* **2.** to sell a software programme at the same time as you sell hardware, both sold together

at a special price ○ *The word-processing package is bundled with the computer.*

bungalow /'bʌŋɡələʊ/ *noun* a house with only a ground floor

burden /'bɜːd(ə)n/ *noun* **1.** a heavy load ○ *He relieved her of her burden.* **2.** something that is hard to deal with ○ *I think he finds running the office at his age something of a burden.*

burger /'bɜːɡə/ *noun* same as **hamburger**

burglar /'bɜːɡlə/ *noun* a person who tries to get into a building to steal things

burn /bɜːn/ *noun* a burnt area of the skin or a surface ○ *She had burns on her face and hands.* ○ *There's a burn on the edge of the table where he left his cigarette.* ■ *verb* **1.** to destroy or damage something by fire ○ *All our clothes were burnt in the fire.* ○ *The hotel was burnt to the ground last year.* ○ *I've burnt the toast again.* **2.** to feel painful, or to make something feel painful ○ *The sun and wind burnt his face.* **3.** to damage part of the body by heat ○ *She burnt her finger on the hot frying pan.* **4.** to be on fire ○ *All the trees were burning.* (NOTE: **burns – burning – burnt** or **burned – has burnt** or **burned**)

burnt /bɜːnt/ *adjective* destroyed or damaged by fire or heat

burst /bɜːst/ *verb* to break open or explode suddenly, or cause something to break open or explode suddenly ○ *A water main burst in the High Street.* ○ *When she picked up the balloon it burst.* (NOTE: **bursts – bursting – burst – has burst**) ■ *noun* **1.** a sudden loud sound ○ *There was a burst of gunfire and then silence.* ○ *Bursts of laughter came from the office.* **2.** a sudden effort or activity ○ *She put on a burst of speed.* ○ *In a burst of energy he cleaned the whole house.*

bury /'beri/ *verb* to put someone or something into the ground ○ *He was buried in the local cemetery.* ○ *Squirrels often bury nuts in the autumn.* (NOTE: **buries – burying – buried**)

bus /bʌs/ *noun* a large motor vehicle which carries passengers ○ *He goes to work by bus.* ○ *She takes the 8 o'clock* *bus to school every morning.* ○ *We missed the last bus and had to walk home.*

bush /'buʃ/ *noun* a small tree ○ *a small bush with red berries* ○ *An animal was moving in the bushes.* (NOTE: The plural is **bushes**.)

business /'bɪznɪs/ *noun* 1. the work of buying and selling things ○ *They do a lot of business with France.* ○ *She works in the electricity business.* □ **on business** working ○ *The sales director is in Holland on business.* 2. a company ○ *She runs a photography business.* ○ *He runs a secondhand car business.* (NOTE: The plural is **businesses**.) 3. something that affects a particular person □ **it's none of your business** it's nothing to do with you

businessperson /'bɪznəs,pɜːs(ə)n/ *noun* a person who works in business, or who runs a business

busy /'bɪzi/ *adjective* 1. working on or doing something ○ *He was busy mending the dishwasher.* ○ *I was too busy to phone my aunt.* ○ *The busiest time for shops is the week before Christmas.* 2. full of people ○ *The shops are busiest during the week before Christmas.* 3. (*of a phone line*) being used by someone else, so you cannot get an answer when you call ○ *His phone's been busy all day.*

but /bət, bʌt/ *conjunction* used for showing a difference ○ *He is very tall, but his wife is quite short.* ○ *We would like to come to your party, but we're doing something else that evening.* ■ *preposition* except ○ *Everyone but me is allowed to go to the cinema.* ○ *They had eaten nothing but apples.*

butcher /'butʃə/ *noun* a person who prepares and sells meat

butter /'bʌtə/ *noun* a yellow fat made from the cream of milk, used on bread or for cooking ○ *Fry the mushrooms in butter.* (NOTE: no plural: *some butter; a knob of butter*) ■ *verb* to spread butter on something ○ *She was busy buttering slices of bread for the sandwiches.*

butterfly /'bʌtəflaɪ/ *noun* an insect with large brightly coloured wings which flies during the day

buttocks /'bʌtəks/ *plural noun* the part of the body on which you sit

button /'bʌt(ə)n/ *noun* 1. a small, usually round piece of plastic, metal or wood that you push through a hole in clothes to fasten them ○ *The wind is cold – do up the buttons on your coat.* ○ *A button's come off my shirt.* 2. a small round object which you push to operate something such as a bell ○ *Press this button to call the lift.* ○ *Push the red button to set off the alarm.* ■ *verb* to fasten something with buttons ○ *He buttoned (up) his coat because it was cold.*

buttonhole /'bʌt(ə)nhəʊl/ *noun* a hole which a button goes through when it is fastened ○ *You've put the button in the wrong buttonhole.*

buy /baɪ/ *verb* to get something by paying money for it ○ *I bought a newspaper on my way to the station.* ○ *She's buying a flat.* ○ *She bought herself a pair of ski boots.* ○ *What did you buy your mother for her birthday?* (NOTE: **buys – buying – bought** /bɔːt/)

buyer /'baɪə/ *noun* a person who buys things

buzz /bʌz/ *noun* a noise like the sound made by a bee ○ *the buzz of an electric saw in the garden next door* ■ *verb* to make a noise like a bee ○ *Wasps were buzzing round the jam.*

by /baɪ/ *preposition* 1. near ○ *The house is just by the bus stop.* ○ *Sit down here by me.* 2. not later than ○ *They should have arrived by now.* ○ *You must be home by eleven o'clock.* ○ *It must be finished by Friday.* 3. used for showing the means of doing something ○ *Send the parcel by airmail.* ○ *Get in touch with the office by phone.* ○ *They came by car.* ○ *She caught a cold by standing in the rain.* ○ *You make the drink by adding champagne to orange juice.* ○ *She paid by cheque, not by credit card.* 4. used for showing the person or thing that did something ○ *a painting by Van Gogh* ○ *a CD recorded by our local group* ○ *'Hamlet' is a play by Shakespeare.* ○ *The postman was bitten by the dog.* ○

She was knocked down by a car. **5.** used for showing amounts ○ *We sell tomatoes by the kilo.* ○ *Eggs are sold by the dozen.* ○ *Prices have been increased by 5%.* ○ *They won by 4 goals to 2.* ■ *ad-*

verb past ○ *She drove by without seeing us.*

bye /baɪ/, **bye-bye** /ˌbaɪ ˈbaɪ/ *interjection* goodbye (*informal*)

C

c /siː/, **C** *noun* the third letter of the alphabet, between B and D

cab /kæb/ *noun* **1.** a taxi ○ *He took a cab to the airport.* ○ *Can you phone for a cab, please?* ○ *Cab fares are very high in New York.* **2.** a separate part of a large vehicle for a driver ○ *The truck driver climbed into his cab and started the engine.*

cabbage /'kæbɪdʒ/ *noun* a vegetable with large pale green or red leaves folded into a tight ball

cabin /'kæbɪn/ *noun* **1.** a small room on a ship ○ *We booked a first-class cabin on the cruise.* **2.** the inside of an aircraft ○ *The aircraft is divided into three separate passenger cabins: first-class, business and tourist.* **3.** a small hut ○ *He has a cabin by a lake where he goes fishing.*

cabinet /'kæbɪnət/ *noun* **1.** a piece of furniture with shelves ○ *a china cabinet* **2.** a committee formed from the most important members of a government ○ *The cabinet met at 10 o'clock this morning.* ○ *There's a cabinet meeting every Tuesday morning.*

cable /'keɪb(ə)l/ *noun* **1.** a wire for carrying electricity or electronic signals ○ *He ran a cable out into the garden so that he could use the lawnmower.* ○ *They've been digging up the pavements to lay cables.* **2.** a thick rope or wire ○ *The ship was attached to the quay by cables.* **3.** same as **cable television**

cable television /,keɪb(ə)l telɪ'vɪʒ(ə)n/, **cable TV** /,keɪb(ə)l tiː'viː/ *noun* a television system where the signals are sent along underground cables

cactus /'kæktəs/ *noun* a plant with thorns which grows in the desert (NOTE: The plural is **cactuses** or **cacti** /'kæktaɪ/.)

café /'kæfeɪ/ *noun* a small restaurant selling drinks or light meals ○ *We had a snack in the station café.*

cage /keɪdʒ/ *noun* a box made of wire or with metal bars for keeping birds or animals in ○ *The rabbit got out of its cage.*

cagey /'keɪdʒi/ *adjective* not wanting to share information (*informal*) ○ *They're being very cagey about their relationship.* (NOTE: **cagier – cagiest**)

cake /keɪk/ *noun* food made by mixing flour, eggs and sugar, and baking it ○ *a piece of cherry cake* ○ *She had six candles on her birthday cake.* ○ *Have another slice of Christmas cake.*

calculate /'kælkjʊ,leɪt/ *verb* to find the answer to a problem using numbers ○ *The bank clerk calculated the rate of exchange for the dollar.* ○ *He calculated that it would take us six hours to finish the job.*

calculation /,kælkjʊ'leɪʃ(ə)n/ *noun* **1.** a series of numbers that you obtain when you are calculating something ○ *According to my calculations, we have enough fuel left to do only twenty kilometres.* **2.** the act of calculating

calculator /'kælkjʊleɪtə/ *noun* a small electronic machine for doing calculations

calendar /'kælɪndə/ *noun* a set of pages showing the days and months of the year

calf /kɑːf/ *noun* **1.** a young cow or bull **2.** the back part of someone's leg between the ankle and the knee (NOTE: The plural is **calves** /kɑːvz/. The meat from a calf is **veal**.)

call /kɔːl/ *verb* **1.** to say something loudly to someone who is some distance away ○ *Call the children when it's time for tea.* **2.** to telephone someone ○ *If he comes back, tell him I'll call him when I'm in the office.* ○ *Mr Smith is out – shall I ask him to call you back?* ○ *Call*

the police – the shop has been burgled!
○ *Can you call me a cab, please?* **3.** to
wake someone ○ *Call me at 7 o'clock.*
4. to give someone or something a name
○ *They're going to call the baby Sam.* ○
*His name is John but everyone calls him
Jack.* ○ *What do you call this computer
programme?* **5. to be called** to have as
a name ○ *Our cat's called Felix.* **6.** to
visit someone or somewhere ○ *We
called at the house, but there was no one
there.* ■ *noun* **1.** a telephone conversation, or an attempt to get in touch with
someone by telephone ○ *Were there any
calls for me while I was out?* □ **to make
a (telephone or phone) call** to make
contact with and speak to someone on
the telephone ○ *She wants to make a
call to Australia.* □ **to take a call** to answer the telephone **2.** a telephone call or
short conversation to wake someone ○
He asked for an early morning call. □ **I
want a call at 7 o'clock** I want someone
to wake me at 7 o'clock **3.** a visit to
someone's home or place of work ○ *The
doctor made three calls on patients this
morning.* □ **to make a call** to visit someone or somewhere, especially on business ◇ **on call** available for duty

call off *phrasal verb* to decide not to do
something which had been planned
call on *phrasal verb* **1.** to visit someone
○ *She called on her mother to see how
she was.* **2.** to ask someone to do something ○ *The police have called on everyone to watch out for the escaped
prisoner.*
call round *phrasal verb* same as **call**
verb **6** ○ *The whole family called round
to see if she was better.*

callbox /ˈkɔːlbɒks/ *noun* a public telephone box ○ *I'm phoning from the callbox outside the station.* (NOTE: The plural is **callboxes**.)

calm /kɑːm/ *adjective* **1.** not anxious or
excited ○ *Keep calm, everything will be
all right.* **2.** not violent or rough ○ *The
sea was perfectly calm and no one was
seasick.* (NOTE: **calmer – calmest**) ■
noun a period of quiet ○ *The calm of the
Sunday afternoon was broken by the
sound of jazz from the house next door.*

■ *verb* to make someone, or a situation,
more peaceful

calm down *phrasal verb* **1.** to become
quieter and less annoyed ○ *After shouting for some minutes he finally calmed
down.* **2.** to make someone quieter ○
*She stroked his hand to try to calm him
down.*

calmly /ˈkɑːmli/ *adverb* in a way that is
not anxious or excited

came /keɪm/ past tense of **come**

camel /ˈkæm(ə)l/ *noun* a desert animal
with long legs and one or two large
round raised parts on its back

camera /ˈkæm(ə)rə/ *noun* a piece of
equipment for taking photographs ○ *He
took a picture of the garden with his new
camera.* ○ *Did you remember to put a
film in your camera?*

camp /kæmp/ *noun* a place where people
live in tents or small buildings in the
open air ○ *We set up camp halfway up
the mountain.* ■ *verb* to spend a period
of time in a tent ○ *They camped for a
week by the side of the lake.* ■ **to go
camping** to spend a holiday in a tent ○
*We go camping in Sweden every sum-
mer.*

campaign /kæmˈpeɪn/ *noun* **1.** an organised attempt to achieve something ○
a publicity campaign ○ *an advertising
campaign* ○ *He's organising a campaign against the new motorway.* ○ *The
government's planning an anti-smoking
campaign.* **2.** an organised military attack ○ *Napoleon's Russian campaign of
1812* ■ *verb* to work in an organised
way to achieve something ○ *The group
has been campaigning for the banning
of landmines.* ○ *They campaign against
nuclear reactors.*

can /kæn/ *noun* a round metal container
for food or drink ○ *He opened a can of
lemonade.* ○ *Empty beer cans were all
over the pavement.* ○ *She opened a can
of beans.* ◇ **tin** ■ *modal verb* **1.** to be
able to do something ○ *He can swim
well but he can't ride a bike.* ○ *She can't
run as fast as I can.* ○ *Can you remember what the doctor told us to do?* ○ *I
can't bear to watch any longer.* **2.** to be
allowed to do something ○ *Children un-*

der 18 can't drive cars. ○ *He says we can go in.* ○ *The policeman says we can't park here.* **3.** to ask politely ○ *Can we come in, please?* ○ *Can you shut the door, please?* (NOTE: The negative is **cannot**, usually **can't**. The past tense is **could**, **could not**, usually **couldn't**. Can and could are only used with other verbs, and are not followed by the word **to**.) ■ *verb* to put food in cans (NOTE: **cans – canning – canned**)

canal /kə'næl/ *noun* an artificial river made between rivers or lakes or from the sea, originally for moving cargo

cancel /'kænsəl/ *verb* to stop something which has been planned ○ *The singer was ill, so the show had to be cancelled.* (NOTE: **cancels – cancelling – cancelled**)

cancellation /ˌkænsə'leɪʃ(ə)n/ *noun* **1.** the act of cancelling something ○ *The event is subject to cancellation if the weather is bad.* **2.** a seat, ticket or appointment which is available again because the person who bought it cannot use it ○ *If we have a cancellation for next week I'll call and let you know.*

cancer /'kænsə/ *noun* a serious disease affecting different parts of the body in which cells grow in a way which is not usual

candidate /'kændɪdeɪt/ *noun* **1.** a person who applies for a job ○ *We interviewed six candidates for the post of assistant manager.* **2.** a person who has entered for an examination ○ *Candidates are given three hours to complete the exam.* **3.** a person who is taking part in an election or competing for a prize ○ *She accompanied the candidate round the constituency.* **4.** someone or something that is likely to be chosen for or be something ○ *a city that is a candidate for the next Olympics*

candle /'kænd(ə)l/ *noun* a stick of wax with a string in the centre, which you burn to give light

candy /'kændi/ *noun* **1.** *US* a sweet food made with sugar ○ *Eating candy is bad for your teeth.* (NOTE: no plural in this sense) **2.** one piece of this food ○ *She bought a box of candies.* (NOTE: The plural in this sense is **candies**.)

cane /keɪn/ *noun* **1.** a strong stem of a plant, especially of tall thin plants like bamboo ○ *a raspberry cane* **2.** a walking stick cut from the stem of some types of plant ○ *She was leaning heavily on a cane as she walked up the path.*

cannot /'kænɒt/ ♦ **can**

canoe /kə'nuː/ *noun* a boat with two pointed ends, which is moved forwards by one or more people using long pieces of wood ○ *She paddled her canoe across the lake.* ■ *verb* to travel in a canoe ○ *They canoed down the river.* (NOTE: **canoes – canoeing – canoed**)

can't /kɑːnt/ ♦ **can**

canvas /'kænvəs/ *noun* a thick cloth for making things such as tents, sails or shoes ○ *He was wearing a pair of old canvas shoes.* (NOTE: The plural is **canvases**.)

cap /kæp/ *noun* **1.** a flat hat with a flat hard piece in front ○ *a baseball cap* ○ *an officer's cap with a gold badge* **2.** a lid which covers something ○ *a red pen with a black cap* ○ *Screw the cap back on the medicine bottle.*

capability /ˌkeɪpə'bɪlɪti/ *noun* the practical ability to do something ○ *We have the capability to produce a better machine than this.*

capable /'keɪpəb(ə)l/ *adjective* able to work well and to deal with problems ○ *She's an extremely capable manager.* □ **capable of** able to do something ○ *The car is capable of very high speeds.* ○ *She isn't capable of running the conference without help.*

capacity /kə'pæsɪti/ *noun* **1.** an amount which something can hold ○ *This barrel has a larger capacity than that one.* ○ *The cinema was filled to capacity.* □ **to work at full capacity** to do as much work as possible **2.** the situation that someone is in or the job they have □ **acting in his capacity as manager** acting as a manager □ **speaking in an official capacity** speaking officially

capital /'kæpɪt(ə)l/ *noun* **1.** the main city of a country, usually where the government is ○ *The capital is in the eastern part of the country.* ○ *Madrid is the capital of Spain.* **2.** money which is invested ○ *a company with £10,000 capital* or *with a capital of £10,000.* **3.** also **capital letter** a letter written as A, B, C, D, etc., rather than a, b, c, d, etc.

captain /ˈkæptɪn/ *noun* **1.** a person in charge of a team ○ *The two captains shook hands at the beginning of the match.* **2.** a person in charge of a ship or aircraft ○ *The captain greeted us as we came on board.* ○ *Captain Smith is flying the plane.* **3.** a rank in the army above a lieutenant and below a major (NOTE: When used as a title before a surname, it is spelt with a capital letter and is often written as **Capt.**)

capture /ˈkæptʃə/ *verb* **1.** to take someone as a prisoner ○ *Four soldiers were captured in the attack.* **2.** to take something by force, especially in war ○ *They captured the enemy capital very quickly.*

car /kɑː/ *noun* **1.** a small private motor vehicle for carrying people ○ *He drove his car into the garage.* ○ *He goes to his office every morning by car.* **2.** *US* a carriage of a railway train ○ *Is there a restaurant car on the train?*

caravan /ˈkærəvæn/ *noun* a vehicle which you can live in, especially on holiday, and which, if small enough, can be attached to a car and pulled along ○ *We got stuck behind a caravan on a narrow road.* ○ *We rent a caravan near the beach every summer.*

card /kɑːd/ *noun* **1.** a flat piece of stiff paper with a picture on one side, which you can send with a message ○ *They sent us a card from Italy.* ○ *How much does it cost to send a card to Australia?* ◊ **postcard 2.** a piece of stiff paper, folded so that a message can be written inside ○ *She sent me a lovely card on my birthday.* **3.** a piece of stiff paper with a picture or pattern on it, used to play games **4.** a piece of stiff paper with your name and address printed on it ○ *He gave me his business card.* ○ *I've lost my membership card.* **5.** a piece of stiff plastic used for payment ○ *Do you want to pay cash or by card?* ■ *plural noun* **cards** the entertainment of playing games with a special set of cards with numbers or patterns on them □ **a game of cards** a period of playing with a special set of cards

cardboard /ˈkɑːdbɔːd/ *noun* thick card, often used for making boxes (NOTE: no plural: *some cardboard*; *a piece of cardboard*)

care /keə/ *noun* **1.** serious and careful attention ○ *He handled the glass with great care.* □ **to take care** to be very careful ○ *Take care when you cross the road.* ○ *He took great care with the box of glasses.* ○ *Take care not to be late.* **2.** looking after someone ○ *the care of the elderly* □ **to take care of someone** to look after someone ○ *Will you take care of the children for the weekend for me?* ■ *verb* to be worried ○ *I don't care if my car is dirty.* ○ *She cares a lot about the environment.* ◊ **someone couldn't care less** used to show that someone does not worry at all about something ○ *Paul couldn't care less about what we think – he's got his own plans.*

care for *phrasal verb* **1.** to like someone or something ○ *I don't care for this music very much.* ○ *I met her once, but I didn't much care for her.* ○ *Would you care for another cup of coffee?* **2.** to look after people ○ *Nurses cared for the injured people after the accident.* ○ *People who have to care for their elderly relatives need extra help.*

career /kəˈrɪə/ *noun* the work someone does throughout their life ○ *She is starting her career as a librarian.* ○ *He gave up his career as a civil servant and bought a farm.*

careful /ˈkeəf(ə)l/ *adjective* **1.** showing attention to details ○ *We are always very careful to include the most recent information.* ○ *The project needs very careful planning.* **2.** taking care not to make mistakes or cause harm ○ *Be careful not to make any noise – the baby is asleep.* ○ *She is very careful about what she eats.*

carefully /ˈkeəf(ə)li/ *adverb* with great care or thought ○ *The holiday had been carefully planned* or *planned carefully.*

careless /ˈkeələs/ *adjective* without any care or thought ○ *He is careless about his work.* ○ *He made several careless mistakes when he took his driving test.*

carelessly /'keələsli/ *adverb* without taking care or thinking carefully

carelessness /'keələsnəs/ *noun* the fact of being careless or not thinking carefully

caretaker /'keəteɪkə/ *noun* a person who looks after a building

cargo /'kɑːgəʊ/ *noun* goods carried on a ship or a plane

caring /'keərɪŋ/ *adjective* kind and helpful ○ *a very caring person*

car park /'kɑː pɑːk/ *noun* a public place where you can leave a car when you are not using it

carpet /'kɑːpɪt/ *noun* thick material for covering floors ○ *He spilt his coffee on our new cream carpet.*

carriage /'kærɪdʒ/ *noun* **1.** one of the vehicles that are joined together to make a train ○ *Where's the first-class carriage on this train?* **2.** a vehicle, especially an old-fashioned one, that is pulled by a horse **3.** the cost of carrying goods, or the action of carrying goods ○ *Carriage is 15% of the total cost.* ○ *How much do they charge for carriage?*

carried /'kærɪd/ past tense and past participle of **carry**

carries /'kæriz/ 3rd person singular present of **carry**

carrot /'kærət/ *noun* **1.** a vegetable with a long orange root **2.** something good that persuades you to do something (*informal*) ○ *He was offered the carrot of a big pay rise to take on the new project.*

carry /'kæri/ *verb* **1.** to take something and move it to another place ○ *There was no lift, so they had to carry the beds up the stairs.* ○ *The plane was carrying 120 passengers.* ○ *That suitcase is too heavy for me to carry.* **2.** (*of sound*) to be heard at a distance ○ *The sound of the bells carries for miles.* (NOTE: **carries – carrying – carried**) ◇ **to get carried away** to become emotional or excited

carry on *phrasal verb* to continue doing something ○ *When the teacher came in, the students all carried on talking.* ○ *They carried on with their work right through the lunch hour.*

carry out *phrasal verb* to do something, especially something that has been planned ○ *Doctors carried out tests on the patients.* ○ *The police are carrying out a search for the missing man.*

cartoon /kɑːˈtuːn/ *noun* **1.** a film made of moving drawings ○ *I like watching Tom and Jerry cartoons.* **2.** a funny, often political, drawing in a newspaper

carve /kɑːv/ *verb* **1.** to cut up a large piece of meat at a meal ○ *Who's going to carve the chicken?* **2.** to make a shape by cutting stone or wood ○ *He carved a bird out of wood.*

case /keɪs/ *noun* **1.** a box with a handle, for carrying things such as your clothes when travelling ○ *She was still packing her case when the taxi came.* ○ *The customs made him open his case.* ◊ **suitcase 2.** a special box for an object ○ *Put the gun back in its case.* ○ *I've lost my red glasses case.* **3.** a large box for a set of goods to be sold ○ *He bought a case of wine.* **4.** a situation, or a way in which something happens ○ *a case of having made a poor choice* ○ *In many cases, we cannot find the owner of the goods.* □ **in that case** if that happens or if that is the situation ○ *There is a strike on the underground – In that case, you'll have to take a bus.* **5.** same as **court case** ◇ **in case** because something might happen ○ *It's still sunny, but I'll take my umbrella just in case.* ◇ **in any case 1.** whatever may happen ○ *We could move the cabinet upstairs or into the dining room, but in any case we'll need some help.* **2.** used to add something to a statement

cash /kæʃ/ *noun* money in coins and notes, not in cheques ○ *We don't keep much cash in the office.* ○ *I'd prefer to use up my spare cash, rather than pay with a credit card.*

cash in *phrasal verb* to make money from something ○ *The company cashed in on the huge interest in computer games.*

cassette /kəˈset/ *noun* a plastic case containing magnetic tape which can be used for listening to words or music, or recording sounds ○ *Do you want it on* *cassette or CD?* ○ *He bought a cassette of folk songs.* ○ *We recorded the poems onto a cassette.*

cast /kɑːst/ *noun* all the actors in a play or film ○ *The film has a large cast.* ■ *verb* to choose actors for a play or film ○ *In his first film, he was cast as a soldier.* (NOTE: **casts – casting – cast**)

castle /'kɑːs(ə)l/ *noun* a large building with strong walls built in the past for protection in war ○ *The soldiers shut the castle gate.*

casually /'kæʒjuəli/ *adverb* in an informal way ○ *He casually mentioned that he had got married last Saturday.*

cat /kæt/ *noun* an animal with soft fur and a long tail, kept as a pet

catalogue /'kæt(ə)lɒg/ *noun* a list of things for sale or in a library or museum ○ *an office equipment catalogue* ○ *Look up the title in the library catalogue.* ■ *verb* to make a list of things that exist somewhere ○ *She spent months cataloguing the novelist's correspondence.*

catch /kætʃ/ *verb* **1.** to take hold of something moving in the air ○ *Can you catch a ball with your left hand?* ○ *He managed to catch the glass before it hit the floor.* **2.** to take hold of something ○ *She caught him by the sleeve as he turned away.* ○ *As he slipped, he caught the rail to stop himself falling.* **3.** to get hold of an animal, especially in order to kill and eat it ○ *He sat by the river all day but didn't catch anything.* ○ *Our cat is no good at catching mice – she's too lazy.* **4.** to get on a vehicle such as a bus, plane or train before it leaves ○ *You will have to run if you want to catch the last bus.* ○ *He caught the 10 o'clock train to Paris.* **5.** to get an illness ○ *He caught a cold from his colleague.* **6.** to find someone doing something wrong ○ *She caught the boys stealing in her shop.* ○ *The police caught the burglar as he was climbing out of the window.* **7.** to hear something ○ *I didn't quite catch what you said.* (NOTE: **catches – catching – caught** /kɔːt/ **– has caught**) ■ *noun* **1.** the action of taking and holding a ball as it moves through the air ○ *He made a marvellous catch.* ○ *I dropped an easy catch.* **2.** a hidden disadvantage ○ *It*

seems such a good deal, but there must be a catch in it somewhere.

catch up *phrasal verb* to move to the same level as someone who is in front of you

catching /'kætʃɪŋ/ *adjective* (*of an illness*) likely to spread from one person to another

category /'kætɪg(ə)ri/ *noun* one of the groups that people, animals or things are divided into in a formal system ○ *We grouped the books into categories according to subject.* (NOTE: The plural is **categories**.)

caterpillar /'kætəpɪlə/ *noun* a small long insect with many legs, which develops into a butterfly ○ *Caterpillars have eaten most of the leaves on our trees.*

cathedral /kə'θiːdrəl/ *noun* the largest and the most important church in an area

cattle /'kæt(ə)l/ *plural noun* animals such as cows and bulls which farmers keep for milk or meat

caught /kɔːt/ past tense and past participle of **catch**

cause /kɔːz/ *noun* **1.** something which makes something else happen ○ *What is the main cause of traffic accidents?* ○ *The police tried to find the cause of the fire.* **2.** an aim, organisation or idea which people support ○ *She is fighting for the cause of working mothers.* ■ *verb* to make something happen ○ *The accident caused a traffic jam on the motorway.* ○ *The sudden noise caused her to drop the cup she was carrying.*

cautious /'kɔːʃəs/ *adjective* not willing to take risks ○ *She's a very cautious driver.*

cave /keɪv/ *noun* a large underground hole in rock or earth

CD *abbr* compact disc ○ *You can get it on CD.*

cease /siːs/ *verb* to stop, or to stop doing something (*formal*)

ceiling /'siːlɪŋ/ *noun* the solid part of a room that is above you ○ *He's so tall, he can easily touch the ceiling.* ○ *He paint-*

ed the kitchen ceiling. ○ *The bedroom has a very low ceiling.*

celebrate /'selɪbreɪt/ *verb* to have a party, or do special things because something good has happened, or because of something that happened at a particular time in the past ○ *Our team won, so we're all going out to celebrate.* ○ *They celebrated their wedding anniversary with their children.*

celebration /ˌselɪ'breɪʃ(ə)n/ *noun* **1.** a party or festival ○ *We had my birthday celebration in the local pub.* ○ *After our team won, the celebrations went on late into the night.* **2.** the activity of celebrating something ○ *a time of celebration* □ **in celebration of something** as an act of celebrating something ○ *an exhibition in celebration of the opening of the new gallery*

cell /sel/ *noun* **1.** a small room in a building such as a prison or monastery ○ *He was arrested and spent the night in the police cells.* **2.** the basic unit of a living thing ○ *You can see the blood cells clearly under a microscope.* (NOTE: Do not confuse with **sell**.)

cellar /'selə/ *noun* an underground room or rooms under a house

cement /sɪ'ment/ *noun* grey powder used in building, which is mixed with water and dries hard ○ *He was mixing cement to make a path round the house.*

cemetery /'semət(ə)ri/ *noun* an area of ground where the bodies of dead people are buried (NOTE: The plural is **cemeteries**.)

cent /sent/ *noun US* a small coin of which there are 100 in a dollar (NOTE: Do not confuse with **sent, scent**. Cent is usually written **c** in prices: **25c**, but not when a dollar price is mentioned: **$1.25**.)

center /'sentə/ *noun, verb US* spelling of **centre**

central /'sentrəl/ *adjective* **1.** in the middle of something ○ *The hall has one central pillar.* **2.** conveniently placed for shops and other facilities ○ *His offices are very central.*

centre /'sentə/ *noun* **1.** the middle of something ○ *chocolates with coffee*

cream centres ○ *They planted a rose bush in the centre of the lawn.* ○ *The town centre is very old.* **2.** a large building containing several different sections ○ *an army training centre* **3.** an important place for something ○ *Nottingham is the centre for the shoe industry.* ■ *verb* **1.** to put something in the middle ○ *Make sure you centre the title on the page.* **2.** to concentrate on something ○ *Our report centres on some aspects of the sales team.*

century /'sentʃəri/ *noun* one hundred years (NOTE: The plural is **centuries**. The number of a century is always one more than the date number, so the period from 1900 to 1999 is the 20th century, and the period starting in the year 2000 is the 21st century.)

cereal /'sɪəriəl/ *noun* **1.** a food made from wheat or similar plants and eaten for breakfast ○ *How much milk do you want on your cereal?* (NOTE: Do not confuse with **serial**.) **2.** a grain crop such as wheat or corn

ceremony /'serɪməni/ *noun* an important official occasion when something special is done in public ○ *They held a short ceremony to remember the victims of the train crash.* ◇ **to stand on ceremony** to be formal and not relaxed ◇ **without ceremony** in an informal and often impolite way

certain /'sɜːt(ə)n/ *adjective* **1.** sure about something ○ *Are you certain that you locked the door?* ○ *I'm not certain where she lives.* **2.** definitely going to happen ○ *Our team is certain to win the prize.* **3.** some ○ *There are certain things I feel I need to say to you.* ○ *Certain plants can make you ill if you eat them.* ◇ **to make certain that** to do something in order that something else will definitely happen ○ *He put the money in his safe to make certain that no one could steal it.*

certainly /'sɜːt(ə)nli/ *adverb* **1.** of course (*after a question or order*) ○ *Can you give me a lift to the station? – Certainly.* ○ *Tell him to write to me immediately. – Certainly, sir.* ○ *Give me a kiss. – Certainly not!* **2.** definitely ○ *She* *certainly impressed the judges.* ○ *He certainly knows how to score goals.*

certificate /sə'tɪfɪkət/ *noun* an official document which proves or shows something ○ *She has been awarded a certificate for swimming.* ○ *He has a certificate of competence in English.*

chain /tʃeɪn/ *noun* **1.** a series of metal rings joined together ○ *She wore a gold chain round her neck.* ○ *He stopped when the chain came off his bike.* **2.** a series of businesses such as shops, restaurants or hotels which belong to the same company ○ *a chain of hotels* or *a hotel chain* ○ *a chain of shoe shops* ■ *verb* to attach with a chain ○ *I chained my bike to the fence.*

chair /tʃeə/ *noun* **1.** a piece of furniture with a back, which you can sit on ○ *He pulled up a chair and started to write.* ○ *These chairs are very hard.* **2.** the person who is in charge of a meeting ○ *Please address all your comments to the chair.* □ **in the chair** the position of controlling what happens at a meeting ○ *Mrs Smith was in the chair for our first meeting.* ■ *verb* to be the person controlling what happens at a meeting ○ *The meeting was chaired by Mrs Smith.*

chairman /'tʃeəmən/ *noun* the person who controls what happens at a meeting ○ *Mrs Jones was the chairman at the meeting.* (NOTE: The plural is **chairmen**. Many people prefer to say **chair** or **chairperson** because **chairman** suggests that the person is a man.)

chairperson /'tʃeəpɜːs(ə)n/ *noun* the person who controls what happens at a meeting

chairwoman /'tʃeəwʊmən/ *noun* a woman who controls what happens at a meeting (NOTE: The plural is **chairwomen**.)

chalk /tʃɔːk/ *noun* **1.** a type of soft white rock **2.** a stick of a hard white or coloured substance used for writing on a board, e.g. in a classroom ○ *He wrote the dates up on the board in coloured chalk.*

chalkboard /'tʃɔːkbɔːd/ *noun* a dark board which you can write on with chalk, especially on the wall of a class-

room (NOTE: Now often preferred to 'blackboard'.)

challenge /'tʃælɪndʒ/ *noun* **1.** a difficult test of someone's skill or strength ○ *It's a difficult job, but I enjoy the challenge.* □ **to pose a challenge to someone** to be extremely difficult to do ○ *Getting the piano up the stairs will pose a challenge to the helpers.* **2.** an invitation to something such as a fight or competition ○ *Our team accepted the challenge to play another game.* **3.** an action that shows there are doubts about the truth, accuracy or legality of something ○ *a challenge over the ownership of the property* ■ *verb* **1.** to accept an invitation to a contest **2.** to ask someone to prove that they are right ○ *When challenged, he admitted that he had seen her get into a car.* ○ *The committee's conclusions have been challenged by other experts.* ◇ **to take up the challenge 1.** to accept an invitation to a contest ○ *Our team took up the challenge to play another game.* **2.** to decide to prove that you are right about something or able to do something difficult ○ *She decided to take up the challenge of being the first woman to complete the course.*

challenged /'tʃælɪndʒd/ *adjective* **1.** unable to do a particular activity easily, especially because of physical or mental disadvantages **2.** not having a particular quality (*humorous*) ○ *a scientifically challenged* (=not accurate according to science) *account of the new cancer treatment*

champion /'tʃæmpiən/ *noun* **1.** the best one in a particular competition ○ *a champion swimmer* ○ *He's the world champion in the 100 metres.* ○ *Their dog was champion two years running.* **2.** a person who strongly supports something or someone ○ *a champion of free city centre transport* ■ *verb* to support something or someone strongly ○ *They have been championing or championing the cause of children's rights for many years.*

championship /'tʃæmpiənʃɪp/ *noun* a contest to find who is the champion ○ *The tennis championship was won by a boy from Leeds.*

chance /tʃɑːns/ *noun* **1.** a possibility ○ *There is little chance of rain in August.* ○ *What are their chances of survival in this weather?* □ **a chance of doing something** a possibility of doing something **2.** an opportunity ○ *I've been waiting for a chance like this for a long time.* ○ *The trip was a good chance for us to meet old friends.* □ **a** *or* **the chance to do something** an opportunity to do something ○ *I wish I'd had the chance to visit South Africa.* **3.** luck or accident ○ *The satisfactory outcome owed more to chance than to good planning.* ○ *It was pure chance that we met at the station.* ◇ **by chance** in a way that was not planned or expected ○ *It was quite by chance that we were travelling on the same bus.* ◇ **by any chance** perhaps ○ *Have you by any chance seen my glasses?*

change /tʃeɪndʒ/ *verb* **1.** to become different, or make something different ○ *She's changed so much since I last saw her that I hardly recognised her.* ○ *Living in the country has changed his attitude towards towns.* **2.** to become different ○ *London has changed a lot since we used to live there.* ○ *He's changed so much since I last saw him.* **3.** to put on different clothes ○ *I'm just going upstairs to change* or *to get changed.* ○ *Go into the bathroom if you want to change your dress.* **4.** to use or have something in place of something else ○ *You ought to change your car tyres if they are worn.* ○ *Can we change our room for one with a view of the sea?* ○ *She's recently changed her job* or *changed jobs.* **5.** to give one country's money for another ○ *I had to change £1,000 into dollars.* ○ *We want to change some traveller's cheques.* ■ *noun* **1.** an occasion on which something is changed ○ *There was a sudden change of plan.* ○ *We've seen a lot of changes over the years.* **2.** something different ○ *We usually go on holiday in summer, but this year we're taking a winter holiday for a change.* ○ *A change of scenery will do you good.* ○ *A glass of water is a nice change after all that coffee.* **3.** money in coins ○ *I need some change for the parking meter.* ○ *Have you got change for a £5 note?* **4.**

money which you get back when you have given more than the correct price ○ *So that's £1.50 change from £5.* ○ *The shopkeeper gave me the wrong change.*

channel /ˈtʃæn(ə)l/ *noun* **1.** a frequency band for radio or TV or a station using this band ○ *We're watching Channel 4.* ○ *Shall we watch the new show on the other channel?* **2.** a way in which information or goods are passed from one place to another ○ *The request will have to be processed through the normal channels.* **3.** a narrow passage along which water can flow **4.** a piece of water connecting two seas ○ *the English Channel* ■ *verb* to send something in a particular direction ○ *They are channelling their funds into research.* (NOTE: **channels – channelling – channelled**. The US spelling is **channeling – channeled**.)

chaos /ˈkeɪɒs/ *noun* a state of confusion ○ *There was total chaos when the electricity failed.*

chap /tʃæp/ *noun* a man (*informal*) ○ *He's a really nice chap.* ○ *I bought it from a chap at work.*

chapel /ˈtʃæp(ə)l/ *noun* **1.** a room used as a church, e.g. in a hospital or airport **2.** a part of a large church ○ *the west chapel of the cathedral* ○ *The west chapel of the cathedral is dedicated to St Teresa.*

chapter /ˈtʃæptə/ *noun* a division of a book ○ *The first chapter is rather slow, but after that the story gets exciting.* ○ *Don't tell me how it finishes – I'm only up to chapter three.*

character /ˈkærɪktə/ *noun* **1.** the part of a person which makes them behave differently from all others ○ *He has a strong, determined character.* **2.** a person in a play or novel ○ *The main character in the film is an old woman with a fascinating history.* **3.** a person with particular qualities ○ *He's an interesting character.* □ **quite a** *or* **a real character** an interesting and unusual person ○ *My first head teacher was quite a character.*

characteristic /ˌkærɪktəˈrɪstɪk/ *adjective* typical ○ *You can recognise her by her characteristic way of walking.* ○ *The shape is characteristic of this type* *of flower.* (NOTE: something is characteristic **of** something) ■ *noun* a typical feature ○ *The two cars have very similar characteristics.*

charge /tʃɑːdʒ/ *noun* **1.** money which you have to pay ○ *There is no charge for delivery.* ○ *We make a small charge for rental.* **2.** a claim by the police that someone has done something wrong ○ *He was in prison on a charge of trying to shoot a neighbour.* **3.** a sudden rush towards someone or something, especially as part of an attack ○ *The police stood firm against the charge of the crowd.* **4.** a statement that someone has done something bad or wrong ○ *I completely reject the charge that I had these facts before I made the decision.* ■ *verb* **1.** to ask someone to pay ○ *The restaurant charged me £10 for two glasses of wine.* ○ *How much did the garage charge for mending the car?* **2.** (*of the police*) to say that someone has done something wrong ○ *She was charged with stealing the jewels.* **3.** to attack someone while running ○ *The police charged the rioters.* ○ *If the bull charges, run as fast as you can for the gate!* **4.** to run quickly and without care ○ *The children charged into the kitchen.* **5.** to put electricity into a battery ○ *You can charge your phone battery overnight.* ◇ **in charge of something** in control of something ○ *Who's in charge here?* ○ *He was put in charge of the sales department.* ◇ **to take charge of something** to start to be responsible for something ○ *She took charge of the class while the teacher was out of the room.*

charity /ˈtʃærɪti/ *noun* an organisation which collects money to help the poor or to support some cause ○ *a medical charity* (NOTE: The plural is **charities**.)

charm /tʃɑːm/ *noun* **1.** attractiveness ○ *the charm of the Devon countryside* ○ *She has great personal charm.* **2.** an object which is supposed to have magical powers ○ *She wears a lucky charm round her neck.* ■ *verb* **1.** to attract someone, or to make someone pleased ○ *He always manages to charm someone into helping him.* ○ *I was charmed*

by the village and surrounding area. **2.** to use magic on someone or something ○ *The fairy charmed the trees to grow golden fruit.*

charming /ˈtʃɑːmɪŋ/ *adjective* attractive

charter /ˈtʃɑːtə/ *noun* a legal document giving rights or privileges to a public organisation, a group of people, or a town ○ *a shoppers' charter* ○ *The university received its charter in 1846.* ■ *verb* to hire an aircraft, bus or boat for a particular trip ○ *We chartered a boat for a day trip to the island.*

chase /tʃeɪs/ *verb* **1.** to go after someone in order to try to catch him or her ○ *The postman was chased by a dog.* ○ *They chased the burglars down the street.* **2.** to find out how work is progressing in order to try to speed it up ○ *We are trying to chase the accounts department for your cheque.* ○ *I will chase up your order with the production department.* ■ *noun* an occasion on which you run after someone to try to catch them ○ *He was caught after a three-hour chase along the motorway.* □ **to give chase** to run after someone in order to try to catch him or her ○ *The robbers escaped and the police gave chase.*

chase up *phrasal verb* to find out how work is progressing in order to try to speed it up ○ *I'll chase it up for you on Monday.*

chat /tʃæt/ *noun* an informal, friendly talk ○ *She likes to drop in for a cup of coffee and a chat.* ○ *I'd like to have a chat with you about your work.*

cheap /tʃiːp/ *adjective* not costing a lot of money ○ *I want to buy a cheap radio.* ○ *Why do you go by bus? – Because it's cheaper than the train.* ○ *Buses are the cheapest way to travel.* ■ *adverb* at a low price ○ *I bought them cheap in the local market.*

cheaply /ˈtʃiːpli/ *adverb* **1.** without spending much money ○ *cheaply made furniture* ○ *You can live quite cheaply if you don't go out to eat in restaurants.* **2.** at a low price ○ *They were selling the last few bottles cheaply.*

cheat /tʃiːt/ *verb* to act unfairly in order to be successful ○ *They are sure he* cheated in his exam, but can't find out how he did it. ■ noun a person who acts unfairly in order to win ○ I won't play cards with him again, he's a cheat.

check /tʃek/ noun **1.** an examination or test ○ The police are carrying out checks on all cars. ○ A routine check of the fire equipment. **2.** US (in a restaurant) a bill ○ I'll ask for the check. ■ verb **1.** to make sure ○ I'd better check with the office if there are any messages for me. ○ Did you lock the door? – I'll go and check. **2.** to examine something to see if it is satisfactory ○ You must have your car checked every 10,000 miles. ◇ in check under control

check in phrasal verb **1.** (at a hotel) to arrive at a hotel and sign for a room ○ He checked in at 12.15. ○ We checked into our hotel and then went on a tour of the town. **2.** (at an airport) to give in your ticket to show you are ready to take the flight ○ Please check in two hours before your departure time.

check out phrasal verb **1.** (at a hotel) to leave and pay for a room ○ We'd better check out before breakfast. **2.** to see if something is all right ○ I thought I heard a noise in the kitchen – I'll just go and check it out.

check-in /'tʃek ɪn/ noun **1.** also **check-in desk** a place where passengers give in their tickets and bags for a flight ○ Where's the check-in? **2.** the procedure of dealing with passengers before a flight ○ Check-in starts at 4.30pm.

checkout /'tʃekaʊt/ noun a cash desk in a supermarket where you pay for the goods you have bought ○ There were huge queues at the checkouts.

cheek /tʃiːk/ noun **1.** the part of the face on each side of the nose and below the eye ○ a baby with red cheeks **2.** rudeness ○ He had the cheek to ask for more money. ○ I didn't like his cheek. (NOTE: no plural in this sense)

cheekily /'tʃiːkɪli/ adverb in a rude way

cheeky /'tʃiːki/ adjective rude (NOTE: **cheekier – cheekiest**)

cheer /tʃɪə/ noun a shout of praise or encouragement ○ When he scored the goal a great cheer went up.

cheer up phrasal verb to become happier, or make someone happier ○ I'm sure I'll cheer up once the treatment is over. ○ She made him a meal to try to cheer him up. □ **cheer up!** stop being unhappy ○ Cheer up! It'll all be over tomorrow.

cheerful /'tʃɪəf(ə)l/ adjective **1.** happy **2.** pleasant ○ a cheerful smile ○ a bright cheerful room

cheese /tʃiːz/ noun a solid food made from milk ○ At the end of the meal we'll have cheese and biscuits.

chef /ʃef/ noun a cook in a restaurant

chemical /'kemɪk(ə)l/ noun a substance which is formed by reactions between chemicals ○ rows of glass bottles containing chemicals ○ Chemicals are widely used in farming and medicine. ■ adjective relating to chemistry ○ If you add acid it sets off a chemical reaction.

chemist /'kemɪst/ noun **1.** a person who prepares and sells medicines ○ Ask the chemist to give you something for the pain. **2.** a scientist who studies chemical substances

chemistry /'kemɪstri/ noun the science of chemical substances and their reactions ○ She's studying chemistry at university. ○ He passed his chemistry exam.

cheque /tʃek/ noun a form asking a bank to pay money from one account to another ○ I paid for the jacket by cheque. ○ He made out the cheque to Mr Smith. ○ He's forgotten to sign the cheque.

cherry /'tʃeri/ noun a small sweet red or black fruit with a single hard seed in the middle, which grows on a tree

chess /tʃes/ noun a game for two people played on a board with sixteen different-shaped pieces on each side (NOTE: no plural)

chest /tʃest/ noun **1.** the top front part of the body, where the heart and lungs are ○ If you have pains in your chest or if you have chest pains, you ought to see a doctor. ○ The doctor listened to the patient's chest. ○ She was rushed to hospital with chest wounds. ○ He has a 48-inch chest. **2.** a measurement around the top part of the body just under the arms ○ *What's his chest size* or *measurement?* **3.** a piece of furniture, like a large box

chew /tʃuː/ *verb* to use your teeth to make something soft, usually so that you can swallow it ○ *You must chew your meat well, or you will get pains in your stomach.* ○ *The dog was lying in front of the fire chewing a bone.*

chick /tʃɪk/ *noun* a baby bird, especially a baby hen

chicken /'tʃɪkɪn/ *noun* **1.** a bird kept for its eggs and meat ○ *Chickens were running everywhere in the farmyard.* (NOTE: The plural is **chickens**.) **2.** meat from a chicken ○ *We're having roast chicken for lunch.* ○ *Would you like another slice of chicken?* ○ *We bought some chicken sandwiches for lunch.* (NOTE: no plural: *some chicken*; *a piece of chicken*; *a slice of chicken*)

chief /tʃiːf/ *adjective* most important ○ *He's our chief adviser.* ○ *What is the chief cause of accidents in the home?* ■ *noun* **1.** the person in control of a group of people or a business ○ *He's been made the new chief of the finance department.* **2.** the leader of a specific group of people who share a culture and social system

chiefly /'tʃiːfli/ *adverb* mainly ○ *The town is famous chiefly for its cathedral.*

child /tʃaɪld/ *noun* **1.** a young boy or girl ○ *There was no TV when my mother was a child.* ○ *A group of children were playing on the beach.* **2.** a son or daughter ○ *Whose child is that?* ○ *They have six children – two boys and four girls.* ○ *We have two adult children.* (NOTE: The plural is **children**.)

childhood /'tʃaɪldhʊd/ *noun* the time when someone is a child

childish /'tʃaɪldɪʃ/ *adjective* **1.** silly or foolish **2.** like a child

children /'tʃɪldrən/ plural of **child**

chill /tʃɪl/ *noun* **1.** a short illness causing a feeling of being cold and shivering ○ *You'll catch a chill if you don't wear a coat in this cold weather.* **2.** coldness ○ *The sun came up and soon cleared away the morning chill.* **3.** an atmosphere of

gloom ○ *The death of the bride's father cast a chill over the wedding.* ■ *verb* to cool ○ *He asked for a glass of chilled orange juice.* □ **chilled to the bone** very cold (*informal*) ○ *They were chilled to the bone when they came back from their walk over the moors.*

chilly /'tʃɪli/ *adjective* quite cold (NOTE: **chillier – chilliest**)

chimney /'tʃɪmni/ *noun* a tall brick tube for taking smoke away from a fire

chin /tʃɪn/ *noun* the front part of the bottom jaw ○ *She suddenly stood up and hit him on the chin.*

china /'tʃaɪnə/ *noun* things such as cups and plates made of decorated fine white clay (NOTE: no plural)

chip /tʃɪp/ *noun* **1.** a long thin piece of potato fried in oil ○ *He ordered chicken and chips.* □ **fish and chips** a traditional British food, obtained from special shops, where portions of fish fried in batter are sold with chips **2.** *US* a thin slice of potato or other food, fried till crisp and eaten cold as a snack ○ *a packet of potato* or *corn chips* **3.** a small piece of something hard, such as wood or stone ○ *Chips of wood flew all over the studio as he was carving the statue.* **4.** a small piece of silicon able to store data, used in a computer ■ *verb* to break a small piece off something hard ○ *He banged the cup down on the plate and chipped it.* (NOTE: **chips – chipping – chipped**) ◇ **to have a chip on your shoulder** to feel constantly annoyed because you feel you have lost an advantage ○ *He's got a chip on his shoulder because his brother has a better job than he has.*

chocolate /'tʃɒklət/ *noun* **1.** a sweet brown food made from the crushed seeds of a tropical tree ○ *a bar of chocolate* ○ *Her mother made a chocolate cake.* **2.** a single sweet made from chocolate ○ *There are only three chocolates left in the box.* **3.** a drink made from chocolate powder and milk ○ *I always have a cup of hot chocolate before I go to bed.* (NOTE: no plural except for sense 2)

choice /tʃɔɪs/ *noun* **1.** something which is chosen ○ *Paris was our first choice* *for our holiday.* **2.** the act of choosing something ○ *You must give customers time to make their choice.* **3.** a range of things to choose from ○ *The store has a huge choice of furniture.* □ **I hadn't any choice, I had no choice** there was nothing else I could do ■ *adjective* (*of food*) specially selected ○ *choice meat* ○ *choice peaches*

choir /kwaɪə/ *noun* a group of people who sing together ○ *He sings in the school choir.*

choke /tʃəʊk/ *verb* **1.** to stop breathing properly because something such as a piece of food is blocking the throat ○ *Don't talk with your mouth full or you'll choke.* ○ *He choked on a piece of bread* or *a piece of bread made him choke.* **2.** to block something such as a pipe ○ *The canal was choked with weeds.* **3.** to squeeze someone's neck so that they cannot breathe ○ *He felt the tight collar was choking him.* □ **to choke someone to death** to squeeze someone's throat until they die **4.** to find it hard to speak because of emotion

choose /tʃuːz/ *verb* **1.** to decide which you want ○ *Have you chosen what you want to eat?* ○ *They chose him as team leader.* ○ *Don't take too long choosing a book to read on holiday.* ○ *There were several good candidates to choose from.* ○ *You must give customers plenty of time to choose.* **2.** to decide to do one thing when there are several things you could do ○ *In the end, they chose to go to the cinema.* ◊ **choice** (NOTE: **chooses – choosing – chose** /tʃəʊz/ – **has chosen** /ˈtʃəʊz(ə)n/)

chop /tʃɒp/ *noun* a piece of meat with a bone attached ○ *We had lamb chops for dinner.* ■ *verb* **1.** to cut something roughly into small pieces with a knife or other sharp tool ○ *He spent the afternoon chopping wood for the fire.* **2.** □ **to chop and change** to do one thing, then another ○ *He keeps chopping and changing and can't make his mind up.* (NOTE: **chops – chopping – chopped**)

chop down *phrasal verb* to cut down a tree with an axe

chop off *phrasal verb* to cut something off, e.g. with an axe or knife

chop up *phrasal verb* to cut something into pieces

chore /tʃɔː/ *noun* a piece of routine work, e.g. cleaning in a house, that you have to do ○ *household chores*

chorus /ˈkɔːrəs/ *noun* **1.** a part of a song which is repeated later in the song ○ *Everybody join in the chorus!* (NOTE: The plural is **choruses**.) **2.** a group of people who sing together ○ *All the members of the chorus were on the stage.*

chose /tʃəʊz/ past tense of **choose**

chosen /ˈtʃəʊz(ə)n/ past participle of **choose**

Christian /ˈkrɪstʃən/ *adjective* relating to the religion based on the teachings of Jesus Christ ■ *noun* a person who believes in the teachings of Jesus Christ and in Christianity

Christmas /ˈkrɪsməs/ *noun* a Christian festival on December 25th, celebrated as the birthday of Jesus Christ, when presents are given

church /tʃɜːtʃ/ *noun* a building where Christians go to pray (NOTE: The plural is **churches**.)

cigarette /ˌsɪɡəˈret/ *noun* a roll of very thin paper containing tobacco, which you can light and smoke ○ *a packet* or *pack of cigarettes* ○ *The room was full of cigarette smoke.*

cinema /ˈsɪnɪmə/ *noun* a building where you go to watch films ○ *We went to the cinema on Friday night to see a French film.*

circle /ˈsɜːk(ə)l/ *noun* **1.** a line forming a round shape ○ *He drew a circle on the blackboard.* **2.** anything forming a round shape ○ *The children sat in a circle round the teacher.* ○ *The soldiers formed a circle round the prisoner.* **3.** a group of people or a society ○ *She went to live abroad and lost contact with her old circle of friends.* ○ *He moves in the highest government circles.* **4.** a row of seats above the stalls in a theatre ○ *We got tickets for the upper circle.* ■ *verb* to make circular movements ○ *Large birds were circling above the dead animals.*

circuit /'sɜːkɪt/ *noun* **1.** a fixed or regular way of travelling from one place to another for a particular activity ○ *a familiar speaker on the lecture circuit* **2.** a path on which competitions take place ○ *a race circuit* **3.** a trip around something ○ *His first circuit of the track was very slow.* **4.** the path that electricity flows around

circular /'sɜːkjʊlə/ *adjective* **1.** round in shape ○ *a circular table* **2.** sent to a number of people ○ *The company sent a circular letter to all employees.* (NOTE: only used before a noun) ■ *noun* a document with one or just a few pages sent to a number of people to inform them about something

circulate /'sɜːkjʊleɪt/ *verb* **1.** to send something round to various people ○ *They circulated a new list of prices to all their customers.* **2.** to move round ○ *Blood circulates round the body.* ○ *Waiters circulated round the room carrying trays of drinks.* **3.** *vi* to talk to different people at a party ○ *Let's talk later – I've got to circulate.*

circulation /ˌsɜːkjʊ'leɪʃ(ə)n/ *noun* **1.** the act of circulating ○ *The circulation of the new price list to all departments will take several days.* **2.** the movement of blood around the body ○ *Rub your hands together to get the circulation going.* ○ *He has poor circulation.*

circumference /sə'kʌmf(ə)rəns/ *noun* the distance round the outside edge of a circle, an object or an area ○ *We walked the dog around the circumference of the field.*

circumstance /'sɜːkəmstəns/ *noun* the set of conditions that affect a situation ○ *The circumstances surrounding the crash led us to believe it was not an accident.* (NOTE: usually plural) □ **in** *or* **under the circumstances** if a particular set of conditions exist ○ *It's hard to do a good job under these circumstances.* ○ *In different circumstances, I'd have been willing to stay longer.* □ **due to circumstances beyond someone's control** because of something which someone has no power to change ○ *The show had to be cancelled due to circumstances beyond our control.*

citizen /'sɪtɪz(ə)n/ *noun* a person who comes from a particular country or has the same right to live there as someone who was born there ○ *All Australian citizens have a duty to vote.* ○ *He was born in Germany, but is now a British citizen.*

city /'sɪti/ *noun* a large town ○ *busy city streets* ○ *Traffic is a problem in big cities.* □ **the city centre** the central part of a town ○ *He has an office in the city centre.*

civil /'sɪv(ə)l/ *adjective* **1.** relating to general public life rather than to the armed forces ○ *He left the air force and became a civil airline pilot.* **2.** polite ○ *She wasn't very civil to the policeman.* **3.** in court, relating to cases brought by one person against another, as opposed to being brought by the police because it is criminal

claim /kleɪm/ *noun* **1.** an occasion on which someone asks for money ○ *His claim for a pay increase was turned down.* **2.** a statement of something which you believe to be true but have no proof ○ *His claim that the car belonged to him was correct.* ■ *verb* to state, but without any proof ○ *He claims he never received the letter.* ○ *She claims that the car belongs to her.*

clap /klæp/ *verb* to beat your hands together to show you are pleased ○ *At the end of her speech the audience stood up and clapped.* ○ *He clapped his hands together in delight.* (NOTE: **claps – clapping – clapped**)

class /klɑːs/ *noun* **1.** a group of children or adults who go to school or college together ○ *There are 30 children in my son's class.* **2.** a lesson ○ *What did you learn in your history class today?* **3.** people of a particular group in society ○ *The college encourages applications from different social classes.* **4.** a group of things, animal or people that share some features ○ *Different standards apply to the five different classes of service you can pay for.* **5.** a particular level of quality ○ *Always buy the best class of product.* ○ *These peaches are Class 1.*

classic /'klæsɪk/ *noun* a great book, play or piece of music ○ *'The Maltese Falcon' is a Hollywood classic.* ○ *We have* to study several classics of English literature for our course. ■ adjective 1. (of a style) elegant and traditional ○ The classic little black dress is always in fashion. ○ The style of the new hotel building is classic, simple and elegant. 2. based on Ancient Greek or Roman architecture 3. typical ○ It was a classic example of his inability to take decisions.

classical /'klæsɪk(ə)l/ adjective 1. elegant and based on the Ancient Greek or Roman style ○ a classical eighteenth century villa 2. referring to Ancient Greece and Rome ○ classical Greek literature 3. referring to traditional serious music ○ a concert of classical music

classification /ˌklæsɪfɪ'keɪʃ(ə)n/ noun a way of arranging things into categories

classify /'klæsɪfaɪ/ verb to arrange things into groups ○ The hotels are classified according to a system of stars. (NOTE: **classifies – classifying – classified**)

classroom /'klɑːsruːm/ noun a room in a school where children are taught ○ When the teacher came into the classroom all the children were shouting.

clause /klɔːz/ noun a paragraph in a legal document ○ According to clause six, payments will not be due until next year.

claw /klɔː/ noun a nail on the foot of an animal or bird ○ The dog dug a hole with its claws.

clay /kleɪ/ noun thick heavy soil ○ The soil in our garden has a lot of clay in it.

clean /kliːn/ adjective 1. not dirty ○ Wipe your glasses with a clean handkerchief. ○ The bedrooms must be spotlessly clean. ○ Tell the waitress these cups aren't clean. 2. not used ○ Take a clean sheet of paper. ○ The maid forgot to put clean towels in the bathroom. ■ verb to take away the dirt from something ○ She was cleaning the car when she saw the damage.

clean up phrasal verb to make everything clean and tidy, e.g. after a party ○ It took us three hours to clean up after her birthday party.

cleaner /'kliːnə/ noun 1. a machine which removes dirt ○ a carpet cleaner 2. a person who cleans a building such as a house or an office ○ The cleaners didn't empty my wastepaper basket.

cleaning /'kliːnɪŋ/ noun 1. the action of making something clean ○ Cleaning the house after the party took hours. 2. clothes which are going to be sent for dry-cleaning or which have been returned after dry-cleaning ○ Could you collect my cleaning for me after work tonight?

clear /klɪə/ adjective 1. with nothing in the way ○ You can cross the road – it's clear now. ○ From the window, she had a clear view of the street. 2. easily understood ○ She made it clear that she wanted us to go. ○ The instructions on the computer screen are not very clear. ○ Will you give me a clear answer – yes or no?

clear away phrasal verb to take something away completely

clear off phrasal verb to go away (informal)

clear out phrasal verb 1. to empty something completely ○ Can you clear out your bedroom cupboard? 2. to leave somewhere quickly (informal) ○ It's time for me to clear out of here completely. □ **Clear out!** used to tell someone to leave (impolite)

clear up phrasal verb 1. to tidy and clean a place completely ○ The cleaners refused to clear up the mess after the office party. 2. (of an illness) to get better ○ He has been resting, but his cold still hasn't cleared up.

clearly /'klɪəli/ adverb 1. in a way which is easily understood or heard ○ He didn't speak clearly, and I couldn't catch the address he gave. 2. obviously ○ He clearly or Clearly he didn't like being told he was too fat.

clergy /'klɜːdʒi/ plural noun priests

clerical /'klerɪk(ə)l/ adjective 1. referring to office work ○ A clerical error made the invoice £300.00 when it should have been £3000.00. ○ He's looking for part-time clerical work. 2. referring to clergy ○ The newspaper sto-

ry has been talked about in clerical circles.

clerk /klɑːk/ *noun* a person who works in an office

clever /'klevə/ *adjective* able to think and learn quickly ○ *Clever children can usually do this by the time they are eight years old.*

cleverly /'klevəli/ *adverb* in a clever way

click /klɪk/ *noun* a short sharp sound ○ *She heard a click and saw the door handle turn.* ■ *verb* to make a short sharp sound ○ *The cameras clicked as the film star came out on to the steps.* ○ *He clicked his fingers to attract the waiter's attention.*

client /'klaɪənt/ *noun* a person who pays for a service

cliff /klɪf/ *noun* a high, steep area of rock usually by the sea

climate /'klaɪmət/ *noun* the general weather conditions in a particular place ○ *The climate in the south of the country is milder than in the north.*

climb /klaɪm/ *verb* **1.** to go up or down something using arms and legs ○ *The cat climbed up the apple tree.* ○ *The boys climbed over the wall.* ○ *He escaped by climbing out of the window.* **2.** to go higher ○ *The road climbs to 500 m above sea level.* ○ *House prices have started to climb again.*

clinic /'klɪnɪk/ *noun* **1.** a medical centre for particular treatment or advice ○ *an eye clinic* **2.** a private hospital

clip /klɪp/ *noun* a small object that holds things together ○ *a paper clip* ■ *verb* to attach things with a clip ○ *She clipped the invoice and the cheque together and put them in an envelope.* (NOTE: **clips – clipping – clipped**)

cloak /kləʊk/ *noun* a long type of coat which hangs from the shoulders and has no sleeves ○ *She wore a long cloak of black velvet.*

clock /klɒk/ *noun* an object which shows the time ○ *Your clock is 5 minutes slow.* ○ *The office clock is fast.* ○ *The clock has stopped.*

clockwise /'klɒkwaɪz/ *adjective, adverb* moving in a circle from left to right, in the same direction as the hands of a clock ○ *Turn the lid clockwise to tighten it.* ○ *He was driving clockwise round the ring road when the accident took place.*

clone /kləʊn/ *noun* an exact genetic copy of an animal or plant ○ *A cutting produces a clone of a plant.* ○ *This sheep was the first mammal to survive as a clone.* ■ *verb* to create an exact genetic copy of an individual animal or plant ○ *Biologists have successfully cloned a sheep.*

close[1] /kləʊs/ *adjective* **1.** very near, or just next to something ○ *Our office is close to the station.* ○ *This is the closest I've ever been to a film star!* **2.** near in time ○ *My birthday is close to Christmas.* ■ *adverb* **1.** very near ○ *Keep close by me if you don't want to get lost.* ○ *Go further away – you're getting too close.* ○ *They stood so close or so close together that she felt his breath on her cheek.* ○ *The sound came closer and closer.* (NOTE: **closer – closest**) **2.** very near in time ○ *The conference is getting very close.* ■ *noun* a short road, especially of houses ○ *They live in Briar Close.*

close[2] /kləʊz/ *verb* **1.** to shut ○ *Would you mind closing the window?* ○ *He closed his book and turned on the TV.* **2.** to come to an end ○ *The meeting closed with a vote of thanks.* (NOTE: **closes – closing – closed**) ■ *noun* an end, the final part ○ *The century was drawing to a close.*

close down *phrasal verb* **1.** to shut a business permanently **2.** (*of a business*) to shut permanently

closed /kləʊzd/ *adjective* **1.** changed from being open by being covered or blocked ○ *Make sure all the windows and doors are tightly closed.* ○ *She sat quietly with closed eyes.* ○ *The object was in a closed box.* **2.** not doing business ○ *The shop is closed on Sundays.* ○ *The office will be closed for the Christmas holidays.* ○ *There was a 'closed' sign hanging in the window.*

closely /'kləʊsli/ *adverb* with a lot of attention ○ *She studied the timetable very closely.* ○ *The prisoners were closely guarded by armed soldiers.*

closeness /'kləʊsnəs/ *noun* the fact of being close to something

close-up /'kləʊs ʌp/ *noun* a photograph taken very close to the subject □ **in close-up** taken very close to the subject ○ *a photo of the leaf in close-up*

cloth /klɒθ/ *noun* **1.** soft material made from woven fibres ○ *Her dress is made of cheap blue cloth.* ○ *This cloth is of a very high quality.* **2.** a piece of material used for cleaning ○ *He wiped up the milk with a damp cloth.* **3.** a piece of material which you put on a table to cover it ○ *The waiter spread a white cloth over the table.*

clothes /kləʊðz/ *plural noun* things which you wear to cover your body and keep you warm, e.g. trousers, socks, shirts and dresses ○ *The doctor asked him to take his clothes off.* ○ *The children haven't had any new clothes for years.* □ **with no clothes on** naked

clothing /'kləʊðɪŋ/ *noun* clothes ○ *a major clothing manufacturer* ○ *Take plenty of warm clothing on your trip to Iceland.* (NOTE: no plural: *some clothing; a piece of clothing*)

cloud /klaʊd/ *noun* a white or grey mass of drops of water floating in the air ○ *Look at those grey clouds – it's going to rain.* ○ *The plane was flying above the clouds.*

cloudy /'klaʊdi/ *adjective* **1.** with clouds ○ *The weather was cloudy in the morning, but cleared up in the afternoon.* **2.** not clear ○ *The liquid turned cloudy when I added the flour.* (NOTE: **cloudier – cloudiest**)

club /klʌb/ *noun* **1.** a group of people who have the same interest or who form a team ○ *a youth club* ○ *I'm joining a tennis club.* ○ *Our town has one of the top football clubs in the country.* **2.** a stick for playing golf (NOTE: A **golf club** can either mean the place where you play golf, or the stick used to hit the ball.) **3.** a large heavy stick ■ *verb* **1.** to hit with a club ○ *She was clubbed to the*

ground. **2.** □ **to club together** (*of several people*) to contribute money jointly ○ *They clubbed together and bought a yacht.* (NOTE: **clubs – clubbing – clubbed**)

clue /kluː/ *noun* information which helps you solve a mystery or puzzle ○ *The detective had missed a vital clue.* ○ *I don't understand the clues to this crossword.* ◊ **to not have a clue** to not know something ○ *The police still haven't a clue who did it.* ○ *I don't have a clue how to get there.*

clumsy /'klʌmzi/ *adjective* tending to break things or knock things over (NOTE: **clumsier – clumsiest**) ■ not expressed or done in a good way ○ *a clumsy apology* ○ *a clumsy attempt to hide the situation*

cluster /'klʌstə/ *noun* a group of objects or people that are close together ○ *a brooch with a cluster of pearls* ○ *He photographed a cluster of stars.*

clutch /klʌtʃ/ *verb* to grip something tightly ○ *She clutched my arm as we stood on the edge of the cliff.* ■ *noun* a tight grip ○ *She felt the clutch of his fingers on her sleeve.* ■ *plural noun* **clutches** the power that a person or group has over someone else ○ *You can't escape the clutches of your family so easily.* □ **in the clutches of, in someone's clutches** under the control of ○ *We want to avoid spending too much and falling into the clutches of the bank* or *the bank's clutches.*

coach /kəʊtʃ/ *noun* **1.** a large bus for travelling long distances ○ *They went on a tour of southern Spain by coach.* ○ *There's an coach service to Oxford every hour.* **2.** one of the vehicles for passengers that is part of a train ○ *The first four coaches are for London.* **3.** a person who trains sports players ○ *The coach told them that they needed to spend more time practising.* ○ *He's a professional football coach.* (NOTE: The plural is **coaches.**) ■ *verb* **1.** to train sports people ○ *She was coached by a former Olympic gold medallist.* **2.** to give private lessons to someone in a particular sport, subject or activity ○ *He coaches young footballers.*

coal /kəʊl/ *noun* a hard black substance which produces heat when burnt

coarse /kɔːs/ *adjective* **1.** consisting of large pieces ○ *coarse grains of sand* **2.** rough and hard ○ *coarse cloth*

coast /kəʊst/ *noun* parts of a country that are by the sea ○ *After ten weeks at sea, Columbus saw the coast of America.* ○ *The south coast is the warmest part of the country.*

coat /kəʊt/ *noun* **1.** a piece of clothing which you wear on top of other clothes when you go outside ○ *a winter coat* **2.** a layer of something ○ *a coat of paint* ○ *a thick coat of dust* **3.** the fur of an animal ○ *These dogs have thick shiny coats.*

cocoa /ˈkəʊkəʊ/ *noun* **1.** a brown chocolate powder ground from the seeds of a tree, used for making a drink ○ *a tin of cocoa* ○ *cocoa powder* **2.** a drink made with cocoa and hot water or milk (NOTE: no plural)

code /kəʊd/ *noun* **1.** secret words or a system agreed as a way of sending messages ○ *We're trying to break the enemy's code.* ○ *He sent the message in code.* **2.** a system of numbers or letters which mean something ○ *The code for Heathrow Airport is LHR.* ○ *What is the code for phoning Edinburgh?* **3.** a set of laws or rules of behaviour ○ *The hotel has a strict dress code, and people wearing jeans are not allowed in.*

coffee /ˈkɒfi/ *noun* **1.** a hot drink made from the seeds of a tropical plant ○ *Would you like a cup of coffee?* ○ *I always take sugar in coffee.* **2.** a cup of coffee ○ *I'd like a white coffee, please.* ○ *Three coffees and two teas, please.*

coffee shop /ˈkɒfi ʃɒp/ *noun* a small restaurant serving drinks and light meals

coffin /ˈkɒfɪn/ *noun* a long box in which a dead person is placed before being buried

coil /kɔɪl/ *noun* a roll of rope, or one loop in something twisted round and round ○ *The sailors stacked the rope in coils on the deck.* ■ *verb* to twist around something or into a coil ○ *The snake had*

coiled itself up in the basket. ○ *The sailor coiled the ropes neatly.*

coin /kɔɪn/ *noun* a piece of metal money ○ *This machine only takes 20p coins.*

cold /kəʊld/ *adjective* **1.** with a low temperature ○ *They say that cold showers are good for you.* ○ *The weather turned colder in January.* ○ *It's too cold to go for a walk.* ○ *If you're hot, have a glass of cold water.* ○ *Start eating, or your soup will get cold.* ○ *He had a plate of cold beef and salad.* **2.** not friendly ○ *He got a very cold reception from the rest of the staff.* ○ *She gave him a cold nod.* (NOTE: **colder – coldest**) ■ *noun* **1.** an illness which makes you blow your nose ○ *He caught a cold from his colleague.* ○ *My sister's in bed with a cold.* ○ *Don't come near me – I've got a cold.* **2.** a cold outdoor temperature ○ *He was in the cold waiting for a bus.* ○ *These plants can't stand the cold.*

coldly /ˈkəʊldli/ *adverb* in an unfriendly way

collapse /kəˈlæps/ *verb* **1.** to fall down suddenly ○ *The roof collapsed under the weight of the snow.* **2.** to fail suddenly ○ *The company collapsed with £25,000 in debts.* **3.** to fall down unconscious ○ *He collapsed after the marathon.* ■ *noun* **1.** a sudden fall ○ *The collapse of the old wall buried two workmen.* **2.** a sudden fall in price ○ *the collapse of the dollar on the foreign exchange markets* **3.** the sudden failure of a company ○ *They lost thousands of pounds in the collapse of the bank.*

collar /ˈkɒlə/ *noun* **1.** the part of a piece of clothing which goes round your neck ○ *I can't wear this shirt – the collar's too tight.* ○ *She turned up her coat collar because the wind was cold.* ○ *He has a winter coat with a fur collar.* **2.** a leather ring round the neck of a dog or cat ○ *The cat has a collar with her name and address on it.*

colleague /ˈkɒliːg/ *noun* a person who works with you, e.g. in the same company or office ○ *His colleagues gave him a present when he got married.* ○ *She was a colleague of mine at my last job.*

collect /kəˈlekt/ *verb* **1.** to bring things or people together, or to come together

○ *We collected information from all the people who offered to help.* ○ *A crowd collected at the scene of the accident.* **2.** to get things and keep them together ○ *Your coat is ready for you to collect from the cleaner's* ○ *The mail is collected from the postbox twice a day.* ○ *I must collect the children from school at 4 p.m.* **3.** to buy things or bring things together as a hobby ○ *He collects stamps and old coins.* **4.** to gather money to give to an organisation that helps people ○ *They're collecting for Oxfam.*

collection /kəˈlekʃən/ *noun* **1.** a group of things that have been brought together ○ *He showed me his stamp collection.* ○ *The museum has a large collection of Italian paintings.* **2.** money which has been gathered ○ *We're making a collection for Oxfam.*

college /ˈkɒlɪdʒ/ *noun* a teaching institution for adults and young people ○ *She's going on holiday with some friends from college.* ○ *He's studying art at the local college.* ○ *The college library has over 20,000 volumes.*

collide /kəˈlaɪd/ *verb* to bump into something ○ *The car collided with a bus.*

collision /kəˈlɪʒ(ə)n/ *noun* **1.** an occasion when someone or something hits against something accidentally ○ *Two people were injured in the collision between a lorry and the bus.* □ **in collision with** involved in hitting into ○ *She was in collision with a bike.* **2.** a disagreement or difference ○ *a collision of ideas*

colon /ˈkəʊlɒn/ *noun* **1.** the main part of the part inside your body that removes waste ○ *The intestines are divided into two parts: the small intestine and the large intestine or colon.* **2.** a printing sign (:)

color /ˈkʌlə/ *noun, verb* US spelling of **colour**

colour /ˈkʌlə/ *noun* **1.** the shade which an object has in light, e.g. red, blue or yellow ○ *What colour is your bathroom?* ○ *I don't like the colour of the carpet.* ○ *His socks are the same colour as his shirt.* **2.** not black or white ○ *The book has pages of colour pictures.* ■ *verb* to add colour to something ○ *The*

children were given crayons and told to colour the trees green and the earth brown.

coloured /ˈkʌləd/ *adjective* in colour ○ *a coloured postcard* ○ *a book with coloured illustrations*

-coloured /kʌləd/ *suffix* with a particular colour ○ *She was wearing a cream-coloured shirt.*

colourful /ˈkʌləf(ə)l/ *adjective* **1.** with bright colours ○ *She tied a colourful silk scarf round her hair.* **2.** full of excitement and adventure ○ *a colourful account of life in Vienna before the First World War*

column /ˈkɒləm/ *noun* **1.** a tall post, especially one made of stone **2.** a narrow block of printing on a page such as in a newspaper ○ *'Continued on page 7, column 4.'* **3.** a regular article in a newspaper ○ *She writes a gardening column for the local newspaper.* **4.** a series of numbers, one written or printed under the other ○ *to add up a column of figures* ○ *Put the total at the bottom of the column.*

comb /kəʊm/ *noun* an object with long pointed pieces that you pull through your hair to make it straight ○ *Her hair is in such a mess that you can't get a comb through it.* ■ *verb* to smooth your hair with a comb ○ *She was combing her hair in front of the mirror.*

combination /ˌkɒmbɪˈneɪʃ(ə)n/ *noun* several things joined or considered together ○ *A combination of bad weather and illness made our holiday a disaster.*

come /kʌm/ *verb* **1.** to move to or towards a place ○ *Come and see us when you're in London.* ○ *The doctor came to see him yesterday.* ○ *Some of the children come to school on foot.* ○ *Don't make any noise – I can hear someone coming.* ○ *Come up to my room and we'll talk about the problem.* **2.** to happen ○ *How did the door come to be open?* **3.** to occur ○ *What comes after R in the alphabet?* ○ *P comes before Q.* ○ *What comes after the news on TV?* (NOTE: **comes – coming – came** /keɪm/ **– has come**) ◇ **how come?** why?, how? ○ *How come the front door was unlocked?*

come across *phrasal verb* to find something by chance ○ *I came across this old photo when I was clearing out a drawer.*

come along *phrasal verb* to go with someone ○ *If you walk, the children can come along with us in the car.*

come back *phrasal verb* to return ○ *They left the house in a hurry, and then had to come back to get their passports.* ○ *They started to walk away, but the policeman shouted at them to come back.*

come in *phrasal verb* to enter a place

come off *phrasal verb* **1.** to stop being attached ○ *The button has come off my coat.* ○ *I can't use the kettle, the handle has come off.* **2.** to be removed ○ *The paint won't come off my coat.*

come on *phrasal verb* to hurry ○ *Come on, or we'll miss the start of the film.*

come out *phrasal verb* **1.** to move outside ○ *Come out into the garden, it's beautifully hot.* **2.** to be removed ○ *The ink marks won't come out of my white shirt.* ○ *Red wine stains don't come out easily.*

come to *phrasal verb* **1.** to add up to a particular amount ○ *The bill comes to £10.* **2.** to become conscious again ○ *When he came to, he was in hospital.*

comedy /ˈkɒmədi/ *noun* **1.** entertainment which makes you laugh **2.** a play or film which makes you laugh (NOTE: The plural is **comedies**.)

comfort /ˈkʌmfət/ *noun* **1.** something which helps to make you feel happier ○ *It was a comfort to know that the children were safe.* ○ *The long-awaited letter gave me some comfort.* **2.** the state of being comfortable ○ *They live in great comfort.* ○ *You expect a certain amount of comfort on a luxury liner.* ○ *She complained about the lack of comfort in the second-class coaches.* ■ *verb* to make someone feel happier ○ *She was comforting the people who had been in the accident.*

comfortable /ˈkʌmf(ə)təb(ə)l/ *adjective* **1.** soft and relaxing ○ *These shoes aren't very comfortable.* ○ *There are more comfortable chairs in the lounge.* **2.** □ **to make yourself comfortable** to relax ○ *She made herself comfortable in the chair by the fire.*

comfortably /ˈkʌmftəbli/ *adverb* in a soft, relaxed or relaxing way ○ *If you're sitting comfortably, I'll explain to you what we have to do.* ○ *Make sure you're comfortably dressed because it is rather cold outside.*

comic /ˈkɒmɪk/ *noun* **1.** a children's magazine with pictures and stories **2.** a person who tells jokes to make people laugh ○ *a well-known TV comic* ■ *adjective* intended to make people laugh, especially as a performance ○ *a comic poem*

comical /ˈkɒmɪk(ə)l/ *adjective* strange or silly in a way that makes people laugh ○ *He looked rather comical wearing his dad's jacket.*

coming /ˈkʌmɪŋ/ *adjective* which is about to happen ○ *The newspaper tells you what will happen in the coming week in parliament.*

comma /ˈkɒmə/ *noun* a punctuation mark (,) showing a break in a sentence

command /kəˈmɑːnd/ *noun* an order ○ *Don't start until I give the command.* ○ *The general gave the command to attack.* □ **in command of** in control of ○ *They are not fully in command of the situation.* ■ *verb* **1.** to order someone to do something ○ *He commanded the troops to open fire on the rebels.* **2.** to be in charge of a group of people, especially in the armed forces ○ *He commands a group of volunteer soldiers.*

comment /ˈkɒment/ *noun* **1.** words showing what you think about something ○ *His comments were widely reported in the newspapers.* ○ *The man made a rude comment accompanied by some very offensive gestures.* **2.** discussion about a particular issue ○ *The scandal aroused considerable comment in the press.* (NOTE: no plural in this meaning) ■ *verb* to say what you think about something ○ *The minister refused to comment.* ○ *The judges commented that the standard had been very high.*

commercial /kəˈmɜːʃ(ə)l/ *adjective* **1.** relating to business ○ *He is a specialist in commercial law.* **2.** used for business purposes and not private or military purposes ○ *The company makes commercial vehicles such as taxis and buses.* (NOTE: [all adjective senses] only used before nouns) ■ *noun* an advertisement on television ○ *Our TV commercial attracted a lot of interest.*

commit /kə'mɪt/ *verb* **1.** to carry out a crime ○ *The gang committed six robberies before they were caught.* ○ *He said he was on holiday in Spain when the murder was committed.* **2.** to promise, or make someone promise, something or to do something ○ *Under my contract I committed to work for them three days a week.* ○ *The agreement commits us to check the machine twice a month.* ○ *They didn't want to commit £5000 all at once.* (NOTE: **commits – committing – committed**)

commitment /kə'mɪtmənt/ *noun* a promise to do something such as pay money ○ *He has difficulty in meeting his commitments.*

committee /kə'mɪti/ *noun* an official group of people who organise or discuss things for a larger group ○ *The company has set up a committee to look into sports facilities.* ○ *Committee members will be asked to vote on the proposal.*

common /'kɒmən/ *adjective* happening often, or found everywhere and so not unusual ○ *It's very common for people to get colds in winter.* ○ *The plane tree is a very common tree in towns.*

commonly /'kɒmənli/ *adverb* often

common sense /ˌkɒmən 'sens/ *noun* the ability to make sensible decisions and do the best thing

commotion /kə'məʊʃ(ə)n/ *noun* noise and confusion

communicate /kə'mjuːnɪkeɪt/ *verb* **1.** to send or give information to someone ○ *Although she is unable to speak, she can still communicate using her hands.* ○ *Communicating with our office in London has been transformed by email.* **2.** to be good at sharing your thoughts or feelings with other people ○ *He finds it difficult to communicate with his children.*

communication /kə,mjuːnɪ'keɪʃ(ə)n/ *noun* the act of passing information on to other people ○ *Email is the most rapid means of communication.* ○ *There is a lack of communication between the head teacher and the other members of staff.* ■ *plural noun* **communications 1.** a system of sending information between people or places ○ *an improved communications network* ○ *Telephone communications have been restored.* **2.** the ways people use to give information or express their thoughts and feelings to each other ○ *There's been a breakdown in communications between the agencies dealing with the case.*

community /kə'mjuːnɪti/ *noun* a group of people living in one area ○ *The local community is worried about the level of violence in the streets.*

compact disc /'kɒmpækt 'dɪsk/ *noun* a hard, round piece of plastic which can hold a large amount of music or computer information ○ *I usually get Dad a CD for his birthday.* Abbreviation **CD**

companion /kəm'pænjən/ *noun* a person who is with someone ○ *She turned to her companion and said a few words.*

company /'kʌmp(ə)ni/ *noun* **1.** an organisation that offers a service or that buys and sells goods ○ *She runs an electrical company.* ○ *He set up a computer company.* ○ *It is company policy not to allow smoking anywhere in the offices.* (NOTE: usually written **Co.** in names: *Smith & Co.* The plural is **companies** in this sense.) **2.** the fact of being together with other people ○ *I enjoy the company of young people.* □ **in company with, in the company of** with ○ *She went to Paris in company with or in the company of three other girls from college.* **3.** a group of people who work together ○ *a theatre company*

comparative /kəm'pærətɪv/ *adjective* to a certain extent, when considered next to something else ○ *Judged by last year's performance it is a comparative improvement.* ■ *noun* the form of an adjective or adverb showing an increase in level or strength ○ *'Happier', 'better' and 'more often' are the comparatives of 'happy', 'good' and 'often.'*

compare /kəm'peə/ *verb* **1.** to look at two things side by side to see how they are different ○ *Compare the front with the back.* ○ *The colour of the paint was compared to the sample.* **2.** □ **to compare something to something else** to say how something is like something else ○ *He compared his mother's home-made bread to a lump of wood.*

comparison /kəm'pærɪs(ə)n/ *noun* the act of comparing two or more things ○ *He made a comparison of the different methods available.* ○ *This year, July was cold in comparison with last year.* □ **there is no comparison between them** one is much better than the other

compass /'kʌmpəs/ *noun* an object with a needle that points to the north ○ *They were lost in the mountains without a compass.*

compensate /'kɒmpənseɪt/ *verb* to make a bad thing seem less serious or unpleasant ○ *The high salary compensates for the long hours worked.* □ **to compensate someone for something** to pay someone for damage or a loss ○ *They agreed to compensate her for damage to her car.* ○ *The airline refused to compensate him when his baggage was lost.*

compensation /ˌkɒmpən'seɪʃ(ə)n/ *noun* **1.** something that makes something bad seem less serious or unpleasant ○ *Working in the centre of London has its compensations.* ○ *Four weeks' holiday is no compensation for a year's work in that office.* **2.** payment for damage or loss ○ *The airline refused to pay any compensation for his lost luggage.*

compete /kəm'piːt/ *verb* to try to win a race or a game ○ *He is competing in both the 100 and 200 metre races.* □ **to compete with someone** *or* **something** to try to be more successful than someone or something in an activity, especially in business ○ *We have to compete with a range of cheap imports.*

competence /'kɒmpɪt(ə)ns/ *noun* **1.** the quality of being able to do a job or task well enough ○ *Does she have the necessary competence in foreign languages?* **2.** the quality of being legally suitable or qualified to do something ○

The case falls within the competence of the tribunal. ○ *This is outside the competence of this court.*

competent /'kɒmpɪt(ə)nt/ *adjective* **1.** efficient ○ *She is a very competent manager.* **2.** legally or officially able to do something ○ *The organisation is not competent to deal with this case.*

competition /ˌkɒmpə'tɪʃ(ə)n/ *noun* **1.** an event in which several teams or people compete with each other ○ *France were the winners of the competition.* ○ *He won first prize in the piano competition.* (NOTE: The plural in this sense is **competitions**.) **2.** a situation in business in which one person or company is trying to do better than another ○ *Our main competition comes from the big supermarkets.* **3.** people or companies who are trying to do better than you ○ *We have lowered our prices to try to beat the competition.* ○ *The competition is* or *are planning to reduce their prices.* (NOTE: singular in this sense, but can take a plural verb)

competitive /kəm'petɪtɪv/ *adjective* **1.** liking to win competitions ○ *He's very competitive.* **2.** having a business advantage, especially by being cheaper ○ *competitive prices* ○ *We must reduce costs to remain competitive.*

competitor /kəm'petɪtə/ *noun* **1.** a person who enters a competition ○ *All the competitors lined up for the start of the race.* **2.** a company which competes with another in the same business ○ *Two German firms are our main competitors.*

complain /kəm'pleɪn/ *verb* to say that something is not good or does not work properly ○ *The shop is so cold the staff have started complaining.* ○ *They are complaining that our prices are too high.* (NOTE: You complain **to** someone **about** something or **that** something is not good enough.)

complaint /kəm'pleɪnt/ *noun* **1.** an occasion when someone says that something is not good enough or does not work properly ○ *She sent her letter of complaint to the directors.* ○ *You must file your complaint with the relevant de-*

partment. **2.** an illness ○ *She was admitted to hospital with a kidney complaint.*

complete /kəm'pliːt/ *adjective* **1.** with all its parts ○ *He has a complete set of the new stamps.* **2.** finished ○ *The building is nearly complete.* (NOTE: used after a verb) **3.** used for emphasis ○ *The trip was a complete waste of money.* ■ *verb* **1.** to finish something ○ *The builders completed the whole job in two days.* **2.** to fill in a form ○ *When you have completed the application form, send it to us in the envelope provided.*

completely /kəm'pliːtli/ *adverb* totally ○ *The town was completely destroyed in the earthquake.* ○ *I completely forgot about my dentist's appointment.*

complex /'kɒmpleks/ *adjective* complicated ○ *This really is a complex problem.* ■ *noun* **1.** a group of buildings ○ *The council has built a new sports complex.* **2.** a worry or an unreasonable fear ○ *He has a complex about going bald.*

complicated /'kɒmplɪkeɪtɪd/ *adjective* difficult to understand, with many small details ○ *It is a complicated subject.* ○ *It's all getting too complicated – let's try and keep it simple.* ○ *Chess has quite complicated rules.* ○ *The route to get to our house is rather complicated, so I'll draw you a map.*

complication /ˌkɒmplɪ'keɪʃ(ə)n/ *noun* **1.** something that causes difficulties **2.** an illness occurring because of or during another illness ○ *She appeared to be getting better, but complications set in.* (NOTE: usually plural)

compliment[1] /'kɒmplɪmənt/ *noun* a nice thing that you say to someone about their appearance or about something good they have done ○ *I've had so many compliments about my new hairstyle today!*

compliment[2] /'kɒmplɪment/ *verb* to praise someone or tell them how nice they look ○ *I would like to compliment the chef on an excellent meal.* ○ *She complimented me on my work.* (NOTE: Do not confuse with **complement**.)

component /kəm'pəʊnənt/ *noun* a small part of something larger, especially a small piece of a machine ○ *a manu-*facturer of computer components ○ *Each section of the plan is broken down into separate components.* ■ *adjective* forming part of something larger

compose /kəm'pəʊz/ *verb* to write something, thinking carefully about it ○ *He sat down to compose a letter to his family.* ○ *It took Mozart only three days to compose his fifth piano concerto.*

composition /ˌkɒmpə'zɪʃ(ə)n/ *noun* **1.** something which has been composed, e.g. a poem or piece of music ○ *We will now play a well-known composition by Dowland.* **2.** an essay or piece of writing on a special subject ○ *We had three hours to write a composition on 'pollution'.*

compound /'kɒmpaʊnd/ *adjective* made up of several parts ○ *The word 'address book' is a compound noun.* ■ *noun* **1.** a chemical made up of two or more elements ○ *Water is a compound of two gases, oxygen and hydrogen.* **2.** buildings and land enclosed by a fence ○ *Soldiers were guarding the prison compound.* ○ *Guard dogs patrol the compound at night.*

compulsory /kəm'pʌlsəri/ *adjective* essential, or required by a rule or law ○ *a compulsory charge for admission* ○ *It is compulsory to complete all pages of the form.*

computer /kəm'pjuːtə/ *noun* an electronic machine which processes and keeps information automatically, and which can be used for connecting to the Internet and sending emails □ **on computer** kept in a computer ○ *All our company records are on computer.*

computing /kəm'pjuːtɪŋ/ *noun* the use of computers

conceal /kən'siːl/ *verb* **1.** to hide something or put it where it cannot be seen ○ *He tried to conceal the camera by putting it under his coat.* **2.** to prevent someone from discovering some information ○ *He concealed the fact that he had a brother in prison.*

conceited /kən'siːtɪd/ *adjective* thinking that you are better, more intelligent, or more talented than other people ○

He's the most conceited and selfish person I've ever known.

concentrate /'kɒnsəntreɪt/ *verb* to give your careful attention to something ○ *The exam candidates were all concentrating on their questions when the electricity went off.*

concentration /ˌkɒnsən'treɪʃ(ə)n/ *noun* **1.** the act of thinking carefully about something ○ *A loud conversation in the next room disturbed my concentration.* ○ *His concentration slipped and he lost the next two games.* **2.** a lot of things together in one area ○ *the concentration of computer companies in the south of Scotland* ○ *The concentration of wild animals round the water hole makes it easy for lions to catch their prey.*

concept /'kɒnsept/ *noun* an idea about something or about how something works ○ *I'll quickly explain the basic concepts of safe working in this environment.* ○ *The concept of punctuation and grammar is completely foreign to her.* ○ *Our children have absolutely no concept of tidiness.*

concern /kən'sɜːn/ *verb* **1.** to have a particular thing as a subject ○ *The film concerns children growing up in the 1950s.* □ **to concern yourself with something** to deal with something ○ *You needn't concern yourself with cleaning the shop.* **2.** to make someone worry ○ *It concerns me that he is always late for work.* ■ *noun* **1.** worry ○ *She's a cause of great concern to her family.* **2.** interest ○ *My main concern is to ensure that we all enjoy ourselves.* ○ *The teachers showed no concern at all for the children's safety.* **3.** a company or business ○ *a big German chemical concern*

concerned /kən'sɜːnd/ *adjective* **1.** worried ○ *She looked concerned.* ○ *I could tell something was wrong by the concerned look on her face.* ○ *We are concerned about her behaviour – do you think she is having problems at school?* **2.** involved in or affected by something ○ *I'll speak to the parents concerned.* **3.** showing interest in something ○ *I'm concerned to know what*

people thought after the information session.

concerning /kən'sɜːnɪŋ/ *preposition* about; on the subject of (*formal*) ○ *He filled in a questionnaire concerning holidays.* ○ *I'd like to speak to Mr Robinson concerning his application for insurance.* ○ *Anyone with information concerning this person should get in touch with the police.*

concert /'kɒnsət/ *noun* an occasion on which music is played in public ○ *I couldn't go to the concert, so I gave my ticket to a friend.*

conclude /kən'kluːd/ *verb* **1.** to end; to come to an end ○ *He concluded by thanking all those who had helped arrange the exhibition.* ○ *The concert concluded with a piece by Mozart.* **2.** to come to an opinion from the information available ○ *The police concluded that the thief had got into the building through the broken kitchen window.*

conclusion /kən'kluːʒ(ə)n/ *noun* **1.** the end of something ○ *At the conclusion of the trial all the accused were found guilty.* **2.** an opinion which you reach after thinking carefully ○ *She came to or reached the conclusion that he had found another girlfriend.* ○ *What conclusions can you draw from the evidence?*

concrete /'kɒŋkriːt/ *noun* a mixture of a grey powder called cement, and sand, used in building ○ *Concrete was invented by the Romans.* ○ *The pavement is made of slabs of concrete.* ■ *adjective* **1.** made of concrete ○ *a concrete path* **2.** firm or definite, rather than vague ○ *The police are sure he is guilty, but they have no concrete evidence against him.* ○ *I need to see some concrete proposals very soon.* **3.** referring to something with a physical structure ○ *A stone is a concrete object.*

condemn /kən'dem/ *verb* **1.** to say strongly that you do not approve of something ○ *She condemned the police for their treatment of the prisoners.* **2.** to sentence a criminal ○ *She was condemned to death.*

condition /kən'dɪʃ(ə)n/ *noun* **1.** a state that something or someone is in ○ *The* car is in very good condition. ○ He was taken to hospital when his condition got worse. **2.** something which has to be agreed before something else is done ○ *They didn't agree with some of the conditions of the contract.* ○ *One of conditions of the deal is that the company pays all travel costs.* ◇ **on condition that** only if ○ *I will come on condition that you pay my fare.*

conduct¹ /'kɒndʌkt/ *noun* a way of behaving ○ *His conduct in class is becoming worse.* ○ *Her conduct during the trial was remarkably calm.*

conduct² /kən'dʌkt/ *verb* **1.** to do something in an organised or particular way (*formal*) ○ *I don't like the way they conduct their affairs.* ○ *They are conducting an experiment into the effect of TV advertising.* □ **to conduct yourself** to behave in a particular way ○ *I was impressed by the calm way in which she conducted herself.* ○ *The children conducted themselves well during the long speeches.* **2.** to direct or take someone to a place ○ *The guests were conducted to their seats.* **3.** to direct the way in which a musician or singer performs ○ *The orchestra was conducted by a Russian conductor.* **4.** to allow electricity or heat to pass through ○ *Copper conducts electricity very well.*

conductor /kən'dʌktə/ *noun* **1.** the person who sells tickets on a bus **2.** the person who directs the way an orchestra plays **3.** a metal or other substance through which electricity or heat can pass ○ *Copper is a good conductor but plastic is not.*

cone /kəʊn/ *noun* a shape which is round at the base, rising to a point above ○ *He rolled the newspaper to form a cone.*

confer /kən'fɜː/ *verb* **1.** to discuss ○ *The leader of the Council conferred with the Town Clerk.* **2.** to give something such as a responsibility, legal right or honour to someone (*formal*) ○ *the powers conferred on the council by law*

conference /'kɒnf(ə)rəns/ *noun* **1.** a large meeting where people who are interested in the same thing come together ○ *The organisation holds an annual conference in Brighton.* **2.** a meeting of

a group or society ○ *The annual conference of the Electricians' Union.* ○ *2000 people attended the conference on genetic engineering.*

confess /kən'fes/ *verb* to admit that you have committed a crime or done something wrong ○ *He confessed to six burglaries.* ○ *She confessed that she had forgotten to lock the door.*

confession /kən'feʃ(ə)n/ *noun* a statement in which someone admits they have committed a crime or done something wrong ○ *The prisoner said his confession had been forced from him by the police.* ○ *I was surprised by her confession of ignorance about the correct procedures to follow.* ○ *I have a confession to make – I forgot to send the cheque.*

confidence /'kɒnfɪd(ə)ns/ *noun* **1.** a feeling of being sure about your own or someone else's abilities ○ *The staff do not have much confidence in their manager.* ○ *I have total confidence in the pilot.* ○ *He hasn't got much confidence in himself.* **2.** the fact of being secret ◇ **in confidence** as a secret ○ *He showed me the report in confidence.*

confident /'kɒnfɪd(ə)nt/ *adjective* sure that you or something will be successful ○ *I am confident (that) the show will go off well.* ○ *She's confident of doing well in the exam.*

confidential /ˌkɒnfɪ'denʃəl/ *adjective* secret or private ○ *This information is strictly confidential.*

confidently /'kɒnfɪdəntli/ *adverb* in a way which shows that you are confident ○ *She walked confidently into the interview room.*

confirm /kən'fɜːm/ *verb* to say that something is certain ○ *The dates of the concerts have been confirmed by the pop group's manager.* ○ *The photograph confirmed that the result of the race was a dead heat.* ○ *We have been told that she left the country last month – can you confirm that?*

conflict¹ /'kɒnflɪkt/ *noun* **1.** a strong disagreement or argument **2.** fighting ○ *The government is engaged in armed conflict with rebel forces.* □ **to come**

into conflict with someone to start to disagree strongly with someone ○ *They soon came into conflict over who should be in charge.*

conflict² /kən'flɪkt/ *verb* to disagree with someone or something ○ *His version of events conflicts with that of his partner.*

confuse /kən'fjuːz/ *verb* **1.** to make someone feel that they cannot understand something ○ *She was confused by all the journalists' questions.* **2.** to mix things or people up ○ *The twins are so alike I am always confusing them.* ○ *I always confuse him with his brother – they are very alike.*

confused /kən'fjuːzd/ *adjective* unable to understand or to think clearly ○ *I'm a bit confused – did we say 8 p.m. or 8.30?* ○ *Grandmother used to get rather confused in her old age.*

confusing /kən'fjuːzɪŋ/ *adjective* difficult to understand ○ *They found the instructions on the computer very confusing.*

confusion /kən'fjuːʒ(ə)n/ *noun* **1.** a state of not knowing what to do or how to decide something ○ *Her reply just created more confusion over who was responsible.* □ **in confusion** not able to decide what is happening or what to do ○ *He was looking at the letter in great confusion.* **2.** a state in which things are not organised in the correct way or are not clear ○ *There were scenes of confusion at the airport when the snow stopped all flights.*

congratulate /kən'grætʃʊleɪt/ *verb* **1.** to tell someone that you are very pleased that they have been successful ○ *I want to congratulate you on your promotion.* **2.** to give someone your best wishes on a special occasion ○ *He congratulated them on their silver wedding anniversary.* (NOTE: You congratulate someone **on** something.)

congratulation /kən,grætʃʊ'leɪʃ(ə)n/ *noun* praise for someone who has done well ○ *His grandparents sent him a letter of congratulation on passing his degree.* ■ *plural noun* **congratulations** an expression of good wishes to someone who has done well or who is cele-brating a special occasion ○ *a congratulations card* ○ *Congratulations – you're our millionth customer!* ○ *Congratulations on passing your exam!* ○ *The office sent him their congratulations on his wedding.*

conjunction /kən'dʒʌŋkʃən/ *noun* **1.** a word which connects different sections of a sentence. 'and' and 'but' are conjunctions. **2.** □ **in conjunction with someone** *or* **something** together with someone or something ○ *The icy road in conjunction with fog made driving very difficult.*

connect /kə'nekt/ *verb* **1.** to join one thing to another ○ *The computer should have been connected to the printer.* ○ *Connect the two red wires together.* **2.** to make it possible for a telephone or a computer to be used for communicating with others ○ *Has the telephone been connected yet?*

connection /kə'nekʃən/ *noun* **1.** a relationship between things ○ *There is a definite connection between smoking and lung cancer.* **2.** a bus, train or plane which you catch after getting off another means of transport ○ *My train was late and I missed my connection to Birmingham.* **3.** a particular way of communicating remotely ○ *a low connection charge* ○ *Is there a reliable phone connection?* **4.** a point at which two different pieces of equipment join ○ *There is a loose connection somewhere.* ■ *plural noun* **connections** people you know ○ *He has business connections in Argentina,* ◇ **in connection with** relating to ○ *I'm writing in connection with your visit.*

conquer /'kɒŋkə/ *verb* **1.** to defeat people by force ○ *The Romans had conquered most of Europe.* **2.** to change a negative emotion or type of behaviour successfully ○ *I eventually conquered my fear of flying.*

conscience /'kɒnʃəns/ *noun* a feeling that you have done right or wrong

conscientious /,kɒnʃi'enʃəs/ *adjective* working carefully and well ○ *She's a very conscientious worker.*

conscious /'kɒnʃəs/ *adjective* awake and able to know what is happening around you ○ *She was conscious during the minor operation on her toe.* □ **a conscious decision** a decision which you have thought carefully about ○ *Refusing the offer was a conscious decision on his part.* ○ *He made a conscious decision to try to avoid her in future.*

consciously /'kɒnʃəsli/ *adverb* in a deliberate or active way ○ *I wasn't consciously ignoring her – I just didn't notice her.* ○ *He doesn't consciously remember locking the door.*

consciousness /'kɒnʃəsnəs/ *noun* the fact of being conscious □ **to lose consciousness** to become unconscious

consecutive /kən'sekjʊtɪv/ *adjective* following one after the other

consequence /'kɒnsɪkwəns/ *noun* **1.** something which happens because of something else ○ *If we lose this order, the consequences for the firm will be disastrous.* ○ *Smoking has serious health consequences.* **2.** importance (*formal*) □ **of no consequence** not important ○ *What he thinks about the situation is of no consequence.* ◇ **as a consequence** as a result ○ *We queued for two hours in the rain, and as a consequence all of us got colds.*

conservation /ˌkɒnsə'veɪʃ(ə)n/ *noun* the careful use of things such as energy or natural resources ○ *The company is spending more money on energy conservation.*

conservative /kən'sɜːvətɪv/ *adjective* not wanting to change ○ *He has very conservative views.*

consider /kən'sɪdə/ *verb* **1.** to think carefully about something ○ *Please consider seriously the offer which we are making.* ○ *We have to consider the position of the children.* **2.** to think ○ *Do you consider him the right man for the job?* ○ *She is considered (to be) one of the best lawyers in town.* **3.** □ **all things considered** used for saying that you have thought about all aspects of a situation, including the bad ones ○ *All things considered, the party went off quite well.*

considerable /kən'sɪd(ə)rəb(ə)l/ *adjective* fairly large ○ *He lost a considerable amount of money at the horse race.*

considerably /kən'sɪd(ə)rəbli/ *adverb* to a fairly large extent

consideration /kənˌsɪdə'reɪʃ(ə)n/ *noun* **1.** careful thought ○ *We are giving serious consideration to the possibility of moving the head office to Scotland.* □ **to take something into consideration** to think about something when making a decision ○ *The age of the children has to be taken into consideration.* □ **under consideration** being thought about ○ *The matter is under consideration.* **2.** something which has an effect on a decision ○ *The safety of the children is more important than all other considerations.*

considering /kən'sɪd(ə)rɪŋ/ *conjunction, preposition* used to say that one thing affects another ○ *He plays the violin extremely well, considering he's only five.* ○ *He ought to be more grateful, considering the amount of help you have given him.*

consonant /'kɒnsənənt/ *noun* a letter representing a sound which is produced by partly stopping the air going out of the mouth

constable /'kʌnstəb(ə)l/ *noun* a police officer of the lowest rank

constant /'kɒnstənt/ *adjective* not changing or stopping ○ *The constant noise of music from the bar next door drives me mad.* ■ *noun* a number or thing which does not change ○ *Death and taxes are the only constants in life.* ○ *The speed of light is a scientific constant.*

constantly /'kɒnstəntli/ *adverb* all the time

construct /kən'strʌkt/ *verb* to build something ○ *The wings are constructed of aluminium.* ○ *The airport was constructed in 1995.*

construction /kən'strʌkʃən/ *noun* **1.** the act of building ○ *The construction of the new stadium took three years.* □ **under construction** being built ○ *The new airport is still under construction.* **2.** something which has been built

consult /kən'sʌlt/ *verb* **1.** to ask someone for advice ○ *He consulted his bank about transferring his account.* **2.** to look at something to get information ○ *After consulting the map they decided to go north.*

consultant /kən'sʌltənt/ *noun* **1.** an expert who gives advice ○ *His tax consultant advised him to sell the shares.* **2.** a senior hospital doctor who is an expert in a particular medical condition or illness ○ *We'll make an appointment for you to see a consultant.*

consume /kən'sjuːm/ *verb* **1.** to eat or drink something ○ *The guests consumed over a hundred hamburgers.* **2.** to use something up ○ *The world's natural resources are being consumed at an alarming rate.* ○ *The new car consumes about half the amount of petrol of an ordinary car.*

consumer /kən'sjuːmə/ *noun* a person or company that buys goods or services ○ *Consumers are buying more from supermarkets and less from small shops.* ○ *Gas consumers are protesting at the increase in prices.*

contact /'kɒntækt/ *noun* **1.** an act of touching ○ *Avoid any contact between the acid and the skin.* ○ *Anyone who has been in physical contact with the patient must consult their doctor immediately.* **2.** the act of communicating with someone ○ *We don't have much contact with our old friends in Australia.* □ **to get in contact with someone** to write to someone or talk to them on the telephone ■ *verb* to write to someone or talk to them on the telephone ○ *He tried to contact his office by phone.* ○ *Can you contact the ticket office immediately?*

contain /kən'teɪn/ *verb* **1.** to hold an amount, or to have an amount inside ○ *The bottle contains acid.* ○ *The envelope contained a cheque for £1,000.* ○ *A barrel contains 250 litres.* ○ *I have lost a briefcase containing important documents.* **2.** to limit or prevent something harmful or unpleasant ○ *The army tried to contain the advance of the enemy forces.* ○ *The party is attempting to contain the revolt among its members.*

container /kən'teɪnə/ *noun* an object such as a box or bottle which holds something else ○ *We need a container for all this rubbish.* ○ *The gas is shipped in strong metal containers.*

contemporary /kən'temp(ə)rəri/ *adjective* of the present time ○ *contemporary art* ■ *noun* a person who lives at the same time as someone ○ *Shakespeare and his contemporaries* ○ *He is one of my contemporaries from school.*

contender /kən'tendə/ *noun* a person who takes part in a competition, especially someone who is likely to win ○ *He's a definite contender for the world title.*

content¹ /'kɒntent/ *noun* the amount of something which is contained in a substance ○ *Dried fruit has a higher sugar content than fresh fruit.* ■ *plural noun* **contents 1.** things which are inside something ○ *The contents of the bottle spilled onto the carpet.* **2.** the list of chapters in a book, usually printed at the beginning

content² /kən'tent/ *adjective* happy with what is happening in your life □ **content to** happy to ○ *She was content to sit in the sun and wait.* □ **content with** satisfied with ○ *If you are not content with the way the car runs, bring it back and we will look at it again.* ■ *noun* a feeling of satisfaction □ **to your heart's content** as much as you want ○ *You can play the piano to your heart's content.* ○ *Living by the sea, they can go sailing to their heart's content.*

contented /kən'tentɪd/ *adjective* satisfied and happy

contest¹ /'kɒntest/ *noun* any event or situation in which people compete with each other ○ *an international sports contest* ○ *Only two people entered the leadership contest.*

contest² /kən'test/ *verb* **1.** to compete with other people to achieve a position ○ *There are four candidates contesting the championship.* **2.** to say that you disagree with what is written in a legal document

contestant /kən'testənt/ *noun* a person who takes part in a competition ○

The two contestants shook hands before the match.

context /'kɒntekst/ *noun* the other words which surround a particular word in a piece of writing and which help to show its meaning ○ *Even if you don't know what a word means, you can sometimes guess its meaning from the context.* □ **taken out of context** showing only part of what someone said or wrote, so that the meaning is changed ○ *My words have been taken out of context – I said the book was 'one of the best' not 'the best' I'd read.*

continent /'kɒntɪnənt/ *noun* one of the seven large land areas in the world, e.g. Africa or Europe

Continent /'kɒntɪnənt/ *noun* the main land area of Europe, as compared with the islands of the United Kingdom ○ *They go to the Continent on holiday each year, sometimes to France, sometimes to Switzerland.* □ **on the Continent** in the main part of Europe

continental /ˌkɒntɪ'nent(ə)l/ *adjective* **1.** referring to a continent **2.** referring to or typical of Europe excluding the United Kingdom

continual /kən'tɪnjuəl/ *adjective* **1.** happening many times in a period of time ○ *We have experienced a period of continual change.* **2.** happening frequently in a way that is annoying ○ *The computer has given us continual problems ever since we bought it.*

continue /kən'tɪnjuː/ *verb* to go on doing something or happening ○ *He continued working, even though everyone else had gone home.* ○ *The engine continued to send out clouds of black smoke.* ○ *The meeting started at 10 a.m. and continued until 6 p.m.* ○ *The show continued with some children's dances.*

continuous /kən'tɪnjuəs/ *adjective* without stopping or without a break ○ *She has been in continuous pain for three days.* ○ *A continuous white line on the road means that you are not allowed to overtake.*

continuously /kən'tɪnjuəsli/ *adverb* without a break

contract[1] /'kɒntrækt/ *noun* a legal agreement ○ *I don't agree with some of the conditions of the contract.* □ **under contract** bound by the conditions of a contract ○ *The company is under contract to a French supermarket.*

contract[2] /kən'trækt/ *verb* **1.** to become smaller ○ *Metal contracts when it gets cold, and expands when it is hot.* **2.** to make an official agreement to do some work ○ *to contract to supply spare parts* or *to contract for the supply of spare parts*

contradict /ˌkɒntrə'dɪkt/ *verb* **1.** to say that what someone else says is not true ○ *They didn't dare contradict their mother.* **2.** to be different from what has been said before ○ *What you have just said contradicts what you said yesterday.*

contrast[1] /'kɒntrɑːst/ *noun* a difference between two things ○ *the contrast in weather between the north and the south of the country* ○ *The two cities are in sharp contrast.* □ **in contrast to** as opposed to ○ *He is quite short, in contrast to his sister who is very tall.* ○ *The north of the country is green and wooded in contrast to the south which is dry and sandy.*

contrast[2] /kən'trɑːst/ *verb* to be obviously different from ○ *His formal letter contrasted with his friendly conversation on the telephone.*

contribute /kən'trɪbjuːt/ *verb* **1.** to help something to happen ○ *The government's policies have contributed to a feeling of anxiety among teachers.* **2.** to give money to help to pay for something, especially when other people are also giving ○ *We were asked to contribute to a charity.* ○ *Everyone was asked to contribute to the receptionist's leaving present.*

contribution /ˌkɒntrɪ'bjuːʃ(ə)n/ something that someone does to help something to happen ○ *I want to thank you for your enormous contribution to the success of the project.* ■ *noun* something, usually money, given to help to pay for something ○ *She makes monthly contributions to the Red Cross.*

contributor /kən'trɪbjʊtə/ *noun* a person or organisation that contributes to something

control /kən'trəʊl/ *noun* **1.** the fact of keeping someone or something in order or being able to direct them ○ *He lost control of his business and resigned.* ○ *The club is under the control of three people.* **2.** the ability to get people to do what you want ○ *The teacher has no control over the class.* ■ *verb* **1.** to keep something in order, to direct or limit something ○ *The police couldn't control the crowds.* ○ *There was nobody there to control the traffic.* ○ *We must try to control the sales of foreign cars.* ○ *The government controls the price of meat.* **2.** □ **to control a business** to have the power to direct the way a business is run ○ *The business is controlled by a company based in Luxembourg.* (NOTE: **controls – controlling – controlled**)

controlled /kən'trəʊld/ *adjective* kept under control

convenient /kən'viːniənt/ *adjective* not causing any practical problems ○ *Six o'clock in the morning is not a very convenient time for a meeting.* ○ *A bank draft is a convenient way of sending money abroad.*

conveniently /kən'viːniəntli/ *adverb* in a convenient way

conventional /kən'venʃ(ə)n(ə)l/ *adjective* ordinary or usual ○ *For your interview it's best to wear a conventional suit.*

conversation /ˌkɒnvə'seɪʃ(ə)n/ *noun* an occasion on which two or more people talk to each other about something ○ *We had a long conversation with the bank manager.* ○ *Why did he suddenly change the subject of the conversation?*

convict¹ /'kɒnvɪkt/ *noun* a criminal who has been sent to prison ○ *The police are searching for two escaped convicts.*

convict² /kən'vɪkt/ *verb* to prove in court that someone is guilty ○ *She was convicted of theft.*

convinced /kən'vɪnst/ *adjective* very certain ○ *She's convinced that she's right.*

cook /kʊk/ *noun* a person who gets food ready ○ *He worked as a cook in a pub during the summer.* ■ *verb* to get food ready for eating, especially by heating it ○ *It's my turn to cook the dinner tonight.* ○ *How do you cook cabbage?*

cooker /'kʊkə/ *noun* a large piece of kitchen equipment, used for cooking food

cookie /'kʊki/ *noun* **1.** *usually US* a small, flat hard sweet cake ○ *She bought a packet of cookies.* (NOTE: The British English term is **biscuit**.) **2.** a computer file sent to your computer by a website when you visit it. It stores information about you which can be used when you next visit the website.

cool /kuːl/ *adjective* **1.** cold in a pleasant way, or colder than you would like or than you expect ○ *It was hot on deck but cool down below.* ○ *Wines should be stored in a cool cellar.* ○ *It gets cool in the evenings in September.* **2.** not friendly or not enthusiastic ○ *I got a cool reception when I arrived half an hour late.* ○ *Their proposal got a cool response.* □ **to be cool towards someone** to be unfriendly to someone or unenthusiastic about something ○ *She was rather cool towards me last time we met.* ○ *My colleagues were cool towards the plan unfortunately.* **3.** calm ○ *The nurses remained cool and professional.* **4.** fashionable (*informal*) ○ *They thought it was cool to wear white trainers.* **5.** good (*informal*) ○ *a cool party* ○ *a really cool idea* (NOTE: **cooler – coolest**) ■ *verb* to make something cool; to become cool ○ *She boiled the jam for several hours and then put it aside to cool.* ■ *noun* **1.** a colder area which is pleasant ○ *After the heat of the town centre, it is nice to sit in the cool of the garden.* **2.** the state of being calm ○ *As soon as the reporters started to ask her questions she lost her cool.* ◇ **to be cool with something** to be satisfied with something (*informal*) ○ *We can go tomorrow – I'm cool with that.*

copper /'kɒpə/ *noun* a reddish metal which turns green when exposed to air ○ *Copper is a good conductor of elec-*

tricity. ○ *The end of the copper wire should be attached to the terminal.*

copy /'kɒpɪ/ *noun* **1.** something made to look the same as something else ○ *This is an exact copy of the painting by Picasso.* **2.** a particular book or newspaper ○ *Where's my copy of today's 'Times'?* ○ *I lent my old copy of the play to my brother and he never gave it back.* (NOTE: [all noun senses] The plural is **copies.**) ■ *verb* **1.** to make something which looks like something else ○ *He stole a credit card and copied the signature* **2.** to do what someone else does (NOTE: **copies – copying – copied**)

cord /kɔːd/ *noun* a strong thin rope ○ *Pull the cord to open the parachute.* ○ *In an emergency, pull the cord to stop the train.*

core /kɔː/ *noun* the central part of an object □ **the core of an apple, an apple core** the hard part in the middle of an apple, containing the seeds ■ the most basic or essential part of something ○ *Lack of resources is the core of the problem.* ■ *adjective* most important ○ *These are the core points of the report.* □ **core values** the things that a group of people think are most important ○ *Honesty and reliability are among our core values.*

cork /kɔːk/ *noun* **1.** a small solid tube, used for closing wine bottles **2.** the very light bark of a type of tree, used for making corks and other things ○ *She placed little cork mats on the table to stop the wine glasses marking it.* ■ *verb* to put a cork into a bottle

corn /kɔːn/ *noun* **1.** cereal plants such as wheat or barley ○ *a field of corn* **2.** maize, a cereal crop which is grown in many parts of the world □ **corn on the cob** the part of maize that has the seeds, boiled and served hot, with butter and salt

corner /'kɔːnə/ *noun* a place where two walls, streets or sides meet ○ *The bank is on the corner of London Road and New Street.* ○ *Put the plant in the corner of the room nearest the window.* ○ *The number is in the top right-hand corner of the page.* ○ *The motorbike went round the corner at top speed.* ◇ **to turn**

the corner 1. to go from one street into another by turning left or right ○ *She turned the corner into the main street.* **2.** to get better after being ill or in a difficult situation ○ *Our business affairs seem to have turned the corner.*

corporate /'kɔːp(ə)rət/ *adjective* relating to a company ○ *Corporate responsibility rests with the whole management.* ○ *Corporate profits are down this year.*

corporation /ˌkɔːpə'reɪʃ(ə)n/ *noun* a large company ○ *Working for a big corporation can be rather impersonal.*

correct /kə'rekt/ *adjective* **1.** without any mistakes ○ *You have to give correct answers to all the questions if you want to win first prize.* ○ *If the information you gave us is correct, we can finish the work by Thursday.* **2.** right according to rules or standards ■ *verb* to take away mistakes in something ○ *You must try to correct your driving mistakes, or you will never pass the test.* ○ *The computer keeps switching itself off – can you correct this fault?*

correction /kə'rekʃən/ *noun* **1.** an action that makes something correct ○ *He made a few small corrections to the letter.* **2.** the process of correcting something ○ *We drew up a timetable for the correction of minor faults.*

correctly /kə'rektlɪ/ *adverb* without making any mistakes

corridor /'kɒrɪdɔː/ *noun* a long narrow passage ○ *The ladies' toilet is straight ahead at the end of the corridor.*

cost /kɒst/ *noun* a price which you have to pay for something ○ *What is the cost of a return ticket to London?* ○ *Computer costs are falling each year.* ■ *verb* to have as a price ○ *Potatoes cost 20p a kilo.* ○ *Petrol seems to cost more all the time.* (NOTE: **costs – costing – cost – has cost**) ◇ **at all costs** no matter what happens ○ *At all costs, we have to be in Trafalgar Square by 12 o'clock.* ◇ **to cost an arm and a leg** to be very expensive ○ *The repairs to his car cost him an arm and a leg.*

costume /'kɒstjuːm/ *noun* a set of clothes worn by an actor or actress ○

The costumes for the film are magnificent.

cosy /'kəʊzi/ *adjective* comfortable and warm ○ *An open log fire always makes a room feel cosy.* ○ *She wrapped herself up in a blanket and made herself cosy on the sofa.* (NOTE: **cosier – cosiest**)

cottage /'kɒtɪdʒ/ *noun* a little house in the country ○ *We have a weekend cottage in the mountains.* ○ *My mother lives in the little cottage next to the post office.*

cotton /'kɒtən/ *noun* **1.** fibres made into thread from the soft seed heads of a tropical plant **2.** cloth made of cotton ○ *I bought some blue cotton to make a skirt.* ○ *He was wearing a pair of cotton trousers.*

cough /kɒf/ *noun* the act of making a noise by sending the air out of your lungs suddenly, e.g. when you are ill ○ *Take some medicine if your cough is bad.* ○ *He gave a little cough to attract the waitress's attention.* ■ *verb* to make a noise by sending air out of your lungs suddenly, e.g. because you are ill ○ *The smoke from the fire made everyone cough.* ○ *People with colds usually cough and sneeze.*

could /kəd, kʊd/ *modal verb* **1.** was or would be able to ○ *The old lady fell down and couldn't get up.* ○ *You could still catch the train if you ran.* **2.** was allowed to ○ *The policeman said he could go into the house.* **3.** used in asking someone to do something ○ *Could you pass me the salt, please?* ○ *Could you shut the window?* **4.** might ○ *The new shopping centre could be finished by Christmas.* **5.** used in making a suggestion ○ *You could always try borrowing money from the bank.* (NOTE: The negative is **could not**, or in speaking, usually **couldn't**. Note also that **could** is the past of **can**; **could** is only used in front of other verbs and is not followed by the word **to**.)

council /'kaʊnsəl/ *noun* **1.** an elected committee **2.** an official group chosen to work on or advise about a specific subject ○ *a council set up to promote the arts in the eastern region*

count /kaʊnt/ *verb* **1.** to say numbers in order, e.g. 1, 2, 3, 4 ○ *She's only two and she can count up to ten.* ○ *Count to five and then start running.* **2.** to find out a total ○ *Did you count how many books there are in the library?* **3.** to include when finding out a total ○ *There were sixty people on the boat if you count the children.* ○ *Did you count my trip to New York as part of my expenses?* □ **not counting** not including ○ *There are three of us, not counting the baby.* ○ *We have three computers, not counting the old ones that don't work any more.* **4.** to be important ○ *Your appearance counts for a lot in an interview.* ■ *noun* **1.** the action of counting or of adding **2.** a large amount of something, calculated scientifically ○ *Today there is a high pollen count.* ◇ **to lose count** to no longer have any idea of a particular number ○ *I tried to add up all the sales figures but lost count and had to start again.* ○ *I've lost count of the number of times he's left his umbrella on the train.*

count on *phrasal verb* to be sure that someone will do something

counter /'kaʊntə/ *noun* **1.** a long flat surface in a shop for showing goods for sale, or in a bank for passing over money ○ *She put her bag down on the counter and took out her cheque book.* ○ *The cheese counter is over there.* **2.** a small round disc used in games ○ *You've thrown a six – you can move your counter six places.* ○ *She placed a pile of counters on the board.* ■ *verb* to act or reply in an opposing way ○ *The adverts are designed to counter familiar opinions about of home and family.* ■ to reply in a way that opposes what has been said ○ *He accused her of laziness and she countered with a list of complaints about his own behaviour.*

country /'kʌntri/ *noun* **1.** an area of land which is has borders and governs itself ○ *the countries of the EU* ○ *Some African countries voted against the plan.* (NOTE: The plural in this sense is **countries**.) **2.** land which is not in a town ○ *He lives in the country.* ○ *We went walking in the country.* ○ *Road travel is difficult in country areas.* (NOTE: no plural in this sense)

countryside /'kʌntrisaɪd/ *noun* land which is not in a town ○ *the beautiful English countryside in spring* ○ *The countryside is in danger of being covered in new houses.* (NOTE: no plural)

county /'kaʊnti/ *noun* a district that has some powers of government over local matters (NOTE: The plural is **counties**.)

couple /'kʌp(ə)l/ *noun* **1.** two things together **2.** two people together ○ *They are a charming couple.* ○ *Several couples strolled past hand in hand.* ■ *verb* **1.** to connect two different things ○ *High tides coupled with strong winds caused flooding along the coast.* **2.** to join two machines together ○ *Couple the trailer to the back of the truck.* ◇ **a couple of 1.** two ○ *They've got a couple of children.* **2.** a few ○ *The film lasted a couple of hours.*

coupon /'kuːpɒn/ *noun* a piece of paper which is used in place of money or in place of a ticket

courage /'kʌrɪdʒ/ *noun* the ability to deal with a dangerous or unpleasant situation ○ *She showed great courage in attacking the burglar.* ○ *I didn't have the courage to disagree with him.* (NOTE: no plural)

course /kɔːs/ *noun* **1.** a series of lessons ○ *I'm taking a maths course.* ○ *She's going on a painting course.* ○ *The hotel offers weekend courses in a variety of subjects.* **2.** a series of medical treatments ○ *He's taking a course of antibiotics.* **3.** a separate part of a meal ○ *a five-course meal* ○ *The first course is soup, and then you can have either fish or roast lamb.* **4.** the direction in which someone or something, especially a vehicle, is moving in, or will move in ◇ **in due course** after a certain amount of time ○ *If you study for several years at college, in due course you will get a degree.* ○ *Put a coin in the slot and in due course the machine will produce a ticket.* ◇ **in the course of** during a period of time ○ *He's got much richer in the course of the last few years.*

court /kɔːt/ *noun* **1.** a room with a judge who tries criminals, sometimes with a jury ○ *The court was packed for the opening of the murder trial.* ○ *Please*

tell the court what you saw when you opened the door.* □ **to take someone to court** to arrange for someone to come to a court to end an argument **2.** an area where sports such as tennis or basketball are played ○ *The tennis courts are behind the hotel.* □ **to be on court** to be playing tennis **3.** a group of people living round a king or queen

court case /'kɔːt keɪs/ *noun* a legal action or trial

courtyard /'kɔːtjɑːd/ *noun* a small square area surrounded by buildings

cousin /'kʌz(ə)n/ *noun* the son or daughter of your uncle or aunt

cover /'kʌvə/ *noun* **1.** something that you put over something else to protect it or keep it clean ○ *Keep a cover over your computer when you are not using it.* ○ *Put a cover over the meat to keep the flies off.* **2.** the front and back of a book or magazine ○ *She read the book from cover to cover.* **3.** a place where you can hide or shelter ○ *They ran for cover when it started to rain.* □ **under cover** under a roof, not in the open air ○ *If it rains the meal will be served under cover.* □ **to take cover** to find a place to shelter from something such as rain ○ *It started to rain and they took cover under a tree.* ○ *When the robbers started shooting, the policeman took cover behind a wall.* ■ *verb* **1.** to put something over something else to keep it clean ○ *You should cover the furniture with sheets before you start painting the ceiling.* **2.** to hide something ○ *He covered the hole in the ground with branches.* ○ *She covered her face with her hands.* **3.** to travel a certain distance ○ *They made good progress, covering twenty miles a day.*

cow /kaʊ/ *noun* a large female farm animal, kept to give milk ○ *a field of cows* ○ *The farmer was milking a cow.*

coward /'kaʊəd/ *noun* a person who is not brave

crack /kræk/ *noun* **1.** a sharp sound ○ *the crack of a whip* ○ *The crack of a twig behind her made her turn round.* **2.** a long thin break in a surface ○ *A crack appeared in the ceiling.* ○ *Her ring fell down a crack in the floorboards.* ○ *The* *field is so dry it is full of cracks.* ■ *verb* **1.** to make a sharp sound ○ *A twig cracked as he stepped on it.* **2.** to make a long thin break in something ○ *The stone cracked the glass.*

crafty /'krɑːfti/ *adjective* good at getting the things you want, often in a way that is not completely honest (NOTE: **craftier – craftiest**)

cramped /kræmpt/ *adjective* too small or too close together ○ *On some planes, the seats are very cramped.*

crane /kreɪn/ *noun* a tall metal piece of equipment for lifting heavy things ○ *The container slipped as the crane was lifting it onto the ship.*

crash /kræʃ/ *noun* **1.** an accident where vehicles are damaged ○ *He was killed in a train crash.* ○ *None of the passengers was hurt in the coach crash.* ○ *His car was badly damaged in the crash.* **2.** a loud noise when something falls over ○ *The ladder fell down with a crash.* ○ *There was a loud crash in the kitchen.* ■ *verb* **1.** (*of vehicles*) to hit something and be damaged ○ *The bus crashed into a wall.* ○ *The plane crashed six kilometres from the airport.* **2.** to fall, making a loud noise ○ *The wall came crashing down.* ○ *The ladder crashed onto the floor.*

crate /kreɪt/ *noun* **1.** a large wooden box ○ *The dinner set arrived safely, carefully packed in a wooden crate.* **2.** a container for bottles ○ *a beer crate* ○ *The office orders a crate of milk every day.*

crawl /krɔːl/ *verb* **1.** to move around on your hands and knees ○ *The baby has just started to crawl.* **2.** to travel along slowly ○ *The traffic was crawling along.* ■ *noun* **1.** a very slow speed ○ *The traffic on the motorway was reduced to a crawl.* **2.** a swimming style where each arm goes over your head in turn ○ *He won the 100m crawl.* (NOTE: no plural)

crayon /'kreɪɒn/ *noun* a coloured wax stick, used especially by children for drawing

crazy /'kreɪzi/ *adjective* not sensible ○ *It was a crazy idea to go mountain-climbing in sandals.*

creak /kriːk/ *verb* to make a squeaky noise ■ *noun* a noise like that of wood moving ○ *She heard a creak on the stairs and sat up in bed.* (NOTE: Do not confuse with **creek**.)

cream /kriːm/ *noun* **1.** the thick yellow part of milk, full of fat ○ *I like strawberries and cream.* **2.** any soft smooth substance used, e.g. for cleaning or for protecting the skin ○ *face cream* ○ *shaving cream* ○ *shoe cream* ■ *adjective* of a yellow-white colour ○ *He was wearing a cream shirt.* ○ *Do you like our new cream carpet?*

crease /kriːs/ *noun* **1.** a mark made in cloth by ironing ○ *Trousers should have a crease in front.* **2.** a mark made by folding accidentally ○ *She ironed his shirts to remove the creases.* ■ *verb* to make folds accidentally in something ○ *After two hours in the car, my skirt was badly creased and had to be pressed.*

create /kri'eɪt/ *verb* to make or invent something ○ *a government scheme which aims at creating new jobs for young people*

creation /kri'eɪʃ(ə)n/ *noun* **1.** the act of making or inventing something ○ *Our aim is the creation of new jobs for young unemployed people.* **2.** something which has been made, especially something artistic or unusual

creature /'kriːtʃə/ *noun* **1.** an animal, especially one that you don't know a name for ○ *Lift any stone and you'll find all sorts of little creatures underneath.* ○ *We try not to harm any living creature.* ○ *Some sea creatures live in holes in the sand.* **2.** an imaginary animal or living being

credit /'kredɪt/ *noun* **1.** praise for something which is well deserved ○ *The professor took all the credit for the invention.* ○ *To his credit, he owned up immediately.* **2.** the length of time given to pay for something ○ *We give purchasers six months' credit.* **3.** the side of an account showing money that you have got or which is owed to you ○ *We paid in £100 to the credit of Mr Smith.* ■ *plural noun* **credits** the list of people who helped to make a film or TV programme ○ *Her name appears in the credits.* ■

verb to pay money into an account ○ *to credit an account with £100* or *to credit £100 to an account*

credit card /'kredɪt kɑːd/ *noun* a plastic card which allows you to borrow money and to buy goods without paying for them immediately

creep /kriːp/ *verb* **1.** to move around quietly ○ *They crept softly down the stairs.* **2.** to move slowly ○ *The traffic was creeping along the motorway because of the fog.* (NOTE: **creeps – creeping – crept**)

crew /kruː/ *noun* the people who work on a vehicle such as boat or aircraft ○ *The lifeboat rescued the crew of the sinking ship.* ○ *The plane was carrying 125 passengers and a crew of six.*

cricket /'krɪkɪt/ *noun* **1.** a game played between two teams of eleven players using bats and a hard ball ○ *We haven't played much cricket this year – the weather has been too bad.* ○ *We are going to a cricket match this afternoon.* **2.** awake and able to know what is happening around you

cried /kraɪd/ past tense and past participle of **cry**

cries /kraɪz/ 3rd person singular present of **cry**

crime /kraɪm/ *noun* **1.** illegal behaviour ○ *We must try to reduce the levels of crime in the inner cities.* ○ *The government is trying to deal with the problem of crime on the streets* or *with the street crime problem.* **2.** a specific illegal act ○ *More crimes are committed at night than during the daytime.*

criminal /'krɪmɪn(ə)l/ *adjective* referring to illegal acts ○ *the criminal justice system* ○ *Stealing is a criminal offence.* ■ *noun* a person who commits a crime

crisis /'kraɪsɪs/ *noun* a serious situation where decisions have to be taken very quickly ○ *an international crisis* ○ *a banking crisis*

crisp /krɪsp/ *adjective* **1.** (*of food*) hard, able to be broken into pieces and making a noise when you bite it ○ *These biscuits are not crisp any more, they have gone soft.* ○ *Pick an apple off the tree, they're really very crisp.* **2.** cold and

sunny ○ *It was a beautiful crisp morning, with frost glinting on the grass.* ○ *She could see her breath in the crisp mountain air.*

criterion /kraɪ'tɪəriən/ *noun* the standard by which things are judged ○ *Does the candidate satisfy all our criteria?*

critic /'krɪtɪk/ *noun* **1.** a person who examines something and comments on it, especially a person who writes comments on new plays and films for a newspaper ○ *She's the TV critic of The Times.* ○ *The film was praised by all the critics.* **2.** a person who says that something is bad or wrong ○ *The chairman tried to answer his critics at the meeting.*

critical /'krɪtɪk(ə)l/ *adjective* **1.** dangerous and difficult ○ *With the enemy attacking on all sides, our position was becoming critical.* **2.** extremely important ○ *He made a critical decision to break off the negotiations.* **3.** very serious ○ *The pilot of the plane was in a critical condition last night.* ○ *The hospital said that her condition was critical.* **4.** criticising someone or something ○ *The report was highly critical of the minister.*

criticise /'krɪtɪsaɪz/, **criticize** *verb* to say that something or someone is bad or wrong ○ *She criticised their lack of interest and enthusiasm.* ○ *The design of the new car has been criticised.*

criticism /'krɪtɪsɪz(ə)m/ *noun* an unfavourable comment or comments ○ *There was a lot of criticism of the government's plan.*

crocodile /'krɒkədaɪl/ *noun* a large reptile which lives in or near rivers and lakes and eats other animals ○ *Crocodiles lay on the banks of the river waiting for the animals to come to drink.*

crooked /'krʊkɪd/ *adjective* bent, not straight ○ *That picture is crooked.*

crop /krɒp/ *noun* plants such as vegetables or cereals grown for food ○ *The bad weather has set the crops back by three weeks.* ○ *We had a wonderful crop of potatoes* or *a wonderful potato crop this year.*

crop up *phrasal verb* to happen suddenly (*informal*)

cross /krɒs/ *verb* **1.** to go across something to the other side ○ *She just crossed the road without looking to see if there was any traffic coming.* **2.** to put one thing across another ○ *He crossed his arms and looked annoyed.* ○ *She sat down and crossed her legs.* ○ *The road crosses the railway line about 10 km from here.* ■ *noun* a shape made where one line has another going across it, especially one which forms the symbol of the Christian Church ○ *Write your name where I have put a cross.* ○ *There is a cross on the top of the church tower.* ■ *adjective* angry ○ *The teacher will be cross with you for missing school.* ○ *Don't be cross – the children were only trying to help.*

cross off, cross out *phrasal verb* to draw a line through something which has been written to show that it should not be there

crossing /'krɒsɪŋ/ *noun* **1.** an occasion of going across to the other side of an area of water ○ *How long is the crossing from England to Germany?* **2.** a place where you go across safely ○ *Cars have to take care at the railway crossing.*

crossword /'krɒswɜːd/ *noun* a puzzle where small squares have to be filled with letters to spell words

crouch /kraʊtʃ/ *verb* to bend down low ○ *He crouched in the bottom of the boat.* ○ *She crouched down to talk to the child.*

crowd /kraʊd/ *noun* a very large number of people together ○ *A crowd of school-children went past.* ○ *Someone in the crowd outside the cinema shouted a warning.* ○ *Let's get an early train home to avoid the crowds after work.* ■ *verb* to group together ○ *All the rugby fans crowded into the pub.* ○ *The children were crowding round their teacher.*

crowded /'kraʊdɪd/ *adjective* full of a large number of people ○ *The town gets very crowded during the holiday season.* ○ *The stands were crowded before the game started.*

crown /kraʊn/ *noun* a round metal decoration that a king or queen wears on his or her head ■ *verb* **1.** to make someone king or queen by placing a crown on his or her head ○ *The Queen was crowned in Westminster Abbey.* **2.** to be a very good end to a set of things that happen ○ *He crowned his career by winning a gold medal.* □ **to crown it all** used to refer to the last of several bad things to happen ○ *To crown it all, he lost his car keys.*

crucial /'kruːʃ(ə)l/ *adjective* extremely important ○ *It is crucial that the story be kept out of the papers.*

cruel /'kruːəl/ *adjective* making a person or animal suffer ○ *Don't be so cruel!* ○ *You must not be cruel to your new puppy.* ○ *It was cruel of him to mention her weight problem.* (NOTE: **crueller – cruellest**)

cruelty /'kruːəlti/ *noun* the act of being cruel

cruise /kruːz/ *noun* a holiday consisting of a long journey in a ship, stopping at different places ○ *When he retired they went on a cruise round the Mediterranean.* ■ *verb* to go in a boat from place to place ○ *They spent May cruising in the Aegean Sea.* ○ *The ship cruised from island to island.*

crumb /krʌm/ *noun* a small piece that has broken off some dry food such as bread, cake or biscuits

crumble /'krʌmbəl/ *verb* to break up into small pieces, or to break something up into small pieces ○ *If you make it too dry it will just crumble when you eat it.* ○ *He picked up a lump of dry earth and crumbled it between his fingers.*

crunch /krʌntʃ/ *verb* **1.** to bite something hard, making a loud noise ○ *She was crunching an apple when the phone rang.* **2.** to crush something dry ○ *The snow crunched under his boots.* ■ *noun* **1.** the sound of something dry being crushed **2.** a situation when something must happen or be decided (*informal*) ○ *The crunch will come when the firm has no cash to pay the wages.* □ **if or when it comes to the crunch** if or when a point of decision is reached ○ *When it came to the crunch, the other side backed down.*

crust /krʌst/ *noun* **1.** a hard outer layer that covers something softer **2.** the hard outside layer of bread ○ *You can cut the crusts off the sandwiches.* **3.** the layer of pastry on top of a pie **4.** the outer layer of the Earth

cry /kraɪ/ *verb* **1.** to have tears coming out of your eyes ○ *The baby cried when her mother took away her toys.* ○ *Cutting up onions makes me cry.* ○ *Many people were crying when they left the cinema.* **2.** to call out ○ *'Hello there,' she cried.* (NOTE: **cries – crying – cried**) ■ *noun* **1.** a loud shout ○ *a cry of pain* ○ *No one heard her cries for help.* **2.** a sound made by a bird or other animal (NOTE: The plural is **cries**.)

crystal /ˈkrɪstəl/ *noun* a solid chemical substance with a regular shape ○ *The salt formed crystals at the bottom of the jar.*

cube /kjuːb/ *noun* **1.** (*in geometry*) a shape like a box, where all six sides are squares of the same size ○ *The design for the library consists of a series of cubes.* **2.** something shaped like a cube ○ *He put two cubes of sugar in his tea.* ○ *The ice cubes chinked in the glasses.* **3.** (*in mathematics*) the result when a number is multiplied by itself twice ○ *27 is the cube of 3.*

cucumber /ˈkjuːkʌmbə/ *noun* a long dark green vegetable used mainly in salads

cuddle /ˈkʌd(ə)l/ *verb* to put your arms round someone and hold them close to you ○ *The little girl was cuddling her teddy bear.* ○ *There was a last chance to cuddle in the taxi that took them to the airport.* ■ *noun* an act of putting your arms round someone and holding them close to you ○ *She picked up her daughter and gave her a cuddle.*

culprit /ˈkʌlprɪt/ *noun* a person or thing that is responsible for a crime, or for something which has gone wrong

cultural /ˈkʌltʃ(ə)rəl/ *adjective* relating to culture ○ *His cultural interests are very wide-ranging – from Mexican art to 12th-century Greek paintings.* ○ *There will be cultural activities available such as a visit to the museum.*

culture /ˈkʌltʃə/ *noun* **1.** activities involving things such as music, art and literature ○ *He is taking a course in Russian culture.* **2.** a country's way of thinking or behaving ○ *Is a TV in every home really what we want from Western culture?*

cunning /ˈkʌnɪŋ/ *adjective* clever at achieving something, especially by tricking people ○ *a cunning plan* ○ *It was cunning of her to ask him to help, as it flattered him.* ■ *noun* cleverness in acting to achieve something ○ *He showed cunning in his attempts to hide his mistake.*

cup /kʌp/ *noun* **1.** a small bowl with a handle, used for drinking from ○ *She put out a cup and saucer for everyone.* **2.** the liquid in a cup ○ *He drank two cups of coffee.* ○ *Can I have a cup of tea?* **3.** a large silver or gold container given as a prize for winning a competition ○ *He has won three cups for golf.*

cupboard /ˈkʌbəd/ *noun* a piece of furniture with shelves and doors ○ *Put the jam in the kitchen cupboard.* ○ *She painted the cupboard doors white.*

cure /kjʊə/ *noun* something which makes a disease better ○ *Doctors are still trying to find a cure for colds.* ■ *verb* to make a patient or a disease better ○ *I don't know what's in the medicine, but it cured my cough very fast.*

curious /ˈkjʊəriəs/ *adjective* **1.** wanting to know things ○ *I'm curious to know what happened at the meeting.* **2.** unusual or strange ○ *We found a curious object that turned out to be an old kitchen tool.* ○ *It's curious that no one knew where he lived.*

curl /kɜːl/ *verb* to twist, or make something twist ○ *My hair curls naturally.* ○ *Some plants have stems that curl round other plants.* ■ *noun* **1.** a piece of hair which grows in a twist ○ *The little girl looked lovely with her golden curls.* **2.** a curved shape of a particular substance ○ *a curl of smoke*

curl up *phrasal verb* to bend your body into a round shape ○ *She curled up in the chair and went to sleep.*

curly /'kɜːli/ *adjective* with natural curves or twists ○ *curly hair*

currency /'kʌrənsɪ/ *noun* the money used in a specific country ○ *I want to change my pounds into French currency.*

current /'kʌrənt/ *adjective* **1.** relating to the present time ○ *What is the current state of the report – will it be finished on time?* ○ *Who is the current prime minister of Japan?* ○ *Do you have a current timetable? – mine is out of date.* **2.** widely accepted at the present time or at a particular time ○ *current ideas about how to treat children* ○ *The idea that the world was flat was current in the Middle Ages.* ■ *noun* **1.** a flow of water or air ○ *Don't go swimming in the river – the current is very strong.* ○ *A warm westerly current of air is flowing across the country.* ○ *Vultures circle in rising currents of warm air.* **2.** a flow of electricity ○ *Switch the current off at the mains.*

currently /'kʌrəntli/ *adverb* at the present time ○ *He is currently the manager of our Paris office.* ○ *We are currently in the process of buying a house.*

curriculum /kə'rɪkjʊləm/ *noun* **1.** the set of subjects studied in school ○ *I am very glad that music and drama have been added to the curriculum.* **2.** the parts of a particular subject that are studied (NOTE: [all senses] The plural is **curriculums** or **curricula**.)

curriculum vitae /kə,rɪkjʊləm 'viːtaɪ/ *noun* full form of **CV**

curry /'kʌri/ *noun* an Indian food prepared with spices ○ *I would like a mild curry, please.* ○ *We ordered chicken curry and rice.* (NOTE: The plural is **curries**.)

cursor /'kɜːsə/ *noun* a small flashing line on a computer screen which shows where the next character will appear

curtain /'kɜːt(ə)n/ *noun* **1.** a long piece of cloth hanging in front of a window ○ *Can you close the curtains, please?* **2.** a long piece of cloth hanging in front of the stage at a theatre

curve /kɜːv/ *noun* a line that is bent like part of a circle ○ *the curve of the coast line* ■ *verb* to be in the shape of a curve ○ *The road curves round the side of the mountain.*

curved /kɜːvd/ *adjective* with a rounded shape

cushion /'kʊʃ(ə)n/ *noun* a bag filled with something soft, e.g. feathers, for sitting or leaning on ○ *Put a cushion behind your back if you find your chair is too hard.* ■ *verb* to make soft something which could be hard or painful ○ *The bushes cushioned his fall.* □ **to cushion somebody** *or* **something from something** to protect someone or something from the bad effects of something □ **to cushion the blow** or **the shock** to reduce the bad effect of something that happens ○ *She made no attempt to cushion the blow, but just told them straight out that they had all lost their jobs.*

custom /'kʌstəm/ *noun* **1.** something that people usually do, or have done for a long time ○ *the local custom of decorating the wells in spring* ○ *It's their custom to invite all their neighbours to a party at New Year.* **2.** the use of a shop or restaurant ○ *If the assistants are rude to me again I will take my custom elsewhere.* □ **to lose someone's custom** to experience a situation in which a regular customer goes to another place of business, e.g. a restaurant or shop ○ *The little shops will lose a lot of custom when the new supermarket opens.*

customary /'kʌstəməri/ *adjective* usual (*formal*) ○ *He handled the situation with his customary efficiency.* ○ *It's customary to give taxi drivers a tip.*

customer /'kʌstəmə/ *noun* **1.** a person who buys something in a shop or restaurant, or from another business ○ *The shops are lowering their prices to attract more customers.* ○ *Customers can order by post or on the Internet.* ○ *His bar is always full of customers.* **2.** a person who uses a service such as a train ○ *We apologise to customers waiting on Platform 5 for the late arrival of their train.*

cut /kʌt/ *verb* **1.** to divide, reduce or remove something using a sharp tool, e.g. a knife or scissors ○ *The meat is very tough – I can't cut it with my knife.* ○ *He needs to get his hair cut.* ○ *There were* *six children, so she cut the cake into six pieces.* **2.** to damage the skin with something sharp ○ *She cut her finger on the broken glass.* ○ *He cut himself while shaving.* **3.** to reduce the size of something ○ *We are trying to cut the number of staff.* ○ *Accidents have been cut by 10%.* ○ *The article is too long, so I asked the author to cut 500 words.* (NOTE: **cuts – cutting – cut – has cut**) ■ *noun* **1.** a place which bleeds when your skin has been broken **2.** a mark made in a surface by something sharp **3.** the sudden lowering of the amount of something ○ *price cuts* ○ *large cuts in spending* ○ *a cut in working hours* **4.** a share of something such as profits ○ *Each salesperson gets a cut of what is sold for cash.*

cut back *phrasal verb* to reduce spending ○ *We are having to cut back on staff costs.*

cut down *phrasal verb* to make a tree fall down with a tool such as a saw ○ *He cut the tree down* or *cut down the tree.*

cut off *phrasal verb* **1.** to take away a small part of something using a sharp tool such as a knife ○ *She cut off a little piece of string.* ○ *He cut off two slices of ham.* **2.** to stop someone from being with someone else, or from or reaching a place ○ *She was cut off from her friends by a crowd of policemen.* ○ *The village was cut off by the snow.*

cut out *phrasal verb* **1.** to remove something from something larger ○ *She cut an advertisement out of the newspaper.* **2.** to remove a part of something larger ○ *We had to cut out all the extras from our order because they cost too much.* **3.** to stop doing or eating something ○ *She's decided to cut out sweet things so as to lose weight.* □ **cut it out!** stop doing that! (*informal*) ◇ **to be cut out for something** to be ideally suited for something ○ *I don't think he's cut out for an office job.*

cut up *phrasal verb* to make something into small pieces by cutting it ○ *She cut the old towel up into little pieces.* ○ *Can you cut up the meat for the children?*

cutlery /ˈkʌtləri/ *noun* knives, forks and spoons (NOTE: no plural)

CV /ˌsiː ˈviː/ *noun* a summary of someone's qualifications and experience. Abbreviation **curriculum vitae**

cycle /ˈsaɪk(ə)l/ *noun* **1.** a period during which something develops and then returns to its starting point ○ *Global warming is starting to affect the natural cycle of the seasons.* ○ *The washing machine broke down in the middle of its cycle.* **2.** a bicycle ■ *verb* to travel on a bicycle ○ *It's hard to cycle into the wind.* (NOTE: **cycles – cycling – cycled**)

cyclist /ˈsaɪklɪst/ *noun* a person who rides a bicycle

cylinder /ˈsɪlɪndə/ *noun* an object shaped like a tube closed at both ends

D

d /diː/, **D** *noun* the fourth letter of the alphabet, between C and E

dad /dæd/ *noun* a father

daily /ˈdeɪli/ *adjective* happening every day ○ *daily newspapers such as the Times and the Daily Mail* ○ *The cooker has been in daily use for ten years.* ○ *There's a daily flight to Washington.* ■ *adverb* every day ○ *We can deliver milk daily.* □ **twice daily** on two occasions every day ■ *noun* a newspaper published every weekday (NOTE: The plural is **dailies**.)

dairy /ˈdeəri/ *adjective* referring to or involved in producing milk and things made from it such as cream or butter ○ *dairy products* ○ *dairy cattle*

dam /dæm/ *noun* a wall which blocks a river to make a lake ○ *After the heavy rain people were afraid the dam would burst.* ■ *verb* to block a river with a wall ○ *When they built the power station, the river had to be dammed.* (NOTE: **dams – damming – dammed**)

damage /ˈdæmɪdʒ/ *noun* **1.** the breaking or physical spoiling of something ○ *The storm did a lot of damage.* ○ *It will take us months to repair the damage to the restaurant.* ○ *The fire caused damage estimated at £100,000.* **2.** emotional harm done to a person ○ *I hope the experience of the crash won't cause the children lasting damage.* ■ *verb* **1.** to break or partially destroy something ○ *A large number of shops were damaged in the fire.* ○ *These glasses are easily damaged.* **2.** to affect someone or something in a negative way

damaged /ˈdæmɪdʒd/ *adjective* broken or spoiled in some way ○ *a damaged book*

damp /dæmp/ *adjective* slightly wet ○ *She'd just had a shower and her hair was still damp.* ○ *The cellar has cold damp walls.* ■ *verb* to wet something slightly

dance /dɑːns/ *noun* **1.** a way of moving in time to music ○ *She teaches dance or is a dance teacher.* ○ *We learnt a new dance today.* ○ *Scottish dances are very lively.* **2.** an entertainment where people can dance ○ *The club is holding a New Year's dance.* ○ *They met at a youth club dance.* ■ *verb* **1.** to move in time to music ○ *There he is – he's dancing with that tall girl.* ○ *She often goes to discos but never dances.* **2.** to move or jump around happily ○ *She danced into the room and announced she'd got the job.* ○ *The football fans were dancing in the streets.*

dancer /ˈdɑːnsə/ *noun* a person who dances

danger /ˈdeɪndʒə/ *noun* the possibility of something bad happening, e.g. damage, failure or getting hurt ○ *When it rains, there's a danger of flooding.* ○ *The terrorist was described as a danger to national security.* ○ *There's no danger he'll find out.* ○ *We were warned of the dangers of travelling alone in the desert.* ◇ **in danger** /ɪn ˈdeɪndʒə/ likely to be harmed or damaged ○ *Get an ambulance – her life is in danger.* ○ *I don't think the children are in any danger.* ○ *The whole building was in danger of catching fire.* ◇ **out of danger** not likely to die ○ *She was very ill, but she's off the danger list now.*

dangerous /ˈdeɪndʒərəs/ *adjective* likely to cause injury or damage ○ *Be careful – that old staircase is dangerous!* ○ *Police warned the public not to approach the man as he was dangerous.* ○ *Children are warned that it is dangerous to go out alone at night.*

dangerously /ˈdeɪndʒərəsli/ *adverb* in a dangerous way

dare /deə/ *verb* **1.** to be brave enough to do something ○ *I wouldn't dare say no – I might lose my job.* □ **I dare say** very probably ○ *I dare say you're right.* □ **to dare not do something** to not be brave enough to do something ○ *I daren't go any faster.* **2.** to try to make someone do something dangerous or unusual in order to see how brave they are ○ *I dared him to go the meeting in his pink track-suit.* ○ *I dare you to jump across that stream.* **3.** used for telling someone how angry you are ○ *Don't you dare do that again!* ○ *How dare you look in my desk drawers!*

dark /dɑːk/ *adjective* **1.** with little or no light ○ *The sky turned dark and it started to rain.* ○ *Can you switch the light on? It's getting too dark to see.* ○ *In Scotland in the summer it gets dark very late.* **2.** not a light colour ○ *Her eyes are dark.* ○ *She was wearing a dark blue coat.* (NOTE: **darker – darkest**)

darkness /'dɑːknəs/ *noun* the fact of not having any light □ **the building was in complete** *or* **total darkness** there were no electric lights on in the building

darling /'dɑːlɪŋ/ *noun* **1.** a name used to talk to someone you love ○ *Darling! I'm back from the shops.* **2.** a lovable person ○ *Be a darling and fetch me the newspaper.*

dart /dɑːt/ *noun* **1.** a small heavy arrow with plastic feathers, used for playing the game of darts ○ *Each player takes a turn to throw his or her three darts.* **2. darts** a game in which players throw small arrows at a round board on a wall, each trying to make their arrow stick closest to the middle ■ *verb* to move quickly ○ *The little boy darted across the street.*

dash /dæʃ/ *noun* **1.** a small line in writing or printing, showing a space or separating items ○ *The reference number is one four six dash seven (146–7).* **2.** a sudden movement towards a place ○ *There was a mad dash to buy tickets.* ○ *While the policeman wasn't looking she made a dash for the door.* (NOTE: The plural is **dashes**.) ■ *verb* to hurry somewhere ○ *I can't stop now – I must dash to catch the last post.* ○ *I dashed*

home to watch the football on television. ○ *She dashed into a shop so that he wouldn't see her.*

data /'deɪtə/ *noun* information involving figures or results of studies ○ *The data is stored in our main computer.* ○ *We spent months gathering data on hospital waiting times.* ○ *The data shows that, on average, flowering takes place after two weeks.* (NOTE: **Data** is often used with a singular verb, except in scientific contexts: *The data is easily available.*)

database /'deɪtəbeɪs/ *noun* a large amount of information stored in a computer in a way that allows particular pieces of information to be found easily

date /deɪt/ *noun* **1.** the number of a day in a month or year, or a day when something will happen or has happened ○ *Put today's date on the document.* ○ *What's the date next Wednesday?* ○ *The dates of the exhibition have been changed.* ○ *The date of the next meeting has been fixed for Wednesday, June 10th.* ○ *Do you remember the date of your girlfriend's birthday?* **2.** a small sweet brown fruit ■ *verb* **1.** to write the date on something ○ *The letter was dated 15 June.* ○ *You forgot to date the cheque.* **2.** □ **to date from** *or* **back to** to exist since ○ *This house dates from* or *dates back to the 17th century.*

daughter /'dɔːtə/ *noun* a female child of a parent ○ *They have two sons and one daughter.* ○ *My daughter Mary goes to the local school.*

dawn /dɔːn/ *noun* the beginning of a day, when the sun rises ○ *We must set off for the Pyramids at dawn, so you'll have to get up very early.* ■ *verb* **(of day)** to begin ○ *The day of the cricket match dawned wet and windy.*

day /deɪ/ *noun* **1.** a period of time lasting 24 hours ○ *There are 365 days in a year and 366 in a leap year.* ○ *New Year's Day is on January 1st.* ○ *They went on a ten-day tour of southern Spain.* ○ *I spoke to him on the phone the day before yesterday.* ○ *We are planning to meet the day after tomorrow.* **2.** the period from morning until night, when it is light ○ *She works all day in the office, and then looks after the children in the* *evening.* ○ *It took the workmen four days to build the wall.*

daylight /'deɪlaɪt/ *noun* light that you see during the daytime □ **in broad daylight** openly, in the middle of the day ○ *Three men robbed the bank in broad daylight.*

daytime /'deɪtaɪm/ *noun* the period of light between morning and night ○ *I watched a lot of daytime television when I lost my job.*

dazzle /'dæz(ə)l/ *verb* to shine a strong light in someone's eyes so that they cannot see for a moment ○ *She was dazzled by the lights of the cars coming towards her.*

dead /ded/ *adjective* **1.** not alive any more ○ *His parents are both dead.* ○ *Dead fish were floating in the water.* **2.** complete ○ *There was dead silence in the exam room.* ○ *The train came to a dead stop.* **3.** not working ○ *We tried to start the car but the battery was dead.* **4.** not lively, not exciting ○ *Seaside towns can be quite dead in winter.* ■ *adverb* **1.** completely ○ *He was dead tired after his long walk.* **2.** exactly ○ *You're dead right.* ○ *The train arrived dead on time.*

deadly /'dedli/ *adjective* likely to kill living things ○ *The terrorists turned the car into a deadly weapon.*

deaf /def/ *adjective* not able to hear, or having difficulty in hearing ○ *My grandma is going deaf.* ○ *He's deafer than he used to be.* (NOTE: Some people avoid this term as it can cause offence and prefer **hearing-impaired**.)

deafening /'def(ə)nɪŋ/ *adjective* so loud as to make you unable to hear

deafness /'defnəs/ *noun* the state of being deaf (NOTE: no plural)

deal /diːl/ *noun* **1.** □ **a good** *or* **great deal** much ○ *He's feeling a good deal better after two days off work.* ○ *She didn't say a great deal.* □ **a good** *or* **great deal of** a lot of ○ *He made a good deal of money from his business.* ○ *There's a great deal of work still to be done.* **2.** a business agreement or contract ○ *We've signed a deal with a German firm.* ○ *They did a deal to supply envelopes.* ○ *The sales director set up a deal with a Russian bank.*

■ *verb* **1.** □ **to deal in something** to buy and sell something ○ *She deals in carpets and rugs imported from India.* **2.** to give out playing cards to players ○ *It's my turn to deal.* ○ *He dealt me two aces.* (NOTE: **deals – dealing – dealt** /delt/)

deal with *phrasal verb* to do what is necessary to complete a job or solve a problem ○ *The job involves dealing with the public.* ○ *Leave it to the filing clerk – he'll deal with it.* ○ *We will deal with your order as soon as we can.* ○ *The government has to deal with the problem of teenage crime.*

dealer /'diːlə/ *noun* a person who buys and sells things

dealt /delt/ past tense and past participle of **deal**

dear /dɪə/ *adjective* **1.** well liked or loved ○ *She's a very dear friend of mine.* (NOTE: **dearer – dearest**) **2.** □ **Dear James** or **Dear Julia** used at the beginning of a letter to a friend or someone you know quite well □ **Dear Sir** *or* **Madam** used at the beginning of a letter to a man or woman whom you do not know **3.** costing a lot of money ○ *Fresh fruit is always dearer in the winter.* ○ *That restaurant is too dear for me.* (NOTE: **dearer – dearest**) ■ *interjection* used when something has gone slightly wrong ○ *Oh dear! It's started to rain.* ○ *Dear me! Is that how late it is!* ■ *noun* a way of referring to someone you like ○ *Did you have a good day, dear?*

death /deθ/ *noun* □ **to death** completely (*informal*) ○ *He was bored to death sitting watching football on television.* ○ *I am sick to death of always having to do the housework.*

debate /dɪ'beɪt/ *noun* **1.** a discussion ○ *After his talk the professor had a lively debate with the students.* **2.** a formal discussion ending with a vote ○ *a debate on increasing student fees* ■ *verb* **1.** to consider or discuss a subject ○ *We sat in the rain and debated what to do next.* **2.** to discuss something formally before coming to a decision

debt /det/ *noun* money owed to someone ○ *After her great success, she was able to repay all her debts.* □ **to be in debt** to owe money ○ *He is in debt to the tune of £2,500.*

decade /'dekeɪd/ *noun* a period of ten years ○ *during the last decade of the 20th century*

decay /dɪ'keɪ/ *noun* the natural process of going bad or of becoming damaged, e.g. when things are not looked after properly ○ *The government has plans to deal with inner city decay.* ○ *Tooth decay is especially bad in children who eat sweets.* ○ *You must treat the wood to prevent decay.* (NOTE: no plural) ■ *verb* to go bad or to become damaged in this way ○ *Sugar makes your teeth decay.* ○ *The jungle path was blocked by decaying branches.*

deceive /dɪ'siːv/ *verb* to make someone believe something which is not true ○ *They had tried to deceive me, but I realised just in time.*

December /dɪ'sembə/ *noun* the twelfth and last month of the year, after November and before January ○ *She was born last December.* ○ *His birthday is on December 25 – Christmas Day!* ○ *They always go on a skiing holiday in December.* ○ *Today is December 6th.* ○ *The cheque was dated December 6.* (NOTE: **December 6th** or **December 6**: say 'the sixth of December' or 'December the sixth' or in US English 'December sixth'.)

decide /dɪ'saɪd/ *verb* to make up your mind to do something ○ *Have you decided which restaurant to go to?* ○ *They decided to stay at home and watch TV.*

decide against *phrasal verb* to make up your mind not to do something ○ *She decided against spending her money on a new car.*

decimal /'desɪm(ə)l/ *noun* a number in a system based on ten ○ *Three-quarters expressed as a decimal is 0.75.*

decision /dɪ'sɪʒ(ə)n/ *noun* an occasion of making up your mind to do something

deck /dek/ *noun* a floor of a ship or bus ○ *I'll stay on deck because I'm feeling seasick.* ○ *Let's go up to the top deck – you can see the sights better from there.*

declare /dɪ'kleə/ *verb* to state something officially ○ *The Senator declared his intention to run for President.* ○ *She was declared dead on arrival at hospital.*

decline /dɪ'klaɪn/ *noun* the fact of going downwards ○ *Sales figures have gone into a sharp decline.* ■ *verb* **1.** to refuse or to turn down an invitation or offer ○ *She declined their request.* ○ *He declined to come to lunch.* **2.** to become weaker ○ *He declined rapidly after he went into hospital.* **3.** to become less in numbers or amount ○ *Our sales declined over the last year.* ○ *The fish population has declined sharply.*

decorate /'dekəreɪt/ *verb* **1.** to put paint or new paper on the walls in a room ○ *She can't come to the phone – she's decorating the kitchen.* **2.** to cover something with pretty or colourful things to make it look attractive or to celebrate an occasion ○ *The streets were decorated with flags.*

decoration /ˌdekə'reɪʃ(ə)n/ *noun* the act of decorating a place ○ *She is in charge of the decoration of the church for the wedding.*

decrease[1] /'diːkriːs/ *noun* the fact of becoming less ○ *a decrease in traffic* ○ *Sales show a 10% decrease on last year.* ○ *There has been a decrease of 20% in applications to join the club.* □ **to be on the decrease** to be becoming less ○ *Road accidents are on the decrease.*

decrease[2] /dɪ'kriːs/ *verb* to become less ○ *The number of road accidents is decreasing.* ○ *Applications to join have decreased by 20%.*

deed /diːd/ *noun* an act, especially a brave one ○ *stories of great deeds performed during the war*

deep /diːp/ *adjective* **1.** going a long way down ○ *The water is very deep in the middle of the river.* ○ *This is the deepest lake in North America.* ○ *In the shallow end of the pool, the water is deep enough to cover your feet.* ◊ **depth 2.** going a long way under the ground ○ *a deep mine* **3.** (*of a voice*) low, not high ○ *Who's been sitting on my chair? said Father Bear in his deep voice.* (NOTE: **deeper – deepest**) ■ *adverb* a long way down ○ *The mine goes deep under the sea.*

deeply /'diːpli/ *adverb* very much ○ *We deeply regret having to make so many people redundant.*

deer /dɪə/ *noun* a wild animal, the male of which has long horns called antlers (NOTE: Do not confuse with **dear**. The plural is **deer**; the female is a **doe**, the male is a **stag**, the young are **fawns**. Note also that the meat from a deer is called **venison**.)

defeat /dɪ'fiːt/ *noun* the loss of a fight, game or vote ○ *The Government suffered a defeat in Parliament last night.* ○ *It was the team's first defeat for two years.* ■ *verb* to succeed against someone in a fight, game or vote ○ *The ruling party was heavily defeated in the presidential election.* ○ *Our team has not been defeated so far this season.* ○ *The proposal was defeated by 10 votes to 3.*

defence /dɪ'fens/ *noun* **1.** protection against something such as attack or infection ○ *Several people ran to her defence when she was attacked.* ○ *These tablets offer some defence against the disease.* **2.** protection provided by the armed forces ○ *Some countries spend more on defence than on education.* **3.** (*in games*) a part of a team whose job is to protect the goal ○ *The England defence came under attack from the other team's forwards.* **4.** (*in a law court*) the lawyers acting on behalf of the accused person

defend /dɪ'fend/ *verb* to protect a person or place that is being attacked ○ *They brought in extra troops to defend the city against attack.*

defense /dɪ'fens/ *noun* US spelling of **defence**

deficiency /dɪ'fɪʃ(ə)nsi/ *noun* not enough of something needed to make someone or something healthy or complete ○ *Their diet has a deficiency of iron* or *has an iron deficiency.*

deficit /'defɪsɪt/ *noun* an amount by which something is less than it should be ○ *The company announced a two-million-pound deficit in its accounts.*

define /dɪ'faɪn/ *verb* to explain something clearly or to give the meaning of something ○ *How would you define the word 'environmental'?* ○ *The memo tried to define the way in which the two departments should work together.*

definite /'def(ə)nət/ *adjective* very sure ○ *I need a definite answer.* ○ *He was quite definite that he had seen the girl at the bus stop.*

definitely /'def(ə)nətli/ *adverb* certainly ○ *I'll definitely be there by 7 o'clock.* ○ *Are you coming? – Definitely not!*

definition /ˌdefɪ'nɪʃ(ə)n/ *noun* an explanation of the meaning of a word ○ *Look up the definition of 'democracy' in the dictionary.*

degree /dɪ'griː/ *noun* **1.** a unit for measuring temperature or angles, shown by the symbol (°) ○ *an angle of eighty degrees* ○ *The temperature of the water is above 20°.* (NOTE: With figures, **degree** is usually written as the symbol °: 25° Celsius.) **2.** a qualification from a university ○ *She has a degree in mathematics from Oxford.* **3.** a small amount of something such as an emotion ○ *I approached the animal with some degree of fear.*

delay /dɪ'leɪ/ *noun* the length of time by which something is late ○ *There will be a delay of ten minutes before the meeting starts.* ○ *We are sorry for the delay in replying to your letter.* ■ *verb* **1.** to make someone or something late ○ *The train has been delayed by fog.* ○ *He was delayed because his taxi had an accident.* **2.** to put something off until later ○ *We will delay making a decision until we see the result of the election.* ○ *The company has delayed payment of all invoices.*

deliberate¹ /dɪ'lɪb(ə)rət/ *adjective* **1.** done on purpose ○ *It was a deliberate attempt to spoil her birthday party.* **2.** slow and thoughtful in speaking or doing something ○ *She has a very deliberate way of signing her name.*

deliberate² /dɪ'lɪbəreɪt/ *verb* to discuss or think carefully about something ○ *The council were deliberating all morning.* ○ *I'll need some time to deliberate* *on the possible ways of solving the problem.*

deliberately /dɪ'lɪb(ə)rətli/ *adverb* on purpose ○ *It was an accident – I didn't hit her deliberately.* ○ *He deliberately left the cage door open.*

delicate /'delɪkət/ *adjective* **1.** made from materials that are thin and light and easily damaged ○ *a delicate china vase* **2.** likely to get ill ○ *Little babies are very delicate.* ○ *She was a delicate child.*

delicious /dɪ'lɪʃəs/ *adjective* tasting very good ○ *Can I have another piece of that delicious cake?*

delight /dɪ'laɪt/ *noun* pleasure ○ *Their singing was a pure delight.* ○ *The news was greeted with delight by the waiting crowd.* □ **to take (great) delight in something** to enjoy something ■ *verb* to give great pleasure to someone ○ *His speech delighted the audience.* □ **to delight in something** to enjoy something ○ *She delights in teasing her little brother.*

delighted /dɪ'laɪtɪd/ *adjective* very pleased

delightful /dɪ'laɪtf(ə)l/ *adjective* very pleasant ○ *What a delightful show of flowers!*

deliver /dɪ'lɪvə/ *verb* to bring something to someone ○ *Has today's newspaper been delivered?* ○ *He delivered the letter himself so as to save buying a stamp.*

delivery /dɪ'lɪv(ə)ri/ *noun* the act of bringing something to someone ○ *There is no charge for delivery within the London area.* ○ *Use the back entrance for deliveries.* ○ *The next delivery will be on Thursday.*

demand /dɪ'mɑːnd/ *noun* **1.** the act of asking for something ○ *a demand for payment* ○ *Her latest demands are quite unreasonable.* **2.** the need for particular goods or services ○ *We can't sell the book, because there is no demand for it.* ○ *We cannot keep up with the demand for our services.* ■ *verb* to ask firmly for something ○ *I demand an explanation.*

democracy /dɪ'mɒkrəsi/ *noun* **1.** a country governed by politicians who have been elected by the people (NOTE: The plural is **democracies.**) **2.** a system of government in which politicians are elected by the people ○ *The people want democracy, not a dictatorship.*

democratic /ˌdemə'krætɪk/ *adjective* relating to democracy ○ *They promised to restore democratic government.*

demonstrate /'demənstreɪt/ *verb* to show something ○ *This incident demonstrates how little he has changed.* ○ *He demonstrated how the machine worked.*

demonstration /ˌdemən'streɪʃ(ə)n/ *noun* **1.** the act of showing how something works ○ *Can you give me a demonstration the new machine?* **2.** a crowd of people who are protesting against something ○ *We went to a demonstration in Trafalgar Square.* ○ *They staged demonstrations against the government in several towns.*

den /den/ *noun* **1.** a place where an animal hides away ○ *a lion's den* **2.** a small room where you can hide away to work ○ *Dad's in his den, so don't disturb him.*

dense /dens/ *adjective* **1.** very thick ○ *Dense fog closed the airport.* **2.** with a lot of trees or plants ○ *They tried to find their way through dense forest.* **3.** containing a lot of information ○ *I find it difficult to read through 100 pages of dense text.* (NOTE: **denser – densest**)

dent /dent/ *noun* a mark that curves inwards, especially in metal, made by hitting something ○ *Someone has made a dent in my car door.* ■ *verb* to make a mark like this in something ○ *He backed into a tree and dented the car.*

dentist /'dentɪst/ *noun* a person whose job is to look after and provide treatment for your teeth

deny /dɪ'naɪ/ *verb* to state that something is not true ○ *You were there, weren't you? – Don't deny it!* ○ *She denied that she had ever seen him.* ○ *He flatly denied stealing the car.* (NOTE: **denies – denying – denied**)

depart /dɪ'pɑːt/ *verb* to go away from a place ○ *The coach departs from Victoria Coach Station at 09.00.*

department /dɪ'pɑːtmənt/ *noun* **1.** a section of a large company ○ *He is in charge of the marketing department.* ○

Write to the complaints department about the service. **2.** one of the sections of the government ○ *the Department for Education and Skills* ○ *the Department of Transport* **3.** a part of a large shop ○ *If you want cheese you'll need to go to the food department.* ○ *You will find beds in the furniture department.*

department store /dɪˈpɑːtmənt stɔː/ *noun* a large shop with several different sections

departure /dɪˈpɑːtʃə/ *noun* the act of leaving a place ○ *The departure time is 3 o'clock.* ○ *The plane's departure was delayed by two hours.*

depend /dɪˈpend/ *verb* **1.** to happen only because of something else happening first ○ *The success of the book will depend on the publicity campaign.* ○ *I can't be sure that we will come to lunch – it depends on what time we get home from the party the night before.* □ **it (all) depends** it is not certain (*informal*) ○ *We may go to France on holiday, or Spain, it all depends.* **2.** □ **to depend on someone** *or* **something** to be sure that someone will do what they say they will do, or that something will happen as expected ○ *You can't depend on Jack – he's always too busy to help.* ○ *You can depend on her to do her best.* ○ *The company depends on government grants.*

dependent /dɪˈpendənt/ *adjective* **1.** needing money from someone else in order to live ○ *She has five dependent relatives.* **2.** needing someone else's help in order to live or succeed ○ *The patients become very dependent on the hospital staff.* **3.** caused or affected by something ○ *The success of the project is dependent on getting a government grant.*

deposit /dɪˈpɒzɪt/ *noun* **1.** money kept in a bank ○ *Her deposits in the bank had grown over the years.* **2.** a particular amount of money that you give someone as a first payment for something expensive ○ *She had to pay a deposit on the watch.* ○ *Can you leave £50 as deposit?* ○ *I paid a 30% deposit and don't have to pay anything more for six months.* ■ *verb* to put money into a bank

account ○ *She deposited £100 in her current account.* ○ *The cheque arrived at long last, and I deposited it immediately.*

depressed /dɪˈprest/ *adjective* so unhappy that you are not able to enjoy life, especially over a long period of time ○ *She's been feeling depressed since the accident.*

depressing /dɪˈpresɪŋ/ *adjective* making you feel sad or unhappy

depth /depθ/ *noun* a measurement of how deep something is ○ *The depth of the lake is 20m.* ○ *The submarine dived to a depth of 200m.*

deputy /ˈdepjʊti/ *noun* **1.** a person who makes decisions when the manager or boss is away ○ *She's acting as deputy while the managing director is in hospital.* **2.** a person who helps someone in their job ○ *He appointed her as his deputy.*

derive /dɪˈraɪv/ *verb* to get something from something ○ *The local people derive a good deal of pleasure from watching the tourists.*

describe /dɪˈskraɪb/ *verb* to say or write what someone or something is like ○ *Can you describe the car which hit the old lady?* ○ *She described how the bus suddenly left the road.* ○ *He described the mugger as a tall man with a black beard.* ○ *The police asked him to describe what happened.*

description /dɪˈskrɪpʃən/ *noun* the act of saying or writing what something or someone is like

desert¹ /ˈdezət/ *noun* a very dry area of the world, usually covered with rocks or sand (NOTE: Do not confuse with **dessert**.)

desert² /dɪˈzɜːt/ *verb* **1.** to leave the armed forces without permission **2.** to leave someone in a difficult situation

deserted /dɪˈzɜːtɪd/ *adjective* with no people ○ *We walked around the deserted town.*

deserve /dɪˈzɜːv/ *verb* to earn something because of what you have done ○ *He didn't deserve to win because he cheated.* ○ *I've been on my feet all day*

– I think I deserve a sit-down. ○ *He deserves a holiday.*

design /dɪ'zaɪn/ *noun* a plan or drawing of something, before it is made or built ○ *Here are the designs for the book cover.* ○ *The architect has produced the designs for the new opera house.* ■ *verb* to draw plans for the shape or appearance of something before it is made or built ○ *He designed the new university library.* ○ *She designs garden furniture.*

designer /dɪ'zaɪnə/ *noun* an artist who plans the shape or appearance of things such as goods, clothes or rooms

desire /dɪ'zaɪə/ *noun* something that you want very much ○ *It's difficult to satisfy the public's desire for information.* ○ *She had a sudden desire to lie down and go to sleep.* ■ *verb* to want something (*formal*) ○ *Most of us desire a large comfortable home.*

desk /desk/ *noun* a table, often with drawers, used for writing ○ *He put the papers away in his desk drawer.* ○ *She was sitting at her desk when the telephone rang.*

despair /dɪ'speə/ *noun* a feeling that a situation is so bad that there is nothing you can do to make it better ○ *When he lost his job and his girlfriend left him, he was filled with despair.* □ **the depths of despair** a situation where there is complete lack of hope ■ *verb* to give up all hope of achieving something ○ *After two months in the jungle, he despaired of ever being rescued.*

desperate /'desp(ə)rət/ *adjective* **1.** having a strong need for something that you are not able to get, and feeling very worried because you do not know how to solve the problem ○ *Food ran out and the people were becoming desperate.* **2.** urgent ○ *There is a desperate need for medical supplies.*

despite /dɪ'spaɪt/ *preposition* although something happened or was done ○ *Despite the wet weather we still enjoyed our holiday.*

dessert /dɪ'zɜːt/ *noun* a sweet dish at the end of a meal ○ *The meal will end with a dessert of strawberries and cream.* ○ *What's for dessert?* (NOTE: Do not confuse with **desert**. The word **dessert** is mainly used in restaurants. At home, this part of the meal is usually called **the sweet** *or* **afters** *or* **pudding**.)

destination /ˌdestɪ'neɪʃ(ə)n/ *noun* the place to which a person or vehicle is going ○ *We reached our destination at eight o'clock.* ○ *The destination is shown on the front of the bus.*

destroy /dɪ'strɔɪ/ *verb* to damage something so badly that it no longer exists ○ *The bomb destroyed several buildings.* ○ *A lot of private property was destroyed in the war.*

destruction /dɪ'strʌkʃən/ *noun* the action of destroying something ○ *the destruction of the village by enemy bombs* ○ *The volcano caused enormous destruction.* (NOTE: no plural)

detail /'diːteɪl/ *noun* a small piece of information ○ *Send in your CV including full details of your past experience.* ○ *Can you give me further details of when the accident took place?* ○ *I can't make out the details in the photo because the light is bad.* ○ *The policeman noted down the details of the incident.* ■ *verb* to list all the facts or items ○ *He detailed the work which had to be done.* ◇ **in detail** with as much information as possible ○ *The catalogue lists all the furniture in detail.* ○ *Please describe the circumstances of the accident in as much detail as possible.*

detailed /'diːteɪld/ *adjective* giving a lot of details ○ *We need a detailed list of the items which have been stolen.* ○ *The police issued detailed descriptions of the two men.*

detective /dɪ'tektɪv/ *noun* a police officer whose job is to try to find out who committed crimes ○ *Detectives have interviewed four suspects.*

determination /dɪˌtɜːmɪ'neɪʃ(ə)n/ *noun* a strong wish to do something, and not to let anyone stop you doing it ○ *They admired his determination to win the prize.* ○ *The government needs to show more determination in its fight against street crime.*

determined /dɪˈtɜːmɪnd/ *adjective* having a strong wish to do something, and not letting anyone prevent you from doing it ○ *She's a very determined young woman, and will go far.* ○ *He had a very determined expression on his face as he entered the ring.* ○ *She is determined to win the prize.*

develop /dɪˈveləp/ *verb* **1.** to grow and change ○ *Eventually, a caterpillar will develop into a butterfly.* **2.** to make something larger ○ *She cycles in order to develop her calf muscles.* **3.** to get an illness ○ *She developed a cold at the weekend.* **4.** to plan and build something ○ *They are planning to develop the site as an industrial estate.* ○ *The company is developing a chain of motorway service stations.*

development /dɪˈveləpmənt/ *noun* **1.** growth ○ *The development of the embryo takes place rapidly.* **2.** the planning and production of a new product ○ *The development of new pesticides will take some time.* **3.** the act of planning and building on an area of land ○ *the development of property on the site of the former docks* **4.** a group of buildings that have been built together at the same time ○ *a new housing development*

device /dɪˈvaɪs/ *noun* a small tool or piece of equipment that is useful for a particular purpose ○ *He invented a device for fixing tops on bottles.* ○ *The engineers brought in a device for taking samples of soil.* ◇ **to be left to your own devices** to be allowed to do whatever you want

diagonal /daɪˈæɡən(ə)l/ *adjective* (*of a line*) going straight from one corner to another ○ *He drew a diagonal line on the floor.* ○ *Areas of the map shaded with diagonal lines indicate cultivated land.* ■ *noun* a diagonal line

diagram /ˈdaɪəɡræm/ *noun* a plan or accurate drawing ○ *She drew a diagram to show how to get to her house.* ○ *The book gives a diagram of the circulation of the blood.*

dial /ˈdaɪəl/ *noun* a round face of a measuring instrument or a old type of telephone ○ *The pilot sits in front of a display of dials.* ■ *verb* to call a telephone

number using the buttons on a telephone ○ *To call the police you must dial 999.* ○ *Dial 9 to get an outside line.* (NOTE: **dials – dialling – dialled**. The US spelling is **dialing – dialed**.)

dialect /ˈdaɪəlekt/ *noun* a variety of a language spoken in a particular area ○ *They were speaking in a local dialect.*

diameter /daɪˈæmɪtə/ *noun* the distance across the centre of a circle

diamond /ˈdaɪəmənd/ *noun* **1.** a very hard, clear, precious stone ○ *He gave her a diamond ring.* ○ *Diamonds sparkled on her crown.* **2.** one of the red sets in a pack of cards, shaped like a square leaning to one side ○ *He held the ten of diamonds.* (NOTE: The other red suit is **hearts**; **clubs** and **spades** are the black suits.)

diary /ˈdaɪəri/ *noun* a description of what has happened in your life day by day ○ *He kept a diary for years.* ○ *She kept a diary of the places she visited on holiday.* (NOTE: The plural is **diaries**.)

dice /daɪs/ *noun* a small block with a different number of spots on each side, used for playing games ○ *Shake the dice in the cup and then throw them onto the board.* (NOTE: The plural is **dice**.)

dictionary /ˈdɪkʃən(ə)ri/ *noun* a book which lists words in alphabetical order, giving their meanings or translations into other languages (NOTE: The plural is **dictionaries**.)

did /dɪd/ past tense of **do**

die /daɪ/ *verb* **1.** to stop living ○ *His mother died last year.* ○ *She died in a car crash.* ○ *If you don't water the plants they'll die.* ◇ **death** (NOTE: **dies – dying – died**) **2.** □ **dying for** *or* **to** wanting something very much ○ *We're dying for a cold drink.* ○ *I'm dying to read his book.*

die away *phrasal verb* to become less noisy

die down *phrasal verb* to get less strong ○ *The wind began to die down.* ○ *The government is waiting for the street protests to die down.*

die out *phrasal verb* to disappear gradually

diet /'daɪət/ *noun* **1.** the kind of food you eat ○ *He lives on a diet of bread and beer.* ○ *These people are healthier than us because their diet is so simple.* **2.** the practice of eating only certain types of food, either in order to become thinner or to cure an illness ○ *The doctor told her to follow a strict diet.* ■ *verb* to eat less food or only one sort of food ○ *He dieted for two weeks before going on holiday.*

differ /'dɪfə/ *verb* **1.** not to be the same as something else ○ *The two machines differ considerably – one has an electric motor, the other runs on oil.* □ **to differ from** to be different from ○ *This car differs from the earlier model.* ○ *Their business differs from ours in one important aspect.* **2.** if people differ, they have different opinions from each other ○ *Our views on education differ.* ○ *Their accounts of what happened differ in several ways.* □ **I beg to differ** I do not agree

difference /'dɪf(ə)rəns/ *noun* a way in which two things are not the same ○ *Can you tell the difference between an apple and a pear with your eyes shut?* ○ *What is the difference in price between these two cars?*

different /'dɪf(ə)rənt/ *adjective* not the same ○ *Living in London is very different from living in the country.* ○ *I went to three different clothes shops but I couldn't find anything in my size.* ○ *He looks different now that he has a beard.*

difficult /'dɪfɪk(ə)lt/ *adjective* not easy to do or achieve ○ *Finding a parking space is difficult on Saturdays.* ○ *I find it difficult to work when I'm tired.*

difficulty /'dɪfɪk(ə)lti/ *noun* **1.** □ **to have difficulty with** *or* **in doing something** to find it hard to do something ○ *She has difficulty in paying the rent.* □ **with difficulty** not easily ○ *She walks with difficulty.* **2.** a problem ○ *The difficulty is that nobody in the group can drive.* ○ *He is in financial difficulties.* ○ *She went swimming in the rough sea and got into difficulties.* (NOTE: The plural is **difficulties**.)

dig /dɪg/ *verb* to make a hole in the ground with a spade ○ *She's been dig-*

ging in the garden all morning. ○ *They dug a big hole in the ground.* ○ *The prisoners dug a tunnel to try to escape.* (NOTE: **digging – dug – has dug**)

dig up *phrasal verb* **1.** to find something by digging ○ *We dug up a Roman coin in the garden.* **2.** to break a solid surface by digging ○ *The workmen had to dig the road up to mend the water main.*

digest /daɪ'dʒest/ *verb* **1.** to break down food in the stomach ○ *I find this meat difficult to digest.* **2.** to think about something and understand it fully ○ *Give me time to digest this news.*

digestion /daɪ'dʒestʃən/ *noun* the process by which food is broken down in the stomach

digital /'dɪdʒɪt(ə)l/ *adjective* **1.** storing information in an electronic form ○ *a digital radio* **2.** (*of a clock or watch*) showing the time as a set of numbers

dim /dɪm/ *adjective* (*of light*) weak ○ *The lights grew dimmer.* (NOTE: **dimmer – dimmed**) ■ *verb* to make a light less bright ○ *They dimmed the cabin lights before takeoff.* (NOTE: **dims – dimming – dimmed**)

dime /daɪm/ *noun US* a coin that is worth ten cents

dimension /daɪ'menʃən/ *noun* the extent of a problem ○ *the international dimension of the refugee problem* ○ *The task is taking on huge dimensions.*

dining room /'daɪnɪŋ ruːm/ *noun* a room in a house or hotel where you usually eat. ◊ **bathroom, bedroom, living room**

dinner /'dɪnə/ *noun* **1.** the main meal of the day, usually eaten in the evening ○ *We were having dinner when the telephone rang.* ○ *Would you like to come to dinner on Saturday?* ○ *What are we having for dinner?* or *What's for dinner?* **2.** a formal evening meal ○ *The club is organising a dinner and dance on Saturday.*

dinosaur /'daɪnəsɔː/ *noun* a large creature that existed on the Earth millions of years ago ○ *At the time when dinosaurs roamed the land, England was covered with tropical forests.*

dip /dɪp/ *noun* **1.** a sudden drop in an area of land ○ *Watch out – there's a dip in the road which makes it difficult to see approaching cars.* **2.** a cold sauce into which you can dip biscuits or raw vegetables ○ *a bowl of cheese dip* ■ *verb* □ **to dip something into something** to put something quickly into a liquid ○ *She dipped the biscuit into her coffee.* ○ *She dipped her hand into the stream.* (NOTE: **dips – dipping – dipped**)

diploma /dɪˈpləʊmə/ *noun* a document which shows that a person has reached a certain level of skill in a subject

direct /daɪˈrekt/ *adjective* straight, without any changes of direction or stops ○ *What's the most direct way of getting to London?* ■ *verb* **1.** to aim something towards a point ○ *I hope you're not directing that gun at me!* **2.** to say something to a particular person ○ *He directed his remarks to the manager.* **3.** to tell someone how to get to a place ○ *Can you direct me to the nearest post office?* ■ *adverb* straight, without stopping ○ *The plane flies direct to Anchorage.*

direction /daɪˈrekʃən/ *noun* the point towards which you are going ○ *You are going in the wrong direction if you want to get to the station.* ○ *The post office is in the opposite direction.* ■ *plural noun* **directions** instructions on how to do something ◇ **in all directions** everywhere ○ *The wind was blowing bits of old newspapers in all directions.*

directly /daɪˈrektlɪ/ *adverb* **1.** straight, without anything or anyone between ○ *This door opens directly into the kitchen.* ○ *She reports directly to the managing director himself.* **2.** soon ○ *I'll be with you directly.* ■ *conjunction* as soon as ○ *I will write the letter directly I get home.*

director /daɪˈrektə/ *noun* **1.** a person who is in charge of all of, or part of, a company ○ *The sales director gave a report on sales to date.* ○ *There are four directors on the board of the company.* **2.** a person who organises the making of a film or play, e.g. giving instructions to the actors, or dealing with the lighting or sound ○ *Who was the first female di-*

rector to win an Oscar? Compare **producer**

dirt /dɜːt/ anything that makes something dirty ○ *a washing powder that removes even the worst kinds of dirt* ■ *noun* mud; earth ○ *Children were playing in the dirt.* ○ *His clothes were covered with dirt from handling potatoes.*

dirty /ˈdɜːtɪ/ *adjective* **1.** not clean ○ *Playing rugby gets your clothes dirty.* ○ *Someone has to wash all the dirty plates.* **2.** not honest, or not done according to the rules (NOTE: **dirtier – dirtied**) ■ *verb* to make something dirty (NOTE: **dirties – dirtying – dirtied**)

disabled /dɪsˈeɪb(ə)ld/ *adjective* not able to use part of your body, e.g. because of long-term illness ○ *an association for disabled riders* ○ *The car crash left him permanently disabled.*

disadvantage /ˌdɪsədˈvɑːntɪdʒ/ *noun* something which makes someone or something less likely to succeed ○ *Her main disadvantage is her lack of experience.* ○ *It was a disadvantage not to be able to get to the airport quickly.* ○ *There are certain disadvantages to leaving at 5.30 in the morning.*

disagree /ˌdɪsəˈɡriː/ *verb* to say that you do not have the same opinion as someone else ○ *We all disagreed with the chairperson.* ○ *They disagreed about what to do next.*

disagreement /ˌdɪsəˈɡriːmənt/ *noun* an argument ○ *They had a disagreement about who should sit in the front row.* ○ *Nothing could be decided because of the disagreement between the chair and the treasurer.*

disappear /ˌdɪsəˈpɪə/ *verb* **1.** to suddenly not be seen any more ○ *He hit the ball hard and it disappeared into the bushes.* ○ *The two boys disappeared on their way home from school.* **2.** to leave a place, often suddenly and without people noticing or knowing where you have gone ○ *Where have the kids disappeared to?* ○ *Half the guests have disappeared already.*

disappointed /ˌdɪsəˈpɔɪntɪd/ *adjective* sad, because things have not happened as you hoped ○ *She is disappointed with* *her exam results.* ○ *He was disappointed because his ticket didn't win a prize.* ○ *You should have seen the disappointed expression on his face.*

disappointing /ˌdɪsə'pɔɪntɪŋ/ *adjective* making you sad because things have not happened as you hoped

disappointment /ˌdɪsə'pɔɪntmənt/ *noun* **1.** a feeling of sadness that you get when things have not happened as you hoped ○ *She tried hard not to show her disappointment.* ○ *To his great disappointment, he didn't win anything on the lottery.* (NOTE: no plural in this sense) **2.** something that disappoints someone ○ *It was a disappointment to his parents when he failed his exam.* ○ *After many disappointments she finally won a prize.*

disapprove /ˌdɪsə'pruːv/ *verb* to show that you do not think something is good ○ *The head teacher disapproves of members of staff wearing jeans to school.*

disaster /dɪ'zɑːstə/ *noun* a very bad accident ○ *The disaster was caused by fog* . ○ *Ten people died in the air disaster.* ○ *We're insured against natural disasters such as hurricanes and earthquakes.*

disastrous /dɪ'zɑːstrəs/ *adjective* extremely bad

disc /dɪsk/ *noun* a round flat object ○ *The setting sun was a huge orange disc on the horizon.* ◊ **disk**

discipline /'dɪsɪplɪn/ *noun* **1.** the practice of keeping people under control ○ *The tour leaders are trying to keep discipline among the teenagers.* ○ *We need to enforce stricter discipline in the school.* (NOTE: no plural in this sense) **2.** a subject that people study ○ *biology and other related disciplines* ■ *verb* to punish someone ○ *As a result of the investigation, one employee was dismissed and three were disciplined.* ○ *She was disciplined for swearing at her supervisor.*

disco /'dɪskəʊ/ *noun* a place or party where people dance to pop music (NOTE: The plural is **discos**.)

discover /dɪ'skʌvə/ *verb* to find something new or to learn something for the first time ○ *Who discovered penicillin?*

The firm discovered some errors in the accounts. ○ *We discovered that the estate agent had sold the house twice.*

discovery /dɪ'skʌv(ə)ri/ *noun* **1.** the act of finding something new or learning something for the first time ○ *her discovery that someone had been in her house while she was away* ○ *They congratulated him on his discovery of a new planet.* **2.** a new thing which has been found ○ *Look at his latest discovery – an antique oak table which he found in a barn.* (NOTE: The plural is **discoveries**.)

discuss /dɪ'skʌs/ *verb* to talk about a serious matter or problem ○ *The point of the meeting is to discuss how to save money.* ○ *They spent hours discussing the details of the wedding.*

discussion /dɪ'skʌʃ(ə)n/ *noun* an occasion on which people talk about a serious matter or problem ○ *Most problems can be solved by discussion.* ○ *The next programme will feature a discussion between environmental experts on climate change.* ○ *She had a heated discussion with the bus driver.*

disease /dɪ'ziːz/ *noun* a serious illness ○ *Hundreds of people caught the disease.* ○ *It is a disease that can be treated with antibiotics.*

disgraceful /dɪs'greɪsf(ə)l/ *adjective* which people should be ashamed of

disguise /dɪs'ɡaɪz/ *noun* a set of clothes or something such as false hair or glasses that a persons wears to make them look like someone else ○ *I didn't recognise him as he was wearing a disguise.* □ **in disguise** dressed to look like someone else ○ *The tramp turned out to be a policeman in disguise.* ■ *verb* **1.** to dress someone or yourself so as to look like someone else ○ *He entered the country disguised as a fisherman.* ○ *She wore a wig to disguise her hair.* **2.** to make something look or sound different

disgust /dɪs'ɡʌst/ *noun* **1.** a feeling of dislike that is so strong that you feel angry or slightly ill ○ *Seeing the dead animals filled her with disgust.* **2.** a strong feeling of annoyance ○ *To my disgust, the examiner passed my friend and failed me.* □ **in disgust** showing that you are upset and annoyed ○ *She walked out of the interview in disgust.* ■ *verb* to give someone a strong feeling of dislike or disapproval ○ *The smell of cooking disgusted her.* ○ *The greediness of these people disgusts me.*

dish /dɪʃ/ *noun* **1.** a large plate for serving food ○ *She carefully arranged the slices of meat on a dish.* **2.** food prepared in a particular way ○ *We are trying a new Mexican dish.* **3.** a round aerial, shaped like a plate, used to get signals from satellites (NOTE: The plural is **dishes.**)

dish out *phrasal verb* to give something out, especially in large quantities (*informal*) ○ *He dished out a piece of bread and a bowl of soup to anyone who asked for it.*

dishonest /dɪsˈɒnɪst/ *adjective* not honest

dishonestly /dɪsˈɒnɪstli/ *adverb* not honestly ○ *They were accused of dishonestly obtaining bank loans.*

disk /dɪsk/ *noun* a round flat piece of metal in a plastic case, used in computers to record information ○ *How much data do these disks hold?* ◊ **disc**

dislike /dɪsˈlaɪk/ *noun* **1.** a feeling of not liking something or someone ○ *She had a great dislike of noisy parties.* **2.** something which you do not like ○ *We try to take account of the likes and dislikes of individual customers.* ■ *verb* not to like something or someone ○ *He particularly disliked the way they spoke to her.* ○ *I dislike it when the people behind me at the cinema start whispering.* ○ *My father dislikes having to get up early on Monday mornings.*

dismay /dɪsˈmeɪ/ *noun* great disappointment ○ *To the dismay of the supporters, the team played extremely badly.* ■ *verb* to make someone very upset or shocked ○ *His reaction to her letter dismayed her.* ○ *She was dismayed to find that her passport had been stolen.*

dismiss /dɪsˈmɪs/ *verb* **1.** to tell someone that they can leave ○ *At the end of the interview he dismissed her with a brief 'good afternoon'.* **2.** to refuse to consider an idea ○ *Her plan was dis-*

missed as being quite impractical. ○ *All his suggestions were dismissed by the MD.* **3.** □ **to dismiss an employee** to remove an employee from a job ○ *He was dismissed for being late.* ○ *When they found him taking money from the petty cash he was dismissed instantly.*

disobey /ˌdɪsəˈbeɪ/ *verb* not to obey someone or something ○ *She would never disobey her parents.*

display /dɪˈspleɪ/ *noun* a show, an exhibition ○ *a display of local crafts* ○ *They have a fine display of Chinese porcelain.* ■ *verb* to put something in a display ○ *She is displaying her collection of Persian carpets at the antiques fair.*

dispute /dɪˈspjuːt, ˈdɪspjuːt/ *noun* an argument ○ *He tried to mediate in the dispute.* ○ *There was some dispute over who would pay the bill.* ■ *verb* to say that you strongly believe that something is not true or correct ○ *I dispute her version of what happened.* ○ *There is no disputing the fact that Sarah is the best player.*

dissatisfied /dɪsˈsætɪsfaɪd/ *adjective* not satisfied ○ *We were dissatisfied with the service we got from our bank.*

dissolve /dɪˈzɒlv/ *verb* to make a solid substance become part of a liquid ○ *Dissolve the sugar in half a litre of boiling water.* ○ *The powder should dissolve in warm water.*

distance /ˈdɪstəns/ *noun* **1.** the space from one point to another ○ *The furthest distance I have travelled by train is 800 km.* ○ *The hotel is only a short distance away.* □ **within walking distance** near enough to walk to ○ *The hotel is within walking distance of the town centre.* **2.** □ **from a distance** seen from some way away ○ *From a distance, the mountain looks like a sleeping animal.* □ **in the distance** a long way away ○ *I caught sight of the mountain in the distance.* ○ *We could hear guns firing in the distance.* ■ *verb* □ **to distance yourself from** to show that you do not agree with someone or something

distant /ˈdɪstənt/ *adjective* far away ○ *We could hear the sound of distant gunfire.* □ **distant relative** a relative who is not a member of the immediate family ○

She's a very distant relative – her grandfather was my grandmother's cousin.

distinct /dɪ'stɪŋkt/ *adjective* **1.** separate ○ *There are two distinct varieties of this plant.* ○ *They keep their printing works quite distinct from their publishing company.* **2.** that you can clearly see, hear or feel ○ *I got the distinct impression that he was carrying a gun.* ○ *Did you notice the distinct tone of anger in his voice?*

distinction /dɪ'stɪŋkʃən/ *noun* **1.** a difference ○ *There is a distinction between being interested in politics and joining a political party.* **2.** the highest mark available in an examination ○ *She got a distinction in her exam.*

distinctly /dɪ'stɪŋktli/ *adverb* clearly

distinguish /dɪ'stɪŋgwɪʃ/ *verb* to see or hear clearly, or to see details ○ *We could easily distinguish houses on the other side of the lake.* ○ *I could distinguish at least two birds calling to each other.*

distract /dɪ'strækt/ *verb* to attract someone's attention when they should be doing something else ○ *The noise of the planes is bound to distract the students.*

distress /dɪ'stres/ *noun* a sad or painful feeling which is very strong ○ *I don't want to cause the family any distress.* ○ *The whole family was in distress at grandmother's death.* ■ *verb* to make someone very sad and worried ○ *The news of her grandmother's death distressed her very much.*

distribute /dɪ'strɪbjuːt/ *verb* to share something between people ○ *She distributed part of her money to the poor.* ○ *The flight attendants came round, distributing immigration forms to non-EU passengers.* ○ *I'll distribute the list to all the committee members.*

district /'dɪstrɪkt/ *noun* an area or region ○ *It's a district of the town well known for its Italian restaurants.*

disturb /dɪ'stɜːb/ *verb* **1.** to interrupt what someone is doing ○ *Sorry to disturb you but there's a phone call.* ○ *Don't disturb your mother – she's resting.* **2.** to make someone feel worried ○ *It disturbed me to see that the wheel was*

wobbling. **3.** to change the order or arrangement of something ○ *The police told us that nothing must be disturbed in the bedroom.*

disturbance /dɪ'stɜːbəns/ *noun* an occasion on which someone is disturbed ○ *I need to work somewhere where there won't be any disturbance.*

ditch /dɪtʃ/ *noun* a long narrow hole cut into the ground for taking away water ○ *After the storm, the ditches were full of rainwater.* ○ *He fell into the ditch beside the road.* (NOTE: The plural is **ditches**.)

dive /daɪv/ *verb* to jump into water head first ○ *He dived in and swam across the pool under water.*

diver /'daɪvə/ *noun* **1.** a person who dives ○ *the Australian Olympic diver* **2.** a person who swims under water, especially as a job ○ *Police divers searched the canal.*

divide /dɪ'vaɪd/ *verb* **1.** to cut something into parts ○ *The cake was divided among the children.* ○ *How can you divide the cake into thirteen pieces?* ○ *The two companies agreed to divide the market between them.* ○ *Our open-plan office is divided up with low partitions.* **2.** to calculate how many times one number fits in another ○ *Ten divided by two gives five.* (NOTE: **Dividing** is usually shown by the sign ÷ : **10 ÷ 2 = 5**: say 'ten divided by two equals five'. Note also **divides – dividing – divided**.)

division /dɪ'vɪʒ(ə)n/ *noun* **1.** an important part of a large organisation ○ *The sales division employs twenty people.* ○ *She is the head of the production division.* **2.** a calculation, where one figure is divided by another ○ *My little sister is just learning how to do division.*

divorce /dɪ'vɔːs/ *noun* a legal separation of a husband and wife where each is free to marry again ○ *Her parents are getting a divorce.* ○ *Since their divorce, they have both married again.* ■ *verb* **1.** to break off a marriage legally ○ *They divorced last year.* **2.** to separate from your husband or wife ○ *She divorced her husband and married the man next door.*

divorced /dɪ'vɔːst/ *adjective* no longer married ○ *They're both divorced, with children from their previous marriages.*

dizzy /'dɪzi/ *adjective* having a feeling that you might fall down, and that everything seems to turn round ○ *Can we stop the car, please, I feel dizzy.* ○ *After standing in the sun, he became dizzy and had to lie down.* ○ *She has started having dizzy spells.* (NOTE: **dizzier – dizziest**)

DJ *abbr* **1.** dinner jacket **2.** disc jockey

do /duː/ *verb* **1.** used with other verbs to make questions ○ *Does this train go to London?* ○ *Did the doctor give you any medicine for your cough?* ○ *Where do they live?* ○ *What did you find there?* **2.** used with other verbs and 'not' to make the negative ○ *They didn't laugh at the film.* ○ *It doesn't matter any more.* ○ *His parents don't live in London.* **3.** used to make a verb stronger ○ *Can I sit down? – Please do!* ○ *Why don't you work harder? – I do work hard!* ○ *Why didn't you tell me? – I did tell you!* **4.** used in place of another verb in short answers to questions using the word 'do' ○ *Do you live in London? – Yes I do.* ○ *But your parents don't live there, do they? – No they don't.* ○ *Does the green colour show? – Yes it does.* ○ *Did you go to the concert after all? – Yes I did.* **5.** used in place of another verb at the end of a question or statement ○ *The Russians live here, don't they?* ○ *It looks very nice, doesn't it?* ○ *It doesn't rain a lot in Spain, does it?* ○ *Can you run as fast as he does?* ○ *He speaks German better than I do.* ○ *She asked me to close the door but I'd already done so.* ○ *They got to the pub before we did.* **6.** telling someone not to do something ○ *Don't throw away that letter!* ○ *Don't put your coffee cups on the computer!* **7.** with nouns ending in -ing ○ *She's doing the shopping.* ○ *He always does the washing-up.* ○ *She was doing the ironing.* **8.** to work at something, to arrange something or to clean something ○ *She's doing her hair.* ○ *Have you done the dishes yet?* ○ *I can't do today's crossword.* ○ *What have you been doing all day?* ○ *They're a difficult company to do busi-*ness with. **9.** to succeed, to continue ○ *She's doing very well in her new job.* ○ *He did badly in the interview.* ○ *How's your business doing?* **10.** to finish cooking something ○ *The carrots aren't done yet.* **11.** to be satisfactory ○ *Will this size do?* **12.** used when greeting someone ○ *How do you do?* (NOTE: **I do**; **you do**; **he/she/it does** /dʌz/; **they do**; **doing – did** /dɪd/ **– has done** /dʌn/; negative: **do not** usually **don't** /dəʊnt/; **does not** usually **doesn't** /'dʌz(ə)nt/; **did not** usually **didn't** /'dɪdn(ə)t/) ◇ **that will do** that's enough ◇ **to make do with** to accept something which is not as good as you wanted ○ *The ordinary plates are all dirty, so we will have to make do with paper ones.*

do away with *phrasal verb* to get rid of something

do up *phrasal verb* **1.** to attach something ○ *He's still a baby and he can't do his buttons up properly.* ○ *Can you do up the zip at the back of my dress?* **2.** to repair something and make it like new ○ *They bought an old cottage and did it up.* ○ *He's looking for an old sports car to do up.*

do with *phrasal verb* **1.** to be related or connected to ○ *It has nothing to do with us.* ○ *It is something to do with my new book.* **2.** to put something somewhere ○ *What have you done with the newspaper?* **3.** to need something ○ *After that long walk I could do with a cup of tea.* ○ *The car could do with a wash.*

do without *phrasal verb* not to have something, to manage without something

dock /dɒk/ *noun* **1.** □ **the docks** a harbour where ships are loaded and unloaded ○ *Cars should arrive at the docks 45 minutes before sailing time.* ○ *We used to go down to the docks to watch the ships come in.* **2.** a place in a law court where the prisoner sits ○ *She was in the dock, facing charges of theft.* ■ *verb (of a ship)* to arrive in a port ○ *The ship docked at 17.00.* ○ *The cruise liner will dock in Bermuda.*

doctor /'dɒktə/ *noun* a person whose job is to look after people who are ill ○ *I* *have a ten o'clock appointment to see the doctor.* ○ *If you have pains in your chest, you ought to see a doctor.* ○ *He went to the doctor's last Friday.*

document[1] /'dɒkjʊmənt/ *noun* **1.** a piece of paper with something official or important printed on it ○ *File all the documents away carefully as we may need them again.* ○ *Please read this document carefully and sign at the bottom of page two.* **2.** a separate file in a computer ○ *The letter was saved as a Word document.*

document[2] /'dɒkjʊ,ment/ *verb* to note something in official writing ○ *Cases of this disease are well documented in Africa.*

documentary /,dɒkjʊ'ment(ə)ri/ *noun* a film which shows facts about a real subject ○ *Did you see the documentary about hippos last night?* ■ *adjective* referring to documents

dodge /dɒdʒ/ *noun* a clever trick ○ *He told me a dodge to avoid paying on the Underground.* ■ *verb* **1.** to avoid something, to get out of the way ○ *He ran across the street, dodging the traffic.* ○ *She dodged behind a parked car hoping he wouldn't see her.* **2.** to avoid doing something you should do, in a dishonest way ○ *to dodge payment of your TV licence fee*

does /dʌz/ 3rd person singular present of **do**

doesn't /'dʌz(ə)nt/ ♦ **do**

dog /dɒg/ *noun* an animal kept as a pet, or used for hunting ○ *Can you take the dog out for a walk?* ○ *Police with dogs were hunting the gang of escaped prisoners.*

doing /'duːɪŋ/ present participle of **do**

doll /dɒl/ *noun* a child's toy which looks like a baby

dollar /'dɒlə/ *noun* **1.** the money system used in the United States ○ *a 5-dollar bill* ○ *The country spends millions of dollars on defence.* ○ *There were two dollars to the pound.* **2.** a similar money system used in many other countries ○ *What is the price in Australian dollars?* (NOTE: usually written $ before figures: $250. The currencies used in different

countries can be shown by the initial letter of the country: *Can$* (Canadian dollar) *Aus$* (Australian dollar).)

dolphin /'dɒlfɪn/ *noun* a large animal with a long nose, that lives in the sea (NOTE: A group of them is a **school of dolphins**.)

dome /dəʊm/ *noun* a round roof shaped like half of a ball

domestic /də'mestɪk/ *adjective* **1.** relating to the home ○ *She hated having to do all the domestic work.* **2.** inside a country ○ *Sales in the domestic market have risen.* ■ *noun* a servant in a house (*old*) ○ *When the fire broke out all the domestics ran into the house to rescue the furniture.*

donate /dəʊ'neɪt/ *verb* to give something, especially money, to a charity or similar organisation ○ *He donated a lot of money to a charity for the homeless.*

done /dʌn/ past participle of **do**

donkey /'dɒŋki/ *noun* a farm animal with long ears, used for riding or pulling carts

don't /dəʊnt/ ♦ **do**

door /dɔː/ *noun* **1.** a solid piece of wood, plastic or metal which closes an entrance ○ *He went into his office and locked the door behind him.* ○ *She opened the car door and hit a passing cyclist.* **2.** used to show where a building is in a street ○ *They live a few doors away from us.*

dot /dɒt/ *noun* **1.** a small round spot ○ *A blue tie with white dots.* **2.** a printing sign (.) used in email addresses ○ *My email address is jane@supertek.com (say 'Jane at Supertek dot com').* ■ *verb* **1.** to mark with a spot **2.** to be or be put in many different parts ○ *Vases of flowers dotted the room.* ○ *The wall was dotted with notices.* (NOTE: **dots – dotting – dotted**)

double /'dʌb(ə)l/ *adjective* **1.** containing two of something ○ *The word 'immeasurable' is spelt with a double 'm'.* ○ *The invoice number is six double five double one.* **2.** with two parts, for two people ○ *double doors* ○ *a double bed* **3.** twice the size of that which is considered normal ○ *She asked for a double portion of* *ice cream.* ■ *plural noun* **doubles** tennis game for two people on either side ■ *verb* to multiply something by two ○ *Think of a number and then double it.*

double figures /ˌdʌb(ə)l ˈfɪgəz/ *plural noun* the numbers with two figures, from 10 to 99

doubt /daʊt/ *noun* **1.** not being sure ○ *Everyone sometimes has doubts about what they really want to do.* □ **to cast doubt on something** to make people feel less sure about something ○ *He cast doubt on the whole proposal.* **2.** □ **no doubt** certainly ○ *No doubt they will be asking for more money soon.* □ **in doubt** not yet known or definite, or not yet sure ○ *The result of the game was in doubt until the last minute.* ○ *I'm in doubt about whether I should take the job or not.* ■ *verb* not to be sure of something ○ *I doubt whether he will want to go to the funeral.* ○ *I doubt her honesty.* ○ *Did you ever doubt that we would win?*

doubtful /ˈdaʊtf(ə)l/ *adjective* not sure that something is right or good, or not likely ○ *I am doubtful about whether we should go.* ○ *It is doubtful whether the race will take place because of the snow.*

down /daʊn/ *preposition* **1.** towards the bottom of ○ *He fell down the stairs and broke his leg.* ○ *The ball ran down the hill.* **2.** away from where the person speaking is standing ○ *He went down the road to the shop.* ○ *The police station is just down the street.* ■ *adverb* **1.** towards the bottom, towards a lower position ○ *Put the box down in the corner.* ○ *I looked in the cellar, but there's no one down there.* **2.** in writing ○ *Did you note down the number of the car?* ○ *The policeman took down her address.* **3.** used for showing criticism ○ *Down with the government!* ○ *Down with exams!* (NOTE: **Down** is often used with verbs, e.g. **to go down, to fall down, to sit down, to lie down.**)

downhill /daʊnˈhɪl/ *adverb* towards the bottom of a hill ○ *The road goes downhill for a while and then crosses the river.*

downstairs /daʊnˈsteəz/ *adverb* on or to the lower part of a building ○ *He heard a noise in the kitchen and went* *downstairs to see what it was.* ○ *I left my cup of coffee downstairs.* ■ *adjective* on the ground floor of a building ○ *The house has a downstairs bedroom.* ○ *You can use the downstairs loo.* ■ *noun* the ground floor of a building ○ *The downstairs has three rooms.* ○ *The downstairs of the house is larger than the upstairs.* Compare **upstairs**

downwards /ˈdaʊnwədz/ *adverb* towards the bottom

doze /dəʊz/ *verb* to sleep a little ○ *She dozed for a while after lunch.* ■ *noun* a short sleep

dozen /ˈdʌz(ə)n/ *noun* **1.** ○ *I need a dozen eggs for this recipe.* ○ *We ordered two dozen (= 24) chairs.* □ **a dozen** twelve □ **half a dozen** six ○ *half a dozen apples* **2.** □ **dozens of** a lot of ○ *Dozens of people visited the exhibition.* ○ *I've been to New York dozens of times.*

Dr *abbr* doctor

draft /drɑːft/ *noun* a rough plan of a document ○ *He quickly wrote out a draft of the agreement.* ○ *It's not the final version, it's just a draft.* ■ *verb* to draw up a rough plan of something

draft in *phrasal verb* to ask someone to do something ○ *The Boy Scouts were drafted in to dig the garden.*

drag /dræg/ *verb* to pull something heavy along the ground ○ *She dragged her suitcase across the floor.* ○ *The police dragged the men away from the gate.* (NOTE: **drags – dragging – dragged**) ■ *noun* a boring thing, which stops you doing things you really want to do ○ *It's a drag, having to write all the Christmas cards.*

drag on *phrasal verb* (*of time or an event*) to seem to pass slowly ○ *The dinner party seemed to drag on for hours.*

drain /dreɪn/ *noun* a pipe for carrying waste water away ○ *In the autumn the drains get blocked by leaves.* ○ *We had to phone the council to come and clear the blocked drain.* ■ *verb* to remove a liquid from something ○ *Boil the potatoes for ten minutes, drain and leave to cool.*

drama /'drɑːmə/ noun **1.** a serious performance in a theatre ○ *a new TV drama series about life in Glasgow* ○ *The 'Globe' has put on an unknown Elizabethan drama.* ○ *I'm reading a book on 19th-century French drama.* ○ *She's a drama student* or *She's studying drama.* **2.** a series of serious and exciting events ○ *a day of high drama in the court* ○ *the drama of the rescue by helicopter* ○ *He always makes a drama out of everything.*

dramatic /drə'mætɪk/ adjective sudden, unexpected and very noticeable ○ *the dramatic moment in the film, when the dinosaurs start to attack them* ○ *The door was thrown open and she made a dramatic entrance.* ○ *The TV news showed dramatic pictures of the disaster.*

drank /dræŋk/ past tense of **drink**

draught /drɑːft/ noun a flow of cool air into a room ○ *Don't sit in a draught.*

draw /drɔː/ noun **1.** a game or competition which ends with both teams having the same number of points ○ *The match was a draw: 2–2.* **2.** a competition in which the winner is chosen by a person who takes a ticket out of a container with a name on it ○ *The draw is held on Saturdays.* ○ *We are holding a draw to raise money for the local hospital.* ■ verb **1.** to make a picture with a pen or pencil ○ *He drew a picture of the house.* ○ *She's drawing a pot of flowers.* **2.** not to have a winner in a game ○ *The teams drew 2 – 2.* **3.** to pull curtains open or closed ○ *She drew the curtains and let in the sun.* ○ *Can you draw the curtains – I don't want anyone to see us in here.* (NOTE: **draws – drawing – drew** /druː/ **– has drawn** /drɔːn/)

draw up phrasal verb **1.** (of a vehicle) to come close and stop ○ *As I was standing at the bus stop, a car drew up and the driver asked if I wanted a lift.* **2.** to write down something, e.g. a plan ○ *They have drawn up a plan to save money.* ○ *Have you drawn up a list of people you want to invite to the party?*

drawer /'drɔːə/ noun a part of a desk or cupboard like an open box which slides in and out when you pull its handle ○ *I keep my cheque book in the top drawer of my desk.*

drawing /'drɔːɪŋ/ noun **1.** a picture that has been drawn ○ *I've bought an old drawing of the church.* **2.** the activity or skill of making pictures with a pencil or pen ○ *He studied drawing in Rome.*

drawn /drɔːn/ adjective tired and ill ○ *She looked drawn after spending all night with her sick baby.* ■ past participle of **draw**

dread /dred/ noun great fear ○ *The sound of her voice filled him with dread.* ○ *She has a dread of meeting him in the street.* □ **in dread of** being very afraid of ○ *They lived in constant dread of being arrested.* ■ verb to fear something very much ○ *I'm dreading taking my driving test.* ○ *She dreads her weekly visit to the doctor.*

dreadful /'dredf(ə)l/ adjective very bad or unpleasant ○ *What a dreadful film!*

dreadfully /'dredf(ə)li/ adverb extremely, in a way that is not good or pleasant

dream /driːm/ noun a story or series of events that you think about while you are sleeping ○ *She had a dream about big pink elephants.* ■ verb to experience a story or series of events while you are sleeping ○ *He was dreaming of white sand and a blue tropical sea.* ○ *I dreamt about you last night.* ○ *Last night I dreamt I was drowning.* (NOTE: **dreams – dreaming – dreamed** or **dreamt** /dremt/) ■ adjective referring to something that is the best you could have ○ *They found their dream house in a small town by the sea.* ○ *Select your dream team for the World Cup.*

dress /dres/ noun a piece of clothing usually worn by women or girls, covering the body and part or all of the legs ○ *She was wearing a blue dress.* (NOTE: The plural is **dresses**.) ■ verb **1.** to put clothes on someone ○ *She dressed her little girl all in blue.* **2. to get dressed** to put clothes on yourself ○ *He got up, got dressed and left the house.* **3.** to clean an injury and cover it with a bandage ○ *The nurse will dress the cut on your knee.*

dressed /drest/ *adjective* wearing clothes ○ *I can't come down to see the visitors – I'm not dressed yet.* ■ **dressed in** wearing a particular colour or type of clothing ○ *She was dressed all in black.* ○ *He was dressed in a tee-shirt and shorts.*

dressing /'dresɪŋ/ *noun* **1.** a sauce for salad **2.** a cover for an injury ○ *The dressings need to be changed every hour.*

drew /druː/ past tense of **draw**

dribble /'drɪb(ə)l/ *verb* **1.** to let liquid flow slowly out of an opening, especially out of your mouth ○ *The baby dribbled over her dress.* **2.** (*of a liquid*) to flow slowly out of an opening ○ *Ketchup dribbled onto the tablecloth.* **3.** to kick a football along as you are running, or to move a ball along with one hand as you are running

dried, drier, dries, driest /draɪd, 'draɪə, draɪz, 'draɪəst/ ♦ **dry**

drill /drɪl/ *noun* **1.** a tool for making holes in a hard substance such as wood or metal ○ *He used an electric drill to make the holes in the wall.* **2.** the action of practising marching, especially in the armed forces ○ *New recruits spend hours practising their drill.* ■ *verb* **1.** to use a drill to make a hole in something ○ *Check how solid the wall is before you drill a hole in it.* ○ *He drilled two holes for the screws.* **2.** to do military practice ○ *The soldiers were drilling on the parade ground.* **3.** to teach someone something by making them do or say it many times

drink /drɪŋk/ *noun* **1.** an amount of liquid such as water, juice, tea or coffee which you swallow ○ *If you're thirsty, have a drink of water.* ○ *She always has a hot drink before she goes to bed.* **2.** an alcoholic drink ○ *Would you like a drink?* ○ *Come and have a drink.* ○ *I'll order some drinks from the bar.* ■ *verb* to swallow liquid ○ *He drank two glasses of water.* ○ *What would you like to drink?* ○ *Do you want something to drink with your meal?* (NOTE: **drinks – drinking – drank** /dræŋk/ **– has drunk** /drʌŋk/)

drink up *phrasal verb* to drink all of a liquid ○ *The baby drank all her milk up.* ○ *Come on, drink up – we're leaving now.*

drip /drɪp/ *noun* a small drop of water ○ *There's a hole in the tent – a drip just fell on my nose.* ■ *verb* **1.** (*of a liquid*) to fall in small drops ○ *Water was slowly dripping from the ceiling.* **2.** (*of e.g. a tap*) to produce small drops ○ *I must fix that tap – it's dripping.* (NOTE: **drips – dripping – dripped**)

drive /draɪv/ *noun* **1.** a journey, especially in a car ○ *Let's go for a drive into the country.* ○ *The baby gets sick on long drives.* ○ *It's a four-hour drive to the coast.* **2.** a part of a computer which makes a disk work ○ *The disk is stuck in the drive.* ■ *verb* to make a motor vehicle travel in a certain direction ○ *I never learnt to drive.* ○ *He was driving a lorry when the accident happened.* ○ *She was driving to work when she heard the news on the car radio.* (NOTE: **drives – driving – drove** /drəʊv/ **– has driven** /'drɪv(ə)n/) ◇ **to drive someone crazy** *or* **mad** to have an effect on someone so that they become very annoyed (*informal*) ○ *The noise is driving me mad.* ○ *All this work is driving her crazy.*

drive away *phrasal verb* **1.** to ride away in a motor vehicle ○ *The bank robbers leapt into a car and drove away at top speed.* **2.** to take someone away in a motor vehicle ○ *The children were driven away in a police car.*

drive back *phrasal verb* to go back or to come back in a motor vehicle ○ *We were driving back to London after a day out.*

drive off *phrasal verb* **1.** to move away in a motor vehicle ○ *The bank robbers leapt into a car and drove off at top speed.* **2.** to force someone or something to go away ○ *They drove off the attackers with shotguns.*

driver /'draɪvə/ *noun* a person who drives a vehicle such as a car or train ○ *He's got a job as a bus driver.* ○ *The drivers of both cars were injured in the accident.*

driving /'draɪvɪŋ/ *adjective* (*of rain or snow*) blown horizontally by the wind ○ *They were forced to turn back because of the driving rain.* ■ *noun* the action of driving a motor vehicle ○ *Driving in the centre of London can be very frustrating.* ○ *She's taking driving lessons.*

driving licence /'draɪvɪŋ ˌlaɪs(ə)ns/ *noun* a permit which allows someone to drive a vehicle on public roads

drizzle /'drɪz(ə)l/ *noun* light rain ○ *A thin drizzle was falling so we took our umbrellas.* ■ *verb* to rain a little ○ *It's drizzling outside, so you need a raincoat.*

drop /drɒp/ *noun* a small amount of liquid which falls ○ *Drops of rain ran down the windows.* ■ *verb* **1.** to fall or let something fall ○ *He dropped the glass and it broke.* ○ *The plate dropped onto the floor.* **2.** to decrease ○ *Prices are dropping.* ○ *Take a warm pullover, because at night the temperature can drop quite sharply.* **3.** to let someone get off a bus or car at a place ○ *I'll drop you at your house.* ○ *The bus dropped her at the school.* (NOTE: **drops – dropping – dropped**)

drop in *phrasal verb* to call on someone, to visit someone

drop off *phrasal verb* **1.** to fall asleep ○ *She dropped off in front of the TV.* ○ *It took me ages to drop off.* **2.** to let someone get off a bus or car at a place ○ *Where would you like me to drop you off?*

drought /draʊt/ *noun* a long period when there is no rain and when the land is dry

drove /drəʊv/ past tense of **drive**

drown /draʊn/ *verb* to die by being unable to breathe in water ○ *He drowned in a shallow pool.*

drudgery /'drʌdʒəri/ *noun* hard boring work ○ *Most of the work in the office is sheer drudgery.*

drug /drʌg/ *noun* **1.** a medicine ○ *They have found a new drug for people with arthritis.* **2.** an illegal substance which affects people physically or mentally when they take it ○ *The customs are looking for such things as drugs or alco-*

hol. ■ *verb* to give a person or animal a drug, or put a drug in their food or drink, to make them unconscious ○ *They drugged him and took him away in a car.* ○ *The dog's food had been drugged with something to make him sleep.* (NOTE: **drugs – drugging – drugged**)

drum /drʌm/ *noun* **1.** a large round musical instrument which you hit with a stick ○ *He plays the drums in the band.* **2.** a large barrel or container shaped like a cylinder ○ *oil drums* ■ *verb* **1.** to play on a drum **2.** to hit something frequently ○ *He drummed his fingers on the table.* (NOTE: **drums – drumming – drummed**)

drum into *phrasal verb* □ **to drum something into someone** to make someone learn something ○ *My grandfather drummed it into me that I had to be polite to customers.*

drunk /drʌŋk/ *adjective* excited or ill from drinking too much alcohol ○ *Do you think she was drunk?* ○ *It doesn't take much for me to get drunk.* ■ *noun* a person who is drunk ■ past participle of **drink**

dry /draɪ/ *adjective* **1.** not wet ○ *Don't touch the door – the paint isn't dry yet.* ○ *The soil is dry because it hasn't rained for weeks.* **2.** (*of wine*) not sweet ○ *A dry white wine is served with fish.* (NOTE: **drier – driest**) ■ *verb* **1.** to become dry ○ *The clothes are drying in the sun.* ○ *Leave the dishes beside the sink to dry.* **2.** to wipe something until it is dry ○ *If I wash up, can you dry or dry the dishes for me?* ○ *He dried himself with a towel.* (NOTE: **dries – drying – dried**)

dubious /'djuːbiəs/ *adjective* thinking that something might not be true or good ○ *Everyone else seems to believe her story, but personally I'm dubious about it.* ○ *I'm dubious about getting involved.*

duck /dʌk/ *noun* **1.** a common water bird ○ *Let's go and feed the ducks in the park.* (NOTE: The male is a **drake**, the female a **duck** and the young are **ducklings**.) **2.** the meat of this bird ○ *We're having roast duck for dinner.* ■ *verb* to lower your head quickly to avoid hitting something ○ *He ducked as he went through the low doorway.*

due /djuː/ *adjective* **1.** expected ○ *When is the baby due?* ○ *We are due to leave London Airport at 5 o'clock.* ○ *The plane is due to arrive at 10.30 or is due at 10.30.* □ **due for** likely to happen ○ *We're due for a thunderstorm after all this hot weather.* **2.** owed ○ *This payment is due now.* ■ *adverb* straight ○ *The plane flew due west.* ■ *noun* what is deserved □ **to give someone their due** to be fair to someone ○ *To give him his due, he works very hard.* ◇ **in due course** later

due to /'djuː tuː/ *preposition* because of ○ *The trains are late due to fog.*

dug /dʌg/ past tense and past participle of **dig**

dull /dʌl/ *adjective* **1.** not exciting or interesting ○ *The story is rather dull.* ○ *What's so interesting about old churches? – I find them dull.* **2.** (*of weather*) grey and cloudy ○ *a dull rainy day* **3.** (*of colours*) not bright ○ *They painted the sitting room a dull green.*

dumb /dʌm/ *adjective* unable to speak (NOTE: Some people avoid this term because it causes offence and prefer to say **speech impaired**.)

dummy /'dʌmi/ *noun* a plastic object, given to a baby to suck in order to stop it from crying ○ *The baby sat sucking a dummy.* (NOTE: The plural is **dummies.**)

dump /dʌmp/ *noun* a large area where rubbish is taken ○ *Take your rubbish to the municipal dump.* ■ *verb* **1.** to put something heavy on the ground, especially in a careless way ○ *She just dumped her suitcases in the hall.* **2.** to throw something away, to get rid of something ○ *Someone has dumped an old pram in the car park.*

duplicate¹ /'djuːplɪkət/ *adjective* made as a copy of something ○ *Put the duplicate invoices in the file.* ■ *noun* a copy ○ *She sent the invoice and filed the duplicate.*

duplicate² /'djuːplɪkeɪt/ *verb* **1.** to make a copy of a document such as a letter ○ *She duplicated the letter and put the copy into a file.* **2.** to do again something which has already been done ○ *Keep a note of where you got to – I don't want to duplicate your work.*

during /'djʊərɪŋ/ *preposition* while something is going on ○ *Conditions were bad during the war.*

dust /dʌst/ *noun* a thin layer of dry dirt ○ *The room had never been cleaned – there was dust everywhere.* ○ *A tiny speck of dust got in my eye.* (NOTE: no plural) ■ *verb* to remove dust from something ○ *Don't forget to dust the Chinese bowls carefully.*

dustbin /'dʌstbɪn/ *noun* a large container for rubbish, kept outside a house

dusty /'dʌsti/ *adjective* covered with dust (NOTE: **dustier – dustiest**)

duty /'djuːti/ *noun* **1.** something which you are legally or morally expected to do ○ *We have a duty to inform the authorities about what we saw.* **2.** □ **on duty** doing official work which you have to do in a job ○ *He's on duty from 9.00 to 6.00.* ○ *She's been on duty all day.* **3.** a tax which has to be paid ■ *plural noun* **duties** different jobs that have to be done as part of your official work ○ *One of his duties is to see that the main doors are locked at night.*

duty-free /ˌdjuːti 'friː/ *adjective, adverb* sold with no tax to be paid ○ *He bought a duty-free watch at the airport* or *he bought the watch duty-free.*

duvet /'duːveɪ/ *noun* a bag full of feathers, used as a covering for a bed

dying /'daɪɪŋ/ present participle of **die**

E

e /iː/, **E** *noun* the fifth letter of the alphabet, between D and F

each /iːtʃ/ *adjective* every ○ *Each five pound note has a number.* ○ *He was holding a towel in each hand.* ○ *Each one of us has a separate office.* ■ *pronoun* **1.** every person ○ *They have two houses each.* or *Each of them has two houses.* ○ *She gave them each five pounds* or *She gave them five pounds each* or *She gave each of them five pounds.* **2.** every thing ○ *Each of the books has three hundred pages* or *The books have three hundred pages each.*

each other /iːtʃ 'ʌðə/ *pronoun* the other one of two people or of two things ○ *They were shouting at each other.* ○ *We always send each other presents on our birthdays.* ○ *The boxes fit into each other.*

eager /'iːgə/ *adjective* wanting to do something very much

eagerly /'iːgəli/ *adverb* in a way that shows that you want something very much

ear /ɪə/ *noun* one of the parts on either side of your head which you hear with ○ *Rabbits have long ears.* ○ *Have you washed behind your ears?*

earlier /'ɜːliə/ *adjective* relating to a time before now or before a time being mentioned ○ *an earlier version of the book* ○ *I'll try to catch an earlier train.* ■ *adverb* before now or before a time being mentioned ○ *Can't you come any earlier than Tuesday?* ○ *I tried to phone earlier but you were out.*

early /'ɜːli/ *adverb* **1.** before the usual time ○ *The plane arrived five minutes early.* ○ *We must get up early tomorrow morning if we want to catch the first boat to France.* **2.** at the beginning of a period of time ○ *We went out early in the evening.* ○ *The snow came early in the year.*

earn /ɜːn/ *verb* to be paid money for working ○ *He earns £20,000 a year.* ○ *How much does a bus driver earn?*

earring /'ɪərɪŋ/ *noun* a piece of jewellery worn attached to part of the ear

earth /ɜːθ/ *noun* **1.** also **Earth** the planet on which we live ○ *The Earth goes round the sun once in twenty-four hours.* **2.** soil, a soft substance in which plants grow ○ *Put some earth in the plant pot and then sow your cucumber seeds.*

earthquake /'ɜːθkweɪk/ *noun* an occasion on which the earth shakes, caused by movement of the earth's surface (NOTE: also called simply a **quake**)

ease /iːz/ *noun* a lack of difficulty ○ *He won the first round with the greatest of ease.* ○ *The bottle has a wide mouth for ease of use.* ■ *verb* to make less painful ○ *A couple of aspirins should ease the pain.*

easily /'iːzɪli/ *adverb* **1.** without any difficulty ○ *I passed my driving test easily.* ○ *I can easily get there by 9 o'clock.* **2.** a lot (*for emphasis before comparatives or superlatives*) ○ *Her work was easily better than yours.* ○ *He is easily the tallest man in the team.* ○ *Our shop is easily the biggest in the High Street.*

east /iːst/ *noun* **1.** the direction of where the sun rises ○ *The sun rises in the east and sets in the west.* ○ *Germany is to the east of France.* ○ *The wind is blowing from the east.* **2.** the part of a country which is to the east of the rest ○ *The east of the country is drier than the west.* ■ *adjective* relating to the east ○ *The east coast is the coldest part of the country.* ■ *adverb* towards the east ○ *The kitchen windows face east, so we get the morning sun.* ○ *Drive east along the motorway for twenty miles.*

Easter /'iːstə/ *noun* a Christian festival, in March or April, celebrating the occasion on which Christ died and then came back to life again

eastern /'iːst(ə)n/ *adjective* from, of or in the east ○ *Bulgaria is part of Eastern Europe.* ○ *The best snow is in the eastern part of the mountains.*

easy /'iːzi/ *adjective* not difficult, or not needing a lot of effort ○ *The test was easier than I expected.* ○ *My boss is very easy to get on with.*

eat /iːt/ *verb* **1.** to put food into your mouth and swallow it ○ *I'm hungry – is there anything to eat?* ○ *We haven't eaten anything since breakfast.* ○ *The children ate all the sandwiches.* ○ *Eat as much as you like for £5.95!* ○ *You'll get thin if you don't eat.* **2.** to have a meal ○ *He was still eating his breakfast when I arrived.* ○ *We are eating at home tonight.* ○ *Have you eaten yet?* (NOTE: **eats – eating – ate** /et/ **– has eaten** /'iːt(ə)n/)

eat out *phrasal verb* to have a meal in a restaurant

eat up *phrasal verb* to eat everything ○ *She ate it all up in a matter of seconds.* ○ *Come on, eat up – it's time to go.*

echo /'ekəʊ/ *noun* a sound which is repeated such as when you shout in a place such as a tunnel ○ *We could hear the echo of voices in the tunnel.* ○ *If you go to the Whispering Gallery in the dome of St Paul's Cathedral you can hear the echo very clearly.* (NOTE: The plural is **echoes**.) ■ *verb* **1.** (*of sound*) to make an echo ○ *Their voices echoed down the tunnel.* **2.** to repeat ○ *The newspaper article echoed the opinions put forward in the minister's speech.* (NOTE: **echoes – echoing – echoed**)

economic /ˌiːkə'nɒmɪk/ *adjective* **1.** relating to the economy ○ *I don't agree with the government's economic policy.* ○ *The government has introduced controls to solve the current economic crisis.* ○ *The country enjoyed a period of economic growth in the 1980s.* **2.** not costing much money ○ *The flat is let at an economic rent.* ○ *It is hardly economic for us to run two cars.* **3.** using money well ○ *It is hardly economic for us to run two cars.*

economy /ɪ'kɒnəmi/ *noun* **1.** the way in which a country makes and uses money, or the financial state of a country ○ *The country's economy is in ruins.* **2.** something you do to avoid wasting money or materials ○ *She tried to make a few economies like buying cheaper brands of washing-up liquid.*

edge /edʒ/ *noun* **1.** a side of something flat ○ *He put his plate down on the edge of the table.* ○ *She lay down on the roof and looked over the edge.* ○ *Can you stand this coin on its edge?* ○ *The axe has a very sharp edge.* **2.** an imaginary line where an area ends ○ *He lived in a house at the edge of the forest.* ○ *The factory is built right on the edge of the town.*

edible /'edɪb(ə)l/ *adjective* which is good enough or safe to eat

edit /'edɪt/ *verb* **1.** to be in charge of a newspaper or magazine ○ *He edited the 'Sunday Express' for more than twenty years.* **2.** to prepare a book for publishing by doing such things as correcting mistakes ○ *I am editing a volume of 20th-century poetry.* **3.** to prepare something such as a film to make it ready to be shown ○ *Once the film has been edited it will run for about 90 minutes.*

editor /'edɪtə/ *noun* **1.** a journalist in charge of a newspaper or part of a newspaper ○ *He wrote to the editor of 'The Times' asking for a job.* ○ *She is the sports editor of the local paper.* **2.** a person who edits books

educate /'edjʊkeɪt/ *verb* to teach someone in a school or college, or give them information that they need ○ *She was educated in Switzerland.* ○ *We need to educate young people about the dangers of alcohol.*

educated /'edjʊkeɪtɪd/ *adjective* having been to school and university

education /ˌedjʊ'keɪʃ(ə)n/ *noun* the system of teaching, or of being taught ○ *Our children deserve the best education.* ○ *We spent a lot of money on his education, and he's got a job as a dustman!*

educational /ˌedjʊ'keɪʃ(ə)nəl/ *adjective* relating to education, teaching and schools ○ *This game for 3 to 5 year-olds is very educational.* ○ *a campaign to improve educational standards.*

effect /ɪ'fekt/ *noun* a result or influence ○ *The cuts in spending will have a serious effect on the hospital.* ○ *The cream has had no effect on her rash.* ○ *The effects of the shock took some time to wear off.* ◇ **with effect from** starting from (*formal*) ○ *Prices will be increased by 10% with effect from January 1st.*

effective /ɪ'fektɪv/ *adjective* **1.** which produces the required result ○ *His method of keeping the children quiet is very effective.* ○ *Advertising on TV is a very effective way of selling.* **2.** which takes effect ○ *an order which is effective from January 1st*

effectively /ɪ'fektɪvli/ *adverb* in a way which produces a good result ○ *The floodlighting worked very effectively.*

effectiveness /ɪ'fektɪvnəs/ *noun* the ability to produce an effective result

efficient /ɪ'fɪʃ(ə)nt/ *adjective* able to work well and do what is necessary without wasting time, money or effort ○ *He needs an efficient assistant to look after him.* ○ *The new system of printing invoices is very efficient.*

efficiently /ɪ'fɪʃ(ə)ntli/ *adverb* in an efficient way

effort /'efət/ *noun* the use of the mind or body to do something ○ *He's made a big effort to learn Spanish.* ○ *Lifting the box took considerable physical effort.* ○ *She's already written to three addresses in an effort to contact the owner.* ○ *Thanks to her efforts, we have collected more than £10,000 for the children's hospital.*

egg /eg/ *noun* **1.** a round object with a hard shell, produced by a female bird or, e.g. snake, in which a baby bird develops ○ *The owl laid three eggs in the nest.* ○ *Turtles lay their eggs in the sand.* **2.** a chicken's egg, used as food ○ *You need three eggs to make this cake.*

eight /eɪt/ *noun* the number 8 ○ *He ate eight chocolates.* ○ *The little girl is eight (years old).* ○ *I usually have breakfast before eight (o'clock).*

eighteen /ˌeɪ'tiːn/ *noun* the number 18 ○ *There are eighteen people in our dance class.* ○ *He will be eighteen (years old) next week.* ○ *The train leaves at eighteen twenty (18:20).*

eighteenth /eɪ'tiːnθ/ *adjective* relating to number 18 in a series ○ *The eighteenth of April* or *April the eighteenth* (*April 18th*). ○ *Today's the seventeenth, so tomorrow must be the eighteenth.* ○ *That's the eighteenth invoice we've sent out today.* ○ *It's his eighteenth birthday next week.* ■ *noun* number 18 in a series ○ *A lot of people have called me today – she's the eighteenth.*

eighth /eɪtθ/, **8th** *adjective* relating to number 8 in a series ○ *The eighth of February* or *February the eighth* (*February 8th*). ○ *His eighth birthday is next Monday.* ■ *noun* number eight in a series ○ *He's the eighth in line to the throne.* ○ *King Henry the Eighth (Henry VIII) had six wives.* (NOTE: **eighth** is usually written **8th** in dates: *April 8th, 1999; September 8th, 1866* (American style is **September 8, 1866**), say 'the eighth of September' or 'September the eighth' (American style is 'September eighth'); with names of kings and queens, **eighth** is usually written **VIII**: *King Henry VIII*, say: 'King Henry the Eighth'.)

eightieth /'eɪtiəθ/, **80th** *adjective* relating to number 80 in a series ○ *Granny's eightieth birthday is next week.* ■ *noun* number 80 in a series ○ *We've had a lot of letters – this is the eightieth.*

eighty /'eɪti/ *noun* the number 80 ○ *It's about eighty miles from London to Dover.* ○ *She's eighty (years old).* □ **the eighties** the numbers between 80 and 89

either /'aɪðə, 'iːðə/ *adjective, pronoun* **1.** one or the other ○ *You can use either computer – it doesn't matter which.* ○ *I don't like either of them.* **2.** each of two; both ○ *There are trees on either side of the road.* ○ *Some people don't take sugar in their coffee, some don't take milk, and some don't take either.* ■ *adverb* used with two negatives to show that two people or things are similar in some way ○ *He isn't Irish and he isn't Scottish either.* ○ *She doesn't want to go,* *and I don't want to go either.* ○ *The report wasn't on the TV news, and it wasn't on the radio either.*

elastic /ɪˈlæstɪk/ *noun* a material which stretches ○ *You'll need to sew this piece of elastic onto the ballet shoes.* ■ *adjective* able to stretch and contract ○ *She was wearing tight shorts made of some elastic material.*

elbow /ˈelbəʊ/ *noun* the joint in the middle of your arm ○ *He sat with his elbows on the table.* ○ *She nudged him with her elbow.*

elderly /ˈeldəli/ *adjective* a more polite word than "old" used for describing someone who has had a long life ○ *An elderly man sat down beside her.* ○ *My mother is now rather elderly and doesn't drive any more.*

elect /ɪˈlekt/ *verb* to choose someone by voting ○ *She was elected MP for the town.* ○ *The president is elected for a term of four years.* ○ *The chairman is elected by the members of the committee.*

election /ɪˈlekʃən/ *noun* the process of choosing by voting ○ *After the election, the crowds were dancing in the streets.* ○ *The next item on the agenda is the election of a new treasurer for the club.*

electric /ɪˈlektrɪk/ *adjective* **1.** worked by electricity ○ *Is your cooker electric or gas?* ○ *He plays an electric guitar.* ○ *He cut the wood with an electric saw.* ○ *She gave me an electric toothbrush for Christmas.* **2.** making or carrying electricity ○ *Don't touch those electric wires.* ○ *Electric plugs in the USA are different from those in Britain.*

electrical /ɪˈlektrɪk(ə)l/ *adjective* relating to electricity ○ *a shop selling electrical appliances* ○ *The college offers courses in electrical engineering.* ○ *They are trying to repair an electrical fault.*

electricity /ɪˌlekˈtrɪsɪti/ *noun* energy used to make light, heat, or power ○ *We haven't paid the electricity bill this month.* ○ *The electricity was cut off this morning.* ○ *The heating is run by electricity.* ○ *The cottage is in the mountains*

and doesn't have any electricity. (NOTE: no plural)

electronic /ˌelekˈtrɒnɪk/ *adjective* using electricity and very small parts which affect the electric current which passes through them ○ *an electronic address book* ○ *My car has an electronic ignition.*

electronics /ˌelekˈtrɒnɪks/ *noun* the science of the movement of electricity in electronic equipment

element /ˈelɪmənt/ *noun* **1.** a basic chemical substance **2.** a basic part of something ○ *I think we have all the elements of a settlement.* **3.** a natural environment ○ *The vicar is in his element when he's talking about cricket.* **4.** a part of a piece of equipment which makes, e.g. water hot ○ *I think the element has burnt out.*

elephant /ˈelɪfənt/ *noun* a very large African or Indian animal, with large ears, a trunk and two long teeth called 'tusks'

elevator /ˈelɪveɪtə/ *noun US* a machine for moving people up or down from floor to floor inside a building ○ *Take the elevator to the 26th floor.*

eleven /ɪˈlev(ə)n/ *noun* the number 11 ○ *When you're eleven (years old) you will go to secondary school.* ○ *Come and see me at eleven (o'clock).*

eleventh /ɪˈlev(ə)nθ/, **11th** *adjective* relating to number 11 in a series ○ *The eleventh of July/July the eleventh (July 11th).* ○ *Today's the tenth, so tomorrow must be the eleventh.* ○ *That's the eleventh complaint we've received this week.* ○ *It's his eleventh birthday next month.*

else /els/ *adverb* other (*used after pronouns*) ○ *What else can I say?* ○ *Everyone else had already left.* ○ *Who else was at the meeting?* ◇ **or else** or if not ○ *We could do it now, or else wait till John comes.* ○ *You must have a ticket, or else you will be thrown off the train by the inspector.*

elsewhere /elsˈweə/ *adverb* somewhere else, in another place ○ *This shop doesn't stock maps, so you'll have to try elsewhere.*

email /'iːmeɪl/, **e-mail** /'iː meɪl/ *noun* **1.** a system of sending messages from one computer to another, using telephone lines ○ *You can contact me by phone or email if you want.* ○ *I'll give you my email address.* **2.** a message sent by email ○ *I had two emails from him this morning.* ■ *verb* to send a message to someone using email ○ *I emailed him about the meeting.*

embarrass /ɪm'bærəs/ *verb* to make someone feel uncomfortable in front of other people, e.g. by talking about something that they would prefer other people not to know about

embarrassed /ɪm'bærəst/ *adjective* uncomfortable or ashamed, and not knowing what to do ○ *She gave an embarrassed laugh, and said she had forgotten to bring the present.* ○ *He was so embarrassed that he turned bright red.*

embarrassing /ɪm'bærəsɪŋ/ *adjective* making a person feel embarrassed ○ *It was very embarrassing when he told everyone about my mistake.*

embryo /'embriəʊ/ *noun* the first state of a living organism ○ *a human embryo*

emerge /ɪ'mɜːdʒ/ *verb* **1.** to come into existence as something ○ *It was only after the election that he emerged as party leader.* **2.** to become known ○ *It soon emerged that the Prime Minister knew nothing about what was happening.*

emergency /ɪ'mɜːdʒənsi/ *noun* a dangerous situation such as a fire or an accident, where decisions have to be taken quickly ○ *Phone for an ambulance – this is an emergency!*

emotion /ɪ'məʊʃ(ə)n/ *noun* a strong feeling ○ *Hatred and love are two of the most powerful emotions.* ○ *He tried to hide his emotions when he made his speech.*

emotional /ɪ'məʊʃ(ə)n(ə)l/ *adjective* causing you to feel emotion, or showing emotion ○ *Saying goodbye was an emotional time for us all.* ○ *The music made her feel very emotional and she started to cry.*

emphasis /'emfəsɪs/ *noun* **1.** the act of showing the importance of something, usually in speech ○ *Don't put too much* emphasis on his age. ○ *She banged the table for emphasis as she spoke.* **2.** how loud your voice is when you pronounce a word or phrase ○ *Everyone noticed the emphasis he put on the word 'peace'.* (NOTE: The plural is **emphases**.)

emphasise /'emfəsaɪz/, **emphasize** *verb* to show how important you feel something is, by saying it more loudly or slowly ○ *Please emphasise that the meeting must start on time.* ○ *He emphasised the importance of everyone working together.* ○ *She kept on emphasising the same point over and over again.*

empire /'empaɪə/ *noun* several separate countries ruled by a central government ○ *We're studying the history of the British Empire.* ○ *The Soviet empire covered a huge area from the Pacific Ocean to the middle of Europe.*

employ /ɪm'plɔɪ/ *verb* **1.** to give someone regular paid work ○ *He is employed as a gardener by the duke.* ○ *She is employed in the textile industry.* **2.** to use something (*formal*) ○ *If we were to employ more up-to-date methods, would we make more money?* ○ *How can we best employ our free time on Sunday?*

employee /ɪm'plɔɪiː/ *noun* a person who is employed ○ *The company has decided to take on twenty new employees.*

employer /ɪm'plɔɪə/ *noun* a person or organisation that gives work to people and pays them ○ *Her employer was a Hong Kong businessman.* ○ *The car factory is the biggest employer in the area.*

employment /ɪm'plɔɪmənt/ *noun* regular paid work

empty /'empti/ *adjective* with nothing inside, or with no people present ○ *When we opened it, the box was empty.* ○ *Take an empty pot and fill it with soil.* ○ *The fridge is empty – we'll have to go out to eat.* ○ *The ski resorts are empty because there is no snow.* (NOTE: **emptier – emptiest**) ■ *verb* to make something empty ○ *She emptied the clothes out of the suitcase.* ○ *He emptied the bottle into the sink.* ○ *They emptied the contents of the petty cash box into a bag.*

(NOTE: **empties – emptying – emptied**)

enable /ɪnˈeɪb(ə)l/ *verb* to make it possible for someone to do something ○ *The dictionary should enable you to understand English better.* (NOTE: **enables – enabling – enabled**)

enclose /ɪnˈkləʊz/ *verb* **1.** to put something inside an envelope with a letter ○ *I am enclosing a copy of our current catalogue.* ○ *Please find our cheque enclosed herewith.* **2.** to put a wall or fence round an area of land ○ *The garden is enclosed by high brick walls.*

enclosed /ɪnˈkləʊzd/ *adjective* surrounded on all sides ○ *an enclosed space*

encounter /ɪnˈkaʊntə/ *verb* to meet someone or something ○ *On the journey we encountered several amusing people.* ○ *I have never encountered such hospitality anywhere else.*

encourage /ɪnˈkʌrɪdʒ/ *verb* **1.** to make it easier for something to happen ○ *Leaving your credit cards on your desk encourages people to steal* or *encourages stealing.* **2.** to help someone to do something by giving them confidence ○ *He encouraged me to apply for the job.* ○ *I always felt encouraged by his interest in what I was doing.*

encyclopedia /ɪnsaɪkləˈpiːdiə/, **encyclopaedia** *noun* **1.** a reference book containing articles on many subjects of human knowledge, usually presented in alphabetical order **2.** a reference book containing articles on a single subject, arranged usually in alphabetical order ○ *a gardening encyclopedia* ○ *the encyclopedia of sport*

end /end/ *noun* **1.** the last part of something ○ *She tied the two ends of the ribbon together.* ○ *The telephone rang and I missed the end of the TV programme.* ○ *Go down to the end of the road and then turn right.* □ **to come to an end** to be finished ○ *The work should come to an end next month.* **2.** the final part of a period of time ○ *Can you wait until the end of the week?* ■ *verb* when something ends, it reaches the point when it stops happening ○ *The film ends with a wedding.* ○ *The meeting ended with eve-*

ryone fighting on the floor. ○ *The concert should end at about 10 o'clock.* ○ *The game ended in a draw.* ◇ **in the end** finally, at last ○ *In the end the teacher let him go home.* ○ *In the end the shop had to call in the police.* ◇ **to make ends meet** to have just enough money to live on ○ *I'm having trouble making ends meet.*

end up *phrasal verb* to finish in a particular situation

endeavour /ɪnˈdevə/ *verb* to try very hard to do something (*formal*) ○ *He endeavoured to contact her by both phone and fax.* (NOTE: The US spelling is **endeavor.**)

ending /ˈendɪŋ/ *noun* the way a story finishes ○ *I like films which have a happy ending.* ○ *He told us so much of the story that we could guess the ending.*

enemy /ˈenəmi/ *noun* a person or country that is not on friendly terms with another, and may try to harm them ○ *Did your husband have many enemies?* (NOTE: The plural is **enemies.**)

energetic /ˌenəˈdʒetɪk/ *adjective* active and lively

energy /ˈenədʒi/ *noun* **1.** the force or strength of a person ○ *He used up a lot of energy rushing around doing the Christmas shopping.* ○ *She put all her energies into her art gallery.* **2.** a power which makes something work ○ *the use of atomic energy* or *nuclear energy to make electricity* ○ *We try to save energy by switching off the lights when the rooms are empty.*

engine /ˈendʒɪn/ *noun* **1.** a machine which powers or drives something ○ *The car may need a new engine, I'm afraid.* ○ *Early industrial equipment was powered by steam engines.* **2.** a vehicle which pulls a train ○ *The engine broke down and the train was stuck in the tunnel.*

engineer /ˌendʒɪˈnɪə/ *noun* **1.** a person who looks after and repairs technical equipment ○ *There are not enough telephone engineers in the area.* ○ *The photocopier's broken down again – we'll have to call the engineer.* **2.** a person whose job is to design mechanical, electrical or industrial equipment

engineering /ˌendʒɪˈnɪərɪŋ/ *noun* the science or study of the design of technical equipment ○ *The college offers courses in electrical engineering.*

England /ˈɪŋlənd/ *noun* a country in the southern part of the island of Great Britain, the largest country in the United Kingdom ○ *How long does it take to cross from England to France?* ○ *A lot of Scottish people live in England.* (NOTE: the word **England** is often used instead of Britain, and this is a mistake, as England is only one part of Great Britain; note also the capital: **London**; people: **the English**; language: **English**; currency: **pound sterling**)

English /ˈɪŋlɪʃ/ *adjective* relating to England ○ *the beautiful English countryside* ○ *Is the English weather really as bad as it is made out to be?* ○ *I think she is English, although she speaks with an Australian accent.* (NOTE: **English** is often used instead of British. This is a mistake as England is only one part of Great Britain. Do not say the **English Prime Minister**, say the **British Prime Minister**.) ■ *noun* the English language as a subject of study in school or university ○ *She's good at maths but not so good at English.* ○ *As well as teaching English, he also teaches drama.* ○ *Mr Smith is our English teacher.* ○ *She gives English lessons at home in the evenings.* ○ *There are twenty students in my English class.*

Englishman /ˈɪŋlɪʃmən/ *noun* a man from England (NOTE: The plural is **Englishmen.**)

Englishwoman /ˈɪŋlɪʃwʊmən/ *noun* a woman from England (NOTE: The plural is **Englishwomen.**)

enhance /ɪnˈhɑːns/ *verb* to increase the value or power of something ○ *Slot in this new memory board to enhance your computer memory.* ○ *He took drugs to enhance his performance as an athlete.*

enjoy /ɪnˈdʒɔɪ/ *verb* to get pleasure from something ○ *Have you enjoyed the holiday so far?* ○ *When he asked them if they had enjoyed the film they all answered 'no'.* ○ *She doesn't enjoy sailing because it make her seasick.*

enjoyable /ɪnˈdʒɔɪəb(ə)l/ *adjective* giving pleasure

enjoyment /ɪnˈdʒɔɪmənt/ *noun* pleasure

enlarge /ɪnˈlɑːdʒ/ *verb* to make something bigger ○ *Could you enlarge this photograph?*

enormous /ɪˈnɔːməs/ *adjective* of an extremely large size ○ *The ballroom is absolutely enormous.* ○ *He ate an enormous lunch.*

enormously /ɪˈnɔːməsli/ *adverb* very much

enough /ɪˈnʌf/ *adjective* as much as is needed ○ *Have you got enough money for your fare* or *to pay your fare?* ○ *There isn't enough light to take photographs.* ■ *pronoun* as much of something as is needed ○ *I had £20 in my purse to pay the taxi, but it wasn't enough.* ○ *Have you all had enough to eat?* ■ *adverb* as much as is needed ○ *This box isn't big enough for all these books.* ○ *He doesn't work fast enough.*

ensure /ɪnˈʃʊə/ *verb* to make sure of something ○ *When taking a shower, please ensure that the shower curtain is inside the bath.* (NOTE: **ensures – ensuring – ensured**)

enter /ˈentə/ *verb* **1.** to go into or to come into a place ○ *He took off his hat as he entered the church.* ○ *Did they stamp your passport when you entered the country?* **2.** to decide to take part in a race or competition ○ *She has entered the 2,000 metres.* **3.** to write information on a book or a form, or to type information into a computer system ○ *We will just enter your name and address on the computer.* ■ *noun* the key on a keyboard which you press when you have finished keying something, or when you want to start a new line ○ *To log on to the system, type your password and press enter.* ◊ **entrance, entry**

entertain /ˌentəˈteɪn/ *verb* **1.** to perform, e.g. by telling stories to people or making them laugh ○ *He entertained us with stories of his life in the army.* ○ *The tourists were entertained by the local dance troupe.* **2.** to have someone as a guest and offer them a meal and drinks, and sometimes a place to sleep ○ *They're entertaining some Swedish friends this evening.*

entertainer /ˌentəˈteɪnə/ *noun* a person who entertains people, especially as a job

entertainment /ˌentəˈteɪnmənt/ *noun* things such as films and shows that people enjoy watching ○ *She sang for their entertainment.* ○ *There's not much entertainment in the village – the nearest cinema is 25km away.*

enthusiasm /ɪnˈθjuːziæz(ə)m/ *noun* great interest and liking ○ *We succeeded, thanks to the enthusiasm and hard work of a small group of members.* ○ *She showed a lot of enthusiasm for our new project.*

enthusiastic /ɪnˌθjuːziˈæstɪk/ *adjective* showing great interest and approval ○ *The editor was very enthusiastic about my book.* ○ *There were enthusiastic cheers at the end of the performance.*

entire /ɪnˈtaɪə/ *adjective* whole ○ *We spent the entire day gardening.* ○ *The entire cast came on the stage and bowed to the audience.*

entirely /ɪnˈtaɪəli/ *adverb* completely ○ *I agree with you entirely.* ○ *This is an entirely separate problem.*

entrance /ˈentrəns/ *noun* a door for going in ○ *She was sitting at the entrance to the museum.* ○ *Let's meet at the side entrance, near the café.*

entrant /ˈentrənt/ *noun* a person who takes part in a race, examination or competition ○ *There are over a thousand entrants for the race.*

entry /ˈentri/ *noun* **1.** the act of going into a place ○ *The sign on the door said 'No Entry'.* **2.** the door or opening where you go into a place ○ *The entry to the cave was blocked by rocks.* **3.** a piece of information in a such as a dictionary, or in a computer system ○ *She looked up the entry on 'roses' in the gardening encyclopaedia.*

envelope /ˈenvələʊp/ *noun* a folded paper cover for sending letters in ○ *She wrote the address on the envelope and sealed it.* ○ *She wrote down all the information on the back of an envelope.*

envious /ˈenviəs/ *adjective* feeling or showing in an unhappy way that you would like to have something that someone else has

environment /ɪnˈvaɪrənmənt/ *noun* the land, the water, the air and the buildings which are around us, and the conditions in which we live ○ *The environment in the office is not good for concentrated work.* ○ *The pollution produced by the factory is causing long-term damage to the environment.*

environmental /ɪnˌvaɪrənˈment(ə)l/ *adjective* relating to the environment ○ *measures taken to protect against environmental pollution* ○ *She's joined an environmental group.*

envy /ˈenvi/ *noun* an unhappy feeling that you would like to have something which someone else has ○ *Her beautiful long dark hair filled us all with envy.* ■ *verb* to have the unhappy feeling that you would like to have something that someone else has ○ *I don't envy him with a job like that!* (NOTE: **envies – envying – envied**)

enzyme /ˈenzaɪm/ *noun* a protein produced by living cells which makes other substances change, as when digestion takes place

equal /ˈiːkwəl/ *adjective* having exactly the same amount as something else ○ *His share is equal to mine.* ○ *Male and female employees must have equal pay.* ○ *The two sticks are of equal length* or *are equal in length.* ■ *verb* **1.** to be exactly the same as ○ *His time for the 100 metres equals the existing record.* **2.** to give a particular result ○ *Two plus two equals four.* ○ *Ten take away four equals six.* (NOTE: **equals – equalling – equalled**. The US spelling is **equaling – equaled**.) ■ *noun* a person who is on the same level as someone else ○ *I don't consider him your equal.* ○ *We're all equals here.*

equally /ˈiːkwəli/ *adverb* in exactly the same way ○ *They are all equally guilty.* ○ *Here men and women are paid equally badly.* ○ *They were both equally responsible for the mistake.*

equipment /ɪˈkwɪpmənt/ *noun* all the things such as tools, arms and machines which are needed for something ○ *He brought all his camera equipment with him.* ○ *Do you really need all this equipment for a short climb?* (NOTE: no plural: for one item say *a piece of equipment*.)

error /'erə/ *noun* something that is wrong, especially a mistake in writing or speaking ○ *There isn't a single error in the whole document.* ○ *The waiter made an error in calculating the bill.*

erupt /ɪ'rʌpt/ *verb* (*of a volcano*) to throw out fire and other very hot substances ○ *The volcano last erupted in 1968.*

escape /ɪ'skeɪp/ *noun* the act of getting away from prison or from a difficult situation ○ *There were three escapes from this jail last year.* ○ *A weekend by the sea was a wonderful escape from the office.*

especially /ɪ'speʃ(ə)li/ *adverb* **1.** used for showing that something is the case to a great degree ○ *This suitcase is especially heavy.* **2.** used for showing that something is more important or true ○ *She does get tired, especially on school day.*

essay /'eseɪ/ *noun* a piece of writing on a specific subject ○ *a collection of the writer's most famous essays* ○ *For our homework, we have to write an essay on pollution.*

essential /ɪ'senʃəl/ *adjective* which is very important or which you must have ○ *You can survive without food for some time, but water is essential.* ○ *It is essential that we get the delivery on time.* ■ *noun* a thing which is very important or which you cannot do without ○ *Sun cream is an essential in the desert.* ○ *We've got all the basic essentials – food, water and fuel.*

essentially /ɪ'senʃəli/ *adverb* used for saying what is the most true, or the most important fact ○ *My new job is essentially not so very different from my old one.* ○ *Although he's essentially a kind man, he does lose his temper sometimes.*

establish /ɪ'stæblɪʃ/ *verb* **1.** to create something, to set something up ○ *The business was established in Scotland in 1823.* ○ *We need to establish a good working relationship with our colleagues.* **2.** to discover or prove something ○ *If only the police could establish where the car was parked that evening.* ○ *It's difficult to establish what her reasons are for resigning.*

establishment /ɪ'stæblɪʃmənt/ *noun* **1.** the act of creating something ○ *She helped them with the establishment of the local drama society.* (NOTE: no plural in this sense) **2.** a business; an organisation ○ *It's an establishment which imports radios from China.* ○ *He runs an important teaching establishment.*

Establishment, the /ɪ'stæblɪʃmənt/ *noun* the most important people in society, especially those who are in authority ○ *He spent a lot of his life fighting against the Establishment.*

estate /ɪ'steɪt/ *noun* **1.** a large area of land belonging to one owner ○ *He owns a 250-acre estate in Norfolk.* **2.** a group of houses on one piece of land, usually all built at the same time

estimate¹ /'estɪmət/ *noun* a calculation or guess which shows the amount of something you think there is, or its worth or cost ○ *I wasn't in when they came to read the gas meter, so this bill is only an estimate.* ○ *Your estimate of two dozen visitors proved to be correct.* □ **she gave me a rough estimate** she gave me an approximate calculation

estimate² /'estɪmeɪt/ *verb* to calculate or guess how much you think something will cost or is worth ○ *I estimate that it will cost £100,000.* ○ *He estimated costs at £50,000.*

etc. /et'setərə/, **etcetera** *adverb* and so on, and other things like this ○ *Fruit such as oranges, bananas, etc.*

euro /'jʊərəʊ/ *noun* the unit of money used by most countries in the European Union ○ *Many articles are priced in euros.* ○ *What's the exchange rate for the euro?* (NOTE: written Ä before numbers: *Ä250:* say: 'two hundred and fifty euros')

Europe /'jʊərəp/ *proper noun* **1.** the continent of Europe, the part of the world to the west of Asia, extending from Russia to Ireland ○ *Most of the countries of Western Europe are members of the EU.* **2.** the same area, but not including the UK ○ *Holidays in Europe are less popular than last year.*

European /ˌjuərə'piːən/ *adjective* relating to Europe

evaluate /ɪ'væljueɪt/ *verb* to make a judgement about something after thinking carefully about it ○ *The students were asked to evaluate the usefulness of the lessons.*

evaluation /ɪˌvælju'eɪʃ(ə)n/ *noun* the act of evaluating something, or the judgement made in this way (NOTE: no plural)

evaporate /ɪ'væpəreɪt/ *verb* (*of liquid*) to turn into steam by being heated ○ *Water gradually evaporates from the soil.*

even /'iːv(ə)n/ *adjective* **1.** flat, level ○ *The road has a smooth, even surface.* **2.** not changing ○ *They kept up an even pace for miles.* ○ *The temperature is an even 28° all through the day.* ■ *adverb* used for showing surprise or making an expression stronger ○ *He doesn't even like strawberries.* ○ *Even the cleverest businessperson can make mistakes.* ○ *She's tall, but her sister is even taller.*

evening /'iːvnɪŋ/ *noun* the late part of the day, when it starts to get dark ○ *I saw her yesterday evening.* ○ *The accident took place at 8.30 in the evening.* ○ *We arrived in London at breakfast time, having left New York the previous evening.* ○ *We always go to a restaurant on Sunday evenings.* ○ *They took an evening flight to Madrid.* ○ *The evening meal is served from 7.30 to 10.30.*

evenly /'iːv(ə)nli/ *adverb* in an equal way

event /ɪ'vent/ *noun* something important which happens ○ *the events leading up to the war* ○ *A baby's first birthday is always a very happy event.*

eventually /ɪ'ventʃuəli/ *adverb* in the end ○ *After weeks of hesitation he eventually decided to sell the cottage.*

ever /'evə/ *adverb* at any time (*used with negatives and in questions*) ○ *Nothing ever happens here.* ○ *Did you ever meet my brother?* ○ *Have you ever been to Germany?*

evergreen /'evəɡriːn/ *noun* a tree which keeps its leaves all winter ○ *Holly and other evergreens can be used as decorations in winter.*

every /'evri/ *adjective* **1.** each ○ *It rained every day during the holidays.* ○ *We have a party every New Year's Day.* ○ *Every Wednesday, he goes for a swim in the local pool.* ○ *Every house in the street has a garden.* **2.** with a particular amount of time or distance in between ○ *The medicine is to be taken every four hours.* ○ *Have your car checked every 10,000 kilometres.*

everybody /'evribɒdi/ *pronoun* same as **everyone**

everyone /'evriwʌn/ *pronoun* all the people involved in a particular situation ○ *Everyone has to die some day.* ○ *If everybody is here, we can start.* ○ *Everyone must show their passport.* (NOTE: **everyone** and **everybody** are followed by **they**, **their**, **themselves**, etc., but the verb stays singular: *Is everyone enjoying themselves? Not everybody likes pop music, do they?*) □ **everyone else** all the other people ○ *Only Maggie could come – everyone else was too busy.*

everything /'evriθɪŋ/ *pronoun* **1.** all things ○ *Did you bring everything you need?* ○ *The burglars stole everything of value.* ○ *Everything he says annoys me.* **2.** things in general ○ *Everything was dark in the street.* ○ *Everything is under control.*

everywhere /'evriweə/ *adverb* in all places ○ *There were papers lying about everywhere.* ○ *We've looked everywhere for the key and can't find it.*

evidence /'evɪd(ə)ns/ *noun* a fact which proves that something really exists or has happened ○ *The bloodstains on his coat were clear evidence of the crime.* ○ *Scientists are looking for evidence of life on Mars.* ○ *There is no evidence that he was ever there.*

evident /'evɪd(ə)nt/ *adjective* obvious

evil /'iːv(ə)l/ *adjective* morally very bad ○ *She's considered to be an evil woman.*

○ *His evil intentions were evident as soon as he locked the door.*

ex- /eks/ *prefix* used for showing that a person used to have a particular job or relationship ○ *an ex-soldier* ○ *Tom's my ex-boyfriend.*

exact /ɪgˈzækt/ *adjective* completely accurate, with no more or no less ○ *What is the exact time of arrival?* ○ *Could you repeat the exact words she used?* ○ *The salesgirl asked me if I had the exact sum, since she had no change.*

exactly /ɪgˈzæktli/ *adverb* not more, not less ○ *That comes to exactly ten dollars and fifty cents.* ○ *The time is exactly 16.24.*

exaggerate /ɪgˈzædʒəreɪt/ *verb* to make things seem, e.g. worse, better, bigger than they really are ○ *The wide black belt exaggerates her small waist.* ○ *She exaggerated the importance of my contribution.*

exam /ɪgˈzæm/ *noun* same as **examination** ○ *The exam was very difficult – half the students failed.* ○ *She passed all her exams.*

examination /ɪgˌzæmɪˈneɪʃ(ə)n/ *noun* **1.** an occasion on which someone looks at something to see if it works properly, or to see if something is wrong ○ *He had to have an X-ray examination.* ○ *The examination of the car showed that its brakes were faulty.* **2.** a written or spoken test ○ *The examination was very difficult – half the students failed.* ○ *He did badly in his English examination.* ○ *She came first in the final examination for the course.* (NOTE: often shortened to **exam** in this sense)

examine /ɪgˈzæmɪn/ *verb* **1.** to look carefully at something to see what is in it, or what it is like ○ *The doctor examined her throat.* ○ *We will have to examine the shop's scales to see if they show the correct weight.* ○ *The customs officials wanted to examine the inside of the car.* ○ *The water samples were examined in the laboratory.* **2.** to test a student ○ *They examined everyone in mathematics and computer skills.*

examiner /ɪgˈzæmɪnə/ *noun* a person who conducts an exam

example /ɪgˈzɑːmpəl/ *noun* something chosen to show something ○ *This is a good example of French architecture of the eleventh century.* □ **to set an example** to do things well or properly yourself, so that other people can copy you ○ *He sets everyone a good example by getting into the office before 8.00 every morning.* □ **to make an example of someone** to punish someone so that others will learn not to do what that person did ○ *Her teacher made an example of her by making her miss the class trip.*

exceed /ɪkˈsiːd/ *verb* to go beyond something ○ *The car was exceeding the speed limit.* ○ *Our expenses have exceeded our income for the first time.* ○ *Did the UN troops exceed their mandate?*

excellent /ˈeksələnt/ *adjective* very good ○ *We had an excellent meal in a Chinese restaurant.* ○ *Her handwriting is excellent – it is much clearer than mine.*

except /ɪkˈsept/ *preposition* not including ○ *She's allowed to eat anything except milk products.* ○ *Everyone was sick on the boat, except (for) me.* ○ *VAT is levied on all goods except books, newspapers, food and children's clothes.* ■ *conjunction* other than; apart from ○ *He doesn't do anything except sit and watch football on the TV.* ○ *Everything went well, except that James was sick.* ○ *Everyone enjoyed the birthday party, except (that) there wasn't enough to eat.* (NOTE: [all senses] Do not confuse with **accept**.)

exception /ɪkˈsepʃən/ *noun* something that is not included ○ *All the students failed, with one exception.* ○ *Are there any exceptions to the rule?*

exceptionally /ɪkˈsepʃən(ə)li/ *adverb* to a very great degree, often so great as to be surprising

exchange /ɪksˈtʃeɪndʒ/ *verb* to give one thing and to get another thing back ○ *The footballers from the two teams exchanged shirts at the end of the match.* ■ *noun* the act of giving one thing for another ○ *the exchange of rings during the wedding ceremony*

excited /ɪkˈsaɪtɪd/ *adjective* lively and happy because you think something good is going to happen ○ *She's excited at* or *by the thought of going on holiday.* ○ *The children are excited because it's the Christmas holidays.* ○ *What's everyone so excited about?* ○ *It was lovely to see the children's happy and excited faces.*

excitement /ɪkˈsaɪtmənt/ *noun* the feeling of being excited ○ *What's all the excitement about?* ○ *The children are always in a state of excitement before the holidays.*

exciting /ɪkˈsaɪtɪŋ/ *adjective* **1.** making you feel excited ○ *The news about the house is really exciting.* **2.** (*of, e.g. a film or an experience*) full of activity, sometimes making you a little scared because you do not know what is going to happen ○ *I couldn't sleep after watching an exciting film on TV.*

exclaim /ɪkˈskleɪm/ *verb* to say something loudly and suddenly

exclude /ɪkˈskluːd/ *verb* not to include someone or something ○ *Damage by fire is excluded from the insurance policy.* ○ *Don't exclude his name from your list.*

excuse[1] /ɪkˈskjuːs/ *noun* a reason given for doing something wrong, or for not doing what was expected ○ *His excuse for not coming was that he forgot the date.*

excuse[2] /ɪkˈskjuːz/ *verb* to forgive someone for making a small mistake ○ *Please excuse my arriving late like this.*

execute /ˈeksɪkjuːt/ *verb* **1.** to kill someone as a punishment ○ *The government's political enemies were executed.* **2.** to do something that has been planned or agreed (*formal*) ○ *As part of the test, drivers are asked to execute an emergency stop.* **3.** in computing, to carry out instructions ○ *Press ENTER to execute the program.*

exercise /ˈeksəsaɪz/ *noun* practice in using physical or mental powers ○ *She does her piano exercises every morning.* □ **to take exercise** to do physical movements, like walking or running, in order to keep fit ○ *You should take some exer-*

cise every day if you want to lose weight.

exercise book /ˈeksəsaɪz bʊk/ *noun* a notebook with lines on each page for writing school work in

exhausted /ɪgˈzɔːstɪd/ *adjective* very tired ○ *I'm exhausted after running three miles.* ○ *They staggered back home very late, with three exhausted children.*

exhibition /ˌeksɪˈbɪʃ(ə)n/ *noun* a public show of things such as paintings or flowers ○ *The exhibition is open from 10 a.m. to 5 p.m.* ○ *We stood in line for half an hour waiting to get into the Picasso exhibition.*

exist /ɪgˈzɪst/ *verb* to be real or present ○ *When I was a child, colour TV didn't exist.* ○ *I don't believe the document exists – I think it has been burnt.*

existence /ɪgˈzɪstəns/ *noun* the state of being a real thing; life ○ *Is there anything which proves the existence of life on Mars?* ○ *They lived a miserable existence in a little coal mining town.*

existing /ɪgˈzɪstɪŋ/ *adjective* in operation at this moment ○ *Can we modify the existing structure in some way?* ○ *Existing regulations do not allow the sale of food in the street.*

exit /ˈegzɪt/ *noun* a way out of a building ○ *The customers all rushed towards the exits when the fire alarm rang.*

expand /ɪkˈspænd/ *verb* to increase the size or extent of something ○ *We have plans to expand our business.*

expect /ɪkˈspekt/ *verb* **1.** to think or to hope that something is going to happen ○ *We expect him to arrive at any moment or he is expected at any moment.* **2.** to think or guess that something is the case ○ *I expect you are tired after your long train journey.* **3.** to think that it is right that someone should do something ○ *He expects me to do all the housework.* **4.** to be waiting for someone ○ *I can't talk for long – we're expecting visitors.*

expectation /ˌekspekˈteɪʃ(ə)n/ *noun* hope; a feeling that something will happen ○ *She lived up to all our expectations.* ○ *We thought our team would do* *well, but in the end they exceeded all our expectations.*

expected /ɪk'spektɪd/ *adjective* **1.** which you think or hope will happen **2.** due to arrive ○ *Our guests are expected at 10 o'clock.*

expedition /ˌekspɪ'dɪʃ(ə)n/ *noun* a journey to explore a place ○ *He set off on an expedition to the South Pole.*

expense /ɪk'spens/ *noun* an amount of money that you have to pay ○ *I can't afford the expense of a holiday just now.* ○ *The expense of running a household seems to increase every week.*

expensive /ɪk'spensɪv/ *adjective* costing a lot of money ○ *Fresh vegetables are more expensive in winter.* ○ *Send your furniture to Australia by sea – it would be much too expensive by air.*

experience /ɪk'spɪəriəns/ *noun* **1.** knowledge obtained by working or living in various situations ○ *I have no experience of travelling in the desert.* ○ *You must write down the full details of your past experience in your CV.* ○ *Some experience of selling is required for this job.* (NOTE: no plural in this sense) **2.** something that happens to you ○ *Going to the top of the Eiffel Tower was a wonderful experience.* ○ *He wrote a book about his experiences in the desert.* ■ *verb* to live through something ○ *I'm surprised she's so cheerful after all she experienced in hospital.* ○ *I have experienced a great deal of pleasure and frustration in my career.* ○ *He is experiencing sharp pains in his tooth.*

experienced /ɪk'spɪəriənst/ *adjective* good at something because you have learnt a lot from particular experiences you have had ○ *She's a very experienced doctor.* ○ *He's the most experienced member of our staff.* ○ *The police are experienced in crowd control.*

experiment[1] /ɪk'sperɪmənt/ *noun* a scientific test; a way of finding out about something ○ *to carry out scientific experiments* ○ *We're offering our customers free samples as an experiment.*

experiment[2] /ɪk'sperɪment/ *verb* to carry out a scientific test ○ *They are experimenting with a new treatment for*

asthma. ○ *The laboratory does not experiment on live animals.*

expert /'ekspɜːt/ *adjective* **1.** knowing a lot about a subject ○ *They can give you expert advice on DIY.* **2.** □ **expert at doing something** very good at doing something ○ *I'm not very expert at making pastry.* ■ *noun* **1.** a person who knows a great deal about a subject ○ *a leading expert in tropical medicine* or *on tropical diseases* ○ *A rose expert was the judge at the flower show.* **2.** a person who is very good at doing something ○ *an expert plumber* ○ *He's an expert at getting the children to go to bed.*

explain /ɪk'spleɪn/ *verb* **1.** to give reasons for something ○ *Can you explain why the weather is cold in winter and warm in summer?* **2.** to make something clear ○ *He tried to explain the new pension scheme to the staff.* ○ *She explained what had happened, but the manager still thought she had tried to steal the watch.*

explanation /ˌeksplə'neɪʃ(ə)n/ *noun* a reason for something ○ *The police officer asked him for an explanation of why the stolen car was in his garage.* ○ *The company has given no explanation for the change of plan.*

explode /ɪk'spləud/ *verb* (of bombs, etc.) to blow up ○ *A bomb exploded in a crowded train.*

explore /ɪk'splɔː/ *verb* to travel and discover place and things that you have not seen before ○ *It is a part of the jungle which has never been explored before.* ○ *We spent our holidays exploring Holland by canal.*

explosion /ɪk'spləuʒ(ə)n/ *noun* an occasion on which something such as a bomb explodes ○ *Several explosions were heard during the night as the army occupied the city.*

explosive /ɪk'spləusɪv/ *noun* a substance used for destroying things by making them explode ○ *Tests revealed traces of explosive on his hands.* ○ *The box contained explosives.* ○ *Police explosives experts defused the bomb.*

export[1] /'ekspɔːt/ *noun* the business of selling products in other countries ○

They make cars for export. ○ *There is a big export trade in wine.* ■ a product sent to a foreign country to be sold ○ *The country's major export is tea.* ○ *Exports to Africa have increased by 25%.*

export² /ɪk'spɔːt/ *verb* to send goods to a foreign country for sale ○ *The company exports half of what it produces.*

express /ɪk'spres/ *verb* to show thoughts or feelings in words, pictures or actions ○ *He expressed his gratitude in a short speech.* ○ *His paintings express his inner thoughts.* ○ *His grief was expressed in fierce anger and constant activity.* ■ *noun* a fast train ○ *We took the express from London to Glasgow.*

expression /ɪk'spreʃ(ə)n/ *noun* **1.** a word, or group of words ○ *'Until the cows come home' is an expression which means 'for a very long time'.* **2.** a look on a person's face which shows a feeling ○ *His expression showed how miserable he was.* ○ *Everyone noticed the expression of surprise on her face.* **3.** the act of expressing thoughts and feelings

extend /ɪk'stend/ *verb* **1.** to stretch something out ○ *She extended both arms in welcome.* **2.** to cover a particular are area of land ○ *The grounds of the house extend over two hectares.* **3.** to make something longer or bigger ○ *We are planning to extend our garden.* ○ *The company has extended my contract for another two years.*

extension /ɪk'stenʃən/ *noun* **1.** the act of extending something ○ *My visa has expired, so I have applied for an extension.* **2.** a telephone in an office which is connected to the company's main line ○ *Can you get me extension 21?* ○ *The manager is on extension 23.*

extensive /ɪk'stensɪv/ *adjective* covering a large area or amount ○ *The grounds of the house are very extensive.* ○ *The church roof needs extensive repair work.*

extent /ɪk'stent/ *noun* the degree, size or area of something ○ *The extent of the earthquake damage was only revealed later.* ○ *He opened up the map to its full extent.*

external /ɪk'stɜːn(ə)l/ *adjective* on the outside ○ *The external walls of the house are quite solid.* ○ *Her injuries were all external.*

extinct /ɪk'stɪŋkt/ *adjective* **1.** (*of a type of animal or plant*) no longer in existence, because all of the same kind have died ○ *These birds are in danger of becoming extinct.* **2.** ((*of a volcano*)) no longer active ○ *The mountain is an extinct volcano.*

extra /'ekstrə/ *adjective* more than usual; additional ○ *We need an extra four teachers* or *four extra teachers for this course.* ○ *The charge for delivery is extra.* ○ *Staff get extra pay for working on Sundays.*

extraordinarily /ɪk'strɔːd(ə)nərəli/ *adverb* extremely ○ *Her action was extraordinarily brave.*

extraordinary /ɪk'strɔːd(ə)n(ə)ri/ *adjective* **1.** wonderful ○ *Seeing her again gave him an extraordinary thrill.* ○ *A peacock's feathers are quite extraordinary.* **2.** very unusual ○ *It's extraordinary weather for June.*

extreme /ɪk'striːm/ *adjective* **1.** very great ○ *The device is made to withstand extreme cold.* ○ *He showed extreme reluctance to get involved.* **2.** considered unreasonable by some people ○ *He holds extreme views.*

extremely /ɪk'striːmli/ *adverb* to a very great degree ○ *It was extremely hot in August.* ○ *The film is extremely long, and some people left before the end.* ○ *It is extremely difficult to spend less than $50.00 a day on meals in New York.*

eye /aɪ/ *noun* **1.** the organ in the head which you see with ○ *He has brown eyes.* ○ *Close your eyes and count to ten while we all hide.* ○ *I've got a bit of dust in my eye.* **2.** a small hole in the end of a needle, through which the thread goes ◇ **to catch someone's eye** to look at someone who is looking at you ○ *She caught his eye and nodded towards the door.* ◇ **to keep an eye on someone or something** to watch someone or something carefully to see that it is safe ○ *Can you keep an eye on the house while we are away?* ◇ **to keep an eye out for someone or something** to watch to see if someone or something is available or nearby ○ *I must keep an eye out for Seville oranges to make some marmalade.* ○ *Can you keep an eye out for the traffic warden while I go into the bank?*

eyebrow /ˈaɪbraʊ/ *noun* the line of hair above each of your eyes

eyelash /ˈaɪlæʃ/ *noun* one of the hairs growing round the edges of your eyes (NOTE: The plural is **eyelashes**.)

eyelid /ˈaɪlɪd/ *noun* a piece of skin which covers the eye

eyesight /ˈaɪsaɪt/ *noun* the ability to see

F

f /ef/, **F** *noun* the sixth letter of the alphabet, between E and G

fabric /ˈfæbrɪk/ *noun* cloth used for making things such as clothes and curtains ○ *The curtains are made of an expensive fabric.*

fabrication /ˌfæbrɪˈkeɪʃ(ə)n/ *noun* an invented story that is not true ○ *The newspaper story was a complete fabrication from start to finish.*

face /feɪs/ *noun* **1.** the front part of your head ○ *Don't forget to wash your face before you go to the party.* **2.** the front part of something ○ *a clock face* ○ *She put the photograph face down on the desk.* ■ *verb* to have the face or front towards ○ *Can everyone please face the camera?* ○ *The house faces north.* ◇ **to show your face** to come to or be in a place where there are other people ○ *After what he said about my mother he doesn't dare show his face here.*

face up to *phrasal verb* to accept an unpleasant situation and try to deal with it

facility /fəˈsɪlɪti/ *noun* **1.** an ability to do something easily ○ *She has a facility for languages.* (NOTE: no plural) **2.** a means of doing something ○ *We offer facilities for payment.* **3.** a large building that enables people to do or have something ○ *We have opened our new warehouse facility.* (NOTE: The plural is **facilities**.)

fact /fækt/ *noun* **1.** something such as a piece of information that is true ○ *He faced up to the fact that he wasn't fit enough for the race.* ○ *Did you check all the facts before you wrote the article?* **2.** □ **in fact**, **in actual fact** really; the truth is that ○ *He told the police he had seen a man steal a car but in fact he made the whole story up.* ○ *It rained a lot last month – in fact it rained all month.* □ **as a matter of fact** actually; used for saying what is really true, especially when

it is surprising ○ *Have you seen John recently? – as a matter of fact I met him yesterday.*

factor /ˈfæktə/ *noun* **1.** a thing which has influence or importance ○ *The key factor is the price.* ○ *The crucial factor for the success of the village fair is the weather.* **2.** one of the numbers which produce a certain other number when multiplied ○ *Four and two are factors of eight.*

factory /ˈfækt(ə)ri/ *noun* a building where things are made in large quantities using machines ○ *She works in a shoe factory.* ○ *He owns a furniture factory.* ○ *The factory makes computer terminals.* (NOTE: The plural is **factories**.)

fade /feɪd/ *verb* **1.** to lose colour ○ *The more you wash your jeans, the more they'll fade.* ○ *This teeshirt has faded in the sun.* **2.** to become less bright or light ○ *As the light faded, bats came out in the garden.* ○ *The light from the torch began to fade as the batteries ran out.* ○ *The islands faded away into the distance.* **3.** to become less noisy ○ *The sound of the music faded away.*

fail /feɪl/ *verb* **1.** not to succeed ○ *The examination was very difficult – half the students failed.* ○ *He passed in maths, but failed his English exam.* ○ *She failed in her attempt to become an MP.* **2.** not to do something ○ *The car failed to stop at the red light.* ○ *She failed to notify the tax office of her change of address.* **3.** not to work properly ○ *The brakes failed and he couldn't stop the car.* ◇ **if all else fails** if you can't do anything else ○ *If all else fails you can always borrow my car.*

failure /ˈfeɪljə/ *noun* **1.** a situation in which something stops working ○ *The accident was caused by brake failure.* ○ *The failure of the plane's engine caused the crash.* **2.** an occasion on a person or event is not successful ○ *His attempts to balance on one leg were a complete failure.* **3.** a person who does not succeed at things ○ *I'm no good at anything – I'm a failure.*

faint /feɪnt/ *adjective* difficult to see or hear ○ *We could just see the faint outline of a man in the fog.* ○ *They could hear a faint tapping under the wreckage.* ■ *verb* to become unconscious for a short time ○ *She fainted when she saw the blood.*

fair /feə/ *adjective* **1.** (*of hair or skin*) light-coloured ○ *Her hair is quite fair.* ○ *Those with fair skin should use a stronger sun cream.* **2.** right, giving someone what they deserve ○ *That's not fair – you must let other children play with the ball too.* ○ *It isn't fair if you go on holiday when we have so much work to do.* ■ *noun* **1.** a group of machines for riding on and stalls where you can win things, set up in one place for a short time ○ *The fair is coming to the village for the Easter Bank Holiday.* **2.** an exhibition for selling and advertising goods ○ *We are going to the car fair tomorrow.* (NOTE: Do not confuse with **fare**.)

fairly /ˈfeəli/ *adverb* **1.** in a way that is right; giving people what they deserve ○ *She complained that she had not been treated fairly in the interview.* **2.** to some degree ○ *I'm fairly certain I have seen this film before.* ○ *She had been working there a fairly short time.* ○ *The hotel is fairly close to the centre of town.* (NOTE: The order of words for **fairly** and **quite** is different: *He's a fairly good worker* but *He's quite a good worker.*)

fairness /ˈfeənəs/ *noun* a tendency or ability to do things in a fair way ○ *Everyone acknowledged her fairness in dealing with staff complaints.*

fairy /ˈfeəri/ *noun* a small imaginary creature who can perform magic (NOTE: The plural is **fairies**.)

faith /feɪθ/ *noun* **1.** belief or trust ○ *I don't have much faith in these new teaching methods.* **2.** a religious belief ○ *We must respect people of other faiths.*

faithful /ˈfeɪθf(ə)l/ *adjective* (*of a person or an animal*) trusting or loyal ○ *his faithful old dog* ○ *We must be faithful to father's last wishes.*

fake /feɪk/ *noun* something which is made or designed to look like something else that is, e.g. more valuable ○ *That picture isn't by Picasso, it's a fake.* ■ *adjective* not real ○ *She was wearing a fake fur coat.*

fall /fɔːl/ *verb* to drop to a lower level ○ *Snow fell all night* ○ *The pound has fallen against the dollar.* ○ *She fell down the stairs.* ○ *He fell off the ladder.* ○ *Did he fall into the river or did someone push him?* (NOTE: **falls – falling – fell** /fel/ – **has fallen**) ■ *noun* **1.** the process of going to a lower level ○ *a welcome fall in the price of oil* ○ *the fall in the exchange rate* **2.** the act of losing your balance ○ *He had a fall and hurt his back.* ○ *She had a bad fall while skiing.*

fall back on *phrasal verb* to do or use something only after all other things have failed

fall behind *phrasal verb* to be late in doing something

fall down *phrasal verb* **1.** to drop to the ground ○ *She fell down and hurt her knee.* **2.** (*of a building*) to become broken down through age ○ *The place has been deserted for so long it's falling down.*

fall off *phrasal verb* to become fewer ○ *The number of customers starts to fall off after 4 o'clock.*

fall out *phrasal verb* **1.** to drop to the ground after having been in something ○ *We put cushions on the floor next to the bed in case she fell out.* **2.** to have an argument ○ *They fell out over the bill for drinks.*

fall over *phrasal verb* to fall down after having been upright

fall through *phrasal verb* not to take place as planned

false /fɔːls/ *adjective* not real; designed to look like something real ○ *a set of false nails*

falsehood /ˈfɔːlshʊd/ *noun* a lie (*literary*) ○ *It appears that he had told several falsehoods under oath.*

familiar /fə'mɪliə/ *adjective* heard or seen before; that you know ○ *The dog wagged its tail as it heard its master's familiar voice at the door.* ○ *He looked round the room, and saw a couple of familiar faces.*

family /'fæm(ə)li/ *noun* **1.** a group of people who are related to each other, especially mother, father and children ○ *The Jones family are going on holiday to Spain.* ○ *He grew up in a big family.* **2.** a group of animals or plants which are closely related ○ *Lions and tigers are members of the cat family.* (NOTE: The plural is **families**. When **family** is used to mean a group of people it can take a singular or plural verb: *The family were out.*)

famine /'fæmɪn/ *noun* a very serious lack of food

famous /'feɪməs/ *adjective* known to many people, especially most people in a place or country ○ *a famous department store* ○ *He's a famous footballer.* ○ *This tea shop is famous for its cakes.*

fan /fæn/ *noun* **1.** a piece of equipment for moving air to make people or things cooler ○ *We put electric fans in the office to try to keep cool.* **2.** an enthusiastic supporter of something or someone, e.g. a team or a pop group ○ *There was a crowd of fans waiting for him outside the theatre.*

fancy /'fænsi/ *verb* **1.** to want to have something (*informal*) ○ *I fancy an ice cream – anyone else want one?* ○ *Do you fancy sharing a taxi to the airport?* **2.** to like someone in a sexual way ○ *I'm sure that guy fancies you.* (NOTE: **fancies – fancying – fancied**) ■ *adjective* attractive or decorated ○ *He wore a fancy tie to the party.*

fantastic /fæn'tæstɪk/ wonderful ○ *We had a fantastic time on holiday.* ■ *adjective* strange; like a dream ○ *His stories are full of fantastic creatures.*

fantasy /'fæntəsi/ *noun* an invented story ○ *Her story of meeting a rich man in Paris is pure fantasy.* (NOTE: The plural is **fantasies**.)

far /fɑː/ *adverb* **1.** a certain distance away ○ *The railway station is not far from here.* ○ *How far away is Paris from London?* ○ *The road was blocked by cars as far as we could see.* **2.** used with comparatives to mean 'much' ○ *It is far cheaper to go by bus than by train.* ○ *Restaurant food is far nicer than the food at college.* ■ *adjective* a long way away; distant ○ *The shop is at the far end of the High Street.* (NOTE: **far – farther** /'fɑːðə/ *or* **further** /'fɜːðə/ - **farthest** /'fɑːðəst/ *or* **furthest** /'fɜːðəst/)

fare /feə/ *noun* a price which you have to pay for a journey ○ *Rail fares have been increased by 10%.* ○ *The tourist-class fare is much less than the first class one.* ○ *If you walk to work, you will save £5 a week on bus fares.* (NOTE: Do not confuse with **fair**.)

farewell /feə'wel/ *interjection, noun* goodbye ○ *It's time to say farewell.* ■ *adjective* (*of an event*) at which you say goodbye ○ *We gave a farewell party for our neighbours who were going to live in Canada.*

far from /'fɑː frɒm/ *adverb* not at all ○ *The food here is far from cheap.*

farm /fɑːm/ *noun* an area of land used for growing crops and raising animals ○ *He runs a pig farm.* ○ *We're going to work on a farm during the holidays.* ○ *You can buy eggs and vegetables at the farm shop.* ■ *verb* to grow crops or raise animals on a farm ○ *He farms dairy cattle in Devon.*

farmer /'fɑːmə/ *noun* a person who manages or owns a farm

farming /'fɑːmɪŋ/ *noun* the work of managing a farm, e.g. growing crops or keeping animals for sale

fascinate /'fæsɪneɪt/ *verb* to make someone very interested

fascinating /'fæsɪneɪtɪŋ/ *adjective* very interesting ○ *A microscope gives you a fascinating glimpse of life in a drop of water.* ○ *The book gives a fascinating description of London in the 1930s.* ○ *It was fascinating to hear her talk about her travels in India.*

fashion /'fæʃ(ə)n/ *noun* the most popular style at a particular time ○ *It was the fashion then to wear your hair very short.* ○ *She always follows fashion.*

fashionable /ˈfæʃ(ə)nəb(ə)l/ *adjective*
1. of a style which is popular at a particular time ○ *These loose trousers are really fashionable at the moment.* **2.** popular with rich or glamorous people ○ *She lives in the fashionable West End of London.* ○ *It's a fashionable restaurant for film stars and journalists.*

fast /fɑːst/ *adjective* **1.** quick ○ *I just love driving fast cars.* ○ *She was driving in the fast lane of the motorway.* **2.** not stopping anywhere ○ *This is the fast train to London.* **3.** (*of a clock*) to show a time which is later than the correct time ○ *Your watch is fast.* ■ *adverb* **1.** quickly ○ *Walk faster if you want to catch up with the children in front.* ○ *Don't go so fast – you almost hit that man on the zebra crossing.* **2.** tightly fixed in a particular position ○ *The window was stuck fast and I couldn't open it.* ■ *verb* to eat nothing for religious or health reasons ○ *Many people fast during Lent.* ○ *He fasted for a week.*

fasten /ˈfɑːs(ə)n/ *verb* to close or attach something tightly ○ *Please fasten your seatbelts.* ○ *These shoes fasten with a buckle.*

fastener /ˈfɑːs(ə)nə/ *noun* an object which fastens something such as a piece of clothing

fat /fæt/ *adjective* having too much flesh or weighing too much ○ *Two fat men got out of the little white car.* ○ *You'll have to eat less – you're getting too fat.* ○ *He's fatter than me.* ■ *noun* a part of meat which is yellowish-white ○ *If you don't like the fat, cut it off.*

fatal /ˈfeɪt(ə)l/ *adjective* which causes death ○ *There were three fatal accidents on this road last year.*

father /ˈfɑːðə/ *noun* a man who has a son or daughter ○ *Ask your father if he will lend you his car.* ○ *She is coming to tea with her mother and father.*

faucet /ˈfɔːsɪt/ *noun US* an object which, when you twist it, lets liquid or gas come out

fault /fɔːlt/ *noun* **1.** the fact of making a mistake or of being to blame for something going wrong ○ *It isn't my fault if there's nothing in the fridge.* ○ *It's all*
your fault – if you hadn't stayed in bed all morning we would be at the seaside by now.* **2.** an instance of something not working properly ○ *The invoice was wrong because of a computer fault.* ○ *The engineers are trying to mend an electrical fault.* **3.** a mistake in serving in tennis ○ *He served two double faults.* ◇ **at fault** having made a mistake ○ *The shop is at fault if they sent you the wrong table.*

faulty /ˈfɔːlti/ *adjective* **1.** not working correctly or not made correctly ○ *The lights are flickering – there must be a faulty connection somewhere.* **2.** with mistakes in planning or judgment ○ *a faulty argument*

favor /ˈfeɪvə/ *noun, verb* US spelling of **favour**

favorable /ˈfeɪv(ə)rəb(ə)l/ *adjective* US spelling of **favourable**

favorite /ˈfeɪv(ə)rət/ *noun, verb* US spelling of **favourite**

favour /ˈfeɪvə/ *noun* **1.** a friendly act done to help someone ○ *Can I ask a favour – will you look after my bike while I'm in the post office?* **2.** approval or popularity ○ *She tried to win the favour of the committee.* ■ *verb* **1.** to like or prefer something ○ *The managers favour moving to a bigger office.* **2.** to make things easier for someone ○ *The conditions favour Australian bowlers.*

favourable /ˈfeɪv(ə)rəb(ə)l/ *adjective* good

favourite /ˈfeɪv(ə)rət/ *adjective* which you like best ○ *Which is your favourite TV programme?* ■ *noun* **1.** something or someone you like best ○ *Which ice cream is your favourite?* ○ *This game is a favourite with the children.* ○ *The singer was a favourite in the fifties.* **2.** someone who is treated better than other people by a particular person ○ *She was always her father's favourite.*

fax /fæks/ *noun* a copy of a document or picture sent to someone using telephone lines ○ *Post it to me, or send a fax.* ○ *Can you confirm the booking by fax?* ■ *verb* to send a document or picture by telephone ○ *I will fax the design to you* or *I will fax you the design as soon as it is ready.*

fear /fɪə/ *noun* the feeling of being afraid ○ *Fear of the dark is common in small children.* ○ *She has no fear of heights.* ■ *verb* to be afraid of something (*formal*) ○ *What do you fear most?*

feast /fiːst/ *noun* **1.** a very large meal for a group of people, especially one eaten to celebrate a special occasion **2.** a special religious day ○ *Today is the Feast of St Nicholas.*

feat /fiːt/ *noun* an particularly difficult act

feather /ˈfeðə/ *noun* one of many light soft parts which cover a bird's body

feature /ˈfiːtʃə/ *noun* **1.** a part of the face such as the nose or mouth ○ *His unusual features make him easy to recognize.* **2.** an important part or aspect of something ○ *The main feature of the castle is its huge tower.* **3.** an important story or article in a TV news programme or in a newspaper ○ *a feature on nuclear power* ○ *Did you see the feature on St Petersburg?* ■ *verb* **1.** to have someone as the main performer of a film, a TV programme or a play ○ *The film featured Charlie Chaplin as the tramp.* ○ *The circus features Russian clowns.* **2.** to have something as the most important part ○ *The tour features a visit to the Valley of the Kings.* ○ *The next programme will feature a discussion between environmental experts.* **3.** to appear as the main actor in, or as the subject of a film or a TV programme ○ *She has featured in many TV series.*

February /ˈfebruəri/ *noun* the second month of the year, between January and March ○ *My birthday is in February.* ○ *He died on February 17th.* ○ *We are moving to new offices next February.* (NOTE: **February 17th:** say 'the seventeenth of February' or 'February the seventeenth', or in US English 'February seventeenth'.)

fed /fed/ past tense and past participle of **feed**

federal /ˈfed(ə)rəl/ *adjective* **1.** relating to the central government of the United States ○ *Most federal offices are in Washington.* ○ *Federal law is more important than state law.* **2.** relating to a system where a group of states exist under a central government ○ *the former Federal Republic of Germany*

fed up /ˌfed ˈʌp/ *adjective* feeling bored and unhappy (*informal*)

fee /fiː/ *noun* money paid to someone such as a doctor or lawyer for work done ○ *Private school fees are very high.* ○ *The lawyer's fee for two days' work was more than I earn in a month!*

feeble /ˈfiːb(ə)l/ *adjective* **1.** physically weak, especially because of illness or age ○ *He gave a feeble wave with his hand.* ○ *The voice on the phone sounded feeble.* (NOTE: **feebler – feeblest**) **2.** not strong or able to be seen or heard well ○ *She replied in a feeble voice.*

feed /fiːd/ *verb* **1.** to give food to a person or an animal ○ *I'd better just feed the baby before we go out.* ○ *Could you feed the cat while we're away?* **2.** (*of a baby or young animal*) to take milk from its mother ○ *Please don't disturb the baby while she's feeding.* (NOTE: **feeds – feeding – fed** /fed/ **– has fed**)

feedback /ˈfiːdbæk/ *noun* information or comments about something which has been done

feel /fiːl/ *verb* **1.** to touch something, usually with your fingers ○ *Feel how soft the bed is.* **2.** to seem soft, cold, etc., when touched ○ *The bed feels hard.* ○ *The stone floor felt cold.* **3.** to experience something with your body or mind ○ *Did you feel the table move?* ○ *I felt the lift go down suddenly.* ○ *Do you feel warmer now that you've had a cup of tea?* ○ *They felt happy when they saw that all was well.* ○ *By twelve o'clock she was feeling hungry.* (NOTE: **feels – feeling – felt** /felt/ **– has felt**)

feel for *phrasal verb* to be sympathetic towards someone

feel up to *phrasal verb* to be strong or well enough to do something

feeling /ˈfiːlɪŋ/ *noun* something which you think you know ○ *I had a feeling that this strange man knew who I was.* ■ **feelings** someone's emotions ○ *I didn't want to hurt her feelings.*

feet /fiːt/ plural of **foot**

fell /fel/ past tense of **fall**

fellow /'feləʊ/ noun **1.** a man ○ *A young fellow came up to me and asked me the time.* ○ *Who's that fellow with a beard?* **2.** a person who belongs to the same group ○ *I was OK on the boat, but several of my fellow passengers were sick.*

felt /felt/ noun a thick material made of wool fibres pressed together

female /'fiːmeɪl/ adjective **1.** relating to women or girls ○ *a female athlete* **2.** relating to the sex of an animal, insect or bird which gives birth to young or produces eggs ○ *a female kitten* **3.** relating to a flower which produces seeds

feminine /'femɪnɪn/ adjective like a woman or suitable for a woman ○ *Her long white silk dress was very feminine.*

fence /fens/ noun a type of wall made of wood or wire, used to keep people or animals in or out of a place ○ *The fence was blown down.* ○ *The boys looked through the hole in the fence.* ○ *The builders put up a fence round the construction site.*

ferocious /fə'rəʊʃəs/ adjective wild and angry ○ *a ferocious dog*

ferry /'feri/ noun a boat which carries cars and trucks or people across a stretch of water ○ *We are going to take the night ferry to Belgium.* ○ *There's a ferry across the Rhine here.*

festival /'festɪv(ə)l/ noun **1.** a religious celebration which is celebrated at the same time each year and is usually a public holiday ○ *The tour will visit Hong Kong for the Lantern Festival.* **2.** an event, often lasting several days, where entertainment is provided ○ *We saw some excellent plays at the Edinburgh Festival this year.*

fetch /fetʃ/ verb to go to a place and bring someone or something back ○ *It's your turn to fetch the children from school.* ○ *Can you fetch me the atlas?*

fever /'fiːvə/ noun a state in which the body's temperature is higher than normal ○ *You must stay in bed until the fever goes down.*

few /fjuː/ adjective, noun not many ○ *She has very few friends at work.* ○ *We go to fewer concerts than last year.*

fib /fɪb/ noun a lie about something unimportant (*informal*) ○ *That was a little fib, wasn't it?*

fibre /'faɪbə/ noun **1.** a small thread of material ○ *From the fibres left at the scene of the murder, the police could work out what the murderer had been wearing.* **2.** thin threads in foods such as vegetables and bread, which cannot be digested, but which helps food to pass through your body ○ *You need to eat more fibre.*

fiction /'fɪkʃən/ noun novels ○ *fiction writers such as Graham Greene* ○ *To find the latest novels you must look in the fiction section of the library.* (NOTE: no plural)

field /fiːld/ noun **1.** a piece of ground on a farm, used for keeping animals or growing crops ○ *a field of potatoes* ○ *The sheep are in the field.* **2.** a piece of ground for playing a game ○ *a football field* ○ *The two teams ran onto the field.*

fierce /fɪəs/ adjective very angry and likely to attack ○ *Watch out – that dog looks fierce.*

fiercely /'fɪəsli/ adverb strongly ○ *She is fiercely independent.*

fifteen /fɪf'tiːn/ noun the number 15 ○ *There are fifteen players in a rugby team.* ○ *She's fifteen (years old).* ○ *Come and see me in fifteen minutes.* ○ *The train leaves at nine fifteen (9.15).*

fifteenth /fɪf'tiːnθ/ adjective relating to number 15 in a series ○ *the fifteenth of July* or *July the fifteenth (July 15th).* ○ *That's the fifteenth phone call I've made this morning.* ○ *It will be her fifteenth birthday next week.* ■ noun number 15 in a series ○ *Our house is the fifth on the right.*

fifth /fɪfθ/ adjective relating to number 5 in a series ○ *The fifth of May* or *May the fifth (May 5th).* ○ *It's his fifth birthday tomorrow.* ■ noun one part of five equal parts

fiftieth /'fɪftiəθ/ adjective relating to number 50 in a series ■ noun the number fifty in a series ○ *He's fiftieth on the waiting list.*

fifty /ˈfɪfti/ *noun* the number 50 ○ *My mother made fifty pots of jam.* ○ *He's fifty (years old).*

fight /faɪt/ *noun* **1.** an occasion on which people try to hurt each other or knock each other down ○ *He got into a fight with boys who were bigger than him.* ○ *Fights broke out between the demonstrators and the police.* **2.** a situation in which people do everything they can to stop something from happening ○ *a fight against the new developments* ■ *verb* **1.** to be involved in a situation in which people try to hurt each other or knock each other down ○ *Rival gangs fought in the street.* **2.** to do everything you can try to stop something from happening ○ *We are committed to fighting crime.* ○ *Doctors are fighting to control the disease.* (NOTE: **fights – fighting – fought** /fɔːt/ **– has fought**)

figure /ˈfɪɡə/ *noun* **1.** a written number, e.g. 35 ○ *I can't read the figure on the order – is it 250?* ○ *He added up the figures on the bill.* ○ *Cheques have to be made out in both words and figures.* ◊ **double, single 2.** the shape of a person ○ *the figures at the front of the painting* ○ *We could see some figures through the mist.* ■ *verb especially US* to consider or think something ○ *I figure the costs will be high.* ○ *We figured that you'd be late because of the show.* ○ *Had you figured on being there before two o'clock?*

figure out *phrasal verb* to try to think of an answer to a problem ○ *Try to figure out the answer yourself, instead of asking someone else.*

file /faɪl/ *noun* **1.** a metal tool used for making rough surfaces smooth ○ *Use a file to round off the edges of the metal.* **2.** a container similar to an envelope, used for keeping documents in ○ *When you have finished with the papers, put them back in the file.* ○ *The police have a file on him.* **3.** a set of information held in a computer ○ *Type the name of the file and then press 'enter'.*

fill /fɪl/ *verb* to make something full; to become full ○ *He filled the bottle with*

water. ○ *She was filling the boxes with presents.* ○ *The bucket filled slowly.*

fill out *phrasal verb* to write in all the empty spaces on a form ○ *Could you please fill out this form?*

fill up *phrasal verb* to make something completely full; to become completely full ○ *He filled the bottle up with fresh water.*

film /fɪlm/ *noun* **1.** moving pictures shown at a cinema or on TV ○ *Have you seen this old Laurel and Hardy film?* ○ *We've seen the film already on TV.* **2.** a roll of material which you put into a camera to take photographs or to record moving pictures ○ *I must buy another film before the wedding.* ○ *Do you want a colour film or a black and white one?* **3.** a thin layer of something ○ *A film of grease had formed on the walls around the oven.* ■ *verb* to take pictures of something or someone with a camera ○ *Security cameras filmed him robbing the bank.* ○ *'Star Wars' was filmed in 1977.*

filthy /ˈfɪlθi/ *adjective* very dirty ○ *Your hands are absolutely filthy!* (NOTE: **filthier – filthiest**)

fin /fɪn/ *noun* a thin part on the body of a fish which sticks out and helps it to swim ○ *From the beach they could see a shark's fin in the sea.*

final /ˈfaɪn(ə)l/ *adjective* last; coming at the end ○ *This is your final warning – if your work doesn't improve you will have to go.* ○ *The competition is in its final stages.* ■ *noun* the last competition in a series between several teams or competitors ○ *I thought they would win a couple of rounds, but I never imagined they would get to the final.*

finally /ˈfaɪn(ə)li/ *adverb* at last; in the end ○ *The police finally cleared up the mystery.* ○ *The little boy finally turned up in Edinburgh.*

finance /ˈfaɪnæns/ *noun* money, especially money which belongs to the public or to a company ○ *How are you going to raise the finance for the project?* ○ *My finances are in a poor state at the moment.* ■ *verb* to provide money for something ○ *How are you going to finance your course at university if you* *don't have a grant?* ○ *The redevelopment of the city centre is being financed locally.*

financial /faɪˈnænʃəl/ *adjective* relating to money ○ *What is our financial position?* ○ *The company has got into financial difficulties.*

find /faɪnd/ *verb* **1.** to see where something hidden or lost is after looking for it ○ *I found a £2 coin behind the sofa.* ○ *Did she find the book she was looking for?* **2.** to discover something which was not known before ○ *No one has found a cure for the common cold yet.* (NOTE: **finds – finding – found** /faʊnd/)

find out *phrasal verb* to discover information ○ *I found out something very interesting last night.* ○ *Where can I find out about my family's history?*

fine /faɪn/ *adjective* **1.** (of the weather) dry and sunny ○ *We'll go for a walk tomorrow if the weather stays fine.* ○ *Let's hope it's fine for the village fair next week.* **2.** well; healthy ○ *I was ill in bed yesterday, but today I'm feeling fine.* **3.** with no problems ○ *How are things at home? – Fine!* **4.** acceptable ○ *It's fine to wear casual clothes for this meeting.* **5.** very thin or very small ○ *Use a sharp pencil if you want to draw fine lines.* ○ *I can't read the notice – the print is too fine.* ■ *adverb* satisfactorily or well ○ *It's working fine.* ■ *noun* money which you have to pay as a punishment for having done something wrong ○ *I had to pay a £25 fine for parking in a No Parking area.* ■ *verb* to make someone pay money as a punishment for having done something wrong ○ *He was fined £25 for parking on double yellow lines.*

finger /ˈfɪŋɡə/ *noun* **1.** one of the parts at the end of your hand, sometimes not including the thumb ○ *He wears a ring on his little finger.* ○ *He pressed the button with his finger.* **2.** one of the parts of a glove that cover the fingers ○ *I must mend my glove – there's a hole in one of the fingers.* ○ *Gloves without fingers are called 'mittens'.* **3.** a piece of food shaped like a finger ○ *a box of chocolate fingers*

fingernail /ˈfɪŋɡəneɪl/ *noun* the hard thin part covering the end of a finger

finish /ˈfɪnɪʃ/ *verb* **1.** to do something completely ○ *Haven't you finished your homework yet?* ○ *Tell me when you've finished reading the paper.* ○ *You can't go out until you've finished doing the washing up.* **2.** to come to an end ○ *The game will finish at about four o'clock.*

finish up *phrasal verb* **1.** to be somewhere in the end ○ *We got lost and finished up miles from our hotel.* **2.** to eat something completely ○ *You must finish up all your vegetables.*

fir /fɜː/ *noun* □ **fir tree** a tree with needle-shaped leaves ○ *Fir trees are often used as Christmas trees.*

fire /faɪə/ *noun* **1.** something which is burning and gives off heat ○ *They burnt the dead leaves on a fire in the garden.* **2.** something which heats ○ *We have an electric fire in the living room.* **3.** an emergency in which something such as a building burns ○ *They lost all their belongings in the fire.* **4.** shooting with guns ○ *The soldiers came under fire.* ■ *verb* **1.** to shoot a gun ○ *The gunmen fired at the police car.* ○ *We could hear guns firing in the distance.* **2.** to tell someone that they must leave their job because of something wrong they have done ○ *She was fired for being late.*

fireplace /ˈfaɪəpleɪs/ *noun* a hole in the wall of a room where you can light a fire for heating

firework /ˈfaɪəwɜːk/ *noun* a small tube holding chemicals which will shine brightly or explode when lit

firm /fɜːm/ *adjective* **1.** solid or fixed ○ *Make sure that the ladder is firm before you climb up.* ○ *My back hurts – I think I need a firmer mattress.* **2.** strong; likely to change ○ *There is no firm evidence that he stole the money.* ○ *She is a firm believer in hard work.* ■ *noun* a business or company ○ *When he retired, the firm presented him with a watch.* ○ *The firm I work for was taken over last year.*

firmly /ˈfɜːmli/ *adverb* in a firm way

firmness /ˈfɜːmnəs/ *noun* **1.** the quality of being strong or firm **2.** determination

first /fɜːst/ *noun* number 1 in a series ○ *Our house is the first on the left.* ■ *adjective* relating to number 1 in a series ○

That was the first time I ever saw him. (NOTE: As a number can be written **1st**.) ■ *adverb* **1.** at the beginning ○ *She came first in the exam.* **2.** before doing anything else ○ *Wash your hands first, and then you can eat.* ◇ **at first** at the beginning ○ *At first he didn't like the work, but later he got used to it.* ◇ **first come, first served** dealing with things such as requests in the order in which they are received ○ *Applications will be dealt with on a first come, first served basis.*

first aid /ˌfɜːst 'eɪd/ *noun* the help given to a person who is hurt before a doctor or the emergency services arrive

first-class /ˌfɜːst 'klɑːs/ *adjective* **1.** very good quality ○ *You can get a first-class meal in that hotel.* **2.** using the most expensive seats on a plane or train ○ *Can I have a first-class return to Paris, please?*

fish /fɪʃ/ *noun* an animal which lives in water and swims; it has fins and no legs, ○ *I sat by the river all day and only caught two little fish.* ■ *verb* to try to catch a fish ○ *We often go fishing in the lake.* ○ *They fished all day but didn't catch anything.*

fishing /'fɪʃɪŋ/ *noun* the sport or industry of catching fish

fist /fɪst/ *noun* a tightly closed hand

fit /fɪt/ *noun* a sudden sharp attack of illness, or of an emotion such as anger ○ *She had a coughing fit* or *a fit of coughing.* ○ *In a fit of anger he threw the plate across the kitchen.* ○ *She's having one of her periodic fits of efficiency.* ■ *adjective* healthy and having a lot of physical energy ○ *He isn't fit enough to go back to work.* ○ *You'll have to get fit if you're going to run in that race.* ■ *verb* to be the right size or shape ○ *He's grown so tall that his jackets don't fit him any more.* ○ *These shoes don't fit me – they're a size too small.* (NOTE: **fits – fitting – fitted**)

fitness /'fɪtnəs/ *noun* **1.** being physically fit ○ *She does fitness exercises every morning.* ○ *Physical fitness is important in the marines.* **2.** being suitable ○ *Doubts were expressed about her fitness for the job.*

five /faɪv/ *noun* the number 5

fix /fɪks/ *verb* **1.** to fasten or to attach one thing to another ○ *Fix one end of the cord to the tree and the other to the fence.* **2.** to organise a time for something such as a meeting ○ *We'll try to fix a time for the meeting.* **3.** to repair something ○ *The telephone people are coming to fix the telephone.* ○ *Someone's coming to fix the telephone this afternoon.* ○ *Can you fix the dishwasher?* ○ *Does anyone know how to fix the photocopier?*

fixed /fɪkst/ *adjective* attached firmly ○ *The sign is fixed to the post with nails.*

fizzy /'fɪzi/ *adjective* full of small balls of gas (NOTE: Drinks which are not fizzy are **still**. A drink which is no longer fizzy is **flat**.)

flag /flæg/ *noun* a piece of brightly coloured material with the symbol of a country or an organisation on it ○ *The French flag has blue, red and white stripes.* ○ *The ship was flying the British flag.* ○ *The flags were blowing in the wind.*

flake /fleɪk/ *noun* **1.** a small, very thin piece of something ○ *The paint came off in little flakes.* **2.** a small piece of snow which falls from the sky ○ *Snow fell in large soft flakes all night.*

flame /fleɪm/ *noun* a brightly burning part of a fire, or the light that burns on a candle ○ *Flames could be seen coming out of the upstairs windows.*

flap /flæp/ *noun* a flat part which is attached to an object and has a special type of fastening allowing it to move up and down ○ *The pilot tested the wing flaps before taking off.* ■ *verb* to move up and down like a bird's wing ○ *Flags were flapping in the breeze.* ○ *The swans stood by the edge of the water, flapping their wings.* (NOTE: **flaps – flapping – flapped**)

flash /flæʃ/ *noun* **1.** a short sudden burst of light ○ *Flashes of lightning lit up the sky.* **2.** a piece of equipment used for making a bright light, allowing you to take photographs in the dark ○ *People sometimes have red eyes in photos taken with a flash.* ■ *verb* **1.** to light up quickly and suddenly ○ *Lightning flashed all around.* **2.** to move or to pass by quickly ○ *The champion flashed past to win in record time.*

flat /flæt/ *adjective* **1.** level, not sloping or curved ○ *a house with a flat roof* **2.** (*of a battery*) with no electric power left ○ *The car wouldn't start because the battery was flat.* ■ *noun* a set of rooms on one floor, usually in a building with several similar sets of rooms ○ *They live in the block of flats next to the underground station.* ○ *Their flat is on the ground floor.*

flatten /'flæt(ə)n/ *verb* to make flat

flatter /'flætə/ *verb* to praise in order to please them ○ *Just flatter the boss a bit, tell him how good his golf is, and he'll give you a rise.*

flavor /'fleɪvə/ *noun, verb* US spelling of **flavour**

flavour /'fleɪvə/ *noun* a particular taste ○ *The tomato soup had an unusual flavour.* ○ *What flavour of ice cream do you want?* ■ *verb* to add things such as salt or pepper to food, to give it a special taste ○ *soup flavoured with herbs* ○ *Use rosemary to flavour lamb.*

flee /fli:/ *verb* to run away from something ○ *As the fighting spread, the village people fled into the jungle.* ○ *She tried to flee but her foot was caught in the rope.* (NOTE: Do not confuse with **flea**. Note also: **flees – fleeing – fled** /fled/.)

fleeting /'fli:tɪŋ/ *adjective* lasting for a very short time only ○ *She only caught a fleeting glimpse of the princess.*

flesh /fleʃ/ *noun* **1.** a soft part of the body covering the bones **2.** a soft part of a fruit ○ *a melon with pink flesh* (NOTE: no plural) ◇ **in the flesh** not on TV or in photographs, but here and now ○ *It was strange to see the TV newsreader in the flesh.*

flew /flu:/ past tense of **fly**

flight /flaɪt/ *noun* a journey in a plane ○ *Go to gate 25 for flight AB198.* ○ *All flights to Paris have been cancelled.* ○ *She sat next to me on a flight to Montreal.*

flimsy /'flɪmzi/ *adjective* likely to break because of being badly made ○ *The shelter was a flimsy construction of branches covered with grass and leaves.*

fling /flɪŋ/ *verb* to throw something carelessly and with a lot of force ○ *He flung the empty bottle into the sea.* (NOTE: **flings – flinging – flung**)

float /fləʊt/ *verb* **1.** to lie on the top of a liquid ○ *Dead fish were floating in the river.* **2.** to put something on the top of a liquid ○ *He floated a paper boat on the lake.*

flock /flɒk/ *noun* a group of similar animals together ○ *a flock of birds* ○ *A flock of sheep were grazing on the hillside.* (NOTE: **flock** is usually used with sheep, goats, and birds such as hens or geese. For cattle, the word to use is **herd**.) ■ *verb* to move in large numbers ○ *Tourists flocked to see the changing of the guard.* ○ *Holidaymakers have been flocking to the resorts on the south coast.*

flood /flʌd/ *noun* a large amount of water over an area of land which is usually dry ○ *The floods were caused by heavy rain.* ■ *verb* **1.** to cover something with water ○ *They are going to build a dam and flood the valley.* ○ *Fields were flooded after the river burst its banks.* ○ *He forgot to turn the tap off and flooded the bathroom.* **2.** to become covered with water ○ *She left the tap on and the bathroom flooded.* **3.** to come in large numbers ○ *The office was flooded with complaints.* or *Complaints came flooding into the office.*

floor /flɔ:/ *noun* **1.** the part of a room on which you walk ○ *He put the books in a pile on the floor.* ○ *If there are no empty chairs left, you'll have to sit on the floor.* **2.** all the rooms on one level in a building ○ *The bathroom is on the ground floor.* ○ *His office is on the fifth floor.* ○ *There is a good view of the town from the top floor.*

flop /flɒp/ *noun* something that is not successful ○ *His new play was a complete flop and closed after only ten performances.* ○ *The film was a big hit in New York but it was a flop in London.* ■ *verb* **1.** to fall or sit down suddenly, with your body relaxed ○ *She got back from the sales and flopped down on the sofa.* **2.** to be unsuccessful ○ *The play was a big hit on Broadway but it flopped in London.* (NOTE: **flops – flopping – flopped**)

flour /flaʊə/ *noun* wheat grain crushed to powder, used for making food such as bread or cakes

flourish /'flʌrɪʃ/ *verb* **1.** to grow well; to be successful ○ *Palms flourish in hot countries.* **2.** to wave something in the air ○ *She came in with a big smile, flourishing a cheque.*

flow /fləʊ/ *verb* to move along smoothly ○ *The river flows into the sea.* ○ *Traffic on the motorway is flowing smoothly.* ■ *noun* the movement of things such as liquid or air, or of people ○ *She tried to stop the flow of blood with a tight bandage.* ○ *There was a steady flow of visitors to the exhibition.*

flower /'flaʊə/ *noun* the colourful part of a plant, which attracts insects and produces fruit or seeds ○ *a plant with bright yellow flowers* □ **in flower** covered with flowers ○ *Go to Japan when the cherry trees are in flower.* ■ *verb* to produce flowers ○ *a plant which flowers in early summer* ○ *The cherry trees flowered very late this year.*

flown /fləʊn/ past participle of **fly**

flu /fluː/ *noun* a common illness like a bad cold, often with a high temperature

fluid /'fluːɪd/ *noun* a liquid ○ *You need to drink plenty of fluids in hot weather.*

flung /flʌŋ/ past tense and past participle of **fling**

fly /flaɪ/ *noun* a small insect with wings which eats food and spreads diseases ○ *He tried to kill the fly with a newspaper.* ○ *Cover the food to protect it from flies.* ■ *verb* **1.** to move through the air using wings ○ *When the cat came into the garden, the birds flew away.* ○ *Some birds fly to Africa for the winter.* **2.** to travel in a plane ○ *I'm flying to China next week.* ○ *He flies across the Atlantic twice a month.* **3.** to be quick ○ *I must fly if I want to get home by 6 o'clock.* (NOTE: **flies – flying – flew** /fluː/ – **has flown** /fləʊn/) ◇ **time flies** time passes

quickly ○ *His daughter is already two – how time flies!*

flying /'flaɪɪŋ/ *adjective* flying in the air ○ *flying ants* ■ *noun* the act of travelling in a plane ○ *He has a fear of flying.*

foam /fəʊm/ *noun* a mass of small bubbles ○ *This soap makes a large amount of foam.*

fog /fɒg/ *noun* a thick mist made up of many tiny drops of water

fold /fəʊld/ *noun* a piece of something such as cloth or skin which hangs down loosely ○ *She wanted the surgeon to remove the folds of skin under her chin.* ■ *verb* to bend something such as a piece of paper so that one part is on top of the other ○ *Fold the piece of paper in half.* ○ *He folded the newspaper and put it into his briefcase.*

folder /'fəʊldə/ *noun* an envelope made of thin card or plastic and used for holding papers

folk /fəʊk/ *noun* people (NOTE: **Folk** takes a plural verb. The plural form **folks** is also used.)

follow /'fɒləʊ/ *verb* **1.** to come after or behind someone or something ○ *What letter follows B in the alphabet?* ○ *The dog followed me all the way home.* **2.** to walk or drive behind someone, e.g. in order to see where they are going ○ *I had the impression I was being followed.* **3.** to do what someone tells you to do ○ *She followed the instructions on the tin of paint.* ○ *He made the cake following a recipe in the newspaper.* ◇ **follow suit** to do what someone else does ○ *She jumped into the pool and everyone else followed suit.*

follower /'fɒləʊə/ *noun* a supporter

following /'fɒləʊɪŋ/ *adjective* which comes next ○ *They arrived on Friday and the following day she became ill.* ○ *Look at the following picture.* ■ *preposition* after ○ *Following his death, his son sold the family house.*

fond /fɒnd/ *adjective* liking someone or something ○ *I'm fond of my sister's children.* ○ *Michael's very fond of playing golf.*

fondly /'fɒndli/ *adverb* in a way which shows you are fond of someone or something

food /fuːd/ *noun* things which you eat ○ *This hotel is famous for its good food.* ○ *Do you like German food?*

foolish /'fuːlɪʃ/ *adjective* showing a lack of intelligence or good judgment ○ *That was a rather foolish thing to do.* ○ *I felt rather foolish.*

foot /fʊt/ *noun* **1.** the part at the end of your leg on which you stand ○ *She has very small feet.* ○ *Watch out, you trod on my foot!* □ **on foot** walking ○ *They completed the rest of the journey on foot.* **2.** the bottom part; the end ○ *There is a door at the foot of the stairs.* ○ *There are traffic lights at the foot of the hill.* ○ *Sign the document at the foot of the page.* **3.** a unit of measurement equal to about 30 centimetres ○ *The table is four foot or four feet long.* ○ *She's almost six foot tall.* ○ *I'm five foot seven (5' 7").* ◊ **inch** (NOTE: The plural is **feet**. As a measurement **foot** often has no plural form: *six foot tall*; *three foot wide*. With numbers **foot** is also often written with the symbol ' *a 6' ladder*; *he is 5' 6*: say 'he's five foot six'.)

football /'fʊtbɔːl/ *noun* **1.** a game played between two teams of eleven players with a round ball which can be kicked or headed, but not carried ○ *They went to a football match.* ○ *The children were playing football in the street.* ○ *Let's have a game of football.* ○ *He spends all his time watching football on TV.* ○ *He's got a new pair of football boots.* **2.** a ball used for kicking; the ball used in the various games of football ○ *They were kicking a football around in the street.*

footballer /'fʊtbɔːlə/ *noun* a person who plays football

footprint /'fʊtprɪnt/ *noun* a mark left by someone's foot on the ground ○ *They followed the footprints in the snow to the cave.*

footstep /'fʊtstep/ *noun* a sound made by a foot touching the ground ○ *We heard soft footsteps along the corridor.*

for /fə, fɔː/ *preposition* **1.** showing the purpose or use of something ○ *This plastic bag is for the apples.* ○ *What's that key for?* **2.** showing the occasion on which or the reason why something is given ○ *What did you get for your birthday?* ○ *What did you win for coming first?* **3.** showing the person who receives something ○ *There was no mail for you this morning.* ○ *I'm making a cup of tea for my mother.* **4.** showing how long something takes ○ *He has gone to France for two days.* ○ *We've been waiting here for hours.* **5.** showing distance ○ *You can see for miles from the top of the hill.* ○ *The motorway goes for kilometres without any service stations.* **6.** showing where someone or something is going ○ *Is this the plane for Edinburgh?* ○ *When is the next bus for Oxford Circus?* **7.** in the place of someone ○ *Can you write this letter for me?*

forbid /fə'bɪd/ *verb* to tell someone that they are not allowed to do something ○ *The staff are forbidden to use the front entrance.* (NOTE: **forbids – forbidding – forbade** /fə'bæd/ – **forbidden** /fə'bɪd(ə)n/)

force /fɔːs/ *noun* **1.** strength or power ○ *The force of the wind blew tiles off the roof.* ○ *The police had to use force to restrain the crowd.* **2.** an organised group of people ○ *He served in the police force for twenty years.* ■ *verb* to make someone do something ○ *He was forced to stop smoking.* ○ *You can't force me to go if I don't want to.*

forecast /'fɔːkɑːst/ *noun* what you think will happen in the future ○ *His forecast of sales turned out to be completely accurate.* ■ *verb* to say what will happen in the future ○ *They are forecasting storms for the south coast.* ○ *They forecast a rise in the number of tourists.* (NOTE: **forecasts – forecasting – forecast**)

foreground /'fɔːgraʊnd/ *noun* a part of a picture which seems nearest the front

forehead /'fɔːhed/ *noun* the part of the front of the head above the eyes and below the line of the hair

foreign /'fɒrɪn/ *adjective* not from your own country ○ *There are lots of foreign medical students at our college.*

foreigner /'fɒrɪnə/ *noun* a person who does not come from the same country as you

forest /'fɒrɪst/ *noun* a large area covered with trees ○ *The country is covered with thick forests.* ○ *In dry weather there's a danger of forest fires.* ○ *In winter bears come out of the forest to search for food.*

forever /fɔːr'evə/, **for ever** /fər 'evə/ *adverb* **1.** always in the future ○ *I will love you forever.* **2.** a very long time ○ *It took us forever to get to the hotel.*

forget /fə'get/ *verb* **1.** not to remember ○ *He's forgotten the name of the restaurant.* ○ *I've forgotten how to play chess.* ○ *She forgot all about her doctor's appointment.* **2.** to leave something behind ○ *When he left the office he forgot his car keys.* (NOTE: **forgets – forgetting – forgot** /fə'gɒt/ **– has forgotten** /fə'gɒtən/)

forgive /fə'gɪv/ *verb* to stop being angry with someone ○ *Don't worry about it – I forgive you!* ○ *Will she ever forgive me for forgetting her birthday?* (NOTE: **forgives – forgiving – forgave** /fə'geɪv/ **– has forgiven**)

forgot /fə'gɒt/ past tense of **forget**

forgotten /fə'gɒt(ə)n/ past participle of **forget**

fork /fɔːk/ *noun* an object with a handle at one end and several sharp points at the other, used for picking up food and putting it in your mouth ○ *Don't try to eat Chinese food with a knife and fork.* ○ *It's polite to use a fork to eat cake – don't use your fingers.* ■ *verb* to become two parts ○ *The railway line forks at Crewe and one branch goes to the coast.*

form /fɔːm/ *noun* **1.** an official paper with spaces, in which you are asked to write information such as your name and address ? Could you please fill in this form with your details? **2.** a state or condition ○ *Their team wasn't in top form and lost.* □ **in good form** in a good mood; well ○ *She's in good form today.* **3.** a class, usually in a secondary school ○ *She's in the third form.* ■ *verb* **1.** to sit or stand with others so as to make a particular shape ○ *The children formed a circle.* ○ *Form a queue here, please.* **2.** □ **formed of** made of ○ *The team is formed of ex-students.*

formal /'fɔːm(ə)l/ *adjective* **1.** done according to certain rules ○ *The formal opening ceremony was performed by the mayor.* **2.** serious in style; suitable for special or official occasions ○ *'Good afternoon' is a formal way of saying 'Hello' in the afternoon.*

formally /'fɔːməli/ *adverb* according to rules; done or spoken in a serious way

formation /fɔː'meɪʃ(ə)n/ *noun* the act of forming something ○ *The formation of ice occurs at temperatures below zero.*

former /'fɔːmə/ *adjective* referring to a person's or a thing's job or position at an earlier time ○ *a former army officer* ○ *The former champion came last in the race.*

formerly /'fɔːməli/ *adverb* at an earlier time ○ *He was formerly head of our department.*

fort /fɔːt/ *noun* a strong army building which can be defended against enemy attacks ○ *The soldiers rode out of the fort.* ○ *He was posted to a fort in the desert.*

forth /fɔːθ/ *adverb* forwards

fortieth /'fɔːtiəθ/ *adjective* relating to the number 40 in a series ○ *her fortieth birthday* ○ *He came fortieth and last in the race.* ○ *It's her fortieth birthday tomorrow.*

fortnight /'fɔːtnaɪt/ *noun* two weeks (NOTE: not used in US English)

fortunate /'fɔːtʃənət/ *adjective* having better things happen to you than happen to other people ○ *You are very fortunate to have such a lovely family.*

fortunately /'fɔːtʃənətli/ *adverb* by good luck ○ *Fortunately, he had remembered to take an umbrella.* ○ *He was late getting to the airport, but fortunately the flight had been delayed.*

fortune /'fɔːtʃən/ *noun* **1.** a large amount of money ○ *He won a fortune on the lottery.* ○ *She made a fortune on* the stock market. ○ *She left her fortune to her three children.* **2.** what will happen in the future ○ *She claims to be able to tell your fortune using cards.*

forty /'fɔːti/ *noun* the number 40 ○ *She's forty (years old).* ○ *He has more than forty pairs of shoes.* □ **forties** the numbers between 40 and 49

forward /'fɔːwəd/ *adjective* confident ○ *She was always very forward as a child.* ■ *adverb* **1.** in the direction that someone or something is facing ○ *She bent forward to hear what he had to say.* ○ *He took two steps forward.* ○ *The policeman made a sign with his hand and the cars began to go forward.* **2.** towards the future ○ *We need to do some forward planning.* □ **to look forward to something** to think happily about something which is going to happen ○ *I'm looking forward to my holidays.* ○ *He isn't looking forward to his exams.* ○ *I'm looking forward to seeing her again.* ■ *noun* a player in a team whose job is to attack the other side ○ *The England defence came under attack from the other team's forwards.*

forwards /'fɔːwədz/ *adverb* in the direction that someone or something is facing ○ *She bent forwards to hear what he had to say.* ○ *He took two steps forwards.* ○ *The policeman made a sign with his hand and the cars began to go forwards.*

fossil /'fɒs(ə)l/ *noun* the mark of an animal or plant left in a rock, formed over millions of years

fought /fɔːt/ past tense and past participle of **fight**

foul /faʊl/ *adjective* **1.** smelling or tasting unpleasant ○ *A foul-smelling drain ran down the centre of the street.* **2.** very unpleasant ○ *What foul weather we're having!* ○ *The boss has been in a foul temper all day.* ■ *noun* an action which is against the rules of a game ○ *The referee gave a free kick for a foul on the goalkeeper.* ○ *Look at the action replay to see if it really was a foul.* (NOTE: Do not confuse with **fowl**.) ■ *verb* to do something to another player which is against the rules of a game ○ *He was*

fouled inside the penalty box so the ref gave a penalty.

found /faʊnd/ *verb* to establish something; to begin something ○ *The business was founded in 1900.* ■ past tense and past participle of **find**

foundation /faʊn'deɪʃ(ə)n/ *noun* **1.** the act of establishing something or of setting something up ○ *Ever since its foundation in 1892, the company has been a great success.* **2.** a charitable organisation which provides money for certain projects ○ *a foundation for educational research*

fountain /'faʊntɪn/ *noun* an object or a structure with a pump which makes a stream of water come out, usually found in a street or a large garden

four /fɔː/ *noun* the number 4 ○ *A square has four corners.* ○ *He's four (years old).* ○ *I have an appointment with the doctor at four (o'clock).*

fourteen /ˌfɔː'tiːn/ *noun* the number 14 ○ *There are fourteen houses in our street.* ○ *He's fourteen (years old) next week.*

fourteenth /ˌfɔː'tiːnθ/ *adjective, noun* relating to the number 14 in a series ○ *She came fourteenth in the race.* ○ *The fourteenth of July* or *July the fourteenth (July 14th).* ○ *It was her fourteenth birthday yesterday.*

fourth /fɔːθ/ *adjective* referring to 4 ○ *the fourth of October* or *October the fourth (October 4th)* ○ *This is the fourth time he's had to go to hospital this year.* ○ *It's her fourth birthday tomorrow.* ■ number 14 in a series ○ *I've had so many letters – this is the fourteenth.*

fox /fɒks/ *noun* a wild animal with reddish fur and a long thick tail (NOTE: The plural is **foxes**.)

fraction /'frækʃən/ *noun* **1.** (*in mathematics*) a unit that is less than a whole number ○ *0.25 and 0.5 are ¼ and ½ expressed as fractions.* **2.** a small part of something ○ *Only a fraction of the stolen money was ever found.*

fracture /'fræktʃə/ *noun* a break, especially in a bone ○ *The X-ray showed up the fracture clearly.* ■ *verb* to break a bone ○ *He fractured his leg in the acci-*

dent. ○ *They put her fractured leg in plaster.*

fragile /'frædʒaɪl/ *adjective* made from materials that are easily broken ○ *Be careful when you're packing these plates – they're very fragile.*

fragment /'frægmənt/ *noun* a small piece ○ *When digging on the site of the house they found fragments of very old glass.*

frail /freɪl/ *adjective* physically weak, especially because of age ○ *His grandmother is now rather frail.*

frame /freɪm/ *noun* a border around something such as a pair of glasses, a picture, a mirror or a window ○ *He has glasses with gold frames.* ○ *I think the frame is worth more than the painting.* ■ *verb* to put a frame round a picture ○ *The photograph has been framed in red.*

free /friː/ *adjective* **1.** not costing any money ○ *Send in four tokens from cereal boxes and you can get a free toy.* ○ *I got a free ticket for the exhibition.* **2.** not busy; available ○ *Will you be free next Tuesday?* ○ *There is a table free in the corner of the restaurant.* ○ *Do you have any free time next week?* **3.** able to do what you want; not forced to do anything ○ *He's free to do what he wants.* **4.** not in prison or a cage ○ *After six years in prison he's a free man again.* □ **to set someone *or* something free** to allow someone to leave prison, or to let an animal out of a cage ○ *The young birds were raised in the zoo and then set free in the wild.* ■ *verb* to release someone who is trapped ○ *It took the fire service some time to free the passengers in the bus.* (NOTE: **frees – freeing – freed**)

freedom /'friːdəm/ *noun* **1.** the state of being free, rather than being forced to stay somewhere or being in prison ○ *She felt a sense of freedom being in the country after working all week in the city.* ○ *His lawyer pleaded for his client's freedom.* **2.** the state of being allowed to do what you want ○ *They are trying to restrict our freedom of movement.*

freeze /friːz/ *verb* **1.** (*of a liquid*) to become solid because of the cold ○ *The winter was mild, and for the first time*

ever *the river did not freeze over.* ○ *It's so cold that the lake has frozen solid.* **2.** to make food very cold so that it does not decay ○ *We froze the raspberries we picked this morning.* **3.** to become very cold ○ *The forecast is that it will freeze tonight.* ○ *Put a hat on or you'll freeze!* (NOTE: **freezes – freezing – froze** /frəʊz/ – **has frozen**)

freezer /'friːzə/ *noun* a piece of equipment like a large box, which is very cold inside, used for freezing food and keeping it frozen

freezing /'friːzɪŋ/ *adjective* very cold

French /frentʃ/ *adjective* referring to France ■ *noun* the language spoken in France

frequency /'friːkwənsi/ *noun* the number of times that something happens over a particular period of time ○ *The government is becoming alarmed at the frequency of accidents in the construction industry.* (NOTE: no plural)

frequent /'friːkwənt/ *adjective* happening or appearing often ○ *He was a frequent visitor to the library.* ○ *Skin cancer is becoming more frequent.* ○ *How frequent are the planes to Birmingham?*

frequently /'friːkwəntli/ *adverb* often ○ *The ferries don't run as frequently in the winter.* ○ *She could frequently be seen walking her dog in the park.*

fresh /freʃ/ *adjective* **1.** not used or not dirty ○ *I'll get you a fresh towel.* **2.** made recently ○ *a basket of fresh rolls* ○ *Let's ask for a pot of fresh coffee.* **3.** new and different ○ *The police produced some fresh evidence.* **4.** (*of food*) not in a tin or frozen ○ *Fresh fruit salad is better than tinned.* ○ *Fresh vegetables are difficult to get in winter.*

Friday /'fraɪdeɪ/ *noun* the fifth day of the week, the day between Thursday and Saturday ○ *We all had a meal together last Friday.* ○ *We always go to the cinema on Friday evenings.* ○ *We normally have our meetings on Fridays.* ○ *Friday is a day of rest for Muslims.* ○ *Today is Friday, June 20th.*

fridge /frɪdʒ/ *noun* a kitchen machine for keeping things cold ○ *The fridge is emp-*

ty – we must buy some more food. ○ Shall I put the milk back in the fridge?

fried /fraɪd/ past tense and past participle of **fry** ■ *adjective* cooked in oil or fat

friend /frend/ *noun* a person that you know well and like ○ *She's my best friend.* ○ *We're going on holiday with some friends from work.*

friendly /'frendli/ *adjective* pleasant and kind, wanting to make friends ○ *Don't be frightened of the dog – he's very friendly.* ○ *We're not on friendly terms with the people who live next door.* (NOTE: **friendlier – friendliest**)

friendship /'frendʃɪp/ *noun* the state of being friends ○ *He formed several lasting friendships at school.*

fries /fraɪz/ 3rd person singular present of **fry**

fright /fraɪt/ *noun* fear

frighten /'fraɪt(ə)n/ *verb* to make someone afraid ○ *Take off that horrible mask – you'll frighten the children.* ○ *The cat has frightened all the birds away.*

frightened /'fraɪt(ə)nd/ *adjective* afraid ○ *The frightened children ran out of the building.*

frightening /'fraɪt(ə)nɪŋ/ *adjective* making you feel afraid ○ *a frightening sound of footsteps in the corridor* ○ *He had a frightening thought – what if no one heard his cries for help?*

frog /frɒg/ *noun* a small greenish-brown animal with long legs, which jumps, and lives both on land and in water ○ *He kept some tadpoles in a jar hoping they would turn into frogs.* ○ *Can you hear the frogs croaking round the pond?*

from /frəm, frɒm/ *preposition* **1.** away **2.** showing the place where something starts or started ○ *He comes from Germany.* ○ *The bees went from flower to flower.* ○ *We've had a letter from the bank.* ○ *He read the book from beginning to end.* ○ *Take three from four and you get one.* ○ *I took a book from the pile on his desk.* **3.** showing the time when something starts or started ○ *I'll be at home from 8 o'clock onwards.* ○ *The hours of work are 9.30 to 5.30, from Monday to Friday.* ○ *From now on I'm going to get up early.* **4.** showing dis-

tance ○ *It is not far from here to the railway station.* **5.** showing difference ○ *Can you tell butter from margarine?* ○ *His job is totally different from mine.* **6.** showing a cause ○ *He died from the injuries he received in the accident.* ○ *He suffers from angina.* ○ *She suffers from coughs every winter.*

front /frʌnt/ *noun* a part of something which is furthest forward ○ *The front of the house is on London Road.* ○ *She spilt coffee down the front of her dress.* ■ *adjective* which is in front ○ *She sat in the front seat, next to the driver.* ◇ **in front** further forwards ○ *Her mother sat in the back seat and she sat in front.* ◇ **in front of someone or something** before or further forwards than something ○ *Don't stand in front of the car – it may start suddenly.* ○ *There are six people in front of me in the queue.* ○ *You can park your car in front of the shop.*

front door /ˌfrʌnt 'dɔː/ *noun* the main door to a house or building

frost /frɒst/ *noun* **1.** a white covering on the ground that appears when the temperature is below freezing ○ *The garden was white with frost.* **2.** an occasion on which the temperature outside is below freezing ○ *There was a hard frost last night.* ○ *There's a touch of frost in the air.* ○ *A late frost can damage young plants.*

frown /fraʊn/ *verb* to make lines in the skin on your forehead because you are concentrating or worried ○ *He frowned as he tried to do the calculation.* ■ *noun* pulling your eyebrows together as a sign that you are angry or worried ○ *Take that frown off your face – everything's going to be all right.*

frown on *phrasal verb* to disapprove of something ○ *The teachers frown on singing in the corridors.* ○ *The company frowns on people who bring food into the office.*

froze /frəʊz/ past tense of **freeze**

frozen /'frəʊz(ə)n/ past participle of **freeze** ■ *adjective* **1.** very cold ○ *Come inside – you must be frozen out there.* **2.** at a temperature below freezing point ○ *We went skating on the frozen lake.*

fruit /fruːt/ noun a food that grows on trees or plants, which is often eaten raw and is usually sweet ○ You should eat five pieces of fruit or vegetables every day. ○ He has six fruit trees in his garden.

fry /fraɪ/ verb to cook something in oil or fat ○ Fry the onions over a low heat so that they don't burn. ○ Fry the eggs in some fat. (NOTE: **fries** /fraɪz/ – **frying** – **fried** /fraɪd/)

frying pan /'fraɪɪŋ pæn/ noun an open pan with low sides, used for frying

fuel /'fjuːəl/ noun a substance such coal, gas, oil, petrol or wood which can be burnt to give heat or power ○ What fuel do you use to heat the house? ○ We ran out of fuel on the motorway.

fulfil /fʊl'fɪl/ verb to complete something in a satisfactory way ○ He died before he could fulfil his ambition to fly a plane. ○ We are so busy that we cannot fulfil any more orders before Christmas. (NOTE: **fulfilling** – **fulfilled**. The US spelling is **fulfill**.)

full /fʊl/ adjective 1. with as much inside as is possible ○ Is the box full? ○ The bag is full of potatoes. ○ We couldn't get on the first bus because it was full. ○ All the hotels were full. 2. complete ○ You must give the police full details of the accident. ○ Write your full name and address at the top of the paper. ■ adverb completely ○ The story has never been told in full.

full stop /ˌfʊl 'stɒp/ noun a punctuation mark like a small dot, showing the end of a sentence or an abbreviation

fully /'fʊli/ adverb completely ○ He was fully aware that he had made a mistake. ○ She still hasn't fully recovered from her accident. ○ The hotel is fully booked for the Christmas week. ○ When fully grown, an elephant can weigh several tons.

fun /fʌn/ noun enjoyment from an activity ○ Having to stay in bed on my birthday is not much fun. □ **to have fun** to enjoy yourself ○ We had a lot of fun on the river. □ **for fun** as a joke or for enjoyment ○ She poured water down his neck for fun. ○ Just for fun, he drove the car

through town dressed as a gorilla. ○ Why did you do that? – Just for the fun of it! ◇ **to make fun of someone, to poke fun at someone** to laugh at someone ○ Don't make fun of her – she's trying her best. ○ He poked fun at the Prime Minister.

function /'fʌŋkʃən/ noun 1. a party, or a gathering of people ○ We have two wedding functions in the main restaurant this weekend. ○ The Prime Minister busy up with official functions all week. 2. the work done by someone or something ○ The function of a goalkeeper is to stop the ball going into the net. ○ What's the function of that red switch? ■ verb to work ○ The computer is still functioning well after years of use.

fund /fʌnd/ noun an amount of money intended for a particular purpose ○ She contributes to a pension fund. ■ verb to provide money for a special purpose ○ We have asked the government to fund the building of the new library. ○ The company is funding her manager's course.

fundamental /ˌfʌndə'ment(ə)l/ adjective basic; essential ○ The fundamental difference between us is that I apologise for my mistakes and you don't. ○ Good air quality is fundamental for children's health.

funds /fʌndz/ noun money which is available for spending ○ He started a course at college and then ran out of funds. ○ The company has the funds to set up the research programme. ○ Funds are available to get the project off the ground.

funeral /'fjuːn(ə)rəl/ noun a ceremony at which a dead person is buried or cremated ○ The church was packed for her funeral. ○ The funeral will take place on Friday morning.

fungus /'fʌŋɡəs/ noun a plant which has no green leaves or flowers and which lives on decaying matter or on other plants (NOTE: The plural is **fungi** /'fʌŋɡaɪ/.)

funnel /'fʌn(ə)l/ noun a tube with a wide opening and a narrow tube, used when pouring liquids from one container into another

funny /'fʌni/ *adjective* **1.** making people laugh ○ *He made funny faces and all the children laughed.* ○ *That joke isn't funny.* **2.** strange ○ *She's been behaving in a funny way recently.* ○ *There's a funny smell in the bathroom.* (NOTE: **funnier – funniest**)

fur /fɜː/ *noun* the soft covering of an animal's body ○ *This type of cat has very short fur.* ○ *She was wearing a fur coat.* ○ *Have you got any fur-lined boots?* (NOTE: Do not confuse with **fir**.)

furious /'fjʊəriəs/ *adjective* very angry

furniture /'fɜːnɪtʃə/ *noun* objects in, e.g. a house or an office such as tables, chairs, beds and cupboards ○ *The burglars stole all our office furniture.* ○ *You should cover up all the furniture before you start painting the ceiling.* (NOTE: no plural: *some furniture; a lot of furniture; a piece of furniture*)

furry /'fɜːri/ *adjective* covered with fur

further /'fɜːðə/ *adverb* at or to a greater distance ○ *Can you all move further back – I can't get you in the picture.* ○ *The police station is quite close, but the post office is further away.* ○ *Edinburgh is further from London than Newcastle.* ■ *adjective* more ○ *The bank needs further information about your salary.* ○ *Please send me further details of holidays in Greece.*

furthest /'fɜːðəst/ *adverb, adjective* at or to the greatest distance ○ *Some of the staff live quite close to the office – James lives furthest away.* ○ *The furthest distance I have ever flown is to Hong Kong.*

fury /'fjʊəri/ *noun* very strong anger ○ *He shouted at us in fury.*

fuse /fjuːz/ *noun* a small piece of wire in an electrical system which breaks if too much power tries to pass through it, so preventing further damage ○ *The plug has a 13-amp fuse.* ○ *If the lights go out, the first thing to do is to check the fuses.*

fuss /fʌs/ *noun* unnecessary excitement or complaints ○ *What's all the fuss about?*

future /'fjuːtʃə/ *noun* a time which has not yet happened ○ *What are his plans for the future?* ○ *You never know what the future will bring.* ○ *Can you imagine what London will be like in the future?* ■ *adjective* which is coming; which has not happened yet ○ *They are spending all their time preparing for their future retirement.* ○ *I try to save something each week for future expenses.*

G

g /dʒiː/, **G** *noun* the seventh letter of the alphabet, between F and H

gadget /'gædʒɪt/ *noun* a small useful tool

gain /geɪn/ *verb* **1.** to achieve something, or get it with some work or effort ○ *The army gained control of the country.* ○ *She gained some useful experience working for a computer company.* **2.** (*of a clock or watch*) to move ahead of the correct time ○ *My watch gains five minutes a day.* ■ *noun* **1.** an increase in weight, quantity or size ○ *There was no gain in weight over three weeks* **2.** benefit or profit ○ *He doesn't do the job for financial gain.*

galaxy /'gæləksi/ *noun* an extremely large group of stars ○ *There are vast numbers of galaxies in the universe.* (NOTE: The plural is **galaxies**.)

Galaxy, the /'gæləksi/ *noun* the large group of stars and planets that the Earth forms part of

gale /geɪl/ *noun* a very strong wind

gallery /'gæləri/ *noun* **1.** □ **(art) gallery** a place where objects such as pictures and sculptures are shown to the public **2.** the highest rows of seats in a theatre or cinema ○ *We managed to get two seats in the gallery.* (NOTE: The plural is **galleries**.)

gallon /'gælən/ *noun* a measure of quantity of liquid, equal to 4.55 litres ○ *The car was empty and I had to put in seven gallons of petrol.*

gallop /'gæləp/ *verb* to go fast, especially on horseback ○ *The riders galloped through the woods.* ○ *He galloped through his lecture.* ■ *noun* the fastest running speed of a horse ○ *The horse went off at a gallop.*

game /geɪm/ *noun* **1.** an activity in which people compete with each other using skill, strength or luck ○ *She's not very good at games like chess.* **2.** a sin-

gle match between two opponents or two opposing teams ○ *Everyone wanted to watch the game of football.* ○ *Do you want a game of snooker?* ○ *Our team have won all their games this year.* **3.** a single session in an activity or sport such as tennis or cards ○ *She's winning by six games to three.* **4.** wild animals and birds such as deer, rabbits and pheasants, which are killed for sport or food ■ *plural noun* **Games** a large organised sports competition ○ *the Olympic Games*

gang /gæŋ/ *noun* **1.** a group of criminals ○ *a drugs gang* **2.** a group of young people who do things together, especially one that causes trouble ○ *Gangs of football fans wandered the streets after the match.* **3.** a group of workers ○ *Gangs of men worked all night to repair the railway track.*

gap /gæp/ *noun* a space between two things or in the middle of something ○ *There's a gap between the two planks.* ○ *The sheep all rushed through the gap in the hedge.*

gape /geɪp/ *verb* **1.** to open your mouth wide in surprise or shock **2.** to be wide open ○ *The entrance to the cave gaped before us.*

garage /'gærɪdʒ, 'gærɑːʒ/ *noun* **1.** a building where you can keep a car ○ *He put the car into the garage overnight.* ○ *She drove the car out of the garage.* ○ *Don't forget to lock the garage door.* ○ *The hotel has garage space for thirty cars.* **2.** a place where petrol is sold and where cars are repaired or sold ○ *Where's the nearest garage? I need some petrol.* ○ *I can't drive you to the station – my car is in the garage for repair.* ○ *You can hire cars from the garage near the post office.*

garbage /'gɑːbɪdʒ/ *noun* **1.** nonsense ○ *I don't believe a word of what he said –*

it's just garbage. (NOTE: no plural) **2.** (*mainly US*) household waste

garden /'gɑːd(ə)n/ *noun* an area of land near a house, used for growing such things as vegetables and flowers ○ *We grow all the vegetables we need in the back garden.* ○ *Your sister's outside, sitting in the garden.*

gardener /'gɑːd(ə)nə/ *noun* a person who looks after a garden either as a hobby or as a job

gardening /'gɑːd(ə)nɪŋ/ *noun* the activity of looking after a garden

garlic /'gɑːlɪk/ *noun* a round white vegetable with a strong smell, which can be separated into sections and used to give flavour to food

gas /gæs/ *noun* **1.** a chemical substance which has no form and which becomes liquid if it is cooled ○ *Air is made up of several gases, mainly nitrogen and oxygen.* ○ *Rubbish gives off a type of gas called methane as it rots.* **2.** a chemical substance which is burnt to make heat, e.g. for cooking

gasoline /'gæsəliːn/ *noun US* a liquid, made from petrol, used to drive a car engine (NOTE: usually shortened to **gas**)

gasp /gɑːsp/ *verb* to take a short deep breath ○ *He gasped when he saw the bill.* ■ *noun* a sudden loud breath that you take when you are surprised or in pain ○ *She gave a gasp when she saw the face at the window.*

gate /geɪt/ *noun* **1.** a low outside door made of bars of wood or metal ○ *Shut the gate – if you leave it open the sheep will get out of the field.* ○ *There is a white gate leading into the garden.* **2.** a door which leads to an aircraft at an airport ○ *Flight AZ270 is now boarding at Gate 23.*

gather /'gæðə/ *verb* **1.** to bring things or people together ○ *He gathered his papers together after the lecture.* ○ *She has been gathering information on the history of the local school.* **2.** (especially of people) to come together in one place, or be brought together by someone ○ *Groups of people gathered outside the Parliament building.* ○ *They gathered together a team of experienced*

people for the new project. **3.** to understand from what someone has told you ○ *I gather that his father is in hospital.* ○ *We gather he has left the office.* **4.** to pick plants, flowers or fruit ○ *The children were gathering blackberries.* ○ *The grape harvest has been gathered.*

gave /geɪv/ past tense of **give**

gay /geɪ/ *adjective* **1.** attracted to people of the same sex, or relating to people like this ○ *It's a club where gay men and women meet.* ○ *They met in a gay bar.* **2.** bright and lively (*dated*) ○ *The houses along the street are all painted in gay colours.* ■ *noun* a person who is attracted to someone of the same sex ○ *a club for gays*

gaze /geɪz/ *verb* to look steadily ○ *She gazed into his eyes.* ○ *He stood on the cliff, gazing out to sea.* ■ *noun* a steady look ○ *She refused to meet his gaze.*

gear /gɪə/ *noun* **1.** equipment for a particular purpose ○ *He took all his climbing gear with him.* ○ *She was carrying her painting gear in a rucksack.* **2.** clothing for a particular purpose ○ *She was putting on her tennis gear.* **3.** a part of an engine that makes it possible to change the amount of work the engine has to do to turn the wheels

gene /dʒiːn/ *noun* a set of chemicals in a cell which carries information about features that are passed from parent to child

general /'dʒen(ə)rəl/ *adjective* not specific; covering a wide range of subjects ○ *He had a good general education, but didn't specialise in any particular field.* ■ *noun* an army officer of high rank ○ *He has only recently been promoted to general.* ◇ **in general** normally ○ *In general, the weather is warmer in the south.*

generally /'dʒen(ə)rəli/ *adverb* usually ○ *The office is generally closed between Christmas and the New Year.*

generate /'dʒenəreɪt/ *verb* to produce something such as power ○ *We use wind to generate electricity.*

generation /ˌdʒenə'reɪʃ(ə)n/ *noun* **1.** the production of something such as power ○ *the generation of electricity* *from waves* **2.** all people born at about the same time ○ *The 1960s generation had an easier life than we did.* ○ *Many people of my father's generation cannot understand computer technology.* **3.** members of a family born at about the same time **4.** a series of machines made at about the same time ○ *They are developing a new type of engine for the next generation of aircraft.*

generous /'dʒen(ə)rəs/ *adjective* **1.** giving more money or presents than people usually do ○ *Thank you! You're so generous!* **2.** large ○ *a generous helping of pudding*

generously /'dʒen(ə)rəsli/ *adverb* in a generous way

genetics /dʒə'netɪks/ *noun* the science and study of the way genes are involved in passing features from parents to children

genre /'ʒɒnrə/ *noun* a type of something artistic such as art, literature or theatre ○ *the three main literary genres of prose, poetry and drama*

gentle /'dʒent(ə)l/ *adjective* **1.** soft and kind ○ *The nurse has gentle hands.* **2.** not very strong ○ *After a little gentle persuasion, she agreed to the plan.* ○ *He gave the door a gentle push.* **3.** not very steep ○ *There is a gentle slope down to the lake.* (NOTE: **gentler – gentlest**)

gentleman /'dʒent(ə)lmən/ *noun* a man, especially a well-behaved or upper-class man ○ *He's such a gentleman; he always opens the door for me.*

gently /'dʒentli/ *adverb* **1.** softly and carefully ○ *He gently put the blanket over her.* **2.** not steeply ○ *The path rises gently to the top of the hill.*

genuine /'dʒenjuɪn/ *adjective* real; true ○ *The painting was not a genuine Picasso.* ○ *A genuine leather purse will cost a lot more than that.*

geography /dʒi'ɒɡrəfi/ *noun* the study of the earth's surface, its climate and the plants and animals that live on it

germ /dʒɜːm/ *noun* an organism which causes disease ○ *Wash your hands after emptying the dustbin so you don't spread any germs.*

German /'dʒɜːmən/ *adjective* referring to Germany or its inhabitants ■ *noun* **1.** the language spoken in Germany, Austria and parts of Switzerland and Italy **2.** a person from Germany

gesture /'dʒestʃə/ *noun* a movement of a part of the body such as the hands to show feeling ○ *She made a slight gesture of impatience with her hand.* ■ *verb* to make a movement with your hands ○ *He gestured to the audience to sit down.*

get /ɡet/ *verb* **1.** to receive something ○ *We got a letter from the bank this morning.* ○ *She gets more money than I do.* **2.** □ **to get to a place** *or* **situation** to arrive at a place or situation ○ *We only got to the hotel at midnight.* ○ *When does your train get to London?* ○ *The plane gets to New York at 4 p.m.* ○ *When you get to my age you'll understand!* **3.** to start to be in a particular state ○ *I'm getting too old for rugby.* ○ *He's got much fatter over the last year or so.* ○ *The sun got hotter and hotter.* ○ *The carpet's getting dirty.* **4.** to have something done ○ *I must get my suit cleaned.* ○ *We got the car mended in time to go on holiday.* **5.** to make someone do something ○ *Can you get them to mend the brakes?* ○ *I'll try and get her to bring some CDs.* (NOTE: **gets – getting – got** /ɡɒt/ – **has got** *or* **gotten**)

get going *phrasal verb* to start doing something, or to leave ○ *Come on, let's get going!*

get across *phrasal verb* **1.** to manage to cross something ○ *They got across the river on rafts.* **2.** to make someone understand something ○ *I'm trying to get across to the people in the office that they all have to work harder.* ○ *We just can't seem to get our message across.*

get along *phrasal verb* to manage ○ *She got along quite well when her mother was away on holiday.* ○ *We seem to get along very happily without the telephone.* ○ *How are you getting along?*

get around *phrasal verb* **1.** to move from place to place ○ *Since he had his accident he gets around on two sticks.* **2.** (*of news*) to be heard by a lot of people ○ *The news soon got around that they were married.*

get at *phrasal verb* to reach something ○ *You'll need to stand on a chair to get at the jam jar on the top shelf.*

get away *phrasal verb* to escape ○ *The robbers got away in a stolen car.*

get back *phrasal verb* **1.** to return ○ *They got back home very late.* ○ *When did they get back from the cinema?* **2.** to get something again which you had before ○ *I got my money back after I had complained to the manager.*

get down *phrasal verb* **1.** to go back down onto the ground ○ *The cat climbed up the tree and couldn't get down.* ○ *He got down off the ladder.* **2.** to bring something down ○ *Can you get my suitcase down for me?*

get in *phrasal verb* **1.** to go inside a place or a vehicle ○ *Get in! – the train's going to leave.* ○ *The burglars must have got in through the bathroom window.* **2.** to arrive home or at the office ○ *What time did you get in last night?* ○ *Because of the train strike, we didn't get in until eleven o'clock.* **3.** to ask someone to come to do a job ○ *We'll get a builder in to mend the wall.*

get into *phrasal verb* to go inside a place or a vehicle ○ *They got into the back of the car.* ○ *I was just getting into bed when the phone rang.* ○ *The burglars got into the building through a window on the ground floor.*

get off *phrasal verb* to come down from or out of a form of transport such as a car, bus, train or plane ○ *She got off her bicycle at the red light.* ○ *If you want the post office, you should get off at the next stop.* ○ *You have to get off the train at South Kensington.*

get on *phrasal verb* **1.** to go onto a form of transport such as a car, bus, train or plane ○ *They got on the bus at the bank.* ○ *The policeman got on his bike and rode away.* **2.** to become old ○ *He's getting on and can't work as hard as he used to.*

get out *phrasal verb* to go out of a place or a vehicle ○ *The bus stopped and the driver got out.* ○ *The burglars got out through the front door.*

get over *phrasal verb* **1.** to climb over something ○ *They got over the wall into the garden.* **2.** to recover from an illness ○ *He's got over his flu.*

get through *phrasal verb* **1.** to manage to go through something ○ *The cows got through the hole in the fence.* **2.** to be successful ○ *He got through his exams, so he is now a qualified engineer.*

get up *phrasal verb* **1.** to get out of bed ○ *He went to bed so late that he didn't get up until 11 o'clock.* **2.** to make someone get out of bed ○ *You must get everyone up by 7.30 if we are going to leave on time.* **3.** to stand up ○ *When he had finished his meal, he got up and walked out of the room.*

get rid of ♦ **rid**

ghost /gəʊst/ *noun* an image of a dead person which some people believe they have seen ○ *They say the house is haunted by the ghost of its former owner.* ○ *Her face is white – she looks as if she has seen a ghost.*

giant /ˈdʒaɪənt/ *noun* (*in fairy tales and myths*) a very large man ○ *a story about a giant who lived in a castle at the top of a mountain* ■ *adjective* very large ○ *He's grown a giant cabbage.* ○ *They are planning to build a giant car factory in South Wales.*

giddy /ˈgɪdi/ *adjective* feeling that everything is turning round, and that you could lose your balance (NOTE: **giddier – giddiest**)

gift /gɪft/ *noun* **1.** a present; something given to someone ○ *The wedding gifts were displayed on a table.* ○ *She was wrapping up gifts to put under the Christmas tree.* **2.** a natural ability for doing something well ○ *She has a gift for making people feel welcome.* ○ *He has a gift for maths.*

gifted /ˈgɪftɪd/ *adjective* with a special talent ○ *He was a gifted musician.*

gigantic /dʒaɪˈgæntɪk/ *adjective* extremely large

giggle /ˈgɪg(ə)l/ *noun* a little laugh, often showing you are embarrassed ■ *verb* to laugh like this ○ *When she saw her mother's hat she started to giggle.* ○ *The class giggled at his accent.*

ginger /'dʒɪndʒə/ *noun* a plant whose root has a sharp burning taste and is used in cooking ○ *Fry the meat with spring onions and slices of ginger.* ○ *Add a pinch of powdered ginger to the cake mixture.* ■ *adjective* (*of hair*) orange in colour ○ *She has ginger hair and green eyes.* ○ *A ginger cat lay sleeping in the sun.*

giraffe /dʒɪ'rɑːf/ *noun* a large African animal with a very long neck

girl /ɡɜːl/ *noun* a female child ○ *a crowd of girls waiting at the bus stop* ○ *They have four children – two boys and two girls.* ○ *My sister goes to the local girls' school.*

girlfriend /'ɡɜːlfrend/ *noun* a girl or woman that someone is having a romantic relationship with ○ *He's broken up with his girlfriend.*

give /ɡɪv/ *verb* **1.** to pass something to someone ○ *Give me another envelope, please.* ○ *Can you give me some information about holidays in Greece?* **2.** to send or pass something to someone as a present ○ *We gave her flowers for her birthday.* ○ *What are you going to give him when he gets married?* ○ *We gave ten pounds to the Red Cross.* **3.** to do something to someone or something ○ *He gave me a broad smile.* ○ *He gave her a kiss.* ○ *She gave the ball a kick.* **4.** to organise something such as a party ○ *They gave a reception for the visiting Foreign Minister.* ○ *We gave a party to celebrate her twenty-first birthday.* (NOTE: **gives – giving – gave** /ɡeɪv/ – **has given** /'ɡɪv(ə)n/)

give back *phrasal verb* to hand something back to someone

give in *phrasal verb* to agree to do something that you had refused to do earlier

give up *phrasal verb* to stop doing something ○ *She's trying to give up smoking.*

give way *phrasal verb* **1.** to let someone go first ○ *Give way to traffic coming from the right.* **2.** to break under a heavy weight ○ *The chair gave way when he sat on it.* **3.** to stop opposing something ○ *In the end, our dad gave*

way and let us go camping by ourselves.

glad /ɡlæd/ *adjective* pleased ○ *Aunt Jane was glad to get your postcard.* ○ *After shopping all day, she was glad to find somewhere to sit down.*

gladly /'ɡlædli/ *adverb* with great pleasure

glance /ɡlɑːns/ *noun* a quick look ○ *She gave him an admiring glance.* ■ *verb* to look quickly ○ *He glanced over his shoulder to see who was following him.* ○ *She glanced suspiciously at the waiter.* ◇ **at a glance** after a quick look at something ○ *At a glance, I'd say these rugs are Chinese.*

glare /ɡleə/ *noun* **1.** a very bright light ○ *The glare of the sun on the wet road blinded me.* **2.** an angry look ○ *He gave her a glare and walked on.* ■ *verb* to look angrily ○ *She glared at me and went on reading her book.*

glass /ɡlɑːs/ *noun* **1.** a hard, smooth material which you can see through, used to make things such as windows, vases and bowls ○ *a bowl made of glass* or *a glass bowl* ○ *They found some very old pieces of glass in the earth.* (NOTE: no plural) **2.** a container to drink out of, usually made of glass ○ *She put the dirty glasses in the dishwasher.* ○ *We took plastic wine glasses on the picnic.* (NOTE: The plural is **glasses**.) **3.** the liquid contained in a glass ○ *She asked for a glass of water.* ○ *He was so thirsty he drank three glasses.* ○ *Add a glass of red wine to the sauce.* (NOTE: The plural is **glasses**.) ■ *plural noun* **glasses** two plastic or glass lenses in a frame which you wear in front of your eyes to help you see better ○ *She has to wear glasses for reading.* (NOTE: no singular: for one item, say 'a pair of glasses'.)

glide /ɡlaɪd/ *verb* to move in a smooth way ○ *Skaters were gliding across the ice.* ○ *A bird went gliding past.*

glimpse /ɡlɪmps/ *noun* a quick sight of something ○ *We caught a glimpse of the princess as she drove past.* ○ *There was a brief glimpse of the sun during the afternoon.* ■ *verb* to catch sight of someone or something ○ *We only glimpsed the back of her head as she was leaving.*

glitter /'glɪtə/ *verb* to shine brightly with small points of light, as the stars in the sky seem to shine ○ *The jewels in her crown were glittering in the light of the candles.* ○ *Her eyes glittered hopefully as she spoke.*

global /'gləʊb(ə)l/ *adjective* **1.** relating to the whole world ○ *We offer a global parcel delivery service.* **2.** relating to the whole of something ○ *We are carrying out a global review of salaries.*

globe /gləʊb/ *noun* **1.** □ **the globe** the world ○ *He is trying to be the first person to fly round the globe in a balloon.* **2.** a map of the world on a ball ○ *He spun the globe round and pointed to Canada.*

gloomy /'gluːmi/ *adjective* **1.** unhappy ○ *She was gloomy about her chances of passing the exam.* ○ *He's very gloomy about his job prospects.* **2.** dark ○ *a gloomy Sunday afternoon in November* (NOTE: **gloomier – gloomiest**)

glossy /'glɒsi/ *adjective* shiny ○ *the glossy coat of a horse* (NOTE: **glossier – glossiest**)

glove /glʌv/ *noun* a piece of clothing worn on your hand

glow /gləʊ/ *verb* to shine in a dull way ○ *The logs glowed in the fireplace.* ○ *Her face glowed with pride.* ■ *noun* a soft bright light ○ *the warm glow of the fire*

glue /gluː/ *noun* a substance which sticks things together ○ *She spread the glue carefully onto the back of the poster.* ○ *The glue on the envelope doesn't stick very well.* ■ *verb* to stick things together ○ *He glued the label to the box.*

gnaw /nɔː/ *verb* to bite something again and again

go /gəʊ/ *verb* **1.** to move from one place to another ○ *The plane goes to Frankfurt, then to Rome.* ○ *She is going to London for the weekend.* ○ *It's time the children went to bed.* ○ *He has gone to work in Washington.* ○ *They are going on a tour of southern Spain.* ○ *She was going downstairs when she fell.* **2.** to leave ○ *Get your coat, it's time to go.* ○ *The last bus goes at half past two.* **3.** to work ○ *Can you phone the garage? – the car won't go.* ○ *He's trying to get his*

motorbike to go. **4.** to fit ○ *It's too big to go into the box.* ○ *This case won't go into the back of the car.* **5.** to be placed ○ *The date should go at the top of the letter.* **6.** to become ○ *Her face went red from sitting in the sun.* ○ *He went pale and rushed out of the room.* ○ *You have to shout, my father's going deaf.* ○ *She's going grey, but it suits her.* **7.** to happen in a particular way ○ *The party went very well.* ○ *Things are going badly at work.* **8.** to make a particular sound ○ *The balloon landed on a candle and went 'pop'.* ○ *Do you remember the song that goes: 'There's no place like home'?* (NOTE: **goes – going – went** /went/ **– has gone** /gɒn/) ■ *noun* a try; an attempt ○ *He won the lottery at the first go.* ○ *She had three goes at the test and still didn't pass.* ○ *We'll give it one more go, and if the car doesn't start I'll call the garage.*

go ahead *phrasal verb* to take place as planned ○ *The project went ahead even though there were not enough staff.*

go away *phrasal verb* to leave

go back *phrasal verb* to return

go back on *phrasal verb* not to do what has been promised

go down *phrasal verb* to go to a lower level ○ *There are thirty-nine steps which go down to the beach.* ○ *Be careful when going down the hill.* ○ *After having a rest in her bedroom, she went down to the hotel bar.* ○ *Prices have gone down.*

go in *phrasal verb* to enter a place ○ *You don't need to knock – just go in.*

go in for *phrasal verb* to take an examination

go into *phrasal verb* **1.** to enter a place ○ *She went into the bedroom.* **2.** to examine something; to look at something carefully ○ *The bank wants to go into the details of his account.*

go off *phrasal verb* **1.** to go to another place ○ *He went off to look for a parking space.* ○ *She went off muttering something about buying cheese.* **2.** (of an alarm) to start making its noise ○ *The burglar alarm went off in the middle of the night.* **3.** to explode ○ *The bomb went off when there were still lots of* people in the building. ○ Fireworks were going off everywhere on Bonfire Night.

go on *phrasal verb* **1.** to continue ○ Please go on, I like hearing you sing. ○ They went on working in spite of the fire. ○ She went on speaking for two hours. **2.** to happen ○ What's been going on here?

go out *phrasal verb* **1.** to leave a building ○ I don't go out often at night. ○ He forgot to lock the door when he went out. **2.** not to be burning or lit any more ○ The fire went out and the room got cold. ○ All the lights in the building suddenly went out.

go round *phrasal verb* **1.** to turn ○ The merry-go-round went round and round. **2.** to visit a place ○ You'll need at least two hours to go round the museum. **3.** to be enough for a particular number of people ○ There wasn't enough ice cream to go round all twelve of us.

go up *phrasal verb* **1.** to go to a higher place ○ Take the lift and go up to the fourth floor. **2.** to increase; to rise to a higher level ○ The price of bread has gone up.

go with *phrasal verb* to match something ○ Blue shoes won't go with a green dress. ○ Red wine goes best with meat.

go without *phrasal verb* not to have something which you usually have ○ We often went without lunch.

goal /gəʊl/ *noun* **1.** (*in games*) two posts between which you have to send the ball to score a point ○ He was unlucky to miss the goal with that shot. **2.** (*in games*) a point scored by sending the ball between the posts ○ He scored a goal before being sent off. ○ Our team scored three goals. **3.** an aim ○ Our goal is to open a new pizza restaurant every month. ○ He achieved his goal of becoming a millionaire before he was thirty.

goalkeeper /'gəʊlkiːpə/ *noun* a player who stands in front of the goal to stop the ball going in

goat /gəʊt/ *noun* a small farm animal with horns and a beard, giving milk and wool ○ a herd of goats

god /gɒd/ *noun* a being with special powers that humans do not have, who is believed in and worshipped by some people ○ Bacchus was the Roman god of wine.

God /gɒd/ *noun* the spiritual Christians, Jews and Muslims believe in and worship ○ Do you believe in God? ○ We pray to God that the children will be found alive. ■ *interjection* used for showing that you are surprised or annoyed ○ God, what awful weather! ○ My God, have you seen how late it is?

goddess /'gɒdes/ *noun* a female god (NOTE: The plural is **goddesses**.)

goes /gəʊz/ 3rd person singular present of **go**

going /'gəʊɪŋ/ present participle of **go**

going to /'gəʊɪŋ tuː/ *phrase* used for showing future ○ We're going to win. ○ I hope it's going to be fine tomorrow. ○ When are you going to wash your hair? ○ He's going to be a great tennis player when he's older. ○ Is she going to sing at the concert?

gold /gəʊld/ *noun* a very valuable yellow-coloured metal ○ That ring isn't made of gold. ○ Gold is worth more than silver. ○ He wears a gold ring on his little finger. (NOTE: no plural: *some gold, a bar of gold*) ■ *adjective* of the colour of gold ○ a gold carpet

golden /'gəʊld(ə)n/ *adjective* coloured like gold; made from gold ○ She has beautiful golden hair.

golf /gɒlf/ *noun* a game played on a large open course, by hitting a small ball into 18 separate holes with a variety of clubs, using as few attempts as possible ○ He plays golf every Saturday. ○ Do you want a game of golf?

gone /gɒn/ past participle of **go**

good /gʊd/ *adjective* **1.** sensible, enjoyable or of a high standard ○ We had a good breakfast and then started work. ○ Did you have a good time at the party? ○ It would be a good idea to invest in these shares. ○ Her Spanish is better than his. **2.** skilful; clever ○ He's good at making things out of wood. ○ She's good with her hands. ○ He is good at football. **3.** well-behaved ○ Be a good *girl and I'll give you a sweet.* ○ *Have you been good while we've been away?* ■ *noun* an advantage or a benefit ○ *The medicine didn't do me any good.* ○ *He decided to give up smoking for the good of his health.* ○ *What's the good of having a big garden if you don't like gardening?* ○ *Governments should work for the good of the people.*

goodbye /ˌɡʊdˈbaɪ/ *noun, interjection* used when leaving someone ○ *Say goodbye to your teacher.* ○ *Goodbye! We'll see you again on Thursday.* (NOTE: often shortened to **bye**)

good evening /ˌɡʊd ˈiːvnɪŋ/ *interjection* used as a greeting when meeting someone or sometimes when leaving someone in the evening

good-looking /ˌɡʊd ˈlʊkɪŋ/ *adjective* (*of a person*) having an attractive face ○ *His sister is a very good-looking girl.* ○ *He's not especially good-looking.*

good morning /ˌɡʊd ˈmɔːnɪŋ/ *interjection* used when meeting someone, or sometimes when leaving someone in the morning

goods /ɡʊdz/ *plural noun* **1.** things that are produced for sale ○ *The company sells goods from various European countries.* **2.** possessions; things which you own ○ *She carried all her worldly goods in a bag.*

gossip /ˈɡɒsɪp/ *noun* stories or news about someone, which may or may not be true ○ *Have you heard the latest gossip about Sue?* ■ *verb* to talk about people's private lives ○ *They spent hours gossiping about the people working in the office.*

got /ɡɒt/ past tense and past participle of **get**

govern /ˈɡʌv(ə)n/ *verb* to rule a country ○ *The country is governed by three generals.*

government /ˈɡʌv(ə)nmənt/ *noun* the people or a political party which rules a country ○ *The president asked the leader of the largest party to form a new government.* ○ *The government controls the price of bread.* ○ *He has an important job in the government.*

grab /ɡræb/ *verb* **1.** to pick something up suddenly ○ *He grabbed his suitcase and ran to the train.* **2.** to get something quickly (*informal*) ○ *Let's grab some lunch before the meeting starts.* (NOTE: **grabs – grabbing – grabbed**)

graceful /ˈɡreɪsf(ə)l/ *adjective* moving in a smooth and beautiful way ○ *She crossed the stage with graceful steps.* ○ *We admired the swimmer's graceful strokes across the pool.*

grade /ɡreɪd/ *noun* **1.** a level of quality ○ *I always buy grade 2 eggs.* ○ *What grade of vegetables do you sell most of?* **2.** an examination mark ○ *She got top grades in maths.* **3.** *US* a class in school ○ *students in fifth grade* ○ *She's a fifth-grade student.* ■ *verb* to sort things according to size or quality ○ *a machine for grading fruit* ○ *Hotels are graded with two, three, four or five stars.* ◇ **to make the grade** to succeed; to do well

gradual /ˈɡrædʒuəl/ *adjective* which changes a little at a time

gradually /ˈɡrædʒuəli/ *adverb* little by little ○ *His condition improved gradually day by day.* ○ *She gradually learnt how to deal with customers' complaints.*

graffiti /ɡrəˈfiːti/ *noun* words which have been written or painted on walls in public places

graft /ɡrɑːft/ *noun* very hard work that needs a lot of physical energy (*informal*) ○ *She has succeeded through sheer hard graft.*

grain /ɡreɪn/ *noun* **1.** a crop such as wheat or corn ○ *a field of grain* ○ *the grain harvest* **2.** a very small piece ○ *a grain of sand*

gram /ɡræm/, **gramme** *noun* a unit of weight; there are 1000 grams in a kilogram (NOTE: usually written **g** after figures: *50 g.*)

grammar /ˈɡræmə/ *noun* **1.** the rules of a language ○ *I'm finding Russian grammar very difficult.* ○ *He's been learning English for years, and still makes basic grammar mistakes.* **2.** a book of rules of a language ○ *I'll look it up in my new German grammar.*

grand /ɡrænd/ *adjective* **1.** big and important ○ *his grand plan for making a* *lot of money* **2.** impressive ○ *We went to a very grand wedding.*

grandad /'grændæd/ *noun* **1.** a grandfather (*informal*) **2.** a common name used for addressing a grandfather

grandchild /'grænt∫aild/ *noun* a child of a son or daughter (NOTE: The plural is **grandchildren** /'grænt∫ildrən/.)

granddaughter /'grændɔ:tə/ *noun* the daughter of a son or daughter

grandfather /'græn,fɑ:ðə/ *noun* the father of your mother or father ○ *Tomorrow is grandfather's hundredth birthday.* ○ *My grandfather always tells us fascinating stories about his childhood.* (NOTE: often called **grandad** or **grandpa** by children)

grandma /'grænmɑ:/ *noun* **1.** a grandmother (*informal*) **2.** a common name used for addressing a grandmother

grandmother /'grænmʌðə/ *noun* the mother of your mother or father ○ *It will be grandmother's ninetieth birthday next month.* ○ *My grandmother taught me how to make bread.* (NOTE: often called **gran** *or* **granny** *or* **grandma** *or* **nan** by children)

grandpa /'grænpɑ:/ *noun* **1.** a grandfather (*informal*) **2.** a common name used for addressing a grandfather

grandparent /'grænpeərənt/ *noun* the mother or father of one of your parents

grandson /'grænsʌn/ *noun* the son of a son or daughter

granny /'græni/ *noun* **1.** a grandmother (*informal*) **2.** a common name used for addressing a grandmother

grant /grɑ:nt/ *noun* an amount of money given to help someone to pay for something, or to live while they are doing something such as studying ○ *Not many students get a full grant.* ○ *My grant only pays for a few books.* ○ *We have applied for a grant to plant trees by the side of the road.* ■ *verb* to give someone something, especially officially (*formal*) ○ *The council has granted the school permission to build a new hall.*

grape /greip/ *noun* a small green or red fruit which grows on low plants, often used to make wine

graph /grɑ:f/ *noun* a chart showing how amounts rise and fall in the form of a line

grasp /grɑ:sp/ *noun* an understanding ○ *She has a good grasp of physics.* ■ *verb* to understand something ○ *They didn't seem to grasp my meaning.*

grass /grɑ:s/ *noun* a low green plant, which is eaten by sheep and cows in fields, or used in gardens to cover the area that you walk or sit on ○ *The grass is getting too long – it needs cutting.*

grate /greit/ *noun* a metal frame for holding coal in a fireplace ■ *verb* to make something into small pieces by rubbing against a grater ○ *She grated nutmeg over the pudding.* ○ *Sprinkle grated cheese over your pasta.* ○ *We made a salad of grated carrots and spring onions.* (NOTE: Do not confuse with **great**.)

grateful /'greitf(ə)l/ *adjective* feeling that you want to thank someone for something that they have done for you ○ *We are most grateful to you for your help.*

grave /grɑ:v/ *noun* a hole in the ground where a dead person is buried ○ *At the funeral, the whole family stood by the grave.* ■ *adjective* serious ○ *She looked at him with a grave expression.* (NOTE: **graver – gravest**)

gravity /'græviti/ *noun* the force which pulls things towards the ground ○ *Apples fall to the ground because of the earth's gravity.*

gravy /'greivi/ *noun* sauce made from the juices of cooked meat (NOTE: no plural)

gray /grei/ *noun, adjective* US spelling of **grey**

graze /greiz/ *noun* a slight skin injury ○ *He had a graze on his knee.* ■ *verb* (*of animals*) to feed on grass ○ *The sheep were grazing on the hillside.*

grease /gri:s/ *noun* **1.** thick oil ○ *Put some grease on the hinge.* **2.** fat that comes from meat when it is cooked ■ *verb* to cover with oil ○ *Don't forget to grease the wheels.* ○ *She greased the pan before cooking the eggs.*

greasy /'gri:si/ *adjective* covered with oil or grease ○ *He wiped his greasy hands on a piece of rag.* ○ *I don't like the chips they serve here – they're too greasy.* (NOTE: **greasier – greasiest**)

great /greɪt/ *adjective* **1.** large ○ *She was carrying a great big pile of sandwiches.* ○ *The guide showed us into the Great Hall.* **2.** important or famous ○ *the greatest tennis player of all time* ○ *New York is a great city.* ○ *Picasso was a great artist.* **3.** wonderful; very good ○ *We had a great time at the party.* ○ *What did you think of the film? – It was great!* ○ *It was great of you to help.* ○ *It was great that they could all get to the picnic.*

greatly /'greɪtli/ *adverb* very much

greedy /'gri:di/ *adjective* wanting more food or other things than you need (NOTE: **greedier – greediest**)

green /gri:n/ *adjective* **1.** of a colour like the colour of grass ○ *He was wearing a bright green shirt.* ○ *They painted the door dark green.* ○ *Go on – the traffic lights are green.* **2.** relating to, interested in or concerned about the environment ○ *She's very worried about green issues.* ○ *He's a leading figure in the green movement.* ■ *noun* **1.** a colour like grass ○ *The door was painted a very dark green.* **2.** an area of public land covered with grass in the middle of a village ○ *They were playing cricket on the village green.*

greet /gri:t/ *verb* to meet someone and say hello

greeting /'gri:tɪŋ/ *noun* the words that people say to each other when they meet

grew /gru:/ past tense of **grow**

grey /greɪ/ *noun* a colour that is a mixture of black and white ○ *He was dressed all in grey.* ■ *adjective* of a colour that is a mixture of black and white ○ *Her hair has turned quite grey.* ○ *She was wearing a light grey suit.* ○ *Look at the grey clouds – I think it is going to rain.*

grief /gri:f/ *noun* a feeling of great sadness ◇ **to come to grief** to have an accident; to fail ○ *His horse came to grief at the first fence.* ○ *The project came to*

grief *when the council refused to renew their grant.*

grill /grɪl/ *noun* a part of a cooker where food is cooked under the heat ○ *Cook the chops under the grill.* ■ *verb* to cook something in this part of the cooker ○ *We're having grilled sardines for dinner.*

grim /grɪm/ *adjective* **1.** serious and not smiling ○ *His expression was grim.* ○ *He gave a grim laugh and went on working.* **2.** grey and unpleasant ○ *The town centre is really grim.*

grimy /'graɪmi/ *adjective* covered with old dirt that is difficult to remove ○ *The furniture was broken and the windows were grimy.*

grin /grɪn/ *verb* to smile widely ○ *He grinned when we asked him if he liked his job.* (NOTE: **grins – grinning – grinned**) ■ *noun* a wide smile ○ *She gave me a big grin.*

grind /graɪnd/ *verb* **1.** to crush something to powder ○ *to grind coffee* **2.** to rub surfaces together (NOTE: **grinds – grinding – ground** /graʊnd/)

grip /grɪp/ *noun* a firm hold ○ *He has a strong firm grip.* ○ *These tyres give a better grip on the road surface.* ■ *verb* **1.** to hold something tight ○ *She gripped the rail with both hands.* **2.** to be very interesting to someone ○ *The story gripped me from the first page.* (NOTE: **grips – gripping – gripped**)

groove /gru:v/ *noun* a wide line cut into a surface

gross /grəʊs/ *adjective* total; with nothing taken away ○ *What's your gross salary?* ■ *adverb* with nothing taken away ○ *His salary is paid gross.*

ground /graʊnd/ *noun* **1.** the surface of the earth ○ *The factory was burnt to the ground.* ○ *There were no seats, so we had to sit on the ground.* ○ *She lay down on the ground and went to sleep.* **2.** soil or earth ○ *You should dig the ground in the autumn.* ○ *The house is built on wet ground.* ○ *It has been so dry that the ground is hard.* **3.** an area of land used for a special purpose ○ *a football ground* ○ *a sports ground* ○ *a cricket ground* ○ *a show ground* ■ *plural noun* **grounds 1.** a large area of land around a big house or institution ○ *The police searched the school grounds for the weapon.* ○ *The village fair is held in the grounds of the hospital.* **2.** reasons ○ *Does he have any grounds for complaint?* ○ *What grounds have you got for saying that?*

ground floor /ˌɡraʊnd 'flɔː/ *noun* a floor in a building which is level with the street

group /ɡruːp/ *noun* **1.** a number of people together ○ *a group of houses in the valley* ○ *Groups of people gathered in the street.* ○ *She is leading a group of businessmen on a tour of Italian factories.* ○ *There are reduced prices for groups of 30 and over.* **2.** a way of classifying things ○ *These drugs belong to the same group.* **3.** people playing music together ○ *He plays in a jazz group.* ○ *She's the lead singer in a pop group.*

grow /ɡraʊ/ *verb* **1.** (*of plants*) to live and develop ○ *There was grass growing in the middle of the road.* ○ *Roses grow well in our garden.* **2.** to make plants grow ○ *He grows all his vegetables in his garden.* ○ *We are going to grow some cabbages this year.* **3.** to become taller or bigger ○ *He's grown a lot taller since I last saw him.* ○ *The profit has grown to £1m.* ○ *The town's population is growing very fast.* (NOTE: **grows – growing – grew** /ɡruː/ **– grown** /ɡraʊn/)

grow up *phrasal verb* to become an adult

growing /ˈɡraʊɪŋ/ *adjective* **1.** becoming bigger in size or amount **2.** becoming stronger or more extreme ○ *growing fear of war*

grown /ɡraʊn/ *adjective* full size ○ *What silly behaviour from a grown man!*

growth /ɡraʊθ/ *noun* an increase in size ○ *the rapid growth of the population since 1980* ○ *They measured the tree's growth over the last fifty years.*

grubby /ˈɡrʌbi/ *adjective* so dirty as to be unpleasant ○ *A grubby little boy asked for money.* ○ *He was wearing a grubby old shirt.* (NOTE: **grubbier – grubbiest**)

grumble /ˈɡrʌmbəl/ to complain in a bad-tempered way, especially regularly and often about unimportant things ○ *He's always grumbling about the music from the flat above.*

guarantee /ˌɡærənˈtiː/ *noun* **1.** a legal document in which someone states that something is going to happen ○ *The travel agent could not give a guarantee that we would be accommodated in the hotel mentioned in the brochure.* **2.** a promise ○ *I can't give you any guarantee of success.* ■ *verb* to give a firm promise that something will work, that something will be done ○ *I can guarantee that the car will give you no trouble.* ○ *We can almost guarantee good weather in the Caribbean at this time of year.* (NOTE: **guarantees – guaranteeing – guaranteed**)

guard /ɡɑːd/ *noun* **1.** a person who protects, often a soldier ○ *Security guards patrol the factory at night.* **2.** the man in charge of a train ○ *The guard helped my put my bike into his van.* ■ *verb* to watch someone or somewhere carefully to prevent attacks or escapes ○ *The prison is guarded at all times.* ◇ **to be on your guard** to try to be ready for an unpleasant surprise ○ *You always have to be on your guard against burglars.*

guerrilla /ɡəˈrɪlə/, **guerilla** *noun* a soldier who is not part of a regular national army

guess /ɡes/ *noun* an attempt to give the right answer or amount ○ *Go on – make a guess!* ○ *At a guess, I'd say it weighs about 10 kilos.* ■ *verb* to try to give the right answer or amount ○ *I would guess it's about six o'clock.* ○ *Neither of them guessed the right answer.* ○ *He guessed right.* ○ *I've bought you a present – shut your eyes and guess what it is.*

guest /ɡest/ *noun* **1.** a person who is invited to come to your home or to an event ○ *We had a very lively party with dozens of guests.* ○ *None of the guests left the party early.* **2.** a person staying in a hotel ○ *Guests are requested to vacate their rooms before midday.*

guidance /ˈɡaɪd(ə)ns/ *noun* advice

guide /ɡaɪd/ *noun* **1.** a person who shows you the way ○ *They used local farmers* as guides through the forest. **2.** a person who shows tourists round a place ○ *The guide showed us round the castle.* ○ *The museum guide spoke so fast that we couldn't understand what she was saying.* **3.** a book which gives information ○ *a guide to Athens* ○ *a guide to the butterflies of Europe* ■ *verb* **1.** to show someone the way to somewhere ○ *She guided us up the steps in the dark.* **2.** to show tourists round a place ○ *He guided us round the castle and told us about its history.*

guidebook /'gaɪdbʊk/ *noun* a book with information about a place

guilty /'gɪlti/ *adjective* **1.** who has committed a crime ○ *He was found guilty of murder.* ○ *The jury decided she was not guilty.* **2.** feeling unhappy because you have done something wrong ○ *I feel very guilty about not having written to you.* (NOTE: **guiltier – guiltiest**)

guitar /gɪ'tɑː/ *noun* a musical instrument with six strings, played with the fingers ○ *He plays the guitar in a pop group.*

gulf /gʌlf/ *noun* an area of sea partly surrounded by land ○ *the Gulf of Mexico*

gum /gʌm/ *noun* **1.** glue ○ *She spread gum on the back of the photo and stuck it onto a sheet of paper.* **2.** the flesh around the base of your teeth ○ *Brushing your teeth every day is good for your gums.* ■ *verb* to stick something with glue ○ *She gummed the pictures onto a sheet of paper.* (NOTE: **gums – gumming – gummed**)

gun /gʌn/ *noun* **1.** a weapon which shoots bullets ○ *The robber pulled out a gun.* ○ *She grabbed his gun and shot*

him dead. **2.** a small piece of equipment which you hold in your hand to spray a substance such as paint or glue ○ *A spray gun gives an even coating of paint.* ◇ **to jump the gun** to start too quickly ○ *The new law comes into effect in a month's time, but some shops have already jumped the gun.*

gunman /'gʌnmən/ *noun* a man armed with a gun ○ *The gunman pulled out a revolver and started shooting.* (NOTE: The plural is **gunmen**.)

gut /gʌt/ *noun* the tube in which food is digested as it passes through the body ○ *He complained of a pain in the gut.*

guts /gʌts/ *plural noun* courage (*informal*) ○ *She had the guts to tell the boss he was wrong.*

gutter /'gʌtə/ *noun* **1.** the side of a road where water can flow ○ *Pieces of paper and leaves were blowing about in the gutter.* **2.** an open pipe under the edge of a roof for catching rain ○ *It rained so hard the gutters overflowed.*

guy /gaɪ/ *noun* **1.** a man (*informal*) ○ *She married a guy from Texas.* ○ *The boss is a very friendly guy.* ○ *Hey, you guys, come and look at this!* **2.** a model of a man burnt on Bonfire Night, November 5th ○ *The children are collecting clothes to make a guy.* ○ *Penny for the guy!*

gym /dʒɪm/ *noun* **1.** a place with special equipment, or a large hall as in a school, for indoor sports and physical training ○ *I go to the gym twice a week to exercise.* **2.** physical exercises, especially as an activity at school

H

h /eɪt ʃ/, **H** *noun* the eighth letter of the alphabet, between G and I

habit /'hæbɪt/ *noun* something that someone does regularly ○ *He has the habit of biting his fingernails.*

had /əd, həd, hæd/ past tense and past participle of **have**

hail /heɪl/ *noun* frozen rain ○ *I thought the hail was going to break the windscreen.* ■ *verb* to fall as frozen rain ○ *It hailed for ten minutes and then the sun came out.*

hair /heə/ *noun* **1.** a mass of long fibres growing on your head ○ *She has long brown hair or her hair is long and brown.* ○ *She always brushes her hair before washing it.* ○ *You must get your hair cut.* ○ *He's had his hair cut short.* ○ *Use some hair spray to keep your hair in place.* **2.** one of the fibres growing on the body of a human or animal ○ *Waiter, there's a hair in my soup!* ○ *The cat has left hairs all over the cushion.* ○ *He's beginning to get some grey hairs.*

hairdresser /'heədresə/ *noun* a person who cuts and washes your hair

hairstyle /'heəstaɪl/ *noun* the way in which your hair has been cut or arranged

half /hɑːf/ *noun* **1.** one of two parts which are the same in size ○ *She cut the orange in half.* ○ *One half of the apple fell on the carpet.* ○ *Half of six is three.* **2.** (in sport) one of two parts of a match ○ *Our team scored a goal in the first half.* ○ *We thought we were going to win, and then they scored in the final minutes of the second half.*

half past /ˌhɑːf 'pɑːst/ *phrase* 30 minutes after an hour

half-term /ˌhɑːf 'tɜːm/ *noun* a short holiday in the middle of a school term

halfway /ˌhɑːf'weɪ/ *adverb* in the middle ○ *Come on, we're more than halfway there!* ○ *The post office is about halfway between the station and our house.*

hall /hɔːl/ *noun* **1.** a room just inside the entrance to a house, where you can leave your coat ○ *Don't wait in the hall, come straight into the dining room.* ○ *She left her umbrella in the hall.* **2.** a large room where large numbers of people can come together ○ *The children have their dinner in the school hall.*

halt /hɔːlt/ *noun* a complete stop ■ *verb* to stop something ○ *The cars halted when the traffic lights went red.* ○ *We are trying to halt experiments on live animals.*

halve /hɑːv/ *verb* to reduce something by half ○ *Because the town has no cash, its budget has been halved.*

ham /hæm/ *noun* meat from a pig which has been treated, e.g. with salt ○ *She cut three slices of ham.* ○ *We had a ham and tomato salad.* ○ *She had a ham sandwich for lunch.*

hamburger /'hæmbɜːgə/ *noun* a piece of minced beef grilled and served in a toasted roll

hammer /'hæmə/ *noun* a tool with a heavy head for knocking nails ○ *She hit the nail hard with the hammer.* ■ *verb* **1.** to knock something such as a nail into something such as a piece of wood with a hammer ○ *It took him a few minutes to hammer the tent pegs into the ground.* **2.** to hit something hard, as with a hammer ○ *He hammered the table with his fist.* ○ *She hammered on the door with her stick.*

hand /hænd/ *noun* **1.** the part of the body at the end of each arm, which you use for holding things ○ *She was carrying a cup of tea in each hand.* ○ *She held out her hand, asking for money.* □ **they walked along hand in hand** they walked holding each other by the hand

2. one of the two long parts on a clock which move round and show the time. The minute hand is longer than the hour hand. ■ *verb* to pass something to someone ○ *Can you hand me that box?* ○ *She handed me all her money.* ◇ **to give *or* lend someone a hand with something** to help someone with something ○ *Can you lend a hand with moving the furniture?* ○ *He gave me a hand with the washing up.* ◇ **to shake hands** to hold someone's hand to show you are pleased to meet them or to show that an agreement has been reached ○ *The visitors shook hands and the meeting started.*

hand in *phrasal verb* to give something to someone such as a teacher or a policeman ○ *We handed in the money we had found.*

hand over *phrasal verb* to give something to someone ○ *She handed over all the documents to the lawyers.*

handbag /'hændbæg/ *noun* a small bag which a woman carries to hold small things such as money or make-up

handicap /'hændikæp/ *noun* **1.** a physical or mental condition which makes ordinary activities difficult (*dated*) **2.** something which puts you at a disadvantage ○ *Not being able to drive is a handicap in this job.*

handkerchief /'hæŋkətʃɪf/ *noun* a piece of cloth or thin paper for wiping your nose (NOTE: The plural is **handkerchiefs** or **handkerchieves**.)

handle /'hænd(ə)l/ *noun* a part of something which you hold in your hand to carry something or to use something ○ *I turned the handle but the door didn't open.* ○ *Be careful, the handle of the frying pan may be hot.* ○ *The handle has come off my suitcase.* ○ *He broke the handle off the cup.* ■ *verb* to move by hand ○ *Be careful when you handle the bottles of acid.*

handsome /'hæns(ə)m/ *adjective* a handsome man or boy has an attractive face ○ *Her boyfriend is very handsome.* (NOTE: usually used of men rather than women)

handwriting /'hændraɪtɪŋ/ *noun* writing done by hand

handy /'hændi/ *adjective* practical and useful ◇ **to come in handy** to be useful ○ *The knife will come in handy when we are camping.*

hang /hæŋ/ *verb* to attach one thing to another so that it does not touch the ground ○ *Hang your coat on the hook behind the door.* ○ *He hung his umbrella over the back of his chair.* ○ *We hung the painting in the hall.* ○ *The boys were hanging upside down from a tree.* (NOTE: **hangs – hanging – hung** /hʌŋ/)

hang around *phrasal verb* to wait in a certain place without doing anything much

hang on *phrasal verb* to wait ○ *If you hang on a few minutes you will be able to see her.*

happen /'hæpən/ *verb* **1.** to take place ○ *The accident happened at the traffic lights.* ○ *How did the accident happen?* ○ *Something happened to make all the buses late.* ○ *He's late – something must have happened to him.* **2.** □ **to happen to someone or something** to have an effect on someone or something ○ *What's happened to his brother since he left school?* ◇ **as it happens, as it happened** completely by chance ○ *As it happens I have the car today and can give you a lift.* ○ *It so happened that my wife bumped into her at the supermarket.*

happily /'hæpɪli/ *adverb* in a happy way

happiness /'hæpinəs/ *noun* a feeling of being happy

happy /'hæpi/ *adjective* **1.** (*of people*) very pleased ○ *I'm happy to say we're getting married next month.* ○ *I'm so happy to hear that you are better.* ○ *She's very happy in her job.* **2.** (*of events*) pleasant ○ *It was the happiest day of my life.*

harbour /'hɑːbə/ *noun* a place where boats can come and tie up ○ *The ship came into harbour last night.*

hard /hɑːd/ *adjective* **1.** not soft ○ *If you have back trouble, you ought to get a hard bed.* ○ *The ice cream is rock hard or hard as a rock.* ○ *The cake she made is so hard I can't bite into it.* **2.** not easy

○ Some of the questions were very hard. ○ It's hard to stay happy when bad things happen. ■ adverb **1.** strongly ○ He hit the nail hard. ○ It's snowing very hard. **2.** with a lot of effort ○ They worked hard to finish the order on time. ○ She always tries hard. ◇ **it's hard to say** it's difficult to know ○ It's hard to say if it's going to rain or not.

hardly /'hɑːdli/ adverb almost not ○ Do you know her? – Hardly at all. ○ We hardly slept a wink last night. ○ She hardly eats anything at all.

hardware /'hɑːdweə/ noun tools and pans used in the home ○ I bought the paint in a hardware shop.

harm /hɑːm/ noun damage done to people or animals ○ He didn't mean to do any harm or He meant no harm. ○ There's no harm in having a little drink before you go to bed. ■ verb to physically affect something or someone in a bad way ○ Luckily, the little girl was not harmed. ○ The bad publicity has harmed our reputation.

harmful /'hɑːmf(ə)l/ adjective which causes damage

harmless /'hɑːmləs/ adjective which does not upset or hurt anyone

harsh /hɑːʃ/ adjective **1.** severe ○ The prosecutor asked for a harsh sentence to fit the crime. **2.** rough ○ He shouted in a harsh voice.

harvest /'hɑːvɪst/ noun picking crops ○ The corn harvest is in August. ■ verb to pick crops ○ The corn will be ready to harvest next week. ○ They have started harvesting the grapes in the vineyard.

has /əz, həz, hæz/ 3rd person singular present of **have**

hat /hæt/ noun a piece of clothing which you wear on your head ○ Take your hat off when you go into a church. ○ He's bought a Russian fur hat for the winter.

hate /heɪt/ verb to dislike someone or something very much ○ I think she hates me, but I don't know why. ○ I hate being late. ■ noun a very strong feeling of not liking someone ○ Her eyes were full of hate.

hatred /'heɪtrɪd/ noun a very strong feeling of not liking someone or some-

thing ○ She had a hatred of unfair treatment.

haul /hɔːl/ verb to pull something with effort ○ They hauled the boat up onto the beach.

have /həv, əv, hæv/ verb **1.** to own something ○ She has a lot of money. ○ They have a new green car. ○ She has long dark hair. ○ The house has no telephone. ○ Do you have a table for three, please? **2.** to take or eat something ○ Have you had any tea? ○ She has sugar in her coffee. ○ They had a meal of bread and cheese. ○ She had her breakfast in bed. **3.** to play a game of something ○ They had a game of tennis. ○ I had a long walk. **4.** to arrange for something to be done for you ○ I must have my hair cut. ○ She's having the house painted. **5.** used to form the present and past perfect form of verbs ○ Have they finished their work? ○ She has never been to Paris. ○ They had finished supper when we arrived. ○ I haven't seen him for two days. ○ If she had asked me I would have said no. **6.** used to introduce good wishes to someone ○ Have a nice day! ○ Have a good trip! (NOTE: **has – having – had**)

have got phrasal verb **1.** to own something ○ She's got dark hair. ○ Have you got a table for three, please? ○ They've got a new green car. ○ The house hasn't got a telephone. ○ They haven't got enough to eat. **2.** used to mean 'must' ○ Why have you got to go so early? ○ She's got to learn to drive.

hay /heɪ/ noun dried grass used to feed animals such as cows

he /hi, hiː/ pronoun referring to a man or boy, and some animals ○ He's my brother. ○ He and I met in Oxford. ○ He's eaten all my pudding. ○ Don't be frightened of the dog – he won't hurt you. ◊ **him, his** (NOTE: When it is the object, **he** becomes **him**: He hit the ball or The ball hit him. When it follows the verb **to be**, **he** usually becomes **him**: Who's that? – It's him, the man who borrowed my knife.)

head /hed/ noun **1.** the top part of the body, where your eyes, nose, mouth and brain are ○ He says he can relax by standing on his head. ○ She hit her head on the cupboard door. **2.** your brain; intelligence ○ She has a good head for figures. ○ He tried to do the sum in his head. ○ If we all put our heads together we might come up with a solution. **3.** the first place ○ An old lady was standing at the head of the queue. ○ His name comes at the head of the list. **4.** the most important person ○ She's head of the sales department. ○ The head waiter showed us to our table. **5.** one person, or one animal, when counting ○ She counted heads as the children got onto the coach. ○ There are fifty head of sheep in the flock. ■ **verb** to go towards something ○ She headed immediately for the manager's office. ○ The car headed east along the motorway. ○ He's heading towards the Channel ports. ○ She's heading for trouble. ◇ **to shake your head** to move your head from side to side to mean 'no' ○ She asked him if he wanted any more coffee and he shook his head.

headache /'hedeɪk/ noun a pain in your head ○ I've got a bad headache.

headline /'hedlaɪn/ noun words in large letters on the front page of a newspaper ○ Did you see the headlines about the accident?

headquarters /hed'kwɔːtəz/ noun the main offices of a large organisation ○ Several people were arrested and taken to police headquarters. Abbreviation **HQ**

head teacher /ˌhed 'tiːtʃə/ noun a man or woman who is in charge of a school

heal /hiːl/ verb to make someone or something healthy again, or to become healthy again ○ She claims to be able to heal people through touch. ○ This should help the wound to heal. (NOTE: Do not confuse with **heel**.)

health /helθ/ noun the fact of being well or being free from any illness ○ He has enjoyed the best of health for years. ○ Smoking is bad for your health.

healthy /'helθi/ adjective **1.** not ill ○ He's healthier than he has ever been. **2.** making you stay fit and well ○ the healthiest place in England ○ She's keeping to a healthy diet. (NOTE: **healthier – healthiest**)

heap /hiːp/ noun a pile ○ a heap of coal ○ Step over that heap of rubbish. ■ **verb** to pile things up ○ A pile of presents were heaped under the Christmas tree. ○ Boxes were heaped up on the station platform.

hear /hɪə/ verb **1.** to notice sounds with your ears ○ He heard footsteps behind him. ○ You could hear the sound of church bells in the distance. ○ I heard her drive up in the car. ○ Can you hear him singing in the bath? **2.** to listen to something ○ Did you hear the talk on the radio? ○ I heard it on the BBC news. **3.** to get information ○ I hear he's got a new job. ○ Have you heard that the manager has resigned? ○ We have not heard from them for some time. (NOTE: **hears – hearing – heard** /hɜːd/)

hearing /'hɪərɪŋ/ noun the ability to hear ○ Bats have a very sharp sense of hearing. ○ She has hearing difficulties. (NOTE: no plural)

heart /hɑːt/ noun **1.** a main organ in the body, which pumps blood around it ○ She isn't dead – her heart's still beating. ○ The doctor listened to his heart. ○ He has had heart trouble for years. **2.** your feelings and emotions ○ My heart sank when I realised that he hadn't read my letter. **3.** a centre or middle ○ The restaurant is in the heart of the old town. **4.** one of the red sets in a game of cards, with a symbol shaped like a heart ○ My last card was the ten of hearts. (NOTE: The other red suit is **diamonds**; **clubs** and **spades** are the black suits.)

heat /hiːt/ noun **1.** the state of being hot ○ The heat of the sun made the ice cream melt. **2.** the amount of heat produced by an oven or heating system ○ Cook the vegetables over a low heat. **3.** one part of a sports competition ○ There are two heats before the final race. ■ **verb** to make something hot ○ Can you heat the soup while I'm getting the table ready? ○ The room was heated by a small electric fire. ○ Heat the milk to room temperature.

heating /'hiːtɪŋ/ noun a way of keeping a place such as a house or an office warm

heaven /'hev(ə)n/ *noun* a beautiful place believed by some people to be where good people go after death ○ *She believes that when she dies she will go to heaven.* ◇ **for heaven's sake** an expression showing you are annoyed, or that something is important ○ *What are you screaming for? – It's only a little mouse, for heaven's sake.* ○ *For heaven's sake try to be quiet, we don't want the guards to hear us!* ◇ **good heavens** an expression showing you are surprised ○ *Good heavens! It's almost 10 o'clock!*

heavily /'hevɪli/ *adverb* **1.** with force ○ *He sat down heavily on the little chair.* **2.** to a great extent; very much ○ *The company was heavily criticised in the press.* ○ *She is heavily in debt.* ○ *It rained heavily during the night.*

heavy /'hevi/ *adjective* **1.** weighing a lot ○ *This suitcase is so heavy I can hardly lift it.* ○ *She's heavier than I am.* **2.** in large amounts ○ *There has been a heavy demand for the book.* ○ *There was a heavy fall of snow during the night.* ○ *The radio says there is heavy traffic in the centre of town.* □ **to be a heavy smoker** to smoke a lot of cigarettes □ **to be a heavy drinker** to drink a lot of alcohol

hedge /hedʒ/ *noun* a row of bushes planted and kept in an even shape to form a screen round a field or garden ○ *There is a thick hedge round the churchyard.*

heel /hi:l/ *noun* **1.** the back part of the foot ○ *After walking, she got sore heels.* **2.** the back part of a sock or shoe ○ *He's got a hole in the heel of his sock.* ○ *She always wears shoes with high heels* or *high-heeled shoes.*

height /haɪt/ *noun* **1.** a measurement of how high something is or how tall someone is ○ *The height of the bridge is only three metres.* **2.** the highest point ○ *looking down on the city from the heights around* **3.** a time of great activity ○ *It is difficult to find hotel rooms at the height of the tourist season.*

held /held/ past tense and past participle of **hold**

helicopter /'helɪkɒptə/ *noun* an aircraft with a set of large flat blades on top that spin round, making it rise straight up in the air

hell /hel/ *noun* **1.** a place where some people believe bad people are sent after they die ○ *Medieval pictures show hell as a burning place.* **2.** a very unpleasant place or experience ○ *It's hell working in the office these days.* **3.** used to emphasise what you are saying (*informal*) ○ *What the hell's been going on here?* ○ *Am I going to lend you £50? Am I hell!* (NOTE: Using expressions that include the word **hell** is offensive to some people.)

he'll /hil, hi:l/ *short form* he will

hello /hə'ləʊ/ *interjection* used as a greeting ○ *She called hello from the other side of the street.* ○ *Hello Mary! I'm glad to see you.* ○ *When you see her, say hello to her from me.* (NOTE: also spelled **hallo, hullo**.)

helmet /'helmɪt/ *noun* a solid hat used as a protection

help /help/ *noun* **1.** something which makes it easier for you to do something ○ *She was washing the floor with the help of a big mop.* ○ *Do you need any help with moving the furniture?* ○ *She finds the word-processor a great help in writing her book.* ○ *Her assistant is not much help in the office – he can't type or drive.* **2.** the act of making it easier for someone to do something ○ *People were calling for help from the ruins of the house.* ○ *The nurses offered help to people injured in the accident.* ■ *verb* to make it easier for someone to do something ○ *He helped the old lady up the steps.* ○ *The government wants to help small businesses.* ○ *Your father can help you with your homework.* ○ *One of my friends helped me move the piano into the bedroom.*

helper /'helpə/ *noun* a person who helps someone do a particular job or task, especially without being paid

helpful /'helpf(ə)l/ *adjective* useful or giving help to someone ○ *She made some helpful suggestions.* ○ *They were very helpful when we moved house.*

helping /'helpɪŋ/ *noun* an amount of food for one person ○ *The helpings in this restaurant are very small.* ○ *Children's helpings are not as large as those for adults.*

helpless /'helpləs/ *adjective* not able to do anything to make a bad situation better

hen /hen/ *noun* an adult female chicken ○ *The hens were scared by the fox.* ○ *Look, one of the hens has laid an egg!*

hence /hens/ *adverb* in the future ○ *Five months hence, the situation should be better.*

her /ə, hə, hɜː/ *object pronoun* referring to a female ○ *There's a parcel for her in reception.* ○ *Did you see her?* ○ *He told her to go away.* ■ *adjective* belonging to a female, a ship or a country ○ *Someone has stolen all her luggage.* ○ *Have you seen her father?* ○ *The dog doesn't want to eat her food.* ○ *France is helping her businesses to sell more abroad.*

herb /hɜːb/ *noun* a plant used to give flavour to food, or as a medicine

herd /hɜːd/ *noun* a group of animals, especially cows ○ *Herds of cattle were grazing on the hillside.* (NOTE: The word **herd** is usually used with cattle; for sheep, goats, and birds, the word to use is **flock**.)

here /hɪə/ *adverb* 1. in this place ○ *I'll sit here in the shade and wait for you.* ○ *Here are the keys you lost.* ○ *I'll put the book down here next to your computer.* ○ *They have been living here in England for a long time.* 2. to this place ○ *Come here at once!* ○ *Can you bring the chairs here, please?* ○ *Here comes the bus!* ◇ **here you are** take this ○ *Here you are, today's newspaper!*

hero /'hɪərəʊ/ *noun* 1. a brave man ○ *The hero of the fire was the man who managed to rescue the children from an upstairs room.* 2. the main male character in something such as a book, play or film ○ *The hero of the story is a little boy.* (NOTE: The plural is **heroes**.)

hers /hɜːz/ *pronoun* belonging to her ○ *That watch is hers, not mine.*

herself /ə'self, hə'self/ *pronoun* used for referring back to a female subject ○ *The manager wrote to me herself.* ○ *Did your sister enjoy herself?* ○ *She's too young to be able to dress herself.*

hesitate /'hezɪteɪt/ *verb* to be slow to speak or make a decision ○ *He hesitated for a moment and then said 'no'.* ○ *She's hesitating about whether to accept the job.*

hiccup /'hɪkʌp/, **hiccough** *noun* 1. a sudden high sound that you sometimes make in your throat, e.g. if you have been eating too quickly ○ *She had an attack of hiccups.* ○ *He got the hiccups from laughing too much.* 2. a small thing which goes wrong ○ *There has been a slight hiccup in the delivery of our supplies.* ■ *verb* to make a hiccup ○ *She patted him on the back when he suddenly started to hiccup.* ○ *He hiccupped so loudly that everyone in the restaurant stared at him.* (NOTE: **hiccups – hiccupping – hiccupped**)

hidden /'hɪd(ə)n/ *adjective* which cannot be seen or found easily ○ *There's a hidden safe in the wall behind his desk.* ○ *They say there's some hidden treasure in the castle.*

hide /haɪd/ *verb* 1. to put something where no one can see or find it ○ *She hid the presents in the kitchen.* ○ *They kept some gold coins hidden under the bed.* ○ *Someone has hidden my car keys.* 2. to put yourself where no one can see or find you ○ *They hid in the bushes until the police car had gone past.* ○ *Quick! Hide behind the door!* (NOTE: **hides – hiding – hid** /hɪd/ **– has hidden** /'hɪd(ə)n/)

hideous /'hɪdiəs/ *adjective* extremely unpleasant to look at ○ *Where did she get that hideous dress?*

hiding /'haɪdɪŋ/ *noun* a situation in which you have put yourself where no one can find you ○ *He stayed in hiding for three days until the soldiers left the village.* ○ *They decided to go into hiding for a time until the police called off their search.*

high /haɪ/ *adjective* 1. far above other things ○ *Everest is the highest mountain in the world.* ○ *The new building is 20 storeys high.* ○ *The kitchen has a high ceiling.* ○ *The door is not high enough* *for us to get the wardrobe into the bedroom.* ◊ **height** (NOTE: **High** is used with figures: *the mountain is 1,000 metres high.* **High** also refers to things that are a long way above the ground: *a high mountain, high clouds.* For people and narrow things like trees use **tall**: *a tall man.*) **2.** large in quantity ○ *the high level of unemployment in the country* ○ *He earns a high income.* ○ *High prices put customers off.* ○ *The car shakes when going at high speeds.* ○ *The price of petrol is higher every year.* ■ *adverb* above; up in the air ○ *The sun rose high in the sky.* ○ *The bird flew higher and higher.* (NOTE: **higher – highest**)

highly /'haɪli/ *adverb* used before some adjectives to mean 'very well' ○ *highly priced meals* ○ *The restaurant has been highly recommended.* ○ *Their employees are not very highly paid.*

highway /'haɪweɪ/ *noun* a main public road ○ *A footbridge was built over the highway.*

hijack /'haɪdʒæk/ *verb* to take control of a vehicle by force ○ *The men hijacked the lorry and left the driver by the road.* ○ *They hijacked an aircraft and ordered the pilot to fly to Moscow.*

hilarious /hɪ'leəriəs/ *adjective* very funny ○ *I thought the play was hilarious.*

hill /hɪl/ *noun* a piece of high land (*informal*) ○ *The hills are covered with spring flowers.* ○ *If you climb to the top of the hill you will get a good view of the valley.*

him /ɪm, hɪm/ *object pronoun* referring to a male ○ *Tell him there's a letter waiting for him.* ○ *Have you spoken to him today?* ○ *That's him! – The man with the beard.*

himself /ɪm'self, hɪm'self/ *pronoun* used for referring back to a male subject ○ *I was served by the manager himself.* ○ *The doctor has got flu himself.* ○ *Did your brother enjoy himself?*

hinge /hɪndʒ/ *noun* a piece of metal used to hold something, e.g. a door, window or lid, so that it can swing open and shut

○ *That hinge squeaks – it needs some oil.* ○ *They lifted the door off its hinges.*

hint /hɪnt/ *noun* **1.** something you say that reveals information in an indirect way ○ *He didn't give a hint as to where he was going on holiday.* **2.** a piece of advice or a suggestion ○ *She gave me some useful hints about painting furniture.* ○ *I don't know what to give her for her birthday – have you any hints?* ■ *verb* to say something in a way that makes people guess what you mean ○ *She hinted that her sister was pregnant.*

hip /hɪp/ *noun* the part of the body where your legs join your waist ○ *The tailor measured him round the hips.* ■ *adjective* very fashionable (*slang*) ○ *That's a very hip shirt she's wearing.*

hire /'haɪə/ *verb* **1.** (*of a borrower*) to pay money to use something for a time ○ *She hired a car for the weekend.* ○ *He was driving a hired car when the accident happened.* **2.** to employ someone to work for you ○ *We've hired three more sales assistants.* ○ *They hired a small company to paint their offices.* ■ *noun* the act of paying money to rent something such as a car, a boat or a piece of equipment

his /ɪz, hɪz/ *adjective* belonging to him ○ *He's lost all his money.* ○ *Have you met his mother?* ○ *Our dog wants his food.* ■ *pronoun* belonging to him ○ *That watch is his, not mine.*

historical /hɪ'stɒrɪk(ə)l/ *adjective* relating to history ○ *He likes books of historical interest.*

history /'hɪst(ə)ri/ *noun* **1.** the study of the past ○ *He is studying Greek history.* ○ *She failed her history exam.* ○ *She teaches history at London University.* **2.** a book which tells the story of what happened in the past ○ *He wrote a history of the French Revolution.*

hit /hɪt/ *noun* someone or something that is very popular, e.g. a song, a film or a performer ○ *The song rapidly became a hit.* ○ *The play was a West End hit.* ○ *She was a hit with the old people's club.* ■ *verb* **1.** to knock something or someone ○ *The car hit the tree.* ○ *She hit him on the head with a bottle.* ○ *She hit the ball so hard that we couldn't find it.* ○ *I* *hit my head on the cupboard door.* **2.** to cause someone to realise something ○ *It suddenly hit her that now she was divorced she would have to live alone.* (NOTE: **hits – hitting – hit**)

hit back *phrasal verb* **1.** to hit someone who has hit you ○ *They hit him so hard that he was unable to hit back.* **2.** to do something as a reaction to something ○ *When the supermarket chain lowered their prices, the other chains hit back by lowering prices too.* ○ *He hit back at the inspectors, saying that their report was biased.*

hoard /hɔːd/ *noun* a store of something such as food or money, which has been collected ○ *They discovered a hoard of gold coins in the field.* ■ *verb* to buy and store supplies of something essential that you think you will need in a crisis ○ *Everyone started hoarding fuel during the strike.*

hobby /ˈhɒbi/ *noun* an enjoyable activity which you do in your spare time (NOTE: The plural is **hobbies**.)

hockey /ˈhɒki/ *noun* a team game played on grass, where you try to hit a small ball into your opponents' goal using a long stick which is curved at the end ○ *He played in the hockey team at school.*

hoist /hɔɪst/ *verb* to lift something or someone using special equipment or a lot of force ○ *The box was hoisted up on a rope.* ○ *It's time to hoist the flag.*

hold /həʊld/ *verb* **1.** to keep something or someone tight, especially in your hand ○ *She was holding the baby in her arms.* ○ *She held her ticket between her teeth as she was carrying suitcases in both hands.* ○ *Hold tight – the machine is going to start.* ○ *He held the bag close to his chest.* **2.** to be large enough to contain a certain quantity of things or people ○ *The bottle holds two litres.* ○ *The box would hold four pairs of shoes.* ○ *Will the car hold eight people?* ○ *The plane holds 250 passengers.* **3.** to make an event happen ○ *They are holding a party for their wedding anniversary.* ○ *The meeting will be held next Tuesday in the town hall.* **4.** to own something ○ *She holds a valid driving licence.* ○ *He holds the record for the 2000 metres.* **5.**

to keep someone inside ○ *The prisoners were held in police cells overnight.* (NOTE: **holds – holding – held** /held/) □ **to hold your breath** to keep air in your lungs, e.g. in order to go under water ○ *She held her breath under water for a minute.* ○ *We're all holding our breath to see if he wins a gold medal.* ■ *noun* **1.** the bottom part of a ship or an aircraft, in which goods or luggage are stored ○ *You can't take all that luggage with you – it has to go in the hold.* **2.** the act of keeping something tightly in your hand ○ *He lost his hold on the ladder.* ○ *Keep tight hold of the bag, we don't want it stolen.* □ **to get hold of someone** to manage to contact someone by telephone ○ *I tried to get hold of the doctor but he was out.*

hold on *phrasal verb* **1.** to hold something tightly ○ *She held on to the rope with both hands.* ○ *Hold on to your purse in the crowd.* ○ *Hold on tight, we're turning!* **2.** to wait ○ *Hold on a moment, I'll get my umbrella.* ○ *Do you want to speak to the manager? Hold on, I'll find him for you.*

hold out *phrasal verb* **1.** to move something towards someone ○ *Hold out your plate to be served.* ○ *He held out his hand but she refused to shake it.* **2.** to manage to be strong enough ○ *The castle held out for ten weeks against a huge enemy army.*

hold up *phrasal verb* **1.** to lift someone or something ○ *He held up his hand.* ○ *He held the little boy up so that he could see the procession.* **2.** to support something ○ *The roof is held up by those pillars.* **3.** to make someone or something late ○ *The planes were held up by fog.* ○ *Government ministers are holding up the deal.* **4.** to use a gun to make someone give up all their money ○ *Six gunmen held up the security van.*

hold-up /ˈhəʊld ʌp/ *noun* **1.** a delay; an occasion on which something is later than planned ○ *Long hold-ups are expected because of road works on the motorway.* ○ *There's been a hold-up and the goods won't arrive till next week.* **2.** an occasion on which a person with a gun steals money from someone

○ *The gang carried out three hold-ups in the same day.*

hole /həʊl/ *noun* an opening or a space in something ○ *You've got a hole in your sock.* ○ *We all peeped through the hole in the fence.* ○ *Rabbits live in holes in the ground.*

holiday /'hɒlɪdeɪ/ *noun* **1.** a period when you do not work, and sometimes go and stay in a different place ○ *When are you taking your holiday* or *When are you planning to go on holiday?* ○ *He's going to Spain on holiday.* ○ *We always spend our holidays in the mountains.* ○ *How many days' holiday do you have each year?* **2.** a day on which most people do not work because of laws or religious rules ○ *The office is closed for the Christmas holiday.*

hollow /'hɒləʊ/ *adjective* with a hole inside ○ *a hollow log* ○ *If you tap the box it sounds hollow.*

holy /'həʊli/ *adjective* relating to religion or the church ○ *They went to ask a holy man his advice.*

home /həʊm/ *noun* **1.** the place where you live or where your parents live ○ *Their home is a flat in the centre of London.* ○ *Will you be at home tomorrow evening?* ○ *When do you leave home for work in the morning?* ○ *I like to go home for the holidays.* □ **to make yourself at home** to behave as if you were in your own home ○ *He lay down on my sofa, opened a bottle of beer, and made himself at home.* **2.** a house ○ *They are building fifty new homes on the edge of the village.* **3.** a house where people are looked after ○ *My aunt has moved to an old people's home.* **4.** □ **at home** (*in sports*) on the local sports ground ○ *Our team is playing at home next Saturday.* ■ *adverb* towards the place where you usually live ○ *We've got to go home now.* ○ *He usually gets home by 7 o'clock.* ○ *Don't send it – I'll take it home with me.* ○ *If you don't want to walk, you can always take the bus home.* (NOTE: used without a preposition: *He went home* or *She's coming home.*) ■ *adjective* referring to where you live or where you were born ○ *My home town*

is Birmingham. ○ *Send the letter to my home address, not to my office.*

homework /'həʊmwɜːk/ *noun* work which you take home from school to do in the evening ○ *Have you finished your maths homework?* ○ *I haven't got any homework today, so I can watch TV.* (NOTE: no plural)

honest /'ɒnɪst/ *adjective* **1.** telling the truth ○ *He was honest with the police and told them what he had done.* **2.** tending to tell people the truth; treating people fairly ○ *I wouldn't buy a car from that garage – I'm not sure they're completely honest.*

honestly /'ɒnɪstli/ *adverb* **1.** in an open and honest way **2.** used to express a feeling of being annoyed ○ *Honestly, you might have told me sooner!*

honesty /'ɒnɪsti/ *noun* the quality of being honest ○ *I admire him for his honesty in saying the job was too difficult for him.*

honey /'hʌni/ *noun* a sweet substance produced by bees ○ *I like honey on toast.* ○ *Greek cakes are often made with honey.*

honeymoon /'hʌnimuːn/ *noun* a holiday taken immediately after a wedding ○ *They went on their honeymoon to Corsica.*

honor /'ɒnə/ *noun, verb* US spelling of **honour**

honour /'ɒnə/ *noun* **1.** the practice of acting according to what you think is right ○ *He's a man of honour.* **2.** something that you are proud of ○ *It is an honour for me to be invited here today.* ■ *verb* **1.** to show your respect for someone ○ *to honour the dead* **2.** to give someone an award to show that you respect them ○ *He was honoured by the university.* **3.** to do what you promised ○ *He honoured the agreement and gave the staff a pay rise.*

hood /hʊd/ *noun* **1.** a loose piece of clothing to cover your head ○ *He has a blue coat with a hood.* **2.** a folding roof on something such as a car or pram ○ *Let's put down the hood, it's very hot.* **3.** *US* a metal cover for the front part of a car, covering the engine ○ *He lifted the* *hood to see what was wrong with the motor.*

hoof /huːf/ *noun* the part of the foot of a horse, cow and many other animals (NOTE: The plural is **hooves** /huːvz/.)

hook /hʊk/ *noun* **1.** a bent piece of metal for hanging things on ○ *Hang your coat on the hook behind the door.* **2.** a very small piece of thin bent metal, attached to a line for catching fish ○ *The fish ate the worm but didn't swallow the hook.*

hop /hɒp/ *verb* **1.** to jump on one leg ○ *He hurt his toe and had to hop around on one foot.* **2.** (of a bird or animal) to jump with both feet together ○ *Magpies were hopping across the grass.* ○ *The frog hopped onto the lily pad.* (NOTE: **hops – hopping – hopped**) ■ *noun* **1.** a little jump ○ *Magpies walk in a series of little hops.* **2.** a short flight ○ *It's only a short hop from London to Paris.*

hope /həʊp/ *verb* to want and expect something to happen ○ *We all hope our team wins.* ○ *She's hoping she will soon be able to drive a car.* ○ *I hope it doesn't rain.* ■ *noun* the fact of wanting and expecting something to happen ○ *Our only hope is that she will get better soon.* ○ *They have given up all hope of rescuing any more earthquake victims.*

hopeful /ˈhəʊpf(ə)l/ *adjective* confident that something will happen ○ *We are hopeful that the company will accept our offer.*

hopeless /ˈhəʊpləs/ *adjective* **1.** unlikely to get better; impossible to improve ○ *The invoices are in a hopeless mess.* **2.** not at all skilful at something ○ *She's hopeless at tennis.* ○ *He's hopeless when it comes to mending cars.*

horizon /həˈraɪz(ə)n/ *noun* the line in the distance where the earth and the sky meet

horizontal /ˌhɒrɪˈzɒnt(ə)l/ *adjective* flat; level with the ground

horn /hɔːn/ *noun* **1.** a sharp pointed bone growing out of an animal's head ○ *That bull's horns look very dangerous.* **2.** a piece of equipment on a car that makes a loud noise to warn people of something **3.** a metal musical instrument

which you blow into ○ *a piece of music for horn and orchestra*

horrible /ˈhɒrɪb(ə)l/ *adjective* extremely unpleasant ○ *The victims of the fire had horrible injuries.* ○ *He's a horrible little boy.* ○ *We had a horrible meal at the restaurant.*

horrified /ˈhɒrɪfaɪd/ *adjective* frightened or shocked

horror /ˈhɒrə/ *noun* the fact or feeling of being very frightened ○ *He couldn't hide his horror at hearing the news.* ○ *She has a horror of spiders.* ○ *Everyone watched in horror as the planes collided.*

horse /hɔːs/ *noun* a large animal used for riding or for pulling vehicles ○ *She was riding a black horse.* ○ *The coach was pulled by six white horses.* ○ *He's out on his horse every morning.*

hospital /ˈhɒspɪt(ə)l/ *noun* a place where sick or hurt people are looked after ○ *She was taken ill at work and sent to hospital.* ○ *When is she due to go into hospital?* ○ *He was in hospital for several days after the accident.*

host /həʊst/ *noun* **1.** a person who has invited guests ○ *The host asked his guests what they wanted to drink.* **2.** the landlord of a hotel or inn, also sometimes of a restaurant **3.** the person who introduces and talks to the guests on a TV or radio show ○ *He had been a host on a Saturday evening TV show.* **4.** □ **a host of** a large number of ○ *We face a host of problems.* ■ *verb* **1.** to act as host at a party ○ *The company hosted a reception for two hundred guests.* **2.** to be the centre where something takes place ○ *Barcelona hosted the Olympic Games.* **3.** to organise and manage websites for other people

hostage /ˈhɒstɪdʒ/ *noun* a person who is captured and held by someone or an organisation, which threatens to kill him or her unless their demands are met ○ *Three of the hostages will be released tomorrow.* ◇ **1. 2.** ○ *He was held hostage for more than a year by the rebels.*

hot /hɒt/ *adjective* **1.** very warm; with a high temperature ○ *The weather is very hot in June, but August is the hottest* month. ○ *If you're too hot, take your coat off.* ○ *Plates should be kept hot before serving the meal.* ◊ **heat 2.** (*of food*) full of spices, giving you a burning feeling in your mouth ○ *This curry is particularly hot.* ○ *He chose the hottest dish on the menu.*

hot dog /'hɒt dɒg/ *noun* a snack consisting of a hot sausage in a long piece of bread

hotel /həʊ'tel/ *noun* a building where travellers can rent a room for the night, eat in a restaurant or drink in a bar ○ *They are staying at the Grand Hotel.* ○ *I'll meet you in the hotel lobby.* ○ *All the hotel rooms in the town are booked.*

hour /aʊə/ *noun* a period of time which lasts 60 minutes ○ *The train journey takes two hours.* ○ *It's a three-hour flight to Greece.* ○ *The train travels at over 150 miles an hour.*

house¹ /haʊs/ *noun* **1.** a building in which someone lives ○ *He has bought a house in London.* ○ *He has a small flat in town and a large house in the country.* ○ *All the houses in our street look the same.* **2.** a part of a Parliament ○ *The British Parliament is formed of the House of Commons and the House of Lords.* ○ *The American Congress is formed of the House of Representatives and the Senate.*

house² /haʊz/ *verb* to provide a place for someone or something to stay or be kept ○ *His collection of old cars is housed in a barn.* ○ *We have been asked if we can house three students for the summer term.* (NOTE: **houses – housing – housed**)

household /'haʊshəʊld/ *noun* the people living together in a house

housework /'haʊswɜːk/ *noun* the work of keeping a house clean (NOTE: no plural)

housing /'haʊzɪŋ/ *noun* houses ○ *Public housing has to meet certain standards.*

hover /'hɒvə/ *verb* to hang in the air without moving forward ○ *flies hovering over the surface of a pool*

how /haʊ/ *adverb* **1.** showing or asking the way in which something is done ○

How do you switch off the cooker? ○ *Can you tell me how to get to the railway station from here?* ○ *I don't know how he does it.* **2.** showing or asking about things such as the age, size or quantity of something ○ *How big is their house?* ○ *How many people are there in your family?* ○ *She showed us how good she was at skiing.* ○ *How old is your little boy?* ○ *How far is it to the church?* **3.** showing surprise ○ *How cold it is outside!* ○ *How different it is from what I remember!*

however /haʊ'evə/ *adverb* but ○ *We never go out on Saturdays – however, this week we're going to a wedding.* ■ *conjunction* in whatever way ○ *Do it however you like.*

howl /haʊl/ *verb* to make a long loud high sound like a wolf ○ *The wolves howled outside the cabin.* ○ *The wind howled in the chimney.* ■ *noun* a long loud cry ○ *Howls of disappointment came from the fans.*

hug /hʌg/ *noun* the act of putting your arms round someone and holding them close to you ○ *She ran to the little girl and gave her a hug.* ■ *verb* to throw your arms around someone ○ *The players hugged each other when the goal was scored.* (NOTE: **hugs – hugging – hugged**)

huge /hjuːdʒ/ *adjective* of a very large size ○ *Huge waves battered the ship.* ○ *The concert was a huge success.* ○ *Failing the test was a huge disappointment for him.*

hum /hʌm/ *verb* **1.** to make a low sound like a bee ○ *Bees were humming around the hive.* **2.** to sing without words ○ *If you don't know the words of the national anthem, you can always hum the tune.* (NOTE: **hums – humming – hummed**)

human /'hjuːmən/ *adjective* relating to people

humble /'hʌmbəl/ *adjective* feeling or acting as if you are not as important as other people ○ *Seeing how much work she does for charity makes me feel very humble.* (NOTE: **humbler – humblest**)

humor /'hjuːmə/ *noun* US spelling of **humour**

humorous /ˈhjuːmərəs/ *adjective* funny in a quiet way, making people smile rather than laugh ○ *humorous stories* ○ *Some of her comments were rather humorous.*

humorously /ˈhjuːmərəsli/ *adverb* in a humorous

humour /ˈhjuːmə/ *noun* **1.** the ability to make situations seem funny ○ *He has a good sense of humour.* ○ *She has absolutely no sense of humour.* ○ *Want to meet male, aged 30 – 35, with a good sense of humour (GSOH).* **2.** a general feeling or mood ○ *I am in no humour to talk about holidays just now.* ○ *His good humour lasted until the end of the party.*

hump /hʌmp/ *noun* **1.** a raised part on the back of a person or animal ○ *Arabian camels have only one hump, while Bactrian camels have two.* **2.** a small raised part in the ground ○ *They have built humps in the road to slow down the traffic.*

hundred /ˈhʌndrəd/ *noun* the number 100 ○ *The church is over a hundred years old.* ○ *My grandfather will be a hundred next month.* ○ *Do I have to tell you a hundred times to stop that noise?* (NOTE: In numbers **hundred** does not change and is followed by **and** when reading: **491** = four hundred and ninety-one; **102** = a hundred and two. Note also: **a hundred and one** (101), **three hundred and six** (306) but **the hundred and first** (101st), **the three hundred and sixth** (306th), etc.) ◇ **hundreds of** very many ○ *Hundreds of birds were killed by the cold weather.* ○ *Hundreds of people caught flu last winter.* ○ *They came in their hundreds to visit the grave.*

hundredth /ˈhʌndrədθ/ *adjective* relating to number 100 in a series ○ *Tomorrow is his hundredth birthday.*

hung /hʌŋ/ past tense and past participle of **hang**

hungry /ˈhʌŋgri/ *adjective* feeling that you need to eat ○ *You must be hungry after that game of football.* ○ *I'm not very hungry – I had a big lunch.* ○ *Hurry up with the food – we're getting hungry.*

hunt /hʌnt/ *verb* **1.** □ **to hunt for something** to search for something ○ *We're hunting for a cheap flat.* ○ *The police are hunting for the driver of the car.* **2.** to chase wild animals for food or sport ○ *Our cat is not very good at hunting mice.* ○ *They go to Scotland every year to hunt deer.* (NOTE: You hunt animals, but you hunt **for** things.) ■ *noun* a search ○ *The hunt for new offices has just started.*

hunter /ˈhʌntə/ *noun* a person who hunts animals

hurricane /ˈhʌrɪkən/ *noun* a tropical storm with strong winds and rain (NOTE: In the Far East called a **typhoon**; in the Indian Ocean called a **cyclone**.)

hurry /ˈhʌri/ *verb* to go somewhere or do something fast ○ *She hurried across the room.* ○ *You'll have to hurry if you want to catch the last post.* ○ *There's no need to hurry – we've got plenty of time.* (NOTE: **hurries – hurrying – hurried**)

hurry up *phrasal verb* to go or do something faster ○ *Hurry up – we'll be late for the film.* ○ *Can't you get the cook to hurry up? I'm getting hungry!*

hurt /hɜːt/ *verb* to have pain, or to cause someone to feel pain ○ *My tooth hurts.* ○ *No one was badly hurt in the accident.* ○ *Where did you hurt yourself?* (NOTE: **hurts – hurting – hurt**)

husband /ˈhʌzbənd/ *noun* a man to whom a woman is married ○ *Her husband is Scottish.* ○ *He's the doctor's husband.*

hut /hʌt/ *noun* a small rough wooden house

hygiene /ˈhaɪdʒiːn/ *noun* the science of being and keeping things clean

hygienic /haɪˈdʒiːnɪk/ *adjective* clean and safe because all germs have been destroyed

hyphen /ˈhaɪf(ə)n/ *noun* a printing sign (-) used to show that two words are joined

I

i /aɪ/, **I** *noun* the ninth letter of the alphabet, between H and J

I[1] /aɪ/ *pronoun* used by a speaker when talking about himself or herself ○ *She said, 'I can do it', and she did it.* ○ *He told me I could go home early.* ○ *She and I come from the same town.* ○ *I said I was going to be late.* (NOTE: When it is the object of a verb, **I** becomes **me**: *I gave it to him – he gave it to me*; *I hit him – he hit me.* When it follows the verb **be**, **I** usually becomes **me**: *Who is it? – It's me!*)

I[2] /aɪ/ *noun* the Roman numeral for one or first ○ *King Charles I*

ice /aɪs/ *noun* water which is frozen and has become solid ○ *When water freezes, it turns into ice.* ○ *Would you like ice in your drink?* (NOTE: no plural: *some ice, a lump of ice*)

ice cream /aɪs ˈkriːm/ *noun* a frozen sweet food made from cream and fruit, chocolate, nuts, etc.

icy /ˈaɪsi/ *adjective* covered with ice ○ *Be careful, the pavement is icy.*

idea /aɪˈdɪə/ *noun* a thought which you have about something

ideal /aɪˈdɪəl/ *adjective* perfect; extremely suitable ○ *This is the ideal site for a factory.* ○ *The cottage is an ideal place for birdwatching.*

identical /aɪˈdentɪk(ə)l/ *adjective* exactly the same ○ *The twins wore identical clothes for the party.* ○ *Their political opinions are identical.*

identify /aɪˈdentɪfaɪ/ *verb* **1.** to recognise a person or thing and to be able to say who or what they are ○ *Can you identify what sort of rock this is?* ○ *She was able to identify her attacker.* **2.** to state that something belongs to you ○ *Each person was asked to identify his or her baggage.* (NOTE: **identifies – identifying – identified**)

identity /aɪˈdentɪti/ *noun* someone's name and personal details ○ *He changed his identity when he went to work for the secret services.*

idle /ˈaɪd(ə)l/ *adjective* not doing anything ○ *He's the idlest man I know – he never does any work at all.*

if /ɪf/ *conjunction* **1.** showing what might happen ○ *If it freezes tonight, the paths will be slippery tomorrow.* ○ *If I'm in London, I'll come and see you.* ○ *If he had told me you were ill, I'd have come to see you in hospital.* ○ *If I won the lottery, I would take a long holiday.* **2.** used in asking questions ○ *Do you know if the plane is late?* ○ *I was wondering if you would like to have some tea.*

ignorance /ˈɪɡnərəns/ *noun* a state of not knowing □ **to keep someone in ignorance of something** not to tell someone about something ○ *The soldiers were deliberately kept in ignorance of the dangers facing them.*

ignorant /ˈɪɡnərənt/ *adjective* not knowing anything

ignore /ɪɡˈnɔː/ *verb* not to notice someone or something deliberately ○ *She ignored the red light and just drove straight through.* ○ *When we met he just ignored me.*

ill /ɪl/ *adjective* sick; not well ○ *Stress can make you ill.* ○ *If you're feeling ill you ought to see a doctor.* □ **to fall ill** to become ill ○ *She fell seriously ill and we thought she was going to die.* □ **to be taken ill** to become ill suddenly ○ *He was taken ill while on holiday in Greece.*

illegal /ɪˈliːɡ(ə)l/ *adjective* against the law ○ *It is illegal to serve alcohol to people under 16.*

illegally /ɪˈliːɡəli/ *adverb* in an illegal way

illness /ˈɪlnəs/ *noun* a medical condition which makes you unwell ○ *She devel-*

oped a serious illness. ○ A lot of the staff are absent because of illness. (NOTE: The plural is **illnesses**.)

illustrate /'ɪləstreɪt/ *verb* to put pictures into a book ○ The book is illustrated with colour photographs of birds.

illustration /ˌɪlə'streɪʃ(ə)n/ *noun* a picture in a book ○ The book has 25 colour illustrations.

image /'ɪmɪdʒ/ *noun* **1.** a picture of someone or something ○ I want the portrait to be a faithful image of my mother. **2.** a picture produced by something such as a mirror or a computer ○ The mirror throws an image onto the paper. ○ Can this software handle images in that format? ○ Can you adjust the projector? The image on the screen is out of focus.

imaginary /ɪ'mædʒɪn(ə)ri/ *adjective* not real; part of a story

imagination /ɪˌmædʒɪ'neɪʃ(ə)n/ *noun* the ability to think of things that are not part of your own immediate life ○ She let her imagination run riot in her stories for children.

imagine /ɪ'mædʒɪn/ *verb* to think of something that is not part of your own immediate life ○ Imagine yourself sitting on a beach in the hot sun. ○ She thought she had heard footsteps, and then decided she had imagined it.

imitate /'ɪmɪteɪt/ *verb* to copy something or someone ○ The company imitates its competitors by making very similar products. ■ to behave as someone else does, often to make other people laugh ○ He made us all laugh by imitating the head teacher's way of walking.

imitation /ˌɪmɪ'teɪʃ(ə)n/ *noun* **1.** a copy made of something **2.** an act of copying someone's behaviour in order to make other people laugh ○ She does a very good imitation of the Queen. ■ *adjective* made to appear to be something else more valuable ○ a necklace of imitation pearls ○ The bag is made of imitation leather.

immediate /ɪ'miːdɪət/ *adjective* **1.** very soon ○ He wrote an immediate letter of complaint. ○ You didn't expect an immediate reply, did you? ○ Your order

will receive immediate attention. **2.** closest, or right next to you ○ He had to share his book with his immediate neighbour.

immediately /ɪ'miːdɪətli/ *adverb* very soon, or very soon after an event ○ He got my letter, and wrote back immediately. ○ As soon as he heard the news he immediately phoned his wife.

immoral /ɪ'mɒrəl/ *adjective* not following the usual principles of good behaviour

impact¹ /'ɪmpækt/ *noun* **1.** a strong effect ○ The TV documentary had an strong impact on the viewers. **2.** an instance of two things coming together with force ○ The car was totally crushed by the impact of the collision. □ **on impact** as soon as contact is made ○ The plane burst into flames on impact with the ground.

impact² /ɪm'pækt/ *verb* □ **to impact on something** to have a strong effect on something ○ The fall in the value of the currency will impact strongly on businesses.

impatience /ɪm'peɪʃ(ə)ns/ *noun* a lack of the ability to wait for things in a calm way

impatient /ɪm'peɪʃ(ə)nt/ *adjective* unable to wait for something in a calm way; in a hurry to do something ○ We were all impatient for the film to start. ○ He's very impatient with anyone who works slowly.

impatiently /ɪm'peɪʃ(ə)ntli/ *adverb* in an impatient way

implication /ˌɪmplɪ'keɪʃ(ə)n/ *noun* **1.** the possible effect of an action ○ What will be the implications of the election results for public spending? **2.** with the fact of being involved in a crime or something that is morally wrong ○ The newspaper revealed his implication in the affair of the stolen diamonds. **3.** a suggestion that something such as a criticism is true although it has not been expressed directly ○ I resent the implication that I knew anything about the report in advance.

imply /ɪm'plaɪ/ *verb* to suggest something without saying it directly ○ He implied that he knew where the papers had been hidden. ○ *The lawyer implied that the witness had not in fact seen the accident take place.* (NOTE: **implies – implying – implied**)

impolite /ˌɪmpəˈlaɪt/ *adjective* rude; not polite

import /ɪmˈpɔːt/ *verb* to bring goods into a country ○ *The company imports television sets from Japan.* ○ *This car was imported from France.*

importance /ɪmˈpɔːtəns/ *noun* the fact of being important ○ *Do not attach too much importance to what he says.* ○ *The bank attaches great importance to the deal.*

important /ɪmˈpɔːtənt/ *adjective* **1.** having a great effect; mattering very much ○ *It's important to be in time for the interview.* ○ *I have to go to London for an important meeting.* ○ *He left a file containing important papers in the taxi.* **2.** (*of a person*) in a high position ○ *He has an important job.* ○ *She's an important government official.* ○ *He was promoted to a more important position.*

impossible /ɪmˈpɒsɪb(ə)l/ *adjective* which cannot be done ○ *It's impossible to do all this work in two hours.* ○ *Getting skilled staff is becoming impossible.*

impress /ɪmˈpres/ *verb* to make someone feel admiration or respect ○ *Her rapid response to the request impressed her boss.* ○ *She was impressed by his skill with the paintbrush.* ○ *The military government organised the display to impress the neighbouring states.*

impression /ɪmˈpreʃ(ə)n/ *noun* an effect on someone's mind ○ *Blue walls create an impression of coldness.* ○ *The exhibition made a strong impression on her.*

impressive /ɪmˈpresɪv/ *adjective* impressing people ○ *He had a series of impressive wins in the chess tournament.* ○ *The government staged an impressive display of military hardware.*

improve /ɪmˈpruːv/ *verb* **1.** to make something better ○ *We are trying to improve our image with a series of TV commercials.* **2.** to get better ○ *The general manager has promised that the bus*

service will improve. ○ *It poured down all morning, but in the afternoon the weather improved a little.*

improvement /ɪmˈpruːvmənt/ *noun* **1.** a process of becoming better, or of making something better ○ *There has been no improvement in the train service since we complained.* **2.** a change that you make so that something is better than before ○ *They carried out some improvements to the house.* ○ *We are planning some home improvements such as a new kitchen.* ○ *The new software is a great improvement on the old version.*

in /ɪn/ *preposition, adverb* **1.** used for showing place ○ *He lives in the country.* ○ *In Japan it snows a lot during the winter.* ○ *She's in the kitchen.* ○ *He's still in bed.* ○ *Don't stand outside in the pouring rain.* **2.** at home, in an office, at a station ○ *Is the boss in?* ○ *He isn't in yet.* ○ *My husband usually gets in from work about now.* ○ *The train from Birmingham is due in at 6.30.* **3.** used for showing time ○ *In autumn the leaves turn brown.* ○ *On holiday there was nothing to do in the evenings.* ○ *She was born in 1999.* ○ *He ate his meal in five minutes.* ○ *We went for a skiing holiday in January.* **4.** used for showing time in the future ○ *I'll be back home in about two hours.* ○ *She should arrive in twenty minutes' time.* **5.** fashionable ○ *This year, short skirts are in.* **6.** used for showing a state or appearance ○ *He was dressed in black.* ○ *She ran outside in her dressing gown.* ○ *We're in a hurry.* ○ *The words are set out in alphabetical order.*

inability /ˌɪnəˈbɪlɪti/ *noun* the state of being unable to do something ○ *His inability to make decisions causes problems.*

inch /ɪntʃ/ *noun* a measure of length equal to 2.54 centimetres ○ *a three-and-a-half-inch disk* ○ *Snow lay six inches deep on the ground.* ○ *She is five foot six inches tall (5'6").* ◊ **foot** (NOTE: The plural is **inches**. With numbers **inch** is usually written with the symbol ": *a 3½" disk; He is 5' 9".*; say: 'a three and a half inch disk', 'He's five foot nine')

incident /'ɪnsɪd(ə)nt/ *noun* **1.** something which happens, especially something unpleasant ○ *Last year six hundred incidents of oil pollution were reported.* **2.** a violent action or disturbance that occurs somewhere ○ *There were several incidents during the demonstration.*

incidentally /ˌɪnsɪ'dent(ə)li/ *adverb* used for mentioning something new in a conversation

include /ɪn'kluːd/ *verb* to count someone or something along with others ○ *The waiter did not include service in the bill.* ○ *The total is £140, not including insurance and handling charges.* ○ *There were 120 people at the wedding if you include the children.*

including /ɪn'kluːdɪŋ/ *preposition* taking something together with something else ○ *The total comes to £25.00 including VAT.*

income /'ɪnkʌm/ *noun* an amount of money which you receive, especially as pay for your work ○ *Their weekly income is not really enough to live on.*

incorrect /ˌɪnkə'rekt/ *adjective* wrong, not correct

increase¹ /ɪn'kriːs/ *noun* an instance of something becoming larger ○ *an increase in tax* or *a tax increase* ○ *an increase in the cost of living*

increase² /ɪn'kriːs/ *verb* **1.** to rise or to grow ○ *The price of oil has increased twice in the past year.* **2.** to make a level or amount higher ○ *The boss increased her salary.* ○ *Rail fares have been increased by 10%.*

increased /ɪn'kriːst/ *adjective* larger or higher than before ○ *These increased rail fares mean that we cannot afford to travel so much.*

increasingly /ɪn'kriːsɪŋli/ *adverb* more and more ○ *He found it increasingly difficult to keep up with the workload at the office.* ○ *His future with the company looks increasingly doubtful.*

indeed /ɪn'diːd/ *adverb* (*for emphasis*) really ○ *Thank you very much indeed for inviting me to stay.* ○ *They have been very kind indeed to their daughter.*

independence /ˌɪndɪ'pendəns/ *noun* **1.** freedom from rule by another country ○ *The colony achieved independence ten years ago.* ○ *Scotland is aiming for independence in the next few years.* **2.** a state of not needing help from anyone else ○ *She's eighteen and is looking forward to a life of independence from her family.*

independent /ˌɪndɪ'pendənt/ *adjective* **1.** free, not ruled by anyone else ○ *Slovenia has been independent since 1991.* **2.** not owned by a group, not controlled by the state ○ *The big chains are forcing the independent shops to close down.* **3.** not needing help from anyone else ○ *She's eighteen and wants to be independent of her family.*

index /'ɪndeks/ *noun* **1.** a list, usually in alphabetical order, showing the pages on which different subjects appear in a book ○ *Look up the references to London in the index.* (NOTE: The plural in this sense is **indexes**) **2.** a regular report which shows rises and falls in things such as prices and unemployment ○ *The economic indices look very promising at the moment.* (NOTE: The plural in this sense is **indices**)

indicate /'ɪndɪkeɪt/ *verb* to show something ○ *Can you indicate the position of the enemy camp on this map?* ○ *The latest figures indicate a fall in the number of unemployed men.*

indignant /ɪn'dɪgnənt/ *adjective* feeling offended or angry because of an unfair situation ○ *I was really indignant when I found out how much my colleague earned.*

indirectly /ˌɪndɪ'rektli/ *adverb* not directly

individual /ˌɪndɪ'vɪdʒuəl/ *noun* a single person ○ *We welcome private individuals as well as groups.* ■ *adjective* single, for a particular person ○ *We treat each individual case on its merits.* ○ *We provide each member of the tour group with an individual itinerary.*

indoor /'ɪndɔː/ *adjective* inside a building ○ *an indoor swimming pool*

indoors /ɪnˈdɔːz/ *adverb* inside a building ○ *Let's go indoors.* ○ *Mum was indoors, reading.*

industrial /ɪnˈdʌstriəl/ *adjective* relating to the production of goods ○ *The Midlands is the main industrial region in Britain.*

industry /ˈɪndəstri/ *noun* the production of goods and the provision of services, or the companies involved in this activity ○ *Oil is a key industry.* ○ *The car industry has had a good year.* ○ *The government is helping industry to sell more products abroad.* ○ *The tourist industry brings in a lot of foreign currency.* (NOTE: The plural is **industries**.)

infamous /ˈɪnfəməs/ *adjective* famous for being bad or unpleasant ○ *Tourists were warned not to go near the infamous back street moneychangers.*

infant /ˈɪnfənt/ *noun* a young baby

infatuation /ɪnˈfætjueɪʃ(ə)n/ *noun* a sudden strong feeling of love for someone, especially someone you do not know very well or someone who does not love you

infect /ɪnˈfekt/ *verb* to pass on a disease or infection to someone ○ *He was infected with the disease when he was abroad on holiday.*

infection /ɪnˈfekʃən/ *noun* a disease which spreads from one person to another ○ *Her throat infection keeps coming back.* ○ *He was sneezing and spreading infection to other people in the office.* ○ *She seems to catch every little infection there is.*

infectious /ɪnˈfekʃəs/ *adjective* (*of an illness or an emotion such as fear*) likely to be passed from one person to another ○ *This strain of flu is highly infectious.* ○ *He's a great music teacher and his enthusiasm for jazz is very infectious.*

infinitive /ɪnˈfɪnɪtɪv/ *noun* the basic form of a verb, usually shown with 'to'

influence /ˈɪnfluəns/ *noun* the ability to change someone or something; an effect ○ *He has had a good influence on the other staff in the department.* ○ *The influence of the moon on the tides.* ○ *He was charged with driving under the in-*

fluence of alcohol. ■ *verb* to make someone or something change ○ *She was deeply influenced by her old teacher.* ○ *The moon influences the tides.* ○ *The price of oil has influenced the price of industrial goods.*

inform /ɪnˈfɔːm/ *verb* to tell someone something officially ○ *Have you informed the police that your watch has been stolen?* ○ *I regret to inform you that your father has died.* ○ *We are pleased to inform you that your offer has been accepted.*

informal /ɪnˈfɔːm(ə)l/ *adjective* **1.** relaxed, not formal ○ *Dress casually – the party will be informal.* ○ *The guide gave us an informal talk on the history of the castle.* **2.** (*of language*) used when talking to friends and family

information /ˌɪnfəˈmeɪʃ(ə)n/ *noun* a set of facts about something ○ *She couldn't give the police any information about how the accident happened.* ○ *She gave me a very useful piece or bit of information.* ○ *For further information, please write to Department 27.*

informed /ɪnˈfɔːmd/ *adjective* having a lot of information, or having the latest information

infuriate /ɪnˈfjʊərieɪt/ *verb* to make someone very angry ○ *Slow service in restaurants always infuriates him.*

ingenious /ɪnˈdʒiːniəs/ *adjective* very clever ○ *It was an ingenious plan.*

ingredient /ɪnˈɡriːdiənt/ *noun* a material or substance which you use to make something ○ *Make sure you've got all your ingredients together before you start cooking.*

inhabit /ɪnˈhæbɪt/ *verb* to live in a place

inhabitant /ɪnˈhæbɪt(ə)nt/ *noun* a person who lives in a particular place

initial /ɪˈnɪʃ(ə)l/ *adjective* first ○ *The initial stage of the project went off smoothly.* ○ *My initial reaction was to say 'no'.* ○ *He started the business with an initial sum of £500.* ■ *verb* to write the first letters of your name on a document to show you have read and approved it ○ *Can you initial each page of the contract to show that you have approved it?* ○ *Please initial the agree-*

ment at the place marked with an X.
(NOTE: **initials** – **initialling** – **initialled**)

initially /ɪ'nɪʃ(ə)li/ *adverb* at the beginning ○ *Initially we didn't like the new flat, but we have got used to it now.*

initiative /ɪ'nɪʃətɪv/ *noun* a decision which is intended to solve a problem ○ *The government has proposed various initiatives to get the negotiations moving again.*

injection /ɪn'dʒekʃən/ *noun* the act of putting a liquid into the body using a needle ○ *The doctor gave him a flu injection.*

injure /'ɪndʒə/ *verb* to cause pain or damage to a part of the body ○ *He injured his back playing rugby.* ○ *He was badly injured in a car accident.*

injured /'ɪndʒəd/ *noun* hurt ○ *The injured girl had fallen off her bike.*

injury /'ɪndʒəri/ *noun* damage to your body ○ *He never really recovered from his football injury.* ○ *She received severe back injuries in the accident.* (NOTE: The plural is **injuries**.)

ink /ɪŋk/ *noun* the liquid in a pen ○ *He has ink marks on his shirt.* ○ *The ink won't come off the tablecloth.* ○ *She wrote comments on his work in red ink.*

inland /'ɪnlənd/ *adverb* away from the coast of a country ○ *If you go inland from the port, you soon get into the forest.*

inn /ɪn/ *noun* a small hotel

inner /'ɪnə/ *adjective* inside ○ *Go through that arch and you will come to the inner courtyard.* ○ *Heat is conducted from the inner to the outer layer of the material.*

innocent /'ɪnəs(ə)nt/ *adjective* not guilty ○ *He was found to be innocent of the crime.* ○ *In English law, the accused is always presumed to be innocent until he is proved to be guilty.*

innovative /'ɪnəveɪtɪv/ *adjective* new in a way that has not been tried before ○ *a very innovative design*

input /'ɪnpʊt/ *noun* information that is put into a computer ○ *The input from the*

various branches is fed automatically into the head office computer.

inquiry /ɪn'kwaɪəri/ *noun* **1.** a formal investigation into a problem ○ *a government inquiry into the police force* ○ *A public inquiry will be held about plans to build another airport.* **2.** a question about something ○ *I refer to your inquiry of May 25th.* ○ *All inquiries should be addressed to this department.* ○ *He made an inquiry about trains to Edinburgh.* (NOTE: also spelt **enquiry**. The plural is **inquiries**.)

insect /'ɪnsekt/ *noun* a small animal with six legs and a body in three parts ○ *A butterfly is a kind of insect.* ○ *Insects have eaten the leaves of the cabbages.* ○ *She was stung by an insect.*

insert¹ /ɪn'sɜːt/ *verb* to put something inside something else ○ *She inserted another sentence into the letter.* ○ *He inserted each leaflet into an envelope.* ○ *Insert a coin into the slot.*

insert² /'ɪnsɜːt/ *noun* a paper which is put inside something ○ *The invitation card had an insert with a map showing how to get to the hotel.*

inside /ɪn'saɪd/ *adverb* in a house or other building ○ *Come on inside – it's cold in the street.* ○ *It rained all afternoon, so we just sat inside and watched TV.* ○ *Is there anyone there? – The house seems quite dark inside.* ■ *preposition* in ○ *There was nothing inside the bottle.* ○ *She was sitting inside the car, reading a book.* ○ *I've never been inside his office.*

insist /ɪn'sɪst/ *verb* to state firmly ○ *He insisted that he had never touched the car.* ○ *She insisted that she should be paid compensation for the delay.*

inspect /ɪn'spekt/ *verb* to look at something closely ○ *She inspected the room to see if it had been cleaned properly.*

inspector /ɪn'spektə/ *noun* a senior official who examines something closely

install /ɪn'stɔːl/ *verb* to put a piece of equipment into the place where it will operate ○ *It took the plumber a week to install the new central heating system.*

instance /'ɪnstəns/ *noun* an example ○ *There have been several instances of* *bullying in our local school.* ○ *In this instance, we will pay for the damage.* ◇ **for instance** as an example ○ *Why don't you take up a new sport – golf, for instance?*

instant /'ɪnstənt/ *noun* a moment or second ○ *For an instant, he stood still and watched the policemen.* ■ *adjective* immediate ○ *A savings account can give you instant access to your money.*

instantly /'ɪnstəntli/ *adverb* so soon after an event that no time appears to have passed in between

instead /ɪn'sted/, **instead of** *adverb* in place of ○ *We haven't any coffee – would you like some tea instead?* ○ *If you can't go, can I go instead?* ○ *I'm going instead of him, because he's ill.* ○ *Instead of stopping when the police officer shouted, he ran away.*

institute /'ɪnstɪtjuːt/ *noun* an organisation set up for a special purpose ○ *They are proposing to set up a new institute of education.* ○ *She goes to the research institute's library every week.*

institution /ˌɪnstɪ'tjuːʃ(ə)n/ *noun* **1.** an organisation or society set up for a special purpose ○ *A prison is an institution which houses criminals.* **2.** a permanent custom ○ *British institutions such as cream teas and the royal family* ○ *The lottery has rapidly become a national institution.* **3.** the process of setting something up ○ *the institution of legal action against the president*

instruct /ɪn'strʌkt/ *verb* to show someone how to do something (*formal*) ○ *We were all instructed in the use of the fire safety equipment.*

instruction /ɪn'strʌkʃən/ *noun* **1.** a statement telling someone what they must do **2.** something which explains how something is to be done or used ○ *She gave us detailed instructions how to get to the church.*

instructor /ɪn'strʌktə/ *noun* a teacher, especially of a sport

instrument /'ɪnstrʊmənt/ *noun* a piece of equipment or a tool ○ *The technical staff have instruments which measure the flow of electricity.*

insult¹ /'ɪnsʌlt/ *noun* a rude word said to or about a person ○ *That is an insult to the government.* ○ *The crowd shouted insults at the police.*

insult² /ɪn'sʌlt/ *verb* to say rude things about someone ○ *He was accused of insulting the president's wife.*

insulting /ɪn'sʌltɪŋ/ *adjective* rude ○ *I'm used to hearing insulting things about my business.*

insurance /ɪn'ʃʊərəns/ *noun* an agreement with a company by which you are paid money for loss or damage in return for regular payments of money ○ *Do you have insurance for your travel?*

intelligence /ɪn'telɪdʒəns/ *noun* **1.** the ability to think and understand ○ *His intelligence is well above average.* **2.** information provided by the secret services ○ *Intelligence gathered by our network of agents is very useful to us in planning future strategy.*

intelligent /ɪn'telɪdʒənt/ *adjective* able to understand and learn things very well ○ *He's the most intelligent child in his class.*

intense /ɪn'tens/ *adjective* very strong or extreme ○ *There was a period of intense activity to try to finish the work before they went on holiday.* ○ *She had an intense period of study before the exams.*

intention /ɪn'tenʃən/ *noun* an aim or plan to do something ○ *I have no intention of going to the party.* ○ *The fans came with the deliberate intention of making trouble.*

interest /'ɪntrəst/ *noun* **1.** special attention to something ○ *She takes a lot of interest in politics.* ○ *He has no interest in what his sister is doing.* ○ *Why doesn't he take more interest in local affairs?* **2.** a thing that you enjoy doing ○ *Her main interest is canoeing.* ○ *List your special interests on your CV.* **3.** a payment made to someone who lends money ○ *Deposit accounts pay more interest.* ○ *How much interest do I have to pay if I borrow £1000?* ■ *verb* to attract someone ○ *He's particularly interested in old cars.* ○ *Nothing seems to interest him very much.* ○ *The book didn't interest me at* *all.* ○ *He tried to interest several companies in his new invention.*

interested /'ɪntrəstɪd/ *adjective* with a personal interest in something ○ *He's interested in old churches.* ○ *She's interested in crime fiction.*

interesting /'ɪntrəstɪŋ/ *adjective* attracting your attention; enjoyable ○ *There's an interesting article in the newspaper on European football.* ○ *She didn't find the TV programme very interesting.* ○ *What's so interesting about old cars? – I find them dull.*

interfere /ɪntə'fɪə/ *verb* □ **to interfere in** *or* **with something** to get in the way of something, to be involved in something in such a way that it does not work well ○ *His mother is always interfering in his private life.* ○ *Stop interfering with the TV controls.*

interference /ɪntə'fɪərəns/ *noun* **1.** an involvement with someone else's life or business ○ *His parents' interference in his travel plans annoyed him.* **2.** a noise which affects radio or TV programmes

interjection /ɪntə'dʒekʃən/ *noun* an exclamation, a word used to show an emotion such as surprise

intermittent /ɪntə'mɪt(ə)nt/ *adjective* stopping and starting in an irregular way ○ *Intermittent showers are expected over the weekend.*

internal /ɪn'tɜːn(ə)l/ *adjective* inside

international /ɪntə'næʃ(ə)nəl/ *adjective* between countries ○ *an international conference on the environment* ○ *an important international company* ■ *noun* a sportsperson who has played for his or her country's team against another country ○ *There are three England internationals in our local team.*

Internet /'ɪntənet/ *noun* an international network allowing people to exchange information on computers using telephone lines ○ *We send messages over the Internet to hundreds of users of our products.* ○ *He searched the Internet for information on cheap plane tickets.* (NOTE: also called simply **the Net**)

interpret /ɪn'tɜːprɪt/ *verb* to translate what someone is saying into a different

language ○ *His brother knows Greek, so he will interpret for us.*

interpretation /ɪnˌtɜːprɪ'teɪʃ(ə)n/ *noun* **1.** a meaning ○ *A poem can have many interpretations.* ○ *The book puts quite a different interpretation on the meaning of the rule.* **2.** the act of translating what someone is saying into a different language **3.** a way of playing a piece of music ○ *Two of the young musicians were praised for their interpretations of Bach.*

interrupt /ɪntə'rʌpt/ *verb* to start talking when someone else is talking ○ *Excuse me for interrupting, but have you seen the office keys anywhere?*

interruption /ɪntə'rʌpʃən/ *noun* something that interrupts or stops you from working

interval /'ɪntəv(ə)l/ *noun* **1.** a period of time between two events or points in time ○ *There will be bright intervals during the morning, but it will rain in the afternoon.* ○ *There will be a short interval during which the table will be cleared.* **2.** a period of time between two acts in a play ○ *Anyone arriving late won't be allowed in until the first interval.*

interview /'ɪntəvjuː/ *noun* **1.** a conversation between a famous or interesting person and a journalist, broadcast on radio or TV, or printed in a newspaper ○ *She gave an interview to the Sunday magazine.* **2.** a formal meeting in which one or more people ask you questions to find out if you are suitable for something such as a particular job or a course at university ○ *We asked six candidates for interview.* ○ *He's had eight interviews, but still no job offers.* ○ *When will you attend your first interview?* ■ *verb* **1.** to ask a famous or interesting person questions about themselves and their work in order to publish or broadcast what they say ○ *The journalist interviewed the Prime Minister.* **2.** to meet a person who is applying for something such as a job or a place on a university course, to see if he or she is suitable ○ *We interviewed ten candidates, but did not find anyone we liked.*

into /'ɪntə, 'ɪntʊ, 'ɪntuː/ *preposition* **1.** used for showing movement towards the inside ○ *She went into the shop.* ○ *He fell into the lake.* ○ *Put the cards back into their box.* ○ *You can't get ten people into a taxi.* ○ *We all stopped talking when he came into the room.* ○ *The bus is going into the town centre.* **2.** hitting against something ○ *The bus drove into a lamp post.* **3.** used for showing a change ○ *The tadpole changed into a frog.* ○ *Water turns into steam when it is heated.* **4.** used for showing that you are dividing something ○ *Try to cut the cake into ten equal pieces.*

introduce /ˌɪntrə'djuːs/ *verb* to tell someone another person's name when they meet for the first time ○ *He introduced me to a friend of his called Anne.* ○ *She introduced me to her new teacher.*

introduction /ˌɪntrə'dʌkʃən/ *noun* **1.** a part at the beginning of a book which describes the subject of the book ○ *Read the introduction which gives an explanation of the book's layout.* **2.** a book which gives basic information about a subject ○ *He's the author of an introduction to mathematics.*

invent /ɪn'vent/ *verb* **1.** to create a new process or a new machine ○ *She invented a new type of computer terminal.* ○ *Who invented this indexing system?* **2.** to make up an excuse ○ *When she asked him why he was late he invented some story about the train not arriving.*

invention /ɪn'venʃən/ *noun* **1.** the act of creating a new process or a new machine ○ *The invention of computers was made possible by developments in electronics.* **2.** a machine or process that someone has invented

inventor /ɪn'ventə/ *noun* a person who invents new processes or new machines

invest /ɪn'vest/ *verb* **1.** to use your money for buying things such as property or shares in a company, so that you will make a profit ○ *She was advised to invest in government bonds.* ○ *He invested all his money in a fish-and-chip restaurant.* **2.** to spend money on something which you believe will be useful ○ *We have invested in a new fridge.*

investigate /ɪn'vestɪgeɪt/ *verb* to try to find out about something ○ *The detective is investigating the details of the case.* ○ *We are investigating the possibility of going to live abroad.*

investigation /ɪnˌvestɪ'geɪʃ(ə)n/ *noun* a close examination ○ *a police investigation into the causes of the crash*

invisible /ɪn'vɪzɪb(ə)l/ *adjective* which cannot be seen ○ *The message was written in invisible ink and hidden inside the pages of a book.*

invitation /ˌɪnvɪ'teɪʃ(ə)n/ *noun* a letter or card, asking someone to do something or go somewhere ○ *He received an invitation to his sister's wedding.* ○ *She had an invitation to dinner.*

invite /ɪn'vaɪt/ *verb* to ask someone to do something, especially to come to a social event such as a party ○ *We invited two hundred people to the party.* ○ *She invited us to come in.* ○ *She's been invited to talk to the club.*

invoice /'ɪnvɔɪs/ *noun* a note sent to ask for payment for services or goods ○ *Our invoice dated November 10th has still not been paid.* ○ *They sent in their invoice six weeks late.* ○ *Ask the sales assistant to make out an invoice for £250.*

involve /ɪn'vɒlv/ *verb* **1.** to include someone or something in an activity or situation ○ *a competition involving teams from ten different countries* ○ *We want to involve the local community in the decision about the bypass.* ○ *Members of the local council are involved in the company which has won the contract for the new road.* **2.** to make an activity necessary ○ *Going to Cambridge from here involves taking a bus and then the train.*

inwards /'ɪnwədz/ *adverb* towards the inside ○ *These doors open inwards.*

Ireland /'aɪələnd/ *noun* a large island forming the western part of the British Isles, containing the Republic of Ireland and Northern Ireland ○ *These birds are found all over Ireland.*

Irish /'aɪrɪʃ/ *adjective* referring to Ireland ○ *The Irish Sea lies between Ireland and Britain.*

iron /'aɪən/ noun **1.** a common grey metal ○ *The old gates are made of iron.* (NOTE: no plural in this sense: *some iron, lumps of iron, pieces of iron*) **2.** an object with a flat metal bottom, which is heated and used to make clothes smooth after washing ○ *Don't leave the iron there – it will burn the clothes.* ○ *If your iron is not hot enough it won't take the creases out.* ■ *verb* to make cloth smooth using an iron ○ *She was ironing shirts when the telephone rang.* ○ *Her skirt doesn't look as if it has been ironed.*

irresponsible /ˌɪrɪ'spɒnsɪb(ə)l/ *adjective* acting or done in a way that shows a lack of good sense

irritable /'ɪrɪtəb(ə)l/ *adjective* easily annoyed ○ *He was tired and irritable, and snapped at the children.*

irritate /'ɪrɪteɪt/ *verb* to make someone feel angry or impatient ○ *It irritates me when the trains run late.*

irritation /ˌɪrɪ'teɪʃ(ə)n/ *noun* a feeling of being annoyed and impatient ○ *She watched with irritation as he tried to fix the wheel again.*

is /ɪz/ 3rd person singular present of **be**

island /'aɪlənd/ *noun* a piece of land with water all around it ○ *They live on a little island in the middle of the river.* ○ *The Greek islands are favourite holiday destinations.*

issue /'ɪʃuː/ *noun* **1.** an occasion when something is officially given out ○ *The issue of identity cards has been delayed.* **2.** a newspaper or magazine which is published at a particular time ○ *We bought the January issue of the magazine.* ■ *verb* **1.** to make something available for use ○ *The new set of stamps will be issued next week.* **2.** to give something out officially ○ *Each soldier was issued with a gun.* **3.** to come out ○ *Smoke began to issue from the hole in the ground.*

it /ɪt/ *pronoun* **1.** used to refer to something which has just been mentioned ○ *What do you want me to do with the box? – Put it down.* ○ *Where's the box? – It's here.* ○ *She picked up a potato and then dropped it on the ground.* ○ *I put my book down somewhere and now I can't find it.* ○ *Where's the newspaper? – It's on the chair.* **2.** used for talking about the weather, the date or time or another situation ○ *Look! – It's snowing.* ○ *It's miles from here to the railway station.* ○ *Is it the 30th today?* ○ *It's almost impossible to get a ticket at this time of year.* ○ *What time is it? – It's ten o'clock.* ○ *It's dangerous to use an electric saw when it's wet.* (NOTE: **It's** = **it is** or **it has**. Do not confuse with **its**.)

IT *abbr* information technology

itch /ɪtʃ/ *noun* a place on the skin where you want to scratch ○ *I've got an itch in the middle of my back that's driving me mad!* (NOTE: The plural is **itches**.) ■ *verb* to make someone want to scratch ○ *The cream made his skin itch more than before.*

item /'aɪtəm/ *noun* a thing shown in a list ○ *We are discussing item four on the agenda.* ○ *Please find enclosed an order for the following items from your catalogue.* ○ *I couldn't buy several items on the shopping list because the shop had sold out.*

its /ɪts/ *adjective* belonging to 'it' ○ *I can't use the car – one of its tyres is flat.* ○ *The company pays its staff very badly.* (NOTE: Do not confuse with **it's**.)

it's /ɪts/ *short for* it is, it has

itself /ɪt'self/ *pronoun* **1.** used for referring back to a thing or an animal ○ *The dog seems to have hurt itself.* ○ *The screw had worked itself loose.* **2.** used for emphasis ○ *If the plug is all right there must be something wrong with the computer itself.*

J

j /dʒeɪ/, **J** *noun* the tenth letter of the alphabet, between I and K

jab /dʒæb/ *verb* to suddenly push something with a sharp object ○ *He jabbed the piece of meat with his fork.* ○ *She jabbed me in the back with her umbrella.* (NOTE: **jabs – jabbing – jabbed**)

jack /dʒæk/ *noun* **1.** a tool for raising something heavy, especially a car ○ *I used the jack to lift the car up and take the wheel off.* **2.** (*in playing cards*) the card with the face of a young man, with a value between the queen and the ten ○ *I won because I had the jack of hearts.*

jacket /'dʒækɪt/ *noun* a short coat ○ *He was wearing a blue jacket and brown trousers.* ○ *Take your jacket off if you are hot.* ○ *This orange jacket shows up in the dark when I ride my bike.*

jail /dʒeɪl/ *noun* a prison ○ *She was sent to jail for three months.* ■ *verb* to put someone in prison ○ *He was jailed for six years.*

jam /dʒæm/ *noun* **1.** a sweet food made by boiling fruit and sugar together ○ *Do you want jam or honey on your bread?* ○ *We made jam with the fruit in the garden.* ○ *Have you any more jam – the jar is empty?* **2.** a situation in which too many things block something ○ *a traffic jam* ○ *There is a paper jam in the printer.* ■ *verb* **1.** (*of machines*) to stick and not be able to move ○ *Hold on – the paper has jammed in the printer.* **2.** to force things into a small space ○ *Don't try to jam all those boxes into the car boot.* ○ *The switchboard was jammed with calls.* (NOTE: **jams – jamming – jammed**)

January /'dʒænjuəri/ *noun* the first month of the year, followed by February ○ *He was born on January 26th.* ○ *It's his birthday on January 26.* ○ *We never go on holiday in January because it's too cold.* ○ *We all went skiing last January.* (NOTE: **January 26th** *or* **January 26**: say 'the twenty-sixth of January' or 'January the twenty-sixth'; American English: 'January twenty-sixth'.)

jar /dʒɑː/ *noun* a container for food such as jam, usually made of glass ○ *There was some honey left in the bottom of the jar.* ○ *Use a jam jar for the water you collect.*

jargon /'dʒɑːɡən/ *noun* a special type of language used by a trade or profession or a particular group of people ○ *People are confused by computers because they don't understand the jargon.*

jaw /dʒɔː/ *noun* the bones in the face which hold the teeth and form the mouth

jazz /dʒæz/ *noun* a type of music with a strong rhythm, and in which the players often make the music up as they play; jazz was first played in the southern United States

jealous /'dʒeləs/ *adjective* feeling annoyed because you want something which belongs to someone else ○ *John was jealous of Mark because all the girls fancied him.* ○ *She was jealous of his new car.* ○ *Her new boyfriend is very handsome – I'm jealous!*

jeans /dʒiːnz/ *plural noun* trousers made of a type of strong cotton, often blue ○ *She came into the office in jeans.* ○ *He bought a new pair of jeans.*

jelly /'dʒeli/ *noun* a type of sweet food made with fruit, which shakes when you touch it or move it ○ *The children had fish fingers and chips followed by jelly and ice-cream.* (NOTE: The plural is **jellies**.)

jerk /dʒɜːk/ *noun* a sudden sharp pull ○ *He felt a jerk on the fishing line.* ■ *verb* to suddenly pull something hard, often causing pain or injury ○ *He jerked the rope.*

jersey /'dʒɜːzi/ *noun* **1.** a warm piece of clothing which covers the top part of your body and your arms ○ *She was knitting a pink jersey for the new baby.* **2.** a special shirt worn by a member of a sports team ○ *After every game the players swapped jerseys with the other team.*

jet /dʒet/ *noun* **1.** a long narrow stream of liquid or gas ○ *A jet of water put out the flames.* **2.** an aircraft with jet engines ○ *Jets flew low overhead.*

jet engine /ˈdʒet ˌendʒɪn/ *noun* an engine which gets its power from a stream of gas

jewel /ˈdʒuːəl/ *noun* a valuable stone such as a diamond

jewellery /ˈdʒuːəlri/ *noun* things that you wear as decoration round your neck, fingers, etc., made from things such as valuable stones, gold and silver ○ *The burglar stole all her jewellery.* (NOTE: no plural)

jigsaw /ˈdʒɪgsɔː/ *noun* □ **jigsaw puzzle** a picture made of shaped pieces of wood or cardboard that you have to try to fit together ○ *As it's raining, let's stay indoors and try to do this huge jigsaw of the Houses of Parliament.*

job /dʒɒb/ *noun* **1.** regular work which you get paid for ○ *She's managed to get a job in the local supermarket.* ○ *When the factory closed, hundreds of people lost their jobs.* **2.** a specific piece of work ○ *Don't sit down, there are a couple of jobs I want you to do.* ○ *He does all sorts of little electrical jobs around the house.* **3.** difficulty (*informal*) ○ *I had a job trying to find your house.* ○ *What a job it was getting a hotel room at the time of the music festival!*

jog /dʒɒg/ *verb* **1.** to run fairly slowly, especially for exercise ○ *He jogged along the river bank for two miles.* ○ *She was listening to her personal stereo as she was jogging.* **2.** to push someone or something slightly ○ *Someone jogged my elbow and I spilt my drink.* (NOTE: **jogs – jogging – jogged**) ◊ **to jog someone's memory** to make someone remember something ○ *The police are hoping that the film from the security camera will jog people's memories.*

join /dʒɔɪn/ *verb* **1.** to come together ○ *Go on for about two hundred metres, until the road joins the motorway.* ○ *The two rivers join about four kilometres beyond the town.* **2.** to become a member of a club or other organisation ○ *After university, he is going to join the police.* ○ *She joined the army because she wanted to travel.* **3.** to do something with someone ○ *We're going to have a cup of coffee – would you like to join us?* ○ *Won't you join us for a game of golf?*

joint /dʒɔɪnt/ *noun* **1.** a place where bones come together and can move, such as the knee or the elbow ○ *Her elbow joint hurt after her game of tennis.* **2.** a large piece of meat, especially for cooking in an oven ○ *The joint of lamb was very tender.* ○ *We all sat round the table while Father carved the joint.* ■ *adjective* combined, with two or more things connected together

joke /dʒəʊk/ *noun* a thing said or done to make people laugh ○ *She poured water down his neck as a joke.* ○ *They all laughed at his jokes.* ○ *He told jokes all evening.*

journal /ˈdʒɜːn(ə)l/ *noun* a book where you write details of things that have happened which you want to remember ○ *He kept a journal during his visit to China.* ○ *She wrote a journal of the gradual progress of her illness.*

journalism /ˈdʒɜːn(ə)lɪz(ə)m/ *noun* the profession of writing for newspapers or magazines, or reporting on events for radio or TV

journalist /ˈdʒɜːn(ə)lɪst/ *noun* a person who writes for newspapers or magazines, or reports on events for radio or TV ○ *Journalists asked the policeman some very awkward questions.* ○ *Film stars were greeted by journalists from around the world at the première of the new film.*

journey /ˈdʒɜːni/ *noun* an occasion when you travel somewhere, usually a long distance ○ *It's at least two days' journey from here.* ○ *They went on a train journey across China.* ○ *She has a difficult journey to work every day – she has to change buses twice.*

joy /dʒɔɪ/ *noun* very great happiness ○ *The birth of our baby son filled us with joy.*

judge /dʒʌdʒ/ *noun* **1.** a person whose job is to make legal decisions in a court of law ○ *He was convicted for stealing, but the judge let him off with a small fine.* **2.** a person who decides who should win a competition ○ *The three judges of the beauty contest couldn't agree.* ■ *verb* to make decisions in situations such as a court of law or a competition ○ *He was judged guilty.* ○ *Her painting was judged the best and she won first prize.*

judgment /'dʒʌdʒmənt/, **judgement** *noun* **1.** a legal decision by a judge or court ○ *We will appeal against the judgment.* **2.** the ability to make good decisions ○ *He trusted his wife's judgment in everything.*

jug /dʒʌg/ *noun* a container with a handle, used for pouring liquids

juice /dʒuːs/ *noun* a liquid from fruit, vegetables or meat ○ *They charged me £1 for two glasses of orange juice.* ○ *She had a glass of grapefruit juice for breakfast.*

juicy /'dʒuːsi/ *adjective* full of juice (NOTE: **juicier – juiciest**)

July /dʒʊ'laɪ/ *noun* the seventh month of the year, between June and August ○ *July 23* ○ *We went to Spain last July. July is always one of the busiest months for holidays.* (NOTE: **July 23rd** or **July 23**: say 'July the twenty-third' or 'the twenty-third of July'; American English: 'July twenty-third'.)

jump /dʒʌmp/ *noun* a sudden movement up or down into the air ○ *The jump was higher than she thought and she hurt her leg.* ■ *verb* **1.** to go suddenly into the air from or towards the ground ○ *Quick, jump on that bus – it's going to Oxford Circus!* ○ *The horse jumped over the fence.* ○ *She jumped down from the chair.* **2.** to make a sudden movement because you are frightened ○ *She jumped when I came up behind her quietly.* ○ *When they fired the gun, it made me jump.*

jumper /'dʒʌmpə/ *noun* a warm piece of clothing, usually made of wool, which covers the top part of your body and your arms

junction /'dʒʌŋkʃən/ *noun* a place where railway lines or roads meet ○ *Go as far as the next junction and you will see the library on your right.* ○ *Leave the motorway at Junction 5.*

June /dʒuːn/ *noun* the sixth month of the year, between May and July ○ *June 17* ○ *Last June we had a holiday in Canada.* (NOTE: **June 17th** or **June 17**: say 'June the seventeenth' or 'the seventeenth of June' or in US English: 'June seventeenth'.)

jungle /'dʒʌŋgəl/ *noun* an area of thick tropical forest which is difficult to travel through

junior /'dʒuːniə/ *adjective* intended for younger children ○ *She sings in the junior choir.* ○ *He plays for the junior hockey team.*

junk /dʒʌŋk/ *noun* useless articles, rubbish ○ *Don't keep that – it's junk.* ○ *You should throw away all that junk you keep under your bed.* (NOTE: no plural)

just /dʒʌst/ *adverb* **1.** exactly ○ *Is that too much sugar? – No, it's just right.* ○ *Thank you, that's just what I was looking for.* ○ *Just how many of students have got computers?* ○ *What time is it? – It's just seven o'clock.* ○ *He's just fifteen – his birthday was yesterday.* **2.** showing the very recent past ○ *The train has just arrived from Paris.* ○ *She had just got into her bath when the phone rang.* **3.** only ○ *We're just good friends, nothing more.* ○ *I've been to Berlin just once.*

justice /'dʒʌstɪs/ *noun* fair treatment in law ○ *Justice must always be seen to be done.*

justify /'dʒʌstɪfaɪ/ *verb* to show that something is fair, to prove that something is right ○ *How can you justify spending all that money?* ○ *How can you justify your behaviour?* (NOTE: **justifies – justifying – justified**)

K

k /keɪ/, **K** *noun* the eleventh letter of the alphabet, between J and L

keen /kiːn/ *adjective* very sensitive ○ *Bats have a keen sense of hearing.* (NOTE: **keener – keenest**)

keep /kiːp/ *verb* **1.** to continue to have something ○ *Can I keep the newspaper I borrowed from you?* ○ *I don't want that book any more, you can keep it.* ○ *The police kept my gun and won't give it back.* **2.** to continue to do something ○ *The clock kept going even after I dropped it on the floor.* ○ *He had to keep smiling so that people would think he was pleased.* ○ *Keep quiet or they'll hear you.* ○ *Luckily the weather kept fine for the fair.* ○ *The food will keep warm in the oven.* **3.** to have or to put something in a particular place ○ *I keep my car keys in my pocket.* ○ *Where do you keep the paper for the laser printer?* **4.** to make someone or something stay in a place or state ○ *It's cruel to keep animals in cages.* ○ *I was kept late at the office.* ○ *They kept us waiting for half an hour.* ○ *We put the plates in the oven to keep them warm.* **5.** to stay ○ *Keep close to me.* (NOTE: **keeps – keeping – kept** /kept/)

keep down *phrasal verb* **1.** to keep at a low level ○ *Keep your voice down, the police will hear us!* **2.** to bend down in order to hide from someone ○ *Keep down behind the wall so that they won't see us.*

keep off *phrasal verb* not to walk on something ○ *Keep off the grass!*

keep on *phrasal verb* to continue to do something ○ *Keep on trying!*

keep out *phrasal verb* **1.** to stop someone going in ○ *We put up notices telling people to keep their dogs out of the field where the lambs are.* **2.** not to go in ○ *There were 'Keep Out!' notices round the building site.* **3.** not to get involved

○ *He kept out of the quarrel.* ○ *Try to keep out of trouble with the police.*

keep up with /ˌkiːp ˈʌp wɪð/ *phrasal verb* to go at the same speed as someone ○ *My foot hurts, that's why I can't keep up with the others.* ○ *His salary hasn't kept up with the cost of living.*

kerb /kɜːb/ *noun* the stone edge of a path along the side of a road

ketchup /ˈketʃəp/ *noun* a type of tomato sauce

kettle /ˈket(ə)l/ *noun* a container used for boiling water

key /kiː/ *noun* **1.** a shaped piece of metal that you use to open a lock or to start a car ○ *I can't start the car, I've lost the key.* ○ *Where did you put the front door key?* **2.** one of the moving parts which you push down with your fingers on a typewriter, a computer or a musical instrument such as a piano ○ *The 'F' key always sticks.* ○ *There are 64 keys on the keyboard.* **3.** a system of musical tones ○ *This piece of music is written in the key of F major.* ■ *adjective* most important ○ *The key person in the team is the goalkeeper.* ○ *The key person in the company is the sales manager.* ○ *Oil is a key industry.*

keyboard /ˈkiːbɔːd/ *noun* a set of keys on something such as a computer or piano ○ *She spilled her coffee on the computer keyboard.* ○ *He practises on the keyboard every day.* ■ *verb* to put information into a computer using a keyboard ○ *She was keyboarding the figures.*

kick /kɪk/ *noun* **1.** the act of hitting something with your foot ○ *The goalkeeper gave the ball a kick.* **2.** a feeling of excitement ○ *He gets a kick out of watching a football match on TV.* ■ *verb* to hit something with your foot ○ *He kicked the ball into the net.* ○ *She kicked her little brother.*

kid /kɪd/ *noun* **1.** a child (*informal*) ○ *There were a few school kids on their bicycles.* ○ *They're married with two kids.* **2.** a young goat ■ *verb* to make someone believe something which is not true ○ *Are you kidding?* ○ *She tried to kid me that she'd had an accident.* (NOTE: **kids – kidding – kidded**)

kidnap /'kɪdnæp/ *verb* to take someone away illegally and keep them prisoner (NOTE: **kidnaps – kidnapping – kidnapped**)

kidney /'kɪdni/ *noun* one of a pair of organs in animals that clean the blood and remove waste from it

kill /kɪl/ *verb* to make someone or something die ○ *Sixty people were killed in the plane crash.* ○ *A long period of dry weather could kill all the crops.*

kilo /'kiːləʊ/ *abbr* kilogram (NOTE: The plural is **kilos**.)

kilogram /'kɪləgræm/ *noun* a measure of weight equal to one thousand grams (NOTE: written **kg** after figures: *20kg*)

kilometre /'kɪlə,miːtə/ *noun* a measure of distance equal to one thousand metres

kind /kaɪnd/ *adjective* friendly and helpful ○ *It's very kind of you to offer to help.* ○ *How kind of you to invite him to your party!* ○ *You should always be kind to little children.* ○ *He's a kind old gentleman.* ■ *noun* a type ○ *A butterfly is a kind of insect.* ○ *We have several kinds of apples in our garden.* ○ *We discussed all kinds of things.* ◇ **of a kind** similar ○ *The three sisters are three of a kind.* ◇ **it's nothing of the kind** that's not correct at all ◇ **kind of** in a certain way (*informal*) ○ *I was kind of annoyed when she told me that.*

kindness /'kaɪndnəs/ *noun* **1.** the quality of being kind ○ *She was touched by his kindness.* **2.** a kind act

king /kɪŋ/ *noun* **1.** a man who governs a country by right of birth ○ *The king and queen came to visit the town.* (NOTE: **king** is spelt with a capital letter when used with a name or when referring to a particular person: *King Henry VIII.*) **2.** (*in cards*) the card with the face of a man, coming before the ace and after the queen in value ○ *He knew he could win when he drew the king of spades.*

kingdom /'kɪŋdəm/ *noun* **1.** the land ruled over by a king or queen ○ *England is part of the United Kingdom.* ○ *He gave her a book of fairy stories about a magic kingdom.* **2.** a part of the world of nature ○ *the animal kingdom*

kiss /kɪs/ *noun* the act of touching someone with your lips to show that you are pleased to see them or that you like them ○ *She gave the baby a kiss.* ■ *verb* to touch someone with your lips to show that you are pleased to see them or that you like them ○ *She kissed her daughter and walked away.* ○ *They kissed each other goodbye.*

kit /kɪt/ *noun* clothes and personal equipment, usually kept in a bag ○ *Did you bring your tennis kit?*

kitchen /'kɪtʃɪn/ *noun* a room where you can cook food ○ *She put the meat down on the kitchen table.* ○ *If you're hungry, have a look in the kitchen to see if there's anything to eat.*

kite /kaɪt/ *noun* a toy made of light wood and paper or cloth which is flown in the wind on the end of a string ○ *He was flying his kite from the top of the hill.*

kitten /'kɪt(ə)n/ *noun* a young cat

knack /næk/ *noun* an ability or tendency to do something, often something wrong (*informal*) ○ *She has a knack for talking to strangers.* ○ *He has this knack of accidentally offending people.*

knee /niː/ *noun* **1.** the part on your body where the upper and the lower leg join, where your leg bends ○ *She sat the child on her knee.* ○ *He was on his knees looking under the bed.* **2.** the part of a pair of trousers that covers the knee ○ *My jeans have holes in both knees.*

kneel /niːl/ *verb* to go down on your knees (NOTE: **kneels – kneeling – kneeled** *or* **knelt** /nelt/)

knew /njuː/ past tense of **know**

knife /naɪf/ *noun* an instrument used for cutting, with a sharp metal blade fixed in a handle ○ *Put out a knife, fork and spoon for each person.* ○ *You need a sharp knife to cut meat.* (NOTE: The plural is **knives**.) ■ *verb* to injure someone using a knife ○ *He was knifed in the back during the fight.* (NOTE: **knifes – knifing – knifed**)

knit /nɪt/ *verb* to make cloth out of wool by joining threads together using two long needles ○ *My mother is knitting me a pullover.* ○ *She was wearing a blue knitted hat.* (NOTE: **knits – knitting – knit** *or* **knitted**)

knives /naɪvz/ plural of **knife**

knob /nɒb/ *noun* **1.** a rounded handle that you turn, e.g. on a door or drawer ○ *To open the door, just turn the knob.* **2.** a round object which you turn to operate a radio or TV, etc. ○ *Turn the knob to increase the volume.*

knock /nɒk/ *noun* a sound made by hitting something ○ *Suddenly, there was a knock at the door.* ■ *verb* to hit something ○ *Knock twice before going in.* ○ *You'll need a heavy hammer to knock that nail in.*

knock down *phrasal verb* **1.** to make something fall down ○ *They are going to knock down the old house to build a factory.* **2.** to hit someone or something ○ *She was knocked down by a car.* **3.** to reduce a price ○ *They knocked the price down to £50.*

knock out *phrasal verb* to hit someone so hard that they are no longer conscious ○ *She was knocked out by a blow on the head.*

knot /nɒt/ *noun* **1.** one or more pieces of string, rope, or other fibre, twisted and fastened together ○ *Boy Scouts are supposed to be able to tie knots.* ○ *Is the knot of my tie straight?* **2.** a measure of the speed of a ship, or of the wind ○ *The ship was doing 22 knots when she hit the rocks.* ○ *There's a wind speed of 60 knots.*

know /nəʊ/ *verb* **1.** to have learned something, to have information about something ○ *Do you know how to start the computer?* ○ *He didn't know she had died.* ○ *How was I to know she wasn't his wife?* ○ *You knew it would be expensive.* ○ *Do you know the Spanish for 'one – two – three'?* ○ *His secretary doesn't know where he is.* **2.** to have met someone ○ *I know your sister – we were at school together.* ○ *I used to know a man called Peter Jones who worked in your company.* **3.** to have been to a place often ○ *I know Paris very well.* ○ *She doesn't know Germany at all.* (NOTE: **knows – knowing – knew** /njuː/ – **has known**)

knowledge /'nɒlɪdʒ/ *noun* the general facts or information that people know ○ *No encyclopedia can contain all human knowledge.*

known /nəʊn/ past participle of **know**

knuckle /'nʌk(ə)l/ *noun* a part where two bones join in a finger

L

l /el/, **L** *noun* the twelfth letter of the alphabet, between K and M

label /ˈleɪb(ə)l/ *noun* a note attached to something to give information about, e.g. its price, its contents or someone's name and address ○ *She stuck a label on the parcel.* ○ *The price on the label is £25.00.* ■ *verb* to put a label on something ○ *All the goods are labelled with the correct price.* (NOTE: **labels – labelling – labelled.** The US spelling is **labeling – labeled.**)

labor /ˈleɪbə/ *noun, verb* US spelling of **labour**

laboratory /ləˈbɒrət(ə)ri/ *noun* a place where scientific experiments, testing and research are carried out ○ *She's working in the university laboratories.* ○ *All our products are tested in our own laboratories.* (NOTE: The plural is **laboratories.**)

labour /ˈleɪbə/ *noun* **1.** work, especially hard work ○ *Does the price include the cost of labour?* **2.** the people who do work ○ *Cheap labour is difficult to find.* **3.** the process of giving birth to a baby ○ *She went into labour at home, and her husband drove her to the hospital.* ○ *She was in labour for 12 hours.* ■ *verb* **1.** to work hard ○ *They laboured night and day to finish the project in time.* **2.** to do something with difficulty ○ *She laboured across the room to me.*

lace /leɪs/ *noun* **1.** a thin strip of material for tying up a shoe or other piece of clothing ○ *His laces kept coming undone.* ○ *She's too little to be able to do up her laces herself.* **2.** cloth made with open patterns of threads, like a net ○ *a lace tablecloth* ○ *Her wedding dress was trimmed with lace.* (NOTE: no plural in this sense)

lack /læk/ *noun* the fact that you do not have something ○ *The children are suffering from a lack of food.* ○ *The project*
was cancelled because of lack of funds. (NOTE: no plural) ■ *verb* not to have enough of something ○ *The sales staff lack interest.*

ladder /ˈlædə/ *noun* an object made of several bars between two posts, used for climbing up to high places ○ *The ladder was leaning against the wall.* ○ *He was climbing up a ladder.* ○ *She got down off the ladder.*

lady /ˈleɪdi/ *noun* a polite way of referring to a woman ○ *There are two ladies waiting to see you.*

laid /leɪd/ past tense and past participle of **lay**

lain /leɪn/ past participle of **lie** *verb* 2

lake /leɪk/ *noun* an area of water surrounded by land ○ *Let's take a boat out on the lake.* ○ *We can sail across the lake.* ○ *The hotel stands on the shores of Lake Windermere.*

lamb /læm/ *noun* **1.** a young sheep ○ *In spring, the fields are full of sheep and their little lambs.* **2.** meat from a lamb or sheep ○ *a leg of lamb* ○ *roast lamb* (NOTE: no plural in this sense)

lamp /læmp/ *noun* an object which produces light ○ *The hall is lit by large electric lamps.*

land /lænd/ *noun* earth, as opposed to water ○ *They were glad to be back on (dry) land again after two weeks at sea.* (NOTE: no plural) ■ *verb* to arrive on the ground, or on another surface ○ *The flight from Amsterdam has landed.* ○ *We will be landing at London Airport in five minutes.* ○ *The ducks tried to land on the ice.*

land up *phrasal verb* to end in a place (*informal*) ○ *I got the wrong train and landed up in Scotland.*

landing /ˈlændɪŋ/ *noun* **1.** (*especially of aircraft*) an instance of arriving on the ground or on a surface ○ *The plane made a smooth landing.* **2.** a flat area at the top of a set of stairs ○ *She was waiting for me on the landing.*

landlady /ˈlændleɪdi/ *noun* a woman from whom you rent a place to live ○ *You must pay your rent to the landlady every month.* (NOTE: The plural is **landladies**.)

landlord /ˈlændlɔːd/ *noun* a man or company from whom you rent property such as a house, room or office ○ *Tell the landlord if your roof leaks.* ○ *The landlord refused to make any repairs to the roof.*

landmark /ˈlændmɑːk/ *noun* a building or large object on land which you can see easily ○ *The statue is a famous landmark.*

landscape /ˈlændskeɪp/ *noun* **1.** the appearance of the countryside ○ *the beautiful landscape of the West Country* **2.** a painting of a country scene ○ *He collects 18th century English landscapes.*

lane /leɪn/ *noun* **1.** a narrow road, often in the country ○ *a lane with hedges on both sides* **2.** a part of a road for traffic going in a particular direction or at a certain speed ○ *Motorways usually have three lanes on either side.* ○ *One lane of the motorway has been closed for repairs.*

language /ˈlæŋgwɪdʒ/ *noun* a way of speaking or writing used in a country or by a group of people ○ *We go to English language classes twice a week.* ○ *She can speak several European languages.*

lap /læp/ *noun* **1.** the part of your body from your waist to your knees when you are sitting ○ *She listened to the story, sitting in her father's lap.* **2.** one turn round a racetrack ○ *He's finished lap 23 – only two laps to go!* ■ *verb* **1.** (*of animals*) to drink with the tongue ○ *The dog lapped the water in the pond.* **2.** to go so fast that you are one whole lap ahead of another person in a race ○ *The winner had lapped three other runners.* (NOTE: **laps – lapping – lapped**)

large /lɑːdʒ/ *adjective* big ○ *She ordered a large cup of coffee.* ○ *Our house has one large bedroom and two very small ones.* ○ *How large is your garden?* ○ *Why has she got an office which is larger than mine?*

largely /ˈlɑːdʒli/ *adverb* mainly, mostly ○ *His farm is largely grazing land.* ○ *The price rises are largely due to increased demand.*

laser /ˈleɪzə/ *noun* an instrument which produces a concentrated beam of light; lasers can be used to cut through hard materials, and to carry out some medical operations

last /lɑːst/ *adjective* **1.** coming at the end of a list, line or period of time ○ *The post office is the last building on the right.* ○ *The invoice must be paid by the last day of the month.* **2.** most recent ○ *She's been ill for the last ten days.* ○ *The last three books I read were rubbish.* ■ *adverb* **1.** at the end ○ *Out of a queue of twenty people, I was served last.* ○ *I'll print the labels last.* **2.** most recently ○ *When did you see her last?* ○ *She was looking ill when I saw her last* or *when I last saw her.* ■ *verb* to continue for some time ○ *The fine weather won't last.* ○ *Our holidays never seem to last very long.* ○ *The storm lasted all night.* ○ *The meeting lasted for three hours.* ◇ **last but one** the one before the last one ○ *My last car but one was a Rolls Royce.*

late /leɪt/ *adjective* **1.** after the usual or expected time ○ *The plane is thirty minutes late.* ○ *It's too late to change your ticket.* ○ *Hurry or you'll be late for the show.* ○ *We apologise for the late arrival of the plane from Amsterdam.* **2.** at the end of a period of time ○ *The traffic was bad in the late afternoon.* ○ *He moved to London in the late 1980s.* **3.** a word used instead of 'dead' in order to be polite ○ *His late father was a director of the company.* (NOTE: only used before a noun in this meaning)

lately /ˈleɪtli/ *adverb* during recent days or weeks

later /ˈleɪtə/ *adverb* at a time after the present; at a time after a time which has been mentioned ○ *The family came to live in England and she was born a month later.* ○ *Can we meet later this evening?*

latest /'leɪtɪst/ *adjective* the most recent (*informal*) ○ *Have you seen his latest film?* ○ *He always drives the latest model car.* ○ *The latest snow reports are published each day in the papers.* ◇ **at the latest** no later than the time stated ○ *I'll ring back before 7 o'clock at the latest.*

latter /'lætə/ *adjective* **1.** used for referring to the second of two people or things mentioned **2.** towards the end of the period of time mentioned ○ *I'm busy on Monday and Tuesday, but I'll be free during the latter part of the week.*

laugh /lɑːf/ *noun* a sound you make when you think something is funny ○ *He's got a lovely deep laugh.* ○ *'That's right,' she said with a laugh.* ■ *verb* to make a sound to show you think something is funny ○ *He was very good last night – he had everyone laughing at his jokes.* ○ *She fell off the ladder and everyone laughed.*

laughter /'lɑːftə/ *noun* the sound or act of laughing ○ *As soon as he opened his mouth, the audience burst into laughter.* (NOTE: no plural)

launch /lɔːntʃ/ *noun* **1.** the act of starting off a boat or a spacecraft ○ *The launch of the new car went off successfully.* ○ *The rocket launch has been delayed by two weeks.* **2.** the act of starting off the sale of a new product ○ *The launch of the new car went off successfully.* ■ *verb* **1.** to put a boat into the water, especially for the first time and with a lot of ceremony ○ *The Queen launched the new ship.* **2.** to send a spacecraft into space ○ *The spacecraft was launched from Cape Kennedy.* **3.** to start selling a new product ○ *We're launching the new perfume just before Christmas.*

laundry /'lɔːndri/ *noun* **1.** clothes that need to be washed ○ *Please put any laundry into the bag provided.* (NOTE: no plural) **2.** a place where clothes are washed ○ *The hotel's sheets and towels are sent to the laundry every day.* (NOTE: The plural is **laundries**.) ◇ **do the laundry** to wash clothes

law /lɔː/ *noun* one of the rules governing a country, usually in the form of an act

of parliament ○ *Parliament has passed a law against the ownership of guns.*

lawful /'lɔːf(ə)l/ *adjective* allowed by the law (*formal*) ○ *Their behaviour was perfectly lawful.*

law-making /'lɔː ˌmeɪkɪŋ/ *noun* the process of making laws

lawn /lɔːn/ *noun* a part of a garden covered with short grass

lawyer /'lɔːjə/ *noun* a person who has studied law and can advise you on legal matters ○ *If you are arrested you have the right to speak to your lawyer.*

lay /leɪ/ *verb* **1.** to put something down flat ○ *He laid the papers on the table.* ○ *A new carpet has been laid in the dining room.* **2.** □ **to lay the table** to arrange knives, fork, spoons, plates and glasses on a table for a meal ○ *The table is laid for four people.* **3.** (*of birds, turtles, etc.*) to produce an egg ○ *The hens laid three eggs.* (NOTE: **lays – laying – laid**)

layer /'leɪə/ *noun* an amount of a substance that lies on a flat surface ○ *She put a layer of chocolate on the cake, then one of cream.*

layout /'leɪaʊt/ *noun* a design, e.g. of a garden or a book

laziness /'leɪzinəs/ *noun* the state of being lazy

lazy /'leɪzi/ *adjective* not wanting to do any work ○ *She's just lazy – that's why the work never gets done on time.* ○ *He is so lazy he does not even bother to open his mail.* (NOTE: **lazier – laziest**)

lead¹ /led/ *noun* **1.** a very heavy soft metal ○ *Tie a piece of lead to your fishing line to make it sink.* **2.** the black part in the middle of a pencil

lead² /liːd/ *noun* **1.** an electric wire which joins a machine to the electricity supply ○ *The lead is too short to go across the room.* **2.** first place during a race ○ *He went into the lead* or *he took the lead.* ○ *Who's in the lead at the halfway mark?* ○ *She has a lead of 20m over her nearest rival.* **3.** a long piece of leather or other material used to hold a dog ○ *All dogs must be kept on a lead in the park.* ■ *verb* **1.** to be in first place during a race or match ○ *Our side was leading at half time.* ○ *They were leading by three*

metres. **2.** to go in front to show someone the way ○ *She led us into the hall.*
3. (*of a path or road*) to go in a particular direction ○ *The road leads you to the
top of the hill.* **4.** to be the main person
in a group ○ *She is leading a group of
businesswomen on a tour of Chinese
factories.* (NOTE: **leads – leading – led**
/led/)

lead up to *phrasal verb* to happen in a
way that makes something else important happen ○ *the events that led up to
the First World War*

leader /'liːdə/ *noun* a person who is in
charge of an organisation such as a political party ○ *He is the leader of the Labour Party.* ○ *The leader of the construction workers' union.*

leadership /'liːdəʃɪp/ *noun* **1.** the ability to manage or direct others ○ *We think
he has certain leadership qualities.* **2.**
the position of a leader ○ *Under his
leadership the party went from strength
to strength.* **3.** a group of leaders of an
organisation ○ *The leadership was
weaker after the president's resignation.*

leading /'liːdɪŋ/ *adjective* most important ○ *He took the leading role in the
play.*

leaf /liːf/ *noun* one of the flat green parts
of a plant ○ *The leaves of the trees turn
brown or red in autumn.* ○ *Caterpillars
have eaten the leaves of the roses.*
(NOTE: The plural is **leaves** /liːvz/.)

leaflet /'liːflət/ *noun* a sheet of paper, often folded, giving information

league /liːg/ *noun* a group of sports clubs
which play matches against each other
○ *He plays for one of the clubs in the local football league.*

leak /liːk/ *noun* **1.** a hole in an object
where liquid or gas can escape ○ *I can
smell gas – there must be a gas leak in
the kitchen.* **2.** an occasion on which secret information is given to the public ○
*She was embarrassed by the leak of the
news.* ○ *The leak of the report led to the
minister's resignation.* ■ *verb* **1.** (*of liquid or gas, etc.*) to flow away, to escape
from its container ○ *Water must have
been leaking through the ceiling for
days.* **2.** to pass on secret information to
the public ○ *Governments don't like*

their plans to be leaked to the press. ○
*We found that the sales director was
leaking information to a rival company.*

lean /liːn/ *adjective* **1.** (*of a person*) thin
○ *He's a lean athletic man.* **2.** (*of meat*)
with little fat ○ *a slice of lean bacon* ■
verb to be in or to put into a sloping position ○ *The ladder was leaning against
the shed.* ○ *She leant her bike against
the wall.* ○ *He leaned over and picked
up the cushion.* ○ *It's dangerous to lean
out of car windows.* (NOTE: **leans –
leaning – leaned** *or* **leant** /lent/)

lean on *phrasal verb* **1.** to try to force
someone to do what you want ○ *They
leant on him to get him to agree.* **2.** to
depend on someone ○ *If things get difficult she always has her father to lean
on.*

leap /liːp/ *verb* to jump ○ *He leapt over
the ditch.* ○ *She leapt with joy when she
heard the news.* ○ *He leapt into the train
as it was leaving.* (NOTE: **leaps – leap-
ing – leaped** *or* **leapt** /lept/)

learn /lɜːn/ *verb* **1.** to find out about
something, or about how to do something ○ *He's learning to ride a bicycle.*
○ *We learn French and German at
school.* **2.** to hear news ○ *Her boss
learned that she was planning to leave
the company.* ○ *How did you come to
learn about the product?* ○ *We learnt of
his death only yesterday.* (NOTE: **learns
– learning – learnt** /lɜːnt/ *or* **learned**)

learner /'lɜːnə/ *noun* a person who is
learning how to do something ○ *The
evening swimming classes are specially
for adult learners.* ○ *The new dictionary
is good for advanced learners of English.*

least /liːst/ *adjective* used for describing
the smallest amount ○ *This car uses by
far the least petrol.* ■ *adverb* less than
everyone or everything else ○ *I liked
that part of the book least.* ○ *He was the
least conceited man she had ever met.*

leather /'leðə/ *noun* the skin of certain
animals used to make things such as
shoes and bags ○ *a leather bag* ○ *My
shoes have leather soles.*

leave /liːv/ *verb* **1.** to go away from a
place ○ *She left home at 9 o'clock this*

morning. ○ *When they couldn't find what they wanted, they left the shop.* ○ *Eurostar leaves Waterloo for Brussels every day at 8.25.* ○ *When does the next bus leave for Oxford?* **2.** to forget to take something with you ○ *I left my toothbrush at home.* **3.** to allow something to stay in a certain condition ○ *Did you leave the light on when you locked up?* ○ *Yesterday she left the iron on, and burnt a hole in the ironing board.* ○ *Someone left the door open and the dog got out.* **4.** to produce a mark that remains ○ *The coffee left a stain on the tablecloth.* **5.** not to take something ○ *Leave some pizza for your brother.* **6.** to choose to stop being in a relationship with someone ○ *She's left her husband.* **7.** not to do something, so that someone else has to do it ○ *She went out leaving me all the washing up to do.* (NOTE: **leaves – leaving – left** /left/)

leave behind *phrasal verb* to not take someone or something with you

leave out *phrasal verb* to forget something or someone

lecture /'lektʃə/ *noun* a talk on a particular subject given to people such as students ○ *She gave a lecture on Chinese art.* ○ *Are you going to the lecture this evening?* ○ *The lecture lasted thirty minutes, and then there was time for questions.* ■ *verb* **1.** to give a lecture on something ○ *He will lecture on Roman history next Thursday.* **2.** to teach a subject, by giving lectures ○ *She lectures on history at Birmingham University.*

lecturer /'lektʃərə/ *noun* **1.** a person who gives a talk on a particular subject ○ *This week's lecturer is talking about modern art.* **2.** a teacher in a university or college ○ *He has been a lecturer in biology for five years.*

led /led/ past tense and past participle of **lead**

ledge /ledʒ/ *noun* a narrow flat part which sticks out from a cliff or a building

left /left/ *adjective* **1.** relating to the side of the body which has the hand that most people do not use for writing ○ *I can't write with my left hand.* ○ *The post office is on the left side of the street as*

you go towards the church. **2.** (*in politics*) relating to people with left-wing opinions ○ *His politics are left of centre.* Compare **right** ■ *noun* the side towards the left ○ *Remember to drive on the left when you are in Britain.* ○ *The school is on the left as you go towards the town centre.* ○ *She was sitting on the chairman's left.* ■ *adverb* towards the left ○ *Go straight ahead and turn left at the traffic lights.*

left-hand /ˌleft 'hænd/ *adjective* on the left side ○ *The book is in the left-hand drawer of his desk.* ○ *In England cars drive on the left-hand side of the road.*

left-handed /ˌleft 'hændɪd/ *adjective* using the left hand more often than the right for doing things ○ *She's left-handed, so we got her a left-handed cup for her birthday.*

left-wing /ˌleft 'wɪŋ/ *adjective* in politics, relating to people who believe that money and property should be shared more equally

leg /leg/ *noun* **1.** one of the parts of the body with which a person or animal walks ○ *The bird was standing on one leg, asleep.* ○ *Some animals can't stand on their back legs.* ○ *She fell down the steps and broke her leg.* **2.** one of the parts of a chair or table which touch the floor ○ *The table has four legs.* **3.** a leg of an animal used for food ○ *roast leg of lamb* ○ *Would you like a chicken leg?* ◇ **to pull someone's leg** to try to make someone believe something that is not true for a joke ○ *Don't worry, she will get here on time – I was only pulling your leg.*

legal /'liːg(ə)l/ *adjective* **1.** allowed by the law ○ *It's legal to drive at 17 years old in the UK* **2.** relating to the law

legally /'liːgəli/ *adverb* according to the law

legislation /ˌledʒɪ'sleɪʃ(ə)n/ *noun* laws, written rules which are passed by Parliament and applied in the courts

legitimate /lɪ'dʒɪtɪmət/ *adjective* fair and reasonable, or allowed by the law ○ *They have legitimate concerns about the project.* ○ *He acted in legitimate defence of his rights.*

lemon /'lemən/ *noun* a pale yellow fruit with a sour taste ○ *Oranges are much sweeter than lemons.*

lend /lend/ *verb* to let someone use something for a certain period of time ○ *He asked me if I would lend him £5 till Monday.* ○ *I lent her my dictionary and now she won't give it back.* Compare **borrow** (NOTE: **lends – lending – lent** /lent/)

length /leŋθ/ *noun* **1.** a measurement of how long something is from end to end ○ *The table is at least twelve feet in length.* **2.** a long piece of something ○ *She bought a length of curtain material in the sale.* ○ *We need two lengths of piping for the new central heating system.*

lens /lenz/ *noun* a curved piece of glass or plastic, used for looking through to make things clearer or bigger ○ *My eyesight is not very good, and I have to have glasses with strong lenses.* ○ *It looks as if the camera lens was scratched.* (NOTE: The plural is **lenses**.)

lent /lent/ past tense and past participle of **lend**

less /les/ *adjective, pronoun* a smaller amount (of) ○ *You will get thinner if you eat less bread.* ○ *The total bill came to less than £10.* ○ *She finished her homework in less than an hour.* ○ *He sold it for less than he had paid for it.* ■ *adverb* not as much ○ *I like that one less than this one.* ○ *The second film was less interesting than the first.* ○ *I want a car which is less difficult to drive.* ■ *preposition* with a certain amount taken away ○ *We pay £10 an hour, less 50p for insurance.* ◇ **more or less** almost ○ *I've more or less finished painting the kitchen.*

lessen /'les(ə)n/ *verb* to become less, or to make something become less ○ *Wearing a seat belt lessens the risk of injury.* (NOTE: Do not confuse with **lesson**.)

lesson /'les(ə)n/ *noun* **1.** a period of time, especially in school, when you are taught something ○ *He went to sleep during the French lesson.* ○ *We have six lessons of history a week.* ○ *She's taking or having driving lessons.* ○ *He gives Spanish lessons at home in the evenings.* **2.** something which you learn from experience and which makes you wiser ○ *He's learnt his lesson, he now knows you shouldn't take such big risks with money.*

let /let/ *verb* **1.** to allow someone to do something ○ *He let her borrow his car.* ○ *Will you let me see the papers?* **2.** to allow someone to use a house or office in return for payment ○ *We're letting our cottage to some friends for the weekend.* (NOTE: **lets – letting – let**) ◇ **let me see** used when you need time to think about something ○ *Let me see what I can do for you.*

let go *phrasal verb* to stop holding on to something

let in *phrasal verb* to allow to come in

let off *phrasal verb* **1.** to make something such as a gun or bomb fire explode ○ *They let off fireworks in the town centre.* **2.** to not punish someone severely ○ *He was charged with stealing, but the judge let him off with a fine.*

let up *phrasal verb* to do less, to become less ○ *The snow didn't let up all day.* ○ *She's working too hard – she ought to let up a bit.*

letter /'letə/ *noun* **1.** a piece of writing sent from one person to another to pass on information ○ *There were two letters for you in the post.* ○ *Don't forget to write a letter to your mother to tell her what we are doing.* ○ *We've had a letter from the bank manager.* **2.** one of the signs which make up the alphabet, a sign used in writing which corresponds to a certain sound ○ *Z is the last letter of the alphabet.* ○ *I'm trying to think of a word with ten letters beginning with A and ending with R.* ◇ **to the letter** exactly as shown or stated ○ *They followed his instructions to the letter.*

lettuce /'letɪs/ *noun* a plant with large green leaves which are used in salads (NOTE: no plural except when referring to several plants: *a row of lettuces*)

level /'lev(ə)l/ *noun* **1.** a position relating to height or amount ○ *I want to lower the level of our borrowings.* ○ *The water reached a level of 5m above normal during the flood.* **2.** a floor in a building ○

Go up to the next level. ○ *The toilets are at street level.* ■ *adjective* **1.** flat, even ○ *Are these shelves level, or do they slope to the left?* **2.** equal, the same ○ *At half-time the scores were level.*

lever /'liːvə/ *noun* an object like a bar, which helps you to lift a heavy object, or to move part of a machine ○ *We used a pole as a lever to lift up the block of stone.* ○ *Lift the lever, then push it down again to make the machine work.*

liberal /'lɪb(ə)rəl/ *adjective* not strict, willing to accept other people's views ○ *The liberal view would be to let the teenagers run the club themselves.*

library /'laɪbrəri/ *noun* **1.** a place where books are kept, especially ones which you can borrow ○ *He forgot to take his books back to the library.* ○ *You can't keep it, it's a library book.* **2.** a collection of things such as books or records ○ *He has a big record library.* (NOTE: The plural is **libraries**.)

licence /'laɪs(ə)ns/ *noun* a document which gives official permission to own something or to do something ○ *She has applied for an export licence for these paintings.*

licensed /'laɪs(ə)nst/ *adjective* given official permission to do something

lick /lɪk/ *verb* to make a gentle movement with your tongue across the surface of something ○ *You shouldn't lick the plate when you've finished your pudding.* ○ *They licked their lips when they saw the cakes.*

lid /lɪd/ *noun* a covering for a container, sometimes with a handle ○ *Where's the lid for the black saucepan?* ○ *He managed to get the lid off the jam jar.*

lie /laɪ/ *verb* **1.** to say something which is not true ○ *She was lying when she said she had been at home all evening.* ○ *He lied about the accident.* (NOTE: in this sense: **lies – lying – lied**) **2.** to be in a flat position ○ *Six soldiers lay dead on the ground.* ○ *The dog spends the evening lying in front of the fire.* (NOTE: **lies – lying – lay – lain**) ■ *noun* something that is not true ○ *That's a lie! – I didn't day that!* ○ *Someone has been telling lies about her.*

lie down *phrasal verb* to put yourself in a flat position, e.g. on a bed

life /laɪf/ *noun* **1.** the period during which you are alive ○ *He spent his whole life working on the farm.* **2.** the fact of being a living person ○ *Life is a precious thing; don't waste it.* **3.** living things ○ *Is there life on Mars?*

lift /lɪft/ *noun* **1.** a machine which takes people up or down from one floor to another in a building ○ *Take the lift to the tenth floor.* ○ *Push the button to call the lift.* ○ *Your room is on the fifteenth floor, so you may wish to use the lift.* **2.** a ride in a car that you give to someone ○ *She gave me a lift to the station.* ■ *verb* to take something, often off the ground, and put it in a higher position ○ *My briefcase is so heavy I can hardly lift it.* ○ *He lifted the little girl up so that she could see the procession.*

light /laɪt/ *noun* **1.** brightness, the opposite of darkness ○ *I can't read the map by the light of the moon.* ○ *There's not enough light to take a photo.* **2.** a piece of electrical equipment which gives light ○ *Turn the light on – I can't see to read.* ○ *It's dangerous to ride a bicycle with no lights.* ○ *In the fog, I could just see the red lights of the car in front of me.* ■ *verb* to start to burn, to make something start to burn ○ *He is trying to get the fire to light.* ○ *Can you light the candles on the birthday cake?* ○ *He couldn't get the fire to light.* ○ *Light a candle – it's dark in the cellar.* (NOTE: **lights – lighting – lit** /lɪt/) ■ *adjective* **1.** not heavy ○ *I can lift this box easily – it's quite light* or *it's as light as a feather.* ○ *You need light clothing for tropical countries.* ○ *She's just been ill, and can only do light work.* **2.** pale ○ *He was wearing a light green shirt.* ○ *I prefer a light carpet to a dark one.* **3.** having a lot of light so that you can see well ○ *The big windows make the kitchen very light.* ○ *It was six o'clock in the morning and just getting light.* ◊ **to cast or throw light on something** to make something easier to understand ○ *The papers throw light on how the minister reached his decision.*

lighten /'laɪt(ə)n/ *verb* **1.** to make or become less dark ○ *You can lighten the room by painting it white.* ○ *The sky lightened as dawn broke.* **2.** to become less heavy, or to make something become less heavy ○ *I'll have to lighten my suitcase – it's much too heavy.*

lightning /'laɪtnɪŋ/ *noun* a flash of electricity in the sky in a storm ○ *The storm approached with thunder and lightning.*

like /laɪk/ *preposition* **1.** similar to, in the same way as ○ *He's like his mother in many ways, but he has his father's nose.* ○ *Like you, I don't get on with the new boss.* ○ *The picture doesn't look like him at all.* ○ *He can swim like a fish.* ○ *It tastes like strawberries.* ○ *What's that record? – it sounds like Elgar.* **2.** used for asking someone to describe something ○ *What was the weather like when you were on holiday?* ○ *What's he like, her new boyfriend?* ■ *verb* **1.** to have pleasant feelings about someone or something ○ *Do you like the new manager?* ○ *She doesn't like eating meat.* ○ *How does he like his new job?* ○ *No one likes driving in rush hour traffic.* ○ *In the evening, I like to sit quietly and read the newspaper.* **2.** to want ○ *Take as many apples as you like.* ◇ **would like** used for telling someone what you want in a polite way ○ *I'd like you to meet one of our sales executives.* ○ *I'd like to go to Paris next week.*

likely /'laɪkli/ *adjective* probably going to happen ○ *It's likely to snow this weekend.* ○ *He's not likely to come to the party.* ○ *Is that at all likely?* (NOTE: **likelier – likeliest**)

liking /'laɪkɪŋ/ *noun* a feeling of enjoying something ○ *She has a liking for chocolate.* ○ *This drink is too sweet for my liking.*

limb /lɪm/ *noun* a leg or arm ○ *He was lucky not to break a limb in the accident.*

limit /'lɪmɪt/ *noun* the furthest point beyond which you cannot go ○ *We were never allowed to go beyond the limits of the garden.* ○ *What's the speed limit on this road?* ■ *verb* not to allow something to go beyond a certain point ○ *Her parents limited the number of evenings she could go out.* ○ *The treasurer wants to limit the amount we spend on flowers.*

limited /'lɪmɪtɪd/ *adjective* which has a limit

limp /lɪmp/ *verb* to walk in a way which is affected by having an injured leg or foot ○ *After the accident she limped badly.* ■ *noun* a way that someone walks, when one leg hurts or is shorter than the other ○ *His limp has improved since his operation.* ■ *adjective* soft, not strong ○ *All we had as a salad was two limp lettuce leaves.* ○ *He gave me a limp handshake.* ○ *She went limp and we had to give her a glass of water.*

line /laɪn/ *noun* **1.** a long thin mark ○ *She drew a straight line across the sheet of paper.* ○ *Parking isn't allowed on yellow lines.* ○ *The tennis ball went over the line.* **2.** a row of written or printed words ○ *He printed the first two lines and showed them to me.* ○ *Can you read the bottom line on the chart?* **3.** a long row of people or things ○ *We had to stand in (a) line for half an hour to get into the exhibition.* ○ *The line of lorries stretched for miles at the frontier.* **4.** a wire along which telephone messages are sent ○ *The snow brought down the telephone lines.* ○ *Can you speak louder – the line is bad.* ◇ **to draw the line at** to refuse to do something ○ *I don't mind having a cup of coffee with the boss, but I draw the line at having to invite him for a meal at home.*

line up *phrasal verb* to stand in a line ○ *Line up over there if you want to take the next boat.*

linen /'lɪnɪn/ *noun* a strong cloth made from natural fibres ○ *a linen tablecloth* ○ *He bought a white linen suit.*

lining /'laɪnɪŋ/ *noun* material sewn onto the inside of something such as a piece of clothing ○ *You'll need a coat with a warm lining if you're going to Canada in winter.* ○ *She has a pair of boots with a fur lining.*

link /lɪŋk/ *noun* **1.** something which connects two things or places ○ *The Channel Tunnel provides a fast rail link between England and France.* **2.** one of the rings in a chain ○ *a chain with solid gold links* ■ *verb* **1.** to join things together ○ *They linked arms and walked down the street.* ○ *All the rooms are linked to the main switchboard.* ○ *Eurostar links London and Paris or Brussels.* **2.** to be related in some way ○ *His salary is linked to the cost of living.*

lion /'laɪən/ *noun* a large wild yellowish-brown animal of the cat family (NOTE: The female is a **lioness** and the young are **cubs.**)

lip /lɪp/ *noun* one of the two pink or red parts forming the outside of the mouth ○ *Put some cream on your lips to stop them getting sore.*

liquid /'lɪkwɪd/ *noun* a substance such as water, which flows easily and which is neither a gas nor a solid ○ *You will need to drink more liquids in hot weather.* ■ *adjective* in a form which flows easily ○ *a bottle of liquid soap*

list /lɪst/ *noun* a number of things such as names or addresses, written or said one after another ○ *We've drawn up a list of people to invite to the party.* ○ *He was ill, so we crossed his name off the list.* ○ *The names on the list are in alphabetical order.* ■ *verb* to say or to write a number of things one after the other ○ *The contents are listed on the label.* ○ *She listed the ingredients on the back of an envelope.* ○ *The catalogue lists twenty-three models of washing machine.*

listen /'lɪs(ə)n/ *verb* to pay attention to someone who is talking or to something which you can hear ○ *Don't make a noise – I'm trying to listen to a music programme.* ○ *Why don't you listen to what I tell you?* ◇ **to listen out for something** to wait to see if you hear something ○ *Can you listen out for the telephone while I'm in the garden?*

lit /lɪt/ past tense and past participle of **light**

liter /'liːtə/ *noun* US spelling of **litre**

literary /'lɪt(ə)rəri/ *adjective* relating to literature

literature /'lɪt(ə)rətʃə/ *noun* **1.** books or writing, especially when considered to be of high quality ○ *She's studying English and American literature.* **2.** written information about something ○ *Do you*

have any literature on holidays in Greece? (NOTE: no plural)

litre /'liːtə/ *noun* a unit of measurement for liquids, equal to 1000 millilitres (NOTE: usually written **l** or **L** after figures: *25 l*, say 'twenty-five litres'.)

litter /'lɪtə/ *noun* **1.** rubbish on streets or in public places ○ *The council tries to keep the main street clear of litter.* (NOTE: no plural in this sense) **2.** a group of young animals born at one time ○ *She had a litter of eight puppies.*

little /'lɪt(ə)l/ *adjective* **1.** small ○ *They have two children – a baby boy and a little girl.* (NOTE: no comparative or superlative forms in this sense) **2.** not much ○ *We drink very little milk.* ○ *A TV uses very little electricity.* ○ *He looked at it for a little while.* (NOTE: **little – less – least** /liːst/) ■ *adverb* not much; not often ○ *It's little more than two miles from the sea.* ○ *We go to the cinema very little these days.*

little by little /ˌlɪt(ə)l baɪ 'lɪt(ə)l/ *adverb* gradually

live¹ /laɪv/ *adjective* **1.** living, not dead ○ *There are strict rules about transporting live animals.* **2.** carrying electricity ○ *Don't touch the live wires.* **3.** not recorded; being broadcast at the same time as events take place ○ *a live radio show* ■ *adverb* at the same time as events take place ○ *The show was broadcast live.*

live² /lɪv/ *verb* **1.** to have your home in a place ○ *They have gone to live in France.* ○ *Do you prefer living in the country to the town?* ○ *He lives next door to a film star.* ○ *Where does your daughter live?* **2.** to be alive ○ *King Henry VIII lived in the 16th century.* ○ *The doctor doesn't think she will live much longer.*

live on *phrasal verb* to use food or money to stay alive ○ *They lived on bread and water for two weeks.*

lively /'laɪvli/ *adjective* very active (NOTE: **livelier – liveliest**)

liver /'lɪvə/ *noun* **1.** a large organ in the body which helps you to process food and cleans the blood **2.** animal's liver used as food ○ *I'll start with chicken liv-*

er pâté. ○ *He looked at the menu and ordered liver and bacon.*

living /'lɪvɪŋ/ *adjective* having the signs such as breathing or growing of not being dead ○ *Does she have any living relatives?* ■ *noun* money that you need for things such as food and clothes ○ *He earns his living by selling postcards to tourists.*

living room /'lɪvɪŋ ruːm/ *noun* (*in a house or flat*) a comfortable room for sitting in

lizard /'lɪzəd/ *noun* a small animal with a long tail and rough skin

load /ləʊd/ *noun* a number of heavy objects which are carried in a vehicle such as truck ○ *The lorry delivered a load of bricks.* ■ *verb* **1.** to put something, especially something heavy, into or on to a vehicle such as a truck or van ○ *They loaded the furniture into the van.* **2.** to put bullets into a gun, or a film into a camera ○ *They loaded their guns and hid behind the wall.* **3.** to put a program into a computer ○ *Load the word-processing program before you start keyboarding.*

loaf /ləʊf/ *noun* bread made in a large round shape, which you can cut into slices before eating it ○ *He bought a loaf of bread at the baker's.* ○ *We eat about 10 loaves of bread per week.*

loan /ləʊn/ *noun* **1.** a thing lent, especially an amount of money ○ *He bought the house with a £100,000 loan from the bank.* **2.** the act of lending something to someone ○ *I had the loan of his car for three weeks.*

local /'ləʊk(ə)l/ *adjective* relating to a place or district near where you are or where you live ○ *She works as a nurse in the local hospital.* ○ *The local paper comes out on Fridays.* ○ *She was formerly the headmistress of the local school.*

locate /ləʊ'keɪt/ *verb* to find the position of something ○ *Divers are trying to locate the Spanish galleon.*

location /ləʊ'keɪʃ(ə)n/ *noun* a place or position ○ *The hotel is in a very central location.*

lock /lɒk/ *noun* a part of a door or container such as a box, used for fastening it so that you can only open it with a key ○ *She left the key in the lock, so the burglars got in easily.* ○ *We changed the locks on the doors after a set of keys were stolen.* ■ *verb* **1.** to close a door or a container such as a box, using a key ○ *I forgot to lock the safe.* ○ *We always lock the front door before we go to bed.* **2.** to fix something or to become fixed in a certain position ○ *The wheels suddenly locked as he went round the corner.*

lock up *phrasal verb* **1.** to close a building by locking the doors ○ *He always locks up before he goes home.* ○ *She was locking up the shop when a man walked in.* **2.** to put someone in prison ○ *They locked him up for a week.*

loft /lɒft/ *noun* the top part of a house right under the roof ○ *They converted their loft into a bedroom.*

log /lɒg/ *noun* a thick piece of a tree ○ *He brought in a load of logs for the fire.*

loneliness /'ləʊnlinəs/ *noun* **1.** a feeling of sadness you can get from being alone ○ *After his wife died it took him a long time to get over his feelings of loneliness.* **2.** the state of being alone ○ *He was attracted by the loneliness of the hotel, all by itself on the top of the cliff.*

lonely /'ləʊnli/ *adjective* **1.** feeling sad because of being alone ○ *It's odd how lonely you can be in a big city full of people.* **2.** (*of a place*) with few or no people around ○ *The cliff top is a lonely place at night.* ○ *We spent the weekend in a lonely cottage in the Welsh hills.* (NOTE: **lonelier – loneliest**)

long /lɒŋ/ *adjective* **1.** not short in length ○ *a long piece of string* ○ *The Nile is the longest river in the world.* ○ *My hair needs cutting – it's getting too long.* **2.** not short in time ○ *What a long programme – it lasted almost three hours.* ○ *They've been waiting for the bus for a long time.* ○ *We don't approve of long holidays in this job.* **3.** used for asking about an amount of time ○ *How long is it before your holiday starts?* ■ *adverb* a long time ○ *Have you been waiting long?* ○ *I didn't want to wait any longer.* ○ *Long ago, before the war, this was a* *wealthy farming area.* ■ *noun* a long time □ **before long** in a short time ○ *She'll be boss of the company before long.* □ **for long** for a long time ○ *He wasn't out of a job for long.* ■ *verb* to want something very much ○ *I'm longing for a cup of tea.* ○ *Everyone was longing to be back home.* ◇ **as long as, so long as** provided that, on the condition that ○ *I like going on picnics as long as it doesn't rain.* ◇ **no longer** not any more ○ *I no longer have that car.*

long-term /ˌlɒŋ ˈtɜːm/ *adjective* planned to last for a long time

loo /luː/ *noun* a toilet or a room in which there is a toilet (*informal*)

look /lʊk/ *noun* the act of seeing something with your eyes ○ *Have a good look at this photograph and tell me if you recognise anyone in it.* ○ *We only had time for a quick look round the town.* ■ *verb* **1.** to turn your eyes to see something ○ *I want you to look carefully at this photograph.* ○ *Look in the restaurant and see if there are any tables free.* ○ *If you look out of the office window you can see our house.* ○ *He opened the lid of the box and looked inside.* **2.** to appear to be ○ *I went to see her in hospital and she looks worse.* ○ *Those pies look good.* ○ *It looks as if it may snow.* ○ *He looks much older than forty.*

look after *phrasal verb* to take care of someone or something

look back *phrasal verb* to turn your head to see what is behind you ○ *He looked back and saw a police car was following him.*

look for *phrasal verb* to search for something, to try to find something

look into *phrasal verb* to try to find out about a matter or problem

look out *phrasal verb* to be careful ○ *Look out! – the car is going backwards!*

look out for *phrasal verb* to try to see or find someone or something ○ *We're looking out for new offices because ours are too small.* ○ *I'll look out for his sister at the party.*

look up *phrasal verb* to try to find some information in a book ○ *I'll look up his address in the telephone book.* ○

Look up the word in the dictionary if you don't know what it means.

loop /luːp/ *noun* a curve formed by a piece of something such as string, which crosses over itself ○ *To tie your laces, start by making a loop.*

loose /luːs/ *adjective* **1.** (*of a garment*) not tight ○ *Wear loose trousers and a teeshirt for the dance class.* (NOTE: **looser – loosest**) **2.** not attached to anything ○ *The front wheel is loose and needs tightening.* ○ *Once he was let loose, the dog ran across the park.*

loosen /ˈluːs(ə)n/ *verb* to make something less tight ○ *He loosened his shoelaces and relaxed.*

lord /lɔːd/ *noun* **1.** a man who has a high social rank ○ *He was born a lord.* ○ *Powerful lords forced King John to sign the Magna Carta.* **2.** an expression of surprise or shock ○ *Good lord! I didn't realise it was so late!*

lorry /ˈlɒri/ *noun* a large motor vehicle for carrying goods

lose /luːz/ *verb* **1.** to put or drop something somewhere and not to know where it is ○ *I can't find my wallet – I think I lost it on the train.* ○ *If you lose your ticket you'll have to buy another one.* **2.** not to have something any longer ○ *We lost money on the lottery.* **3.** not to win ○ *We lost the match 10 – 0.* ○ *Did you win? – No, we lost.* (NOTE: **loses – losing – lost** /lɒst/) ◇ **to lose your way** to not know where you are or which direction to go in ○ *They lost their way in the fog on the mountain.*

loss /lɒs/ *noun* **1.** the state of no longer having something ○ *He was very unhappy at the loss of his house.* ○ *The loss of a child is almost unbearable to a parent.* **2.** money which you have spent and have not got back through earnings ○ *Companies often make losses in their first year of operations.*

lost /lɒst/ past tense and past participle of **lose**

lot /lɒt/ *noun* □ **a lot of, lots of** a large number or a large quantity ○ *There's lots of time before the train leaves.* ○ *What a lot of cars there are in the car park!* ○ *I've been to the cinema quite a* *lot recently.* ○ *She's feeling a lot better now.* ○ *Lots of people are looking for jobs.* ◇ **the lot** everything ○ *That's the lot – there's nothing left.* ○ *There were old pots and books and newspapers – we sold the lot for £50.* ○ *We picked 2 kilos of beans and ate the lot for dinner.*

lottery /ˈlɒtəri/ *noun* a game of chance in which tickets with numbers on are sold with prizes given for certain numbers (NOTE: The plural is **lotteries**.)

loud /laʊd/ *adjective* very easy to hear ○ *Can't you stop your watch making such a loud noise?* ○ *Turn down the radio – it's too loud.* ■ *adverb* loudly ○ *I can't sing any louder.* ○ *She laughed out loud in church.*

loudly /ˈlaʊdli/ *adverb* in a way which is easy to hear

loudness /ˈlaʊdnəs/ *noun* the state of being loud, being noisy

lounge /laʊndʒ/ *noun* a comfortable room for sitting in ○ *Let's go and watch TV in the lounge.*

love /lʌv/ *noun* 1. a strong feeling of liking someone or something very much ○ *his love for his children* ○ *I had never felt true love like this before.* □ **to be in love** to love someone or to love each other ○ *They seem to be very much in love.* ○ *I told her I was in love with her.* □ **to fall in love with someone** to start to feel very strong affection for someone ○ *They fell in love at first sight.* 2. (*in games such as tennis*) a score of zero points ○ *She lost the first set six – love (6–0).* ■ *verb* 1. to have strong feelings of affection for someone or something ○ *'I love you!,' he said.* ○ *She loves little children.* ○ *The children love their teacher.* 2. to like something very much ○ *We love going on holiday by the seaside.* ○ *I'd love to come with you, but I've got too much work to do.*

lovely /ˈlʌvli/ *adjective* 1. very pleasant to look at ○ *She looks lovely in that dress.* ○ *There's a lovely garden behind the house.* 2. pleasant or enjoyable ○ *I had a lovely time on holiday.* ○ *It was lovely to have all those visitors when I was in hospital.* (NOTE: **lovelier – loveliest**)

low /ləʊ/ *adjective* not high ○ *She hit her head on the low branch.* ○ *The town is surrounded by low hills.* ○ *We shop around to find the lowest prices.* ○ *The engine works best at low speeds.* ○ *The temperature here is too low for oranges to grow.* ○ *Sales were lower in December than in November.* ■ *adverb* towards the bottom; not high up ○ *The plane was flying too low – it hit the trees.*

lower /ˈləʊə/ *adjective* not as high ○ *They booked a cabin on the lower deck.* ■ *verb* to make something go down ○ *They lowered the boat into the water.*

loyal /ˈlɔɪəl/ *adjective* who supports someone or something for along time without changing ○ *Dogs are very loyal to their owners.*

loyalty /ˈlɔɪəlti/ *noun* the quality of being loyal

luck /lʌk/ *noun* something, usually good, which happens to you ○ *The bus is empty – that's a bit of luck!* ◇ **bad luck** used for telling someone that you feel sorry that they were not successful ◇ **good luck** used for telling someone that you hope they will be successful

luckily /ˈlʌkɪli/ *adverb* used for showing that you think an event was lucky

lucky /ˈlʌki/ *adjective* 1. having good things happening to you, especially if they are unexpected ○ *He's lucky not to have been sent to prison.* ○ *How lucky you are to be going to Spain!* 2. bringing good luck ○ *Fifteen is my lucky number.* (NOTE: **luckier – luckiest**)

luggage /ˈlʌɡɪdʒ/ *noun* suitcases or bags for carrying your clothes and other things when travelling

lump /lʌmp/ *noun* a piece of something, often with no particular shape ○ *a lump of coal* ○ *a lump of sugar*

lunch /lʌntʃ/ *noun* the meal eaten in the middle of the day ○ *Come on – lunch will be ready soon.* ○ *We always have lunch at 12.30.* ○ *We are having fish and chips for lunch.* ○ *I'm not hungry so I don't want a big lunch.* ○ *The restaurant serves 150 lunches a day.*

lung /lʌŋ/ *noun* one of two organs in the chest with which you breathe

luxury /'lʌkʃəri/ *noun* **1.** great comfort ○ *He lived a life of great luxury.* ○ *A hot bath is a real luxury after two weeks camping in the mountains.* **2.** a thing which is pleasant to have, but not neces- sary ○ *She often buys little luxuries for dessert on Friday nights.* (NOTE: The plural in this sense is **luxuries**)

lying /'laɪɪŋ/ present participle of **lie**

M

m /em/, **M** *noun* the thirteenth letter of the alphabet, between L and N

machine /mə'ʃiːn/ *noun* a piece of equipment that uses power ○ *We have bought a machine for putting leaflets in envelopes.* ○ *There is a message on my answering machine.* ○ *She made her dress on her sewing machine.* ○ *The washing machine has broken and flooded the kitchen.*

machinery /mə'ʃiːnəri/ *noun* machines in general ○ *The factory has got rid of a lot of old machinery.* (NOTE: no plural: *some machinery, a piece of machinery*)

mad /mæd/ *adjective* **1.** having a serious medical condition which affects the brain (*offensive*) **2.** silly or crazy ○ *Everyone thought he was mad to try to cross the Atlantic in a rowing boat.* **3.** very angry (*informal*) ○ *She's mad at or with him for borrowing her car.* ○ *He was hopping mad when they told him his car had been stolen.* (NOTE: **madder – maddest**) ◇ **to drive someone mad** to make someone crazy or upset ○ *The noise is driving her mad.*

madam /'mædəm/ *noun* **1.** a polite way of addressing a woman, often used by people who are providing a service such as waiters or shop assistants ○ *After you, madam.* ○ *Can I help you, madam?* **2.** used when writing a letter to a woman whom you do not know ○ *Dear Madam*

made /meɪd/ past tense and past participle of **make**

magazine /mægə'ziːn/ *noun* a large thin book with a paper cover, which is published regularly ○ *The gardening magazine comes out on Fridays.*

magic /'mædʒɪk/ *noun* **1.** tricks such as making things appear and disappear, performed by an entertainer called a 'magician' ○ *The magician made a rabbit appear in his hat.* **2.** a power that some people believe they have, which makes them able to make impossible things happen ○ *She claimed to be a witch and able to perform magic.*

magician /mə'dʒɪʃ(ə)n/ *noun* **1.** a wizard ○ *Merlin was the great magician in medieval legends.* **2.** a conjuror ○ *They hired a magician to entertain the children at the party.*

magnet /'mægnɪt/ *noun* a piece of metal which attracts iron and steel ○ *She has a Mickey Mouse which sticks to the fridge door with a magnet.*

magnetic /mæg'netɪk/ *adjective* which attracts metal

magnificent /mæg'nɪfɪs(ə)nt/ *adjective* very impressive or beautiful

mail /meɪl/ *noun* **1.** letters which are delivered or which are sent ○ *The mail hasn't come yet.* ○ *The receipt was in this morning's mail.* **2.** a service provided by the post office ○ *We sent the parcel by sea mail.* ○ *It's cheaper to send the order by surface mail than by air.*

main /meɪn/ *adjective* most important ○ *The main thing is to get to work on time.* ○ *Their main factory is in Scotland.* ○ *January is the main month for skiing holidays.* ○ *A car will meet you at the main entrance.*

mainly /'meɪnli/ *adverb* most often ○ *We sell mainly to businesses.* ○ *People mainly go on holiday in the summer.*

maintain /meɪn'teɪn/ *verb* **1.** to make something stay the same ○ *We like to maintain good relations with our customers.* **2.** to keep something in good working order ○ *The boiler needs to be regularly maintained.* **3.** to continue to state something as a fact ○ *Throughout the trial he maintained that the car was not his.*

major /'meɪdʒə/ *adjective* important ○ *Smoking is a major cause of lung cancer.* ○ *Computers are a major influence* on modern industrial society. ○ *Many small roads are blocked by snow, but the major roads are open.* ■ *noun* a rank of an officer in the army below colonel ○ *A major came up in a truck with six soldiers.* (NOTE: also used as a title before a surname: *Major Smith*)

majority /məˈdʒɒrɪti/ *noun* **1.** the larger part of a group ○ *The majority of the members of the club don't want to change the rules.* **2.** a number of voters which is larger than half ○ *She was elected with a majority of 10,000.* **3.** the age when you become legally adult

make /meɪk/ *verb* **1.** to put something together or build something ○ *He made a boat out of old pieces of wood.* ○ *These knives are made of steel.* **2.** to get something ready ○ *She is making a Christmas cake.* ○ *Do you want me to make some tea?* **3.** to add up to a total ○ *Six and four make ten.* **4.** to give someone a feeling ○ *The smell of curry makes me hungry.* ○ *The rough sea made him feel sick.* ○ *Looking at old photographs made her sad.* ○ *He made himself comfortable in the armchair.* **5.** to force someone to do something ○ *His mother made him clean his room.* ○ *The teacher made us all stay in after school.* ○ *I can't make the car go any faster.* ○ *What on earth made you do that?* (NOTE: **makes – making – made** /meɪd/) ◊ **to make sense 1.** to be understood ○ *The message doesn't make sense.* **2.** to be a good idea ○ *It makes sense to put a little money into your savings account every week.*

make for *phrasal verb* to go towards a place ○ *The army was making for the capital.* ○ *As soon as the film started, she made straight for the exit.*

make out *phrasal verb* **1.** to be able to see clearly ○ *Can you make out the house in the dark?* **2.** to claim something which is probably not true ○ *The English weather isn't really as bad as it is made out to be.* ○ *She tries to make out that she's very poor.*

make up *phrasal verb* to invent a story ○ *He said he had seen a man climbing into the house, but in fact he made the*

whole story up.

makeup /ˈmeɪkʌp/ *noun* substances, e.g. face powder and lipstick, which people put on their face to make it more beautiful or change their appearance in some way ○ *She wears no makeup apart from a little eye shadow.* ○ *He spent hours over his makeup for the part of the monster.*

making /ˈmeɪkɪŋ/ present participle of **make**

male /meɪl/ *adjective* relating to the sex which does not give birth to young ○ *A male deer is called a stag.* (NOTE: Do not confuse with **mail**.)

mammal /ˈmæm(ə)l/ *noun* a type of animal which gives birth to live young and feeds them with milk

man /mæn/ *noun* a male human being ○ *That tall man is my brother.* ○ *There's a young man at reception asking for Mr Smith.* (NOTE: The plural is **men** /men/.) ■ *verb* to provide staff to work something ○ *The switchboard is manned all day.* ○ *She sometimes mans the front desk when the receptionist is ill.* (NOTE: **mans – manning – manned**)

manage /ˈmænɪdʒ/ *verb* to be in charge of something ○ *She manages all our offices in Europe.* ○ *We want to appoint someone to manage the new shop.*

management /ˈmænɪdʒmənt/ *noun* **1.** a group of people who direct workers ○ *The management has decided to move to new offices.* **2.** the practice of directing and controlling work ○ *He's taking a course in management.* ○ *If anything goes wrong now it's just a case of bad management.*

manager /ˈmænɪdʒə/ *noun* **1.** the person in charge of a department in a shop or in a business ○ *The bank manager wants to talk about your account.* ○ *The sales manager organised a publicity campaign.* ○ *She's the manager of the shoe department.* **2.** a person in charge of a sports team ○ *The club have just sacked their manager.*

mane /meɪn/ *noun* the long hair on the neck of a lion or horse (NOTE: Do not confuse with **main**.)

manner /'mænə/ *noun* a way of behaving ○ *She has a very unpleasant manner.* ○ *The staff don't like the new manager's manner.*

manufacture /ˌmænjʊ'fæktʃə/ *verb* to make products for sale ○ *We no longer manufacture tractors here.*

manufacturer /ˌmænjʊ'fæktʃərə/ *noun* a person or company producing industrial products

many /'meni/ *adjective* **1.** a large number of things or people ○ *Many old people live on the south coast.* ○ *So many people wanted rooms that the hotel was booked up.* ○ *She ate twice as many cakes as her sister did.* **2.** asking a question ○ *How many times have you been to France?* ○ *How many passengers were there on the plane?* ■ *pronoun* a large number of people ○ *Many of the students knew the lecturer when he was a student himself.* ○ *Many would say that smoking should be banned in all public places.*

map /mæp/ *noun* a drawing which shows a place, e.g. a town, a country or the world, as if it is seen from the air ○ *Here's a map of Europe.* ○ *The village where they live is so small I can't find it on the map.* ○ *Show me on the map where the mountains are.* ○ *They lost their way because they'd forgotten to take a map.*

marathon /'mærəθ(ə)n/ *noun* a race, often run on roads in a city, covering a distance of 42 kilometres ○ *She's training for the New York marathon.*

marble /'mɑːb(ə)l/ *noun* a very hard type of stone which can be polished so that it shines ○ *The entrance hall has a marble floor.* ○ *The table top is made from a single slab of green marble.*

march /mɑːtʃ/ *noun* the act of walking so that your legs move at exactly the same times as everyone else's, especially by soldiers ○ *The soldiers were tired after their long march through the mountains.* ■ *verb* **1.** to walk in this way ○ *The guards marched after the band.* ○ *We were just in time to see the soldiers march past.* **2.** to walk in a protest march ○ *Thousands of workers marched to the parliament building.*

March /mɑːtʃ/ *noun* the third month of the year, between February and April (NOTE: **March 6th** or **March 6**: say 'March the sixth' or 'the sixth of March' or in US English: 'March sixth'.)

margarine /ˌmɑːdʒə'riːn/ *noun* a substance made from animal or vegetable oil which is used instead of butter

margin /'mɑːdʒɪn/ *noun* a white space at the edge of a page of writing ○ *Write your comments in the margin.* ○ *We left a wide margin so that you can write notes in it.*

marine /mə'riːn/ *adjective* referring to the sea ○ *marine plants and animals*

mark /mɑːk/ *noun* **1.** a small spot of a different colour ○ *The red wine has made a mark on the tablecloth.* ○ *She has a mark on her forehead where she hit her head.* **2.** the points given to a student ○ *She got top marks in English.* ○ *What sort of mark did you get for your homework?* ○ *No one got full marks – the top mark was 8 out of 10.* ■ *verb* **1.** to make a mark on something **2.** to correct and give points to work ○ *The teacher hasn't finished marking our homework.* ○ *Has the English exam been marked yet?*

market /'mɑːkɪt/ *noun* a place where products, e.g. fruit and vegetables, are sold from small tables, often in the open air ○ *We buy all our vegetables and fish at the market.* ○ *Market day is Saturday, so parking will be difficult.*

marketing /'mɑːkɪtɪŋ/ *noun* the methods used by a company to encourage people buy a product

marriage /'mærɪdʒ/ *noun* **1.** the state of being legally joined as husband and wife ○ *A large number of marriages end in divorce.* ○ *She has two sons by her first marriage.* **2.** a wedding, the ceremony of being married ○ *They had a simple marriage, with just ten guests.*

married /'mærɪd/ *adjective* joined as husband and wife ○ *Are you married or single?* ○ *Married life must suit him – he's put on weight.*

marry /'mæri/ *verb* **1.** to make two people husband and wife ○ *They were married in church.* **2.** to become the husband or wife of someone ○ *She married the boy next door.* (NOTE: **marries – marrying – married**) ◇ **to get married to someone** to be joined as husband and wife in a ceremony ○ *They're getting married next Saturday.*

marsh /mɑːʃ/ *noun* an area of wet land (NOTE: The plural is **marshes**.)

masculine /'mæskjʊlɪn/ *adjective* suitable for or typical of a man ○ *She had a very masculine hair style.*

mask /mɑːsk/ *noun* something which covers or protects your face ○ *The burglars wore black masks.* ○ *He wore a mask to go diving.*

mass /mæs/ *noun* 1. a large number or large quantity of things ○ *Masses of people went to the exhibition.* ○ *A mass of leaves blew onto the pavement.* ○ *I have a mass of letters or masses of letters to write.* 2. a Catholic church service ○ *She's a strict Catholic and goes to mass every week.* ■ *adjective* involving a large number of people ○ *They found a mass grave on the hillside.* ○ *The group is organising a mass protest to parliament.*

massive /'mæsɪv/ *adjective* very large ○ *He had a massive heart attack.* ○ *The company has massive losses.* ○ *A massive rock came hurtling down the mountainside towards them.*

mast /mɑːst/ *noun* 1. a tall pole on a ship which carries the sails ○ *The gale was so strong that it snapped the ship's mast.* 2. a tall metal structure for broadcasting TV, radio or mobile phone signals ○ *They have put up a television mast on top of the hill.*

master /'mɑːstə/ *verb* to become skilled at something ○ *She has mastered the art of TV newscasting.* ○ *Although he passed his driving test some time ago, he still hasn't mastered the art of motorway driving.*

mat /mæt/ *noun* a small piece of something such as carpet, used as a floor covering ○ *Wipe your shoes on the mat before you come in.*

match /mætʃ/ *noun* 1. a single occasion when two teams or players compete with each other in a sport ○ *We watched* the football match on TV. ○ *He won the last two table tennis matches he played.* 2. a small piece of wood with a one end which catches fire when you rub it against a special surface ○ *He bought a packet of cigarettes and a box of matches.* ○ *She struck a match and lit a candle.* ■ *verb* to fit or to go with something ○ *The yellow wallpaper doesn't match the bright green carpet.*

mate /meɪt/ *noun* 1. a friend, especially a man's friend ○ *He's gone down to the pub with his mates.* 2. one of a pair of people or animals, especially where these can produce young together ■ *verb* (*of animals*) to breed ○ *A mule is the result of a donkey mating with a horse.*

material /mə'tɪəriəl/ *noun* 1. something which can be used to make something ○ *You can buy all the materials you need in the DIY shop.* (NOTE: The plural is **materials**.) 2. cloth ○ *I bought three metres of material to make curtains.* ○ *What material is your coat made of?* (NOTE: no plural) 3. facts or information ○ *She's gathering material for a TV programme on drugs.* (NOTE: no plural)

mathematics /ˌmæθə'mætɪks/, **maths** /mæθs/ *noun* the science of numbers and measurements

matter /'mætə/ *noun* 1. a problem or difficulty ○ *What's the matter?* ○ *This is a matter for the police.* 2. a concern or business ■ *verb* to be important ○ *It doesn't matter if you're late.* ○ *His job matters a lot to him.* ○ *Does it matter if we sit by the window?*

mattress /'mætrəs/ *noun* a thick pad forming the part of a bed that you lie on

maximum /'mæksɪməm/ *adjective* the greatest possible ○ *What is the maximum number of guests the hotel can take?* ■ *noun* the greatest possible number or amount ○ *The maximum we are allowed to charge per person is £10.* (NOTE: The plural is **maximums** or **maxima**.) □ **at the maximum** not more than ○ *We can seat 15 at the maximum.*

may /meɪ/ *modal verb* 1. it is possible ○ *If you don't hurry you may miss the train.* ○ *Take your umbrella, they say it may rain.* ○ *Here we are sitting in the* bar, and he may be waiting for us out-side. **2.** it is allowed ○ *Guests may park in the hotel car park free of charge.* ○ *You may sit down if you wish.* **3.** asking questions politely ○ *May I ask you a question?* ○ *May we have breakfast early tomorrow as we need to leave the hotel before 8 o'clock?*

May /meɪ/ *noun* the fifth month of the year, after April and before June ○ *Her birthday's in May.* ○ *Today is May 15th.* ○ *She was born on May 15.* ○ *We went on holiday last May.* (NOTE: **May 15th** or **May 15**: say 'the fifteenth of May' or 'May the fifteenth' or in US English: 'May fifteenth'.)

maybe /'meɪbi/ *adverb* possibly, perhaps ○ *Maybe the next bus will be the one we want.* ○ *Maybe you should ask a policeman.* ○ *Maybe the weather forecast was right after all.* □ **maybe not** possibly not ○ *Are you coming? – Maybe not.*

mayor /meə/ *noun* a person who is chosen as the official head of a town, city or local council

me /miː/ *pronoun* used by the person who is speaking to talk about himself or herself ○ *give me that book* ○ *Could you give me that book, please?* ○ *I'm shouting as loud as I can – can't you hear me?* ○ *She's much taller than me.* ○ *Who is it? – It's me!* ○ *Can you hear me?* ○ *She's taller than me.*

meadow /'medəʊ/ *noun* a large field of grass

meal /miːl/ *noun* an occasion when people eat food, or the food that is eaten ○ *Most people have three meals a day – breakfast, lunch and dinner.* ○ *You sleep better if you only eat a light meal in the evening.* ○ *When they had finished their evening meal they watched TV.* ○ *You can have your meals in your room at a small extra charge.*

mean /miːn/ *adjective* **1.** not liking to spend money or to give people things ○ *Don't be mean – let me borrow your car.* ○ *She's very mean with her money.* **2.** nasty or unpleasant ○ *He played a mean trick on his mother.* ○ *That was a mean thing to say.* ■ *verb* **1.** used when you have not understood something ○ *Did*

he mean me when he was talking about fat old men? ○ *What do you mean when you say she's old-fashioned?* **2.** to show or represent something ○ *His family means a lot to him.* ○ *When a red light comes on it means that you have to stop.* ○ *'Zimmer' means 'room' in German.* (NOTE: **means – meaning – meant** /ment/)

meaning /'miːnɪŋ/ *noun* what something represents ○ *If you want to find the meaning of the word, look it up in a dictionary.* ○ *The meaning of a red light is pretty clear to me.*

means /miːnz/ *noun* **1.** a way or method of doing something ○ *Is there any means of sending the message to London this afternoon?* ○ *Do we have any means of copying all these documents quickly?* ○ *The bus is the cheapest means of getting round the town.* □ **by means of** by using something ○ *He got her money by means of a trick.* **2.** money ○ *They don't have the means to buy a flat in London.*

meanwhile /'miːnwaɪl/ *adverb* during this time ○ *She hid under the table – meanwhile, the footsteps were coming nearer.*

measure /'meʒə/ *noun* a piece of equipment which shows the size or quantity of something ■ *verb* **1.** to be of a certain size or quantity ○ *a package which measures* or *a package measuring 10cm by 25cm* ○ *How much do you measure round your waist?* ○ *The table measures four foot long by three foot wide.* **2.** to find out the length or quantity of something ○ *She measured the window for curtains.* ○ *He measured the size of the garden.*

measurement /'meʒəmənt/ *noun* a quantity or size, found by measuring ○ *He took the measurements of the room.* ○ *The piano won't go through the door – are you sure you took the right measurements?* ○ *The measurements of the box are 25cm x 20cm x 5cm.*

meat /miːt/ *noun* food from an animal or bird ○ *Can I have some more meat, please?* ○ *Would you like meat or fish for your main course?* ○ *I like my meat very well cooked.*

mechanical /mɪ'kænɪk(ə)l/ *adjective* relating to machines ○ *Engineers are trying to fix a mechanical fault.*

medal /'med(ə)l/ *noun* a round metal object, made to represent an important occasion or battle, and given to people who have performed well

medical /'medɪk(ə)l/ *adjective* relating to medicine ○ *She's a medical student.* ○ *The Red Cross provided medical help.*

medicine /'med(ə)s(ə)n/ *noun* 1. a drug taken to treat a disease ○ *If you have a cough you should take some cough medicine.* ○ *The chemist told me to take the medicine four times a day.* ○ *Some cough medicines make you feel sleepy.* 2. the study of diseases and how to cure or prevent them ○ *He went to university to study medicine.* (NOTE: no plural in this sense)

medium /'miːdiəm/ *adjective* middle, average ○ *He is of medium height.*

meet /miːt/ *verb* 1. to come together with someone ○ *He met her at the railway station.* ○ *We'll meet for lunch before we go to the cinema.* 2. to come together ○ *Several streets meet at the Arc de Triomphe.* ○ *If you draw a diagonal line from each corner of a square to the opposite corner, the two lines will meet in the centre.* 3. to get to know someone ○ *I've never met your sister. – Come and meet her then!* ○ *Have you met our sales manager? – Yes, we have already met.* (NOTE: **meets – meeting – met** /met/)

meeting /'miːtɪŋ/ *noun* an occasion on which people come together, especially in order to discuss something ○ *The next meeting of the club will be on Tuesday.* ○ *There were only four people at the committee meeting.*

melon /'melən/ *noun* a large round fruit which grows on a plant which grows near the ground

melt /melt/ *verb* to change from a solid to a liquid by heating, or to cause a solid to do this ○ *If the sun comes out your snowman will melt.* ○ *The heat of the sun melted the road.* ○ *Glass will melt at very high temperatures.*

member /'membə/ *noun* a person who belongs to a group ○ *The two boys went* swimming while the other members of the family sat on the beach. ○ *Three members of staff are away sick.*

membership /'membəʃɪp/ *noun* 1. the state of belonging to a group ○ *I must remember to renew my membership.* ○ *Membership costs £50 a year.* 2. the members of a group ○ *The club has a membership of five hundred.* ○ *The membership voted to go on strike.*

memorise /'meməraɪz/, **memorize** *verb* to learn something thoroughly so that you know and can repeat all of it

memory /'mem(ə)ri/ *noun* 1. (*in people*) the ability to remember ○ *He recited the poem from memory.* 2. an event that you remember ○ *We have a lot of happy memories of our time in France.* 3. (*in computers*) the capacity for storing information ○ *This computer has a much larger memory than the old one.*

men /men/ plural of **man**

mend /mend/ *verb* to make something work which has a fault ○ *She's trying to mend the washing machine.*

mental /'ment(ə)l/ *adjective* relating to the mind ○ *I've lost my calculator – how's your mental arithmetic?*

mentally /'ment(ə)li/ *adverb* concerning the brain ○ *mentally ill*

mention /'menʃən/ *verb* to refer to something ○ *The press has not mentioned the accident.* ○ *Can you mention to everyone that the date of the next meeting has been changed?*

menu /'menjuː/ *noun* 1. a list of food available in a restaurant ○ *The lunch menu changes every week.* ○ *Some dishes are not on the menu, but are written on a blackboard.* 2. a list of choices available on a computer program

merely /'mɪəli/ *adverb* simply, only ○ *I'm not criticising you – I merely said I would have done it differently.*

mess /mes/ *noun* dirt or disorder ○ *We had to clear up the mess after the party.* ○ *The milk bottle broke and made a mess on the floor.*

mess up *phrasal verb* to spoil something ○ *I'm sorry we can't come – I hope it doesn't mess up your arrange-*

ments.

message /'mesɪdʒ/ *noun* information which is sent to someone ○ *I will leave a message with his secretary.* ○ *Can you give the director a message from his wife?* ○ *We got his message by e-mail.*

messenger /'mesɪndʒə/ *noun* a person who brings a message

met /met/ past tense and past participle of **meet**

metal /'met(ə)l/ *noun* a material, such as iron, which can carry heat and electricity and is used for making things ○ *a metal frying pan* ○ *These spoons are plastic but the knives are metal.*

meter /'miːtə/ *noun* 1. a piece of equipment for counting how much of something such as time, water or gas has been used ○ *He came to read the gas meter.* 2. US spelling of **metre**

method /'meθəd/ *noun* a way of doing something ○ *We use the most up-to-date manufacturing methods.* ○ *What is the best method of payment?*

metre /'miːtə/ *noun* a standard measurement of length, equal to 100 centimetres

mice /maɪs/ plural of **mouse**

microchip /'maɪkrəʊtʃɪp/ *noun* a very small part, used in computers, with electronic connections on it

microphone /'maɪkrəfəʊn/ *noun* a piece of electrical equipment used for making someone's voice louder, or for recording sound ○ *He had difficulty in making himself heard without a microphone.*

microscope /'maɪkrəskəʊp/ *noun* a piece of equipment which makes things look much bigger than they really are, allowing you to examine things which are very small

microscopic /,maɪkrə'skɒpɪk/ *adjective* extremely small, or so small that you need to use a microscope to see it

microwave /'maɪkrəweɪv/ *noun* a small oven which cooks very quickly using very short electric waves ○ *Put the dish in the microwave for three minutes.* ■ *verb* to cook something in a microwave ○ *You can microwave those potatoes.*

midday /,mɪd'deɪ/ *noun* twelve o'clock in the middle of the day

middle /'mɪd(ə)l/ *adjective* in the centre; halfway between two ends ○ *They live in the middle house, the one with the green door.* ◇ **in the middle 1.** in the centre ○ *She was standing in the middle of the road, trying to cross over.* ○ *Chad is a country in the middle of Africa.* **2.** halfway through a period of time ○ *We were woken in the middle of the night by a dog barking.* ○ *We were just in the middle of eating our supper when they called.* ○ *His telephone rang in the middle of the meeting.* ○ *The house was built in the middle of the eighteenth century.*

middle class /,mɪd(ə)l 'klɑːs/ *noun* a social or economic group of people who usually have more than enough money to live on, and who often own their own property

midnight /'mɪdnaɪt/ *noun* twelve o'clock at night ○ *I must go to bed – it's after midnight.* ○ *We only reached the hotel at midnight.*

might /maɪt/ *noun* strength ○ *She pulled at it with all her might, and still could not move it.* ○ *All the might of the armed forces is displayed during the National Day parade.* ■ *modal verb* **1.** it is possible ○ *Take an umbrella – it might rain.* ○ *If he isn't here, he might be waiting outside.* ○ *I might call in to see you tomorrow if I have time.* ○ *That was a stupid thing to do – you might have been killed!* ○ *They might win, but I wouldn't bet on it.* **2.** should (have done) ○ *You might try and stay awake next time.* □ **he might have done something to help** it would have been better if he had done something to help □ **you might have told me** I wish you had told me ○ *You might have told me you'd invited her as well.* **3.** making a request politely ○ *Might I have another cup of tea?* (NOTE: The negative is **might not**, usually **mightn't**. Note also that **might** is always used with other verbs and is not followed by **to**.)

mighty /'maɪti/ *adjective* having a lot of force or strength (*literary*) ○ *With one mighty heave he lifted the sack onto the* *lorry.* ○ *All she could remember was getting a mighty blow on the head, and then everything went black.* (NOTE: **mightier – mightiest**)

migrate /maɪˈɡreɪt/ *verb* to move from one place to another as the weather becomes warmer or colder

mild /maɪld/ *adjective* **1.** not severe ○ *There was some mild criticism, but generally the plan was welcomed.* ○ *He had a mild heart attack and was soon back to work again.* **2.** not strong-tasting ○ *We'll choose the mildest curry on the menu.*

mile /maɪl/ *noun* a measure of length, equal to 1.61 kilometres ○ *The car can't go any faster than sixty miles per hour.* ○ *The line of cars stretched for three miles from the road works.*

military /ˈmɪlɪt(ə)ri/ *adjective* relating to the armed forces ○ *The two leaders discussed the possibility of military intervention.* ○ *Military spending has fallen over the past three years.*

milk /mɪlk/ *noun* a white liquid produced by some female animals to feed their young, especially the liquid produced by cows ○ *Do you want milk with your coffee?* ○ *Can we have two glasses of milk, please?* ○ *Don't forget to buy some milk, there's none in the fridge.*

mill /mɪl/ *noun* **1.** a small machine for turning seeds into powder ○ *There is a pepper mill on the table.* **2.** a large factory ○ *a paper mill*

millimetre /ˈmɪlɪmiːtə/ *noun* one of a thousand parts of a metre (NOTE: usually written **mm** after figures: *35mm*. The US spelling is **millimeter**.)

million /ˈmɪljən/ *noun* the number 1,000,000 ○ *The population of Great Britain is just over 58 million.*

millionaire /ˌmɪljəˈneə/ *noun* a person who has more than a million pounds or a million dollars (NOTE: To show the currency in which a person is a millionaire, say 'a dollar millionaire', 'a sterling millionaire', etc.)

mind /maɪnd/ *noun* the part of the body which controls memory and reasoning ○ *His mind always seems to be on other things.* ○ *I've forgotten her name – it*

just slipped my mind. ○ *I think about her night and day – I just can't get her out of my mind.* ○ *My mind went blank as soon as I saw the exam paper.* □ **to bear in mind** to remember something that might change a decision ○ *Bear in mind that it takes 2 hours to get there.* ○ *Bear me in mind when you're looking for help.* ■ *verb* **1.** to be careful, to watch out ○ *Mind the steps – they're slippery!* ○ *Mind you get back early.* ○ *Mind the plate – it's hot!* **2.** to worry about ○ *Don't mind me, I'm used to working with children.* **3.** to look after someone or something for someone, or while the owner is away ○ *Who will be minding the house while you're on holiday?* ○ *Have you got anyone to mind the children when you start work?* **4.** to be annoyed by something ○ *Nobody will mind if you're late.* ○ *There aren't enough chairs, but I don't mind standing up.* ◇ **never mind** don't worry ○ *Never mind – you'll get another chance to enter the competition next year.*

mindful /ˈmaɪndf(ə)l/ *adjective* remembering or thinking about something carefully when doing something ○ *He is mindful of his responsibilities as a parent, even though his job often takes him away from home.* ○ *You should be mindful of the risks you are taking in not following the guidelines.*

mine /maɪn/ *pronoun* belonging to me ○ *That book is mine.* ○ *Can I borrow your bike, mine's been stolen.* ○ *She's a great friend of mine.* ■ *noun* a deep hole in the ground from which substances such as coal are taken ○ *The coal mine has stopped working after fifty years.* ○ *He has shares in an African gold mine.*

miner /ˈmaɪnə/ *noun* a person who works in a mine (NOTE: Do not confuse with **minor**.)

mineral /ˈmɪn(ə)rəl/ *noun* a substance, such as rock, which is dug out of the earth, or which is found in food ○ *What is the mineral content of spinach?* ○ *The company hopes to discover valuable minerals in the mountains.*

miniature /ˈmɪnɪtʃə/ *adjective* much smaller than the usual size ○ *He has a miniature camera.*

minimum /'mɪnɪməm/ *adjective* smallest possible ○ *The minimum amount you can save is £25 per month.* ○ *The minimum age for drivers is 18.* ■ *noun* the smallest possible amount ○ *We try to keep expenditure to a minimum.* ○ *She does the bare minimum of study, just enough to pass her exams.*

minister /'mɪnɪstə/ *noun* **1.** the member of a government in charge of a department ○ *The inquiry is to be headed by a former government minister.* ○ *He was the Minister of Defence in the previous government.* **2.** a clergyman

ministry /'mɪnɪstri/ *noun* a government department ○ *He works in the Ministry of Defence.* (NOTE: The plural is **ministries**. In the UK and the USA, important ministries are also called **departments**: *the Department of Work and Pensions, the Commerce Department.*)

minor /'maɪnə/ *adjective* not very serious or important ○ *It was just a minor injury.* ○ *She has a minor role in the film.* ○ *He played a minor part in the revolution.* (NOTE: Do not confuse with **miner.**) ■ *noun* a person under the age of 18, who is not considered to be an adult ○ *We are forbidden to serve alcohol to minors.*

minority /maɪ'nɒrɪti/ *noun* **1.** a number or quantity which is less than half of a total ○ *A large minority of members voted against the proposal.* **2.** the period when a person is less than 18 years old ○ *During the king's minority the country was ruled by his uncle.*

minus /'maɪnəs/ *preposition* **1.** reduced by ○ *Ten minus eight equals two (10 − 8 = 2).* ○ *Net salary is gross salary minus tax and National Insurance deductions.* **2.** below ○ *It was minus 10 degrees (-10°) outside.*

minute[1] /'mɪnɪt/ *noun* **1.** one of 60 parts of an hour ○ *There are sixty minutes in an hour, and sixty seconds in a minute.* ○ *The doctor can see you for ten minutes only.* ○ *The house is about ten minutes' walk* or *is a ten-minute walk from the office.* **2.** a very short space of time ○ *I'll be ready in a minute.* ○ *Why don't*

you wait for a minute and see if the dentist is free?

minute[2] /maɪ'njuːt/ *adjective* extremely small ○ *A minute piece of dust must have got into the watch.*

miracle /'mɪrək(ə)l/ *noun* **1.** a very lucky event ○ *It was a miracle she was not killed in the accident.* **2.** an event which you cannot explain, and which people believe happens by the power of God ○ *She went to the shrine and was cured – it must have been a miracle.*

mirror /'mɪrə/ *noun* a piece of glass with a metal backing which reflects an image ○ *They looked at themselves in the mirror.*

mischief /'mɪstʃɪf/ *noun* behaviour, especially by children, which causes trouble

mischievous /'mɪstʃɪvəs/ *adjective* a mischievous person enjoys annoying people and causing trouble ○ *He's a very mischievous little boy.* ○ *She had a mischievous look in her eyes.*

miserable /'mɪz(ə)rəb(ə)l/ *adjective* **1.** very sad ○ *He's in a very miserable state of mind.* ○ *She's really miserable since her boyfriend left her.* **2.** (of weather) bad or unpleasant ○ *What miserable weather – will it ever stop raining?*

misery /'mɪzəri/ *noun* great unhappiness

miss /mɪs/ *verb* **1.** not to hit something that you are trying to hit ○ *He missed the target.* ○ *She tried to shoot the rabbit but missed.* **2.** not to see, hear or notice someone or something ○ *We missed the road in the dark.* ○ *I missed the article about books in yesterday's evening paper.* ○ *I arrived late, so missed most of the discussion.* **3.** not to catch something that you are trying to catch ○ *He tried to catch the ball but he missed it.* ○ *She missed the last bus and had to walk home.* ■ *noun* an instance of not hitting something that you are trying to hit ○ *He hit the target twice and then had two misses.*

miss out on *phrasal verb* not to enjoy something because you are not there

Miss /mɪs/ *noun* a polite title given to a girl or woman who is not married ○ *Have you met Miss Jones, our new sales manager?* ○ *The letter is addressed to Miss Anne Smith.* (NOTE: used before a surname, or a first name and surname)

missile /'mɪsaɪl/ *noun* a weapon which is sent or thrown ○ *They think the plane was brought down by an enemy missile.* ○ *They threw missiles at the police.*

missing /'mɪsɪŋ/ *adjective* lost, which is not there ○ *I'm looking for my missing car keys.* ○ *They found there was a lot of money missing.* ○ *The police searched everywhere for the missing children.*

mission /'mɪʃ(ə)n/ *noun* **1.** an aim or purpose for which someone is sent ○ *The students were sent on a mission to find the best place to camp.* **2.** a group of people sent somewhere with a particular aim ○ *a United Nations peace mission* ○ *Several firms took part in a business mission to Japan.* ○ *A rescue mission was sent out into the mountains.*

mist /mɪst/ *noun* tiny drops of water that hang in the air ○ *Early morning mist covered the fields.*

mistake /mɪ'steɪk/ *noun* an act or belief that is wrong ○ *There are lots of mistakes in this essay.* ○ *You've made a mistake – my name is David, not John.* ■ *verb* to not understand or not realise something ○ *There's no mistaking him, with his red hair and purple anorak.* (NOTE: **mistakes – mistaking – mistook** /mɪs'tʊk/ **– has mistaken** /mɪs 'teɪkən/) ◇ **by mistake** as an accident ○ *They sent the wrong items by mistake.* ○ *By mistake she put my letter into an envelope for the chairman.* ○ *We took the wrong bus by mistake.* ○ *He put my coat on by mistake in the cloakroom.*

mix /mɪks/ *verb* **1.** to combine things ○ *She made the cake by mixing eggs and flour.* **2.** to come together and become a different substance ○ *Oil and water do not mix.*

mix up *phrasal verb* to think that a person or thing is someone or something else ○ *I always mix her up with her sis-*

ter.

mixed /mɪkst/ *adjective* **1.** made up of different things put together ○ *I'll have the mixed salad, please.* **2.** not completely for or against an idea ○ *The reaction to the proposal has been rather mixed – some people approve, but others disapprove.*

mixture /'mɪkstʃə/ *noun* **1.** a number of things mixed together ○ *a mixture of flour, fat and water* **2.** something made up of different types of thing ○ *His latest paintings are a strange mixture of shapes and colours.*

moan /məʊn/ *noun* a low sound made by someone who is in pain or upset ○ *The rescue team could hear moans from under the wreckage.* ○ *When she read the news she gave a loud moan.* ■ *verb* to make a low sound as if you are in pain ○ *I could hear someone moaning in the bathroom.* ○ *They could hear someone moaning in the cellar.*

mob /mɒb/ *noun* a large number of people behaving in a noisy, angry or uncontrolled way ○ *An angry mob surged towards the factory gates.*

mobile /'məʊbaɪl/ *adjective* able to move or be moved ○ *a mobile library* ■ *noun* **1.** a mobile phone ○ *I'll call him on his mobile.* ○ *He gave me the number of his mobile.* **2.** an object made of small pieces of metal, card etc., which when hung up move around with the movements of the air ○ *They bought a mobile of clowns to hang over the baby's cot.*

mobile phone /ˌməʊbaɪl 'fəʊn/ *noun* a small telephone which you can carry around

model /'mɒd(ə)l/ *noun* **1.** a small version of something larger ○ *The exhibition has a model of the new town hall.* ○ *He spends his time making model planes.* **2.** a person who wears new clothes to show them to customers ○ *He used only top models to show his designs during the London Fashion Week.*

modern /'mɒd(ə)n/ *adjective* referring to the present time ○ *It is a fairly modern invention – it was patented only in the 1980s.* ○ *You expect really modern offices to have air-conditioning systems.*

modest /'mɒdɪst/ *adjective* not telling other people about your achievements ○ *He was very modest about his gold medal.*

modify /'mɒdɪfaɪ/ *verb* to change something to suit a different situation ○ *The design was modified to make the car faster.*

module /'mɒdjuːl/ *noun* a part of something such as a course of study, which is made up of various sections ○ *The science course is made up of a series of modules.*

moist /mɔɪst/ *adjective* slightly wet, often in a pleasant way ○ *To clean the oven, just wipe it with a moist cloth.* ○ *The cake should be moist, not too dry.*

moisture /'mɔɪstʃə/ *noun* small drops of water in the air or on a surface (NOTE: no plural)

mole /məʊl/ *noun* **1.** a small animal with soft dark grey fur, which lives under the ground **2.** a small dark spot on the skin ○ *She has a little mole on her cheek.* ○ *The doctor removed a mole from the back of her hand.*

molecule /'mɒlɪkjuːl/ *noun* the smallest unit in a substance that can exist by itself.

moment /'məʊmənt/ *noun* a very short time ○ *Can you please wait a moment – the doctor is on the phone?* ○ *I only saw her for a moment.* ◇ **in a moment** in a short time from now

Monday /'mʌndeɪ/ *noun* the first day of the working week, the day between Sunday and Tuesday ○ *Some stores are shut on Mondays.* ○ *She had to go to the doctor last Monday.* ○ *The 15th is a Sunday, so the 16th must be a Monday.*

money /'mʌni/ *noun* **1.** coins or notes which are used for buying things ○ *How much money have you got in the bank?* ○ *He doesn't earn very much money.* ○ *We spent more money last week than in the previous month.* ○ *We ran out of money in Spain and had to come home early.* **2.** the type of coins and notes used in a country ○ *I want to change my British pounds into Mexican money.* **3.** □ **to make money** to make a profit

monitor /'mɒnɪtə/ *noun* the screen of a computer, or a small television screen used for checking what is happening ○ *My computer has a colour monitor.* ○ *Details of flight arrivals and departures are displayed on monitors around the airport.* ■ *verb* to check or to watch over the progress of something ○ *Doctors are monitoring her heart condition.* ○ *How do you monitor the performance of the sales staff?*

monk /mʌŋk/ *noun* a man who is a member of a religious group who live together in a monastery, away from other people (NOTE: The equivalent women are **nuns.**)

monkey /'mʌŋki/ *noun* a tropical animal which lives in trees and normally has a long tail ○ *Monkeys ran up the trees looking for fruit.*

monster /'mɒnstə/ *noun* a strange and frightening animal ○ *The Loch Ness Monster is said to be a large dinosaur.* ○ *She drew a picture of a green monster with purple horns and huge teeth.* ■ *adjective* very large ○ *Look at the monster cabbage Dad's grown in the garden.* ○ *What a monster sandwich!*

month /mʌnθ/ *noun* one of the twelve parts that a year is divided into ○ *December is the last month of the year.* ○ *What day of the month is it today?* ○ *There was a lot of hot weather last month, in fact it was hot all month long.* ○ *She's taken a month's holiday to visit her parents in Australia.* ○ *We haven't had any homework for months.*

monthly /'mʌnθli/ *adjective, adverb* happening every month ○ *He is paying for his car by monthly instalments.* ○ *My monthly salary cheque is late.* ○ *She gets paid monthly.*

monument /'mɒnjʊmənt/ *noun* a stone, building or statue, built in memory of someone who is dead ○ *They put up a monument to the people from the village who died in the war.*

mood /muːd/ *noun* the way you are feeling at a particular time ○ *Wait until she's in a good mood and then ask her.* ○ *The boss is in a terrible mood this morning.* ○ *Her mood changed as soon as she* *opened the letter.* ○ *A mood of gloom fell over the office.*

moon /muːn/ *noun* an object in the sky like a planet which goes round the Earth and shines at night ○ *The first man walked on the moon in 1969.* ○ *The moon is shining very brightly tonight.* ○ *There's no moon because it's cloudy.*

moonlight /'muːnlaɪt/ *noun* the light from the moon ○ *We could see the path clearly in the moonlight.*

moor /mʊə/ *noun* a large area of poor land covered with grass and small bushes ○ *The horsemen galloped across the moor.* ○ *The Lake District is wild country, full of moors and forests.* ■ *verb* to attach a boat to something ○ *The boat was moored to the river bank.* ○ *He moored his boat with a piece of rope.*

moral /'mɒrəl/ *adjective* **1.** relating to right and wrong behaviour ○ *Judges have a moral obligation to be impartial.* ○ *He refused to join the army on moral grounds.* **2.** relating to good behaviour ○ *She's a very moral person.* ■ *noun* something which you can learn from a story ○ *There must be a moral in this somewhere.* ○ *The moral of the story is that if you always tell lies, no one will believe you when you tell the truth.*

morally /'mɒrəli/ *adverb* according to the principles of correct human behaviour

more /mɔː/ *adjective* extra, which is added ○ *Do you want any more tea?* ○ *There are many more trains during the week than at the weekend.* ■ *adverb* used with adjectives to make the comparative form ○ *The dog was more frightened than I was.* ○ *She is much more intelligent than her sister.* ○ *The dinner was even more unpleasant than I had thought it would be.* ■ *pronoun* an extra thing or amount ○ *Is there any more of that soup?* ○ *£300 for that suit – that's more than I can afford!* ○ *We've only got nine men, we need two more to make a football team.*

moreover /mɔːr'əʊvə/ *adverb* in addition ○ *Its freezing cold, and moreover you're too young to go out in the dark.*

morning /'mɔːnɪŋ/ *noun* the first part of the day, before 12 o'clock ○ *Every morning he took his briefcase and went to the office.* ○ *Tomorrow morning we will be meeting our Japanese agents.* ○ *Have you read the morning paper?* ○ *If we want to be in Paris for lunch you have to get the early morning train.*

mortal /'mɔːt(ə)l/ *adjective* **1.** human and therefore bound to die ○ *He suffered a mortal blow in the fight.* **2.** causing death ○ *a mortal wound*

mosque /mɒsk/ *noun* a building where Muslims meet for prayer

mosquito /mɒ'skiːtəʊ/ *noun* a small flying insect which bites people and animals and sucks their blood

most /məʊst/ *adjective* the largest number of ○ *Most people go on holiday in the summer.* ○ *He spends most evenings watching TV.* ○ *Most apples are sweet.* ■ *pronoun* a very large number or amount ○ *Most of the work was done by my wife.* ○ *She spent most of the evening on the phone to her sister.* ○ *It rained for most of our holiday.* ○ *Most of the children in the group can ride bikes.* ■ *adverb* used with adjectives and 'the' for making the superlative form ○ *She's the most intelligent child in the class.* ○ *The most important thing if you are a sales representative is to be able to drive a car.* (NOTE: **Most** is used to form the superlative of adjectives which do not take the ending **-est**.)

mostly /'məʊstli/ *adverb* **1.** usually, most often ○ *We sometimes go to France for our holidays, but we mostly stay in Britain.* **2.** almost all ○ *The staff are mostly women of about twenty.*

moth /mɒθ/ *noun* a flying insect similar to a butterfly, but which has brown wings and flies mainly at night

mother /'mʌðə/ *noun* a woman who has children ○ *He's twenty-two but still lives with his mother.* ○ *Her mother's a dentist.* ○ *Mother! There's someone asking for you on the telephone.*

motion /'məʊʃ(ə)n/ *noun* the act of moving ○ *The motion of the ship made him feel ill.* ◇ **in motion** moving ○ *Do not try to get on or off while the train is* *in motion.* ◊ **to set something in motion** to make something start to happen ○ *Now that we have planning permission for the new sports hall, we can set things in motion to get the foundations laid.*

motive /'məʊtɪv/ *noun* a reason for doing something ○ *The police are trying to find a motive for the murder.*

motor /'məʊtə/ *noun* the part of a machine which makes it work ○ *The model plane has a tiny electric motor.*

motorbike /'məʊtəbaɪk/ *noun* a motorcycle

motorcycle /'məʊtəsaɪk(ə)l/ *noun* a type of large bicycle driven by a motor

motorway /'məʊtəweɪ/ *noun* a road with several lanes, on which traffic can travel at high speeds

mount /maʊnt/ *verb* **1.** to climb on to something; to climb up something ○ *They mounted their horses and rode off.* ○ *He mounted the stairs two at a time.* ○ *The car turned, mounted the pavement, and hit a wall.* **2.** to increase ○ *Tension is mounting as the time for the football final approaches.*

mountain /'maʊntɪn/ *noun* a very high piece of land, rising much higher than the land which surrounds it ○ *Everest is the highest mountain in the world.* ○ *Every weekend we go climbing in the Scottish mountains.*

mountainous /'maʊntɪnəs/ *adjective* with many high mountains ○ *It is a mountainous region, and very difficult for tanks and artillery.* ○ *Parts of Scotland are very mountainous.*

mouse /maʊs/ *noun* **1.** a small animal with a long tail, often living in holes in the walls of houses ○ *I saw a mouse sitting in the middle of the kitchen floor.* ○ *Our cat is good at catching mice.* (NOTE: The plural is **mice** /maɪs/.) **2.** a piece of computer equipment which is held in the hand and moved across a flat surface, used to control activity on the screen ○ *You can cut, paste and copy using the mouse.* ○ *Using the mouse, move the mouse pointer to the start button and click twice.* ○ *Click twice on the mouse to start the program.*

mouth¹ /maʊθ/ *noun* **1.** the opening in your face through which you take in food and drink, and which has your teeth and tongue inside ○ *It's not polite to talk with your mouth full.* ○ *He snored because he slept with his mouth open.* ○ *The cat was carrying a mouse in its mouth.* **2.** a wide or round entrance ○ *The mouth of the cave is hidden by bushes.* ○ *The train came out of the mouth of the tunnel.* ○ *New York is built on the mouth of the Hudson river.* (NOTE: The plural is **mouths** /maʊðz/.)

mouth² /maʊð/ *verb* to speak without making any sound ○ *She mouthed 'No' across the room.*

move /muːv/ *noun* a change in position ○ *The police were watching every move he made.* ■ *verb* **1.** to change the place of something ○ *Move the chairs to the side of the room.* ○ *Who's moved my drink?* ○ *He moved his hand to show he had heard.* **2.** to change your position ○ *Some animal was moving about outside the tent.* ○ *The only thing moving was the tip of the cat's tail.* ◊ **on the move** moving ○ *After I've been on the move all day I just want to get home and go to bed.*

movement /'muːvmənt/ *noun* an act of moving, not being still ○ *There was hardly any movement in the trees.* ○ *All you could see was a slight movement of the tiger's tail.*

movie /'muːvi/ *noun especially US* a cinema film ○ *We watch a movie most weekends.*

moving /'muːvɪŋ/ *adjective* making you feel emotion ○ *a moving story* ○ *The funeral was very moving.*

MP *abbr* member of parliament (NOTE: The plural is **MPs** /ˌem 'piːz/.)

Mr /'mɪstə/ *noun* the polite title given to a man ○ *Mr Jones is our new sales manager.* ○ *Here are Mr and Mrs Smith.* ○ (at the beginning of a letter) *Dear Mr Smith, .* (NOTE: used before a surname, sometimes with both the first name and surname)

Mrs /'mɪsɪz/ *noun* the title given to a married woman ○ *Mrs Jones is our manager.* ○ (at the beginning of a letter) *Dear*

Mrs Jones, . (NOTE: used before a surname, sometimes with both the first name and surname.)

Ms /məz, mɪz/ *noun* (*at the beginning of a letter*) a way of referring to a woman without saying whether or not she is married (NOTE: **Ms** is used with a surname, sometimes with both the first name and surname.)

much /mʌtʃ/ *adjective* a lot of ○ *with much love from Aunt Mary* ○ *How much sugar do you need?* ○ *I never take much money with me when I go on holiday.* ○ *She eats too much meat.* ■ *adverb* a lot ○ *He's feeling much better today.* ○ *It's much less cold in the south of the country.* ○ *Does it matter very much?* ○ *Much as I like her, I don't want to share an office with her.* ■ *pronoun* a lot ○ *He didn't write much in his exam.* ○ *Much of the work has already been done.*

mud /mʌd/ *noun* wet earth

muddy /'mʌdi/ *adjective* full of mud; covered with mud (NOTE: **muddier – muddiest**)

mug /mʌg/ *noun* a large cup with a handle ○ *She passed round mugs.* ■ *verb* to attack and steal from someone in the street ○ *She was mugged as she was looking for her car keys.* ○ *She's afraid of going out at night for fear of being mugged.* ○ *The gang specialises in mugging tourists.* (NOTE: **mugs – mugging – mugged**)

multiple /'mʌltɪp(ə)l/ *adjective* involving many people or things ○ *She was taken to hospital suffering from multiple injuries.*

multiply /'mʌltɪplaɪ/ *verb* to calculate the result when several numbers are added together a certain number of times ○ *Square measurements are calculated by multiplying length by width.* ○ *Ten multiplied by five gives fifty.* (NOTE: **multiplies – multiplying – multiplied**.)

mumble /'mʌmbəl/ *verb* to speak in a low voice which is not clear ○ *He mumbled an excuse and left the room.* ○ *She mumbled something about the telephone and went to the back of the shop.*

munch /mʌntʃ/ *verb* to eat noisily something such as an apple or raw carrot, with a regular movement of your mouth

murder /'mɜːdə/ *noun* the act of deliberately killing someone ○ *The murder was committed during the night.* ○ *She was accused of murder.* ○ *They denied the murder charge.* ■ *verb* to kill someone deliberately ○ *He was accused of murdering a policeman.*

murderer /'mɜːdərə/ *noun* a person who has committed a murder

murmur /'mɜːmə/ *noun* a low sound of people talking ○ *There was a murmur of voices in the hall.* ■ *verb* to speak very quietly ○ *She murmured something and closed her eyes.*

muscle /'mʌs(ə)l/ *noun* one of the part of the body which makes other parts move ○ *He has very powerful arm muscles.*

museum /mjuˈziːəm/ *noun* a building which you can visit to see a collection of valuable or rare objects ○ *The museum has a rich collection of Italian paintings.* ○ *The Natural History Museum is always very popular with school parties who go to see the dinosaurs.*

mushroom /'mʌʃruːm/ *noun* a round white or brown fungus which can be eaten ○ *Do you want fried mushrooms with your steak?* ○ *She ordered a mushroom omelette.* (NOTE: Fungi which are poisonous are called **toadstools**.)

music /'mjuːzɪk/ *noun* **1.** the sound made when you sing or play an instrument ○ *Do you like Russian music?* ○ *She's taking music lessons.* ○ *Her music teacher says she plays the violin very well.* **2.** written signs which you read to play an instrument ○ *Here's some music, see if you can play it on the piano.* ○ *He can play the piano by ear – he doesn't need any music.*

musical /'mjuːzɪk(ə)l/ *adjective* relating to music ○ *Do you play any musical instrument?*

musician /mjuˈzɪʃ(ə)n/ *noun* a person whose job is to play music ○ *a group of young musicians playing the street* ○ *The actors applauded the group of mu-*

sicians who had played during 'Twelfth Night'.

Muslim /'mʊzlɪm/ *adjective* relating to the religion of the prophet Muhammad ■ *noun* a person who follows the religion of the prophet Muhammad

must /məst, mʌst/ *modal verb* **1.** it is necessary that ○ *You must go to bed before eleven, or your mother will be angry.* ○ *We mustn't be late or we'll miss the last bus.* ○ *You must hurry up if you want to see the TV programme.* ○ *Must you really go so soon?* (NOTE: The negative is **mustn't, needn't**. Note also the meanings: **mustn't** = not allowed; **needn't** = not necessary: *we mustn't be late; you needn't hurry*) **2.** used for showing that you think something is very likely ○ *I must have left my briefcase on the train.* ○ *There is someone knocking at the door – it must be the postman.* ○ *You must be wet through after walking in the rain.* (NOTE: The negative is **can't**: *It can't be the doctor.* The past tense is **had to**: *I must go to the dentist, Yesterday I had to go to the dentist*; negative: **didn't have to**. The perfect tense is **must have**: *I must have left it on the train*; negative: **can't have**: *I can't have left it on the train.* Note also that **must** is only used with other verbs and is not followed by **to**.) ■ *noun* something important ○ *When in Florida, a trip to the Everglades is a must.*

my /maɪ/ *adjective* belonging to me ○ *Is that my pen you're using?* ○ *Have you seen my glasses anywhere?* ○ *We went skiing and I broke my leg.*

myself /maɪ'self/ *pronoun* used for referring back to 'I' ○ *I hurt myself climbing down the ladder.* ○ *It's true – I saw it myself.* ○ *I enjoyed myself a lot at the party.*

mysterious /mɪ'stɪəriəs/ *adjective* which cannot be explained

mystery /'mɪst(ə)ri/ *noun* something that cannot be explained ○ *The police finally cleared up the mystery of the missing body.* ○ *It's a mystery how the box came to be hidden under her bed.* (NOTE: The plural is **mysteries**.)

myth /mɪθ/ *noun* an ancient story about gods ○ *poems based on the myths of Greece and Rome*

N

n /en/, **N** *noun* the fourteenth letter of the alphabet, between M and O

nail /neɪl/ *noun* **1.** a small thin metal object which you use for attaching two pieces of a hard material such as wood ○ *Hit the nail hard with the hammer.* ○ *You need a hammer to knock that nail in.* **2.** the hard part at the end of your fingers and toes ○ *She painted her nails red.* ■ *verb* to attach something with nails ○ *He nailed the notice to the door.*

naked /ˈneɪkɪd/ *adjective* not wearing clothes ○ *The little children were playing in the river stark naked.* ○ *A naked man was standing on the balcony.*

name /neɪm/ *noun* a way of calling someone or something ○ *Hello! My name's James.* ○ *What's the name of the shop next to the post office?* ■ *verb* to call someone or something by a name ○ *They named him Nicholas.* ○ *They have a black cat named Jonah.*

narrow /ˈnærəʊ/ *adjective* not wide ○ *Why is your bicycle seat so narrow?* ○ *We went down a narrow passage to the shop.* ■ *verb* to become less wide ○ *The road narrows suddenly, and there is hardly enough room for two cars to pass.*

nasty /ˈnɑːsti/ *adjective* unpleasant

nation /ˈneɪʃ(ə)n/ *noun* **1.** a country ○ *the member nations of the EU* **2.** the people living in a country ○ *The whole nation was shocked by the terrible events.*

national /ˈnæʃ(ə)nəl/ *adjective* belonging to a country ○ *This is in our national interest.* ○ *The story even appeared in the national newspapers.* ○ *We need to protect our national culture.*

native /ˈneɪtɪv/ *noun* **1.** a person born in a place ○ *She's a native of Cornwall.* **2.** something such as a flower or a bird, which has always been in a particular place ■ *adjective* belonging to a country ○ *The tiger is native to India.*

natural /ˈnætʃ(ə)rəl/ *adjective* **1.** ordinary, not unusual ○ *Her behaviour at the meeting was quite natural.* ○ *It's natural to worry about your first baby.* **2.** coming from nature, and not produced or caused by people ○ *Do you think the colour of her hair is natural?* ○ *Yes, she's a natural blonde.* ○ *The inquest decided that he died from natural causes.*

naturally /ˈnætʃ(ə)rəli/ *adverb* of course ○ *Naturally the top team beat the bottom team.* ○ *Do you want to watch the game? – Naturally!*

nature /ˈneɪtʃə/ *noun* **1.** plants and animals ○ *We must try to protect nature and the environment.* **2.** the character of a person, thing, animal ○ *He has a very aggressive nature.*

naughty /ˈnɔːti/ *adjective* (*usually of a child*) a naughty child causes trouble and is not obedient ○ *Children who are naughty should be punished.* ○ *It was very naughty of you to put glue on your daddy's chair.* (NOTE: **naughtier – naughtiest**)

navy /ˈneɪvi/ *noun* a military force which fights battles at sea ○ *He left school and joined the navy.* ○ *The navy has many ships.* ■ *adjective* □ **navy (blue)** of a dark blue colour ○ *She was wearing a navy skirt.* ○ *He's bought a navy blue pullover.*

near /nɪə/ *adverb, preposition, adjective* **1.** close to, not far away from ○ *Our house is near the post office.* ○ *Bring your chair nearer to the table.* ○ *He lives quite near or quite near here.* ○ *Which is the nearest chemist's?* **2.** soon, not far off in time ○ *Her birthday is on December 21st – it's quite near to Christmas.* ○ *Can you phone again nearer the day and I'll see if I can find a* *few minutes to see you?* ■ *verb* to get closer to a place or time ○ *We're nearing the end of the year.*

nearby /nɪə'baɪ/ *adverb, adjective* not far away ○ *He lives just nearby.* ○ *They met in a nearby restaurant.*

nearly /'nɪəli/ *adverb* almost ○ *He's nearly 18 – he'll be going to university next year.* ○ *The film lasted nearly three hours.* ○ *The book isn't nearly as good as the last one I read.* ○ *Hurry up, it's nearly time for breakfast.* ○ *We haven't got nearly enough time to get to London.*

neat /niːt/ *adjective* tidy, without any mess ○ *a blouse with a neat lace collar* ○ *Leave your bedroom neat and tidy.* ○ *Her handwriting is very neat.*

necessarily /ˌnesɪ'serɪli/ *adverb* which cannot be avoided ○ *Going to Newcastle from here necessarily means changing trains twice.*

necessary /'nesɪs(ə)ri/ *adjective* which has to be done ○ *Don't phone me in the evening unless it's absolutely necessary.* ○ *Is it necessary to finish the work today?*

neck /nek/ *noun* **1.** a part which joins your head to your body ○ *She was sitting in a draught and got a stiff neck.* ○ *The mayor wears a gold chain round his neck.* **2.** the part of a piece of clothing which goes round your neck ○ *I can't wear this shirt – the neck is too tight.*

necklace /'nekləs/ *noun* a piece of jewellery which you wear round your neck

need /niːd/ *verb* **1.** to require something, or have to have something ○ *We shall need some euros for our holiday in Spain.* ○ *Painting needs a lot of skill.* ○ *I need someone to help me with the cooking.* **2.** to want something ○ *Does anyone need any more coffee?* ■ *modal verb* used with other verbs meaning to be necessary ○ *Need you make so much noise in the bath?* ○ *Need you go now?* ○ *The living room needs painting* or *needs to be painted.* ○ *You don't need to come if you have a cold.* ○ *The police need to know who saw the accident.* ○ *You needn't bother waiting for me.* ■ *noun* what is necessary or wanted ○

There's no need for you to wait – I can find my own way.

needle /'niːd(ə)l/ *noun* **1.** a long thin sharp object with a hole at one end, used for sewing ○ *This needle hasn't got a very sharp point.* ○ *You must try to put the piece of wool through the hole in the needle.* □ **knitting needle** a thin pointed plastic or metal stick used for knitting **2.** a long thin sharp piece of medical equipment, used for putting medicine into your body **3.** a small thin part on a piece of equipment, which points to something such as a number ○ *He looked at the dial and saw the needle was pointing to zero.* **4.** one of the thin leaves of a pine tree ○ *She had lots of pine needles stuck in her hair.*

negative /'negətɪv/ *noun* developed film with an image where the light parts are dark and dark parts light ○ *Don't touch the negatives with your dirty fingers.* ■ *adjective* showing that something is not there ○ *Her blood test was negative.*

negotiation /nɪˌgəʊʃi'eɪʃ(ə)n/ *noun* the process of discussing something

neighbor /'neɪbə/ *noun* US spelling of **neighbour**

neighbour /'neɪbə/ *noun* **1.** a person who lives near you ○ *He doesn't get on with his neighbours.* **2.** a person who is sitting next to you ○ *Help yourself and then pass the plate on to your neighbour.* **3.** another person (*old*) ○ *'Love of your neighbour' is one of the essentials of Christian doctrine.*

neighbouring /'neɪbərɪŋ/ *adjective* which is close to you (NOTE: The US spelling is **neighboring**.)

neither /'naɪðə, 'niːðə/ *adjective, pronoun* not either of two people or things ○ *Neither car* or *neither of the cars passed the test.* ○ *Neither sister is dark* or *neither of the sisters is dark.* ■ *adverb* not either; used for showing that a negative statement applies to two things or people ○ *He doesn't eat meat and neither does his wife.* ○ *She isn't fat but neither is she really very thin.*

nephew /'nefjuː/ *noun* a son of your sister or brother, or a son of your husband's or wife's brother or sister

nerve /nɜːv/ *noun* **1.** one of the fibres in your body which take messages to and from the brain ○ *Nerves are very delicate and easily damaged.* **2.** over-confidence or rude behaviour ○ *He's got a nerve to ask for a day off, when he was away all last week.* **3.** the ability to keep your fear under control in order to achieve something ○ *It takes a lot of nerve to disagree with your friends.* ○ *He went over to speak to her but at the last minute he lost his nerve.*

nervous /'nɜːvəs/ *adjective* **1.** worried and easily frightened ○ *She gets nervous if she is alone in the house at night.* ○ *He's nervous about driving in London.* **2.** referring to the nerves ○ *the nervous system*

nervousness /'nɜːvəsnəs/ *noun* a state of worry and tension

nervous system /'nɜːvəs ˌsɪstəm/ *noun* the system of nerves in the body

nest /nest/ *noun* a structure built by birds, and by some animals and insects, to lay their eggs in ○ *an ants' nest* ○ *The birds built their nests among the trees.* ○ *The blackbirds have laid three eggs in their nest.*

net /net/ *noun* **1.** a woven material with large holes ○ *A long skirt made of pink net.* **2.** a piece of this material used for a special purpose ○ *a fishing net* **3.** same as **Internet** ■ *adjective* after all payments such as tax have been considered ○ *That figure is net, not gross.*

network /'netwɜːk/ *noun* **1.** a system of things such as roads or railways connecting different places ○ *the British rail network* ○ *a satellite TV network* ○ *There is a network of tunnels under the castle.* **2.** a system of computers which are connected together ○ *How does this network operate?* ○ *You can book at any of our hotels throughout the country using our computer network.* **3.** a group of people connected with each other ○ *His rapidly developing network of contacts in government.* ■ *verb* to connect two or more computers in order to allow them to exchange information ○ *Workstations*

within an office are usually networked and share resources.

never /'nevə/ *adverb* not at any time; not ever ○ *We'll never forget that restaurant.* ○ *I've never bought anything in that shop although I've often been inside it.* ○ *He never eats meat.*

nevertheless /ˌnevəðə'les/ *adverb* although a particular situation exists ○ *I know it is raining, but nevertheless I'd like to go for a walk along the beach.* ○ *She had a cold, but went to the meeting nevertheless.*

new /njuː/ *adjective* **1.** made very recently, or never used before ○ *Put some new paper in the printer.* ○ *The new version of the software is now available.* **2.** which arrived recently ○ *There are two new secretaries in the office.* **3.** completely different from what was before ○ *We need someone with new ideas.* ○ *They put some new wallpaper in the bedroom.*

news /njuːz/ *noun* spoken or written information about what has happened ○ *What's the news of your sister?* ○ *She told me all the latest news about the office.* ○ *He was watching the 10 o'clock news on TV.* ○ *I don't want to hear any bad news.*

newspaper /'njuːzpeɪpə/ *noun* a set of loose folded sheets of paper, containing news of what has happened, especially in the last 24 hours ○ *He was so absorbed in his newspaper that he didn't notice that the toast had burnt.* ○ *We saw your picture in the local newspaper.* ○ *The newspapers are full of news of the election.*

New Year's Day /ˌnjuː jɪəz 'deɪ/ *noun* 1st January

New Year's Eve /ˌnjuː jɪəz 'iːv/ *noun* 31st December

next /nekst/ *adjective, adverb* **1.** coming after in time ○ *On Wednesday we go to Paris, and the next day we travel to Italy.* ○ *First you put the eggs into a bowl and next you add some sugar.* ○ *Don't forget to give me a call when you're next in town.* ○ *Next week is the start of our holiday.* ○ *The next time you go to the supermarket, can you get some coffee?* **2.**

nearest in place ○ *The ball went over the fence into the next garden.* ○ *She took the seat next to mine.* ■ *pronoun* the thing or person following ○ *After two buses went past full, the next was almost empty.* ○ *I'll be back from holiday the week after next.* ○ (asking the next person in the queue to come) *Next, please!*

nibble /'nɪb(ə)l/ *verb* to take small bites from something ○ *She was nibbling a biscuit.* ○ *The mice have nibbled into the flour sacks.*

nice /naɪs/ *adjective* **1.** pleasant, enjoyable ○ *We had a nice time at the seaside.* ○ *If the weather's nice let's have a picnic.* ○ *The nicest thing about the town is that it is on the sea.* **2.** pleasant, polite ○ *That wasn't a very nice thing to say.* ○ *Try and be nice to your grandfather.* (NOTE: **nicer – nicest**)

nickname /'nɪkneɪm/ *noun* a short or informal name given to someone ○ *Her real name's Henrietta, but everyone calls her by her nickname 'Bobbles'.* ■ *verb* to give a nickname to someone ○ *He was nicknamed 'Camel' because of his big nose.*

niece /niːs/ *noun* a daughter of a brother or sister, or a daughter of your husband's or wife's brother or sister

night /naɪt/ *noun* the time when it is dark ○ *It's dangerous to walk alone in the streets at night.* ○ *Burglars got into the office during the night.* ○ *He is on night duty three days a week.* ○ *They're planning to have a night out tomorrow.*

nightmare /'naɪtmeə/ *noun* a very frightening dream ○ *I had a nightmare that I was drowning.*

nine /naɪn/ *noun* the number 9 ○ *She's nine (years old) tomorrow.* ○ *The shop opens at 9 o'clock.*

nineteen /ˌnaɪn'tiːn/ *noun* the number 19 ○ *He's nineteen (years old) tomorrow.*

nineteenth /naɪn'tiːnθ/, **19th** *adjective* relating to number 19 in a series ○ *It's his nineteenth birthday tomorrow.* ○ *The nineteenth of August* or *August the nineteenth (August 19th).* ■ *noun* number nineteen in a series ○ *He's the nineteenth in the queue.*

ninetieth /'naɪntiəθ/, **90th** *adjective* relating to number 90 in a series ○ *It's his ninetieth birthday tomorrow.* ■ *noun* number ninety in a series ○ *I've had so many calls – this is the ninetieth.*

ninety /'naɪnti/ *noun* number 90 ○ *My old aunt will be ninety (years old) next week and her husband is ninety-two: they are both in their nineties.*

ninth /naɪnθ/, **9th** *adjective* relating to number 9 in a series ○ *You're the ninth person in the queue.* ■ *noun* number nine in a series ○ *A lot of people have cancelled – he's the ninth.*

no /nəʊ/ *adjective, adverb* **1.** used for giving a negative answer ○ *I asked my mother if we could borrow her car but she said 'no'.* ○ *Do you want another cup of coffee? – No, thank you.* **2.** not any ○ *There's no milk left in the fridge.* ○ *We live in a little village, and there's no post office for miles around.* ○ *We had no reply to our fax.* ◇ **no entry** you may not go in this way ◇ **no exit** you may not go out this way ◇ **no parking** you may not park ◇ **no smoking** you may not smoke

nobody /'nəʊbədi/ *pronoun* same as **no one**

nocturnal /nɒk'tɜːn(ə)l/ *adjective* relating to the night ○ *The nocturnal habits of the badger.*

nod /nɒd/ *verb* to move the head slightly up and down, meaning 'yes' ○ *When he asked her if she understood, she nodded (her head).* ○ *He nodded to show his agreement.* (NOTE: The opposite is to **shake** your head, meaning 'no'. Note also: **nods – nodding – nodded**.) ■ *noun* a movement of the head up and down, meaning 'yes' ○ *He gave me a nod as I came in.*

noise /nɔɪz/ *noun* **1.** a loud or unpleasant sound ○ *The workmen are making such a lot of noise that we can't use the telephone.* ○ *Let's not invite the children – I can't stand noise.* **2.** a sound ○ *The baby made a little gurgling noise.* ○ *Is there anything the matter with the washing machine? It's making a funny noise.* ○ *There was a noise of running water in the bathroom.* ○ *He woke up when he heard a noise in the kitchen.* ○ *Don't* make a noise – the guards might hear you.

noisily /'nɔɪzɪli/ *adverb* making a lot of noise

noisy /'nɔɪzi/ *adjective* who or which makes a lot of noise ○ *a crowd of noisy little boys* ○ *Unfortunately, the hotel overlooks a noisy crossroads.* (NOTE: **noisier – noisiest**)

none /nʌn/ *pronoun* **1.** not any ○ *How many dogs have you got? – None.* ○ *Can you buy some milk? We've none left in the fridge?* ○ *A little money is better than none at all.* **2.** not one ○ *None of my friends smokes.* ○ *None of the group can speak Chinese.*

nonsense /'nɒnsəns/ *noun* silly ideas ○ *I'm too fat – nonsense!* ○ *He talked a lot of nonsense.* ○ *It's nonsense to expect people to pay money for that.* (NOTE: no plural)

non-stop /,nɒn 'stɒp/ *adjective* which does not stop ○ *a non-stop train to Paris* ○ *They took a non-stop flight to Australia.* ○ *All our flights to Toronto are non-stop.* ■ *adverb* without stopping ○ *The planes flies to Hong Kong non-stop.* ○ *They worked non-stop to finish the job on time.*

noon /nuːn/ *noun* twelve o'clock in the middle of the day

no one /'nəʊ wʌn/ *pronoun* no person ○ *We met no one we knew.* ○ *No one here takes sugar in their tea.* ○ *There was nobody in the café.* ○ *Nobody wants to do her job.* □ **no one else** no other person ○ *No one else's child behaved as badly as ours on the plane!*

nor /nɔː/ *conjunction* and not ○ *'I don't want to go' – 'Nor me!'* ○ *I did not meet him that year nor in subsequent years.* ○ *I never went there again, nor did my wife.* ◊ **neither**

normal /'nɔːm(ə)l/ *adjective* usual or expected ○ *We hope to restore normal service as soon as possible.* ○ *Look at the rain – it's just a normal British summer.* ○ *What's the size of a normal swimming pool?* ○ *At her age, it's only normal for her to want to go to parties.*

normally /'nɔːm(ə)li/ *adverb* usually ○ *The bus is normally late.* ○ *She doesn't normally drink wine.*

north /nɔːθ/ *noun* the direction to your left when you are facing the direction in which the sun rises ○ *There will be snow in the north of the country.* ○ *It's cold when the wind blows from the north.* ■ *adjective* relating to the north ○ *We went on holiday to the north coast of Scotland.* ○ *The north side of our house never gets any sun.* ○ *When the north wind blows, you can expect snow.* ■ *adverb* towards the north ○ *They were travelling north at the time.* ○ *Go north for three miles and then you'll see the road to London.* ○ *Our office windows face north.*

north-east /,nɔːθ 'iːst/ *adverb* the direction between north and east ○ *They were travelling north-east at the time.* ○ *Go north-east for three miles and then you'll come to our village.* ○ *Our office windows face north-east.* ■ *noun* the part of a country to the north and east ○ *The North-East of England will have snow showers.* ○ *It's cold when the wind blows from the north-east.*

northern /'nɔːð(ə)n/ *adjective* relating to the north ○ *Northern countries have more rain.* ○ *They live in the northern part of the country.*

north-west /,nɔːθ 'west/ *adverb* the direction between west and north ○ *They were travelling north-west at the time.* ○ *Go north-west for a few miles and then you'll come to our house.* ■ *noun* the part of a country to the north and west ○ *The North-West of England is wetter than the east coast.* ○ *We can expect rain when the wind blows from the north-west.* ○ *The old castle stood to the north-west of the cathedral.*

nose /nəʊz/ *noun* a part of the body on your face which you breathe through and smell with ○ *He has a cold, and his nose is red.* ○ *Dogs have wet noses.* ○ *She's got flu – her nose is running.* ○ *Don't wipe your nose on your sleeve, use a tissue.* ◊ **under his, her, etc. very nose** in front of him, her, etc. ○ *I did it under his very nose and he didn't notice a thing.*

nostril /'nɒstrɪl/ *noun* one of the two holes in your nose, which you breathe through

not /nɒt/ *adverb* used with verbs to show the negative ○ *A service charge is not included.* ○ *It isn't there.* ○ *She can't come.* ○ *He didn't want any meat.* ○ *We couldn't go home because of the fog.* ○ *Don't you like coffee?* ◇ **not exactly 1.** not completely ○ *Was it a disaster? – Not exactly a disaster, but it didn't go very well.* ○ *It's not exactly the colour I wanted.* **2.** used for emphasising a negative ○ *He's not exactly pleased at having to pay out so much money.* ◇ **not...either** and not...also ○ *She doesn't eat meat, and she doesn't eat fish either.* ○ *It wasn't hot, but it wasn't very cold either.* ◇ **not only...but also** not just this...but this as well ○ *The film wasn't only very long, but it was also very bad.*

note /nəʊt/ *noun* **1.** a few words that you write to tell someone something or to help you to remember something ○ *She made a few notes before she gave her speech.* ○ *She made a note of what she needed to buy before she went to the supermarket.* ○ *He left us a note before he went out.* **2.** a piece of paper money ○ *I tried to pay with a £10 note.* **3.** a musical sound, or a written sign representing a musical sound ○ *He can't sing high notes.* ■ *verb* to write down something in a few words ○ *The policeman noted in his notebook all the details of the accident.* ◇ **to take note of** to pay attention to ○ *We have to take note of public opinion.*

notebook /'nəʊtbʊk/ *noun* a small book for making notes ○ *The policeman wrote down the details in his notebook.*

nothing /'nʌθɪŋ/ *pronoun* not anything ○ *There's nothing interesting on TV.* ○ *She said nothing about what she had seen.* ○ *There's nothing more we can do.* ◇ **for nothing** free, without having to pay ○ *We're friends of the woman running the show and she got us in for nothing.*

notice /'nəʊtɪs/ *noun* **1.** a piece of writing giving information, usually put in a place where people can see it ○ *He*

pinned up a notice about the staff tennis match.* **2.** an official warning that something has to be done, or that something is going to happen ○ *They gave us five minutes' notice to leave the office.* ○ *If you want to resign, you have to give a month's notice.* ○ *The train times were changed without notice.* ■ *verb* to see and take note of something ○ *I wore one blue and one white sock all day and nobody noticed.* ○ *I didn't notice you had come in.* ○ *Did you notice if John was sitting next to Sarah?* ◇ **at short notice** with very little warning ○ *It had to be done at short notice.* ○ *The bank manager will not see anyone at such short notice.* ◇ **until further notice** until different instructions are given ○ *You must pay £200 on the 30th of each month until further notice.*

noticeable /'nəʊtɪsəb(ə)l/ *adjective* which is easily noticed

notion /'nəʊʃ(ə)n/ *noun* an idea ○ *She has this strange notion that she ought to be a TV star.*

notorious /nəʊ'tɔːriəs/ *adjective* well known for bad qualities, or for doing bad things

noun /naʊn/ *noun* (*in grammar*) a word which can be the subject or object of a verb and is used to refer to a person, thing or animal ○ *nouns such as 'brick' and 'elephant'* ○ *In 'the cat caught a mouse', 'cat' and 'mouse' are both nouns.*

novel /'nɒv(ə)l/ *noun* a long story with imaginary characters and events ○ *'Pickwick Papers' was Dickens' first major novel.* ■ *adjective* new and unusual ○ *Visiting New York is a novel experience for me.*

November /nəʊ'vembə/ *noun* the eleventh month of the year, the month after October and before December ○ *November 5* ○ *Today is November 5th.* ○ *She was born in November.* ○ *We never go on holiday in November.* (NOTE: **November 5th** *or* **November 5**: say 'November the fifth' or 'the fifth of November' or in US English: 'November fifth'.)

novice /'nɒvɪs/ *noun* a person who has very little experience or skill, e.g. in a job or sport ○ *He's still a novice at row-*

ing. ○ *A competition like this is not for novices.*

now /naʊ/ *adverb* at or around this point in time ○ *I can hear a train coming now.* ○ *Please can we go home now?* ○ *The flight is only two hours – he ought to be in Berlin by now.* ○ *Now's the best time for going skiing.* ○ *A week from now we'll be sitting on the beach.* ■ *interjection* showing a warning ○ *Now then, don't be rude to the teacher!* ○ *Come on now, work hard!* ○ *Now, now! Nobody wants to hear you crying.* ◇ **now and then** from time to time, not continuously ◇ **until now, up to now** until this point in time ○ *Until now, I've never had to see a doctor.*

nowhere /'nəʊweə/ *adverb* not in or to any place ○ *My wallet was nowhere to be found.* ○ *Where are you going? – Nowhere.* ○ *There is nowhere else for them to live.* ◇ **to get nowhere** not to have any success ○ *I rang six shops to try and find a spare part, but got nowhere.*

nuclear /'njuːkliə/ *adjective* relating to energy made from parts of atoms ○ *a nuclear power station*

nude /njuːd/ *adjective* not wearing clothes, especially in situations where people are expected to wear some clothes ○ *Nude sunbathing is not allowed on this beach.* ○ *She has appeared nude on stage several times.*

nudge /nʌdʒ/ *noun* a little push, usually with the elbow ○ *She gave me a nudge to wake me up.* ■ *verb* to give a little push, usually with the elbow ○ *He nudged me when it was my turn to speak.*

nuisance /'njuːs(ə)ns/ *noun* a thing which annoys people ◇ **to make a nuisance of yourself** to do something annoying ○ *The children made a nuisance of themselves running round the restaurant and throwing bits of bread.*

numb /nʌm/ *adjective* not able to feel things that you touch ○ *The tips of his fingers went numb.* ○ *His hands were numb with cold.*

number /'nʌmbə/ *noun* **1.** a sign that represents an amount ○ *13 is not a lucky number.* ○ *They live on the opposite side of road at number 49.* ○ *Can you give me your telephone number?* ○ *A number 6 bus goes to Oxford Street.* ○ *Please quote your account number.* **2.** a quantity of people or things ○ *The number of tickets sold was disappointing.* ○ *A large number of children or large numbers of children will be sitting the exam.* ○ *There were only a small number of people at the meeting.* ■ *verb* to give something a number ○ *The raffle tickets are numbered 1 to 1000.* ○ *I refer to our invoices numbered 234 and 235.* ○ *All the seats are clearly numbered.*

numerous /'njuːm(ə)rəs/ *adjective* very many ○ *He has been fined for speeding on numerous occasions.*

nun /nʌn/ *noun* a woman member of a religious group who live together (NOTE: Do not confuse with **none**. Note: the equivalent men are **monks**.)

nurse /nɜːs/ *noun* a person who looks after sick people (*woman or man*) ○ *She has a job as a nurse in the local hospital.* ■ *verb* to look after people who are ill ○ *When she fell ill her daughter nursed her until she was better.*

nursery /'nɜːs(ə)ri/ *noun* a school for very young children, or a place where very young children are looked after ○ *My sister went to a nursery every day from the age of 18 months.* (NOTE: The plural is **nurseries**.)

nut /nʌt/ *noun* **1.** a dry fruit with a hard shell, that grows on trees **2.** a metal ring which screws on a bolt to hold it tight ○ *Screw the nut on tightly.*

O

o /əʊ/, **O** *noun* the fifteenth letter of the alphabet, between N and P

oak /əʊk/ *noun* **1.** a type of large tree which loses its leaves in winter ○ *a forest of oak trees* ○ *Oaks produce thousands of acorns each year.* **2.** wood from this tree ○ *an oak table*

obedient /ə'biːdiənt/ *adjective* doing what you are told to do ○ *Our old dog is very obedient – he always comes when you call him.*

obese /əʊ'biːs/ *adjective* someone who is obese is so fat that it is dangerous for their health

obey /ə'beɪ/ *verb* to do what someone tells you to do ○ *If you can't obey orders you shouldn't be a policeman.* ○ *Everyone must obey the law.*

object¹ /'ɒbdʒekt/ *noun* **1.** a thing ○ *They thought they saw a strange object in the sky.* **2.** an aim ○ *Their object is to take control of the radio station.* **3.** a noun, pronoun or phrase which follows directly from a verb or preposition ○ *In the phrase 'the cat caught the mouse', the word 'mouse' is the object of the verb 'caught'.*

object² /əb'dʒekt/ *verb* to say that you do not like something or you do not want something to happen ○ *He objected that the pay was too low.*

objective /əb'dʒektɪv/ *adjective* considering things from a general point of view and not from your own ○ *You must be objective when planning the future of your business.* ■ *noun* an aim ○ *Our long-term objective is to make the company financially sound.* ○ *The company has achieved its main objectives.*

obligation /ˌɒblɪ'geɪʃ(ə)n/ *noun* something that you must do, e.g. for legal reasons ○ *You have an obligation to attend the meeting.*

oblong /'ɒblɒŋ/ *noun* a shape with two pairs of equal sides, one pair being longer than the other ○ *The screen is an oblong, approximately 30cm by 40cm.*

observation /ˌɒbzə'veɪʃ(ə)n/ *noun* **1.** the act of observing ○ *By careful observation, the police found out where the thieves had hidden the money.* **2.** a remark ○ *He made several observations about the government.*

observe /əb'zɜːv/ *verb* **1.** to follow or to obey something such as a law, rule or custom ○ *His family observes all the religious festivals strictly.* ○ *The local laws must be observed.* **2.** to watch something with a lot of attention ○ *They observed and recorded all the changes carefully.* **3.** to make a remark ○ *I merely observed that the bus was late as usual.*

obtain /əb'teɪn/ *verb* to manage to get something ○ *She obtained a copy of the will.* ○ *He obtained control of the business.*

obvious /'ɒbviəs/ *adjective* clear; easily seen ○ *It's obvious that we will have to pay for the damage.* ○ *It was obvious to everyone that the shop was not making any money.*

obviously /'ɒbviəsli/ *adverb* clearly ○ *Obviously we will need to borrow various pieces of equipment.*

occasion /ə'keɪʒ(ə)n/ *noun* **1.** □ **a special occasion** a special event such as a wedding ○ *The baby's first birthday was a special occasion.* **2.** a happening, a time when something happens ○ *She claimed that she hadn't seen anything on that particular occasion.* ◇ **on occasion** from time to time ○ *On occasion, we spend a weekend in the country.*

occasional /ə'keɪʒ(ə)n(ə)l/ *adjective* happening sometimes, but not very often ○ *He was an occasional visitor to my parents' house.* ○ *We make the occasional trip to London.*

occasionally /əˈkeɪʒ(ə)nəli/ *adverb* sometimes, not very often ○ *Occasionally he has to work late.* ○ *We occasionally go to the cinema.*

occupation /ˌɒkjʊˈpeɪʃ(ə)n/ *noun* **1.** the act of taking control of a place, or the fact of being in such a situation ○ *the occupation of the country by enemy soldiers* ○ *The city had been under enemy occupation for a week.* **2.** a job, position, employment ○ *What is her occupation?* ○ *His main occupation is running a small engineering works.*

occupied /ˈɒkjʊpaɪd/ *adjective* **1.** being used ○ *All the rooms in the hotel are occupied.* ○ *All the toilets are occupied, so you'll have to wait.* **2.** busy ○ *The manager is occupied just at the moment.* ○ *Keeping a class of 30 little children occupied is difficult.*

occupy /ˈɒkjʊpaɪ/ *verb* **1.** to live in or work in ○ *They occupy the flat on the first floor.* ○ *The firm occupies offices in the centre of town.* **2.** (*of time, thoughts or attention*) to use or fill ○ *Dealing with the office occupies most of my time.* **3.** to keep someone busy ○ *Could you occupy him for five minutes while I wrap his present?* (NOTE: **occupies – occupying – occupied**)

occur /əˈkɜː/ *verb* **1.** to happen ○ *When did the accident occur?* **2.** to come to your mind ○ *Did it never occur to you that she was lying?* (NOTE: **occurs – occurring – occurred**)

ocean /ˈəʊʃ(ə)n/ *noun* a very large area of sea surrounding the large areas of land on the Earth ○ *Ocean currents can be very treacherous.*

o'clock /əˈklɒk/ *adverb* used with numbers to show the time ○ *Get up – it's 7 o'clock.* ○ *We never open the shop before 10 o'clock.* ○ *By 2 o'clock in the morning everyone was asleep.* (NOTE: **O'clock** is only used for the exact hour, not for times which include minutes. It can also be omitted: *We got home before eight.* or *We got home before eight o'clock.*)

October /ɒkˈtəʊbə/ *noun* the tenth month of the year, between September and November ○ *October 18* ○ *Do you ever go on holiday in October?* ○ *Today*

is October 18th. ○ *Last October we moved to London.* (NOTE: **October 18th** or **October 18**: say 'October the eighteenth' or 'the eighteenth of October'; in US English: 'October eighteenth'.)

octopus /ˈɒktəpəs/ *noun* a sea animal with eight long arms called 'tentacles' (NOTE: The plural is **octopuses**.)

odd /ɒd/ *adjective* **1.** unusual and not normal ○ *It's odd that she can never remember how to get to their house.* ○ *He doesn't like chocolate – Really, how odd!* **2.** □ **odd numbers** numbers such as 17 or 33 which cannot be divided by two ○ *The buildings with odd numbers are on the opposite side of the street.* **3.** (*of an amount*) almost, not exact or accurate ○ *She had 200 odd records in cardboard boxes* **4.** one forming part of a pair **5.** done only rarely or occasionally ○ *I've only been to the odd concert in the last few years.* ○ *On the odd occasions I've met him, he's seemed very nice.*

odour /ˈəʊdə/ *noun* a smell, especially an unpleasant smell ○ *the odour of rotten eggs* (NOTE: The US spelling is **odor**.)

of /əv, ɒv/ *preposition* **1.** used for showing a connection ○ *She's the sister of the girl who you met at the party.* ○ *Where's the top of the jam jar?* ○ *What are the names of Henry VIII's wives?* **2.** used for showing a part or a quantity ○ *a litre of orange juice* ○ *How much of the cloth do you need?* ○ *Today is the sixth of March.* ○ *There are four boys and two girls – six of them altogether.* ○ *Half of the staff are on holiday.* **3.** used for giving a specific age, amount, etc ○ *The school takes children of ten and over.* ○ *He earns a salary of over £30,000.* **4.** showing position, material, cause ○ *He lives in the north of the town.* ○ *The jumper is made of cotton.* ○ *She died of cancer.* (NOTE: **Of** is often used after verbs or adjectives: *to think of, to be fond of, to be tired of, to smell of, to be afraid of,* etc.)

of course /əv ˈkɔːs/ *adverb* **1.** used to say 'yes' or 'no' more strongly ○ *Are you coming with us? – Of course I am!* ○ *Do you want to lose all your money?*

– *Of course not!* **2.** used for stating something that is not surprising ○ *He is rich, so of course he lives in a big house.*

off /ɒf/ *adverb, preposition* **1.** showing movement or position away from a place ○ *We're off to the shops.* ○ *The office is just off the main road.* ○ *They spent their holiday on an island off the coast of Wales.* ○ *The children got off the bus.* ○ *Take your boots off before you come into the house.* **2.** away from work ○ *She took the week off.* ○ *It's my day off today.* ○ *Half the staff are off with flu.* **3.** not switched on ○ *Is the TV off?*

off and on /ˌɒf ənd 'ɒn/ *adverb* not continuously, with breaks in between

offence /ə'fens/ *noun* **1.** the state of being offended ○ *He took offence when I said he looked bigger than before.* **2.** a crime, an act which is against the law ○ *He was charged with committing an offence.* ○ *Since it was his first offence, he was let off with a fine.*

offend /ə'fend/ *verb* **1.** to be or to go against public opinion, someone's feelings ○ *He offended the whole village by the article he wrote in the paper.* ○ *That wallpaper offends my sense of taste.* **2.** to commit a crime ○ *He was released from prison and immediately offended again.*

offense /ə'fens/ *noun* US spelling of **offence**

offensive /ə'fensiv/ *adjective* **1.** unpleasant ○ *What an offensive smell!* **2.** not polite; rude ○ *The waiter was quite offensive.*

offer /'ɒfə/ *noun* a suggestion to someone that you will give them something or do something for them ○ *He turned down her offer to drive him to the station.* ○ *She accepted his offer of a job in Paris.* ■ *verb* to suggest doing something for someone or giving someone something ○ *She offered to drive him to the station.* ◇ **on offer** which has been offered ○ *There are several good holiday bargains on offer.*

office /'ɒfɪs/ *noun* a room or building where you do work such as writing, telephoning and working at a computer ○ *I'll be working late at the office this*

evening. ○ *We bought some new office furniture.* ○ *Dad has his office at the top of the house.*

officer /'ɒfɪsə/ *noun* a person who holds an official position ○ *The customs officer asked me to open my suitcase.*

official /ə'fɪʃ(ə)l/ *adjective* **1.** relating to an organisation, especially one which is part of a government or some other authority ○ *He left official papers in his car.* ○ *We had an official order from the local authority.* ○ *He represents an official body.* **2.** done or approved by someone in authority ○ *She received an official letter of explanation.* ○ *The strike was made official by the union headquarters.* ■ *noun* a person holding a recognised position ○ *They were met by an official from the embassy.* ○ *I'll ask an official of the social services department to help you.*

officially /ə'fɪʃ(ə)li/ *adverb* **1.** in an official way ○ *He has been officially named as a member of the British team.* ○ *She has been officially named as our representative at the meeting.* **2.** according to what is said in public ○ *Officially, you are not supposed to go in through this door, but everyone does.* ○ *Officially he knows nothing about the problem, but unofficially he has given us a lot of advice about it.*

often /'ɒf(ə)n/ *adverb* on many occasions ○ *I often have to go to town on business.* ○ *Do you eat beef often?* ○ *How often is there a bus to Richmond?* ◇ **every so often** from time to time ○ *We go to the cinema every so often.*

oil /ɔɪl/ *noun* **1.** a liquid taken from plants and animals, which flows smoothly and is used in cooking ○ *Cook the vegetables in hot oil.* **2.** a thick mineral liquid found mainly underground and used as a fuel or to make something move smoothly ○ *The door squeaks – it needs some oil.* ○ *Some of the beaches are covered with oil.* ○ *The company is drilling for oil in the desert.*

OK /əʊ'keɪ/, **okay** *interjection* **1.** used for answering 'yes' to a question ○ *Would you like a coffee? – OK!* **2.** used for starting to talk about something after a pause ○ *'It's ten o'clock' – 'OK, let's* *get going'.* ■ *adjective* all right ○ *He was off ill yesterday, but he seems to be OK now.* ○ *Is it OK for me to bring the dogs?*

old /əʊld/ *adjective* **1.** having had a long life ○ *My uncle is an old man – he's eighty-four.* ○ *She lives in an old people's home.* **2.** having existed for a long time ○ *He collects old cars.* ○ *Play some old music, I don't like this modern stuff.* ○ *She's an old friend of mine.* **3.** relating to something which has been used for a long time ○ *Put on an old shirt if you're going to wash the car.* ○ *He got rid of his old car and bought a new one.* **4.** used with a number to talk about someone's age ○ *He's six years old today.* ○ *How old are you?*

old-fashioned /ˌəʊld ˈfæʃ(ə)nd/ *adjective* no longer in fashion ○ *She wore old-fashioned clothes.*

olive /ˈɒlɪv/ *noun* a small black or green fruit from which oil is made for use in cooking ○ *Olives are grown in Mediterranean countries like Spain, Greece and Italy.* ○ *Which do you prefer – green or black olives?*

omit /əʊˈmɪt/ *verb* to leave something out ○ *She omitted the date when she signed the contract.*

on /ɒn/ *preposition* **1.** on the top or surface of something ○ *Put the box down on the floor.* ○ *Flies can walk on the ceiling.* **2.** hanging from ○ *Hang your coat on the hook.* **3.** showing movement or place ○ *A crowd of children got on the train.* ○ *The picture's on page three.* ○ *The post office is on the left-hand side of the street.* **4.** doing something ○ *I have to go to Germany on business.* ○ *We're off on holiday tomorrow.* **5.** referring to a time, date or day ○ *The shop is open on Sundays.* ○ *We went to see my mother on my birthday.* **6.** a means of travel ○ *You can go there on foot – it only takes five minutes.* ○ *She came on her motorbike.* **7.** using an instrument or machine ○ *He played some music on the piano.* ○ *The song is available on CD.* ○ *He was on the telephone for most of the morning.* ○ *The film was on TV last night.* ■ *adverb* **1.** being worn ○ *Have you all got your wellingtons on?* ○ *The*

central heating was off, so he kept his coat on in the house. **2.** operating ○ *Have you put the kettle on?* ○ *The heating is on.* ○ *She left all the lights on.* ○ *She turned the engine on.* ○ *He switched the TV on.* **3.** being shown or played ○ *What's on at the theatre this week?*

on and off /ˌɒn ənd ˈɒf/ *adverb* not continuously but with breaks in between

once /wʌns/ *adverb* **1.** one time ○ *Take the tablets once a day.* ○ *The magazine comes out once a month.* ○ *'How many times did you go to the cinema last year?' – 'Only once'.* **2.** at a time in the past ○ *Once, when it was snowing, the car skidded into a ditch.* ○ *He's someone I knew once when I worked in London.* ■ *conjunction* as soon as ○ *Once he starts talking you can't get him to stop.* ○ *Once we've moved house I'll give you a phone call.* ◇ **once and for all** finally ○ *I'll tell you once and for all 'stop talking!'.* ○ *The government wants to eradicate poverty once and for all.* ◇ **once in a while** from time to time ○ *It's nice to go and have an Indian meal once in a while.*

one /wʌn/ *noun* **1.** the number 1 ○ *One plus one makes two.* ○ *Our grandson is one year old today.* ○ *His grandmother is a hundred and one.* **2.** a single item ○ *Have a toffee – oh dear, there's only one left!* ■ *pronoun* a single thing ○ *All the china plates were dirty so we made do with* ○ *Which hat do you like best – the black one or the red one?* ○ *One of the staff will help you carry the box to your car.* ○ *I've lost my map – have you got one?* ○ *Small cars use less petrol than big ones.*

onion /ˈʌnjən/ *noun* a round, strong-tasting vegetable which is made up of many layers

only /ˈəʊnli/ *adjective* without others of the same type ○ *Don't break it – it's the only one I've got.* ■ *adverb* **1.** with no one or nothing else ○ *We've only got ten pounds between us.* ○ *This lift is for staff only.* **2.** as recently as ○ *We saw her only last week.* ○ *Only yesterday the bank phoned for information.* ■ *conjunction* but, except ○ *I would have arrived on* *time, only the train was late.* ◇ **only just** almost not ◇ **only too** very much

onto /'ɒntə, 'ɒntʊ, 'ɒntuː/ *preposition* on or to something ○ *The speaker went up onto the platform.* ○ *The door opens directly onto the garden.* ○ *Turn the box onto its side.*

open /'əʊpən/ *adjective* **1.** not shut ○ *The safe door is open.* ○ *Leave the window open – it's very hot in here.* **2.** available for use by or the enjoyment of the public ○ *Is the supermarket open on Sundays?* ○ *The show is open from 9 a.m. to 6 p.m.* ○ *The competition is open to anyone over the age of fifteen.* ■ *verb* **1.** to make something open ○ *Can you open the door for me, I'm trying to carry these heavy boxes?* ○ *Don't open the envelope until tomorrow.* **2.** to start doing something, to start a business ○ *A new restaurant is going to open next door to us.* ○ *Most shops open early in the morning.*

opener /'əʊp(ə)nə/ *noun* a piece of equipment for opening things such as tins or bottles

opening /'əʊp(ə)nɪŋ/ *noun* **1.** an occasion or time at which something opens ○ *The opening of the exhibition has been postponed.* ○ *The office opening times are 9.30 to 5.30.* **2.** a hole or space ○ *The cows got out through an opening in the wall.*

opera /'ɒp(ə)rə/ *noun* a performance on a stage with music in which the words are sung and not spoken

operate /'ɒpəreɪt/ *verb* **1.** to make something work ○ *He knows how to operate the machine.* ○ *She is learning how to operate the new telephone switchboard.* **2.** to treat a patient by cutting open the body ○ *She was operated on by Mr Jones.* ○ *The surgeon decided she would have to operate on the patient.*

operation /ˌɒpə'reɪʃ(ə)n/ *noun* **1.** an organised activity carried out to achieve a specific aim ○ *The rescue operation was successful.* **2.** a medical treatment, usually involving cutting open a person's body ○ *She's had three operations on her leg.* ○ *The operation lasted almost two hours.*

opinion /ə'pɪnjən/ *noun* what someone thinks about a subject ○ *Ask the lawyer for his opinion about the letter.* ○ *In my opinion, we should wait until the weather gets warmer before we go on holiday.* ○ *Tell me what in your opinion we should do.*

opponent /ə'pəʊnənt/ *noun* **1.** a person or group which is against something ○ *Opponents of the planned motorway have occupied the site.* **2.** (in boxing, an election, etc.) a person who fights someone else ○ *His opponent in the election is a local councillor.* ○ *He knocked out his last three opponents.*

opportunity /ˌɒpə'tjuːnɪti/ *noun* a chance allows you to do something ○ *When you were in London, did you have an opportunity to visit St Paul's Cathedral?* ○ *I'd like to take this opportunity to thank all members of staff for the work they have done over the past year.*

oppose /ə'pəʊz/ *verb* **1.** to put yourself against someone in an election ○ *She is opposing him in the election.* **2.** to try to prevent something happening ○ *Several groups oppose the new law.*

opposed to /ə'pəʊzd tuː/ *adjective* not agreeing with ○ *He is opposed to the government's policy on education.*

opposite /'ɒpəzɪt/ *preposition* on the other side of, facing ○ *I work in the offices opposite the railway station.* ○ *She sat down opposite me.* ■ *adjective* which is on the other side ○ *The shop's not on this side of the street – it's on the opposite side.* ○ *Her van hit a tree on the opposite side of the road.* ○ *Her van was hit by a lorry going in the opposite direction.* ■ *noun* something which is completely different ○ *'Black' is the opposite of 'white.'* ○ *She's just the opposite of her brother – he's tall and thin, she's short and fat.* ○ *He likes to say one thing, and then do the opposite.*

opposition /ˌɒpə'zɪʃ(ə)n/ *noun* **1.** the act of opposing something ○ *There was a lot of opposition to the company's plans to build a supermarket.* **2.** (in politics) the party or group which opposes the government ○ *The leader of the opposition rose to speak.* ○ *The party lost the election and is now in opposition.*

optician /ɒpˈtɪʃ(ə)n/ *noun* a person who tests your eyes and sells glasses

option /ˈɒpʃən/ *noun* a choice ○ *One option would be to sell the house.* ○ *The tour offers several options as half-day visits.*

or /ɔː/ *conjunction* **1.** used for joining two parts of a sentence which show two possibilities ○ *You can come with us in the car or just take the bus.* ○ *Do you prefer tea or coffee?* ○ *Was he killed in an accident or was he murdered?* ○ *The film starts at 6.30 or 6.45, I can't remember which.* **2.** used for showing that you are not sure about an amount ○ *Five or six people came into the shop.* ○ *It costs three or four dollars.*

oral /ˈɔːrəl/ *adjective* spoken rather than written down ○ *There is an oral test as well as a written one.*

orange /ˈɒrɪndʒ/ *noun* a sweet, brightly coloured Mediterranean fruit ○ *roast duck and orange sauce* ○ *She had a glass of orange juice and a cup of coffee for breakfast.* ■ *adjective* of the colour of an orange ○ *That orange tie is awful.* ○ *She wore a dark orange dress.*

orbit /ˈɔːbɪt/ *noun* the curved path of something moving through space ○ *The rocket will put the satellite into orbit round the earth.* ■ *verb* to move in a curved path round something ○ *The satellite orbits the earth once every five hours.*

orchestra /ˈɔːkɪstrə/ *noun* a large group of musicians who play together ○ *the London Symphony Orchestra*

order /ˈɔːdə/ *noun* **1.** an instruction to someone to do something ○ *He shouted orders to the workmen.* ○ *If you can't obey orders you can't be a soldier.* **2.** (*of a customer*) the act of asking for something to be served or to be sent ○ *We've had a large order for books from Russia.* ○ *She gave the waitress her order.* **3.** a special way of organising things according to date, alphabet, etc ○ *Put the invoices in order of their dates.* **4.** □ **in order to** used for showing why something is done ○ *She called out all their names in order to check who was there.* ○ *He looked under the car in order to see if there was an oil leak.* ■ *verb* **1.** to tell someone to do something ○ *They ordered the protesters out of the building.* ○ *The doctor ordered him to take four weeks' holiday.* **2.** (*of a customer*) to ask for something to be served or to be sent ○ *They ordered chicken and chips and some wine.* ○ *I've ordered a new computer for the office.* ○ *They ordered a Rolls Royce for the managing director.*

ordinary /ˈɔːd(ə)n(ə)ri/ *adjective* not special ○ *I'll wear my ordinary suit to the wedding.* ○ *They lead a very ordinary life.* ◇ **out of the ordinary** unusual or different ○ *Their flat is quite out of the ordinary.*

organ /ˈɔːgən/ *noun* **1.** a part of the body with a special function, such as the heart or liver ○ *He was badly injured and some of his organs had stopped functioning.* **2.** a musical instrument which is often played in churches with one or more keyboards and many pipes through which air is pumped to make a sound ○ *She played the organ at our wedding.*

organic /ɔːˈgænɪk/ *adjective* relating to living things

organisation /ˌɔːgənaɪˈzeɪʃ(ə)n/, **organization** *noun* **1.** the act of arranging something ○ *The organisation of the meeting is done by the secretary.* **2.** an organised group or institution ○ *He's chairman of an organisation which looks after blind people.* ○ *International relief organisations are sending supplies.*

organisational /ˌɔːgənaɪˈzeɪʃ(ə)n(ə)l/, **organizational** *adjective* relating to the way in which something is organised

organise /ˈɔːgənaɪz/, **organize** *verb* **1.** to arrange something ○ *She is responsible for organising the meeting.* ○ *We organised ourselves into two groups.* ○ *The company is organised in three sections.* **2.** to put into good order ○ *We have put her in charge of organising the city archives.*

organised /ˈɔːgənaɪzd/, **organized** *adjective* **1.** (*of a person*) working efficiently and according to a plan **2.** (*of an activity*) planned carefully, and involving many different people or elements

organiser /'ɔːgənaɪzə/, **organizer** *noun* a person who arranges things

origin /'prɪdʒɪn/ *noun* where something or someone comes from ○ *What is the origin of the word 'taboo'?* ○ *His family has French origins.*

original /ə'rɪdʒən(ə)l/ *adjective* 1. new and interesting ○ *The planners have produced some very original ideas for the new town centre.* 2. not a copy ○ *They sent a copy of the original invoice.* ○ *He kept the original receipt for reference.* ■ *noun* a thing from which other things are copied ○ *Send the police a copy, but make sure you keep the original.*

originally /ə'rɪdʒən(ə)lɪ/ *adverb* in the beginning ○ *Originally it was mine, but I gave it to my brother.* ○ *The family originally came from France in the 18th century.*

ornament /'ɔːnəmənt/ *noun* a small object used as decoration ○ *There's a row of china ornaments on the mantelpiece.*

other /'ʌðə/ *adjective, pronoun* 1. a different person or thing ○ *We went swimming while the other members of the group sat and watched.* ○ *I don't like chocolate cakes – can I have one of the others?* ○ *I'm fed up with that restaurant – can't we go to some other place?* 2. second one of two ○ *He has two cars – one is red, and the other one is blue.* ○ *One of their daughters is fat, but the other is quite thin.* ■ *pronoun* □ **others** other people or things ○ *I'll have to ask the others if they agree.* ○ *Are there any others in the box?*

otherwise /'ʌðəwaɪz/ *adverb* 1. apart from something just mentioned ○ *Your little boy can be noisy sometimes, but otherwise he's an excellent pupil.* 2. if not, or else ○ *Are you sure you can come on Tuesday? – Otherwise I'll have to give the tickets to someone else.*

ought /ɔːt/ *modal verb* 1. it would be a good thing to ○ *You ought to go swimming more often.* ○ *You ought to see the doctor if your cough doesn't get better.* ○ *He oughtn't to eat so much – he'll get fat.* ○ *The travel agent ought to have told you the hotel was full before you went on holiday.* 2. used for showing that you expect something to happen or to be the case ○ *She ought to pass her driving test easily.* ○ *He left his office at six, so he ought to be home by now.* (NOTE: The negative is **ought not**, shortened to **oughtn't**. Note also that **ought** is always followed by **to** and a verb in the infinitive.)

ounce /aʊns/ *noun* a measure of weight, equal to 28 grams (NOTE: usually written **oz** after figures: *3oz of butter*, say 'three ounces of butter')

our /aʊə/ *adjective* belonging to us ○ *Our office is near the station.* ○ *Our cat is missing again.* ○ *Two of our children caught flu.* (NOTE: Do not confuse with **hour**.)

ours /aʊəz/ *pronoun* a thing or person that belongs to us ○ *That house over there is ours.* ○ *Friends of ours told us that the restaurant was good.* ○ *Can we borrow your car, because ours is being serviced?* (NOTE: Do not confuse with **hours**.)

ourselves /aʊə'selvz/ *pronoun* to for referring back to the subject pronoun 'we' ○ *We all organised ourselves into two teams.* ○ *We were enjoying ourselves when the police came.*

out /aʊt/ *adverb* 1. away from inside ○ *How did the tiger get out of its cage?* ○ *She pulled out a box of matches.* ○ *Take the computer out of its packing case.* 2. not at home ○ *No one answered the phone – they must all be out.*

outcome /'aʊtkʌm/ *noun* a result ○ *The outcome of the match was in doubt until the final few minutes.* ○ *What was the outcome of the appeal?*

outdoor /aʊt'dɔː/ *adjective* in the open air

outdoors /aʊt'dɔːz/ *adverb* in the open air, not inside a building ○ *The ceremony is usually held outdoors.* ○ *Why don't we take our coffee outdoors and sit in the sun?* ○ *The concert will be held outdoors if the weather is good.* (NOTE: You can also say **out of doors**.)

outer /'aʊtə/ *adjective* on the outside ○ *Though the outer surface of the pie was hot, the inside was still cold.*

outfit /ˈautfɪt/ *noun* a set of clothes, often worn for a particular purpose ○ *She bought a new outfit for the wedding.* ○ *For the fancy dress party she wore a nurse's outfit.*

outing /ˈautɪŋ/ *noun* a short trip ○ *The children went on an outing to the seaside.*

outline /ˈautlaɪn/ *noun* a line showing the outer edge of something ○ *He drew the outline of a car on the paper.*

out of date /ˌaut əv ˈdeɪt/ *adjective* **1.** without recent information **2.** no longer in fashion ○ *Flared trousers are rather out of date.*

outside /ˈautsaɪd/ *noun* the outer surface or the part which is not inside ○ *He polished the outside of his car.* ○ *The apple was red and shiny on the outside, but rotten inside.* ■ *adjective* which is on the outer surface ○ *The outside walls of the house are made of brick.* ■ *adverb* not inside a building ○ *It's beautiful and warm outside in the garden.* ○ *The dog's all wet – it must be raining outside.*

outstanding /autˈstændɪŋ/ *adjective* excellent or of a very high standard or quality ○ *an antique Chinese vase of outstanding quality* ○ *Her performance was outstanding.*

outwards /ˈautwədz/ *adverb* towards the outside or away from the centre or starting point

oval /ˈəuv(ə)l/ *noun* a long round shape similar to an egg, but flat ■ *adjective* with this shape ○ *The pie was cooked in an oval bowl.*

oven /ˈʌv(ə)n/ *noun* a metal box with a door, used for cooking ○ *Don't put that plate in the oven – it's made of plastic.* ○ *Supper is cooking in the oven.* ○ *Can you look in the oven and see if the meat is cooked?*

over /ˈəuvə/ *preposition* **1.** above or higher than ○ *He put a blanket over the bed.* ○ *Planes fly over our house every minute.* ○ *The river rose over its banks.* **2.** on the other side or to the other side ○ *Our office is just over the road from the bank.* ○ *He threw the ball over the wall.* ○ *The children ran over the road.* **3.**

from the top of ○ *He fell over the cliff.* ○ *She looked over the edge of the balcony.* **4.** during ○ *Over the last few weeks the weather has been cold and wet.* ○ *Let's discuss the problem over lunch.* **5.** more than ○ *Children over 16 years old have to pay full price.* ○ *The car costs over £40,000.* ○ *We had to wait for over two hours.* ■ *adverb* **1.** down from being upright ○ *The bottle fell over and all the contents poured out.* ○ *She knocked over the plant pot.* ○ *He leaned over and picked up a pin from the floor.* **2.** more than ○ *Children of 16 and over pay full price.* ○ *There are special prices for groups of 30 and over.* **3.** not used, left behind ○ *Any food left over after the meal can be given to the poor.* ■ *adjective* finished ○ *Is the match over yet?* ○ *When the civil war was over everyone had more food to eat.*

overall /ˌəuvərˈɔːl/ *adjective* covering or taking in everything ○ *The overall impression was favourable.*

overcome /ˌəuvəˈkʌm/ *verb* **1.** to deal with a difficult situation ○ *Do you think the drugs problem can ever be overcome?* **2.** to make someone helpless ○ *She was overcome by fear.* ○ *Two people were overcome by smoke.* **3.** to gain victory over an enemy ○ *The army quickly overcame the invaders.* (NOTE: **overcomes – overcoming – overcame** /ˌəuvəˈkeɪm/ **– has overcome**)

overgrown /ˌəuvəˈgrəun/ *adjective* (*of e.g. a garden*) covered with plants and long grass because of not being looked after

overhead /ˌəuvəˈhed/ *adverb* above you ○ *Look at that plane overhead.*

overhear /ˌəuvəˈhɪə/ *verb* to hear accidentally something which you are not meant to hear ○ *I couldn't help overhearing what you said just then.* (NOTE: **overhears – overhearing – overheard** /ˌəuvəˈhɜːd/)

overlap¹ /ˈəuvəlæp/ *verb* to cover part of something else ○ *Try not to let the pieces of wallpaper overlap.* (NOTE: **overlaps – overlapping – overlapped**)

overlap² /ˌəuvəˈlæp/ *noun* an amount by which something overlaps

overlook /ˌəʊvə'lʊk/ *verb* not to notice something ○ *She overlooked several mistakes when she was correcting the exam papers.*

overseas¹ /ˌəʊvə'siːz/ *adverb* in or to a foreign country ○ *He went to work overseas for some years.* ○ *Sue's gone overseas for a few weeks.*

overseas² /'əʊvəsiːz/ *adjective* relating to foreign countries ○ *Overseas sales are important for our company.*

overtake /ˌəʊvə'teɪk/ *verb* to go past someone travelling in front of you (NOTE: **overtakes – overtaking – overtook – has overtaken**)

overweight /əʊvə'weɪt/ *adjective* having a body that weighs too much

owe /əʊ/ *verb* **1.** to be in a situation where you will have to pay someone money, either because you have borrowed some from them, or because you have bought something from them ○ *He still owes me the £50 he borrowed last month.* **2.** to feel that something should be done ○ *He owes her an apology.* ○ *I owe my sister a letter.*

owing to /'əʊɪŋ tuː/ *preposition* because of ○ *The plane was late owing to fog.*

owl /aʊl/ *noun* a large bird which hunts small animals, mainly at night

own /əʊn/ *adjective* belonging to you alone ○ *I don't need to borrow a car – I have my own car.* ○ *He has his own book shop.* ■ *noun* □ **on my** *or* **his** *or* **her, etc own** alone ○ *He built the house all on his own.* ○ *I'm on my own this evening – my girlfriend's gone out with her family.* ■ *verb* to have or to possess ○ *There's no sense in owning a car, since there's nowhere to park.*

owner /'əʊnə/ *noun* a person who owns something ○ *The police are trying to find the owner of the stolen car.* ○ *Insurance is necessary for all house owners.*

oxygen /'ɒksɪdʒən/ *noun* a common gas which is present in the air and is essential for plant and animal life

ozone /'əʊzəʊn/ *noun* a harmful form of oxygen, which is found in the atmosphere and which is poisonous to humans when concentrated

P

p /piː/, **P** *noun* the sixteenth letter of the alphabet, between O and Q

pace /peɪs/ *noun* **1.** the distance covered by one step ○ *Walk thirty paces to the north of the stone.* ○ *Step three paces back.* **2.** speed ○ *The car was travelling at quite a pace.* ■ *verb* to measure by walking ○ *He paced out the distance between the tree and the house.*

pack /pæk/ *noun* **1.** a set of things put together in a box ○ *He bought a pack of chewing gum.* **2.** a set of playing cards ○ *a pack of cards* ○ *Shuffle the pack.* **3.** a group of wild animals together ○ *a pack of wild dogs* **4.** a bag which you can carry on your back ○ *Will you be able to manage this walk with a heavy pack on your back?* ■ *verb* **1.** to put things into a suitcase ready for travelling ○ *The taxi's arrived and she hasn't packed her suitcase yet.* ○ *I've finished packing, so we can start.* ○ *He packed his toothbrush at the bottom of the bag.* **2.** to put things in containers ready for sending ○ *The books are packed in boxes of twenty.* ○ *Fish are packed in ice.* **3.** to put a lot of people or things into something ○ *How can you pack ten adults into one tent?* ○ *The streets are packed with Christmas shoppers.* ○ *The supermarket shelves are packed with fruit and vegetables.*

pack off *phrasal verb* to send someone away (*informal*) ○ *We've packed the children off to their grandparents for the summer holidays.*

pack up *phrasal verb* **1.** to put things into a box before going away ○ *They packed up all their equipment and left.* **2.** to stop working ○ *I'll pack up now and finish the job tomorrow morning.*

package /ˈpækɪdʒ/ *noun* **1.** a parcel which has been wrapped up for sending ○ *There was a package for you in the post.* ○ *We mailed the package to you yesterday.* **2.** a box or bag in which goods are sold ○ *Instructions for use are printed on the package.* **3.** a set of goods or services offered together at one time ○ *a software package*

package holiday /ˌpækɪdʒ ˈhɒlɪdeɪ/ *noun* a holiday where everything including a hotel, food and travel is arranged and paid for before you leave

packaging /ˈpækɪdʒɪŋ/ *noun* **1.** paper, cardboard or plastic used to wrap goods ○ *The boxes are sent in plastic packaging.* **2.** the act of wrapping of goods ○ *The packaging is all done by machines.*

packed /pækt/ *adjective* **1.** full of people ○ *The restaurant was packed and there were no free tables.* **2.** put in a container ○ *a packed lunch*

packet /ˈpækɪt/ *noun* a small bag, parcel or box ○ *a packet of cigarettes* ○ *a packet of soup*

pad /pæd/ *noun* **1.** a soft cushion which protects a person or thing from something ○ *Put a pad of cotton on your knee.* **2.** a set of sheets of paper attached together ■ *verb* to walk softly with regular steps ○ *The tiger was padding up and down in its cage.* (NOTE: **pads – padding – padded**)

padlock /ˈpædlɒk/ *noun* a small lock with a hook ○ *The gate is fastened with a padlock.*

page /peɪdʒ/ *noun* a side of a sheet of paper used in a book, newspaper or magazine ○ *It's a short book, it only has 64 pages.* ○ *The crossword is on the back page.* ○ *Start reading at page 34.* ○ *Look at the picture on page 6.* (NOTE: With numbers the word **the** is left out: *on the next page* but *on page 50.*) ■ *verb* to call someone by radio, over a loudspeaker, etc. ○ *Mr Smith isn't in his office at the moment – I'll page him for you.*

paid /peɪd/ past tense and past participle of **pay**

pail /peɪl/ *noun* an old-fashioned word for a bucket (NOTE: Do not confuse with **pale**.)

pain /peɪn/ *noun* a feeling in your body of being hurt or ill ○ *If you have a pain in your chest, you ought to see a doctor.* ○ *She had to take drugs because she could not stand the pain.* ○ *I get pains in my teeth when I eat ice cream.*

painful /'peɪnf(ə)l/ *adjective* hurting, causing pain ○ *She got a painful blow on the back of the head.* ○ *I have very painful memories of my first school.*

painstaking /'peɪnzteɪkɪŋ/ *adjective* (*of a person*) done slowly and carefully in order to avoid mistakes ○ *The design is the result of years of painstaking effort.*

paint /peɪnt/ *noun* a coloured liquid which you use to give something a colour or to make a picture ○ *We gave the ceiling two coats of paint.* ○ *I need a two-litre tin of green paint.* ○ *The paint's coming off the front door.* (NOTE: no plural) ■ *verb* 1. to cover something with paint ○ *We got someone in to paint the house.* ○ *They painted their front door blue.* ○ *She painted her toenails bright red.* 2. to make a picture of something using paint ○ *She painted a picture of the village.* ○ *He's painting his mother.* ○ *The sky is not easy to paint.*

paintbrush /'peɪntbrʌʃ/ *noun* a brush used to put paint on something (NOTE: The plural is **paintbrushes**.)

painter /'peɪntə/ *noun* 1. a person who paints something such as a house ○ *The painter is coming next week to paint the kitchen.* 2. a person who paints pictures ○ *He collects pictures by 19th-century French painters.*

painting /'peɪntɪŋ/ *noun* 1. the act of putting paint on something or of making pictures with paint ○ *Painting and decorating is my trade* 2. a picture done with paints ○ *Do you like this painting of the old church?*

pair /peə/ *noun* 1. two things taken together ○ *a pair of socks* ○ *a pair of gloves* ○ *She's bought a new pair of boots.* 2. two things joined together to make a single one ○ *I'm looking for a clean pair of trousers.* ○ *Where's my pair of green shorts?* ○ *This pair of scissors is blunt.*

pal /pæl/ *noun* a friend (*informal*)

palace /'pælɪs/ *noun* a large building where a king, queen, president, etc., lives

pale /peɪl/ *adjective* 1. light-coloured ○ *What colour is your hat? – It's a pale blue colour.* 2. not looking healthy, with a white face ○ *She's always pale and that worries me.* ○ *When she read the letter she went pale.* (NOTE: **paler – palest**. Do not confuse with **pail**.)

palm /pɑːm/ *noun* 1. the soft inside surface of your hand ○ *She held out some crumbs in the palm of her hand and the birds came and ate them.* 2. a tall tropical tree with long leaves ○ *an oasis surrounded by date palms* ○ *The boy climbed a coconut palm and brought down a nut.*

pan /pæn/ *noun* a metal cooking container with a handle ○ *Boil the potatoes in a pan of water.* ○ *She burnt her hand on the hot frying pan.* ◊ **frying pan, saucepan**

panel /'pæn(ə)l/ *noun* 1. a flat piece of something such as wood or metal, which forms part of something ○ *Unscrew the panel at the back of the washing machine.* 2. a group of people who answer questions or who judge a competition ○ *She's on the panel that will interview candidates for the post.*

panic /'pænɪk/ *noun* sudden great fear ○ *The forecast of flooding caused panic in towns near the river.* ■ *verb* to become very frightened ○ *Don't panic, the fire engine is on its way.* (NOTE: **panics – panicking – panicked**)

pant /pænt/ *verb* to breathe fast ○ *He was red in the face and panting as he crossed the finishing line.*

paper /'peɪpə/ *noun* 1. thin, often white, material, which you write on, and which is used for wrapping or to make books, newspapers and magazines ○ *He got a letter written on pink paper.* ○ *I need another piece of paper* or *sheet of paper to finish my letter.* ○ *There was a box of paper handkerchiefs by the bed.* (NOTE: no plural for this meaning: *some paper, a piece of paper, a sheet of paper*) **2.** a newspaper ○ *I buy the paper to read on the train every morning.* ○ *My photo was on the front page of today's paper.* ○ *Our local paper comes out on Fridays.* ○ *The Sunday papers are so big that it takes me all day to read them.* (NOTE: The plural is **papers**.) **3.** an exam ○ *The English paper was very difficult.* (NOTE: The plural is **papers**.)

parade /pə'reɪd/ *noun* a public display of soldiers ○ *A sergeant inspects the men before they go on parade.*

paragraph /'pærəgrɑːf/ *noun* a section of several written sentences starting on a new line ○ *to answer the first paragraph of your letter* or *paragraph one of your letter* ○ *Please refer to the paragraph headed 'Shipping Instructions'.*

parallel /'pærəlel/ *adjective* (*of lines*) which are side by side and remain the same distance apart without ever touching ○ *Draw two parallel lines three millimetres apart.* ○ *The road is parallel to* or *with the railway.*

parcel /'pɑːs(ə)l/ *noun* something that is wrapped in paper and sent by post ○ *The postman has brought a parcel for you.* ○ *The parcel was wrapped up in brown paper.* ○ *If you're going to the post office, can you post this parcel for me?*

pardon /'pɑːd(ə)n/ *noun* the act of forgiving someone ■ *verb* to forgive someone for having done something wrong ○ *Pardon me for interrupting, but you're wanted on the phone.* ○ *Please pardon my rudeness in not answering your call earlier.*

parent /'peərənt/ *noun* **1.** a father or mother **2.** an organisation which owns or rules another ○ *Our parent company is based in Switzerland.*

parents /'peərənts/ *noun* your mother and father ○ *His parents live in Manchester.* ○ *Did your parents tell you I had met them in London?*

park /pɑːk/ *noun* an open space with grass and trees ○ *Hyde Park and Regents Park are in the middle of London.* ○ *You can ride a bicycle across the park but cars are not allowed in.* ■ *verb* to

leave your car somewhere while you are not using it ○ *You can park your car in the street next to the hotel.* ○ *You mustn't park on a double yellow line.*

parking /'pɑːkɪŋ/ *noun* the act of leaving a car somewhere when you are not using it

parliament /'pɑːləmənt/ *noun* a group of elected representatives who decide on the laws of a country ○ *Parliament has passed a law forbidding the sale of these drugs.*

parrot /'pærət/ *noun* a brightly coloured tropical bird with a large curved beak ○ *He keeps a green parrot in a cage in his living room.*

part /pɑːt/ *noun* **1.** a piece or section ○ *Parts of the film were very good.* ○ *They live in the downstairs part of a large house.* ○ *They spend part of the year in France.* **2.** a person that an actor plays, e.g. in a play or film ○ *He played the part of Hamlet.* □ **to take part in something** to join in an activity ○ *They all took part in the game.* ○ *Did he take part in the concert?* ■ *verb* to separate or move apart ○ *The curtains parted and the show began.*

part with *phrasal verb* to give or sell something to someone ○ *He refused to part with his old bicycle.*

participle /pɑː'tɪsɪp(ə)l/ *noun* a word formed from a verb, used either to form perfect or progressive forms or as an adjective or noun. The present participle of 'to go' is 'going' and the past participle is 'gone'.

particle /'pɑːtɪk(ə)l/ *noun* a very small piece

particular /pə'tɪkjʊlə/ *adjective* special, referring to one thing or person and to no other ○ *The photocopier only works with one particular type of paper.*

particularly /pə'tɪkjʊləli/ *adverb* specially ○ *I particularly asked them not to walk on the lawn.* ○ *It's a particularly difficult problem.* ○ *He isn't particularly worried about the result.*

partly /'pɑːtli/ *adverb* not completely ○ *The house is partly furnished.* ○ *I'm only partly satisfied with the result.* ○ *We're selling our house in London,* *partly because we need the money, but also because we want to move nearer to the sea.*

partner /'pɑːtnə/ *noun* **1.** a person who plays games or dances with someone ○ *Take your partners for the waltz.* ○ *Sally is my usual tennis partner.* **2.** a person with whom you are in a relationship, especially one you live with ○ *We invited him and his partner for drinks.* **3.** a person who owns and works in a business together with one or more others ○ *He became a partner in a firm of solicitors.*

partnership /'pɑːtnəʃɪp/ *noun* a business relationship between two or more people in which the risks and profits are shared according to a letter of agreement between the partners

party /'pɑːti/ *noun* a special occasion when several people meet, usually in someone's house, in order to celebrate something such as a birthday ○ *We're having a party on New Year's Eve.* ○ *Our family Christmas party was a disaster as usual.* ○ *She invited twenty friends to her birthday party.*

pass /pɑːs/ *noun* (*in football, etc.*) the act of sending the ball to another player ○ *He sent a long pass across the field and Smith headed it into goal.* ■ *verb* **1.** to move something towards someone ○ *Can you pass me the salt, please?* ○ *He passed the ball back to the goalkeeper.* **2.** to be successful in a test or examination ○ *He passed in English, but failed in French.* ○ *She passed her driving test first time!*

pass out *phrasal verb* to become unconscious for a short time ○ *He passed out when he saw the blood.*

pass round *phrasal verb* to hand something to various people ○ *She passed the box of chocolates round the table.*

passage /'pæsɪdʒ/ *noun* **1.** a long narrow space with walls on either side ○ *She hurried along the passage.* ○ *There's an underground passage between the two railway stations.* **2.** a section of a piece of writing ○ *She quoted passages from the Bible.* ○ *I photocopied a particularly interesting passage from the textbook.*

passenger /'pæsɪndʒə/ *noun* a person who is travelling, e.g. in a car, bus, train or plane, but who is not the driver or one of the people who works on it ○ *His car's quite big – it can take three passengers on the back seat.* ○ *The plane was carrying 104 passengers and a crew of ten.*

passing /'pɑːsɪŋ/ *adjective* **1.** existing for a short time only ○ *It's just a passing fashion.* **2.** which is going past ○ *The driver of a passing car saw the accident.*

passion /'pæʃ(ə)n/ *noun* a very strong feeling of love, especially sexual love ○ *He couldn't hide the passion he felt for her.*

passive /'pæsɪv/ *adjective* allowing things to happen to you and not taking any action yourself ○ *He wasn't one of the ringleaders, he only played a passive role in the coup.* ■ *noun* the form of a verb which shows that the subject is being acted upon (NOTE: If you say 'the car hit him' the verb is active, but 'he was hit by the car' is passive.)

passport /'pɑːspɔːt/ *noun* an official document allowing you to travel from one country to another ○ *If you are going abroad you need to have a valid passport.* ○ *We had to show our passports at customs.* ○ *His passport is out of date.*

password /'pɑːswɜːd/ *noun* a secret word which you need to know to be allowed to do something such as use a particular computer

past /pɑːst/ *preposition* **1.** later than, after ○ *It's past the children's bedtime.* ○ *It's ten past nine (9.10) – we've missed the TV news.* **2.** passing in front of something ○ *If you go past the bank, you'll see the shop on your left.* ○ *She walked past me without saying anything.* ○ *The car went past at at least 60 miles an hour.* (NOTE: **Past** is used for times between o'clock and the half-hour: **3.05** = five past three; **3.15** = a quarter past three; **3.25** = twenty-five past three; **3.30** = half past three. For times after **half past** see **to. Past** is also used with many verbs: **to go past, to drive past, to fly past**, etc.) ■ *adjective* happening in a time which his finished ○ *He has spent the past year working in France.* ○ *The time for talking is past – what we need is action.* ■ *noun* the time before now ○ *In the past we always had an office party just before Christmas.*

paṣta /'pæstə/ *noun* an Italian food made of flour and water, and sometimes eggs, cooked by boiling, and eaten with oil or sauce (NOTE: no plural: *some pasta, a bowl of pasta;* note that **pasta** takes a singular verb: *the pasta is very good here*)

paste /peɪst/ *noun* **1.** a thin liquid glue ○ *Spread the paste evenly over the back of the wallpaper.* **2.** soft food ○ *Mix the flour, eggs and milk to a smooth paste.* ○ *Add tomato paste to the soup.* ■ *verb* to glue something such as paper ○ *She pasted a sheet of coloured paper over the front of the box.* ○ *He pasted the postcards into his scrapbook.* ◊ **cut**

pastry /'peɪstri/ *noun* a mixture of flour, fat and water, used to make pies ○ *She was in the kitchen making pastry.*

pat /pæt/ *noun* a gentle touch with the hand ○ *I didn't hit her – I just gave her a little pat.* ■ *verb* to give someone or something a pat ○ *He patted his pocket to make sure that his wallet was still there.* (NOTE: **pats – patting – patted**) ◇ **to pat someone on the back** to praise someone ◇ **a pat on the back** praise ○ *The committee got a pat on the back for having organised the show so well.*

patch /pætʃ/ *noun* **1.** a small piece of material used for covering up a hole, e.g. in clothes ○ *His mother sewed a patch over the hole in his trousers.* **2.** a small area of something ○ *They built a shed on a patch of ground by the railway line.* ○ *There's a patch of rust on the car door.*

path /pɑːθ/ *noun* a narrow track for walking ○ *There's a path across the field.* ○ *Follow the path until you get to the sea.*

pathetic /pə'θetɪk/ *adjective* making you feel either sympathy or a lack of respect ○ *He made a pathetic attempt at a joke.* ○ *She looked a pathetic figure standing in the rain.*

patience /'peɪʃ(ə)ns/ *noun* the quality of being patient ○ *With a little patience, you'll soon learn how to ride a bike.* ○ *I don't have the patience to wait that long.*

patient /'peɪʃ(ə)nt/ *adjective* the ability to wait a long time without getting annoyed ○ *You must be patient – you will get served in time.* ■ *noun* a sick person who is in hospital or who is being treated by a doctor, dentist, psychiatrist, etc. ○ *There are three other patients in the ward.* ○ *The nurse is trying to take the patient's temperature.*

patiently /'peɪʃ(ə)ntli/ *adverb* without getting annoyed

patrol /pə'trəʊl/ *noun* **1.** the act of keeping guard by walking or driving in one direction and then back again ○ *They make regular patrols round the walls of the prison.* ○ *He was on patrol in the centre of town when he saw some youths running away from a bank.* **2.** a group of people keeping guard ○ *Each time a patrol went past we hid behind a wall.* ■ *verb* to keep guard on a place by walking or driving up and down ○ *Armed security guards are patrolling the warehouse.* (NOTE: **patrols – patrolling – patrolled**)

pattern /'pæt(ə)n/ *noun* **1.** instructions which you follow to make something ○ *She copied a pattern from a magazine to knit her son a pullover.* **2.** a design of something, e.g. lines or flowers, repeated again and again on cloth, wallpaper, etc. ○ *She was wearing a coat with a pattern of black and white spots.* ○ *Do you like the pattern on our new carpet?*

pause /pɔːz/ *noun* a short stop during a period of activity such as work ○ *He read his speech slowly, with plenty of pauses.* ○ *Take a short pause after every 100 steps.* ■ *verb* to stop or rest for a short time before continuing ○ *She paused for a second to look at her watch.*

pavement /'peɪvmənt/ *noun* **1.** a hard path for people to walk on at the side of a road ○ *Walk on the pavement, not in the road.* ○ *Look out; the pavement is covered with ice!* **2.** *US* a hard road surface

paw /pɔː/ *noun* the foot of an animal such as a cat or dog ○ *The bear held the fish in its paws.*

pay /peɪ/ *noun* the money you receive for working ○ *They're on strike for more pay.* ○ *I can't afford luxuries on my miserable pay.* ■ *verb* 1. to give someone money for something ○ *How much did you pay for your car?* ○ *We pay £100 a week in rent.* ○ *Please pay the waiter for your drinks.* ○ *She paid him £10 for his old bike.* 2. to give money to someone for doing something ○ *We pay secretaries £10 an hour.* ○ *I paid them one pound each for washing the car.* ○ *I'll pay you a pound to wash my car.* (NOTE: You **pay someone to wash the car** before he or she washes it, but you **pay someone for washing the car** after he or she has washed it. **pays – paying – paid** /peɪd/)

pay back *phrasal verb* to give someone money which you owe them ○ *He borrowed £10 last week and hasn't paid me back.*

pay up *phrasal verb* to pay all the money which you owe ○ *The tourist paid up quickly when the taxi driver called the police.*

payment /ˈpeɪmənt/ *noun* the fact of giving money for something ○ *I make regular monthly payments into her account.* ○ *She made a payment of £10,000 to the solicitor.*

pea /piː/ *noun* a climbing plant of which the round green seeds are eaten as vegetables

peace /piːs/ *noun* 1. the state of not being at war ○ *The UN troops are trying to keep the peace in the area.* ○ *Both sides are hoping to reach a peace settlement.* 2. a calm quiet state ○ *Noisy motorcycles ruin the peace and quiet of the village.*

peaceful /ˈpiːsf(ə)l/ *adjective* enjoyable because there is very little noise or activity ○ *We spent a peaceful afternoon by the river.*

peach /piːtʃ/ *noun* a sweet fruit with a large stone and very soft skin ○ *We had peaches and cream for dessert.*

peak /piːk/ *noun* 1. the top of a mountain ○ *Can you see that snow-covered peak in the distance?* 2. the highest point ○ *The team has to reach a peak of fitness before the match.* ○ *The graph shows the peaks and troughs of pollution over the last month.* 3. the front part of a cap, which sticks out ○ *He wore a white cap with a dark blue peak.*

peanut /ˈpiːnʌt/ *noun* a nut which grows under the ground in a shell

pear /peə/ *noun* a fruit like a long apple, with one end wider than the other

pearl /pɜːl/ *noun* a valuable round white jewel formed inside an oyster ○ *She wore a string of pearls which her grandmother had given her.*

pebble /ˈpeb(ə)l/ *noun* a small round stone

peculiar /pɪˈkjuːliə/ *adjective* strange ○ *There's a peculiar smell coming from the kitchen.* ○ *It's peculiar that she never opens the curtains in her house.*

pedal /ˈped(ə)l/ *noun* 1. an object worked by the foot to make a machine operate ○ *If you want to stop the car put your foot down on the brake pedal.* 2. a flat rest which you press down on with your foot to make a bicycle go forwards ○ *He stood up on the pedals to make the bike go up the hill.* ■ *verb* to make a bicycle go by pushing on the pedals ○ *He had to pedal hard to get up the hill.* (NOTE: **pedals – pedalling – pedalled**)

pedestrian /pəˈdestriən/ *noun* a person who walks, rather than drives along, in a street ○ *Two pedestrians were also injured in the accident.*

peel /piːl/ *noun* the outer skin of a fruit or a vegetable ○ *Throw the banana peel into the rubbish bin.* ○ *This orange has got very thick peel.* (NOTE: no plural) ■ *verb* to take the outer skin off a fruit or a vegetable ○ *He was peeling a banana.* ○ *If the potatoes are very small you can boil them without peeling them.*

peer /pɪə/ *noun* a member of the a high social class in the UK ○ *Peers sit in the House of Lords.*

peg /peg/ *noun* 1. a small wooden or metal object used for holding something in place ○ *The children hang their coats on pegs in the cloakroom.* ○ *They used no nails in building the roof – it is all held together with wooden pegs.* **2.** □ **clothes peg** little wooden clip, used to attach wet clothes to a washing line ■ *verb* to attach something with a peg ○ *She pegged the washing out on the line.* (NOTE: **pegs – pegging – pegged**)

pen /pen/ *noun* an object for writing with, using ink ○ *I've lost my red pen – can I borrow yours?* ○ *If you haven't got a pen you can always write in pencil.*

penalty /'pen(ə)lti/ *noun* a punishment ○ *The maximum penalty for this offence is two years' imprisonment.* (NOTE: The plural is **penalties**.)

pencil /'pensəl/ *noun* an object for writing or drawing with, made of wood, with a long piece of black or coloured material through the middle

penny /'peni/ *noun* the smallest British coin, one hundredth of a pound ○ *It cost £4.99, so I paid with a £5 note and got a penny change.* ○ *I came out without my purse and I haven't got a penny on me.* (NOTE: The plural is **pennies** or **pence**. **Pennies** is used to refer to several coins, but **pence** refers to the price. In prices, **pence** is always written **p** and often said as /piː/ : *This book only costs 60p.*: say 'sixty p' or 'sixty pence'.) ◇ **not have a penny** not have any money

pension /'penʃən/ *noun* money paid regularly, e.g. to someone who has retired from work ○ *He has a good pension from his firm.* ○ *She finds her pension is not enough to live on.*

people /'piːp(ə)l/ *noun* men, women or children considered as a group ○ *There were at least twenty people waiting to see the doctor.* ○ *So many people wanted to see the film that there were queues every night.* ○ *A group of people from our office went to Paris by train.*

pepper /'pepə/ *noun* **1.** a strong-tasting powder used in cooking, made from the whole seeds of a plant (black pepper) or from seeds with the outer layer removed (white pepper) ○ *Add salt and pepper to taste.* (NOTE: no plural in this sense) **2.** a hollow green, red or yellow fruit used

as a vegetable ○ *We had stuffed peppers for lunch.*

per /pɜː, pə/ *preposition* for each ○ *I can't cycle any faster than fifteen miles per hour.* ○ *Potatoes cost 10p per kilo.* ○ *We paid our secretaries £10 per hour.*

perceive /pə'siːv/ *verb* to notice or realise something ○ *The changes are so slight that they're almost impossible to perceive with the naked eye.* ○ *I perceived a worsening in his condition during the night.*

per cent /pə 'sent/, **percent** *noun* out of each hundred ○ *Fifty per cent of staff are aged over 40.* (NOTE: The symbol % is used after numbers: 50%.)

percentage /pə'sentɪdʒ/ *noun* an amount considered in relation to 100 ○ *A low percentage of the population voted.* ○ *'What percentage of businesses are likely to be affected?'* – *'Oh, about 40 per cent'.*

perfect¹ /'pɜːfɪkt/ *adjective* **1.** good in every way ○ *Your coat is a perfect fit.* ○ *Don't change anything – the room is perfect as it is.* **2.** completely suitable ○ *She's the perfect secretary.* ○ *George would be perfect for the job of salesman.* ○ *I was in a perfect position to see what happened.*

perfect² /pə'fekt/ *verb* to make something new and perfect ○ *She perfected a process for speeding up the bottling system.*

perfectly /'pɜːfɪktli/ *adverb* very well ○ *That dress fits you perfectly.*

perform /pə'fɔːm/ *verb* **1.** to do an action ○ *She performed a perfect dive.* ○ *It's the sort of task that can be performed by any computer.* **2.** to do something such as acting, dancing or singing in public ○ *The dance group will perform at the local theatre next week.* ○ *The play will be performed in the village hall.*

performance /pə'fɔːməns/ *noun* **1.** the way in which someone or something works, e.g. how successful they are or how much they achieve ○ *We're looking for ways to improve our performance.* ○ *After last night's miserable performance I don't think the team is likely to* *reach the semi-finals.* **2.** a public show for entertainment ○ *The next perform-ance will start at 8 o'clock.* ○ *There are three performances a day during the summer.*

performer /pə'fɔːmə/ *noun* a person who gives a public show in order to en-tertain people

perfume /'pɜːfjuːm/ *noun* **1.** a liquid which smells nice, and which you put on your skin **2.** a pleasant smell, espe-cially of flowers ○ *the strong perfume of the roses*

perhaps /pə'hæps/ *adverb* possibly ○ *Perhaps the train is late.* ○ *They're late – perhaps the snow's very deep.* ○ *Is it going to be fine? – Perhaps not, I can see clouds over there.*

period /'pɪəriəd/ *noun* **1.** an amount of time ○ *She swam under water for a short period.* ○ *The offer is open for a limited period only.* ○ *It was an unhap-py period in her life.* **2.** the time during which a lesson is given in school ○ *We have three periods of English on Thurs-days.*

periodic /ˌpɪəri'ɒdɪk/ *adjective* repeat-ed after a regular period of time ○ *peri-odic attacks of the illness* ○ *We carry out periodic reviews of the company's fi-nancial position.*

permanent /'pɜːmənənt/ *adjective* lasting or intended to last, for ever ○ *He has found a permanent job.* ○ *She is in permanent employment.* ○ *They are liv-ing with her parents temporarily – it's not a permanent arrangement.*

permanently /'pɜːmənəntli/ *adverb* for ever; always

permission /pə'mɪʃ(ə)n/ *noun* the free-dom which you are given to do some-thing by someone in authority ○ *You need permission from the boss to go into the storeroom.* ○ *He asked the manag-er's permission to take a day off.*

permit[1] /'pɜːmɪt/ *noun* an official paper which allows you to do something ○ *You have to have a permit to sell ice cream from a van.*

permit[2] /pə'mɪt/ *verb* to allow someone to do something ○ *This ticket permits three people to go into the exhibition.* ○

Smoking is not permitted in under-ground stations. (NOTE: **permits – per-mitting – permitted**)

person /'pɜːs(ə)n/ *noun* a man or wom-an ○ *The police say a person entered the house by the window.* ○ *His father's a very interesting person.* ◇ **in person** used to emphasise that someone is phys-ically present ○ *Several celebrities were at the first night in person.*

personal /'pɜːs(ə)n(ə)l/ *adjective* **1.** be-longing or referring to a particular per-son or people ○ *They lost all their per-sonal property in the fire.* **2.** private; that you would not like to discuss with most people ○ *Can I ask you a personal ques-tion?* ○ *That's personal – I'd rather not answer that.*

personality /ˌpɜːsə'næliti/ *noun* **1.** character ○ *He has a strange personali-ty.* **2.** a famous person, especially a TV or radio star ○ *The new supermarket is going to be opened by a famous sporting personality.*

persuade /pə'sweɪd/ *verb* to get some-one to do what you want by explaining or asking ○ *She managed to persuade the bank manager to give her a loan.* ○ *After ten hours of discussion, they per-suaded him to leave.*

pest /pest/ *noun* **1.** a plant, animal or in-sect which causes problems ○ *Many farmers look on rabbits as a pest.* **2.** a person who annoys someone ○ *That lit-tle boy is an absolute pest – he won't stop whistling.*

pet /pet/ *noun* an animal kept in the home ○ *The family has several pets – two cats, a dog and a hamster.*

petal /'pet(ə)l/ *noun* the colourful part of a flower

petrol /'petrəl/ *noun* a liquid used as a fuel for engines ○ *This car doesn't use very much petrol.* ○ *The bus ran out of petrol on the motorway.* ○ *Petrol prices are lower at supermarkets.* (NOTE: no plural: *some petrol, a litre of petrol*)

phase /feɪz/ *noun* a stage in the develop-ment of something ○ *The project is now in its final phase.* ○ *It's a phase she's going through and hopefully she will* *grow out of it.* ○ *I'm sure dyeing his hair green is just a phase.*

philosophy /fɪˈlɒsəfi/ *noun* **1.** the study of the meaning of human existence ○ *He's studying philosophy.* **2.** a general way of thinking ○ *My philosophy is that you should treat people as you would want them to treat you.*

phone /fəʊn/ *noun* a telephone ○ *If someone rings, can you answer the phone for me?* ○ *She lifted the phone and called the ambulance.* ■ *verb* to speak to someone using a telephone ○ *Your wife phoned when you were out.* ○ *Can you phone me at ten o'clock tomorrow evening?* ○ *I need to phone our office in New York.*

phone back *phrasal verb* to reply by telephone; to call again ○ *The manager is out – can you phone back in about fifteen minutes?* ○ *She phoned back three minutes later to ask me my address.*

phone book /ˈfəʊn bʊk/ *noun* a book which gives the names of people and businesses in a town in alphabetical order, with their addresses and phone numbers

phone call /ˈfəʊn kɔːl/ *noun* an occasion on which you speak to someone by telephone

phone number /ˈfəʊn ˌnʌmbə/ *noun* a series of numbers that you press on a telephone to contact a particular person

photo /ˈfəʊtəʊ/ *noun* a photograph; a picture taken using a camera ○ *Here's a photo of the village in the snow.* ○ *I've brought some holiday photos to show you.* (NOTE: The plural is **photos**.)

photograph /ˈfəʊtəgrɑːf/ *noun* a picture taken with a camera ○ *I've found an old black and white photograph of my parents' wedding.* ○ *She's trying to take a photograph of the cat.* ○ *He kept her photograph in his wallet.* ○ *You'll need two passport photographs to get your visa.* ■ *verb* to take a picture with a camera ○ *She was photographing the flowers in the public gardens.*

photographer /fəˈtɒgrəfə/ *noun* a person who takes photographs, especially as a job

photography /fəˈtɒgrəfi/ *noun* the practice of taking pictures on sensitive film with a camera

phrasal verb /ˌfreɪz(ə)l ˈvɜːb/ *noun* a type of verb which has two or three parts, which together have a meaning different from that of the main verb, such as 'tell off', 'look after' and 'put up with'

phrase /freɪz/ *noun* a short sentence or group of words ○ *Try to translate the whole phrase, not just one word at a time.* ○ *I'm trying to remember a phrase from 'Hamlet'.*

physical /ˈfɪzɪk(ə)l/ *adjective* relating to the human body ○ *The illness is mental rather than physical.* ○ *He has a strong physical attraction for her.*

physically /ˈfɪzɪkli/ *adverb* **1.** relating to the body ○ *I find him physically very attractive.* ○ *One of the children is physically handicapped.* **2.** relating to the laws of nature ○ *It is physically impossible to get a piano into that little car.*

physics /ˈfɪzɪks/ *noun* the study of things such as heat, light and sound, and the way in which they affect objects ○ *She teaches physics at the local college.* ○ *It's a law of physics that things fall down to the ground and not up into the sky.*

piano /piˈænəʊ/ *noun* a large musical instrument with black and white keys which you press to make music ○ *She's taking piano lessons.* ○ *She played the piano while her brother sang.*

pick /pɪk/ *verb* **1.** to choose something ○ *The captain picks the football team.* ○ *She was picked to play the part of the victim's mother.* ○ *The Association has picked Paris for its next meeting.* **2.** to take fruit or flowers from plants ○ *They've picked all the strawberries.* ○ *Don't pick the flowers in the public gardens.* ◇ **take your pick** choose which one you want ○ *We've got green, red and blue balloons – just take your pick!*

pick up *phrasal verb* **1.** to take something that is lying on a surface and lift it in your hand ○ *She dropped her handkerchief and he picked it up.* ○ *He bent down to pick up a pound coin which he* *saw on the pavement.* **2.** to learn something easily without being taught ○ *She never took any piano lessons, she just picked it up.* ○ *He picked up some German when he was working in Germany.* **3.** to give someone a lift in a vehicle ○ *We will pick you up from the hotel.* ○ *Can you send a taxi to pick us up at seven o'clock?*

picnic /'pɪknɪk/ *noun* a meal eaten outdoors away from home ○ *If it's fine, let's go for a picnic.* ○ *They stopped by a wood, and had a picnic lunch.* ■ *verb* to eat a picnic ○ *People were picnicking on the bank of the river.* (NOTE: **picnics – picnicking – picnicked**)

picture /'pɪktʃə/ *noun* a drawing, a painting or a photograph ○ *She drew a picture of the house.* ○ *The book has pages of pictures of wild animals.* ○ *She cut out the picture of the President from the magazine.*

pie /paɪ/ *noun* meat or fruit cooked in a pastry case ○ *For pudding, there's apple pie and ice cream.* ○ *If we're going on a picnic, I'll buy a big pork pie.*

piece /piːs/ *noun* a bit of something or one of a number of similar things ○ *Would you like another piece of cake?* ○ *I need two pieces of black cloth.*

pierce /pɪəs/ *verb* to make a hole in something

piercing /'pɪəsɪŋ/ *adjective* (*of a sound*) unpleasantly high and loud ○ *They suddenly heard a piercing cry.* ○ *He let out a piercing yell.*

pig /pɪg/ *noun* a pink or black farm animal with short legs kept for its meat (NOTE: Fresh meat from a **pig** is called **pork**. **Bacon**, **gammon** and **ham** are types of smoked or cured meat from a **pig**.)

pigeon /'pɪdʒən/ *noun* a fat grey bird which is common in towns

pile /paɪl/ *noun* a large mass of things ○ *Look at that pile of washing.* ○ *The pile of plates crashed onto the floor.* ○ *The wind blew piles of dead leaves into the road.* ○ *He was carrying a huge pile of books.*

pill /pɪl/ *noun* medicine in solid form, usually in a small round shape ○ *Take two pills before breakfast.*

pillow /'pɪləʊ/ *noun* a cloth bag full of soft material which you put your head on in bed

pilot /'paɪlət/ *noun* a person who flies a plane or other aircraft ○ *He's training to be an airline pilot.* ○ *He's a helicopter pilot for an oil company.*

pin /pɪn/ *noun* a small thin sharp metal object with a round piece at the top, used for fastening things such as pieces of cloth or paper ○ *She fastened the ribbons to her dress with a pin before sewing them on.* ■ *verb* to attach something with a pin ○ *She pinned up a notice about the meeting.* ○ *He pinned her photograph on the wall.* ○ *He pinned the calendar to the wall by his desk.* (NOTE: **pins – pinning – pinned**)

pinch /pɪntʃ/ *noun* **1.** the action of squeezing something between your finger and thumb ○ *He gave her arm a pinch.* **2.** a small quantity of something held between finger and thumb ○ *Add a pinch of salt to the boiling water.* (NOTE: The plural is **pinches**.) ■ *verb* **1.** to squeeze something tightly, using the finger and thumb ○ *Ow! You're pinching me!* **2.** to steal something, especially something that is not very valuable (*informal*) ○ *Someone's pinched my pen!*

pine /paɪn/ *noun* **1.** □ **pine (tree)** a type of evergreen tree with needle-shaped leaves ○ *They planted a row of pines along the edge of the field.* **2.** wood from a pine tree ○ *We've bought a pine table for the kitchen.* ○ *There are pine cupboards in the children's bedroom.* ■ *verb* □ **to pine for something** to feel sad because you do not have something any more ○ *She's miserable because she's pining for her cat.*

pineapple /'paɪnæp(ə)l/ *noun* a large sweet tropical fruit, with stiff leaves with sharp points on top

pink /pɪŋk/ *adjective* pale red or flesh coloured ○ *Your cheeks look pink and healthy now.* ■ *noun* a pale red colour ○ *The bright pink of those flowers shows clearly across the garden.*

pint /paɪnt/ *noun* a liquid measure, equal to 0.568 of a litre

pipe /paɪp/ *noun* **1.** a tube, especially one that carries a liquid or a gas from one place to another ○ *He's clearing a blocked pipe in the kitchen.* ○ *The water came out of the hole in the pipe.* **2.** a tube for smoking tobacco, with a small bowl at one end in which the tobacco burns

pit /pɪt/ *noun* **1.** a deep dark hole in the ground ○ *They dug a pit to bury the rubbish.* **2.** a mine; a place where substances such as coal are dug out of the ground ○ *My grandfather spent his whole life working down a pit.*

pitch /pɪtʃ/ *noun* **1.** the ground on which a game is played ○ *I'll time you, if you run round the football pitch.* ○ *The pitch is too wet to play on.* ○ *He kept the ball the whole length of the pitch and scored.* (NOTE: The plural is **pitches**.) **2.** the level of a period of anger or excitement ○ *Excitement was at fever pitch.* ■ *verb* to put up a tent ○ *They pitched their tent in a field by the beach.*

pity /'pɪti/ *noun* a feeling of sympathy for someone who is in a bad situation ○ *Have you no pity for the homeless?* ■ *verb* to feel sympathy for someone ○ *I pity those children.* (NOTE: **pities – pitying – pitied**) ◇ **what a pity** used for showing that you are disappointed, or for showing that you feel sympathy for someone who is disappointed

pizza /'piːtsə/ *noun* an Italian food, consisting of a flat round piece of bread cooked with things such as cheese, tomatoes and onions on top

place /pleɪs/ *noun* **1.** where something is, or where something happens ○ *Here's the place where we saw the cows.* ○ *We found a nice place for a picnic.* **2.** where something is usually kept ○ *Make sure you put the file back in the right place.* **3.** a seat ○ *I'm keeping this place for my sister.* ○ *I'm sorry, but this place has been taken.* **4.** a position in a race ○ *The British runners are in the first three places.* ■ *verb* to put something somewhere ○ *The waitress placed the teapot on the table.* ○ *Please place the envelope in the box.*

plain /pleɪn/ *adjective* **1.** simple and not complicated ○ *We put plain wallpaper in the dining room.* ○ *The outside is decorated with leaves and flowers, but the inside is quite plain.* **2.** easy to understand ○ *The instructions are written in plain English.* **3.** obvious ○ *It's perfectly plain what he wants.* ○ *We made it plain to them that this was our final offer.* **4.** a more polite word than "unattractive", used for describing a person ○ *His two daughters are rather plain.* ■ *noun* a flat area of country ○ *a broad plain bordered by mountains* (NOTE: Do not confuse with **plane**.)

plainly /'pleɪnli/ *adverb* **1.** in a way that is easy to see ○ *He's plainly bored by the French lesson.* ○ *Plainly, the plan is not working.* **2.** clearly ○ *It is plainly visible from here.* ○ *The sounds of a violent argument could be heard plainly from behind the door.* **3.** without much decoration ○ *plainly-decorated wallpaper*

plan /plæn/ *noun* **1.** an organised way of doing things ○ *He made a plan to get up earlier in future.* ○ *She drew up plans for the village fair.* □ **according to plan** in the way it was arranged ○ *The party went off according to plan.* **2.** a drawing showing how something is arranged ○ *Here are the plans for the kitchen.* ○ *The fire exits are shown on the plan of the office.* ■ *verb* **1.** to arrange how you are going to do something ○ *She's busy planning her holiday in Greece.* **2.** to intend to do something ○ *They are planning to move to London next month.* ○ *We weren't planning to go on holiday this year.* ○ *I plan to take the 5 o'clock flight to New York.* (NOTE: **plans – planning – planned**)

plane /pleɪn/ *noun* **1.** an aircraft with wings ○ *When is the next plane for Glasgow?* ○ *How are you getting to Paris? – We're going by plane.* ○ *Don't panic, you've got plenty of time to catch your plane.* ○ *He was stuck in a traffic jam and missed his plane.* **2.** a tool with a sharp blade for making wood smooth ○ *He smoothed off the rough edges with a plane.*

planet /'plænɪt/ *noun* **1.** one of the objects in space which move round the Sun ○ *Is there life on any of the planets?* ○ *Earth is the third planet from the Sun.* **2. the planet** the planet Earth ○ *an environmental disaster which could affect the whole planet*

plank /plæŋk/ *noun* a long flat piece of wood used in building

planning /'plænɪŋ/ *noun* the act or practice of making plans ○ *The trip will need very careful planning.* ○ *The project is still in the planning stage.*

plant /plɑːnt/ *noun* **1.** a living thing which grows in the ground and has leaves, a stem and roots ○ *He planted a row of cabbage plants.* ○ *Sunflower plants grow very tall.* **2.** a large factory ○ *They are planning to build a car plant near the river.* ■ *verb* to put a plant in the ground ○ *We've planted two pear trees and a peach tree in the garden.*

plaster /'plɑːstə/ *noun* **1.** a mixture of sand and a white substance called 'lime', which is mixed with water and used for covering the inside walls of houses ○ *The flat hasn't been decorated yet and there is still bare plaster in most of the rooms.* **2.** a white substance which becomes hard when it dries, used to cover a broken arm or leg and hold it in place ○ *He had an accident skiing and now has his leg in plaster.* **3.** □ **sticking plaster** adhesive tape used for covering small wounds ○ *She put a piece of sticking plaster on my cut.*

plastic /'plæstɪk/ *noun* a strong material made from chemicals, used to make many things ○ *We take plastic plates when we go to the beach.* ○ *The supermarket gives you plastic bags to put your shopping in.* ○ *We cover our garden furniture with plastic sheets when it rains.* (NOTE: no plural: *a bowl made of plastic*)

plate /pleɪt/ *noun* **1.** a flat round dish for putting food on ○ *Put one pie on each plate.* ○ *Pass all the plates down to the end of the table.* **2.** a flat piece of something such as metal or glass ○ *The dentist has a brass plate on his door.*

platform /'plætfɔːm/ *noun* **1.** a high flat structure by the side of the railway lines at a station, to help passengers get on or off the trains easily ○ *Crowds of people were waiting on the platform.* ○ *The train for Liverpool will leave from platform 10.* **2.** a high wooden floor for someone to stand on when they are speaking in public ○ *The main speakers sat in a row on the platform.*

play /pleɪ/ *noun* a story which is acted in a theatre or on TV ○ *Did you see the play on TV last night?* ○ *We went to the National Theatre to see the new play.* ○ *Two of Shakespeare's plays are on the list for the English exam.* ■ *verb* **1.** to take part in a game ○ *He plays rugby for the university.* ○ *Do you play tennis?* **2.** to make music on a musical instrument or to put a recording on a machine such as a CD player ○ *He can't play the violin very well.* ○ *Let me play you my new Bach CD.* **3.** to enjoy yourself ○ *When you've finished your lesson you can go out to play.* ○ *He doesn't like playing with other children.*

play back *phrasal verb* to listen to something which you have just recorded

player /'pleɪə/ *noun* **1.** a person who plays a game ○ *You only need two players for chess.* ○ *Rugby players have to be fit.* ○ *Four of the players in the opposing team are ill.* **2.** a person who plays a musical instrument ○ *a famous horn player*

playground /'pleɪɡraʊnd/ *noun* a place, at a school or in a public area, where children can play

pleasant /'plez(ə)nt/ *adjective* enjoyable or attractive ○ *What a pleasant garden!* ○ *How pleasant it is to sit here under the trees!*

please /pliːz/ *interjection* used when you are making a polite request or accepting an offer ○ *Can you close the window, please?* ○ *Please sit down.* ○ *Can I have a ham sandwich, please?* ○ *Do you want some more tea? – Yes, please!* Compare **thank you** ■ *verb* to make someone happy or satisfied ○ *She's not difficult to please.* □ **please yourself** do as you like ○ *Shall I take the red one or the green one? – Please yourself.*

pleased /pliːzd/ *adjective* happy ○ *We're very pleased with our new house.*

○ *I'm pleased to hear you're feeling better.* ○ *He wasn't pleased when he heard his exam results.*

pleasure /'pleʒə/ *noun* a pleasant feeling ○ *His greatest pleasure is sitting by the river.* ○ *It gives me great pleasure to be able to visit you today.* ◇ **with pleasure** used for saying that you are happy to do something for someone ○ *I'll do the job with pleasure.*

plenty /'plenti/ *noun* a large quantity ○ *You've got plenty of time to catch the train.* ○ *Plenty of people complain about the bus service.* ○ *Have you got enough bread? – Yes, we've got plenty.* (NOTE: no plural)

plot /plɒt/ *noun* 1. a small area of land, e.g. used for building or for growing vegetables ○ *They own a plot of land next to the river.* ○ *The plot isn't big enough to build a house on.* 2. the basic story of a book, play or film ○ *The novel has a complicated plot.* ○ *I won't tell you the plot of the film – I don't want to spoil it for you.* 3. a secret plan to do something illegal or wrong ○ *They hatched a plot to hold up the security van.*

pluck /plʌk/ *verb* 1. to pull out feathers from a bird ○ *Ask the butcher to pluck the pheasants for you.* 2. to pull and let go of the strings of a guitar or other musical instrument, in order to make a sound ○ *He was gently plucking the strings of his guitar.*

plug /plʌg/ *noun* 1. a flat round rubber object which covers the hole in a bath or sink ○ *Can you call reception and tell them there's no plug in the bath?* ○ *She pulled out the plug and let the water drain away.* 2. an object attached to the end of a wire, which you push into a hole in the wall to make a piece of electrical equipment work ○ *The vacuum cleaner is supplied with a plug.*

plug in *phrasal verb* to connect a piece of electrical equipment to an electricity supply by pushing the plug into a hole in the wall ○ *The computer wasn't plugged in – that's why it wouldn't work.*

plum /plʌm/ *noun* a gold, red or purple fruit with a smooth skin and a large stone ○ *She bought a pound of plums to make a pie.*

plumber /'plʌmə/ *noun* a person whose job is to install or repair things such as water pipes and heating systems

plump /plʌmp/ *adjective* (of a person) slightly fat in an attractive way ○ *He's a short man with a plump red face.* ○ *Is she pregnant or is she just plumper than she was?*

plunge /plʌndʒ/ *verb* 1. to throw yourself into water ○ *He plunged into the river to rescue the little boy.* 2. to fall sharply ○ *Share prices plunged on the news of the devaluation.*

plural /'plʊərəl/ *adjective, noun* (in grammar) (which is) the form of a word showing that there is more than one ○ *Does 'government' take a singular or plural verb?* ○ *What's the plural of 'mouse'?* ○ *The verb should be in the plural after 'programs'.*

plus /plʌs/ *preposition* 1. added to ○ *His salary plus bonus comes to more than £30,000.* (NOTE: In calculations **plus** is usually shown by the sign + : 10 + 4 = 14: say 'ten plus four equals fourteen'.) 2. more than ○ *houses valued at £200,000 plus*

pocket /'pɒkɪt/ *noun* a small bag sewn into the inside of a piece of clothing such as a coat, in which you can keep things such as money or keys ○ *She looked in all her pockets but couldn't find her keys.* ○ *He was leaning against a fence with his hands in his pockets.*

pod /pɒd/ *noun* a long green case in which some small vegetables such as peas or beans grow ○ *Mangetout peas are eaten in their pods.*

poem /'pəʊɪm/ *noun* a piece of writing with words carefully chosen to sound attractive or interesting, set out in lines usually of a regular length which sometimes end in words which sound the same ○ *He wrote a long poem about an old sailor.* ○ *The poem about the First World War was set to music by Britten.*

poet /'pəʊɪt/ *noun* a person who writes poems

poetry /'pəʊɪtri/ *noun* poems in general ○ *Reading poetry makes me cry.* ○ *This* *is a good example of German poetry.* (NOTE: no plural)

point /pɔɪnt/ *noun* **1.** a sharp end of something long ○ *The point of my pencil has broken.* ○ *The stick has a very sharp point.* **2.** a particular place ○ *The path led us for miles through the woods and in the end we came back to the point where we started from.* ○ *We had reached a point 2,000m above sea level.* **3.** a particular moment in time ○ *From that point on, things began to change.* ○ *At what point did you decide to resign?* **4.** a meaning or reason ○ *The main point of the meeting is to see how we can continue to run the centre without a grant.* □ **there's no point** there's no good reason for doing something ○ *There's no point in asking them to pay – they haven't any money.* □ **what's the point?** why? ○ *What's the point of doing the same thing all over again?* **5.** a score in a game ○ *Their team scored three points.* ○ *In rugby, a try counts as five points.* ■ *verb* to aim a gun or your finger at something ○ *The teacher is pointing at you.* ○ *It's rude to point at people.* ○ *Don't point that gun at me – it might go off.* ○ *The guide pointed to the map to show where we were.* ◇ **it's beside the point** it's got nothing to do with the main subject ○ *Whether or not the coat matches your hat is beside the point – it's simply too big for you.*

pointed /'pɔɪntɪd/ *adjective* with a sharp point at one end ○ *a pointed stick*

poison /'pɔɪz(ə)n/ *noun* a substance which kills you or makes you ill if it is swallowed or if it gets into the blood ○ *There's enough poison in this bottle to kill the whole town.* ○ *Don't drink that – it's poison.*

poisonous /'pɔɪz(ə)nəs/ *adjective* able to kill or harm people or animals with poison

poke /pəʊk/ *noun* a quick push with a finger or something sharp ○ *He got a poke in the eye from someone's umbrella.* ■ *verb* to push something or someone quickly with a finger or with something sharp ○ *He poked the heap with his stick.* □ **to poke about for something** to search for something among

other things ○ *She poked about in her desk to see if she could find the papers.* □ **to poke out of somewhere** to appear through a hole or small space ○ *A red-faced man poked his head out of the window.* ○ *A red handkerchief was poking out of his pocket.* ◇ **to poke fun at someone** *or* **something** to laugh at someone *or* something in an unkind way ○ *He poked fun at the maths teacher.* ○ *She poked fun at his odd hat.*

pole /pəʊl/ *noun* a long wooden or metal stick

Pole /pəʊl/ *noun* a person from Poland

police /pə'liːs/ *noun* the people whose job is to control traffic, to try to stop crime and to catch criminals ○ *The police are looking for the driver of the car.* ○ *The police emergency number is 999.* ○ *Call the police – I've just seen someone drive off in my car.*

policeman /pə'liːsmən, pə'liːswʊmən/ *noun* a man who is an ordinary member of the police (NOTE: The plural is **policemen**.)

police officer /pə'liːs ˌɒfɪsə/ *noun* a member of the police

policy /'pɒlɪsi/ *noun* decisions on the way of doing something ○ *government policy on wages* or *government wages policy* ○ *It is not our policy to give details of employees over the phone.* ○ *People voted Labour because they liked their policies.*

polish /'pɒlɪʃ/ *noun* a substance used to make things shiny ○ *Wash the car thoroughly before you put the polish on.* ■ *verb* to rub something in order to make it shiny ○ *He polished his shoes until they shone.*

Polish /'pəʊlɪʃ/ *adjective* relating to Poland ○ *The Polish Army joined in the manoeuvres.* ■ *noun* the language spoken in Poland ○ *I know three words of Polish.* ○ *You will need an English-Polish phrasebook if you're visiting Warsaw.*

polite /pə'laɪt/ *adjective* pleasant towards other people, not rude ○ *Sales staff should be polite to customers.* (NOTE: **politer – politest**)

politely /pə'laɪtli/ *adverb* in a polite way ○ *Ask the lady politely if you can have a sweetie.*

politeness /pə'laɪtnəs/ *noun* the practice of being polite

political /pə'lɪtɪk(ə)l/ *adjective* referring to government or to party politics ○ *I don't want to get involved in a political argument.* ○ *She gave up her political career when she had the children.*

politician /ˌpɒlɪ'tɪʃ(ə)n/ *noun* a person who works in politics, especially a member of parliament ○ *Politicians from all parties have welcomed the report.*

politics /'pɒlɪtɪks/ *plural noun* the ideas and methods used in governing a country ■ *noun* the study of how countries are governed ○ *He studied politics and economics at university.* (NOTE: takes a singular verb)

pollen /'pɒlən/ *noun* a yellow powder on the stamens of a flower which touches part of a female flower and so creates seeds

polluted /pə'luːtɪd/ *adjective* made dirty

pollution /pə'luːʃ(ə)n/ *noun* **1.** the process of making the environment dirty ○ *Pollution of the atmosphere has increased over the last 50 years.* **2.** chemicals and other substances that harm people and the environment ○ *It took six months to clean up the oil pollution on the beaches.* ○ *The pollution in the centre of town is so bad that people have started wearing face masks.*

pond /pɒnd/ *noun* a small lake

pony /'pəʊni/ *noun* a small horse (NOTE: The plural is **ponies**.)

pool /puːl/ *noun* **1.** a very small lake ○ *He dived in and swam across the mountain pool.* ○ *We looked for shrimps in the rock pools.* **2.** a large bath of water for swimming in ○ *an outdoor pool* ○ *a heated pool* ○ *We have a little swimming pool in the garden.* ○ *He swam two lengths of the pool.* **3.** a game rather like snooker, where you hit balls into pockets using a long stick called a 'cue' ○ *We were playing pool in the bar.*

poor /pɔː/ *adjective* **1.** with little or no money ○ *The family is very poor now that both parents have no work.* ○ *This is one of the poorest countries in Africa.* **2.** of not very good quality ○ *Vines can grow even in poor soil.* ○ *They were selling off poor quality vegetables at a cheap price.* ○ *She's been in poor health for some months.* **3.** used for showing you are sorry ○ *Poor old you, having to stay at home and finish your homework while we go to the cinema.* ○ *My poor legs, after climbing up the mountain!*

pop /pɒp/ *noun* a noise like a cork coming out of a bottle ○ *There was a 'pop' as she lit the gas.* ■ *verb* **1.** to go somewhere quickly ○ *I'll just pop down to the town.* ○ *He popped into the chemist's.* ○ *I'm just popping round to Jane's.* ○ *I'd only popped out for a moment.* **2.** to put something somewhere quickly (*informal*) ○ *Pop the pie in the microwave for three minutes.* (NOTE: **pops – popping – popped**)

popular /'pɒpjʊlə/ *adjective* liked by a lot of people ○ *The department store is popular with young mothers.* ○ *The South Coast is the most popular area for holidays.*

popularity /ˌpɒpjʊ'lærɪti/ *noun* the fact of being liked by a lot of people

population /ˌpɒpjʊ'leɪʃ(ə)n/ *noun* the number of people who live in a place ○ *The population of the country is 60 million.* ○ *Paris has a population of over three million.*

pork /pɔːk/ *noun* fresh meat from a pig, eaten cooked (NOTE: no plural. Note also that salted or smoked meat from a pig is **ham** or **bacon**.)

port /pɔːt/ *noun* **1.** a place along a coast where boats can stop, or a town with a place like this ○ *a fishing port* ○ *The ship is due in port on Tuesday.* ○ *We left port at 12.00.* **2.** an opening in a computer for plugging in an attachment ○ *a mouse port*

portable /'pɔːtəb(ə)l/ *adjective* which can be carried ○ *He used his portable computer on the plane.* ○ *Portable phones won't work in the Underground.*

portion /'pɔːʃ(ə)n/ *noun* **1.** a part ○ *This is only a small portion of the material we collected.* ○ *Our carriage was in the rear portion of the train.* **2.** an amount of food, usually for one person ○ *The portions in that restaurant are tiny.* ○ *Ask the waiter if they serve children's portions.*

portrait /'pɔːtrɪt/ *noun* a painting or photograph of a person ○ *He has painted a portrait of the Queen.* ○ *Old portraits of members of the family lined the walls of the dining room.*

posh /pɒʃ/ *adjective* expensive and attractive; suitable for special occasions ○ *I decided I'd better wear my poshest frock to the wedding.* ○ *We ate in a really posh restaurant.*

position /pə'zɪʃ(ə)n/ *noun* **1.** a place where someone or something is ○ *From his position on the roof he can see the whole of the street.* ○ *The ship's last known position was 200 miles east of Bermuda.* **2.** a job ○ *The sales manager has a key position in the firm.* ○ *He's going to apply for a position as manager.* ○ *We have several positions vacant.* **3.** a situation or state of affairs ○ *What is the company's cash position?*

positive /'pɒzɪtɪv/ *adjective* **1.** certain or sure ○ *I'm positive I put the key in my pocket.* ○ *Are you positive he said six o'clock?* **2.** (*in a test*) showing that the person tested has a particular condition ○ *The cancer test was positive.*

possess /pə'zes/ *verb* to own something ○ *They possess several farms in the south of the country.* ○ *He lost all he possessed in the fire.*

possession /pə'zeʃ(ə)n/ *noun* the fact of owning something ○ *When he couldn't keep up the mortgage payments the bank took possession of the house.*

possibility /ˌpɒsɪ'bɪlɪti/ *noun* the fact of being likely to happen ○ *Is there any possibility of getting a ticket to the show?* ○ *There is always the possibility that the plane will be early.* ○ *There is no possibility of the bank lending us any more money.*

possible /'pɒsɪb(ə)l/ *adjective* able to be done ○ *She agreed that the changes were possible.*

possibly /'pɒsɪbli/ *adverb* **1.** perhaps ○ *The meeting will possibly finish late.* ○ *January had possibly the worst snowstorms we have ever seen.* **2.** used with 'can' or 'can't' to make a phrase stronger ○ *You can't possibly eat 22 pancakes!* ○ *How can you possibly expect me to do all that work in one day?*

post /pəʊst/ *noun* **1.** a long piece of wood or metal put in the ground ○ *The fence is attached to concrete posts.* ○ *His shot hit the goalpost.* **2.** a job ○ *He applied for a post in the sales department.* ○ *We have three posts vacant.* ○ *They advertised the post in 'The Times'.* **3.** letters and parcels that are sent and received ○ *The morning post comes around nine o'clock.* ○ *There were no cheques in this morning's post.* ○ *Has the post arrived yet?* **4.** the system of sending letters and parcels ○ *It is easier to send the parcel by post than to deliver it by hand.* ■ *verb* to send a letter or parcel ○ *Don't forget to post your Christmas cards.* ○ *The letter should have arrived by now – we posted it ten days ago.*

postbox /'pəʊstbɒks/ *noun* a box into which you can put letters, which will then be collected and sent on by the post office

postcard /'pəʊstkɑːd/ *noun* a piece of card often with a picture on one side, which you send to someone with a short message on it

postcode /'pəʊstkəʊd/ *noun* a series of letters and numbers given at the end of an address, to help the people whose job is to sort letters

poster /'pəʊstə/ *noun* a large notice, picture or advertisement stuck on a wall

postman /'pəʊstmən/ *noun* a person who delivers letters to houses (NOTE: The plural is **postmen**.)

post office /'pəʊst ˌɒfɪs/ *noun* a building where you can do such things as buying stamps, sending letters and parcels and paying bills ○ *The main post* *office is in the High Street.* ○ *There are two parcels to be taken to the post office.*

postpone /pəʊsˈpəʊn/ *verb* to change the time or date of an event so that it will happen a later date or time ○ *The meeting has been postponed until next week.*

pot /pɒt/ *noun* **1.** a glass or china container, usually without a handle ○ *The plant is too big – it needs a bigger pot.* ○ *She made ten pots of strawberry jam.* ◊ **teapot 2.** a deep metal container with a long handle, used for cooking ○ *Do I have to wash all the pots and pans by hand?*

potato /pəˈteɪtəʊ/ *noun* a common white or yellow root vegetable which grows under the ground ○ *boiled potatoes* ○ *mashed potatoes* ○ *roast potatoes* ○ *Do you want any more potatoes?* ○ *We're having roast lamb and potatoes for Sunday lunch.*

potential /pəˈtenʃəl/ *adjective* possible ○ *He's a potential world champion.* ○ *The potential profits from the deal are enormous.* ■ *noun* the possibility of developing into something useful or valuable ○ *The discovery has enormous potential.* ○ *She doesn't have much experience, but she has a lot of potential.* ○ *The whole area has great potential for economic growth.*

pottery /ˈpɒtəri/ *noun* **1.** a place where pots are made ○ *There are several local potteries where you can buy dishes.* ○ *I bought this vase from the pottery where it was made.* (NOTE: The plural in this sense is **potteries**.) **2.** objects such as pots and plates, made of clay ○ *There's a man in the market who sells local pottery.* ○ *She brought me some Spanish pottery as a present.*

pouch /paʊtʃ/ *noun* **1.** a small bag for carrying objects such as coins ○ *She carried the ring in a small leather pouch round her neck.* **2.** a bag in the skin in front of some animals, where the young are carried ○ *The kangaroo carries its young in its pouch.* (NOTE: The plural is **pouches**.)

pound /paʊnd/ *noun* **1.** a measure of weight, equal to about 450 grams (NOTE: **pound** is usually written **lb** after figures: *It weighs 26lb.*; *Take 6lb of sugar.*

say 'twenty-six pounds, six pounds'.) **2.** a unit of money used in Britain and several other countries ○ *He earns more than six pounds an hour.* ○ *The price of the car is over £50,000 (fifty thousand pounds).* ○ *He tried to pay for his bus ticket with a £20 note (twenty-pound note).* (NOTE: **pound** is usually written **£** before figures: *£20, £6,000:* say 'twenty pounds, six thousand pounds'. With the word **note**, **pound** is singular: *twenty pounds* but *a twenty-pound note*.) ■ *verb* **1.** to hit something hard ○ *He pounded the table with his fist.* **2.** to smash something into little pieces ○ *The ship was pounded to pieces by heavy waves.*

pour /pɔː/ *verb* **1.** to make a liquid flow ○ *The waiter poured water all over the table.* ○ *He poured the wine into the glasses.* ○ *She poured water down his neck as a joke.* **2.** to flow out or down ○ *Clouds of smoke poured out of the house.* ○ *There was a sudden bang and smoke poured out of the engine.* ○ *Water was pouring through the ceiling.*

pour down *phrasal verb* to rain very hard ○ *Don't go out without an umbrella – it's pouring down.*

poverty /ˈpɒvəti/ *noun* the fact of being poor ○ *He lost all his money and died in poverty.* ○ *Poverty can drive people to crime.*

powder /ˈpaʊdə/ *noun* a substance like flour with very small dry grains ○ *The drug is available in the form of a white powder.* ○ *This machine grinds pepper corns to powder.*

power /ˈpaʊə/ *noun* **1.** the ability to control people or events ○ *He is the official leader, but his wife has all the real power.* ○ *I haven't the power or it isn't in my power to ban the demonstration.* **2.** physical force ○ *They use the power of the waves to generate electricity.* ○ *The engine is driven by steam power.* **3.** electricity used to drive machines or devices ○ *Turn off the power before you try to repair the TV set.* **4.** political control ○ *During the period when he was in power the country's economy was ruined.* **5.** a powerful country ○ *China is one of the great powers.*

powerful /'pauəf(ə)l/ *adjective* having a lot of force, influence or capability ○ *This model has a more powerful engine.* ○ *The treasurer is the most powerful person in the organisation.* ○ *The raft was swept away by the powerful current.* ○ *This is the most powerful personal computer on the market.*

practical /'præktɪk(ə)l/ *adjective* **1.** referring to real actions and events rather than ideas or plans ○ *She needs some practical experience.* ○ *I need some practical advice on how to build a wall.* **2.** possible or sensible ○ *It isn't practical to plug the computer into the same socket as the TV.* ○ *Has anyone got a more practical suggestion to make?* ○ *You need practical clothing for camping.* ○ *We must be practical and not try anything too ambitious.*

practically /'præktɪkli/ *adverb* almost ○ *Practically all the students passed the test.* ○ *The summer is practically over.* ○ *His suit is such a dark grey it is practically black.*

practice /'præktɪs/ *noun* **1.** the act of doing something, as opposed to thinking about it or planning it **2.** a repeated activity done so that you can improve ○ *You need more practice before you're ready to enter the competition.* ○ *He's at football practice this evening.* ○ *The cars make several practice runs before the race.* **3.** a way of doing something, especially a way that is regularly used ○ *It's a standard practice for shops to open late one day a week for staff training.* ○ *It's been our practice for many years to walk the dogs before breakfast.* ■ *verb* US spelling of **practise** ◇ **in practice** when something is done or carried out ○ *The plan seems very interesting, but what will it cost in practice?*

practise /'præktɪs/ *verb* **1.** to do something many times in order to become better at it ○ *He's practising catching and throwing.* **2.** to work as a doctor, dentist or lawyer ○ *He's officially retired but still practises part-time.*

praise /preɪz/ *noun* admiration, the act of showing approval ○ *The rescue team earned the praise of the survivors.* ■ *verb* to express strong approval of

something or someone ○ *The mayor praised the firemen for their efforts in putting out the fire.*

pray /preɪ/ *verb* to speak to God or some other religious being, asking for something or saying thank you for something ○ *Farmers prayed for rain.*

prayer /preə/ *noun* the words that someone says when they are speaking to God ○ *She says her prayers every night before going to bed.* ○ *They said prayers for the sick.*

precious /'preʃəs/ *adjective* **1.** worth a lot of money ○ *a precious stone* **2.** of great value to someone ○ *All her precious photographs were saved from the fire.* ○ *The memories of that holiday are very precious to me.*

precise /prɪ'saɪs/ *adjective* exact ○ *We need to know the precise measurements of the box.* ○ *At that precise moment my father walked in.* ○ *Can you be more precise about what the men looked like?*

precisely /prɪ'saɪsli/ *adverb* exactly ○ *The train arrived at 12.00 precisely.* ○ *I don't know precisely when it was, but it was about three months ago.* ○ *How, precisely, do you expect me to cope with all this work?*

predict /prɪ'dɪkt/ *verb* to say what will happen ○ *The weather forecasters have predicted rain.* ○ *He predicted correctly that the deal would not last.* ○ *Everything happened exactly as I had predicted.*

prefix /'priːfɪks/ *noun* a group of letters put in front of another to form a new word (NOTE: The plural is **prefixes**.)

pregnant /'pregnənt/ *adjective* (*of a woman or female animal*) carrying a developing baby inside the body ○ *Don't carry heavy weights when you're pregnant.* ○ *She hasn't told her family yet that she's pregnant.* ○ *There are three pregnant women in my office.*

preparation /ˌprepə'reɪʃ(ə)n/ *noun* **1.** the things that you do in order to get ready for something ○ *The preparations for the wedding went on for months.* ○ *We've completed our preparations and now we're ready to start.* **2.** a substance which has been mixed ○ *a chemical preparation*

prepare /prɪ'peə/ *verb* **1.** to get something ready ○ *We have prepared the hall for the school play.* ○ *I have some friends coming to dinner and I haven't prepared the meal.* **2.** to get ready for something ○ *He is preparing for his exam.* ○ *You'd better prepare yourself for some bad news.*

prepared /prɪ'peəd/ *adjective* ready ○ *Be prepared, you may get quite a shock.* ○ *Six people are coming to dinner and I've got nothing prepared.*

preposition /ˌprepə'zɪʃ(ə)n/ *noun* a word used with a noun or pronoun to show place or time

presence /'prez(ə)ns/ *noun* **1.** the fact of being present ○ *The presence of both his wives in court was noted.* ○ *Your presence is requested at a meeting of the committee on June 23rd.* **2.** an effect you have on other people ○ *The general has a commanding presence.*

present¹ /'prez(ə)nt/ *noun* **1.** something which you give to someone, e.g. on their birthday ○ *I got a watch as a Christmas present.* ○ *How many birthday presents did you get?* ○ *Her colleagues gave her a present when she got married.* **2.** the time we are in now ○ *The novel is set in the present.* **3.** the form of a verb showing that the action is happening now ○ *The present of the verb 'to go' is 'he goes' or 'he is going'.* ■ *adjective* at a place when something happens there ○ *How many people were present at the meeting?* ◇ **at present** now ○ *The hotel still has some vacancies at present.* ◇ **for the present** for now ○ *That will be enough for the present.*

present² /prɪ'zent/ *verb* **1.** to give something formally to someone as a present ○ *When he retired after thirty years, the firm presented him with a large clock.* **2.** to introduce a show on TV or radio ○ *She's presenting a programme on gardening.*

presentation /ˌprez(ə)n'teɪʃ(ə)n/ *noun* **1.** the act of giving something to someone ○ *The chairman will make the presentation to the retiring sales man-*

ager. **2.** a formal occasion on which something is given to someone **3.** a formal occasion on which someone tells other people about their work ○ *The company made a presentation of the services they could offer.*

presently /'prez(ə)ntli/ *adverb* **1.** soon ○ *I'll be there presently.* ○ *He'll be making a speech presently.* **2.** *US* now, at the present time ○ *He's presently working for a chemical company.* ○ *She's presently in England.* ○ *What is presently being done to correct the problem?*

preserve /prɪ'zɜːv/ *verb* **1.** to look after something and keep it in the same state ○ *Our committee aims to preserve the wildlife in our area.* ○ *The doctors' aim is to preserve the life of the unborn child.* ○ *They would like to preserve their own alphabet rather than use the Roman one.* **2.** to treat something so that it does not decay ○ *Meat can be preserved in salt.* ○ *Freezing is a common method of preserving meat.*

president /'prezɪd(ə)nt/ *noun* the head of a republic ○ *President Bush was elected in 2000.* ○ *The French president came on an official visit.* (NOTE: also used as a title before a surname: *President Wilson*)

presidential /ˌprezɪ'denʃəl/ *adjective* relating to a president

press /pres/ *noun* newspapers taken as a group ○ *The election wasn't reported in the British press.* ○ *There has been no mention of the problem in the press.* (NOTE: no plural) ■ *verb* to push something ○ *Press '12' for room service.*

pressure /'preʃə/ *noun* **1.** something which forces you to do something ○ *Pressure from farmers forced the minister to change his mind.* □ **to put pressure on someone to do something** to try to force someone to do something ○ *They put pressure on the government to build a new motorway.* **2.** the force of something such as air which is pushing or squeezing ○ *There is not enough pressure in your tyres.* ◇ **under pressure** feeling that you are being forced to do something ○ *He did it under pressure.* ○ *We're under pressure to agree to a postponement.*

pretend /prɪ'tend/ *verb* to make someone believe something that is not true ○ *He got into the house by pretending to be a telephone engineer.* ○ *She pretended she had flu and phoned to say she was having the day off.*

pretty /'prɪti/ *adjective* 1. a pretty woman or girl has a face that is quite attractive ○ *Her daughters are very pretty.* (NOTE: **prettier – prettiest**. Usually **pretty** is used of things or girls, not of boys or men.) 2. quite pleasant to look at ○ *That's a pretty necklace.* ■ *adverb* fairly (*informal*) ○ *The patient's condition is pretty much the same as it was yesterday.* ○ *I'm pretty sure I'm right.* ○ *You did pretty well, considering it was the first time you had tried rock-climbing.*

prevent /prɪ'vent/ *verb* to stop something happening ○ *We must try to prevent any more flooding.*

previous /'priːviəs/ *adjective* happening or existing at an earlier time ○ *The letter was sent to my previous address.* ○ *The gang of workers had arrived the previous night and started work first thing in the morning.* ○ *I had spent the previous day getting to know my way round the town.*

previously /'priːviəsli/ *adverb* at a time before ○ *This is my first train trip to Paris – previously I've always gone by plane.* ○ *The arrangements had been made six weeks previously.* ○ *At that time they were living in New York, and previously had lived in London.*

prey /preɪ/ *noun* an animal eaten by another animal ○ *Mice and small birds are the favourite prey of owls.*

price /praɪs/ *noun* money which you have to pay to buy something ○ *The price of petrol is going up.* ○ *I don't want to pay such a high price for a hotel room.* ○ *There has been a sharp increase in house prices during the first six months of the year.*

prick /prɪk/ *verb* to make a very small hole with a sharp point in the outer layer of something such as skin ○ *She pricked her finger when she was picking roses.* ○ *Prick the sausages before you fry them to stop them from bursting.*

prickle /'prɪk(ə)l/ *noun* a sharp point on a plant or animal

pride /praɪd/ *noun* 1. a pleasure in your own ability or possessions ○ *He takes great pride in his garden.* 2. a feeling of respect for yourself that is sometimes too strong, making you behave wrongly ○ *His pride would not let him admit that he had made a mistake.*

priest /priːst/ *noun* a person who carries out formal religious duties

primary /'praɪməri/ *adjective* main, basic ○ *Our primary concern is the safety of our passengers.*

primary school /'praɪməri skuːl/ *noun* a school for children up to the age of eleven

prime /praɪm/ *adjective* 1. most important ○ *The prime suspect in the case is the dead woman's husband.* ○ *This is a prime example of what is wrong with this country.* 2. most likely to be chosen ○ *She is a prime target for any kidnapper.*

prime minister /ˌpraɪm 'mɪnɪstə/ *noun* the head of the government in Britain and other countries ○ *the Australian Prime Minister* or *the Prime Minister of Australia* ○ *She cut out the picture of the Prime Minister from the newspaper.* ○ *The Prime Minister will address the nation at 6 o'clock tonight.* ○ *He was determined to become prime minister before the age of 40.* (NOTE: Use initial capitals when you are talking about a particular prime minister.)

prince /prɪns/ *noun* the son of a king or queen

princess /prɪn'ses/ *noun* the daughter of a king or queen ○ *Once upon a time a beautiful princess lived in a castle by the edge of the forest.* (NOTE: also used as a title before a name: *Princess Sophia*. The plural is **princesses**.)

principal /'prɪnsɪp(ə)l/ *adjective* most important ○ *The country's principal products are paper and wood.* ○ *She played a principal role in setting up the organisation.* ■ *noun* the head of a school or college ○ *The principal wants to see you in her office.* (NOTE: Do not confuse with **principle**.)

principle /'prɪnsɪp(ə)l/ *noun* a general rule ○ *the principles of nuclear physics* ○ *It is a principle in our system of justice that a person is innocent until he is proved guilty.*

print /prɪnt/ *verb* **1.** to mark letters or pictures on paper with a machine, e.g. to make a book ○ *The book is printed directly from a computer disk.* ○ *We had five hundred copies of the leaflet printed.* **2.** to write capital letters or letters which are not joined together ○ *Print your name in the space below.* ■ *noun* **1.** letters printed on a page ○ *I can't read this book – the print is too small.* **2.** a photograph ○ *If you are not happy with your prints, we can guarantee a full refund.*

print out *phrasal verb* to print information from a computer through a printing machine ○ *She printed out three copies of the letter.*

printer /'prɪntə/ *noun* **1.** a person or company that prints things such as books and newspapers ○ *The book has gone to the printer, and we should have copies next week.* **2.** a machine for printing documents

printout /'prɪntaʊt/ *noun* paper printed with information from a computer

prior /'praɪə/ *adjective* before; previous ○ *The house can be visited by prior arrangement with the owner.*

priority /praɪ'ɒrɪti/ *noun* **1.** a right to be first ○ *Children have priority in the waiting list.* **2.** a thing which has to be done first ○ *Finding somewhere to stay the night was our main priority.*

prison /'prɪz(ə)n/ *noun* a building where people are kept when they are being punished for a crime ○ *The judge sent him to prison for five years.* ○ *His father's in prison for burglary.* (NOTE: **Prison** is often used without the article **the.**)

prisoner /'prɪz(ə)nə/ *noun* a person who is in prison ○ *The prisoners were taken away in a police van.*

private /'praɪvət/ *adjective* **1.** which belongs to one person, and is not available to everyone ○ *He flew there in his private jet.* **2.** that you would not like to discuss with most people ○ *You have no right to interfere in my private affairs.* ○ *This is a private discussion between me and my son.* ◇ **in private** away from other people ○ *She asked to see the teacher in private.*

prize /praɪz/ *noun* a reward given to someone who has won a competition ○ *He won first prize in the music competition.* ○ *He answered all the questions correctly and claimed the prize.* ○ *The prize was awarded jointly to the young British and Russian competitors.*

probable /'prɒbəb(ə)l/ *adjective* likely ○ *It's probable that the ship sank in a storm.*

probably /'prɒbəbli/ *adverb* used for saying that something is likely to happen ○ *We're probably going to Spain for our holidays.* ○ *My father is probably going to retire next year.* ○ *Are you going to Spain as usual this year? – Very probably.*

problem /'prɒbləm/ *noun* **1.** something or someone that causes difficulty ○ *We're having problems with the new computer system.* □ **to solve a problem** to find an answer to a problem ○ *The police are trying to solve the problem of how the thieves got into the house.* ○ *We have called in an expert to solve our computer problem.* **2.** a question in a test, especially in mathematics ○ *Most of the students could do all the problems in the maths test.* ◇ **no problem** used for giving an informal agreement to a request

procedure /prə'si:dʒə/ *noun* **1.** the way in which something should be carried out ○ *To obtain permission to build a new house you need to follow the correct procedure.* **2.** a medical treatment ○ *a new procedure for treating burns*

proceed /prə'si:d/ *verb* **1.** to go further ○ *He proceeded down the High Street towards the river.* **2.** to do something after something else ○ *The students then proceeded to shout and throw bottles at passing cars.*

process /prəʊ'ses/ *noun* **1.** the way in which something is done, or the fact of it being done ○ *a new process for extracting oil from coal* (NOTE: The plural is **processes**.) **2.** □ **in the process of doing something** while doing something ○ *She interrupted me while I was in the process of writing my report.* ○ *We were in the process of moving to London when I had the offer of a job in Australia.* ■ *verb* **1.** to make goods from raw materials ○ *The uranium has to be processed before it can be used in a nuclear reactor.* **2.** to deal with a claim or bill in the usual way ○ *to process an insurance claim* ○ *Orders are processed in our warehouse.*

procession /prəˈseʃ(ə)n/ *noun* a group of people walking in line, sometimes with music playing

produce¹ /prəˈdjuːs/ *verb* **1.** to show something or bring something out of e.g. your pocket ○ *The tax office asked him to produce the relevant documents.* ○ *He produced a bundle of notes from his inside pocket.* ○ *The factory produces cars and trucks.* **2.** to organise a play or film ○ *She is producing 'Hamlet' for the local drama club.* **3.** to make something, especially in a factory **4.** to give birth to young ○ *Our cat has produced six kittens.* **5.** to grow crops ○ *The region produces enough rice to supply the needs of the whole country.*

produce² /ˈprɒdjuːs/ *noun* things that have been grown in a garden or on a farm ○ *vegetables and other garden produce* (NOTE: Do not confuse with **product**.)

producer /prəˈdjuːsə/ *noun* a company or country which makes or grows something ○ *an important producer of steel* ○ *The company is a major car producer.*

product /ˈprɒdʌkt/ *noun* a thing which is made in a factory ○ *The government is helping industry to sell more products abroad.* (NOTE: Do not confuse with **produce**.)

production /prəˈdʌkʃən/ *noun* **1.** the process of making of something ○ *We are trying to step up production.* ○ *Production will probably be held up by the strike.* **2.** organising a play or film ○ *The film is currently in production.*

profession /prəˈfeʃ(ə)n/ *noun* work which needs special training, skill or knowledge ○ *the legal profession* ○ *the*

medical profession ○ *the teaching profession*

professional /prəˈfeʃ(ə)n(ə)l/ *adjective* **1.** relating to a profession ○ *He keeps his professional life and his private life completely separate.* **2.** expert or skilled ○ *They did a very professional job in designing the new office.* **3.** (*of sportsmen*) who is paid to play ○ *a professional footballer* ■ *noun* an expert ○ *Don't try to deal with the problem yourself – get a professional in.*

professor /prəˈfesə/ *noun* **1.** the most senior teacher in a particular subject at a university ○ *a professor of English* ○ *an economics professor* **2.** the title taken by some teachers of music and art ○ *She goes to Professor Smith for piano lessons.* (NOTE: used as a title before a name: *Professor Smith*.)

profit /ˈprɒfɪt/ *noun* money you gain from selling something ○ *The sale produced a good profit* or *a handsome profit.*

program /ˈprəʊɡræm/ *noun* a set of instructions given to a computer ○ *to load a program* ○ *to run a program* ○ *a word-processing program* ■ *verb* to give instructions to a computer ○ *They program computers for a living.* (NOTE: **programs – programming – programmed**)

programme /ˈprəʊɡræm/ *noun* **1.** a TV or radio show ○ *We watched a programme on life in the 17th century.* ○ *There's a football programme on after the news.* ○ *I want to listen to the phone-in programme at 9.15.* ○ *There are no good television programmes tonight.* ○ *The programme gives a list of the actors.* **2.** a paper in a theatre or at a sports event, which gives information about the show ■ *verb* to arrange programmes on TV or radio ○ *The new chat show is programmed to compete with the gardening programme on the other channel.*

progress¹ /ˈprəʊɡres/ *noun* **1.** a movement forwards ○ *We are making good progress towards finishing the house.* (NOTE: no plural) **2.** □ **in progress** which is happening or being done ○ *The* *meeting is still in progress.* ○ *We still have a lot of work in progress.*

progress[2] /prəʊˈgres/ *verb* to develop or move forwards ○ *Work on the new road is progressing slowly.*

project[1] /ˈprɒdʒekt/ *noun* work planned by students on their own ○ *She asked her teacher for some pointers to help her with her project.*

project[2] /prəˈdʒekt/ *verb* to send a picture onto a screen ○ *The lecturer projected slides of his visit to the Arctic.*

projector /prəˈdʒektə/ *noun* a machine which sends pictures onto a screen

promise /ˈprɒmɪs/ *noun* the act of saying that you will definitely do something ○ *But you made a promise not to tell anyone else and now you've told my mother!* ○ *I'll pay you back on Friday – that's a promise.* ■ *verb* to give your word that you will definitely do something ○ *They promised to be back for supper.* ○ *You must promise to bring the computer back when you have finished with it.* ○ *He promised he would look into the problem.* ○ *She promised the staff an extra week's holiday but it never materialised.*

promote /prəˈməʊt/ *verb* **1.** to give someone a better job ○ *He was promoted from salesman to sales manager.* **2.** to make sure that people know about a product or service, by advertising it ○ *There are posters all over the place promoting the new night club.* **3.** to encourage something ○ *The club's aim is to promote gardening.*

promotion /prəˈməʊʃ(ə)n/ *noun* **1.** a move to a better job ○ *He ruined his chances of promotion when he argued with the boss.* **2.** the process of advertising a new product ○ *We're giving away small bottles of shampoo as a promotion.*

prompt /prɒmpt/ *adjective* done immediately ○ *Thank you for your prompt reply.* ■ *verb* to tell an actor words which he or she has forgotten ○ *He had to be prompted in the middle of a long speech.*

promptly /ˈprɒmptli/ *adverb* very soon after an event, in a way that is helpful or efficient

pronoun /ˈprəʊnaʊn/ *noun* a word used instead of a noun, such as 'I', 'you', 'he', 'she' and 'it'

pronounce /prəˈnaʊns/ *verb* **1.** to speak sounds, especially in a particular way ○ *How do you pronounce 'Paris' in French?* **2.** to state something officially ○ *He was pronounced dead on arrival at hospital.* ○ *The priest pronounced them man and wife.*

pronunciation /prəˌnʌnsiˈeɪʃ(ə)n/ *noun* a way of saying words ○ *What's the correct pronunciation of 'controversy'?* ○ *You should try to improve your pronunciation by taking lessons from native speakers.*

proof /pruːf/ *noun* something which proves that something is true ○ *The police have no proof that he committed the murder.*

prop /prɒp/ *noun* a support or stick which holds something up ○ *I used a piece of wood as a prop to keep the window open.*

proper /ˈprɒpə/ *adjective* right and correct; in the way that things are normally done ○ *She didn't put the sugar back into its proper place in the cupboard.* ○ *This is the proper way to use a knife and fork.* ○ *The parcel wasn't delivered because it didn't have the proper address.*

properly /ˈprɒpəli/ *adverb* correctly ○ *The accident happened because the garage hadn't fitted the wheel properly.* ○ *The parcel wasn't properly addressed.*

property /ˈprɒpəti/ *noun* **1.** something that belongs to a particular person ○ *The furniture is the property of the landlord.* ○ *The hotel guests lost all their property in the fire.* ○ *The management is not responsible for property left in the restaurant.* **2.** buildings and land ○ *The family owns property in West London.* ○ *A lot of industrial property was damaged in the war.* (NOTE: [all senses] no plural)

proportion /prəˈpɔːʃ(ə)n/ *noun* a part of a whole ○ *Only a small proportion of his income comes from his TV appearances.*

proposal /prəˈpəʊz(ə)l/ *noun* a plan which has been suggested ○ *The committee made a proposal to rebuild the* clubhouse. ○ *His proposal was accepted by the committee.* ○ *She put forward a proposal but it was rejected.*

propose /prə'pəʊz/ *verb* to make a suggestion ○ *I propose that we all go for a swim.*

prosecute /'prɒsɪkjuːt/ *verb* to bring someone to court to answer a criminal charge ○ *People found stealing from the shop will be prosecuted.*

prospect /'prɒspekt/ *noun* a future possibility ○ *There is no prospect of getting her to change her mind.* ○ *Faced with the grim prospect of two weeks at home he decided to go on holiday.* ■ *plural noun* **prospects** future opportunities, especially in your work ○ *His job prospects are very good.* ○ *What are our prospects of success in this business deal?*

protect /prə'tekt/ *verb* to keep someone or something safe from harm or danger ○ *The cover protects the machine against dust.* ○ *The injection is supposed to protect you against the disease.*

protection /prə'tekʃən/ *noun* shelter, the process of being protected ○ *The trees give some protection from the rain.* ○ *The legislation offers no protection to temporary workers.* ○ *The injection gives some protection against cholera.*

protein /'prəʊtiːn/ *noun* a substance in food such as meat, eggs and nuts which is one of the elements in food which you need to keep your body working properly

protest¹ /'prəʊtest/ *noun* a statement saying that you object or disapprove of something ○ *The new road went ahead despite the protests of the local inhabitants.* ○ *She resigned as a protest against the change in government policy.*

protest² /prə'test/ *verb* **1.** to say or show that you do not approve of something ○ *After being stuck in the train for twenty minutes, the passengers began to protest.* □ **to protest against something** to object strongly to something ○ *Everyone has protested against the increase in fares.* **2.** to insist that something is true, when others think it isn't ○ *She*

went to prison still protesting her innocence.

protester /prə'testə/ *noun* a person who protests in a public way about something they don't agree with ○ *Several protesters stood outside the bank's offices handing out leaflets.*

proud /praʊd/ *adjective* showing pleasure in what you or someone else has done or in something which belongs to you ○ *We're proud of the fact we did it all without help from anyone else.*

proudly /'praʊdli/ *adverb* showing that you are proud of something

prove /pruːv/ *verb* to show that something is true ○ *The police think he stole the car but they can't prove it.* ○ *I was determined to prove him wrong or that he was wrong.* ◊ **proof** (NOTE: **proves – proving – proved**)

proverb /'prɒvɜːb/ *noun* a saying which teaches you something

provide /prə'vaɪd/ *verb* to supply something ○ *Medical help was provided by the Red Cross.* ○ *Our hosts provided us with a car and driver.*

provided (that) /prə'vaɪdɪd ðæt/, **providing** /prə'vaɪdɪŋ/ *conjunction* on condition that; as long as, so long as ○ *It's nice to go on a picnic provided it doesn't rain.* ○ *You can all come to watch the rehearsal providing you don't interrupt.*

prudent /'pruːdənt/ *adjective* showing good sense and using good judgement ○ *It would be prudent to consult a lawyer before you sign the contract.*

pub /pʌb/ *noun* a place where you can buy beer and other alcoholic drinks, and sometimes meals ○ *I happened to meet him at the pub.* ○ *We had a sandwich and some beer in the pub.*

public /'pʌblɪk/ *adjective* relating to the people in general ○ *The crown jewels are on public display in the Tower of London.* ○ *It's in the public interest that the facts should be known.* ■ *noun* people in general ○ *The public have the right to know what is going on.*

publication /ˌpʌblɪ'keɪʃ(ə)n/ *noun* **1.** the process of making something public ○ *The publication of the official figures* *has been delayed.* **2.** a book or newspaper which has been published ○ *He asked the library for a list of gardening publications.*

publicity /pʌ'blɪsɪti/ *noun* advertising which attracts people's attention to something ○ *We're trying to get publicity for our school play.* ○ *The failure of the show was blamed on bad publicity.*

publicly /'pʌblɪkli/ *adverb* in public ○ *The Prime Minister publicly denied the accusations.*

publish /'pʌblɪʃ/ *verb* **1.** to bring out a book or newspaper for sale ○ *The company publishes six magazines for the business market.* ○ *We publish dictionaries for students.* **2.** to make something publicly known ○ *The government has not published the figures yet.*

publisher /'pʌblɪʃə/ *noun* a person or company that produces books or newspapers for sale

pudding /'pʊdɪŋ/ *noun* **1.** a sweet dish at the end of the meal ○ *I'll have ice cream for my pudding.* **2.** a sweet cooked food

puddle /'pʌd(ə)l/ *noun* a small pool of water, e.g. on the ground after it has rained

pull /pʊl/ *verb* to move something towards you or after you ○ *Pull the door to open it, don't push it.* ○ *The truck was pulling a trailer.* ○ *She pulled an envelope out of her bag.*

pull off *phrasal verb* **1.** to take off a piece of clothing by pulling ○ *He sat down and pulled off his dirty boots.* **2.** to succeed in doing something very good, especially if it is unexpected ○ *The deal will be great for the company, if we can pull it off.*

pull out *phrasal verb* **1.** to take something out by pulling ○ *They used a rope to pull the car out of the river.* **2.** to drive a car away from the side of the road ○ *He forgot to signal as he was pulling out.* ○ *Don't pull out into the main road until you can see that there is nothing coming.*

pull over *phrasal verb* to drive a car towards the side of the road and stop ○ *The police car signalled to him to pull over.*

pull up *phrasal verb* **1.** to bring something closer ○ *Pull your chair up to the window.* **2.** (*of a vehicle*) to stop ○ *A car pulled up and the driver asked me if I wanted a lift.* ○ *He didn't manage to pull up in time and ran into the back of the car in front.*

pullover /'pʊləʊvə/ *noun* a piece of clothing made of wool, which covers the top part of your body

pulse /pʌls/ *noun* a regular beat of your heart ○ *The doctor took his pulse.* ○ *Her pulse is very weak.*

pump /pʌmp/ *noun* a machine for forcing liquids or air into something ○ *a bicycle pump* ■ *verb* to force in something such as liquid or air with a pump ○ *Your back tyre needs pumping up.* ○ *The heart pumps blood round the body.*

punch /pʌntʃ/ *noun* **1.** a blow with the fist ○ *She landed two punches on his head.* **2.** a metal tool for making holes ○ *The holes in the belt are made with a punch.* (NOTE: The plural is **punches**.) ■ *verb* **1.** to hit someone with your fist ○ *He punched me on the nose.* **2.** to make holes in something with a punch ○ *The conductor punched my ticket.*

punctual /'pʌŋktʃuəl/ *adjective* on time ○ *He was punctual for his appointment with the dentist.*

punctuation /ˌpʌŋktʃu'eɪʃ(ə)n/ *noun* the practice of dividing up groups of words using special printed symbols

puncture /'pʌŋktʃə/ *noun* a hole in a tyre ○ *I've got a puncture in my back tyre.* ■ *verb* to make a small hole in something ○ *The tyre had been punctured by a nail.*

punish /'pʌnɪʃ/ *verb* to make someone suffer because of something they have done ○ *The children must be punished for stealing apples.* ○ *The simplest way to punish them will be to make them pay for the damage they caused.*

punishment /'pʌnɪʃmənt/ *noun* a treatment given to punish someone ○ *As a punishment, you'll wash the kitchen floor.*

pupil /'pjuːp(ə)l/ *noun* **1.** a child at a school ○ *There are twenty-five pupils in the class.* ○ *The piano teacher thinks* *she is her best pupil.* **2.** a black hole in the central part of the eye, through which the light passes ○ *The pupil of the eye grows larger when there is less light.*

puppet /'pʌpɪt/ *noun* a doll which moves, used to give a show

puppy /'pʌpi/ *noun* a young dog ○ *Our dog has had six puppies.* (NOTE: The plural is **puppies**.)

purchase /'pɜːtʃɪs/ *noun* something that has been bought ○ *She had difficulty getting all her purchases into the car.* □ **to make a purchase** to buy something ○ *We didn't make many purchases on our trip to Oxford Street.* ■ *verb* to buy something ○ *They purchased their car in France and brought it back to the UK*

purchaser /'pɜːtʃɪsə/ *noun* a person who buys something

pure /pjʊə/ *adjective* **1.** not spoiled by being mixed with other things or substances of a lower quality ○ *a bottle of pure water* ○ *a pure silk blouse* ○ *a pure mountain stream* **2.** total, complete ○ *This is pure nonsense.* ○ *It is pure extortion.* ○ *It is pure spite on his part.* ○ *It was by pure good luck that I happened to find it.* (NOTE: **purer – purest**)

purple /'pɜːp(ə)l/ *adjective* blue-red in colour ○ *The sky turned purple as night approached.* ○ *His face was purple with fury.* ■ *noun* a blue-red colour ○ *They painted their living room a deep purple.*

purpose /'pɜːpəs/ *noun* an aim or plan ○ *The purpose of the meeting is to plan the village fair.*

purse /pɜːs/ *noun* a small bag for carrying money ○ *I know I had my purse in my pocket when I left home.* ○ *She put her ticket in her purse so that she wouldn't forget where it was.*

pursue /pə'sjuː/ *verb* to go after someone in order to try to catch him or her (*formal*) ○ *The police pursued the stolen car across London.* ○ *The boys fled, pursued by their older brother.*

push /pʊʃ/ *noun* the action of making something move forwards ○ *Can you give the car a push? – It won't start.* ■ *verb* to make something move away from you or in front of you ○ *We'll have to push the car to get it to start.* ○ *The*

piano is too heavy to lift, so we'll have to push it into the next room. ○ *Did she fall down the stairs or was she pushed?*

put /pʊt/ *verb* to place something somewhere ○ *Did you remember to put the milk in the fridge?* ○ *Where do you want me to put this book?* (NOTE: **puts – putting – put – has put**)

put back *phrasal verb* to put something where it was before

put down *phrasal verb* **1.** to place something lower down onto a surface ○ *He put his suitcase down on the floor beside him.* **2.** to kill an animal that is old or ill, painlessly using drugs ○ *The cat will have to be put down.*

put in *phrasal verb* **1.** to place something inside something ○ *I forgot to put in my pyjamas when I packed the case.* **2.** to fix something such as a system or a large piece of equipment in place so that it can be used ○ *The first thing we have to do with the cottage is to put in central heating.*

put off *phrasal verb* **1.** to arrange for something to take place later ○ *We have put the meeting off until next month.* **2.** to take someone's attention so that they cannot do things properly ○ *Stop making that strange noise, it's putting me off my work.* **3.** to say something that makes someone decide not to do something ○ *He told a story about cows that put me off my food.* ○ *I was going to see the film, but my brother said something which put me off.*

put on *phrasal verb* **1.** to place something on top of something, on a surface ○ *Put the lid on the saucepan.* ○ *He put his hand on my arm.* ○ *Put the suitcases down on the floor.* **2.** to dress yourself in a certain piece of clothing ○ *I put a clean shirt on before I went to the party.* ○ *Put your gloves on, it's cold outside.* ○ *Put on your wellies if you're going out in the rain.* **3.** to switch something on ○ *Can you put the light on, it's getting dark?* ○ *Put on the kettle and we'll have some tea.*

put out *phrasal verb* **1.** to place something outside ○ *Did you remember to put the cat out?* **2.** to switch something off ○ *He put the light out and went to bed.*

put up *phrasal verb* **1.** to attach something to a wall, to attach something high up ○ *I've put up the photos of my family over my desk.* ○ *They are putting up Christmas decorations all along Regent Street.* **2.** to build something ○ *They put up a wooden shed in their garden.* **3.** to increase something, to make something higher ○ *The shop has put up all its prices by 5%.* **4.** to give someone a place to sleep in your house ○ *They've missed the last train, can you put them up for the night?*

put up with *phrasal verb* to accept someone or something unpleasant ○ *I don't think I can put up with that noise any longer.*

puzzle /'pʌz(ə)l/ *noun* **1.** a game where you have to find the answer to a problem ○ *I can't do today's crossword puzzle.* **2.** something that is hard to understand ○ *It's a puzzle to me why they don't go to live in the country.* ■ *verb* to be difficult to understand ○ *It puzzles me how the robbers managed to get away.*

pyramid /'pɪrəmɪd/ *noun* a shape with a square base and four sides rising to meet at a point

Q

q /kjuː/, **Q** *noun* the seventeenth letter of the alphabet, between P and R

qualification /ˌkwɒlɪfɪˈkeɪʃ(ə)n/ *noun* **1.** something necessary for a job, e.g. proof that you have completed a particular course of study ○ *Does she have the right qualifications for the job?* **2.** something which limits the meaning of a statement, or shows that you do not agree with something completely ○ *I want to add one qualification to the agreement: if the goods are not delivered by the 30th of June, then the order will be cancelled.* **3.** success in a test or competition which takes you on to the next stage ○ *She didn't reach the necessary standard for qualification.*

qualify /ˈkwɒlɪfaɪ/ *verb* to attach conditions to something ○ *I must qualify the offer by saying that your proposals still have to be approved by the chairman.* (NOTE: **qualifies – qualifying – qualified**)

quality /ˈkwɒlɪti/ *noun* **1.** how good something is ○ *We want to measure the air quality in the centre of town.* ○ *There are several high-quality restaurants in the West End.* (NOTE: no plural) **2.** something which is part of a person's character ○ *She has many good qualities, but unfortunately is extremely lazy.* ○ *What qualities do you expect in a good salesman?* (NOTE: The plural is **qualities**.)

quantity /ˈkwɒntɪti/ *noun* how much of something there is (NOTE: The plural is **quantities**.)

quarrel /ˈkwɒrəl/ *noun* an occasion when people argue about something ○ *They have had a quarrel and aren't speaking to each other.* ○ *I think the quarrel was over who was in charge of the cash desk.*

quarter /ˈkwɔːtə/ *noun* one of four equal parts of something ○ *She cut the pear into quarters.* ○ *The jar is only a quarter empty.* ○ *He paid only a quarter of the normal fare because he works for the airline.*

quay /kiː/ *noun* the part of a harbour or port where boats stop (NOTE: Do not confuse with **key**.)

queen /kwiːn/ *noun* **1.** the wife of a king ○ *King Charles I's queen was the daughter of the king of France.* **2.** a woman who rules a country ○ *The Queen sometimes lives in Windsor Castle.* ○ *Queen Victoria was queen for many years.* (NOTE: **queen** is spelt with a capital letter when used before a name or when referring to a particular person: *Queen Elizabeth I.*) **3.** in the game of chess, the second most important piece, after the king ○ *In three moves he had captured my queen.*

query /ˈkwɪəri/ *noun* a question ○ *She had to answer a mass of queries about the tax form.* (NOTE: The plural is **queries**.)

question /ˈkwestʃ(ə)n/ *noun* **1.** a sentence which needs an answer ○ *The teacher couldn't answer the children's questions.* ○ *Some of the questions in the exam were too difficult.* ○ *The manager refused to answer questions from journalists about the fire.* **2.** a problem or matter ○ *The question is, who do we appoint to run the shop when we're on holiday?* ○ *The main question is that of cost.* ○ *He raised the question of moving to a less expensive part of town.* ■ *verb* to ask questions ○ *The police questioned the driver for four hours.* ◇ **in question** under discussion ○ *Please keep to the matter in question.*

question mark /ˈkwestʃən mɑːk/ *noun* a sign (?) used in writing to show that a question is being asked

questionnaire /ˌkwestʃəˈneə/ *noun* a printed list of questions given to people to answer, usually questions about what they like or what they buy

queue /kjuː/ *noun* a line of people or things such as cars, waiting one behind the other for something ○ *There was a queue of people waiting to get into the exhibition.* ○ *We joined the queue at the entrance to the stadium.* ■ *verb* to stand in a line and wait for something ○ *We spent hours queuing for tickets.* (NOTE: **queues – queuing – queued**)

quick /kwɪk/ *adjective* done with speed or in a short time ○ *I'm trying to work out the quickest way to get to the Tower of London.* ○ *We had a quick lunch and then went off for a walk.* ○ *He is much quicker at calculating than I am.* ○ *I am not sure that going by air to Paris is quicker than taking the train.*

quickly /ˈkwɪkli/ *adverb* very fast, without taking much time ○ *He ate his supper very quickly because he wanted to watch the match on TV.* ○ *The firemen came quickly when we called 999.*

quiet /ˈkwaɪət/ *adjective* **1.** without any noise ○ *a house in a quiet street* ○ *I wish the children would be quiet. – I'm trying to work.* **2.** with no great excitement ○ *We had a quiet holiday by the sea.* ○ *It's a quiet little village.* ○ *The hotel is in the quietest part of the town.*

quietly /ˈkwaɪətli/ *adverb* without making any noise ○ *The burglar climbed quietly up to the window.* ○ *She shut the door quietly behind her.*

quit /kwɪt/ *verb* **1.** to leave something such as a job or a place and not return ○ *When the boss criticised her, she quit.* ○ *I'm fed up with the office, I'm thinking of quitting.* **2.** *US* to stop doing something ○ *Will you quit bothering me!* ○ *He quit smoking.* (NOTE: **quits – quitting – quit** or **quitted**)

quite /kwaɪt/ *adverb* **1.** to some degree ○ *It's quite a long play.* ○ *She's quite a good writer.* ○ *The book is quite amusing but I liked the TV play better.* **2.** to a great degree ○ *You're quite mad to go walking in a snowstorm.* ○ *He's quite right.* ○ *I don't quite understand why you want to go China.*

quiz /kwɪz/ *noun* a game where you are asked a series of questions ○ *She got all the questions right in the quiz.* ○ *They organised a general knowledge quiz.* (NOTE: The plural is **quizzes**.)

quotation /kwəʊˈteɪʃ(ə)n/ *noun* the words of one person which are repeated by another person ○ *The article ended with a quotation from one of Churchill's speeches.*

quote /kwəʊt/ *noun* a quotation ○ *I need some good quotes from his speech to put into my report.* ■ *verb* to repeat what someone has said or written ○ *He started his speech by quoting lines from Shakespeare's 'Hamlet'.*

R

r /ɑː/, **R** *noun* the eighteenth letter of the alphabet, between Q and S

rabbit /'ræbɪt/ *noun* a common wild animal with grey fur, long ears and a short white tail ○ *The rabbit ran down its hole.* ○ *She keeps a pet rabbit in a cage.*

race /reɪs/ *noun* a competition to see which person, animal or vehicle is the fastest ○ *She was second in the 200 metres race.* ○ *The bicycle race goes round the whole country.* ■ *verb* **1.** to run fast ○ *They saw the bus coming and raced to the bus stop.* ○ *He snatched some watches from the shop window and then raced away down the street.* **2.** to run with someone in order to find out who is fastest ○ *I'll race you to see who gets to school first.*

rack /ræk/ *noun* a frame for holding things, e.g. letters, tools or suitcases ○ *He put the envelope in the letter rack on his desk.*

racket /'rækɪt/ *noun* **1.** a light frame with tight strings, used for hitting the ball in games ○ *She bought a new tennis racket at the start of the summer season.* ○ *She asked if she could borrow his badminton racket for the tournament.* **2.** a loud noise (*informal*) ○ *Stop that racket at once!* ○ *The people next door make a terrible racket when they're having a party.*

radiator /'reɪdieɪtə/ *noun* **1.** a metal object, usually fixed to a wall, which is filled with hot water for heating a room ○ *Turn the radiator down – it's boiling in here.* ○ *When we arrived at the hotel our room was cold, so we switched the radiators on.* **2.** a metal container filled with cold water for preventing a car engine from becoming too hot ○ *The radiator overheated causing the car to break down.*

radio /'reɪdiəʊ/ *noun* **1.** a method of sending out and receiving messages us-ing air waves ○ *They got the news by radio.* ○ *We always listen to BBC radio when we're on holiday.* **2.** a machine which sends out and receives messages using air waves ○ *Turn on the radio – it's time for the weather forecast.* ○ *I heard the news on the car radio.* ○ *Please, turn the radio down – I'm on the phone.*

radius /'reɪdiəs/ *noun* **1.** a line from the centre of a circle to the outside edge ○ *We were all asked to measure the radius of the circle.* **2.** the distance in any direction from a particular central point ○ *People within a radius of twenty miles heard the explosion.* ○ *The school accepts children living within a two-mile radius.* (NOTE: The plural is **radii** or **radiuses**.)

rag /ræg/ *noun* a piece of torn cloth ○ *He used an old oily rag to clean his motorbike.*

rage /reɪdʒ/ *noun* sudden extreme anger ○ *Her face was red with rage.* ■ *verb* to be violent ○ *The storm raged all night.*

raid /reɪd/ *noun* a sudden attack; a sudden visit by the police ○ *Robbers carried out six raids on post offices during the night.* ○ *Police carried out a series of raids on addresses in London.* ■ *verb* to make a sudden attack on a place ○ *The police raided the club.* ○ *We caught the boys raiding the fridge.*

rail /reɪl/ *noun* **1.** a straight metal or wooden bar ○ *The pictures all hang from a picture rail.* ○ *Hold onto the rail as you go down the stairs.* ○ *There is a heated towel rail in the bathroom.* **2.** one of two parallel metal bars on which trains run ○ *Don't try to cross the rails – it's dangerous.* **3.** the railway, a system of travel using trains ○ *Six million commuters travel to work by rail each day.* ○ *We ship all our goods by rail.* ○ *Rail travellers are complaining about rising* fares. ○ *Rail travel is cheaper than air travel.*

railway /'reɪlweɪ/ *noun* a way of travelling which uses trains to carry passengers and goods ○ *The railway station is in the centre of town.* ○ *The French railway system has high-speed trains to all major cities.*

rain /reɪn/ *noun* drops of water which fall from the clouds ○ *The ground is very dry – we've had no rain for days.* ○ *Yesterday we had 3cm of rain* or *3cm of rain fell here yesterday.* ○ *If you have to go out in the rain take an umbrella.* ○ *All this rain will help the plants grow.* ■ *verb* to fall as drops of water from the clouds ○ *As soon as we sat down and took out the sandwiches it started to rain.* ○ *Look at the clouds, it's going to rain.*

rainbow /'reɪnbəʊ/ *noun* a shape like half a circle which shines with many colours in the sky when it is sunny and raining at the same time

raincoat /'reɪnkəʊt/ *noun* a coat which keeps off water, which you wear when it is raining

rain forest /'reɪn ˌfɒrɪst/ *noun* a thick forest which grows in tropical regions where there is a lot of rain

raise /reɪz/ *verb* **1.** to put something in a higher position or at a higher level ○ *He picked up the flag and raised it over his head.* ○ *Air fares will be raised on June 1st.* **2.** to mention a subject which could be discussed ○ *No one raised the subject of politics.* ○ *The manager tried to prevent the question of pay being raised.* **3.** to obtain money ○ *The hospital is trying to raise £2m to finance its building programme.* ○ *Where will he raise the money from to start up his business?* **4.** to look after a child ○ *She was raised by her aunt in Canada.* (NOTE: **raises – raising – raised**)

rally /'ræli/ *noun* a large meeting of members of a group or political party ○ *We are holding a rally to protest against the job cuts.*

ran /ræn/ past tense of **run**

ranch /rɑːntʃ/ *noun* a farm where horses or cows are kept, especially in North or South America ○ *The cowboys returned to the ranch each evening.* ○ *They left the city and bought a ranch in Colorado.*

rang /ræŋ/ past tense of **ring**

range /reɪndʒ/ *noun* **1.** a choice or series of things which are available ○ *We have a range of holidays at all prices.* ○ *I am looking for something in the £20–£30 price range.* **2.** a distance which you can go; a distance over which you can see or hear ○ *The missile only has a range of 100 km.* ○ *The police said the man had been shot at close range.* ○ *The optician told her that her range of vision would be limited.* **3.** a series of buildings or mountains in line ○ *There is a range of outbuildings next to the farmhouse which can be converted into holiday cottages.* ○ *They looked out at the vast mountain range from the plane window.* ■ *verb* □ **to range from** include all types between two limits ○ *The sizes range from small to extra large.* ○ *Holidays range in price from £150 to £350 per person.* ○ *The quality of this year's examination papers ranged from excellent to very poor.*

rank /ræŋk/ *noun* an official position in the army, the police force or a similar organisation ○ *She rose to the rank of captain.*

rapid /'ræpɪd/ *adjective* done very quickly or happening very quickly ○ *There has been a rapid rise in property prices this year.* ○ *The rapid change in the weather forced the yachts to turn for home.*

rapidly /'ræpɪdli/ *adverb* quickly

rare /reə/ *adjective* not usual or common ○ *It's very rare to meet a foreigner who speaks perfect Chinese.* ○ *Experienced sales staff are rare these days.* ○ *The woodland is the habitat of a rare species of frog.* (NOTE: **rarer – rarest**)

rarely /'reəli/ *adverb* almost never ○ *I rarely buy a Sunday newspaper.* ○ *He is rarely in his office on Friday afternoons.*

rash /ræʃ/ *noun* a mass of red spots on your skin, which stays for a time and then disappears ○ *She had a rash on her arms.* ■ *adjective* done without thinking carefully or sensibly ○ *It was a bit rash of him to suggest that he would pay for everyone.*

rat /ræt/ *noun* a small furry animal like a large mouse which has a long tail and can carry disease

rate /reɪt/ *noun* **1.** a number shown as a proportion of another **2.** how frequently something is done or how often something happens ○ *a sharp increase in the country's birth rate* ○ *His heart was beating at a rate of only 59 per minute.* **3.** a level of payment ○ *He immediately accepted the rate offered.* ○ *Before we discuss the project further, I would like to talk about the rates of payment.* ○ *Their rate of pay is lower than ours.* **4.** speed ○ *At the rate he's going, he'll be there before us.* ○ *If you type at a steady rate of 70 words per minute you'll finish copying the text today.*

rather /'rɑːðə/ *adverb* to a slight degree ○ *Their house is rather on the small side.* ○ *Her dress is a rather pretty shade of blue.*

ratio /'reɪʃiəʊ/ *noun* an amount of something measured in relation to another amount ○ *the ratio of successes to failures* ○ *Our athletes beat theirs by a ratio of two to one (2:1).* (NOTE: The plural is **ratios**.)

rattle /'ræt(ə)l/ *verb* to make a repeated noise like two pieces of wood hitting each other ○ *The wind made the windows rattle.*

raw /rɔː/ *adjective* not cooked ○ *Don't be silly – you can't eat raw potatoes!* ○ *We had a salad of raw cabbage and tomatoes.* ○ *Sushi is a Japanese dish of raw fish.* ○ *They served the meat almost raw.*

ray /reɪ/ *noun* a beam of light or heat ○ *A ray of sunshine hit the window pane and lit up the gloomy room.*

razor /'reɪzə/ *noun* an instrument with a very sharp blade for removing hair from the face or body

reach /riːtʃ/ *noun* how far you can stretch out your hand ○ *Keep the medicine bottle out of the reach of the children.* ■ *verb* **1.** to stretch out your hand in order to touch or take something ○ *She reached across the table and took*

some meat from my plate. ○ *He's quite tall enough to reach the tool cupboard.* ○ *Can you reach me down the suitcase from the top shelf?* **2.** to arrive at a place ○ *We were held up by fog and only reached home at midnight.* ○ *The plane reaches Hong Kong at midday.* ○ *We wrote to tell her we were coming to visit, but the letter never reached her.* **3.** to get to a certain level ○ *The amount we owe the bank has reached £100,000.*

react /ri'ækt/ *verb* to do or to say something as a result of something that someone else does or says ○ *How will he react when we tell him the news?* ○ *When she heard the rumour she didn't react at all.*

reaction /ri'ækʃən/ *noun* **1.** a thing done or said as a result of something else ○ *His immediate reaction to the news was to burst into laughter.* ○ *There was a very negative reaction to the proposed building development.* **2.** a process of chemical change ○ *A chemical reaction takes place when the acid is added.*

read /riːd/ *verb* **1.** to look at and understand written words ○ *She was reading a book when I saw her.* ○ *What are you reading at the moment?* ○ *We're reading about the general election.* **2.** to look at and understand written music ○ *She can play the piano by ear, but can't read music.* **3.** to understand the meaning of data from something such as a computer disk or a piece of electronic equipment ○ *My PC cannot read these old disks.* ○ *The scanner reads the code on each product.* **4.** to speak the words of something which is written ○ *The chairman read a message from the president during the meeting.* ○ *She reads a story to the children every night.* ○ *Can you read the instructions on the medicine bottle? – The print is too small for me.* (NOTE: **reads – reading – read**)

read aloud, read out *phrasal verb* to speak the words you are reading

reader /'riːdə/ *noun* **1.** a person who reads, especially a person who reads regularly or who reads a particular newspaper or type of book ○ *a message from the editor to all our readers* ○ *She's a great reader of science fiction.*

2. a school book to help children to learn to read ○ *The teacher handed out the new readers to the class.* ○ *I remember one of my first readers – it was about pirates.*

reading /'riːdɪŋ/ *noun* **1.** the act of looking at and reading written words ○ *Reading and writing should be taught early.* **2.** an occasion when someone speaks the words of something which is written ○ *They gave a poetry reading in the bookshop.*

ready /'redi/ *adjective* **1.** prepared for something ○ *Hold on – I'll be ready in two minutes.* ○ *Are all the children ready to go to school?* ○ *Why isn't the coach here? – The group are all ready and waiting to go.* **2.** available and suitable to be used or eaten ○ *Don't sit down yet – the meal isn't ready.* ○ *Is my dry cleaning ready yet?*

real /rɪəl/ *adjective* **1.** not false or artificial ○ *Is that watch real gold?* ○ *That plastic apple looks very real* or *looks just like the real thing.* ○ *He has a real leather case.* **2.** used for emphasising something ○ *That car is a real bargain at £300.* ○ *Their little girl is going to be a real beauty.* ○ *Wasps can be a real problem on picnics.* ○ *There's a real danger that the shop will be closed.* **3.** which exists in the world, not only in someone's imagination or in stories ○ *She believes fairies are real.*

realise /'rɪəlaɪz/, **realize** *verb* **1.** to understand clearly something that you did not understand before ○ *He didn't realise what he was letting himself in for when he said he would paint the house.* ○ *We soon realised we were on the wrong road.* ○ *When she went into the manager's office she did not realise she was going to be sacked.* **2.** to make something become real ○ *After four years of hard work, the motor racing team realised their dream of winning the Grand Prix.* ○ *By buying a house by the sea he realised his greatest ambition.*

reality /ri'ælɪti/ *noun* situations which are real and not imaginary ○ *the grim realities of life in an industrial town* ○ *He worked hard, and his dreams of wealth soon became a reality.* (NOTE:

The plural is **realities**.) ◇ **in reality** in fact ○ *She always told people she was poor, but in reality she was worth millions.*

really /'rɪəli/ *adverb* **1.** in fact ○ *The building really belongs to my father.* **2.** used to show surprise ○ *She's not really French, is she?* ○ *She doesn't like apples. – Really, how strange!* ○ *Did you really mean what you said?*

rear /rɪə/ *noun* the part at the back ○ *The rear of the car was damaged in the accident.* ○ *They sat towards the rear of the cinema.* ■ *adjective* at the back ○ *The children sat in the rear seats in the car.* ○ *He wound down the rear window.* ■ *verb* **1.** to look after animals or children as they are growing up ○ *They rear horses on their farm.* ○ *They stopped rearing pigs because of the smell.* **2.** to rise up, or to lift something up ○ *A rhino suddenly reared up out of the long grass.* ○ *The walls of the castle reared up before them.*

reason /'riːz(ə)n/ *noun* **1.** a thing which explains why something has happened ○ *The airline gave no reason for the plane's late arrival.* ○ *The boss asked him for the reason why he was behind with his work.* **2.** the ability to make sensible judgments ○ *She wouldn't listen to reason.* ■ *verb* to think or to plan something carefully and sensibly ○ *He reasoned that any work is better than no work, so he took the job.* ○ *If you take the time to reason it out, you'll find a solution to the problem.* ◇ **it stands to reason** it is reasonable ○ *It stands to reason that he wants to join his father's firm.* ◇ **to see reason** to see that someone's argument is right or reasonable ○ *She was going to report her neighbours to the police, but in the end we got her to see reason.* ◇ **within reason** to a sensible degree, in a sensible way ○ *The children get £5 pocket money each week, and we let them spend it as they like, within reason.*

reasonable /'riːz(ə)nəb(ə)l/ *adjective* **1.** sensible ○ *The manager of the shop was very reasonable when she tried to explain that she had left her credit cards at home.* **2.** not expensive ○ *The hotel's* charges are quite reasonable. ○ The restaurant offers good food at reasonable prices.

rebel¹ /'reb(ə)l/ noun a person who fights against a government or against those who are in authority ○ The rebels fled to the mountains after the army captured their headquarters. ○ He considers himself something of a rebel because he wears his hair in a ponytail.

rebel² /rɪ'bel/ verb to fight against someone or something ○ The peasants are rebelling against the king's men. ○ The class rebelled at the idea of doing extra homework. (NOTE: **rebels – rebelling – rebelled**)

recall¹ /'riːkɔːl/ noun the act of asking for products to be returned, or the act of ordering someone to return ○ The recall of the faulty goods caused the manufacturers some serious 3problems.

recall² /rɪ'kɔːl/ verb **1.** to remember something ○ I don't recall having met her before. ○ She couldn't recall any details of the accident. **2.** (of a manufacturer) to ask for products to be returned because of possible faults ○ They recalled 10,000 washing machines because of a faulty electrical connection. ○ They have recalled all their 2001 models as there is a fault in the steering. **3.** to tell a government official to come home from a foreign country ○ The United States recalled their representatives after the military coup.

receipt /rɪ'siːt/ noun a piece of paper that shows you have paid for something or shows you have received something ○ We can't give you your money back if you don't have a receipt.

receive /rɪ'siːv/ verb **1.** to get something which has been sent ○ We received a parcel from the supplier this morning. ○ We only received our tickets the day before we were due to leave. ○ The staff have not received any wages for six months. **2.** to meet or to welcome a visitor ○ The group was received by the mayor.

recent /'riːs(ə)nt/ adjective something which is recent took place not very long ago ○ We will mail you our most recent

catalogue. ○ The changes are recent – they were made only last week.

recently /'riːs(ə)ntli/ adverb only a short time ago ○ I've seen him quite a lot recently. ○ They recently decided to move to Australia.

reception /rɪ'sepʃən/ noun **1.** the way in which people react to something that happens or to someone who arrives ○ The committee gave the proposal a favourable reception. ○ The critics gave the play a warm reception. **2.** the place in a hotel where guests go when they arrive or leave, e.g. to get the key to their room ○ Let's meet at reception at 9.00 am tomorrow. **3.** a place in a large building where visitors go when they arrive and say who they have come to see ○ There's a parcel waiting for you in reception. **4.** a big party held to welcome special guests ○ He hosted a reception for the prince. **5.** the quality of the sound on a radio or the sound and picture of a TV broadcast ○ Perhaps you'd get better reception if you moved the aerial.

receptionist /rɪ'sepʃənɪst/ noun a person in a place such as a hotel or doctor's office who meets visitors and answers the telephone

recipe /'resəpi/ noun instructions for cooking food ○ I copied the recipe for leek soup from the newspaper. ○ You can buy postcards with recipes of local dishes.

reckon /'rekən/ verb **1.** to calculate something or to estimate something ○ We reckon the costs to be about £25,000. ○ We reckon we'll be there before lunch. **2.** to have an opinion about something or to make a judgment about something ○ I reckon we should have stayed at home.

recognisable /'rekəgnaɪzəb(ə)l/ adjective who can be recognised

recognise /'rekəgnaɪz/, **recognize** verb **1.** to know someone or something because you have seen him or her or it before ○ He'd changed so much since I last saw him that I hardly recognised him. ○ He didn't recognise his father's voice over the phone. ○ Do you recognise the handwriting on the letter? **2.** to admit something that has gone wrong or is bad ○ *I recognise that we should have acted earlier.* **3.** to approve of something or someone officially ○ *The language school has been recognised by the Ministry of Education.* ○ *She is recognised as an expert in the field of genetics.* **4.** to express praise for something which has been done ○ *They recognised her years of service.*

recognition /ˌrekəgˈnɪʃ(ə)n/ *noun* praise expressed for something that someone has done ○ *In recognition of his services he was given a watch.*

recommend /ˌrekəˈmend/ *verb* **1.** to tell someone that it would be good to do something ○ *I would recommend that you talk to the bank manager.* ○ *This restaurant was recommended by a friend.* **2.** to praise something or someone ○ *She was highly recommended by her boss.* ○ *I certainly would not recommend Miss Smith for the job.* ○ *Can you recommend a good hotel in Amsterdam?*

record¹ /ˈrekɔːd/ *noun* **1.** a success in sport which is better than any other performance ○ *She holds the world record for the 100 metres.* ○ *He broke the world record* or *he set up a new world record at the last Olympics.* ○ *The college team is trying to set a new record for eating tins of beans.* **2.** written evidence of something which has happened ○ *We have no record of the sale.* **3.** a flat round piece of usually black plastic on which sound is stored ○ *She bought me an old Elvis Presley record for Christmas.* ○ *Burglars broke into his flat and stole his record collection.* ◇ **off the record** in private and not to be made public ○ *She spoke off the record about her marriage.*

record² /rɪˈkɔːd/ *verb* **1.** to report something or to make a note of something ○ *First, I have to record the sales, then I'll post the parcels.* **2.** to put sounds or images onto something such as a film, tape or disc ○ *The police recorded the whole conversation on a hidden tape-recorder.* ○ *This song has been badly recorded.*

recorder /rɪˈkɔːdə/ *noun* **1.** an instrument which records sound ○ *My tape recorder doesn't work, so I can't record*

the concert. **2.** a musical instrument that you play by blowing ○ *Like most children, I learnt to play the recorder at school.*

recording /rɪˈkɔːdɪŋ/ *noun* **1.** the action of putting sounds or images onto something such as a film, tape or disc ○ *the recording of a video* ○ *The recording session starts at 3pm.* **2.** music or speech which has been recorded ○ *Did you know there was a new recording of the concerto?*

recover /rɪˈkʌvə/ *verb* **1.** to feel healthy again after being ill ○ *Has she recovered from her operation?* **2.** to get back something which has been lost or stolen ○ *You must work much harder if you want to recover the money you invested in your business.* ○ *She's trying to recover damages from the driver of the car.*

recovery /rɪˈkʌv(ə)ri/ *noun* **1.** the process of becoming healthy again after being ill ○ *She made a quick recovery and is now back at work.* **2.** the act of getting back something which has been lost or stolen ○ *The TV programme led to the recovery of all the stolen goods.* ○ *We are aiming for the complete recovery of the money invested.*

recreation /ˌrekriˈeɪʃ(ə)n/ *noun* enjoyable activities that people do for fun ○ *The park is used for sport and recreation.*

rectangle /ˈrektæŋgəl/ *noun* a shape with four sides and right angles at the corners, with two long sides and two short sides

recycle /riːˈsaɪk(ə)l/ *verb* to process waste material so that it can be used again

red /red/ *adjective* coloured like the colour of blood ○ *She turned bright red when we asked her what had happened to the money.* ○ *Don't start yet – the traffic lights are still red.* ■ *noun* a colour like the colour of blood ○ *I would like a darker red for the door.* ○ *Don't start yet – the traffic lights are still on red.*

reduce /rɪˈdjuːs/ *verb* to make something smaller or less ○ *The police are* *fighting to reduce traffic accidents.* ○ *Prices have been reduced by 15 per cent.* ○ *I'd like to reduce the size of the photograph so that we can use it as a Christmas card.*

reduction /rɪˈdʌkʃən/ *noun* the act of making something smaller in size or number ○ *Price reductions start on 1st August.* ○ *The company was forced to make job reductions.*

reef /riːf/ *noun* a long line of rocks just above or below the surface of the sea ○ *The yacht hit a reef and sank.*

refer /rɪˈfɜː/ *verb* **1.** to be about something or someone ○ *Do you think he was referring to me when he said some staff would have to leave?* **2.** to look into something for information ○ *He referred to his diary to see if he had a free afternoon.* **3.** to pass a problem to someone to decide ○ *We have referred your complaint to our head office.* ○ *He was referred to an ear specialist by his GP.* (NOTE: **refers – referring – referred**)

referee /ˌrefəˈriː/ *noun* (*in sports*) a person who makes sure that a game is played according to the rules ○ *When fighting broke out between the players, the referee stopped the match.* ○ *The referee sent several players off.*

reference /ˈref(ə)rəns/ *noun* an act of mentioning something or someone ○ *She made a reference to her brother-in-law.* ○ *The report made no reference to the bank.* ◇ **with reference to** concerning something ○ *With reference to your letter of May 25th.*

refill[1] /riːˈfɪl/ *verb* to fill a container that has become empty ○ *The waiter refilled our glasses.* ○ *We stopped twice to refill the car on the way to Scotland.*

refill[2] /ˈriːfɪl/ *noun* another amount of a drink that you have finished ○ *Your glass is empty – can I get you a refill?*

reflect /rɪˈflekt/ *verb* to send back light, heat or an image of something ○ *a picture of snow-capped mountains reflected in a clear blue lake* ○ *The light reflected on the top of the car.* ○ *White surfaces reflect light better than dark ones.*

reform /rɪˈfɔːm/ *noun* the act of changing something in order to make it better ○ *The government is planning a series of reforms to the benefit system.* ■ *verb* **1.** to change something in order to make it better ○ *They want to reform the educational system.* **2.** to stop committing crimes, or to stop having bad habits and to become good ○ *After her time in prison she became a reformed character.* ○ *He used to drink a lot, but since he got married he has reformed.*

refreshing /rɪˈfreʃɪŋ/ *adjective* something which is refreshing makes you feel fresh or full of energy again ○ *I had a refreshing drink of cold water.* ○ *A refreshing shower of rain cooled the air.*

refrigerator /rɪˈfrɪdʒəreɪtə/ *noun* an electrical machine used in the kitchen for keeping food and drink cold ○ *There's some orange juice in the refrigerator.* (NOTE: often called a **fridge**)

refugee /ˌrefjʊˈdʒiː/ *noun* a person who has left his or her country because of war or because the government did not like allow his or her religious or political beliefs

refusal /rɪˈfjuːz(ə)l/ *noun* an act of saying that you do not accept something ○ *His refusal to help was unexpected.* ○ *Did you accept? – no! I sent a letter of refusal.*

refuse[1] /rɪˈfjuːz/ *verb* **1.** to say that you will not do something ○ *His father refused to lend him any more money.* ○ *He asked for permission to see his family, but it was refused.* **2.** □ **the car refused to start** the car would not start ○ *Once again this morning the car refused to start.*

refuse[2] /ˈrefjuːs/ *noun* rubbish and things which are not wanted ○ *Please put all refuse in the bin.* ○ *Refuse collection on our road is on Thursdays.* (NOTE: no plural)

regard /rɪˈgɑːd/ *noun* **1.** care or concern for something ○ *She had no regard for the safety of her children.* **2.** an opinion of someone ○ *He is held in high regard by his staff.* **3.** □ **regards** best wishes ○ *She sends her (kind) regards.* ○ *Please give my regards to your mother.* ■ *verb* to have an opinion about someone ○ *She* is highly regarded by the manager. ◇ **as regards** relating to ○ *As regards the cost of the trip, I'll let you know soon what the final figure is.* ◇ **with regard to** relating to ○ *With regard to your request for extra funds.*

region /ˈriːdʒən/ *noun* a large area of a country ○ *The South-West region is well known for its apples.*

regional /ˈriːdʒ(ə)nəl/ *adjective* relating to a region ○ *The recession has not affected the whole country – it is only regional.* ○ *After the national news, here is the regional news for the South West.*

register /ˈredʒɪstə/ *noun* **1.** a list of names ○ *I can't find your name in the register.* ○ *His name was struck off the register.* **2.** a book in which you sign your name ○ *Please sign the hotel register when you check in.* ■ *verb* to write a name officially in a list ○ *If you don't register, we won't be able to get in touch with you.* ○ *Babies have to be registered with the registrar as soon as they are born.*

regret /rɪˈgret/ *noun* the feeling of being sorry that something has happened ○ *I have absolutely no regrets about what we did.* ■ *verb* to be sorry that something has happened ○ *I regret to say that you were not successful.* ○ *I regret the trouble this has caused you.* ○ *We regret the delay in the arrival of our flight from Amsterdam.* (NOTE: **regrets – regretting – regretted**)

regular /ˈregjʊlə/ *adjective* **1.** done at the same time each day ○ *His regular train is the 12.45.* ○ *The regular flight to Athens leaves at 06.00.* **2.** usual or standard ○ *The regular price is £1.25, but we are offering them at 99p.*

regularly /ˈregjʊləli/ *adverb* on most occasions ○ *She is regularly the first person to arrive at the office each morning.*

regulation /ˌregjʊˈleɪʃ(ə)n/ *noun* an official rule about how to do something ○ *safety regulations* ■ *plural noun* **regulations** laws or rules controlling something ○ *The restaurant broke the fire regulations.* ○ *Safety regulations were not being properly followed.*

rehearsal /rɪˈhɜːs(ə)l/ *noun* a practice of a play or concert before the first public performance

reign /reɪn/ *noun* a period when a king, queen or emperor rules ○ *during the reign of Elizabeth I* ■ *verb* to rule ○ *Queen Victoria reigned between 1837 and 1901.* ○ *She reigned during a period of great prosperity.* (NOTE: Do not confuse with **rain**.)

reject¹ /rɪˈdʒekt/ *verb* **1.** to refuse to accept something ○ *She rejected my suggestion that we changed our plans.* ○ *The proposals for the new project were rejected.* **2.** to refuse to accept something because it is not satisfactory ○ *Poles shorter than the standard size are rejected.*

reject² /ˈriːdʒekt/ *noun* something which is not accepted because it is not satisfactory

relate /rɪˈleɪt/ *verb* **1.** to be concerned with something ○ *The regulations relate to the movement of boats in the harbour.* **2.** to tell a story ○ *It took him half an hour to relate what had happened.*

related to /rɪˈleɪtɪd tʊ/ *adjective* **1.** belonging to the same family as ○ *Are you related to the Smith family in London Road?* **2.** connected in some way with ○ *The disease is related to the weakness of the heart muscle.* ○ *There are several related items on the agenda.*

relating to /rɪˈleɪtɪŋ tuː/ *adverb* relating to or connected with ○ *documents relating to the sale of the house*

relation /rɪˈleɪʃ(ə)n/ *noun* **1.** a member of a family ○ *All my relations live in Canada.* ○ *Laura's no relation of mine, she's just a friend.* **2.** a link between two things ○ *Is there any relation between his appointment as MD and the fact that his uncle owns the business?* □ **in relation to** relating to or connected with ○ *Documents in relation to the sale.* ■ *plural noun* **relations** the way that people or organizations behave towards each other ○ *We try to maintain good relations with our customers.* ○ *Relations between the two countries have become tense.*

relationship /rɪˈleɪʃ(ə)nʃɪp/ *noun* **1.** a close friendship, especially one in which two people are involved in a romantic or sexual way with each other ○ *She decided to end the relationship when she found he had been seeing other women.* **2.** the way that people or organizations behave towards each other ○ *We try to have a good working relationship with our staff.* **3.** a link or connection ○ *There is a proven relationship between smoking and lung cancer.*

relative /ˈrelətɪv/ *noun* a person who is related to someone ○ *We have several relatives living in Canada.* ○ *He has no living relatives.*

relatively /ˈrelətɪvli/ *adverb* to some extent ○ *The children have been relatively free from colds this winter.* ○ *We are dealing with a relatively new company.*

relax /rɪˈlæks/ *verb* to rest from work or to be less tense ○ *They spent the first week of their holiday relaxing on the beach.* ○ *Guests can relax in the bar before going to eat in the restaurant.* ○ *Just lie back and relax – the injection won't hurt.*

relaxed /rɪˈlækst/ *adjective* not upset or nervous ○ *Even if he failed his test, he's still very relaxed about the whole thing.*

relaxing /rɪˈlæksɪŋ/ *adjective* which makes you less tense

release /rɪˈliːs/ *verb* **1.** to stop holding something, or to stop keeping someone prisoner ○ *Pull that lever to release the brakes.* ○ *The hostages were released last night.* **2.** to make something public ○ *The government has released figures about the number of people out of work.*

relevant /ˈreləv(ə)nt/ *adjective* if something is relevant, it has something to do with the thing being mentioned ○ *Which is the relevant government department?* ○ *Can you give me the relevant papers?* ○ *Is this information at all relevant?*

reliable /rɪˈlaɪəb(ə)l/ *adjective* which can be relied on or which can be trusted ○ *It is a very reliable car.* ○ *The sales manager is completely reliable.*

relief /rɪˈliːf/ *noun* **1.** the pleasant feeling you get when pain has stopped or when you are no longer nervous or worried ○ *An aspirin should bring relief.* ○ *He breathed a sigh of relief when the police car went past without stopping.* ○ *What a relief to have finished my exams!* **2.** help for people in a difficult or dangerous situation ○ *The Red Cross is organising relief for the flood victims.*

relieved /rɪˈliːvd/ *adjective* glad to be rid of a problem

religion /rɪˈlɪdʒən/ *noun* a belief in gods or in one God ○ *Does their religion help them to lead a good life?* ○ *It is against my religion to eat meat on Fridays.*

religious /rəˈlɪdʒəs/ *adjective* relating to religion ○ *There is a period of religious study every morning.*

reluctant /rɪˈlʌktənt/ *adjective* not willing to do something ○ *He seemed reluctant to help.*

reluctantly /rɪˈlʌktəntli/ *adverb* not willingly

rely *verb*

rely on *phrasal verb* to believe or know that something will happen or that someone will do something ○ *We can rely on him to finish the work on time.* ○ *Can these machines be relied on?*

remain /rɪˈmeɪn/ *verb* **1.** to continue to be in a particular place or state, with no changes ○ *We expect it will remain fine for the rest of the week.* ○ *She remained behind at the office to finish her work.* **2.** to be left ○ *Half the food remained uneaten and had to be thrown away.* ○ *After the accident not much remained of the car.*

remainder /rɪˈmeɪndə/ *noun* what is left after everything else has gone ○ *What shall we do for the remainder of the holidays?*

remark /rɪˈmɑːk/ *noun* something that someone says ○ *I heard his remark even if he spoke in a low voice.* ■ *verb* to notice and comment on ○ *She remarked on how dirty the café was.*

remarkable /rɪˈmɑːkəb(ə)l/ *adjective* very unusual ○ *She's a remarkable woman.* ○ *It's remarkable that the bank has not asked us to pay back the money.*

remarkably /rɪˈmɑːkəbli/ *adverb* to an unusually great degree, or in an unusual way ○ *She remained remarkably calm.*

remedy /'remədi/ *noun* a thing which may cure an illness or may solve a problem ○ *It's an old remedy for hayfever.*

remember /rɪ'membə/ *verb* to bring back into your mind something which you have seen or heard before ○ *Do you remember when we got lost in the fog?* ○ *My grandmother can remember seeing the first television programmes.* ○ *She can't remember where she put her umbrella.* ○ *I don't remember having been in this hotel before.* ○ *I remember my grandmother very well.* ○ *Did you remember to switch off the kitchen light?* (NOTE: You **remember doing something** which you did in the past; you **remember to do something** in the future.)

remind /rɪ'maɪnd/ *verb* to make someone remember something ○ *Now that you've reminded me, I do remember seeing him last week.* ○ *Remind me to book the tickets for New York.* ○ *She reminded him that the meeting had to finish at 6.30.*

remote /rɪ'məʊt/ *adjective* **1.** far away from towns and places where there are lots of people ○ *The hotel is situated in a remote mountain village.* **2.** not very likely ○ *There's a remote chance of finding a cure for his illness.* ○ *The possibility of him arriving on time is remote.* (NOTE: **remoter – remotest**)

remote control /rɪ,məʊt kən'trəʊl/ *noun* a small piece of electronic equipment which you use for controlling something such as a TV or CD player from a distance

remotely /rɪ'məʊtli/ *adverb* **1.** very slightly, or not even very slightly ○ *I'm not remotely interested in meeting him.* **2.** at a great distance from a town ○ *a remotely situated farm* **3.** without direct physical contact ○ *They were able to set the controls remotely.*

removal /rɪ'muːv(ə)l/ *noun* **1.** taking something or someone away ○ *the removal of the ban on importing computers* ○ *Refuse collectors are responsible for the removal of household waste.* ○ *The opposition called for the removal of the Foreign Secretary.* **2.** the act of moving to a new home, new office, etc. ○ *a removal van*

remove /rɪ'muːv/ *verb* to take something away ○ *You can remove his name from the mailing list.* ○ *The waitress removed the dirty plates and brought us some tea.*

renowned /rɪ'naʊnd/ *adjective* known and admired by many people ○ *the renowned Italian conductor* ○ *Rome is renowned as the centre of Catholicism.*

rent /rent/ *noun* money paid to live in a flat or house or to use an office or car ○ *Rents are high in the centre of the town.* ○ *The landlord asked me to pay three months' rent in advance.* ■ *verb* to pay money to use a house, flat, office or car ○ *He rents an office in the centre of town.* ○ *He rented a villa by the beach for three weeks.*

repair /rɪ'peə/ *verb* to make something work which is broken or damaged ○ *I dropped my watch on the pavement, and I don't think it can be repaired.* ○ *She's trying to repair the washing machine.* ○ *The photocopier is being repaired.* ■ *noun* the act of making something which is broken or damaged work again ○ *His car is in the garage for repair.* ○ *The hotel is closed while they are carrying out repairs to the kitchens.*

repeat /rɪ'piːt/ *verb* to say something again ○ *Could you repeat what you just said?* ○ *He repeated the address so that the policeman could write it down.* ○ *She kept on repeating that she wanted to go home.*

repeatedly /rɪ'piːtɪdli/ *adverb* very many times, often so many that it is annoying

replace /rɪ'pleɪs/ *verb* to put something back where it was before ○ *Please replace the books correctly on the shelves.*

replacement /rɪ'pleɪsmənt/ *noun* **1.** a thing which is used to replace something ○ *An electric motor was bought as a replacement for the old one.* **2.** the act of replacing something with something else ○ *The mechanics recommended the replacement of the hand pump with an electric model.*

replicate /'replɪkeɪt/ *verb* to do or make something in exactly the same way as before

reply /rɪ'plaɪ/ *noun* **1.** an answer, especially to a letter or telephone call ○ *We wrote last week, but haven't had a reply yet.* ○ *We had six replies to our advertisement.* (NOTE: The plural is **replies**.) **2.** □ **in reply** as an answer ○ *In reply to my letter, I received a fax two days later.* ○ *She just shook her head in reply and turned away.* ■ *verb* to give or send an answer to something such as a message or letter ○ *He never replies to my letters.* ○ *We wrote last week, but he hasn't replied yet.* ○ *He refused to reply to questions until his lawyer arrived.* (NOTE: **replies – replying – replied**)

report /rɪ'pɔːt/ *noun* a description of what has happened or what will happen ○ *We read the reports of the accident in the newspaper.* ○ *Can you confirm the report that the council is planning to sell the old town hall?* ■ *verb* to go somewhere officially, or to say that you have arrived somewhere ○ *to report for work* ○ *Candidates should report to the office at 9.00.*

reporter /rɪ'pɔːtə/ *noun* a journalist who writes reports of events for a newspaper or for a TV news programme

represent /ˌreprɪ'zent/ *verb* **1.** to speak or act on behalf of someone or of a group of people ○ *He asked his solicitor to represent him at the meeting.* **2.** to mean something, or to be a symbol of something g ○ *The dark green on the map represents woods.*

representative /ˌreprɪ'zentətɪv/ *adjective* typical of all the people or things in a group ○ *The sample isn't representative of the whole batch.* ■ *noun* a person who represents, who speaks on behalf of someone else ○ *He asked his solicitor to act as his representative.* ○ *Representatives of the workforce have asked to meet the management.*

reproduce /ˌriːprə'djuːs/ *verb* to make a copy of something ○ *His letters have been reproduced in the biography.* ○ *It is very difficult to reproduce the sound of an owl accurately.*

reptile /'reptaɪl/ *noun* a cold-blooded animal which has skin covered with scales and which lays eggs

republic /rɪ'pʌblɪk/ *noun* a system of government in which elected representatives have power and the leader is an elected or nominated president ○ *France is a republic while Spain is a monarchy.*

reputation /ˌrepjʊ'teɪʃ(ə)n/ *noun* an opinion that people have of someone ○ *He has a reputation for being difficult to deal with.* ○ *His bad reputation won't help him find a suitable job.*

request /rɪ'kwest/ *noun* asking for something ○ *Your request will be dealt with as soon as possible.* ■ *verb* to ask for something politely or formally ○ *I am enclosing the leaflets you requested.* ○ *Guests are requested to leave their keys at reception.* ◇ **on request** if asked for ○ *'catalogue available on request'*

require /rɪ'kwaɪə/ *verb* to need something ○ *The disease requires careful nursing.* ○ *Writing the program requires a computer specialist.*

required /rɪ'kwaɪəd/ *adjective* which must be done or provided ○ *We can cut the wood to the required length.* ○ *We can't reply because we don't have the required information.*

requirement /rɪ'kwaɪəmənt/ *noun* what is necessary ○ *It is a requirement of the job that you should be able to drive.*

rescue /'reskjuː/ *verb* to save someone from a dangerous or difficult situation ○ *When the river flooded, the party of tourists had to be rescued by helicopter.* ○ *The company nearly collapsed, but was rescued by the bank.* ■ *noun* the action of saving someone or something in a difficult or dangerous situation ○ *No one could swim well enough to go to her rescue.*

research /rɪ'sɜːtʃ/ *noun* scientific study which tries to find out facts ○ *The company is carrying out research to find a cure for colds.* ○ *The research laboratory has come up with encouraging results.* ○ *Our researches proved that the* *letter was a forgery.* ■ *verb* to study something in order to find out facts ○ *Research your subject thoroughly before you start writing about it.*

resent /rɪˈzent/ *verb* to feel annoyed because of something that you think is unfair ○ *She resents having to do other people's work.*

resentment /rɪˈzentmənt/ *noun* the feeling of being angry and upset about something that someone else has done ○ *The decision caused a lot of resentment among local people.*

reservation /ˌrezəˈveɪʃ(ə)n/ *noun* the act of booking something, e.g. a seat or table ○ *I want to make a reservation on the train to Plymouth tomorrow evening.*

reserve /rɪˈzɜːv/ *verb* to book a seat or a table ○ *I want to reserve a table for four people.* ○ *Can you reserve two seats for me for the evening performance?* ○ *We're very busy this evening. Have you reserved?* ■ *noun* an amount kept back in case it is needed in the future ○ *Our reserves of coal were used up during the winter.* ◇ **in reserve** waiting to be used ○ *We're keeping the can of petrol in reserve.*

reservoir /ˈrezəvwɑː/ *noun* a large, usually artificial, lake where drinking water is kept for supplying a city

resident /ˈrezɪd(ə)nt/ *noun* a person who lives in a place, e.g. a country or a hotel ○ *You need an entry permit if you're not a resident of the country.* ○ *Only residents are allowed to park their cars here.* ■ *adjective* who lives permanently in a place ○ *There is a resident caretaker.*

resign /rɪˈzaɪn/ *verb* to give up a job ○ *He resigned with effect from July 1st.* ○ *She has resigned (her position) as finance director.*

resist /rɪˈzɪst/ *verb* to oppose or fight against something ○ *He resisted all attempts to make him sell the house.* ○ *Bands of guerrillas resisted doggedly in the mountains.* ○ *They resisted the enemy attacks for two weeks.*

resistance /rɪˈzɪstəns/ *noun* opposition to or fighting against something ○ *The*

patients had no resistance to disease. ○ *Skiers crouch down low to minimise wind resistance.* ○ *There was a lot of resistance to the new plan from the local residents.*

resolve /rɪˈzɒlv/ (*formal*) *verb* to strongly decide to do something ○ *We all resolved to avoid these mistakes next time.* ■ *noun* a strong decision to do something ○ *The head teacher encouraged him in his resolve to go to university.*

resource /rɪˈzɔːs/ *noun* a source of supply for what is needed or used ○ *financial resources* ○ *The country is rich in oil, minerals and other natural resources.*

respect /rɪˈspekt/ *noun* admiration for someone ○ *No one deserves more respect than her mother for the way she coped with the bad news.* ○ *He showed very little respect for his teacher.* ■ *verb* to admire someone, especially because of his or her achievements or status ○ *Everyone respected her for what she did.*

respectable /rɪˈspektəb(ə)l/ *adjective* considered by people to be good, and deserving to be respected ○ *She's marrying a very respectable young engineer.* ○ *I don't want to bring up my children here, it is not a respectable area.*

respond /rɪˈspɒnd/ *verb* **1.** to give a reply ○ *She shouted at him, but he didn't respond.* **2.** to show that you like or approve of something ○ *I hope the public will respond to our new advertisement.* ○ *The government has responded to pressure from industry.*

response /rɪˈspɒns/ *noun* something that you do or say as a reaction to something ○ *There was no response to our call for help.* ○ *The changes provoked an angry response from customers.* □ **in response to something** as an answer or reaction to something ○ *In response to the United Nations' request for aid, the government has sent blankets and tents.*

responsibility /rɪˌspɒnsɪˈbɪlɪti/ *noun* **1.** the position of someone who must look after or deal with something ○ *The management accepts no responsibility for customers' property.* ○ *There is no responsibility on his part for the poor* *results.* ○ *Who should take responsibility for the students' welfare?* **2.** something that someone is responsible for

responsible /rɪ'spɒnsɪb(ə)l/ *adjective* **1.** looking after something and so likely to be blamed if something goes wrong ○ *He is not responsible for the restaurant next door to his hotel.* ○ *Customers are responsible for all breakages.* ○ *He is responsible for a class of 25 children.* □ **responsible to someone** under the authority of someone ○ *She's directly responsible to the sales manager.* **2.** (*of a person*) reliable and able to be trusted to be sensible

rest /rest/ *noun* **1.** a period of being quiet and peaceful, being asleep or doing nothing ○ *All you need is a good night's rest and you'll be fine again tomorrow.* ○ *We took a few minutes' rest and started running again.* ○ *I'm having a well-earned rest after working hard all week.* **2.** what is left ○ *Here are the twins, but where are the rest of the children?* ○ *I drank most of the milk and the cat drank the rest.* ○ *Throw the rest of the food away – it will go bad.* (NOTE: **Rest** takes a singular verb when it refers to a singular: *Here's the rest of the milk; Where's the rest of the string? The rest of the money has been lost.* It takes a plural verb when it refers to a plural: *Here are the rest of the children; Where are the rest of the chairs? The rest of the books have been lost.*) ■ *verb* **1.** to spend time relaxing or not using energy ○ *Don't disturb your father – he's resting.* ○ *They ran for ten miles, rested for a few minutes, and then ran on again.* **2.** to lean something against something ○ *She rested her bike against the wall.*

restaurant /'rest(ə)rɒnt/ *noun* a place where you can buy and eat a meal ○ *I don't want to stay at home tonight – let's go out to the Italian restaurant in the High Street.* ○ *She's was waiting for me at the restaurant.*

restful /'restf(ə)l/ *adjective* which makes you feel calm and relaxed

restless /'restləs/ *adjective* too nervous, worried or full of energy to keep still

restore /rɪ'stɔː/ *verb* to repair something and make it seem new again ○ *The old house has been restored and is now open to the public.*

restrain /rɪ'streɪn/ *verb* to prevent or try to stop someone doing something ○ *It took six policemen to restrain him.* □ **to restrain yourself** to keep your temper under control ○ *Next time, I won't restrain myself: I'll tell him exactly what I think of him.*

restrict /rɪ'strɪkt/ *verb* to limit someone or something ○ *You are restricted to two bottles per person.*

result /rɪ'zʌlt/ *noun* **1.** something which happens because of something else ○ *What was the result of the police investigation?* □ **as a result (of something)** because of something ○ *There was a traffic jam and as a result, she missed her plane.* **2.** the final score in a game, the final marks in an exam, etc. ○ *She isn't pleased with her exam results.* ○ *I had great fun making the rug but I'm only partly happy with the result.* ○ *He listened to the football results on the radio.*

retire /rɪ'taɪə/ *verb* **1.** to stop work and take a pension ○ *He will retire from his job as manager next April.* ○ *She's retiring this year.* **2.** to make an employee stop work and take a pension ○ *They decided to retire all staff over 50.*

retreat /rɪ'triːt/ *verb* to pull back from a battle ○ *Napoleon retreated from Moscow in 1812.* ■ *noun* the act of pulling back an army from a battle ○ *The army's retreat was swift and unexpected.*

return /rɪ'tɜːn/ *noun* **1.** the act of going or coming back to a place ○ *It snowed on the day of her return from Canada.* ○ *I'll come and see you on my return.* **2.** the key on a keyboard which you press when you have finished keying something, or when you want to start a new line ○ *To change directory, type C: and press return.* ■ *verb* **1.** to come back or go back ○ *When she returned from lunch she found two messages waiting for her.* ○ *When do you plan to return to Paris?* **2.** to give or send something back ○ *The letter was returned to the sender.* ◇ **many happy returns of the day**

greetings said to someone on his or her birthday

reveal /rɪ'viːl/ *verb* to show or mention something which was hidden ○ *He revealed his ignorance about cars.* ○ *An unexpected fault was revealed during the test.* ○ *The X-ray revealed a brain tumour.*

revenge /rɪ'vendʒ/ *noun* the act of punishing someone in return for harm he or she has caused you ○ *They attacked the police station in revenge for the arrest of three members of the gang.* ○ *All the time he spent in prison, his only thought was of revenge.* ○ *He had his revenge in the end, when her car broke down and she had to phone for help.*

reverse /rɪ'vɜːs/ *adjective* opposite to the front ○ *The reverse side of the carpet is made of foam rubber.* ○ *The conditions are printed on the reverse side of the invoice.* □ **in reverse order** backwards ○ *They called out the names of the prize-winners in reverse order.* ■ *noun* **1.** the opposite side ○ *Didn't you read what was on the reverse of the label?* **2.** a car gear which makes you go backwards ○ *Put the car into reverse and back very slowly into the garage.* ○ *The car's stuck in reverse!* ■ *verb* **1.** to make something do the opposite ○ *The page order was reversed by mistake.* ○ *Don't try to reverse the trend, go along with it.* **2.** to make a car go backwards ○ *Reverse as far as you can, then go forward.* ○ *Be careful not to reverse into that lamppost.*

review /rɪ'vjuː/ *noun* **1.** written comments on something, e.g. a book, play or film, published in a newspaper or magazine ○ *Did you read the review of her latest film in today's paper?* ○ *His book got some very good reviews.* **2.** a monthly or weekly magazine which contains articles of general interest ○ *His first short story appeared in a Scottish literary review.* **3.** an examination of several things together ○ *The company's annual review of each department's performance.* ■ *verb* **1.** to read a book, see a film, etc., and write comments about it in a newspaper or magazine ○ *Her exhibition was reviewed in today's paper.* ○

Whoever reviewed her latest book, obviously didn't like it. **2.** to examine something in a general way ○ *The bank will review our overdraft position at the end of the month.* ○ *Let's review the situation in the light of the new developments.* **3.** *US* to study a lesson again ○ *You must review your geography before the exam.*

revise /rɪ'vaɪz/ *verb* **1.** to study a lesson again ○ *There isn't enough time to revise before the exam.* ○ *I'm revising for my history test.* **2.** to change something or make something correct ○ *He is revising the speech he is due to give this evening.* ○ *These figures will have to be revised, there seems to be a mistake.*

revision /rɪ'vɪʒ(ə)n/ *noun* the action of revising something

revolting /rɪ'vəʊltɪŋ/ *adjective* extremely unpleasant, often so unpleasant as to make you feel ill ○ *a revolting smell*

revolution /ˌrevə'luːʃ(ə)n/ *noun* **1.** a violent attempt to get rid of a government or ruler ○ *He led an unsuccessful revolution against the last president.* **2.** a change in the way things are done ○ *a revolution in data processing*

reward /rɪ'wɔːd/ *noun* money given to someone for work done or as a prize for finding something, or for information about something ○ *When she took the purse she had found to the police station she got a £25 reward.* ○ *He is not interested in money – the Olympic gold medal will be reward enough.* ■ *verb* to give someone money as a prize for finding something, or for doing something ○ *He was rewarded for finding the box of papers.* ○ *All her efforts were rewarded when she won first prize.*

rhyme /raɪm/ *noun* the way in which some words end in the same sound ○ *Can you think of a rhyme for 'taught'?* ■ *verb* □ **to rhyme with something** to end with the same sound as another word ○ *'Mr' rhymes with 'sister'*

rhythm /'rɪð(ə)m/ *noun* a strong regular beat in music or poetry ○ *They stamped their feet to the rhythm of the music.*

rib /rɪb/ *noun* one of 24 curved bones which protect your chest ○ *He fell down while skiing and broke two ribs.*

ribbon /'rɪbən/ *noun* a long thin piece of material for tying things or used as decoration

rice /raɪs/ *noun* the seeds of a tropical plant which are cooked and eaten ○ *She only had a bowl of rice for her evening meal.* (NOTE: no plural: *some rice, a bowl of rice, a spoonful of rice*)

rich /rɪtʃ/ *adjective* **1.** who has a lot of money ○ *If only we were rich, then we could buy a bigger house.* ○ *He never spends anything, and so he gets richer and richer.* **2.** made with a lot of cream, butter, or eggs ○ *This cream cake is too rich for me.*

rid /rɪd/ *adjective* □ **to get rid of something** to throw something away ○ *Do you want to get rid of that old bookcase?* ○ *We have been told to get rid of twenty staff.* ○ *She doesn't seem able to get rid of her cold.*

ride /raɪd/ *noun* a pleasant trip, e.g. on a horse or a bike or in a car ○ *Does anyone want to come for a bike ride?* ○ *Can I have a ride on your motorbike?* ○ *He took us all for a ride in his new car.* ○ *The station is only a short bus ride from the college.* ■ *verb* to go on a horse, on a bike, etc. ○ *He rode his bike across the road without looking.* ○ *She's never ridden (on) an elephant.* ○ *My little sister is learning to ride, but she's frightened of big horses.* (NOTE: **rides – riding – rode** /rəʊd/ **– ridden** /'rɪd(ə)n/)

rider /'raɪdə/ *noun* a person who rides ○ *The rider of the black horse fell at the first fence.* ○ *Motorcycle riders must wear helmets.*

ridiculous /rɪ'dɪkjʊləs/ *adjective* extremely silly or unreasonable

rifle /'raɪf(ə)l/ *noun* a gun with a long barrel which you hold with two hands, against your shoulder ○ *The gunman was on a roof with a rifle.* ○ *He was shooting at a target with an air rifle.*

right /raɪt/ *adjective* **1.** correct ○ *She didn't put the bottles back in the* ○ *You're right – the number 8 bus doesn't go to Marble Arch.* ○ *She gave the right*

answer every time. ○ *He says the answer is 285 – quite right!* ○ *Is the station clock right?* ○ *Is this the right train for Manchester?* ◊ **all right 2.** on the same side as the hand which most people use to write with ○ *In England cars don't drive on the right side of the road.* ○ *The keys are in the top right drawer of my desk.* ○ *He was holding the suitcase in his right hand.* ■ *noun* the side opposite to the left ○ *When driving in France remember to keep to the right.* ○ *When you get to the next crossroads, turn to the right.* ○ *Who was that girl sitting on the right of your father?* ○ *Go straight ahead, and take the second road on the right.* ■ *adverb* **1.** directly, or in a straight line ○ *Instead of stopping at the crossroads, he drove right on across the main road and* ○ *To get to the police station, keep right on to the end of the road, and then turn left.* ○ *Go right along to the end of the corridor, you'll see my office in front of you.* **2.** exactly ○ *The pub is right at the end of the road.* ○ *The phone rang right in the middle of the TV programme.* ○ *She stood right in front of the TV and no one could see the screen.* **3.** towards the right-hand side ○ *To get to the station, turn right at the traffic lights.* ○ *Children should be taught to look right and left before crossing the road.* ■ *interjection* agreed, OK ○ *Right, so we all meet again at 7 o'clock?*

right-hand /ˌraɪt 'hænd/ *adjective* on the right side

right-handed /ˌraɪt 'hændɪd/ *adjective* using the right hand more often than the left for things like writing and eating

right-wing /ˌraɪt 'wɪŋ/ *adjective* belonging or relating to the conservative political parties

rigid /'rɪdʒɪd/ *adjective* stiff and not bending much

rim /rɪm/ *noun* **1.** the edge of something round, like a wheel or a cup ○ *The rim of the glass is chipped.* **2.** a frame of a pair of spectacles ○ *He wears glasses with steel rims.*

ring /rɪŋ/ *noun* **1.** a round object, especially a piece of jewellery ○ *She has a gold ring in her nose.* ○ *He wears a ring on his little finger.* **2.** a circle of people or things ○ *The teacher asked the children to sit in a ring round her.* **3.** the noise of an electric bell ○ *There was a ring at the door.* **4.** a space where a circus show takes place or where a boxing match is held ○ *The horses galloped round the ring the ring.* ○ *The ringmaster came into the ring with his top hat and whip.* ■ *verb* **1.** to make a sound with a bell ○ *The postman rang the doorbell.* ○ *Is that your phone ringing?* **2.** to telephone someone ○ *He rang me to say he would be late.* ○ *Don't ring tomorrow afternoon – the office will be closed.* ○ *Don't ring me, I'll ring you.* (NOTE: **rings – ringing – rang** /ræŋ/ – **rung** /rʌŋ/) ◇ **to ring a bell** to remind someone of something ○ *The name rings a bell.* ○ *Does the name Arbuthnot ring any bells?*

ring up *phrasal verb* to speak to someone using a telephone

rinse /rɪns/ *verb* to put things covered with soap or dirty things into clean water to remove the soap or the dirt ○ *Rinse the dishes before putting them on the draining board to dry.* ■ *noun* the act of washing something in clean water to get rid of soap ○ *Give your shirt a good rinse.*

riot /'raɪət/ *noun* noisy and usually violent behaviour by a crowd of people ○ *The protesters started a riot.*

rip /rɪp/ *noun* a tear in cloth ○ *He lost the race because of a rip in his sail.* ■ *verb* **1.** to tear something roughly ○ *I ripped my sleeve on a nail.* ○ *She ripped open the parcel to see what he had given her.* ○ *The old bathroom is being ripped out and new units put in.* **2.** to go through something violently ○ *The fire ripped through the building.* (NOTE: **rips – ripping – ripped**)

ripe /raɪp/ *adjective* ready to eat or to be picked ○ *Don't eat that apple – it isn't ripe yet.*

ripple /'rɪp(ə)l/ *noun* a little wave ○ *Even a little stone thrown into the water will make ripples.* ○ *In the desert, the wind creates ripples on the sand.*

rise /raɪz/ *noun* a movement or slope upwards ○ *There is a gentle rise until you get to the top of the hill.* ○ *Salaries are increasing to keep up with the rise in the cost of living.* ○ *The recent rise in interest rates has made mortgages more expensive.* ■ *verb* to go up ○ *The sun always rises in the east.* ○ *The road rises steeply for a few miles.* ○ *Prices have been rising steadily all year.* ○ *If you open the oven door, the cake won't rise properly.* (NOTE: **rises – rising – rose** /rəʊz/ – **risen** /'rɪz(ə)n/)

risk /rɪsk/ *noun* a possible bad result ○ *There is not much risk of rain in August.* ○ *The risk of going blind is very remote.* ○ *There is a financial risk attached to this deal.* ○ *At the risk of looking foolish, I'm going to ask her to come out with me.* ■ *verb* to do something which may possibly harm you ○ *The fireman risked his life to save her.* ○ *He risked all his savings on buying the bookshop.*

risky /'rɪski/ *adjective* which is dangerous (NOTE: **riskier – riskiest**)

rival /'raɪv(ə)l/ *adjective* who competes ○ *Two rival companies are trying to win the contract.* ○ *Is this the rival product you were talking about?* ○ *Simon and I are friends but we play for rival teams.* ■ *noun* a person or a company that competes ○ *Do you know if he has any rivals?* ○ *We keep our prices low to undercut our biggest rival.* ○ *We keep our prices low to compete with our rivals.*

river /'rɪvə/ *noun* a large mass of fresh water which runs across the land and goes into the sea or into a large lake ○ *London is on the River Thames.* ○ *The river is very deep here, so it's dangerous to swim in it.* (NOTE: With names of rivers, you usually say **the River**: *the River Thames*; *the River Amazon*; *the River Nile*.)

road /rəʊd/ *noun* a hard surface which vehicles travel on ○ *The road to York goes directly north from London.* ○ *Drivers must be careful because roads are icy.* ○ *Children are taught to look both ways before crossing the road.* ○ *Our office address is: 26 London Road.* (NOTE: often used in names: *London Road, York Road*, etc., and usually written **Rd**: *London Rd*, etc.)

roar /rɔː/ *verb* to make a deep loud noise ○ *He roared with laughter at the film.* ○ *The lion roared and then attacked.*

roast /rəʊst/ *verb* to cook food over a fire or in an oven ○ *You can either roast pigeons or cook them in a casserole.* ■ *adjective* which has been roasted ○ *What a lovely smell of roast meat!* ○ *We had roast chicken for dinner.*

rob /rɒb/ *verb* to attack and steal from someone (NOTE: **robs – robbing – robbed**)

robber /'rɒbə/ *noun* a person who attacks and steals from someone

robot /'rəʊbɒt/ *noun* a machine which is designed to work like a person automatically

rock /rɒk/ *noun* **1.** a large stone or a large piece of stone ○ *The ship was breaking up on the rocks.* **2.** a hard pink sweet shaped like a stick, often with the name of a town printed in it, bought mainly by tourists ○ *a stick of Brighton rock* **3. rock music** loud popular music with a strong rhythm ○ *Rock is the only music he listens to.* ■ *verb* to move from side to side, or to make something move from side to side ○ *The little boat rocked in the wake of the ferry.* ○ *The explosion rocked the town.*

rocket /'rɒkɪt/ *noun* **1.** a type of space vehicle that looks like a tall tower **2.** a type of firework which flies up into the sky ○ *We stood in the square and watched the rockets lighting up the sky.* **3.** a type of bomb which is shot through space at an enemy ○ *They fired a homemade rocket into the police station.*

rod /rɒd/ *noun* a long stick ○ *You need something rigid like a metal rod to hold the tent upright.*

rode /rəʊd/ past tense of **ride**

role /rəʊl/ *noun* **1.** a part played by someone in a play or film ○ *He plays the role of the king.* **2.** the purpose of someone or something in real life ○ *He played an important role in getting the project off the ground.* (NOTE: Do not confuse with **roll**.)

roll /rəʊl/ *noun* **1.** a tube of something which has been turned over and over on itself ○ *a roll of fax paper* ○ *a roll of toilet paper* or *a toilet roll* **2.** a very small loaf of bread for one person, sometimes cut in half and used to make a sandwich ○ *a bowl of soup and a bread roll* ■ *verb* **1.** to make something go forward by turning it over and over ○ *He rolled the ball to the other player.* **2.** to go forward by turning over and over ○ *The ball rolled down the hill.* ○ *My pound coin has rolled under the piano.* **3.** to make something move on wheels or rollers ○ *The table is fitted with wheels, just roll it into the room.* ○ *The patient was rolled into the operating theatre ten minutes ago.* **4.** to turn something flat over and over ○ *He rolled the poster into a tube.*

roller /'rəʊlə/ *noun* **1.** a heavy round object which rolls, e.g. one used for making lawns or cricket pitches flat ○ *The ground is so bumpy, you'll need a roller to flatten it.* ○ *They used the roller just before the match started.* **2.** a plastic tube used for rolling hair into curls

romantic /rəʊ'mæntɪk/ *adjective* **1.** full of mystery and love ○ *romantic music* ○ *The atmosphere in the restaurant was very romantic.* **2.** used to describe something, often a literary or artistic style, which is based on personal emotions or imagination ○ *His style is too romantic for my liking.* ○ *She has a romantic view of life.*

roof /ruːf/ *noun* **1.** a part of a building which covers it and protects it ○ *The cat walked across the roof of the greenhouse.* ○ *She lives in a little cottage with a thatched roof.* **2.** the top of the inside of the mouth ○ *I burnt the roof of my mouth drinking hot soup.* **3.** the top of a vehicle, e.g. a car, bus or lorry ○ *We had to put the cases on the roof of the car.*

room /ruːm/ *noun* **1.** a part of a building, divided from other parts by walls ○ *The flat has six rooms, plus kitchen and bathroom.* ○ *We want an office with at least four rooms.* **2.** a bedroom in a hotel ○ *Your room is 316 – here's your key.* ○ *His room is just opposite mine.* **3.** space for something ○ *The table is too big – it takes up a lot of room.* ○ *There isn't enough room in the car for six people.* ○

We can't have a piano in our flat – there just isn't enough room.

root /ruːt/ *noun* **1.** a part of a plant which goes down into the ground, and which takes nourishment from the soil ○ *I'm not surprised the plant died – it has hardly any roots.* **2.** the part of a hair or a tooth which goes down into the skin ○ *He pulled her hair out by the roots.*

rope /rəʊp/ *noun* a very thick cord ○ *You'll need a rope to pull the car out of the ditch.* ○ *The burglar climbed down from the balcony on a rope.* ■ *verb* to tie together with a rope ○ *The climbers roped themselves together.* ○ *We roped the sofa onto the roof of the car.*

rose /rəʊz/ *noun* a common garden flower with a strong pleasant smell ○ *He gave her a bunch of red roses.* ○ *These roses have a beautiful scent.* ■ past tense of **rise**

rot /rɒt/ *verb* to decay ○ *The wooden fence is not very old but it has already started to rot.* ◊ **rotten** (NOTE: **rots – rotting – rotted**)

rotate /rəʊˈteɪt/ *verb* to turn round or turn something round an axis like a wheel

rotten /ˈrɒt(ə)n/ *adjective* **1.** decayed ○ *The apple looked nice on the outside, but inside it was rotten.* ○ *Don't walk on that plank, I think it is rotten.* **2.** unpleasant ○ *I had a rotten time at the party – no one would dance with me.* ○ *We had rotten weather on holiday.*

rough /rʌf/ *adjective* **1.** not smooth ○ *Rub down any rough edges with sandpaper.* **2.** not very accurate ○ *I made some rough calculations on the back of an envelope.* **3.** not finished, or with no details ○ *He made a rough draft of the new design.* **4.** not gentle ○ *Don't be rough when you're playing with the puppy.*

roughly /ˈrʌfli/ *adverb* **1.** in a way that is not gentle enough ○ *Don't play so roughly with the children.* ○ *The men threw the boxes of china roughly into the back of their van.* **2.** approximately ○ *There were roughly one hundred people in the audience.* ○ *Ten euros make roughly six pounds.* ○ *The cost of building the new kitchen will be roughly £25,000.*

round /raʊnd/ *adjective* **1.** with a shape like a circle ○ *In Chinese restaurants, you usually sit at round tables.* **2.** with a shape like a sphere ○ *Soccer is played with a round ball, while a Rugby ball is oval.* ○ *People used to believe that the Earth was flat, not round.* ■ *adverb, preposition* **1.** in a circular way or movement ○ *The wheels of the lorry went round and round.* ○ *The Earth goes round the Sun.* ○ *He was the first person to sail round the world single-handed.* ○ *We all sat round the table chatting.* ○ *He ran down the street and disappeared round a corner.* **2.** towards the back ○ *She turned round when he tapped her on the shoulder.* ○ *Don't look round when you're driving on the motorway.* **3.** from one person to another ○ *They passed round some papers for everyone to sign.* ○ *Can you pass the plate of cakes round, please?* **4.** in various places ○ *They spent the afternoon going round the town.*

round up *phrasal verb* to gather people or animals together ○ *The secret police rounded up about fifty suspects and took them off in vans.* ○ *She rounded up the children and took them into the museum.* ○ *The farmer is out in the fields rounding up his sheep.*

roundabout /ˈraʊndəbaʊt/ *noun* **1.** a place where several roads meet, and traffic has to move in a circle ○ *When you get to the next roundabout, turn right.* **2.** a heavy wheel which turns, and which children ride on in a park ○ *The children all ran to get on the roundabout.* ○ *A small child fell from the roundabout and hurt his leg badly.* **3.** (*in a fairground*) a large machine in a fairground which turns round and plays music, usually with horses to sit on which move up and down

route /ruːt/ *noun* a way to be followed to get to a destination ○ *We still have to decide which route we will take.*

routine /ruːˈtiːn/ *noun* the usual, regular way of doing things ○ *He doesn't like his daily routine to be disturbed.* ○ *A change of routine might do you good.* ■

adjective done as part of a regular pattern of activities ○ *He went to the doctor for a routine examination.*

row¹ /rəʊ/ *noun* a line of things, side by side or one after the other ○ *He has a row of cabbages in the garden.* ○ *They pulled down an old house to build a row of shops.* ○ *I want two seats in the front row.*

row² /raʊ/ *noun* (*informal*) **1.** a serious argument ○ *They had a row about who was responsible for the accident.* **2.** a loud noise ○ *Stop making that dreadful row!*

royal /'rɔɪəl/ *adjective* relating to a king or queen

rub /rʌb/ *verb* to move something across the surface of something else ○ *He rubbed his hands together to get them warm.* ○ *These new shoes have rubbed against my heel and given me a blister.* ○ *The cat rubbed herself against my legs.* (NOTE: **rubs – rubbing – rubbed**)

rub out *phrasal verb* to remove a pencil mark with a rubber

rubber /'rʌbə/ *noun* **1.** a strong substance that bends easily, made from the sap of a tropical tree ○ *Car tyres are made of rubber.* ○ *Many years ago, we visited a rubber plantation in Malaysia.* **2.** a piece of rubber used for removing pencil marks ○ *He used a rubber to try to rub out what he had written.*

rubbish /'rʌbɪʃ/ *noun* **1.** waste, things which are no use and are thrown away ○ *We had to step over heaps of rubbish to get to the restaurant.* **2.** worthless nonsense ○ *Have you read his new book? – It's rubbish!* ○ *He's talking rubbish, don't listen to him.* (NOTE: no plural)

rude /ruːd/ *adjective* not polite and likely to offend people ○ *Don't point at people – it's rude.* ○ *The teacher asked who had written rude words on the board.* ○ *He was rude to the teacher.*

rudely /'ruːdli/ *adverb* in a rude way

rug /rʌg/ *noun* **1.** a small carpet ○ *This beautiful rug comes from the Middle East.* **2.** a thick blanket, especially one used when travelling ○ *Put a rug over your knees if you're cold.* ○ *We spread rugs on the grass to have our picnic.*

rugby /'rʌgbi/, **rugby football** /ˌrʌgbi 'fʊtbɔːl/ *noun* a type of football played with an oval ball which is thrown as well as kicked

ruin /'ruːɪn/ *verb* to spoil something completely ○ *The rain spoiled our picnic.*

rule /ruːl/ *noun* a strict order telling people the way to behave ○ *There are no rules that forbid parking here at night.* ○ *According to the rules, your ticket must be paid for two weeks in advance.* ■ *verb* to govern or to control a place or a people ○ *The president rules the country according to very old-fashioned principles.*

ruler /'ruːlə/ *noun* **1.** a person who governs ○ *A ruler should be fair.* ○ *He's the ruler of a small African state.* **2.** a long piece of wood or plastic with measurements marked on it, used for measuring and drawing straight lines ○ *You need a ruler to draw straight lines.*

run /rʌn/ *verb* **1.** to go quickly on foot ○ *When she heard the telephone, she ran upstairs.* ○ *Children must be taught not to run across the road.* ○ *She's running in the 200 metre race.* **2.** (*of buses, trains, etc.*) to be operating ○ *All underground trains are running late because of the accident.* ○ *This bus doesn't run on Sundays.* **3.** (*of vehicles*) to work ○ *He left his car in the street with the engine running.* ○ *My car's not running very well at the moment.* **4.** to direct the way an organisation operates ○ *He runs a chain of shoe shops.* ○ *I want someone to run the sales department for me when I'm away on holiday.* ○ *He runs the local youth club.* ○ *The country is run by the army.* **5.** to drive someone by car ○ *Let me run you to the station.* **6.** (*of liquid*) to flow somewhere ○ *The river runs past our house.* (NOTE: **runs – running – ran – run**) ■ *noun* **1.** the act of going quickly on foot, usually as a sport ○ *She entered for the 10-mile run.* ○ *I always go for a run before breakfast. You must be tired out after that long run.* **2.** a score of 1 in cricket ○ *He made 45 runs before he was out.*

run away *phrasal verb* to escape or to go away fast ○ *They were running away* *from the police.* ○ *She ran away from school when she was 16.* ○ *The youngsters ran away to Paris.*

run into *phrasal verb* **1.** to go into a place fast ○ *She ran into the street, shouting 'Fire!'.* **2.** to go fast and hit something, usually in a vehicle ○ *He didn't look where he was going and ran into an old lady.* ○ *The bus turned the corner too fast and ran into a parked van.* **3.** to amount to something ○ *Costs have run into thousands of pounds.* ○ *Her income runs into five figures.* **4.** to find someone by chance ○ *I ran into him again in a café on the South Bank.*

run out *phrasal verb* to have nothing left of something ○ *The car ran out of petrol on the motorway.* ○ *I must go to the supermarket – we're running out of butter.*

run over *phrasal verb* to knock someone down by hitting them with a vehicle ○ *She was run over by a taxi.* ○ *The car ran over a dog.*

rung /rʌŋ/ *noun* one of the bars on a ladder ○ *Put your foot on the bottom rung to hold the ladder steady.* ■ past participle of **ring**

runner /'rʌnə/ *noun* a person or horse running in a race ○ *My horse came in last of seven runners.* ○ *There are 30,000 runners in the London Marathon.*

running /'rʌnɪŋ/ *adjective* □ **for three days running** one day after another for three days ○ *The company have made a profit for six years or the sixth year running.* ■ *noun* **1.** the activity of running, as a sport or a leisure activity **2.** the action of managing ○ *I now leave the running of the firm to my daughter.* ◇ **to be**

in the running to be a candidate for something ○ *Three people are in the running for the post of chairperson.* ◇ **to be out of the running** to no longer be a candidate for something ○ *She's out of the running for the job in France.*

runway /'rʌnweɪ/ *noun* a track on which planes land and take off at an airport

rural /'rʊərəl/ *adjective* relating to the countryside ○ *Rural roads are usually fairly narrow.* ○ *We live quite close to a town but the country round us still looks very rural.*

rush /rʌʃ/ *noun* a fast movement ○ *There was a rush of hot air when they opened the door.* ○ *There has been a rush to change pounds to euros.* ○ *When the film ended there was a rush for the toilets.* ■ *verb* to hurry, to go forward fast ○ *The ambulance rushed to the accident.* ○ *Crowds of shoppers rushed to the shops on the first day of the sales.*

rustle /'rʌs(ə)l/ *verb* to make a soft noise like dry surfaces rubbing against each other ○ *Her long skirt rustled as she sat down.* ○ *Don't rustle the newspaper when the radio is on, I can't hear it properly.* ■ *noun* the noise of dry leaves or pieces of paper rubbing together ○ *Listen to the rustle of the dry leaves in the hedge.*

rusty /'rʌsti/ *adjective* covered with rust ○ *She tried to cut the string with a pair of rusty old scissors.* ○ *He has a rusty old fridge in his front garden.* (NOTE: **rustier – rustiest**)

rut /rʌt/ *noun* a deep track made in soft earth by the wheels of vehicles ○ *The front wheel of the car was stuck in a deep rut.*

S

s /es/, **S** *noun* the nineteenth letter of the alphabet, between R and T

sack /sæk/ *noun* a large bag made of strong cloth or paper, used for carrying heavy things ○ *He hurt his back lifting up the sack of potatoes.* ■ *verb* to force someone to leave his or her job ○ *He was sacked because he was always late for work.*

sad /sæd/ *adjective* not happy ○ *He's sad because the holidays have come to an end.* ○ *What a sad film – everyone was crying.* ○ *Reading his poems makes me sad.* ○ *It was sad to leave the house for the last time.* ○ *He felt sad watching the boat sail away.* ○ *It's sad that he can't come to see us.* (NOTE: **sadder – saddest**)

saddle /'sæd(ə)l/ *noun* **1.** a rider's seat on a bicycle or motorbike **2.** a rider's seat on a horse ○ *He leapt into the saddle and rode away.*

sadly /'sædli/ *adverb* **1.** in a sad way ○ *She smiled sadly.* **2.** used for saying that something makes you sad ○ *Sadly, John couldn't join us for my birthday party.*

sadness /'sædnəs/ *noun* a feeling of being very unhappy

safe /seɪf/ *adjective* not in danger, or not likely to be hurt ○ *In this cave, we should be safe from the thunderstorm.* ○ *All the children are safe, but the school was burnt down.* ○ *Is it safe to touch this snake?* ■ *noun* a strong box for keeping things such as documents, money or jewels in ○ *Put your valuables in the hotel safe.* ○ *The burglars managed to open the safe.*

safely /'seɪfli/ *adverb* without being hurt ○ *The rescue services succeeded in getting all the passengers safely off the burning train.* ○ *We were shown how to handle explosives safely.* ○ *'Drive safely!' she said as she waved goodbye.*

safety /'seɪfti/ *noun* **1.** the fact of being safe ○ *The police tried to ensure the safety of the public.* ○ *I am worried about the safety of air bags in cars.* **2.** □ **for safety** in order to make something safe ○ *Put the money in the office safe for safety.* ○ *Keep a note of the numbers of your traveller's cheques for safety.*

said /sed/ past tense and past participle of **say**

sail /seɪl/ *noun* a piece of cloth which catches the wind and drives a boat along ○ *The wind dropped so they lowered the sail and started to row.* ○ *They hoisted the sail and set out across the Channel.* ■ *verb* **1.** to travel on water ○ *The ship was sailing towards the rocks.* ○ *We were sailing east.* ○ *He was the first person to sail across the Atlantic single-handed.* ○ *She's planning to sail round the world.* **2.** to leave a harbour ○ *The ferry sails at 12.00.*

sailing /'seɪlɪŋ/ *noun* travel in a ship

sailor /'seɪlə/ *noun* a person who works on a ship ○ *The sailors were washing down the deck of the ship.*

sake /seɪk/ *noun* □ **for the sake of something, for something's sake** for certain reasons or purposes, or because of something ○ *They gave the children sweets, just for the sake of a little peace and quiet.* ○ *The muggers killed the old lady, just for the sake of £20.* □ **for the sake of someone, for someone's sake** because you want to help someone or to please someone ○ *Will you come to the party for my sake?* ○ *The president decided to resign for the sake of the country.* □ **for old times' sake** in order to remember a relationship or activity from the past ○ *We always send them a Christmas card, just for old times' sake.* □ **for heaven's sake, for goodness' sake** used for showing you are annoyed or worried ○ *What's all the fuss? It's* *only a little scratch, for heaven's sake. ○ For goodness' sake try to be quiet, we don't want wake everyone!*

salad /'sæləd/ *noun* a mixture of cold vegetables eaten raw, or a meal that includes such a mixture ○ *a chicken salad sandwich* ○ *We found some ham, tomatoes and lettuce in the fridge, and made ourselves a salad.*

salary /'sæləri/ *noun* payment for work, especially in a professional or office job ○ *She started work at a low salary, but soon went up the salary scale.* ○ *I expect a salary increase as from next month.*

sale /seɪl/ *noun* **1.** the act of selling something ○ *The sale of the house produced £200,000.* ○ *The shop only opened this morning and we've just made our first sale.* **2.** an occasion when things are sold at cheaper prices ○ *There's a sale this week in the department store along the High Street.* ○ *I bought these plates for £1 in a sale.* ○ *The sale price is 50% of the normal price.*

salesperson /'seɪlz,pɜːs(ə)n/ *noun* a person who sells goods in a shop

salt /sɔːlt/ *noun* a white substance that you put on food to make it taste better or put on roads to make snow or ice melt

salute /sə'luːt/ *noun* a movement which expresses respect or recognition, especially the movement of putting your right hand up to touch the side of your forehead ○ *The officer returned the soldier's salute.* ■ *verb* to give a salute to someone ○ *Ordinary soldiers must salute their officers.*

same /seɪm/ *adjective, pronoun* **1.** being, looking, sounding, etc. exactly alike ○ *These two beers taste the same.* ○ *You must get very bored doing the same work every day.* ○ *She was wearing the same dress as me.* ○ *This book is not the same size as that one.* **2.** showing that two or more things are in fact one ○ *They all live in the same street.* ○ *Should we all leave at the same time?* ○ *Our children go to the same school as theirs.*

sample /'sɑːmpəl/ *noun* a small part which is used to show what the whole is like ○ *a sample of the cloth* or *a cloth*

sample ○ *Try a sample of the local cheese.* ○ *He gave a blood sample.* ○ *We interviewed a sample of potential customers.*

sand /sænd/ *noun* a mass of very small bits of rock found on beaches and in the desert ○ *a beach of fine white sand* ○ *the black sand beaches of the Northern coast of New Zealand*

sandal /'sænd(ə)l/ *noun* a light shoe with an open top

sandwich /'sænwɪdʒ/ *noun* a light meal made with two pieces of bread with other food between them ○ *She ordered a cheese sandwich and a cup of coffee.* ○ *What sort of sandwiches do you want to take for your lunch?* ○ *I didn't have a big meal – just a sandwich with some beer in the pub.*

sang /sæŋ/ past tense of **sing**

sank /sæŋk/ past tense of **sink**

sat /sæt/ past tense and past participle of **sit**

satellite /'sætəlaɪt/ *noun* **1.** an object in space which goes round the Earth and sends and receives signals, pictures and data ○ *The signals are transmitted by satellite all round the world.* **2.** an object like a planet which goes round a planet ○ *The Moon is the only satellite of the Earth.*

satisfaction /,sætɪs'fækʃən/ *noun* a feeling of comfort or happiness ○ *After finishing his meal he gave a deep sigh of satisfaction.* ○ *I get no satisfaction from telling you this – you're fired.*

satisfactory /,sætɪs'fækt(ə)ri/ *adjective* good enough, or quite good

satisfied /'sætɪsfaɪd/ *adjective* accepting that something is enough, is good or is correct

satisfy /'sætɪsfaɪ/ *verb* to make someone pleased with what he or she has received or achieved ○ *The council's decision should satisfy most people.* ○ *Our aim is to satisfy our customers.* (NOTE: **satisfies – satisfying – satisfied**)

Saturday /'sætədeɪ/ *noun* the sixth day of the week, the day between Friday and Sunday ○ *He works in a shop, so Saturday is a normal working day for him.* ○ *We go shopping in London most Satur-*

days. ○ *Saturday is the Jewish day of rest.* ○ *Today is Saturday, November 15th.* ○ *The 15th is a Saturday, so the 16th must be a Sunday.* ○ *We arranged to meet up on Saturday.*

sauce /sɔːs/ *noun* a liquid with a particular taste, poured over food ○ *ice cream with chocolate sauce* ○ *We had chicken with a barbecue sauce.* ○ *The waitress put a bottle of tomato sauce on the table.*

saucepan /'sɔːspən/ *noun* a deep metal cooking pan with a lid and a long handle

saucer /'sɔːsə/ *noun* a shallow dish which a cup stands on

sausage /'sɒsɪdʒ/ *noun* a food which is a tube of skin full of a mixture of meat and spices

save /seɪv/ *verb* **1.** to stop something from being damaged ○ *We managed to save most of the paintings from the fire.* **2.** to keep things such as money, food or other articles so that you can use them later ○ *If you save £10 a week, you'll have £520 at the end of a year.* ○ *They save old pieces of bread to give to the ducks in the park.* ○ *He saves bits of string in case he may need them later.* **3.** not to waste something such as time or money ○ *By walking to work, he saves £25 a week in bus fares.* ○ *She took the parcel herself so as to save the cost of postage.* ○ *If you have your car checked regularly it will save you a lot of expense in the future.* ○ *Going by air saves a lot of time.* **4.** to stop someone from being hurt or killed ○ *The firefighters saved six people from the burning house.* ○ *How many passengers were saved when the ferry sank?* **5.** to store information on a computer disk ○ *Don't forget to save your files when you have finished working on them.*

saving /'seɪvɪŋ/ *noun* the act of using less of something ○ *We are aiming for a 10% saving in fuel.* ■ *suffix* which uses less ○ *energy-saving light bulbs*

saw /sɔː/ past tense of **see** ■ *noun* a tool with a long metal blade with teeth along its edge, used for cutting ○ *He was cutting logs with a saw.* ■ *verb* to cut something with a saw ○ *She was sawing wood.* ○ *You will need to saw that piece*

of wood in half. (NOTE: **saws – sawing – sawed – has sawn** /sɔːn/)

say /seɪ/ *verb* **1.** to speak words ○ *What's she saying? – I don't know, I don't understand Dutch.* ○ *She says the fee is £3 per person.* ○ *Don't forget to say 'thank you' after the party.* ○ *The weather forecast said it was going to rain and it did.* ○ *I was just saying that we never see James any more.* **2.** to give information in writing ○ *The letter says that we owe the bank £200.* ○ *The notice says that you are not allowed to walk on the grass.* (NOTE: **says** /sez/ – **saying** – **said** /sed/)

saying /'seɪɪŋ/ *noun* a phrase which is often used to describe an aspect of everyday life

scale /skeɪl/ *noun* **1.** the size of a smaller form of something compared to the real size ○ *a map with a scale of 1 to 100,000* ○ *a scale model of the new town centre development* ○ *The architect's design is drawn to scale.* **2.** a measuring system in which there are several levels ○ *The Richter scale is used to measure earthquakes.*

scar /skɑː/ *noun* a mark left on the skin after a wound has healed ○ *He still has the scars of his operation.* ■ *verb* **1.** to leave a mark on the skin after a wound has healed ○ *His arm was scarred as a result of the accident.* **2.** to affect someone's feelings badly ○ *The bullying she received at school has scarred her for life.* (NOTE: **scars – scarring – scarred**)

scarce /skeəs/ *adjective* if something is scarce, there is much less of it than you need ○ *This happened at a period when food was scarce.* ○ *Good designers are getting scarce.*

scare /skeə/ *verb* to make someone feel fear ○ *The thought of travelling alone across Africa scares me.* ○ *She was scared by the spider in the bathroom.* ■ *noun* a fright ○ *What a scare you gave me – jumping out at me in the dark like that!*

scared /skeəd/ *adjective* feeling or showing fear ○ *Don't be scared – the snake is harmless.* ○ *She was too scared to answer the door.* ○ *I'm scared at the* *idea of driving in London's rush-hour traffic.* ○ *She looked round with a scared expression.*

scarf /skɑːf/ *noun* a long piece of cloth which is worn round your neck to keep yourself warm ○ *Take your scarf – it's snowing.* (NOTE: The plural is **scarves** /skɑːvz/.)

scatter /'skætə/ *verb* **1.** to throw something in various places ○ *The crowd scattered flowers all over the path.* **2.** to run in different directions ○ *When the police arrived, the children scattered.*

scene /siːn/ *noun* **1.** a place where something has happened ○ *It took the ambulance ten minutes to get to the scene of the accident.* ○ *A photographer was at the scene to record the ceremony.* **2.** a short part of a play or film ○ *Did you like the scene where he is trying to climb up the skyscraper?* ○ *It was one of the funniest scenes I have ever seen.*

scenery /'siːnəri/ *noun* **1.** the features of the countryside ○ *the beautiful scenery of the Lake District* **2.** the objects and backgrounds on a theatre stage that make it look like a real place ○ *They lowered the scenery onto the stage.* ○ *In between the acts all the scenery has to be changed.* (NOTE: no plural)

scent /sent/ *noun* **1.** a pleasant smell of a particular type ○ *the scent of roses in the cottage garden* **2.** perfume ○ *That new scent of yours makes me sneeze.* (NOTE: Do not confuse with **cent, sent.**)

sceptical /'skeptɪk(ə)l/ *adjective* thinking that something is probably not true or good ○ *You seem sceptical about his new plan.* ○ *I'm sceptical of the need for these changes.*

scheme /skiːm/ *noun* a plan for making something work ○ *She joined the company pension scheme.* ○ *He has thought up some scheme for making money very quickly.*

school /skuːl/ *noun* **1.** a place where students, usually children, are taught ○ *Our little boy is four, so he'll be going to school this year.* ○ *Some children start school younger than that.* ○ *What did the children do at school today?* ○ *When*

he was sixteen, he left school and joined the army. ○ *Which school did you go to?* **2.** a section of a college or university ○ *The school of medicine is one of the largest in the country.* ○ *She's studying at law school.* ■ *verb* to train someone in a particular skill

science /'saɪəns/ *noun* the study of natural physical things ○ *She took a science course* or *studied science.* ○ *We have a new science teacher this term.* ○ *He has a master's degree in marine science.*

scientific /ˌsaɪən'tɪfɪk/ *adjective* relating to science ○ *We employ hundreds of people in scientific research.* ○ *He's the director of a scientific institute.*

scientist /'saɪəntɪst/ *noun* a person who studies a science, often doing research ○ *Scientists have not yet found a cure for the common cold.* ○ *Space scientists are examining the photographs of Mars.*

scissors /'sɪzəz/ *plural noun* a tool for cutting things such as paper and cloth, made of two blades attached in the middle, with handles with holes for the thumb and fingers ○ *These scissors aren't very sharp.* ○ *Have you got a pair of scissors I can borrow?*

scoop /skuːp/ *noun* **1.** a deep round spoon with a short handle, for serving soft food such as ice cream ○ *You must wash the scoop each time you use it.* **2.** a portion of soft food such as ice cream ○ *I'll have one scoop of strawberry and one scoop of vanilla, please.* ■ *verb* to lift something or someone up in a single quick movement ○ *She scooped up the babies into her arms and ran upstairs.* ○ *He scooped all the newspapers off the floor.*

scooter /'skuːtə/ *noun* **1.** a child's two-wheeled vehicle which is pushed along with one foot while the other foot is on the board **2.** a vehicle like a small motorbike with a platform for the feet ○ *She dodged through the traffic on her scooter.*

score /skɔː/ *noun* the number of goals or points made in a match ○ *The final score in the rugby match was 22–10.* ○ *I didn't see the beginning of the match –*

what's the score? ■ *verb* to make a goal or point in a match ○ *They scored three goals in the first twenty minutes.* ○ *She scored sixty-five!*

Scot /skɒt/ *noun* a person from Scotland

Scotch /skɒtʃ/ *adjective* used for referring to some things, especially food and drink, from Scotland

Scotland /'skɒtlənd/ *noun* a country to the north of England, forming part of the United Kingdom ○ *He was brought up in Scotland.* ○ *Scotland's most famous export is whisky.*

Scots /skɒts/ *adjective* Scottish ○ *'Not proven' is a decision in Scots Law.*

Scottish /'skɒtɪʃ/ *adjective* relating to Scotland

scramble /'skræmbəl/ *verb* **1.** to climb using your hands and knees ○ *He scrambled up the steep bank.* **2.** to hurry to do something ○ *They scrambled to get a seat.*

scrap /skræp/ *noun* **1.** a little piece ○ *a scrap of paper* ○ *There isn't a scrap of evidence against him.* ○ *She is collecting scraps of cloth to make a quilt.* **2.** waste materials ○ *to sell a car for scrap* ○ *The scrap value of the car is £200.* ■ *verb* **1.** to throw something away as useless ○ *They had to scrap 10,000 faulty spare parts.* **2.** to give up or stop working on a plan ○ *We've scrapped our plans to go to Greece.* (NOTE: **scraps – scrapping – scrapped**)

scrape /skreɪp/ *verb* **1.** to scratch something with a hard object which is pulled across a surface ○ *She scraped the paint off the door.* ○ *He fell off his bike and scraped his knee on the pavement.* **2.** to remove something from the surface of something ○ *She scraped the paint off the door.*

scratch /skrætʃ/ *noun* **1.** a long wound on the skin ○ *Put some antiseptic on the scratches on your arms.* **2.** a long mark made by a sharp point ○ *I will never be able to cover up the scratches on the car door.* ■ *verb* **1.** to make a long wound on the skin ○ *His legs were scratched by the bushes along the path.* **2.** to make a mark on something with a sharp point ○ *I must touch up the car where it has*

been scratched. **3.** to rub a part of the body which itches with your fingernails ○ *He scratched his head as he wondered what to do next.* ○ *Stop scratching – it will make your rash worse!*

scream /skriːm/ *noun* a loud cry of pain or excitement ○ *He let out a scream of pain.* ■ *verb* to make a loud cry of pain or excitement ○ *People on the third floor were screaming for help.* ○ *They screamed with pain.* ○ *She screamed at the class to stop singing.*

screen /skriːn/ *noun* **1.** a flat surface which acts as protection against something, e.g. fire or noise ○ *a screen decorated with flowers and birds* ○ *The hedge acts as a screen against the noise from the motorway.* **2.** a flat glass surface on which a picture is shown ○ *a computer screen* ○ *a TV screen* ○ *I'll call the information up on the screen.* **3.** a flat white surface on which things such as films or slides are shown ○ *a cinema complex with four screens* ○ *We'll put up the screen on the stage.* ■ *verb* to show a film in a cinema or on TV ○ *Tonight's film will be screened half an hour later than advertised.*

screw /skruː/ *noun* a type of nail which you twist to make it go into a hard surface ○ *I need some longer screws to go through this thick plank.* ○ *The plate was fixed to the door with brass screws.* ■ *verb* **1.** to attach something with screws ○ *The picture was screwed to the wall.* **2.** to attach something by twisting ○ *He filled up the bottle and screwed on the top.* ○ *Screw the lid on tightly.*

scribble /'skrɪb(ə)l/ *verb* **1.** to make marks which don't have any meaning ○ *The kids have scribbled all over their bedroom walls.* **2.** to write something hurriedly and badly ○ *She scribbled a few notes in the train.*

scrub /skrʌb/ *verb* to clean something by rubbing it with a brush ○ *a well-scrubbed kitchen table* ○ *Scrub your fingernails to get rid of the dirt.* (NOTE: **scrubs – scrubbing – scrubbed**) ■ *noun* **1.** an area of land with a few small bushes ○ *They walked for miles through the scrub until they came to a river.* **2.**

the action of scrubbing ○ *After a game of rugby you will need a good scrub.*

sculpture /'skʌlptʃə/ *noun* a piece of art that is a figure carved out of stone or wood or made out of metal

sea /siː/ *noun* an area of salt water between continents or islands which is large but not as large as an ocean ○ *Swimming in the sea is more exciting than swimming in a river.* ○ *The sea's too rough for the ferries to operate.* ○ *His friends own a house by the sea.* ○ *The North Sea separates Britain from Denmark and Germany.*

seagull /'siːgʌl/ *noun* a large white sea bird

seal /siːl/ *noun* a large animal with short smooth fur which eats fish and lives near or in the sea ■ *verb* to close something tightly ○ *a box carefully sealed with sticky tape*

search /sɜːtʃ/ *noun* the action of trying to find something ○ *Our search of the flat revealed nothing.* ○ *They carried out a search for the missing children.* ○ *I did a quick search on the Internet for references to Proust.* ■ *verb* **1.** to examine something or someone very carefully ○ *The police searched the house but didn't find any weapons.* ○ *She was stopped and searched by customs.* **2.** to look carefully to try to find something ○ *The police searched the house for weapons.* □ **to search for someone** *or* **something** to try to find someone or something ○ *The police searched for the missing children.* ○ *I searched the Internet for references to Ireland.*

seaside /'siːdsaɪd/ *noun* an area near the sea where people go to have a holiday

season /'siːz(ə)n/ *noun* **1.** one of four parts of a year ○ *Autumn is her favourite season.* **2.** a part of the year when something usually happens ○ *The tourist season is very long here – from March to September.* ○ *The football season lasts from September to May.* ○ *London is very crowded during the school holiday season.*

seat /siːt/ *noun* a chair or similar object which you sit on ○ *He was sitting in the* driver's seat. ○ *Can we have two seats in the front row?* ○ *Our kitchen chairs have wooden seats.* ○ *Bicycle seats are narrow.* ◇ **to take a seat** to sit down ○ *Please take a seat, the dentist will see you in a few minutes.* ○ *Please take your seats, the play is about to begin.* ○ *All the seats on the bus were taken so I had to stand.*

second /'sekənd/ *noun* **1.** one of sixty parts which make up a minute ○ *I'll give you ten seconds to get out of my room.* ○ *They say the bomb will go off in twenty seconds.* **2.** a very short time ○ *Please wait a second.* ○ *Wait here, I'll be back in a second.* **3.** the thing which is number 2 in a series ○ *Today is the second of March* or *March the second (March 2nd).* ○ *The Great Fire of London took place when Charles the Second (Charles II) was king.* (NOTE: In dates **second** is usually written **2nd** or **2**: *August 2nd, 1932, 2 July, 1666* (American style is **July 2, 1666**), say 'the second of July' or 'July the second' (American style is 'July second'). With names of kings and queens **second** is usually written **II**: *Queen Elizabeth II* (say 'Queen Elizabeth the Second').) ■ *adjective* **1.** coming after the first and before the third ○ *February is the second month of the year.* ○ *It's his second birthday next week.* ○ *Women's clothes are on the second floor.* ○ *That's the second time the telephone has rung while we're eating.* **2.** next after the longest, best, tallest etc. (*followed by a superlative*) ○ *This is the second longest bridge in the world.* ○ *He's the second highest paid member of staff.*

secondary /'sekənd(ə)ri/ *adjective* less important

second-class /,sekənd 'klɑːs/ *adjective, adverb* **1.** less expensive and less comfortable than first-class ○ *I find second-class hotels are perfectly adequate.* ○ *We always travel second-class because it is cheaper.* **2.** less expensive and slower than the first-class postal service ○ *A second-class letter is cheaper than a first-class.* ○ *Send it second-class if it is not urgent.*

secrecy /'si:krəsi/ *noun* the fact of being secret or keeping something secret

secret /'si:krət/ *adjective* not known about by other people ○ *There is a secret door into the cellar.* ■ *noun* something which other people do not know about ○ *Have I told you my secret?*

secretary /'sekrət(ə)ri/ *noun* a person who does work such as writing letters, answering the phone and filing documents for someone (NOTE: The plural is **secretaries**.)

secretive /'si:krətɪv/ *adjective* liking to keep things secret ○ *She's very secretive about her holiday plans.*

secretly /'si:krətli/ *adverb* without anyone knowing

section /'sekʃən/ *noun* a part of something which, when joined to other parts, makes up a whole ○ *the brass section of the orchestra* ○ *the financial section of the newspaper* ○ *He works in a completely different section of the organisation.*

sector /'sektə/ *noun* **1.** a part of the economy or of the business organisation of a country ○ *All sectors of industry suffered from the rise in the exchange rate.* ○ *Computer technology is a booming sector of the economy.* **2.** a part of a circle between two lines drawn from the centre to the outside edge ○ *The circle had been divided into five sectors.*

secure /sɪ'kjʊə/ *adjective* firmly fixed ○ *Don't step on that plank, it's not secure.* ■ *verb* to be successful in getting something important ○ *He secured the support of a big bank.* ○ *They secured a valuable new contract.*

securely /sɪ'kjʊəli/ *adverb* in a secure way

security /sɪ'kjʊəriti/ *noun* **1.** safety or protection against harm ○ *There were worries about security during the prince's visit.* ○ *Security in this office is nil.* ○ *Security guards patrol the factory at night.* **2.** a thing given to someone who has lent you money and which is returned when the loan is repaid ○ *He uses his house as security for a loan.* ○ *The bank lent him £20,000 without security.*

see /si:/ *verb* **1.** to use your eyes to notice something ○ *Can you see that tree in the distance?* ○ *They say eating carrots helps you to see in the dark.* ○ *We ran because we could see the bus coming.* **2.** to watch something such as a film ○ *I don't want to go to the cinema this week, I've seen that film twice already.* ○ *We saw the football match on TV.* **3.** to understand something ○ *I can't see why they need to borrow so much money.* ○ *You must see that it's very important for everything to be ready on time.* ○ *Don't you see that they're trying to trick you?* ○ *I see – you want me to lend you some money.* **4.** to visit someone, e.g. a lawyer or doctor ○ *If your tooth aches that badly you should see a dentist.* ○ *He went to see his bank manager to arrange a mortgage.* (NOTE: **sees – seeing – saw** /sɔ:/ – **seen** /si:n/)

see off *phrasal verb* to go to the airport or station with someone who is leaving on a journey

see through *phrasal verb* **1.** to see from one side of something to the other ○ *I can't see through the window – it's so dirty.* **2.** not to be tricked by something or someone ○ *Won't they quickly see through such a poor excuse?* ○ *He pretended he was helping me, but I soon saw through him.*

see to *phrasal verb* to arrange something or make sure that something is done

seed /si:d/ *noun* a part of a plant which is formed after the flowers die and from which a new plant will grow ○ *a packet of carrot seed* ○ *Sow the seeds in fine earth.* ○ *Can you eat pumpkin seeds?*

seek /si:k/ *verb* to look for someone or something (*formal*) ○ *The police are seeking a group of teenagers who were in the area when the attack took place.* (NOTE: **seeks – seeking – sought** /sɔ:t/ – **has sought**)

seem /si:m/ *verb* to give the appearance of being something ○ *She seems to like* or *It seems that she likes her new job. Everyone seemed to be having a good time at the party.* ○ *The new boss seems very nice.* ○ *It seems to me that the parcel has gone to the wrong house.* ○ *It* *seemed strange to us that no one answered the phone.*

seize /siːz/ *verb* to grab something and hold it tight ○ *She seized the bag of sweets in both hands and would not let go.*

seldom /'seldəm/ *adverb* not often (NOTE: Note the word order when **seldom** is at the beginning of a phrase: *you seldom hear* or *seldom do you hear*)

select /sɪ'lekt/ *verb* to choose something or someone carefully ○ *She looked carefully at the shelves before selecting a book.* ○ *He was selected for the England squad.* ○ *Selected items are reduced by 25%.*

selection /sɪ'lekʃən/ *noun* **1.** a range ○ *There is a huge selection of hats to choose from.* **2.** a thing which has or things which have been chosen ○ *a selection of our product line* ○ *a selection of French cheeses*

self /self/ *noun* your own person or character ○ *She was ill for some time, but now she's her old self again.* ○ *She's not her usual happy self today – I think she's got something on her mind.* (NOTE: The plural is **selves**.)

selfish /'selfɪʃ/ *adjective* doing things only for yourself and not for other people

sell /sel/ *verb* **1.** to give something to someone for money ○ *He sold his house to my father.* ○ *She sold him her bicycle for next to nothing.* ○ *We managed to sell the car for £500.* ○ *The shop sells vegetables but not meat.* **2.** to be sold ○ *Those packs sell for £25 a dozen.* ○ *Her latest book is selling very well.* (NOTE: **sells – selling – sold** /səʊld/)

sell off *phrasal verb* to sell goods quickly and cheaply to get rid of them ○ *At the end of the day the market stalls sell off their fruit and vegetables very cheaply.*

sell out *phrasal verb* **1.** to sell every item of a particular type ○ *Have you got the dress in a size 12? – No, I'm afraid we've sold out.* ○ *We're selling out of these hats fast.* **2.** *US* to sell a business

to someone ○ *He sold out to his partner and retired.* **3.** to give in to a group of influential people ○ *The environmental group has accused the government of selling out to the oil companies.*

sell up *phrasal verb* to sell a business ○ *He sold up and retired.*

semicolon /ˌsemi'kəʊlɒn/ *noun* a punctuation mark (;) used to separate two parts of a sentence and also used to show a pause

semi-final /ˌsemi 'faɪn(ə)l/ *noun* one of the last two matches in a competition, the winners of which go into the final game

senate /'senət/ *noun* the upper house of the legislative body in some countries ○ *She was first elected to the Senate in 2001.*

senator /'senətə/ *noun* a member of a senate (NOTE: written with a capital letter when used as a title: *Senator Jackson*)

send /send/ *verb* **1.** to make someone or something go from one place to another ○ *My mother sent me to the baker's to buy some bread.* ○ *I was sent home from school because I had a headache.* ○ *He sent the ball into the net.* ○ *The firm is sending him out to Australia for six months.* **2.** to use the postal services to get something to someone ○ *The office sends 200 Christmas cards every year.* ○ *Send me a postcard when you get to Russia.* ○ *Send the letter by air if you want it to arrive next week.* ○ *Send your donations to the following address.* (NOTE: **sends – sending – sent** /sent/)

send for *phrasal verb* to ask someone to come

senior /'siːniə/ *adjective* **1.** older ○ *the senior members of the tribe* **2.** more important, e.g. in rank ○ *A sergeant is senior to a corporal.* ○ *My senior colleagues do not agree with me.*

sensation /sen'seɪʃ(ə)n/ *noun* **1.** a general feeling ○ *I felt a curious sensation as if I had been in the room before.* **2.** a physical feeling ○ *She had a burning sensation in her arm.* **3.** a thing or person that causes great excitement ○ *The* *new ballet was the sensation of the season.*

sense /sens/ *noun* **1.** one of the five ways in which you notice something (sight, hearing, smell, taste, touch) ○ *He may be 93, but he still has all his senses.* ○ *His senses had been dulled by the drugs he was taking.* ○ *Dogs have a good sense of smell.* **2.** a meaning ○ *He was using 'bear' in the sense of 'to carry'.* **3.** the fact of being sensible ○ *At least someone showed some sense and tried to calm the situation.* ○ *She didn't have the sense to refuse.* ○ *I thought Patrick would have had more sense than that.*

senseless /'sensləs/ *adjective* done for no good reason ○ *a senseless attack on a little old lady* ○ *It's senseless to buy clothes you don't need, just because they are in the sales.*

sensible /'sensɪb(ə)l/ *adjective* **1.** showing good judgment and wisdom ○ *Staying indoors was the sensible thing to do.* ○ *Try and be sensible for once!* **2.** (*of shoes*) strong and comfortable for walking, rather than fashionable

sensitive /'sensɪtɪv/ *adjective* **1.** easily upset ○ *She's a very sensitive young woman.* ○ *Some actors are extremely sensitive to criticism.* **2.** which measures very accurately ○ *a very sensitive light meter*

sent /sent/ past tense and past participle of **send**

sentence /'sentəns/ *noun* **1.** a series of words put together to make a complete statement, usually ending in a full stop ○ *I don't understand the second sentence in your letter.* ○ *Begin each sentence with a capital letter.* **2.** a judgment of a court ○ *He was given a six-month prison sentence.* ○ *The judge passed sentence on the accused.* ■ *verb* to give someone an official legal punishment ○ *She was sentenced to three weeks in prison.* ○ *He was sentenced to death for murder.*

separate¹ /'sep(ə)rət/ *adjective* not together or attached ○ *They are in separate rooms.* ○ *The house has one bathroom with a separate toilet.* ○ *The dogs were kept separate from the other pets.*

○ *Can you give us two separate invoices?*

separate² /'sepəreɪt/ *verb* **1.** to divide people or things ○ *The employees are separated into permanent and temporary staff.* ○ *The teacher separated the class into two groups.* **2.** to keep people or things apart ○ *The police tried to separate the two gangs.* ○ *Is it possible to separate religion and politics?*

separately /'sep(ə)rətli/ *adverb* individually, rather than together or as a group

September /sep'tembə/ *noun* the ninth month of the year, between August and October ○ *September 3* ○ *The weather is usually good in September.* ○ *Her birthday is in September.* ○ *Today is September 3rd.* ○ *We always try to take a short holiday in September.* (NOTE: **September 3rd** or **September 3**: say 'September the third' or 'the third of September' or in US English 'September third'.)

sequence /'siːkwəns/ *noun* a series of things which happen or follow one after the other ○ *The sequence of events which led to the accident.*

sergeant /'sɑːdʒənt/ *noun* a non-commissioned officer in the army, or an officer of low rank in the police (NOTE: also used as a title before a surname: *Sergeant Jones*)

serial /'sɪəriəl/ *noun* a story that is broadcast on TV or radio in separate parts ○ *an Australian police serial* (NOTE: Do not confuse with **cereal**.)

series /'sɪəriːz/ *noun* **1.** a group of things which come one after the other in order ○ *We had a series of phone calls from the bank.* **2.** TV or radio programmes which are broadcast at the same time each week ○ *There's a new wildlife series starting this week.* (NOTE: The plural is **series**.)

serious /'sɪəriəs/ *adjective* **1.** not funny or not joking ○ *a very serious play* ○ *He's such a serious little boy.* ○ *Stop laughing – it's very serious.* ○ *He's very serious about the proposal.* ○ *The doctor's expression was very serious.* **2.** important and possibly dangerous ○ *There* was a serious accident on the motorway. ○ The storm caused serious damage. ○ There's no need to worry – it's nothing serious. **3.** carefully planned ○ The management is making serious attempts to improve working conditions.

seriously /'sɪəriəsli/ adverb **1.** in a serious way ○ She should laugh more – she mustn't always take things so seriously. **2.** to a great extent ○ The cargo was seriously damaged by water. ○ Her mother is seriously ill.

seriousness /'sɪːriəsnəs/ noun the fact of being serious

servant /'sɜːvənt/ noun a person who is paid to work for a family ○ They employ two servants in their London home. ○ Get it yourself – I'm not your servant!

serve /sɜːv/ verb **1.** to give food or drink to someone ○ She served the soup in small bowls. ○ Just take a plate and serve yourself. ○ Has everyone been served? **2.** to go with a dish ○ Fish is served with a white sauce. ○ You usually serve red wine with meat. **3.** to help a customer, e.g. in a shop ○ Are you being served? ○ The manager served me himself. ○ Will you serve this lady next, please? **4.** (in games like tennis) to start the game by hitting the ball ○ She served two faults in a row. ○ He served first.

service /'sɜːvɪs/ noun **1.** a facility which the public needs ○ Our train service to London is very bad. ○ The postal service is efficient. ○ The bus service is very irregular. ○ The hotel provides a laundry service. **2.** the act of serving or helping someone in a shop or restaurant ○ The food is good here, but the service is very slow. ○ The bill includes an extra 10% for service. ○ Is the service included? ○ The bill does not include service. **3.** a regular check of a machine ○ The car has had its 20,000-kilometre service. **4.** a group of people working together ○ the ambulance service **5.** a time when you work for a company or organisation or in the armed forces ○ Did he enjoy his service in the army? ○ She did six years' service in the police. ○ He was awarded a gold watch for his long service to the company. ○ He saw

service in Northern Ireland. **6.** a religious ceremony ○ My mother never misses the nine o'clock service on Sundays. **7.** (in games like tennis) the action of hitting the ball first ○ She has a very powerful service. ■ verb to keep a machine in good working order ○ The car needs to be serviced every six months.

session /'seʃ(ə)n/ noun the time when an activity is taking place ○ All these long sessions in front of the computer screen are ruining my eyesight.

set /set/ noun a group of things which go together, which are used together or which are sold together ○ He carries a set of tools in the back of his car. ○ The six chairs are sold as a set. ■ verb **1.** to put something in a special place ○ She set the plate of biscuits down on the table next to her chair. **2.** to fix something ○ When we go to France we have to set our watches to French time. ○ The price of the new computer has been set at £500. **3.** to make something happen ○ He went to sleep smoking a cigarette and set the house on fire. ○ All the prisoners were set free. ○ I had been worried about her, but her letter set my mind at rest. **4.** when the sun sets, it goes down ○ The sun rises in the east and sets in the west. (NOTE: **sets – setting – set**) ■ adjective ready ○ We're all set for a swim. ○ My bags are packed and I'm all set to leave. ○ Her latest novel is set to become the best-selling book of the year.

set off phrasal verb **1.** to begin a trip ○ We're setting off for Germany tomorrow. ○ They all set off on a long walk after lunch. **2.** to start something happening ○ They set off a bomb in the shopping centre. ○ If you touch the wire it will set off the alarm. ○ Being in the same room as a cat will set off my asthma.

set out phrasal verb to begin a journey ○ The hunters set out to cross the mountains. ○ We have to set out early tomorrow.

settee /se'tiː/ noun a long seat with a soft back where several people can sit

setting /'setɪŋ/ *noun* the background for a story ○ *The setting for the story is Hong Kong in 1935.*

settle /'set(ə)l/ *verb* **1.** to arrange or agree something ○ *Well, I'm glad everything's settled at last.* ○ *Have you settled the title for the new film yet?* ○ *It took six months of negotiation for the union and management to settle their differences.* **2.** to place yourself in a comfortable position ○ *She switched on the television and settled in her favourite armchair.* **3.** to fall to the ground, or to the bottom of something, gently ○ *Wait for the dust to settle.* ○ *A layer of mud settled at the bottom of the pond.*

settle down *phrasal verb* **1.** to place yourself in a comfortable position ○ *After dinner, she likes to settle down in a comfortable chair with a good book.* **2.** to change to a calmer way of life without many changes of house or much travelling ○ *He has worked all over the world, and doesn't seem ready to settle down.* ○ *She had lots of boyfriends, and then got married and settled down in Surrey.*

seven /'sev(ə)n/ *noun* the number 7 ○ *There are only seven children in his class.* ○ *She's seven (years old) next week.* ○ *The train is supposed to leave at seven (o'clock).*

seventeen /ˌsev(ə)n'tiːn/ *noun* the number 17 ○ *He will be seventeen (years old) next month.* ○ *The train leaves at seventeen sixteen (17.16).*

seventeenth /ˌsev(ə)n'tiːnθ/ *adjective, noun* number 17 in a series ○ *Today is October the seventeenth or the seventeenth of October (October 17th).* ○ *Q is the seventeenth letter of the alphabet.* ○ *It's his seventeenth birthday next week.* ○ *He came seventeenth out of thirty.* ■ *noun* the thing that is number 17 in a series ○ *Today is October the seventeenth or the seventeenth of October (October 17th).*

seventh /'sevənθ/ *adjective, noun* number 7 in a series ○ *His office is on the seventh floor.* ○ *It's her seventh birthday on Saturday.* ○ *What is the seventh letter of the alphabet?* ○ *She came seventh in the race.* ■ *noun* **1.** the thing that is number 7 in a series ○ *Today is June the seventh or the seventh of June (June 7th).* **2.** one of seven equal parts

seventieth /'sevəntiəθ/ *adjective* number 70 in a series ○ *It's his seventieth birthday next week* ○ *He came seventieth out of a hundred.* ■ *noun* the thing that is number 70 in a series

seventy /'sev(ə)nti/ *noun* the number 70 ○ *She will be seventy (years old) on Tuesday.* ○ *That shirt cost him more than seventy dollars.*

several /'sev(ə)rəl/ *adjective, pronoun* more than a few, but not a lot ○ *Several buildings were damaged in the storm.* ○ *We've met several times.* ○ *Several of the students are going to Italy.* ○ *Most of the guests left early but several stayed on till midnight.*

severe /sɪ'vɪə/ *adjective* **1.** very strict ○ *He was very severe with any child who did not behave.* ○ *Discipline in the school was severe.* **2.** having a very bad effect ○ *The government imposed severe financial restrictions on importers.* ○ *The severe weather has closed several main roads.* (NOTE: **severer – severest**)

severely /sɪ'vɪəli/ *adverb* **1.** strictly ○ *She was severely punished for being late.* **2.** to a great extent ○ *a severely injured survivor* ○ *Train services have been severely affected by snow.*

sew /səʊ/ *verb* to attach, make or repair something by using a needle and thread (NOTE: Do not confuse with **sow**. Note also: **sews – sewing – sewed – sewn** /səʊn/.)

sex /seks/ *noun* **1.** one of two groups, male and female, into which animals and plants can be divided ○ *They've had a baby, but I don't know what sex it is.* **2.** physical activity which, between a man and a woman, could cause a baby to develop ○ *a film full of sex and violence* ○ *Sex was the last thing on her mind.*

sexual /'sekʃuəl/ *adjective* relating to the activity of having sex ○ *Their relationship was never sexual.*

sexually /'sekʃuəli/ *adverb* in a sexual way

shabby /'ʃæbi/ *adjective* (*of clothes*) used about clothes which are of poor quality or look worn out ○ *He wore a shabby coat with two buttons missing.*

shade /ʃeɪd/ *noun* **1.** a variety of a particular colour ○ *Her hat is a rather pretty shade of green.* **2.** a dark place which is not in the sun ○ *Let's try and find some shade – it's too hot in the sun.* ○ *The sun's so hot that we'll have to sit in the shade.*

shadow /'ʃædəʊ/ *noun* a dark place behind an object where light is cut off by the object ○ *In the evening, the trees cast long shadows across the lawn.* ○ *She saw his shadow move down the hall.* ○ *They rested for a while, in the shadow of a large tree.*

shaft /ʃɑːft/ *noun* **1.** the long handle of a tool such as a spade ○ *The shaft of the spade was so old it snapped in two.* **2.** a thin beam of light ○ *Tiny particles of dust were dancing in a shaft of sunlight.* **3.** a deep hole connecting one place to another ○ *The shaft had become blocked with rubbish.*

shake /ʃeɪk/ *verb* to move something from side to side or up and down ○ *Shake the bottle before pouring.* ○ *The house shakes every time a train goes past.* ○ *His hand shook as he opened the envelope.* (NOTE: **shakes – shaking – shook /ʃʊk/ – shaken**)

shall /ʃəl, ʃæl/ *modal verb* **1.** used to make the future tense ○ *We shall be out on Saturday evening.* ○ *I shan't say anything – I shall keep my mouth shut!* ○ *Tomorrow we shan't be home until after 10 o'clock.* **2.** used to show a suggestion ○ *Shall we open the windows?* ○ *Shall I give them a ring?* (NOTE: **shall** is mainly used with **I** and **we**. The negative is **shan't** /ʃɑːnt/. The past tense is **should**, **should not** usually **shouldn't**.)

shallow /'ʃæləʊ/ *adjective* not far from top to bottom ○ *Children were playing in the shallow end of the pool.* ○ *The river is so shallow in summer that you can walk across it.*

shame /ʃeɪm/ *noun* the feeling you have when you know you have done something bad or wrong ○ *She went bright red with shame.* ○ *To my shame, I did nothing to help.*

shampoo /ʃæm'puː/ *noun* **1.** liquid soap for washing your hair or for washing things such as carpets or cars **2.** the action of washing the hair ○ *She went to the hairdresser's for a shampoo.*

shape /ʃeɪp/ *noun* the form of how something looks ○ *A design in the shape of a letter S.* ○ *The old table was a funny shape.* ■ *verb* to make into a certain form ○ *He shaped the pastry into the form of a little boat.*

shaped /ʃeɪpt/ *adjective* with a certain shape

share /ʃeə/ *noun* a part of something that is divided between two or more people ○ *Did he get his share of the prize?* ○ *Take your share of the cake and leave me the rest.* ○ *She should have paid her share of the food bill.* ○ *There's a lot of work to do, so everyone must do their share.* ■ *verb* **1.** also **share out** to divide up something among several people ○ *Let's share the bill.* ○ *In her will, her money was shared out among her sons.* **2.** to use something which someone else also uses ○ *We share an office.* ○ *We shared a taxi to the airport.*

shark /ʃɑːk/ *noun* a large dangerous fish which lives in the sea and can kill people

sharp /ʃɑːp/ *adjective* **1.** with an edge or point which can easily cut or pass through something ○ *For injections, a needle has to have a very sharp point.* ○ *The beach is covered with sharp stones.* ○ *This knife is useless – it isn't sharp enough.* **2.** sudden and great ○ *There was a sharp drop in interest rates.* ○ *The road makes a sharp right-hand bend.* ○ *He received a sharp blow on the back of his head.* ○ *We had a sharp frost last night.* **3.** bitter ○ *Lemons have a very sharp taste.* **4.** quick to notice things ○ *He has a sharp sense of justice.* ○ *She has a sharp eye for a bargain.* ○ *He's pretty sharp at spotting mistakes.* ■ *adverb* **1.** exactly ○ *The coach will leave the hotel at 7.30 sharp.* **2.** suddenly, at an angle ○ *The road turned sharp right.*

sharpen /'ʃɑːpən/ *verb* to make something sharp

shave /ʃeɪv/ *noun* the act of cutting off the hair on your face with a razor ○ *He decided to have a shave before going out to dinner.* ■ *verb* **1.** to cut off the hair on your face with a razor ○ *He cut himself shaving.* **2.** to cut the hair on your head or, on a part of your body, so that it is very short ○ *I didn't recognise him with his head shaved.*

she /ʃiː/ *pronoun* used for referring to a female person, a female animal and sometimes to cars, ships and countries ○ *She's my sister.* ○ *She and I are going on holiday to France together.* ○ *I'm angry with her – she's taken my motorbike.* ○ *She's a sweet little cat, but she's no good at catching mice.* ○ *The customs officers boarded the ship when she docked.* (NOTE: When it is the object, **she** becomes **her**: *She hit the ball* or *the ball hit her.* When it follows the verb to **be**, **she** usually becomes **her**: *Who's that? – It's her, the girl we met yesterday.*)

shed /ʃed/ *noun* a small wooden building ○ *They kept the mower in a shed at the bottom of the garden.* ■ *verb* to lose something which you are carrying or wearing ○ *In autumn, the trees shed their leaves as soon as the weather turns cold.* ○ *A lorry has shed its load of wood at the roundabout.* ○ *We shed our clothes and dived into the cool water.* (NOTE: **sheds – shedding – shed**)

sheep /ʃiːp/ *noun* a common farm animal, which gives wool and meat ○ *a flock of sheep* ○ *The sheep are in the field.* (NOTE: The plural is **sheep.**)

sheer /ʃɪə/ *adjective* **1.** used for emphasizing something ○ *It was sheer heaven to get into a hot bath after skiing.* ○ *She was crying out of sheer frustration.* ○ *It's sheer madness to go out without a coat in this weather.* **2.** very steep ○ *It was a sheer drop to the beach below.*

sheet /ʃiːt/ *noun* **1.** a large piece of thin cloth which is put on a bed, either to lie on or to cover you ○ *She changed the sheets on the bed.* **2.** a large flat piece of something such as paper, metal, ice or plastic ○ *Can you give me another sheet of paper?*

shelf /ʃelf/ *noun* a flat piece of wood attached to a wall or in a cupboard on which things can be put ○ *He put up* or *built some shelves in the kitchen.* ○ *The shelves were packed with books.* ○ *Put that book back on the shelf.* ○ *Can you reach me down the box from the top shelf?* ○ *The plates are on the top shelf in the kitchen cupboard.* (NOTE: The plural is **shelves.**)

shell /ʃel/ *noun* **1.** the hard outside part which covers some animals such as snails or tortoises ○ *The children spent hours collecting shells on the beach.* **2.** the hard outside part of an egg or a nut ○ *I found a big piece of shell in my omelette.* **3.** a metal tube which is fired from a gun and explodes when it hits something ○ *A shell landed on the hospital.*

shelter /ˈʃeltə/ *noun* **1.** protection ○ *We stood in the shelter of a tree waiting for the rain to stop.* ○ *On the mountain there was no shelter from the pouring rain.* □ **to take shelter** to go somewhere for protection ○ *When the gunmen started to shoot we all took shelter behind a wall.* **2.** a structure or building which protects you from bad weather or danger ○ *People stood in the bus shelter out of the rain as they waited for the bus to come.* ■ *verb* to go somewhere for protection ○ *Sheep were sheltering from the snow beside the hedge.*

shelves /ʃelvz/ plural of **shelf**

sheriff /ˈʃerɪf/ *noun US* an official in charge of justice in a particular part of a state ○ *the sheriff of Orange County*

shield /ʃiːld/ *noun* a large plate held in one hand, carried by people such as police as a protection ○ *The policemen cowered behind their plastic shields.* ■ *verb* to protect someone or something from being reached or seen ○ *He tried to shield her from the wind.*

shift /ʃɪft/ *noun* a change of something such as position or direction ○ *The company is taking advantage of a shift in the market towards higher priced goods.* ○ *There has been a shift of emphasis from opposition to partnership.* ○ *I don't understand this shift in attitude.* ■ *verb* to change position or direction ○ *We've shifted the television from the kitchen* *into the dining room.* ○ *My opinion has shifted since I read the official report.*

shin /ʃɪn/ *noun* the front part of your leg below the knee ○ *He scraped his shin climbing over the wall.* ○ *They kicked him in the shins.*

shine /ʃaɪn/ *verb* **1.** to be bright with light ○ *The sun is shining and they say it'll be hot today.* ○ *She polished the table until it shone.* ○ *The wine glasses shone in the light of the candles.* ○ *Why do cats' eyes shine in the dark?* ○ *The moon shone down on the waiting crowd.* **2.** to make light fall on something ○ *He shone his torch into the cellar.* (NOTE: **shines – shining – shone** /ʃɒn/)

shiny /ˈʃaɪni/ *adjective* which shines (NOTE: **shinier – shiniest**)

ship /ʃɪp/ *noun* a large boat for carrying passengers and goods on the sea ○ *She's a fine ship.* ○ *How many ships does the Royal Navy have?* ○ *The first time we went to the United States, we went by ship.* (NOTE: A **ship** is often referred to as **she** or **her**.)

shirt /ʃɜːt/ *noun* a light piece of clothing which you wear on the top part of the body ○ *The teacher wore a blue suit and a white shirt.* ○ *When he came back from the trip he had a suitcase full of dirty shirts.* ○ *It's so hot that the workers in the fields have taken their shirts off.*

shiver /ˈʃɪvə/ *verb* to shake with cold or fear ○ *She shivered in the cold night air.* ○ *He was coughing and shivering, so the doctor told him to stay in bed.* ■ *noun* the action of shaking because of feeling cold or frightened

shock /ʃɒk/ *noun* a sudden unpleasant surprise ○ *It gave me quite a shock when you walked in.* ○ *He's in for a nasty shock.* □ **in a state of shock** reacting badly to a sudden unpleasant surprise ○ *She was in a state of shock after hearing of the accident.* ■ *verb* to give someone a sudden unpleasant surprise ○ *The conditions in the hospital shocked the inspectors.*

shocked /ʃɒkt/ *adjective* having an unpleasant surprise

shocking /ˈʃɒkɪŋ/ *adjective* very unpleasant, which gives someone a sudden surprise

shoe /ʃuː/ *noun* a piece of clothing which is worn on your foot ○ *She's bought a new pair of shoes.* ○ *He put his shoes on and went out.* ○ *Take your shoes off if your feet hurt.* (NOTE: The plural is **shoes**.)

shone /ʃɒn/ past tense and past participle of **shine**

shook /ʃʊk/ past tense of **shake**

shoot /ʃuːt/ *noun* a new growth of a plant, growing from a seed or from a branch ○ *One or two green shoots are already showing where I sowed my lettuces.* ○ *After pruning, the roses will send out a lot of strong new shoots.* ■ *verb* **1.** to fire a gun ○ *Soldiers were shooting into the woods.* **2.** to hit or kill a person or animal by firing a gun ○ *One of the robbers was shot by a policeman when he tried to run away.* ○ *We went out hunting and shot two rabbits.* **3.** to go very fast ○ *When the bell rang she shot down the stairs.* ○ *He started the engine and the car shot out of the garage.* **4.** in some sports, to aim a ball at the goal ○ *He shot, and the ball bounced off the post.* (NOTE: **shoots – shooting – shot** /ʃɒt/)

shop /ʃɒp/ *noun* a place where you can buy things ○ *Quite a few shops are open on Sundays.* ○ *I never go to that shop – it's much too expensive.* ○ *The sweet shop is opposite the fire station.* ■ *verb* to look for and buy things in shops ○ *She's out shopping for his birthday present.* ○ *Mum's gone shopping in town.* ○ *They went shopping in Oxford Street.* ○ *Do you ever shop locally?* (NOTE: **shops – shopping – shopped**)

shopkeeper /ˈʃɒpkiːpə/ *noun* a person who owns a shop

shopping /ˈʃɒpɪŋ/ *noun* **1.** the activity of buying things in a shop ○ *We do all our shopping at the weekend.* ○ *He's gone out to do the weekly shopping.* **2.** things which you have bought in a shop ○ *Put all your shopping on the table.* ○ *She was carrying two baskets of shop-*

ping. (NOTE: no plural: *some shopping, a lot of shopping*)

shore /ʃɔː/ *noun* land at the edge of the sea or a lake ○ *She stood on the shore waving as the boat sailed away.*

short /ʃɔːt/ *adjective* **1.** not long ○ *Have you got a short piece of wire?* **2.** (*of distance*) not far ○ *She only lives a short distance away.* ○ *The taxi driver wanted to take me through the high street, but I told him there was a shorter route.* ○ *The shortest way to the railway station is to go through the park.* **3.** (*of time*) not lasting a long time ○ *He phoned a short time ago.* ○ *We had a short holiday in June.* ○ *She managed to have a short sleep on the plane.* **4.** not tall ○ *He is only 1m 40 – much shorter than his brother.*

shortage /ˈʃɔːtɪdʒ/ *noun* the fact that you do not have something you need ○ *a shortage of skilled staff* ○ *During the war, there were food shortages.*

shortly /ˈʃɔːtli/ *adverb* soon

shot /ʃɒt/ *noun* **1.** the action of shooting ○ *The police fired two shots at the car.* ○ *Some shots were fired during the bank robbery.* **2.** a kick or hit to try to score a goal ○ *He kicked but his shot was stopped by the goalkeeper.* ■ *past tense and past participle of* **shoot**

should /ʃʊd/ *modal verb* **1.** used in giving advice or warnings for saying what is the best thing to do ○ *You should go to the doctor if your cough gets worse.* ○ *I should have been more careful.* ○ *She shouldn't eat so much if she's trying to lose weight.* ○ *Should I ask for more coffee?* ○ *Why should I clean up your mess?* (NOTE: **Ought to** can be used instead of **should**.) **2.** used to say what you expect to happen ○ *If you leave now you should be there by 4 o'clock.* ○ *Their train should have arrived by now.* ○ *There shouldn't be any more problems now.* (NOTE: **Ought to** can be used instead of **should**.) **3.** used to show a possibility ○ *If the President should die in office, the Vice-President automatically takes over.* ○ *I'll be in the next room should you need me.* **4.** same as **would** (*dated*) ○ *We should like to offer you our congratulations.* ○ *If I had*

enough money I should like to buy a new car.

shoulder /ˈʃəʊldə/ *noun* the part of the body at the top of the arm ○ *The policeman hurt me on the shoulder.* ○ *Look over your shoulder, he's just behind you.*

shout /ʃaʊt/ *noun* a loud cry ○ *She gave a shout and dived into the water.* ○ *People came running when they heard the shouts of the children.* ■ *verb* to make a loud cry or to speak very loudly ○ *They stamped on the floor and shouted.* ○ *I had to shout to the waitress to get served.* ○ *They were shouting greetings to one another across the street.*

shove /ʃʌv/ *noun* a sudden push ○ *She gave the car a shove and it rolled down the hill.* ■ *verb* to push someone or something roughly ○ *He shoved the papers into his pocket.* ○ *Stop shoving – there's no more room on the bus.*

show /ʃəʊ/ *noun* **1.** an exhibition ○ *The Hampton Court Flower Show opens tomorrow.* ○ *She has entered her two cats for the local cat show.* **2.** a play or other performance which is on at a theatre ○ *'Cats' is a wonderful show.* ○ *We're going to a show tonight.* ○ *The show starts at 7.30, so let's have dinner early.* ■ *verb* **1.** to let someone see something ○ *He wanted to show me his holiday photos.* ○ *She proudly showed me her new car.* ○ *You don't have to show your passport when you're travelling to Ireland.* **2.** to point something out to someone ○ *Show me where the accident happened.* ○ *He asked me to show him the way to the railway station.* ○ *The salesman showed her how to work the photocopier.* ○ *My watch shows the date as well as the time.* **3.** to be seen, or to be obvious ○ *The repairs were badly done and it shows.* ○ *Her rash has almost disappeared and hardly shows at all.* (NOTE: **shows – showing – showed – shown** /ʃəʊn/) ◇ **on show** arranged for everyone to see ○ *Is there anything new on show in this year's exhibition?*

show off *phrasal verb* **1.** to show how much better than other people you think you are ○ *Don't watch her dancing about like that – she's just showing off.* **2.** to let a lot of people see something which you are proud of ○ *He drove past with the radio on very loud, showing off his new car.*

show up *phrasal verb* **1.** to do something which shows other people to be worse than you ○ *She dances so well that she shows us all up.* **2.** to be seen clearly ○ *When I ride my bike at night I wear an orange jacket because it shows up clearly in the dark.* **3.** to come to or arrive in a place (*informal*) ○ *We invited all our friends to the picnic but it rained and only five of them showed up.*

shower /ˈʃaʊə/ *noun* **1.** a slight fall of rain or snow ○ *In April there's usually a mixture of sunshine and showers.* ○ *There were snow showers this morning, but it is sunny again now.* **2.** a piece of equipment in a bathroom, usually fixed high up on the wall, which sends out water to wash your whole body **3.** an occasion when you wash your body with a shower ○ *She went up to her room and had a shower.* ○ *He has a cold shower every morning.* ○ *You can't take a shower now, there's no hot water.* ■ *verb* to wash yourself under a shower ○ *He showered and went down to greet his guests.*

shown /ʃəʊn/ past participle of **show**

shrank /ʃræŋk/ past tense of **shrink**

shred /ʃred/ *noun* a long narrow piece torn off something ○ *She tore his newspaper to shreds.* ○ *The curtains were on the floor in shreds.* ■ *verb* **1.** to tear or cut paper into long thin pieces, which can then be thrown away or used as packing material ○ *They sent a pile of old invoices to be shredded.* ○ *She told the police that the manager had told her to shred all the documents in the file.* **2.** to cut something into very thin pieces ○ *Here's a utensil for shredding vegetables.* ○ *Add a cup of shredded carrot.* (NOTE: **shreds – shredding – shredded**)

shrink /ʃrɪŋk/ *verb* **1.** to make smaller ○ *The water must have been too hot – it's shrunk my shirt.* **2.** to get smaller ○ *My shirt has shrunk in the wash.* ○ *The market for typewriters has shrunk almost to nothing.* (NOTE: **shrinks – shrinking – shrank** /ʃræŋk/ **– shrunk** /ʃrʌŋk/)

shrivel /ˈʃrɪv(ə)l/ *verb* to make the surface of something become dry and creased, or to become like this (NOTE: **shrivels – shrivelling – shrivelled**)

shrunk /ʃrʌŋk/ past participle of **shrink**

shuffle /ˈʃʌf(ə)l/ *verb* **1.** to walk dragging your feet along the ground ○ *He shuffled into the room in his slippers.* **2.** to mix the playing cards before starting a game ○ *I think he must have done something to the cards when he was shuffling them.*

shut /ʃʌt/ *adjective* not open ○ *Some shops are shut on Sundays, but most big stores are open.* ○ *We tried to get into the museum but it was shut.* ○ *She lay with her eyes shut.* ○ *Come in – the door isn't shut!* ■ *verb* **1.** to close something which is open ○ *Can you please shut the window – it's getting cold in here.* ○ *Here's your present – shut your eyes and guess what it is.* **2.** to close for business ○ *In Germany, shops shut on Saturday afternoons.* ○ *The restaurant shuts at midnight.* (NOTE: **shuts – shutting – shut**)

shut down *phrasal verb* **1.** to close completely ○ *The factory shut down for the holiday weekend.* **2.** to switch off an electrical system ○ *They had to shut down the factory because pollution levels were too high.*

shut in *phrasal verb* to lock someone inside a place

shut off *phrasal verb* **1.** to switch something off ○ *Can you shut off the water while I mend the tap?* **2.** to stop access to ○ *We can shut off the dining room with folding doors.* ○ *The house is shut off from the road by a high wall.*

shut out *phrasal verb* **1.** to lock someone outside a place ○ *I was shut out of the house because I'd left my keys inside.* ○ *If the dog keeps on barking you'll have to shut him out.* **2.** to stop light getting inside, or to stop people seeing inside ○ *Those thick curtains should shut out the light from the children's room.* ○ *A high wall shuts out the view of the factory.* **3.** to stop thinking about something ○ *Try to shut out the memory of the accident.*

shut up *phrasal verb* **1.** to close something inside a place ○ *I hate being shut up indoors on a sunny day.* **2.** an impolite way of telling someone to stop talking or to stop making a noise ○ *Tell those children to shut up – I'm trying to work.* ○ *Shut up! – we're tired of listening to your complaints.* ○ *Once he starts talking it's impossible to shut him up.*

shutter /'ʃʌtə/ *noun* **1.** a folding wooden or metal cover for a window ○ *Close the shutters if the sunlight is too bright.* **2.** the part of a camera which opens and closes very quickly to allow the light to go on to the film ○ *He released the shutter and took the picture.*

shy /ʃaɪ/ *adjective* nervous and afraid to speak or do something ○ *He's so shy he sat in the back row and didn't speak to anyone.*

sick /sɪk/ *adjective* **1.** not in good health ○ *He's been sick for months.* ○ *We have five staff off sick.* **2.** □ **to be sick** to bring up food from the stomach into the mouth ○ *The last time I ate oysters I was sick all night.* □ **to feel sick** to feel ill because you want to bring up food from the stomach ○ *When I got up this morning I felt sick and went back to bed.* ○ *The greasy food made her feel sick.* **3.** □ **to make someone sick** to make someone very annoyed ○ *All my friends earn more than I do – it makes me sick!* **4.** involving subjects or behaviour that many people are upset or offended by ○ *a sick joke* ■ *noun* the contents of the stomach when they come out through the mouth (*informal*)

side /saɪd/ *noun* **1.** one of the four parts which with the top and bottom make a solid object such as a box ○ *Stand the box upright – don't turn it onto its side.* **2.** one of the two parts which with the front and back make a building ○ *The garage is attached to the side of the house.* **3.** one of the surfaces of a flat object ○ *Please write on both sides of the paper.* **4.** one of two or more parts or edges of something ○ *Our office is on the opposite side of the street to the bank.* ○ *London's Heathrow Airport is on the west side of the city.* ○ *The hitchhikers were standing by the side of the*
road. ○ *She sat to one side of the fireplace.* **5.** one of two parts separated by something ○ *She jumped over the fence to get to the other side.* ○ *In the UK, cars drive on the left-hand side of the road.* **6.** a sports team ○ *The local side was beaten 2 – 0.* **7.** the part of the body between the top of the legs and the shoulder ○ *I can't sleep when I'm lying on my right side.* ○ *The policemen stood by the prisoner's side.* ○ *They all stood side by side.* ■ *adjective* which is at the side ○ *There is a side entrance to the shop.* ○ *Can you take that bucket round to the side door?*

sidewalk /'saɪdwɔːk/ *noun US* a pavement ○ *A girl was walking slowly along the sidewalk.* ○ *We sat at a sidewalk café.*

sideways /'saɪdweɪz/ *adverb* to the side or from the side ○ *Crabs walk sideways.* ○ *Take a step sideways and you will be able to see the castle.* ○ *If you look at the post sideways you'll see how bent it is.*

sigh /saɪ/ *noun* a long deep breath, showing feelings such as sadness or showing that you feel tired ○ *She gave a deep sigh and put the phone down.* ○ *You could hear the sighs of relief from the audience when the hero was saved.* ■ *verb* to breathe with a sigh ○ *He sighed and wrote out another cheque.*

sight /saɪt/ *noun* **1.** the sense that is the ability to see ○ *My grandfather's sight isn't very good any more.* **2.** the fact of being able to see something ○ *He can't stand the sight of blood.* ○ *We caught sight of an eagle up in the mountains.* ○ *She kept waving until the car disappeared from sight.* ○ *The fog cleared and the mountains came into sight.* ○ *They waved until the boat was out of sight.* **3.** something, especially something famous, which is interesting to see ○ *They went off on foot to see the sights of the town.* ○ *The guidebook lists the main tourist sights in Beijing.* (NOTE: Do not confuse with **site**.)

sign /saɪn/ *noun* **1.** a movement of the hand which means something ○ *He made a sign to us to sit down.* **2.** something such as a drawing or a notice which advertises something ○ *The shop* has a big sign outside it saying 'for sale'. ○ A 'no smoking' sign hung on the wall. **3.** something which shows that something is happening or has happened ○ There is no sign of the rain stopping. ○ The economy is showing signs of improvement. ○ The police can find no sign of how the burglars got into the office. ○ He should have arrived by now, but there's no sign of him. **4.** a printed character ○ the pound sign (£) ○ the dollar sign ($) ■ *verb* to write your name in a special way on a document to show that you have written it or that you have approved it ○ Sign on the dotted line, please. ○ The letter is signed by the managing director. ○ A cheque is not valid if it has not been signed.

signal /'sɪgn(ə)l/ *noun* **1.** a sign or movement which tells someone to do something ○ I'll give you a signal to start singing. **2.** a piece of equipment used to tell someone to do something ○ The signal was at red so the train had to stop. ■ *verb* to make signs to tell someone to do something ○ The driver signalled to show that he was turning right. ○ She signalled to me that we were running out of time. (NOTE: **signals – signalling – signalled**. The US spelling is **signaling – signaled**.)

signature /'sɪgnɪtʃə/ *noun* a name written in a special way by someone to show that a document has been officially accepted ○ He found a pile of cheques on his desk waiting for his signature. ○ Her signature doesn't look like her name at all. ○ The shopkeeper looked very closely at her signature and compared it with the one on the credit card.

significant /sɪg'nɪfɪkənt/ *adjective* important or noticeable ○ It is highly significant that everyone else was asked to the meeting, but not the finance director. ○ There has been a significant improvement in his condition.

silence /'saɪləns/ *noun* a situation which is quiet, without any noise ○ I love the silence of the countryside at night. ○ The crowd of tourists waited in silence. ○ The mayor held up his hand and asked for silence. ○ There was a sudden si-

lence as she came in. ○ There will be a minute's silence at 11 o'clock.

silent /'saɪlənt/ *adjective* not talking or making any noise ○ He kept silent for the whole meeting. ○ This new washing machine is almost silent. ○ They showed some old silent films.

silk /sɪlk/ *noun* cloth made from fibres produced by insects ○ She was wearing a beautiful silk scarf. ○ I bought some blue silk to make a dress.

silly /'sɪli/ *adjective* stupid in an annoying way ○ Don't be silly – you can't go to the party dressed like that! ○ She asked a lot of silly questions. ○ Of all the silly newspaper articles that must be the silliest. (NOTE: **sillier – silliest**)

silver /'sɪlvə/ *noun* a precious white metal often used for making jewellery ○ Gold is worth more than silver. ○ How much is an ounce of silver worth? ■ *adjective* of a shiny white colour, like silver ○ The car has been resprayed with silver paint. ○ She wore silver sandals to match her handbag.

similar /'sɪmɪlə/ *adjective* very much like someone or something but not exactly the same ○ The two cars are very similar in appearance. ○ Our situation is rather similar to yours.

similarity /ˌsɪmɪ'lærɪti/ *noun* being similar (NOTE: The plural is **similarities**.)

similarly /'sɪmɪləli/ *adverb* in a similar way ○ All these infections must be treated similarly. ○ He always writes a nice thank you letter, and similarly so does his sister.

simple /'sɪmpəl/ *adjective* **1.** easy to do or understand ○ The machine is very simple to use. **2.** not unusual, special or complicated ○ They had a simple meal of bread and soup. ○ It's a very simple pattern of lines and squares.

simply /'sɪmpli/ *adverb* **1.** in a simple way ○ He described very simply how the accident had happened. ○ She always dresses very simply. **2.** only ○ He did it simply to annoy everyone. ○ She gave a new look to the room simply by painting one wall red. **3.** used for emphasis ○ Your garden is simply beauti-

ful. ○ *It's simply terrible – what shall we do?*

since /sɪns/ *preposition* during the period after ○ *She's been here since Monday.* ○ *We've been working non-stop since four o'clock – can't we have a rest?* ■ *conjunction* **1.** during the period after ○ *He has had trouble borrowing money ever since he was rude to the bank manager.* ○ *Since we got to the hotel, it has rained every day.* **2.** because ○ *Since he's ill, you can't ask him to help you.* ○ *Since it's such a fine day, let's go for a walk.* ■ *adverb* during the period until now ○ *She phoned on Sunday and we haven't heard from her since.* ○ *He left England in 1990 and has lived abroad ever since.*

sincere /sɪn'sɪə/ *adjective* very honest and real, not false or pretended

sincerely /sɪn'sɪəli/ *adverb* honestly or really

sing /sɪŋ/ *verb* to make music with your voice ○ *She was singing as she worked.* ○ *Please sing another song.* ○ *He always sings in the bath.* ○ *She sang a funny song about elephants.* ○ *The birds were singing in the garden.* (NOTE: **sings – singing – sang** /sæŋ/ **– sung** /sʌŋ/)

singer /'sɪŋə/ *noun* a person who sings

single /'sɪŋg(ə)l/ *adjective* **1.** one alone ○ *He handed her a single sheet of paper.* ○ *There wasn't a single person I knew at the party.* ○ *The single most important fact about him is that he has no money.* **2.** for one person only ○ *Have you got a single room for two nights, please?* ○ *We prefer two single beds to a double bed.* **3.** not married ○ *She's twenty-nine and still single.* ○ *Are there any single men on the course?*

singular /'sɪŋgjʊlə/ *adjective* showing that there is only one thing or person ○ *'She' is a singular pronoun.*

sink /sɪŋk/ *noun* a fixed container for water in which you wash things such as dishes in a kitchen ○ *The sink was piled high with dirty dishes.* ○ *He was washing his hands at the kitchen sink.* ■ *verb* **1.** to go down to the bottom of something such as water or mud ○ *The ferry*

sank *in 30m of water.* ○ *The paper boat floated for a few minutes, then sank.* ○ *You should tie a piece of lead to your fishing line to make it sink.* **2.** to fall suddenly ○ *She was so upset that she just sank into an armchair and closed her eyes.* ○ *My heart sank when I heard the news.* (NOTE: **sinks – sinking – sank** /sæŋk/ **– sunk** /sʌŋk/)

sip /sɪp/ *noun* the act of drinking a small amount ○ *She took a sip of water, and went on with her speech.* ■ *verb* to drink something taking only a small amount at a time ○ *The girl was sipping her drink quietly.* (NOTE: **sips – sipping – sipped**)

sir /sɜː/ *noun* **1.** a polite way of speaking to a man, e.g. a man who is a customer in a shop ○ *Would you like a drink with your lunch, sir?* ○ *Please come this way, sir.* **2.** □ **Dear Sir** a polite way of beginning a letter to a man you do not know **3.** the title given to a baronet or knight

siren /'saɪrən/ *noun* a piece of equipment which makes a loud warning signal

sister /'sɪstə/ *noun* **1.** a girl or woman who has the same father and mother as someone else ○ *His three sisters all look alike.* ○ *My younger sister Louise works in a bank.* ○ *Do you have any sisters?* **2.** a senior female nurse in charge of a ward ○ *The sister told me my son was getting better.* (NOTE: The male equivalent is **charge nurse.**)

sit /sɪt/ *verb* **1.** to be resting with your bottom on something ○ *Mother was sitting in bed eating her breakfast.* **2.** (*of a bird*) to rest on something ○ *The robin always comes and sits on the fence when I'm digging.* (NOTE: **sits – sitting – sat** /sæt/)

sit down *phrasal verb* to sit on a seat
sit up *phrasal verb* **1.** to sit with your back straight ○ *Sit up straight!* **2.** to move from a lying to a sitting position ○ *He's too weak to sit up.* ○ *He sat up in bed to eat his breakfast.* **3.** to delay going to bed or to go to bed later than usual ○ *We sat up playing cards until 2 a.m.*

site /saɪt/ *noun* **1.** a place where something is or will be ○ *This is the site for the new factory.* **2.** a place where something happened, or where something once existed ○ *This was the site of the Battle of Hastings in 1066.* ○ *They're trying to locate the site of the old Roman fort.*

sitting room /'sɪtɪŋ ruːm/ *noun* a comfortable room in a house for sitting in

situation /ˌsɪtʃu'eɪʃ(ə)n/ *noun* **1.** the position which someone or something is in because of things which have happened ○ *What's your opinion of the company's present situation?* ○ *I wonder how she got herself into this situation?* **2.** a place where something is ○ *The hotel is in a very pleasant situation by the sea.*

six /sɪks/ *noun* the number 6 ○ *He's six (years old).* ○ *We're having some people round for drinks at six (o'clock).* ○ *There are only six chocolates left in the box – who's eaten the rest?*

sixteen /ˌsɪks'tiːn/ *noun* the number 16 ○ *He'll be sixteen next month.* ○ *The train leaves at seventeen sixteen (17.16).*

sixteenth /sɪks'tiːnθ/ *adjective* number 16 in a series ○ *She came sixteenth in the race.* ○ *Her sixteenth birthday is on Tuesday.* ■ *noun* the thing that is number 16 in a series ○ *Today is July the sixteenth* or *the sixteenth of July (July 16th).*

sixth /sɪksθ/ *adjective* number 6 in a series ○ *His office is on the sixth floor.* ○ *What is the sixth letter of the alphabet?* ○ *Tomorrow is her sixth birthday.* ■ *noun* **1.** the thing that is number 6 in a series ○ *Today is September the sixth* or *the sixth of September (September 6th).* **2.** one part of six equal parts ○ *Ten minutes is a sixth of an hour.*

sixtieth /'sɪkstɪəθ/ *adjective* number sixty in a series ○ *his sixtieth birthday* ■ *noun* the thing that is number sixty in a series

sixty /'sɪksti/ *noun* the number 60 ○ *She's sixty (years old).* ○ *Over sixty players took part in the competition.*

size /saɪz/ *noun* the measurements of something, or how big something is ○ *Their garage is about the same size as our house.* ○ *The school has an Olympic size swimming pool.* ○ *He takes size ten in shoes.* ○ *What size collars do you take?* ○ *The size of the staff has doubled in the last two years.*

sizzle /'sɪz(ə)l/ *verb* to make a sound like food cooking in oil or fat

skate /skeɪt/ *noun* a boot with a blade attached to the bottom which you wear for sliding over ice ○ *a pair of skates* ■ *verb* to move wearing skates ○ *She skated across the frozen lake.* (NOTE: **skates – skating – skated**)

skateboard /'skeɪtbɔːd/ *noun* a board with two pairs of wheels underneath, which you stand on to move about

skeleton /'skelɪt(ə)n/ *noun* all the bones which make up a body ○ *They found the skeleton of a rabbit in the garden shed.* ○ *He demonstrated joints using the skeleton in the biology lab.*

skeptical /'skeptɪk(ə)l/ *adjective* US spelling of **sceptical**

sketch /sketʃ/ *noun* a rough quick drawing ○ *He made a sketch of the church.* ■ *verb* to make a rough quick drawing of something ○ *She was sketching the old church.* ○ *He sketched out his plan on the back of an envelope.*

sketchbook /'sketʃbʊk/ *noun* a book of drawing paper for sketching

ski /skiː/ *noun* one of two long flat objects which are attached to your boots for sliding over snow ○ *We always hire skis when we get to the ski resort.* ○ *Someone stole my new pair of skis.* ■ *verb* to travel on skis ○ *The mountain rescue team had to ski to the site of the avalanche.* ○ *We skied down to the bottom of the slope without falling.* ○ *She broke her arm skiing.* (NOTE: **skis – skiing – skied**)

skiing /'skiːɪŋ/ *noun* the sport of sliding on skis

skilful /'skɪlf(ə)l/ *adjective* showing a lot of skill

skilfully /'skɪlfʊli/ *adverb* in a skilful way ○ *It was difficult but he did it very skilfully.*

skill /skɪl/ *noun* the ability to do something well as a result of training or experience ○ *Portrait painting needs a lot of* *skill.* ○ *This job will help you develop management skills.*

skilled /skɪld/ *adjective* **1.** able to do something well, using a particular skill ○ *She's a skilled therapist.* ○ *We need skilled programmers.* **2.** needing a particular skill ○ *nursing and other skilled professions*

skillful /'skɪlf(ə)l/ *adjective* US spelling of **skilful**

skim /skɪm/ *verb* **1.** to remove things floating on a liquid ○ *Skim the soup to remove the fat on the surface.* **2.** to move quickly over the surface of something ○ *Flies skimmed across the surface of the lake.* (NOTE: **skims – skimming – skimmed**)

skin /skɪn/ *noun* **1.** the outer surface of the body ○ *The baby's skin is very smooth.* **2.** the outer surface of a fruit or vegetable ○ *This orange has a very thick skin.* ○ *You can cook these new potatoes with their skins on.*

skinny /'skɪni/ *adjective* too thin to be attractive ○ *A tall skinny guy walked in.* ○ *She has very skinny legs.* (NOTE: **skinnier – skinniest**)

skip /skɪp/ *verb* **1.** to run along partly hopping and partly jumping ○ *The children skipped happily down the lane.* **2.** to jump over a rope which you turn over your head ○ *The boys played football and the girls were skipping.* **3.** to miss part of something (*informal*) ○ *She skipped the middle chapters and went on to read the end of the story.* ○ *I'm not hungry, I'll skip the pudding.* (NOTE: **skips – skipping – skipped**)

skirt /skɜːt/ *noun* a piece of clothing worn by women over the lower part of the body from the waist down ○ *She started wearing jeans to work, but was told to wear a skirt.*

skull /skʌl/ *noun* the bones which are joined together to form the head

sky /skaɪ/ *noun* a space above the earth which is blue during the day and where the moon and stars appear at night ○ *What makes the sky blue?* ○ *It's going to be a beautiful day – there's not a cloud in the sky.* ○ *The wind carried the glider high up into the sky.*

skyscraper /'skaɪskreɪpə/ *noun* a very tall building

slab /slæb/ *noun* a flat square or rectangular block of stone or concrete

slack /slæk/ *adjective* **1.** not pulled tight or not fitting tightly ○ *The wind had dropped and the sails were slack.* ○ *The ropes are slack – pull on them to make them tight.* **2.** not busy ○ *Business is slack at the end of the week.* ○ *January is always a slack period for us.*

slam /slæm/ *verb* **1.** to bang a door shut ○ *When he saw me, he slammed the door in my face.* **2.** to shut with a bang ○ *The door slammed and I was locked out.* **3.** to move, or to hit something, with great force ○ *The car slammed into a tree.* ○ *He slammed his fist on the desk.* (NOTE: **slams – slamming – slammed**)

slang /slæŋ/ *noun* popular words or phrases used by certain groups of people, but which are not used in formal situations ○ *Don't use slang in your essay.* ○ *Slang expressions are sometimes difficult to understand.*

slant /slɑːnt/ *noun* a slope ○ *The garden is on a slant, which makes cutting the lawn difficult.* ■ *verb* to slope ○ *The path slants down the side of the hill.* ○ *The picture seems to be slanting to the right.*

slap /slæp/ *noun* a blow given with your hand flat ○ *She gave him a slap in the face.* ■ *verb* **1.** to hit someone or something with your hand flat ○ *She slapped his face.* **2.** to hit someone or something gently with your open hand as a sign of friendship ○ *They all slapped him on the back to congratulate him.* (NOTE: **slaps – slapping – slapped**)

slash /slæʃ/ *verb* to make a long cut in something with a knife, often violently ○ *He slashed the painting with a kitchen knife.*

slate /sleɪt/ *noun* a thin piece of this stone used to cover a roof ○ *The slates were already piled up on the roof ready for fixing.*

slaughter /'slɔːtə/ *noun* **1.** the killing of many people ○ *the terrible slaughter of innocent people in the riots* **2.** the killing of animals ○ *These lambs will be ready for slaughter in a week or so.* ■ *verb* **1.** to kill many people or animals at the same time ○ *Thousands of civilians were slaughtered by the advancing army.* **2.** to kill animals for their meat

sleek /sliːk/ *adjective* smooth and shiny ○ *the cat's sleek coat* ○ *After dinner we walked across the sleek lawns to the river.*

sleep /sliːp/ *verb* to rest with your eyes closed in an unconscious state ○ *She never sleeps for more than six hours each night.* ○ *He slept through the whole of the TV news.* ○ *Don't make any noise – Daddy's trying to sleep.* (NOTE: **sleeps – sleeping – slept** /slept/)

sleepy /'sliːpi/ *adjective* feeling ready to go to sleep ○ *The children had a busy day – they were very sleepy by 8 o'clock.* ○ *The injection will make you feel sleepy.* ○ *If you feel sleepy, don't try to drive the car.* ○ *Sitting in front of the TV made him sleepier and sleepier.* (NOTE: **sleepier – sleepiest**)

sleet /sliːt/ *noun* snow mixed with rain ○ *The temperature fell and the rain turned to sleet.*

sleeve /sliːv/ *noun* the part of a piece of clothing which covers your arm ○ *The sleeves on this shirt are too long.* ○ *He was wearing a blue shirt with short sleeves.*

slender /'slendə/ *adjective* long and thin, or tall and slim ○ *slender fingers* ○ *a slender flower stem* ○ *a girl with a slender figure*

slept /slept/ past tense and past participle of **sleep**

slice /slaɪs/ *noun* a thin piece cut off something to eat ○ *Can you cut some more slices of bread?* ○ *Have a slice of chocolate cake.* ○ *Would you like another slice of chicken?* ■ *verb* to cut something into thin pieces ○ *She stood at the table slicing the joint for lunch.*

slide /slaɪd/ *noun* **1.** a slippery metal or plastic structure for children to slide down ○ *There are swings and a slide in the local playground.* **2.** a small piece of film which can be shown on a screen ○ *She put the screen up and showed us the*

slides of her last trip. ○ *There will be a slide show in the village hall.* ■ *verb* to move smoothly over a slippery surface ○ *The drawer slides in and out easily.* ○ *The car slid to a stop.* ○ *The children were sliding on the ice when it broke.* (NOTE: **slides – sliding – slid** /slɪd/)

slight /slaɪt/ *adjective* not very big or noticeable ○ *a slight difference* ○ *She wasn't the slightest bit nervous.*

slightly /'slaɪtli/ *adverb* to only a small extent ○ *He was only slightly hurt in the car crash.* ○ *The American bank is offering a slightly better interest rate.* ○ *I only know him slightly.*

slim /slɪm/ *adjective* with a body that is thin in an attractive way ○ *How do you manage to stay so slim?* ○ *She looks slimmer in that dress.* (NOTE: **slimmer – slimmest**) ■ *verb* to eat less food, or eat only special foods, in order to become thin ○ *She started slimming before her summer holidays.* (NOTE: **slims – slimming – slimmed**)

slime /slaɪm/ *noun* a slippery substance, which covers surfaces

slimy /'slaɪmi/ *adjective* covered with something that is unpleasant and slippery ○ *Watch out, the rocks are slimy.* ○ *What's this slimy mess at the bottom of the fridge?* (NOTE: **slimier – slimiest**)

slip /slɪp/ *verb* **1.** to push something without being seen ○ *The postman slipped the letters through the letter box.* ○ *He slipped the keys into his pocket.* **2.** to go quickly ○ *I'll just slip down to the post office with this letter.* (NOTE: **slips – slipping – slipped**) ■ *noun* a small, often careless mistake ○ *Don't worry about that. It was just a slip.* ○ *He made a few slips in his calculations.*

slippers /'slɪpəz/ *noun* light comfortable shoes worn indoors ○ *They put their slippers on when they come into the house.*

slippery /'slɪp(ə)ri/ *adjective* so smooth that one can easily slip and fall

slit /slɪt/ *noun* a long cut or narrow opening ○ *She peeped through a slit in the curtains.*

slope /sləʊp/ *noun* a surface or piece of ground that has one end higher than the other ○ *The land rises in a gentle slope to the church.* ○ *They stopped halfway down the slope.* ■ *verb* to have one end higher than the other ○ *The road slopes down to the sea.*

slot /slɒt/ *noun* a long thin hole ○ *A coin has got stuck in the slot of the parking meter.* ○ *Put the system disk into the slot on the front of your computer.*

slow /sləʊ/ *adjective* **1.** needing a long time to do something ○ *Luckily, the car was only going at a slow speed.* ○ *She is the slowest walker of the group.* ○ *The company is very slow at answering my letters.* ○ *Sales got off to a slow start but picked up later.* **2.** showing a time which is earlier than the right time ○ *The office clock is four minutes slow.*

slow down *phrasal verb* **1.** to go more slowly ○ *The van had to slow down as it came to the traffic lights.* ○ *Please slow down, I can't keep up with you.* **2.** to make something go more slowly ○ *The snow slowed the traffic down on the motorway.*

slowly /ˈsləʊli/ *adverb* at a slow speed ○ *Luckily, the car was going very slowly when it hit the fence.* ○ *The group walked slowly round the exhibition.* ○ *Speak more slowly so that everyone can understand.*

sly /slaɪ/ *adjective* good at doing secret or slightly dishonest things

smack /smæk/ *verb* to hit someone or something with your hand flat ○ *She smacked the little girl for being rude.* ■ *noun* an act of hitting someone, especially a child, with your hand flat ○ *If you pull the cat's tail you'll get a smack.*

small /smɔːl/ *adjective* not large in size or amount ○ *Small cars are more economical than large ones.* ○ *The house is too big for us, so we're selling it and buying a smaller one.* ○ *She only paid a small amount for that clock.* ○ *The guidebook isn't small enough to carry in your pocket.* ○ *These trousers are already too small for him.*

smart /smɑːt/ *adjective* **1.** having a neat appearance ○ *A smart young man asked me if he could use my mobile phone.* ○ *He looked very smart in his uniform.* **2.** intelligent ○ *It was smart of her to note the car's number plate.* ■ *verb* if something smarts, it hurts with a burning feeling ○ *The place where I burnt my hand is still smarting.*

smash /smæʃ/ *verb* **1.** to break into pieces ○ *He dropped the plate and it smashed to pieces.* **2.** to break something into pieces, often using force or violence ○ *Demonstrators smashed the windows of police cars.* **3.** to do better than the previous best performance ○ *She smashed the world record.* ○ *Six records were smashed at the Olympics.* **4.** to hit against something violently ○ *The train smashed into the car.* ○ *The crowd smashed through the railings.*

smell /smel/ *noun* **1.** the sense that allows you to be aware of something through your nose ○ *Animals have a better sense of smell than humans.* ○ *These dogs have a very keen sense of smell and can sniff out even a minute quantity of drugs.* **2.** something which you can sense with your nose ○ *I love the smell of coffee.* ○ *She noticed a smell of gas downstairs.* ■ *verb* **1.** to notice the smell of something ○ *Can you smell gas?* ○ *Wild animals can smell humans.* ○ *My nose is blocked – I can't smell anything.* **2.** to make a smell ○ *I don't like cheese which smells too strong.* ○ *What's for dinner? – it smells very good!* ○ *There's something which smells funny in the bathroom.* ○ *It smelt of gas in the kitchen.* **3.** to bring your nose close to something to smell it ○ *She bent down to smell the snowdrops.* (NOTE: **smells – smelling – smelled** or **smelt** /smelt/)

smile /smaɪl/ *noun* an act of turning your mouth up at the corners to show that you are pleased ○ *The dentist gave me a friendly smile.* ○ *She had a big smile as she told them the good news.* ■ *verb* to show that you are pleased by turning your mouth up at the corners ○ *That girl has just smiled at me.* ○ *Everyone smile please – I'm taking a picture!*

smoke /sməʊk/ *noun* a white, grey or black substance produced by something that is burning ○ *The restaurant was full of cigarette smoke.* ○ *Clouds of smoke* *were pouring out of the upstairs windows.* ○ *Two people died from inhaling toxic smoke.* ○ *Smoke detectors are fitted in all the rooms.* ■ *verb* **1.** to produce smoke ○ *Two days after the fire, the ruins of the factory were still smoking.* **2.** to breathe in smoke from something such as a cigarette ○ *Everyone was smoking even though the signs said 'no smoking'.* ○ *She doesn't smoke much.* ○ *You shouldn't smoke if you want to play football.* (NOTE: **smokes – smoking – smoked**)

smooth /smuːð/ *adjective* **1.** with no bumps or rough parts ○ *the smooth surface of a polished table* ○ *The baby's skin is very smooth.* ○ *Velvet has a smooth side and a rough side.* **2.** with no sudden unpleasant movements ○ *Dirt in the fuel tank can prevent the smooth running of the engine.* ○ *We had a very smooth ride.*

smoothly /'smuːðli/ *adverb* in a smooth way

smoothness /'smuːðnəs/ *noun* the state of being smooth ○ *The fabric has all the smoothness of a baby's skin.* ○ *The smoothness of the ride makes up for the high fare.*

smother /'smʌðə/ *verb* **1.** to kill someone by stopping them from breathing ○ *They took the kittens and smothered them.* ○ *Never put a pillow over someone's face – you may smother them!* **2.** to cover something completely ○ *a chocolate cake simply smothered in cream* ○ *The firemen put out the fire by smothering it with foam.*

smudge /smʌdʒ/ *noun* a dirty mark ○ *There is a smudge on the top corner of the photograph.* ○ *He had a black smudge on his cheek.* ■ *verb* to make a dirty mark, e.g. by rubbing ink which is not dry ○ *Don't touch the print with your wet hands, or you'll smudge it.*

smug /smʌg/ *adjective* pleased about something, especially your own achievements, in a way that is annoying (NOTE: **smugger – smuggest**)

smuggle /'smʌg(ə)l/ *verb* **1.** to take goods into a country secretly and illegally ○ *They tried to smuggle cigarettes into the country.* ○ *We had to smuggle*

the spare parts over the border. **2.** to take something into or out of a place secretly and dishonestly ○ *The knives were smuggled into the prison by a someone visiting a prisoner.* ○ *We'll never know how they smuggled the letter out.*

snack /snæk/ *noun* a light meal, or a small amount of food eaten between meals ○ *We didn't have time to stop for a proper lunch, so we just had a snack on the motorway.*

snag /snæg/ *noun* a little problem which prevents you from doing something ○ *We've run into a snag: there are no flights to the island on Sundays.* ○ *The only snag is that he's not a very good driver.*

snail /sneɪl/ *noun* a small animal which moves slowly along the ground, which has a soft body and a spiral-shaped shell on its back

snake /sneɪk/ *noun* a long thin animal which has no legs and moves along the ground by wriggling ○ *Is this snake safe to handle?*

snap /snæp/ *noun* a photograph taken quickly (*informal*) ○ *She showed me an old black-and-white snap of the house.* ○ *He took a lot of snaps of his children.* ■ *adjective* sudden ○ *They carried out a snap check* or *a snap inspection of the passengers' luggage.* ○ *The government called a snap election.* ■ *verb* **1.** to break sharply with a dry noise ○ *He snapped a branch off the bush.* **2.** to break and make a loud high noise ○ *The handle snapped off.* (NOTE: **snaps – snapping – snapped**)

snarl /snɑːl/ *verb* to growl angrily ○ *The leopard snarled as he approached its cage.* ○ *'Take your money, and get out' he snarled.* ■ *noun* an angry growl ○ *As she opened the door of the cage she heard a snarl.*

snatch /snætʃ/ *verb* to grab something suddenly and quickly ○ *He came beside her on his bike and snatched her handbag.*

sneak /sniːk/ *verb* to go somewhere quietly without being seen ○ *She sneaked* *into the room.* ○ *The burglar sneaked up to the house, hidden by the trees.*

sneer /snɪə/ *noun* an unpleasant smile ○ *He held the whip in his hand and looked at her with a sneer.* ■ *verb* to give someone a sarcastic smile or to speak in a contemptuous way ○ *He sneered at her attempts to speak French.* ○ *You shouldn't sneer at her clothes – they're by the best designers and are very expensive.*

sneeze /sniːz/ *noun* the uncontrolled action of blowing air suddenly out through your mouth and nose because of an irritation inside your nose ○ *Coughs and sneezes spread diseases.* ■ *verb* to make a sneeze ○ *The smell of roses makes me sneeze.*

sniff /snɪf/ *noun* the act of breathing in air through your nose ○ *The dog gave a sniff at the plate before licking it.* ○ *He gave a little sniff and walked out of the shop.* ■ *verb* to breathe in air through your nose ○ *He sniffed and said 'I can smell fish and chips'.* ○ *The customs inspection is very strict, a dog is taken round to sniff (at) each bag and suitcase.*

snooker /'snuːkə/ *noun* a game for two players played on a table with twenty-two balls of different colours which you hit with a long thin stick

snore /snɔː/ *noun* a loud noise which someone who is sleeping produces in his or her nose and throat ○ *His snores kept her awake.* ■ *verb* to make a snore ○ *I can't get to sleep because my husband snores.*

snow /snəʊ/ *noun* water which falls as light white pieces of ice in cold weather ○ *Two metres of snow fell during the night.* ○ *The highest mountains are always covered with snow.* ○ *Children were out playing in the snow.* ○ *We went for a skiing holiday and there was hardly any snow.* ■ *verb* to fall as snow ○ *Look – it's started to snow!* ○ *It snowed all day, and the streets were blocked.* ○ *It hardly ever snows here in March.* (NOTE: The verb **snow** is always used with the subject **it**.)

snug /snʌɡ/ *adjective* warm and comfortable (NOTE: **snugger – snuggest**)

snuggle /'snʌɡ(ə)l/ *verb* to curl your body into a warm comfortable position ○ *They snuggled under their blankets.*

so /səʊ/ *adverb* **1.** showing how much ○ *It's so cold that the lake is covered with ice.* ○ *We liked Greece so much that we're going there again on holiday next year.* ○ *The soup was so salty that I couldn't eat it.* **2.** also ○ *She was late and so was I.* ○ *The children all caught flu, and so did their teacher.* ○ *I like apples. – So do I.* ○ *He's a good cook and so is his wife.* ○ *The teacher will be late and so will everyone else.* **3.** showing that the answer is 'yes' ○ *Does this train go to London? – I think so.* ○ *Was your car completely smashed? – I'm afraid so.* ○ *Will you be coming to the party? – I hope so!* ○ *Are they going to be at the meeting? – I suppose so.* ■ *conjunction* and this is the reason why ○ *It was snowing hard so we couldn't go for a walk.* ○ *She's got flu so she can't come to the office.* ◇ **so what** what does it matter?

soak /səʊk/ *verb* **1.** to put something in a liquid for a time ○ *Dry beans should be soaked in cold water for 24 hours.* **2.** to become very wet, or to make something very wet ○ *I forgot my umbrella and got soaked.* ○ *The rain soaked the soil.*

soaking /'səʊkɪŋ/ *adjective, adverb* very wet ○ *Don't let the dog into the kitchen – he's soaking* or *he's soaking wet.*

soap /səʊp/ *noun* a substance which you wash with, made from oils and usually with a pleasant smell ○ *There's no soap left in the bathroom.* ○ *I've put a new bar of soap in the kitchen.* (NOTE: no plural: *some soap, a bar* or *a cake* or *a piece of soap*)

soar /sɔː/ *verb* **1.** to go up very quickly ○ *Food prices soared during the cold weather.* **2.** to fly high up into the sky ○ *The rocket went soaring into the night sky.* (NOTE: Do not confuse with **sore**.)

sob /sɒb/ *verb* to cry, taking short breaths like hiccups ○ *She lay sobbing on the bed.* ○ *The little girl sobbed herself to sleep.* (NOTE: **sobs – sobbing – sobbed**) ■ *noun* a short breath like a hiccup, made by someone who is crying

○ *You could hear the sobs as she lay on her bed.* ○ *He gave a sob, and put the phone down.*

soccer /'sɒkə/ *noun* a game played between two teams of eleven players with a round ball which can be kicked or hit with the head, but not carried (NOTE: The game is called **football** in most countries, but is generally called **soccer** in the USA to distinguish it from American football.)

social /'səʊʃ(ə)l/ *adjective* relating to people as a group, or to human society in general ○ *an area with very serious social problems*

socially /'səʊʃ(ə)li/ *adverb* **1.** in a friendly situation ○ *I know her from work but I've never met her socially.* ○ *They get on very well socially.* **2.** with respect to other people or society ○ *the socially unacceptable behaviour of some football fans* ○ *These policies are socially divisive.*

society /sə'saɪəti/ *noun* **1.** a large group of people, usually all the people living in a country, considered as an organised community ○ *a free and democratic society* ○ *a member of society* ○ *Society needs to be protected against these criminals.* (NOTE: no plural) **2.** a club or association of people who have the same interests ○ *He belongs to the local drama society.* (NOTE: The plural is **societies**.)

sock /sɒk/ *noun* a piece of clothing worn on your foot inside a shoe ○ *a pair of socks*

sofa /'səʊfə/ *noun* a long comfortable seat with a soft back

so far /səʊ 'fɑː/ *adverb* until now

soft /sɒft/ *adjective* **1.** which moves easily when pressed ○ *I don't like soft seats in a car.* ○ *Do you like soft ice cream?* **2.** not loud ○ *When she spoke, her voice was so soft that we could hardly hear her.* ○ *Soft music was playing in the background.* **3.** not bright ○ *Soft lighting makes a room look warm.*

software /'sɒftweə/ *noun* computer programs which are put into a computer to make it work, as opposed to the computer itself ○ *What word-processing*

software do you use? Compare **hardware** (NOTE: no plural)

soggy /'sɒgi/ *adjective* wet and soft to an unpleasant degree (NOTE: **soggier – soggiest**)

soil /sɔɪl/ *noun* the earth in which plants grow ○ *Put some soil in the plant pot and then sow your flower seeds.* ○ *This soil's too poor for growing fruit trees.* ○ *The farm has fields of rich black soil.*

solar /'səʊlə/ *adjective* relating to the sun (NOTE: The similar word relating to the moon is **lunar** and to the stars is **stellar**.)

sold /səʊld/ past tense and past participle of **sell**

soldier /'səʊldʒə/ *noun* a member of an army ○ *Here's a photograph of my father as a soldier.* ○ *We were just in time to see the soldiers march past.* ○ *Enemy soldiers blew up the bridge.* ○ *The children are playing with their toy soldiers.*

sole /səʊl/ *adjective* only; belonging to one person ○ *Their sole aim is to make money.* ○ *She was the sole survivor from the crash.* ○ *I have sole responsibility for what goes on in this office.* ■ *noun* **1.** the underneath side of your foot ○ *He tickled the soles of her feet.* **2.** the main underneath part of a shoe, but not the heel ○ *These shoes need mending – I've got holes in both soles.* (NOTE: Do not confuse with **soul**.)

solemn /'sɒləm/ *adjective* **1.** serious and formal ○ *The doctor looked very solemn and shook his head.* ○ *At the most solemn moment of the ceremony someone's mobile phone rang.* **2.** which should be treated as very serious ○ *He made a solemn promise never to smoke again.*

solicitor /sə'lɪsɪtə/ *noun* a lawyer who gives advice to members of the public and acts for them in legal matters

solid /'sɒlɪd/ *adjective* **1.** hard and not liquid ○ *a solid lump of fat* ○ *She is allowed some solid food.* **2.** firm or strong ○ *Is the table solid enough to stand on?* ○ *His wealth is built on a solid base of property and shares.* **3.** not hollow ○ *Cricket is played with a solid ball.* **4.** made only of one material ○ *The box is made of solid silver.* ■ *noun* a hard substance which is not liquid ○ *Many solids melt when heated and become liquids.*

solo /'səʊləʊ/ *noun* a piece of music played or sung by one person alone ○ *She played a violin solo.* (NOTE: The plural is **solos**.) ■ *adjective* done by one person alone ○ *a piece for solo trumpet* ○ *She gave a solo performance in the Albert Hall.* ○ *He crashed on his first solo flight.*

solution /sə'luːʃ(ə)n/ *noun* **1.** a way of solving a problem ○ *It took us weeks to find a solution.* **2.** a mixture of a solid substance dissolved in a liquid ○ *Bathe your eye in a weak salt solution.*

solve /sɒlv/ *verb* to find an answer to a problem or question ○ *The loan will solve some of his financial problems.* ○ *He tried to solve the riddle.*

some /səm, sʌm/ *adjective, pronoun* **1.** a certain number of ○ *Some young drivers drive much too fast.* ○ *Some books were damaged in the fire.* ○ *Some days it was so hot that we just stayed by the swimming pool all day.* ○ *Can you cut some more slices of bread?* ○ *She bought some oranges and bananas.* ○ *We've just picked some strawberries.* **2.** a certain amount of ○ *Can you buy some bread when you go to town?* ○ *Can I have some more coffee?* ○ *Her illness is of some concern to her family.* **3.** used for referring to a person or thing you cannot identify (*followed by a singular noun*) ○ *Some man just knocked on the door and tried to sell me a magazine.* ○ *I read it in some book I borrowed from the library.* ○ *We saw it in some shop or other in Regent Street.* **4.** relating to a period of time or a distance ○ *Don't wait for me, I may be some time.* ○ *Their house is some way away from the railway station.*

somebody /'sʌmbədi/ *pronoun* **1.** same as **someone 2.** someone who is considered to be important

some day /'sʌm deɪ/ *adverb* at a time in the future that is not specified ○ *Some day I'll get round to cleaning out the garage.*

somehow /'sʌmhaʊ/ *adverb* by some means that are not yet known ○ *Some-*

how we must get back home by 6 o'clock.

someone /'sʌmwʌn/ *pronoun* a person who is not identified or referred to in particular way ○ *Can someone answer the phone?* ○ *I know someone who can fix your car.* ○ *I need someone tall who can reach the top shelf for me.* □ **someone else** an extra person, or a different person ○ *I've got four volunteers already, but I still need someone else.* ○ *If Jo is ill, could someone else help you?*

somersault /'sʌməsɔːlt/ *noun* a movement in which you roll over, head first ○ *He did a couple of somersaults on the mat.*

something /'sʌmθɪŋ/ *pronoun* **1.** a thing which is not identified or referred to in particular ○ *There's something soft at the bottom of the bag.* ○ *Something's gone wrong with the TV.* ○ *Can I have something to drink, please?* ○ *There's something about her that I don't like.* **2.** an important thing ○ *Come in and sit down, I've got something to tell you.*

sometimes /'sʌmtaɪmz/ *adverb* on some occasions but not on others ○ *Sometimes the car starts easily, and sometimes it won't start at all.* ○ *She sometimes comes to see us when she's in town on business.*

somewhat /'sʌmwɒt/ *adverb* to a fairly great degree (*formal*)

somewhere /'sʌmweə/ *adverb* in or at a place which is not identified ○ *I left my umbrella somewhere when I was in London.* ○ *Let's go somewhere else, this pub is full.* ○ *His parents live somewhere in Germany.*

son /sʌn/ *noun* a male child ○ *They have a large family – two sons and four daughters.* ○ *Her son has got married at last.* ○ *Their youngest son is in hospital.*

song /sɒŋ/ *noun* a set of words which are sung, usually to music ○ *She was singing a song in the bath.* ○ *The group's latest song has just come out on CD.* ○ *The soldiers marched along, singing a song.*

soon /suːn/ *adverb* in a short time from now ○ *Don't worry, we'll soon be in Ox-*

ford. ○ *It will soon be time to go to bed.* ○ *The fire started soon after 11 o'clock.*

sooner /'suːnə/ *adverb* earlier ○ *Can't we meet any sooner than that?*

soprano /sə'prɑːnəʊ/ *adjective* relating to a high-pitched woman's singing voice ○ *She sings soprano in the local choir.* ■ *noun* a woman with a high-pitched singing voice ○ *The sopranos are too feeble – I can hardly hear them.* (NOTE: The plural is **sopranos**.)

sore /sɔː/ *adjective* rough and swollen or painful ○ *He can't play tennis because he has a sore elbow.*

sorry /'sɒri/ *adjective* feeling unhappy, ashamed or disappointed about something ■ *interjection* used to excuse yourself ○ *Sorry! I didn't see that table had been reserved.* ○ *Can I have another mint, please? – sorry, I haven't any left.*

sort /sɔːt/ *noun* a type ○ *There were all sorts of people at the meeting.* ○ *I had an unpleasant sort of day at the office.* ○ *What sorts of ice cream have you got?* ○ *Do you like this sort of TV show?* ■ *verb* to arrange things in order or groups ○ *The apples are sorted according to size before being packed.* ○ *The votes are sorted then counted.*

sought /sɔːt/ past tense and past participle of **seek**

soul /səʊl/ *noun* the spirit in a person, which is believed by some people to go on existing after the person dies ○ *Do you believe your soul lives on when your body dies?* ○ *From the depths of his soul he longed to be free.* (NOTE: Do not confuse with **sole**.)

sound /saʊnd/ *noun* something which you can hear ○ *Sounds of music came from the street.* ○ *I thought I heard the sound of guns.* ○ *Please can you turn down the sound on the TV when I'm on the phone?* ○ *She crept out of her bedroom and we didn't hear a sound.* ■ *verb* **1.** to make a noise with something ○ *Sound your horn when you come to a corner.* ○ *They sounded the alarm after two prisoners escaped.* **2.** to seem to be the case ○ *It sounds as if he's made an unfortunate choice.* ○ *The book sounds interesting according to what I've heard.* ■ *adverb* deeply ○ *The children were sound asleep when the police came.*

soup /suːp/ *noun* a liquid food which you eat hot from a bowl at the beginning of a meal, usually made from meat, fish or vegetables ○ *We have onion soup or mushroom soup today.* ○ *Does anyone want soup?* ○ *A bowl of hot soup is always welcome on a cold day.* ○ *If you're hungry, open a tin of soup.*

sour /'saʊə/ *adjective* with a sharp bitter taste ○ *If the cooked fruit is too sour, you can add some sugar.* ○ *Nobody likes sour milk.*

source /sɔːs/ *noun* a place where something comes from ○ *I think the source of the infection is in one of your teeth.* ○ *The source of the river is in the mountains.* ○ *You must declare income from all sources to the tax office.*

sourness /'saʊənəs/ *noun* the state of being sour

south /saʊθ/ *noun* **1.** the direction facing towards the sun at midday ○ *Look south from the mountain, and you will see the city in the distance.* ○ *The city is to the south of the river.* ○ *The wind is blowing from the south.* **2.** the part of a country to the south of the rest ○ *The south of the country is warmer than the north.* ○ *She went to live in the south of England.* ■ *adjective* relating to the south ○ *The south coast is popular for holidaymakers.* ○ *Cross to the south side of the river.* ■ *adverb* towards the south ○ *Many birds fly south for the winter.* ○ *The river flows south into the Mediterranean.*

southern /'sʌð(ə)n/ *adjective* of the south ○ *The southern part of the country is warmer than the north.*

souvenir /ˌsuːvə'nɪə/ *noun* a thing bought to remind you of the place where you bought it

sow /səʊ/ *verb* to put seeds into soil so that they become plants ○ *Peas and beans should be sown in April.* ○ *Sow the seed thinly in fine soil.* (NOTE: Do not confuse with **sew**. Note also: **sows – sowing – sowed – sown** /səʊn/.)

space /speɪs/ *noun* **1.** an empty place between other things ○ *There's a space to park your car over there.* ○ *Write your name and reference number in the space at the top of the paper.* **2.** an area which is available for something ○ *His desk takes up too much space.* **3.** also **outer space** the area beyond the earth's atmosphere ○ *exploring outer space* ○ *space vehicles*

spade /speɪd/ *noun* **1.** a tool with a wide square blade at the end of a long handle, used for digging or moving something such as soil or sand **2.** a similar small plastic tool, used by children ○ *The children took their buckets and spades to the beach.*

spaghetti /spə'geti/ *noun* long thin strips of pasta, cooked and eaten with a sauce

span /spæn/ *noun* the width of wings or of an arch ○ *Each section of the bridge has a span of fifty feet.* ■ *verb* to stretch across space or time ○ *Her career spanned thirty years.* ○ *A stone bridge spans the river.* (NOTE: **spans – spanning – spanned**)

spare /speə/ *adjective* available but not being used ○ *I always take a spare pair of shoes when I travel.* ■ *plural noun* **spares** spare parts or pieces used to mend broken parts of a car or other machine ○ *We can't get spares for that make of washing machine.* ○ *It's difficult to get spares for the car because they don't make this model any more.* ■ *verb* to give something or to do without something ○ *Can you spare your assistant to help me for a day?* ○ *Can you spare about five minutes to talk about the problem?* ○ *If you have a moment to spare, can you clean the car?*

spark /spɑːk/ *noun* a little flash of fire or of light ○ *Sparks flew as the train went over the junction.* ■ *verb* **1.** to send out sparks or to make electric sparks **2.** to make something start ○ *The proposed closure of the station sparked anger amongst travellers.* ○ *The shooting of the teenager sparked off a riot.*

spark off *phrasal verb* same as **spark** *verb* 2

sparkle /'spɑːk(ə)l/ *verb* to shine brightly ○ *Her jewels sparkled in the light of the candles.* ○ *His eyes sparkled when he heard the salary offered.*

speak /spiːk/ *verb* **1.** to say words ○ *She spoke to me when the meeting was over.* ○ *He walked past me without speaking.* ○ *He was speaking to the postman when I saw him.* ○ *The manager wants to speak to you about sales in Africa.* **2.** to be able to say things in a particular language ○ *We need someone who can speak Russian.* ○ *He speaks English with an American accent.* ○ *You will have to brush up your Japanese as my mother speaks hardly any English.* (NOTE: **speaks – speaking – spoke** /spəʊk/ **– has spoken** /'spəʊkn/) ◊ **to speak your mind** to say exactly what you think

speak out *phrasal verb* to make your opinions or feelings known strongly

speak up *phrasal verb* to speak louder; to say what you have to say in a louder voice ○ *Can you speak up please – we can't hear you at the back!*

speaker /'spiːkə/ *noun* **1.** a person who speaks ○ *We need an English speaker to help with the tour.* **2.** a loudspeaker ○ *One of the speakers doesn't work.*

spear /spɪə/ *noun* a long pointed throwing stick, formerly used as a weapon ○ *They kill fish with spears.* ■ *verb* to push something sharp into something to catch it ○ *Spearing fish is not easy.* ○ *She managed to spear a sausage on the barbecue with her fork.*

special /'speʃ(ə)l/ *adjective* having a particular importance or use ○ *This is a very special day for us – it's our twenty-fifth wedding anniversary.* ○ *He has a special pair of scissors for cutting metal.*

specialise /'speʃəlaɪz/, **specialize** *verb* **1.** to study one particular subject ○ *At university, she specialised in marine biology.* **2.** to produce one thing in particular ○ *The company specialises in electronic components.*

specialist /'speʃəlɪst/ *noun* **1.** a person who knows a lot about something ○ *You should go to a tax specialist for advice.* **2.** a doctor who specialises in a certain branch of medicine ○ *He was referred to a heart specialist.*

species /'spiːʃiːz/ *noun* a group of living things such as animals or plants which can breed with each other ○ *Several species of butterfly are likely to become extinct.*

specific /spəˈsɪfɪk/ *adjective* relating to something in particular ○ *Can you be more specific about what you're trying to achieve?* ○ *I gave specific instructions that I was not to be disturbed.* ○ *Is the money intended for a specific purpose?*

specifically /spəˈsɪfɪkli/ *adverb* particularly ○ *I specifically said I didn't want a blue door.* ○ *The advertisement is specifically aimed at people over 50.*

specimen /'spesɪmɪn/ *noun* an example of something ○ *The bank asked for a specimen signature for their records.*

spectator /spekˈteɪtə/ *noun* a person who watches an event like a football match or a horse show

speech /spiːtʃ/ *noun* **1.** a formal talk given to an audience ○ *She made some notes before giving her speech.* ○ *He wound up his speech with a story about his father.* ○ *Who will be making the speech at the prize giving?* **2.** the ability to say words, or the act of saying words ○ *His speech has been affected by brain damage.* ○ *Some of these expressions are only used in speech, not in writing.*

speed /spiːd/ *noun* the rate at which something moves or is done ○ *The coach was travelling at a high speed when it crashed.* ○ *The speed with which they repaired the gas leak was incredible.* ■ *verb* to move quickly ○ *The ball sped across the ice.* (NOTE: **speeds – speeding – sped** /sped/ *or* **speeded**)

spell /spel/ *verb* to write or say correctly the letters that make a word ○ *W-O-R-R-Y spells 'worry'* ○ *How do you spell your surname?* ○ *We spelt his name wrong on the envelope.* (NOTE: **spells – spelling – spelled** *or* **spelt** /spelt/ – **has spelled** *or* **has spelt**) ■ *noun* words which are intended to have a magic effect when they are spoken ○ *The wicked witch cast a spell on the princess.*

spelling /'spelɪŋ/ *noun* the correct way in which words are spelt

spelt /spelt/ past tense and past participle of **spell**

spend /spend/ *verb* **1.** to pay money ○ *I went shopping and spent a fortune.* ○ *Why do we spend so much money on food?* **2.** to use time doing something ○ *He wants to spend more time with his family.* ○ *She spent months arguing with the income tax people.* ○ *Don't spend too long on your homework.* ○ *Why don't you come and spend the weekend with us?* (NOTE: **spends – spending – spent** /spent/)

sphere /sfɪə/ *noun* an object which is perfectly round like a ball ○ *The earth is not quite a perfect sphere.*

spice /spaɪs/ *noun* a substance made from the roots, flowers, seeds or leaves of plants, which is used to flavour food ○ *Add a blend of your favourite spices.* ○ *You need lots of different spices for Indian cookery.*

spider /'spaɪdə/ *noun* a small animal with eight legs which makes a web and eats insects

spike /spaɪk/ *noun* a piece of metal or wood wit ha sharp point ○ *The wall was topped with a row of metal spikes.*

spill /spɪl/ *verb* to pour a liquid or a powder out of a container by mistake ○ *That glass is too full – you'll spill it.* ○ *He spilt soup down the front of his shirt.* ○ *She dropped the bag and some of the flour spilled out onto the floor.* (NOTE: **spills – spilling – spilled** *or* **spilt** /spɪlt/) ■ *noun* the act of pouring a liquid by accident ○ *The authorities are trying to cope with the oil spill from the tanker.*

spin /spɪn/ *verb* **1.** to move round and round very fast ○ *The earth is spinning in space.* ○ *The plane was spinning out of control.* **2.** to make something turn round and round ○ *The washing machine spins the clothes to get the water out of them.* ○ *He spun the wheel to make sure it turned freely.* **3.** (*of a spider*) to make a web ○ *The spider has* *spun a web between the two posts.* (NOTE: **spins – spinning – spun** /spʌn/) ■ *noun* the turning movement of a ball as it moves ○ *He put so much spin on the ball that it bounced sideways.* ○ *He jammed on the brakes and the car went into a spin.*

spin out *phrasal verb* to make something last as long as possible

spine /spaɪn/ *noun* **1.** a series of bones joined together from your skull down the middle of your back ○ *He injured his spine playing rugby.* (NOTE: The bones in the spine are the **vertebrae**.) **2.** a sharp part like a pin, on a plant, animal or fish ○ *Did you know that lemon trees had spines?* **3.** the back edge of a book, which usually has the title printed on it ○ *The title and the author's name are printed on the front of the book and also on the spine.*

spiral /'spaɪrəl/ *noun* a shape which is twisted round and round like a spring ○ *He drew a spiral on the sheet of paper.* ■ *adjective* which twists round and round ○ *A spiral staircase leads to the top of the tower.*

spirit /'spɪrɪt/ *noun* **1.** the mental attitude which controls how someone behaves generally ○ *She has a great spirit of fun.* ○ *He had an independent spirit.* **2.** feelings which are typical of a particular occasion **3.** the part of a person that is said to still exist after death **4.** alcohol (NOTE: usually plural)

spiritual /'spɪrɪtʃuəl/ *adjective* relating to the spirit or the soul ○ *The church's main task is to give spiritual advice to its members.*

spite /spaɪt/ *noun* **1.** bad feeling ○ *They sprayed his car with white paint out of spite.* **2.** □ **in spite of** although something happened or was done ○ *In spite of all his meetings, he still found time to ring his wife.* ○ *We all enjoyed ourselves, in spite of the awful weather.* ■ *verb* to annoy someone on purpose ○ *He did it to spite his sister.*

spiteful /'spaɪtf(ə)l/ *adjective* full of a nasty feelings against someone

splash /splæʃ/ *noun* a sound made when something falls into a liquid or when a liquid hits something hard ○ *She fell into the pool with a loud splash.* ○ *Listen to the splash of the waves against the rocks.* ■ *verb* **1.** (*of liquid*) to make a noise when something is dropped into it or when it hits something ○ *I missed the ball and it splashed into the pool.* ○ *The rain splashed against the windows.* **2.** to make someone wet by sending liquid on to him or her ○ *The car drove past through a puddle and splashed my trousers.* **3.** to move through water, making a noise ○ *He splashed his way through the shallow water to the rocks.* ○ *The little children were splashing about in the paddling pool.*

splendid /'splendɪd/ *adjective* extremely good or impressive

split /splɪt/ *verb* **1.** to divide something into parts ○ *He split the log into small pieces with an axe.* **2.** to divide or come apart ○ *My trousers were too tight – they split when I bent down.* ○ *After they lost the election, the party split into various factions.* (NOTE: **splits – splitting – split**)

spoil /spɔɪl/ *verb* **1.** to change something which was good so that it is no longer good ○ *We had such bad weather that our camping holiday was spoilt.* ○ *Half the contents of the warehouse were spoiled by floodwater.* **2.** to be too kind to someone, especially a child, so that he or she sometimes becomes badly behaved ○ *You'll spoil that child if you always give in to him.* ○ *Grandparents are allowed to spoil their grandchildren a little.* (NOTE: **spoils – spoiling – spoilt** /spɔɪlt/ or **spoiled**)

spoke /spəʊk/ past tense of **speak**

spoken /'spəʊkən/ past participle of **speak**

sponge /spʌndʒ/ *noun* **1.** a soft material full of small holes used to make things like cushions ○ *The sofa has sponge cushions.* **2.** a sea animal with a skeleton which is full of holes ○ *Diving down into the Red Sea you could see sponges on the sea floor.* ■ *verb* to wipe clean with a sponge ○ *He sponged the kitchen table.*

spoon /spuːn/ *noun* an object used for eating liquids and soft food, or for stirring food which is being cooked, with a handle at one end and a small bowl at the other, ○ *Use a spoon to eat your pudding.* ○ *We need a big spoon to serve the soup.*

sport /spɔːt/ *noun* a game or games involving physical activity and competition ○ *Do you like watching sport on TV?* ○ *The world of sport is mourning the death of the racing driver.* ○ *The only sport I play is tennis.* ○ *She doesn't play any sport at all.*

spot /spɒt/ *noun* **1.** a coloured mark, usually round ○ *Her dress has a pattern of white and red spots.* ○ *He wore a blue tie with white spots.* **2.** a particular place ○ *This is the exact spot where the queen died.* **3.** a small round mark or pimple on the skin ○ *She suddenly came out in spots after eating fish.* ■ *verb* to notice something or someone ○ *The teacher didn't spot the mistake.* ○ *We spotted him in the crowd.* (NOTE: **spots – spotting – spotted**)

spotless /ˈspɒtləs/ *adjective* completely clean, with no dirty marks at all

spout /spaʊt/ *noun* a tube on a container which is shaped for pouring liquid out of the container ○ *You fill the kettle through the spout.* ○ *Cut here and pull out to form a spout.*

sprain /spreɪn/ *verb* to damage a joint of the body by twisting it suddenly and violently ○ *He sprained his ankle jumping over the fence.* ■ *noun* a condition where a joint is injured because of a sudden violent movement ○ *He is walking with a stick because of an ankle sprain.*

sprang /spræŋ/ past tense of **spring**

sprawl /sprɔːl/ *verb* to lie with your arms and legs spread out ○ *He sprawled in his armchair and turned on the TV.* ○ *The boy on the bike hit her and sent her sprawling.*

spray /spreɪ/ *noun* a mass of tiny drops of liquid ○ *The waves crashed against the sea wall sending spray over the road.* ○ *She uses a nasal spray to clear her catarrh.* ■ *verb* to send out liquid in fine drops ○ *He sprayed water all over the garden with the hose.* ○ *They sprayed the room with disinfectant.*

spread /spred/ *verb* **1.** to arrange something over a wide area ○ *Spread the paper flat on the table.* **2.** to move over a wide area ○ *The fire started in the top floor and soon spread to the roof.* ○ *The flu epidemic spread rapidly.* **3.** to cover a surface with a layer of something ○ *She spread a white cloth over the table.* ○ *He was spreading butter on a piece of bread.* (NOTE: **spreads – spreading – spread**) ■ *noun* **1.** the action of moving over a wide area ○ *Doctors are trying to check the spread of the disease.* **2.** a soft food consisting of meat, fish or cheese, which you can spread on something such as bread ○ *As snacks, they offered us water biscuits with cheese spread.*

spring /sprɪŋ/ *noun* **1.** the season of the year between winter and summer ○ *In spring all the trees start to grow new leaves.* ○ *We always go to Greece in the spring.* ○ *They started work last spring* or *in the spring of last year and they still haven't finished.* **2.** a wire which is twisted round and round and which goes back to its original shape after you have pulled it or pushed it ○ *The mattress is so old the springs have burst through the cover.* ○ *There's a spring to keep the door shut.* **3.** a place where a stream of water rushes out of the ground ○ *The town of Bath was built in Roman times around hot springs.* ■ *verb* to move suddenly ○ *Everyone sprang to life when the officer shouted.* ○ *The door sprang open without anyone touching it.* (NOTE: **springs – springing – sprang** /spræŋ/ **– has sprung** /sprʌŋ/)

sprinkle /ˈsprɪŋkəl/ *verb* to put small amounts of a liquid or powder over a surface by shaking

sprint /sprɪnt/ *verb* to run very fast over a short distance ○ *I had to sprint to catch the bus.* ○ *She sprinted down the track.*

sprout /spraʊt/ *noun* a new shoot of a plant ○ *The vine is covered with new sprouts.* ■ *verb* to produce new shoots ○ *Throw those old potatoes away, they're starting to sprout.* ○ *The bush had begun to sprout fresh green leaves.*

spun /spʌn/ past participle of **spin**

spurt /spɜːt/ *verb* **1.** □ **to spurt out** to come out in a strong jet ○ *Oil spurted out of the burst pipe.* **2.** to run fast suddenly ○ *He spurted past two runners and came in first.* ■ *noun* a strong flow of liquid ○ *They tried to block the spurts of water coming out of the pipe.*

spy /spaɪ/ *noun* a person who is paid to try to find out secret information about the enemy or a rival group ○ *He was executed as a Russian spy.* (NOTE: The plural is **spies**.) ■ *verb* to work as a spy (NOTE: **spies – spying – spied**) □ **to spy on someone** to watch someone in secret, to find out what they are planning to do ○ *We discovered that our neighbours had been spying on us.*

squalid /ˈskwɒlɪd/ *adjective* a squalid room or building is dirty and unpleasant ○ *The prisoners are kept in squalid conditions.*

square /skweə/ *noun* **1.** a shape with four equal sides and four right-angled corners ○ *The board on which you play chess is made up of black and white squares.* ○ *Graph paper is covered with small squares.* **2.** an open space in a town, with big buildings all round ○ *The hotel is in the main square of the town, opposite the town hall.* ○ *Red Square is in the middle of Moscow.* **3.** a number that is the result of multiplying another number by itself ○ *9 is the square of 3.* ■ *adjective* **1.** shaped like a square, with four equal sides and four right-angled corners ○ *You can't fit six people round a small square table.* ○ *An A4 piece of paper isn't square.* **2.** multiplied by itself

squash /skwɒʃ/ *verb* to crush or to squeeze something ○ *Hundreds of passengers were squashed into the train.* ○ *He sat on my hat and squashed it flat.* ■ *noun* a fast game for two players played in an enclosed court, with a small, squashy rubber ball and light, long-handled rackets ○ *He plays squash to unwind after a day at the office.* ○ *Let's play a game of squash.*

squat /skwɒt/ *verb* to move your body close to the ground so that you are sitting on your heels ○ *She squatted on the floor, trying to get the stains out of the carpet.* (NOTE: **squats – squatting – squatted**)

squeak /skwiːk/ *noun* a quiet high sound like the sound that a mouse makes ○ *You can tell when someone comes into the garden by the squeak of the gate.* ■ *verb* to make a squeak ○ *That door squeaks – the hinges need oiling.*

squeal /skwiːl/ *noun* a loud high noise ○ *The children let out squeals of delight when they saw the presents under the Christmas tree.* ○ *The car turned the corner with a squeal of tyres.* ■ *verb* to make a loud high-pitched noise ○ *She squealed when she heard she had won first prize.* ○ *As the car turned the corner its tyres squealed.*

squeeze /skwiːz/ *noun* the act of pressing or crushing ○ *I gave her hand a squeeze.* ■ *verb* **1.** to press on something or to press or crush something like a fruit or a tube to get something out of it ○ *She squeezed my arm gently.* ○ *He squeezed an orange to get the juice.* ○ *She squeezed some toothpaste out onto her brush.* **2.** to force something, or to force your own body, into a small space ○ *You can't squeeze six people into that little car.* ○ *More people tried to squeeze on the train even though it was full already.* ○ *The cat managed to squeeze through the window.*

squirrel /ˈskwɪrəl/ *noun* a small red or grey wild animal with a large tail which lives in trees and eats nuts ○ *The squirrel sat up on a branch nibbling a nut.* ○ *Squirrels hoard nuts for the winter.*

squirt /skwɜːt/ *verb* to send out a thin powerful flow of liquid ○ *Don't squirt so much washing-up liquid into the bowl.* ○ *She squeezed the tube hard and masses of toothpaste squirted out.*

St *abbr* **1.** street **2.** saint

stab /stæb/ *verb* to push a sharp knife with force into someone or something ○ *He was stabbed in the chest.* (NOTE: **stabs – stabbing – stabbed**) ■ *noun* a deep wound made by the point of a knife ○ *He died of stab wounds.* ◇ **to have a stab at something** to try to do something ○ *I'm keen to have a stab at driving the tractor.*

stable /'steɪb(ə)l/ *adjective* which does not change ○ *The hospital said his condition was stable.* ■ *noun* a building for keeping a horse ○ *My horse is not in his stable, who's riding him?*

stack /stæk/ *noun* a pile or heap of things one on top of the other ○ *a stack of books and papers* ■ *verb* to pile things on top of each other ○ *The skis are stacked outside the chalet.* ○ *She stacked up the dirty plates.* ○ *The warehouse is stacked with boxes.*

stadium /'steɪdiəm/ *noun* a large building where crowds of people watch sport, with seats arranged around a sports field (NOTE: The plural is **stadiums** or **stadia**.)

staff /stɑːf/ *noun* all the people who work in a company, school, college, or other organisation ○ *She's on the school staff.* ○ *Only staff can use this lift.* ○ *A quarter of our staff are ill.* ○ *That firm pays its staff very badly.* ○ *He joined the staff last Monday.* ○ *Three members of staff are away sick.* (NOTE: **staff** refers to a group of people and so is often followed by a verb in the plural.)

stage /steɪdʒ/ *noun* **1.** a raised floor, especially where the actors perform in a theatre ○ *The pop group came onto the stage and started to sing.* **2.** one of several points of development ○ *the different stages of a production process* ○ *The first stage in the process is to grind the rock to powder.* **3.** a section of a long journey ○ *Stage one of the tour takes us from Paris to Bordeaux.* ■ *verb* to put on or arrange a play, a show, a musical or other performance or event ○ *The exhibition is being staged in the college library.*

stagger /'stægə/ *verb* **1.** to walk in way that is not steady or controlled, almost falling down ○ *She managed to stagger across the road and into the police station.* ○ *Three men staggered out of the pub.* **2.** to surprise someone very much ○ *I was staggered at the amount they charge for service.* **3.** to arrange something such as holidays or working hours, so that they do not all begin and end at the same time ○ *We have to stagger the lunch hour so that there is always some-*

one on the switchboard. ■ *noun* the movement of someone who is staggering ○ *He walked with a noticeable stagger.*

stain /steɪn/ *noun* a mark which is difficult to remove, e.g. ink or blood ○ *It is difficult to remove coffee stains from the tablecloth.* ○ *There was a round stain on the table where he had put his wine glass.* ■ *verb* to make a mark of a different colour on something ○ *If you eat those berries they will stain your teeth.* ○ *His shirt was stained with blood.*

stair /steə/ *noun* one step in a series of steps, going up or down inside a building ○ *He was sitting on the bottom stair.*

staircase /'steəkeɪs/ *noun* a set of stairs which go from one floor in a building to another

stake /steɪk/ *noun* a strong pointed piece of wood or metal, pushed into the ground to mark something, or to hold something up ○ *They hammered stakes into the ground to put up a wire fence.* ○ *The apple trees are attached to stakes.*

stale /steɪl/ *adjective* food which is stale is old and no longer fresh

stalk /stɔːk/ *noun* the stem of a plant which holds a leaf, a flower or a fruit ○ *Roses with very long stalks are more expensive.* ■ *verb* to stay near someone and watch him or her all the time, especially in a way that is frightening or upsetting ○ *She told the police that a man was stalking her.* ○ *The hunters stalked the deer for several miles.*

stall /stɔːl/ *noun* a place in a market where one person sells his or her goods ○ *He has a flower stall at Waterloo Station.* ○ *We wandered round the market looking at the stalls.* ■ *verb* (*of a car engine*) to stop unintentionally, often when trying to drive off without accelerating ○ *If he takes his foot off the accelerator, the engine stalls.* ○ *The car stalled at the traffic lights and he couldn't restart it.*

stammer /'stæmə/ *verb* to repeat sounds when speaking, e.g. because of feeling nervous ○ *He stammers badly when making speeches.* ○ *She rushed into the police station and stammered* *out 'he's – he's – he's after me, he's got – got – a knife'.* ■ *noun* a speech problem that involves hesitating and repeating sounds when speaking ○ *Because of his stammer he was shy and reserved at school.*

stamp /stæmp/ *noun* **1.** a little piece of paper with a price printed on it which you stick on a letter to show that you have paid for it to be sent by post ○ *a first-class stamp* ○ *She forgot to put a stamp on the letter before she posted it.* ○ *He wants to show me his stamp collection.* **2.** a mark made on something ○ *The invoice has the stamp 'received with thanks' on it.* ○ *The customs officer looked at the stamps in his passport.* ■ *verb* **1.** to mark something with a stamp ○ *They stamped my passport when I entered the country.* **2.** to walk, or to put your feet down, with loud or forceful steps ○ *They stamped on the ants to kill them.* ○ *He was so angry that he stamped out of the room.*

stand /stænd/ *verb* **1.** to be upright on your feet and not sitting or lying down ○ *She stood on a chair to reach the top shelf.* ○ *They were so tired they could hardly keep standing.* ○ *If there are no seats left, we'll have to stand.* ○ *Don't just stand there doing nothing – come and help us.* **2.** to be upright ○ *Only a few houses were still standing after the earthquake.* ○ *The jar was standing in the middle of the table.* **3.** to accept something bad that continues ○ *The office is filthy – I don't know how you can stand working here.* ○ *She can't stand all this noise.* ○ *He stopped going to French lessons because he couldn't stand the teacher.* (NOTE: **stands – standing – stood** /stʊd/) ■ *noun* something which holds something up ○ *The pot of flowers fell off its stand.*

stand for *phrasal verb* to have a meaning ○ *What do the letters BBC stand for?*

stand out *phrasal verb* to be easily seen ○ *Their house stands out because it is painted pink.* ○ *Her red hair makes her stand out in a crowd.*

stand up *phrasal verb* to get up from sitting ○ *When the teacher comes into* the room all the children should stand up. ○ *He stood up to offer his seat to the old lady.*

stand up for *phrasal verb* to try to defend someone or something in a difficult situation ○ *He stood up for the rights of children.*

stand up to *phrasal verb* **1.** to oppose someone bravely ○ *No one was prepared to stand up to the head of department.* **2.** to be able to resist difficult conditions ○ *A carpet in a shop has to stand up to a lot of wear.*

standard /'stændəd/ *noun* **1.** the level of quality something has ○ *The standard of service in this restaurant is very high.* ○ *This piece of work is not up to your usual standard.* **2.** an excellent quality which something or someone is expected to achieve ○ *This product does not meet our standards.* ○ *She has set a standard which it will be difficult to match.* **3.** a large official flag ○ *The royal standard flies over Buckingham Palace.* ■ *adjective* **1.** usual, not special ○ *She joined on a standard contract.* ○ *You will need to follow the standard procedure to join the association.* **2.** on a tall pole

stank /stæŋk/ past tense of **stink**

staple /'steɪp(ə)l/ *noun* a piece of wire which is pushed through papers and bent over to hold them together ○ *He used some scissors to take the staples out of the papers.* ■ *verb* to fasten papers together with a staple or with staples ○ *Don't staple the cheque to the order form.*

star /stɑː/ *noun* **1.** a bright object which can be seen in the sky at night like a very distant bright light ○ *On a clear night you can see thousands of stars.* ○ *The pole star shows the direction of the North Pole.* **2.** a shape that has several points like a star ○ *Draw a big star and colour it red.* **3.** a famous person who is very well known to the public ○ *football stars* ○ *Who is your favourite film star?* ■ *verb* to appear as a main character in a film or play ○ *She starred in 'Gone with the Wind'.* ○ *He has a starring role in the new play.* (NOTE: **stars – starring – starred**)

stare /steə/ *verb* to look at someone or something for a long time ○ *She stared sadly out of the window at the rain.* ■ *noun* a long fixed look ○ *He gave her a stare and walked on.*

start /stɑːt/ *noun* the beginning of something ○ *Building the house took only six months from start to finish.* ○ *Things went wrong from the start.* ○ *Let's forget all you've done up to now, and make a fresh start.* ■ *verb* **1.** to begin to do something ○ *The babies all started to cry* or *all started crying at the same time.* ○ *He started to eat* or *he started eating his dinner before the rest of the family.* ○ *Take an umbrella – it's starting to rain.* ○ *When you learn Russian, you have to start by learning the alphabet.* **2.** (*of a machine*) to begin to work ○ *The car won't start – the battery must be flat.* ○ *The engine started beautifully.* ◇ **to start with** first of all ○ *We have lots to do but to start with we'll do the washing up.*

start off *phrasal verb* **1.** to begin ○ *We'll start off with soup and then have a meat dish.* **2.** to leave on a journey ○ *You can start off now, and I'll follow when I'm ready.*

startle /ˈstɑːt(ə)l/ *verb* to make someone suddenly surprised

starve /stɑːv/ *verb* not to have enough food ○ *Many people starved to death in the desert.*

state /steɪt/ *noun* **1.** the way something or someone is at a specific time ○ *The children are in a state of excitement.* ○ *They left the flat in a terrible state.* ○ *She's not in a fit state to receive visitors.* **2.** the government of a country ○ *We all pay taxes to the state.* ○ *The state should pay for the upkeep of museums.* **3.** an independent country ○ *The member states of the European Union.* **4.** one of the parts into which some countries are divided ○ *the State of Arizona* ○ *New South Wales has the largest population of all the Australian states.* ■ *verb* to give information clearly ○ *Please state your name and address.* ○ *It states in the instructions that you must not open the can near a flame.* ○ *The document states that all revenue has to be declared to the*

tax office. ◇ **in a state 1.** in a very unhappy, worried or upset condition ○ *She's in such a state that I don't want to leave her alone.* ○ *He was in a terrible state after the phone call.* **2.** in a dirty or bad condition ○ *Look at the state of your trousers.* ○ *They left our flat in a terrible state.*

statement /ˈsteɪtmənt/ *noun* **1.** something that is spoken or written publicly ○ *a statement about or on the new procedures* ○ *She refused to issue a statement to the press.* **2.** a written document from a bank showing how much money is in an account

station /ˈsteɪʃ(ə)n/ *noun* **1.** a place where trains stop and passengers get on or off ○ *The train leaves the Central Station at 14.15.* ○ *This is a fast train – it doesn't stop at every station.* ○ *We'll try to get a sandwich at the station buffet.* **2.** a large main building for a service ○ *The fire station is just down the road from us.* ○ *He was arrested and taken to the local police station.*

stationary /ˈsteɪʃ(ə)n(ə)ri/ *adjective* not moving (NOTE: Do not confuse with **stationery**.)

stationery /ˈsteɪʃ(ə)n(ə)ri/ *noun* things such as paper, envelopes, pens and ink which you use for writing (NOTE: no plural. Do not confuse with **stationary**.)

statue /ˈstætʃuː/ *noun* a solid image of a person or animal made from a substance such as stone or metal

status /ˈsteɪtəs/ *noun* **1.** social importance when compared to other people ○ *He has a low-status job on the Underground.* ○ *His status in the company has been rising steadily.* **2.** a general position

stay /steɪ/ *verb* **1.** not to change ○ *The temperature stayed below zero all day.* ○ *In spite of the fire, he stayed calm.* ○ *I won't be able to stay awake until midnight.* **2.** to stop in a place ○ *They came for lunch and stayed until after midnight.* ○ *I'm rather tired so I'll stay at home tomorrow.* ○ *He's ill and has to stay in bed.* **3.** to stop in a place as a visitor ○ *They stayed two nights in Edinburgh on their tour of Scotland.* ○

Where will you be staying when you're in New York? ○ *My parents are staying at the Hotel London.*

stay up *phrasal verb* not to go to bed

steadily /'stedɪli/ *adverb* regularly or continuously

steady /'stedi/ *adjective* **1.** firm and not moving or shaking ○ *You need a steady hand to draw a straight line without a ruler.* ○ *He put a piece of paper under the table leg to keep it steady.* **2.** continuing in a regular way ○ *There is a steady demand for computers.* ○ *The car was doing a steady seventy miles an hour.* ○ *She hasn't got a steady boyfriend.* (NOTE: **steadier – steadiest**) ■ *verb* to keep something firm ○ *He put out his hand to steady the ladder.* (NOTE: **steadies – steadying – steadied**)

steak /steɪk/ *noun* **1.** a thick piece of meat, usually beef ○ *He ordered steak and chips.* ○ *I'm going to grill these steaks.* **2.** a thick piece of a big fish ○ *A grilled salmon steak for me, please!* (NOTE: Do not confuse with **stake**.)

steal /stiːl/ *verb* **1.** to take and keep something that belongs to another person without permission ○ *Someone tried to steal my handbag.* ○ *He was arrested for stealing cars.* **2.** to move quietly ○ *He stole into the cellar and tried to find the safe.* (NOTE: Do not confuse with **steel**. Note also: **steals – stealing – stole** /stəʊl/ **– stolen** /'stəʊlən/)

steam /stiːm/ *noun* the substance like clouds which comes off hot or boiling water ○ *Clouds of steam were coming out of the kitchen.*

steel /stiːl/ *noun* a strong metal made from iron and carbon ○ *Steel knives are best for the kitchen.* ○ *The door is made of solid steel.*

steep /stiːp/ *adjective* **1.** which rises or falls quickly ○ *The car climbed the steep hill with some difficulty.* ○ *The steps up the church tower are steeper than our stairs at home.* **2.** very sharply increasing or falling ○ *a steep increase in interest charges* ○ *a steep fall in share prices*

steer /stɪə/ *verb* to make a vehicle go in a particular direction ○ *She steered the car into the garage.*

stem /stem/ *noun* the tall thin part of a plant which holds a leaf, a flower or a fruit ○ *Trim the stems before you put the flowers in the vase.*

step /step/ *noun* **1.** a movement of your foot when walking ○ *I wonder when the baby will take his first steps.* ○ *Take a step sideways and you will be able to see the castle.* **2.** a regular movement of feet at the same time as other people **3.** one stair in a set of stairs ○ *There are two steps down into the kitchen.* ○ *I counted 75 steps to the top of the tower.* ○ *Be careful, there's a step up into the bathroom.* **4.** an action which is done or has to be done out of several ○ *The first and most important step is to find out how much money we can spend.* ■ *verb* to move forwards, backwards or sideways on foot ○ *He stepped out in front of a bicycle and was knocked down.* ○ *She stepped off the bus into a puddle.* ○ *Don't step back, there's a child behind you.* (NOTE: **steps – stepping – stepped**) ◇ **in step** moving your feet at the same rate as everybody else ○ *I tried to keep in step with him as we walked along.* ○ *The recruits can't even march in step.* ◇ **out of step** moving your feet at a different rate from everyone else ○ *One of the squad always gets out of step.* ◇ **to take steps to** to act to encourage or prevent something ○ *We should take steps to encourage female applicants.* ○ *The museum must take steps to make sure that nothing else is stolen.*

stereo /'steriəʊ/ *noun* a machine which plays music or other sound through two different loudspeakers ○ *I bought a new pair of speakers for my stereo.* □ **in stereo** using two speakers to produce sound

stern /stɜːn/ *adjective* serious and strict ○ *The judge addressed some stern words to the boys.*

stew /stjuː/ *noun* a dish of meat and vegetables cooked together for a long time ○ *This lamb stew is a French recipe.* ■ *verb* to cook food for a long time in liquid ○ *Stew the apples until they are completely soft.*

stick /stɪk/ *noun* **1.** a thin piece of wood ○ *He jabbed a pointed stick into the hole.* ○ *I need a strong stick to tie this plant to.* **2.** a thin branch of a tree **3.** anything long and thin ○ *carrots cut into sticks* ■ *verb* **1.** to attach something with glue ○ *Can you stick the pieces of the cup together again?* ○ *She stuck the stamp on the letter.* ○ *They stuck a poster on the door.* **2.** to be fixed or not to be able to move ○ *The car was stuck in the mud.* ○ *The door sticks – you need to push it hard to open it.* ○ *The cake will stick if you don't grease the tin.* ○ *He was stuck in Italy without any money.* **3.** to push something into something ○ *He stuck his hand into the hole.* ○ *She stuck her finger in the jam to taste it.* ○ *She stuck the ticket into her bag.* ○ *She stuck a needle into her finger.* **4.** to stay in a place ○ *Stick close to your mother and you won't get lost.* **5.** to accept something bad that continues ○ *I don't know how she can stick working in that office.* ○ *I'm going, I can't stick it here any longer.* (NOTE: **sticks – sticking – stuck** /stʌk/) ◇ **to stick together** to stay together ○ *If we stick together they should let us into the club.*

stick out *phrasal verb* **1.** to push something out **2.** to be further forward or further away from something ○ *Your wallet is sticking out of your pocket.* ○ *The balcony sticks out over the road.*

sticker /ˈstɪkə/ *noun* a small piece of paper or plastic which you can stick on something to show a price, as a decoration or to advertise something

sticky /ˈstɪki/ *adjective* **1.** covered with something which sticks like glue ○ *My fingers are all sticky.* ○ *This stuff is terribly sticky – I can't get it off my fingers.* **2.** with glue on one side so that it sticks easily (NOTE: **stickier – stickiest**)

stiff /stɪf/ *adjective* **1.** which does not move easily ○ *The lock is very stiff – I can't turn the key.* ○ *I've got a stiff neck.* ○ *She was feeling stiff all over after running in the race.* **2.** with hard bristles ○ *You need a stiff brush to get the mud off your shoes.*

stiffness /ˈstɪfnəs/ *noun* **1.** having muscle pains after doing exercise, or being unable to move easily because of damaged joints ○ *Arthritis accompanied by a certain amount of stiffness in the joints.* **2.** the quality of being stiff ○ *The stiffness of the material makes it unsuitable for a dress.*

still /stɪl/ *adjective* not moving ○ *Stand still while I take the photo.* ○ *There was no wind, and the surface of the lake was completely still.* ■ *adverb* **1.** continuing until now or until then ○ *I thought he had left, but I see he's still there.* ○ *They came for lunch and were still sitting at the table at eight o'clock in the evening.* ○ *Weeks afterwards, they're still talking about the accident.* **2.** in spite of everything ○ *It wasn't sunny for the picnic – still, it didn't rain.* ○ *He still insisted on going on holiday even though he had broken his leg.*

stimulus /ˈstɪmjʊləs/ *noun* an encouragement or incentive that leads to greater activity

sting /stɪŋ/ *noun* a wound made by an insect or plant ○ *Bee stings can be very painful.* ○ *Have you anything for wasp stings?* ■ *verb* **1.** to wound someone with an insect's or plant's sting ○ *I've been stung by a wasp.* ○ *The plants stung her bare legs.* **2.** to give a burning feeling ○ *The antiseptic may sting a little at first.* (NOTE: **stings – stinging – stung** /stʌŋ/)

stink /stɪŋk/ (*informal*) *noun* a very unpleasant smell ○ *the stink of cigarette smoke* ■ *verb* to make an unpleasant smell ○ *The office stinks of gas.* (NOTE: **stinks – stinking – stank** /stæŋk/ – **stunk** /stʌŋk/)

stir /stɜː/ *verb* to move a liquid or powder or something which is cooking, to mix it up ○ *He was stirring the sugar into his coffee.* ○ *Keep stirring the porridge, or it will stick to the bottom of the pan.* (NOTE: **stirs – stirring – stirred**)

stirring /ˈstɜːrɪŋ/ *adjective* making you feel strong emotions, especially pride or enthusiasm

stitch /stɪtʃ/ *noun* **1.** a little loop of thread made with a needle in sewing or with knitting needles when knitting ○ *She used very small stitches in her embroidery.* ○ *Very fine wool will give you* more stitches than in the pattern. **2.** a small loop of thread used by a surgeon to attach the sides of a wound together to help it to heal ○ *She had three stitches in her arm.* ○ *Come back in ten days' time to have the stitches removed.* ■ *verb* to attach something with a needle and thread ○ *She stitched the badge to his jacket.*

stock /stɒk/ *noun* **1.** a supply of something kept to use when needed ○ *I keep a good stock of printing paper at home.* ○ *Our stocks of food are running low.* ○ *The factory has large stocks of coal.* **2.** a liquid made from boiling bones in water, used as a base for soups and sauces ○ *Fry the onions and pour in some chicken stock.* ■ *verb* to keep goods for sale in a shop or warehouse ○ *They don't stock this book.* ○ *We try to stock the most popular colours.*

stocking /'stɒkɪŋ/ *noun* a long light piece of women's clothing which covers all of a leg and foot

stole /stəʊl/ past tense of **steal**

stolen /'stəʊlən/ past participle of **steal**

stomach /'stʌmək/ *noun* **1.** a part of the body shaped like a bag, into which food passes after being swallowed and where it continues to be digested ○ *I don't want anything to eat – my stomach's upset* or *I have a stomach upset.* ○ *He has had stomach trouble for some time.* **2.** the front of your body between your chest and your waist ○ *He had been kicked in the stomach.*

stone /stəʊn/ *noun* **1.** a very hard material, found in the earth, used for building ○ *All the houses in the town are built in the local grey stone.* ○ *The stone carvings in the old church date from the 15th century.* ○ *Stone floors can be very cold.* (NOTE: no plural: *some stone, a piece of stone, a block of stone*) **2.** a small piece of stone ○ *The children were playing at throwing stones into the pond.* ○ *The beach isn't good for bathing as it's covered with very sharp stones.* **3.** a British measure of weight equal to 14 pounds or 6.35 kilograms ○ *She's trying to lose weight and so far has lost a stone and a half.* ○ *He weighs twelve stone ten*

(*i.e. 12 stone 10 pounds*). (NOTE: no plural in this sense: *He weighs ten stone.* In the USA, human body weight is always given only in pounds.)

stony /'stəʊni/ *adjective* made of lots of stones ○ *They walked carefully across the stony beach.*

stood /stʊd/ past tense and past participle of **stand**

stool /stuːl/ *noun* a small seat with no back ○ *When the little girl sat on the piano stool her feet didn't touch the floor.*

stoop /stuːp/ *verb* to bend forward ○ *She stooped and picked something up off the carpet.* ○ *I found him standing at the table, stooped over a spreadsheet.*

stop /stɒp/ *verb* **1.** not to move any more ○ *The motorcycle didn't stop at the red lights.* ○ *This train stops at all stations to London Waterloo.* **2.** to make something not move any more ○ *The policeman stopped the traffic to let the lorry back out of the garage.* ○ *Stop that boy! – he's stolen my purse.* **3.** not to do something any more ○ *The office clock has stopped at 4.15.* ○ *At last it stopped raining and we could go out.* ○ *She spoke for two hours without stopping.* ○ *We all stopped work and went home.* ○ *The restaurant stops serving meals at midnight.* **4.** □ **to stop someone** *or* **something (from) doing something** to make someone *or* something not do something any more ○ *The rain stopped us from having a picnic.* ○ *How can the police stop people stealing cars?* ○ *Can't you stop the children from making such a noise?* ○ *The plumber couldn't stop the tap dripping.* **5.** to stay as a visitor in a place ○ *They stopped for a few days in Paris.* ○ *I expect to stop in Rome for the weekend.* (NOTE: **stops – stopping – stopped**) ■ *noun* **1.** the end of something, especially of movement ○ *The police want to put a stop to car crimes.* **2.** a place where you break a journey ○ *We'll make a stop at the next service station.* **3.** a place where a bus or train lets passengers get on or off ○ *We have been waiting at the bus stop for twenty minutes.* ○ *There are six stops between here and Marble Arch.*

stopper /'stɒpə/ *noun* an object that you put into the mouth of a bottle or jar to close it

store /stɔː/ *noun* a shop, usually a big shop ○ *You can buy shoes in any of the big stores in town.* ○ *Does the store have a food department?* ■ *verb* **1.** to keep food etc. to use later ○ *We store (away) all our vegetables in the garden shed.* **2.** to keep something in a computer file ○ *We store all our personnel records on computer.*

storey /'stɔːri/ *noun* a whole floor in a building

storm /stɔːm/ *noun* a high wind and very bad weather ○ *Several ships got into difficulties in the storm.* ○ *How many trees were blown down in last night's storm?*

stormy /'stɔːmi/ *adjective* when there are storms ○ *They are forecasting stormy weather for the weekend.* (NOTE: **stormier – stormiest**)

story /'stɔːri/ *noun* **1.** a description that tells things that did not really happen but are invented by someone ○ *The book is the story of two children during the war.* ○ *She writes children's stories about animals.* **2.** a description that tells what really happened ○ *She told her story to the journalist.* (NOTE: The plural is **stories**.)

stout /staʊt/ *adjective* **1.** (*of a person*) quite fat ○ *He has become much stouter and has difficulty going up stairs.* **2.** (*of material*) strong or thick ○ *Take a few sheets of stout paper.* ○ *Find a stout branch to stand on.*

stove /stəʊv/ *noun* a piece of equipment for heating or cooking

straight /streɪt/ *adjective* **1.** not curved ○ *a long straight street* ○ *The line isn't straight.* ○ *She has straight black hair.* ○ *Stand up straight!* **2.** not sloping ○ *Is the picture straight?* ○ *Your tie isn't straight.* ■ *adverb* **1.** in a straight line, not curving ○ *The road goes straight across the plain for two hundred kilometres.* ○ *She was sitting straight in front of you.* **2.** immediately ○ *Wait for me here – I'll come straight back.* ○ *If there is a problem, you should go straight to the manager.* **3.** without stopping or

changing ○ *She drank the milk straight out of the bottle.* ○ *The cat ran straight across the road in front of the car.* ○ *He looked me straight in the face.* ○ *The plane flies straight to Washington.*

straighten /'streɪt(ə)n/ *verb* to make something straight

straightforward /streɪt'fɔːwəd/ *adjective* easy to understand or carry out ○ *The instructions are quite straightforward.*

strain /streɪn/ *noun* **1.** nervous feelings caused by a busy or difficult situation ○ *Can she stand the strain of working in that office?* **2.** a variety of a living thing ○ *They are trying to find a cure for a new strain of the flu virus.* ○ *He crossed two strains of rice to produce a variety which is resistant to disease.* ■ *verb* **1.** to injure part of your body by pulling too hard ○ *He strained a muscle in his back* or *he strained his back.* ○ *The effort strained his heart.* **2.** to make great efforts to do something ○ *They strained to lift the piano into the van.* **3.** to pour liquid through a sieve to separate solid parts in it ○ *Boil the peas for ten minutes and then strain.*

strange /streɪndʒ/ *adjective* **1.** not usual ○ *Something is the matter with the engine – it's making a strange noise.* ○ *She told some very strange stories about the firm she used to work for.* ○ *It felt strange to be sitting in the office on a Saturday afternoon.* ○ *It's strange that no one spotted the mistake.* **2.** which you have never seen before or where you have never been before ○ *I find it difficult getting to sleep in a strange room.* ○ *We went to Korea and had lots of strange food to eat.*

stranger /'streɪndʒə/ *noun* **1.** a person whom you have never met ○ *He's a complete stranger to me.* ○ *Children are told not to accept lifts from strangers.* **2.** a person in a place where he or she has never been before ○ *I can't tell you how to get to the post office – I'm a stranger here myself.*

strap /stræp/ *noun* a long flat piece of material used to attach something ○ *Can you do up the strap of my bag for me?* ○ *I put a strap round my suitcase to* *make it more secure.* ■ *verb* to fasten something with a strap ○ *He strapped on his rucksack.* ○ *The patient was strapped to a stretcher.* ○ *Make sure the baby is strapped into her seat.* (NOTE: **straps – strapping – strapped**)

strategy /ˈstrætədʒi/ *noun* the decisions you make about how you are going to do something ○ *Their strategy is to note which of their rival's models sells best and then copy it.* ○ *The government has no long-term strategy for dealing with crime.* (NOTE: The plural is **strategies**.)

straw /strɔː/ *noun* **1.** dry stems and leaves of crops, used for animals to sleep on ○ *You've been lying on the ground – you've got bits of straw in your hair.* ○ *The tractor picked up bundles of straw and loaded them onto a truck.* **2.** a thin plastic tube for sucking up liquids ○ *She was drinking orange juice through a straw.*

strawberry /ˈstrɔːb(ə)ri/ *noun* a common soft red summer fruit which grows on low plants (NOTE: The plural is **strawberries**.)

stray /streɪ/ *verb* to move away from the usual or expected place ○ *The sheep strayed onto the golf course.* ○ *The children had strayed too far and couldn't get back.* ■ *noun* a pet animal which is lost or without a home ○ *We have two female cats at home and they attract all the strays in the district.* ■ *adjective* **1.** not where it should be ○ *He was killed by a stray bullet from a sniper.* **2.** ((*of a pet animal*)) lost or without a home ○ *We found a stray cat and brought it home.*

stream /striːm/ *noun* **1.** a small river ○ *Can you jump across that stream?* **2.** a number of things which pass in a continuous flow ○ *Crossing the road is difficult because of the stream of traffic.* ○ *We had a stream of customers on the first day of the sale.* ○ *Streams of refugees tried to cross the border.*

street /striːt/ *noun* **1.** a road in a town, usually with houses on each side ○ *It is difficult to park in our street on Saturday mornings.* ○ *Her flat is on a noisy street.* ○ *The school is in the next street.*

2. used with names ○ *What's your office address? – 16 Cambridge Street.* ○ *Oxford Street, Bond Street and Regent Street are the main shopping areas in London.* (NOTE: When used in names, **street** is usually written **St**: *Oxford St.*)

strength /streŋθ/ *noun* the fact that something or someone is physically strong ○ *She hasn't got the strength to lift it.* ○ *You should test the strength of the rope before you start climbing.*

strenuous /ˈstrenjuəs/ *adjective* requiring a lot of physical effort or energy ○ *The doctor has told him to avoid strenuous exercise.* ○ *It's a very strenuous job.*

stress /stres/ *noun* **1.** nervous strain caused by an outside influence ○ *the stresses of working in a busy office* ○ *She's suffering from stress.* **2.** the force or pressure on something ○ *Stresses inside the earth create earthquakes.* ■ *verb* to put emphasis on something ○ *I must stress the importance of keeping the plan secret.*

stretch /stretʃ/ *verb* **1.** to spread out for a great distance ○ *The line of cars stretched for three miles from the accident.* ○ *The queue stretched from the door of the cinema right round the corner.* ○ *White sandy beaches stretch as far as the eye can see.* **2.** to push out your arms or legs as far as they can go ○ *The cat woke up and stretched.* ○ *The monkey stretched out through the bars and grabbed the little boy's cap.* **3.** to pull something out so that it becomes loose, or to become loose by pulling ○ *Don't hang your jumper up like that – you will just stretch it.* ○ *These trousers are not supposed to stretch.* ■ *noun* **1.** a long piece of land, water or road ○ *Stretches of the river have been so polluted that bathing is dangerous.* **2.** a long period of time ○ *For long stretches we had nothing to do.* ◇ **at a stretch** without a break ○ *He played the piano for two hours at a stretch.* ◇ **to stretch your legs** to go for a short walk after sitting for a long time ○ *In the coffee break I went out into the garden to stretch my legs.*

strict /strɪkt/ *adjective* **1.** which must be obeyed ○ *I gave strict instructions that no one was to be allowed in.* ○ *The rules are very strict and any bad behaviour will be severely punished.* **2.** expecting people to obey rules ○ *Our parents are very strict with us about staying up late.*

strictly /ˈstrɪktli/ *adverb* in a strict way ○ *All staff must follow strictly the procedures in the training manual.*

stride /straɪd/ *noun* a long step ○ *In three strides he was across the room and out of the door.* ■ *verb* to walk with long steps ○ *He strode into the room.* ○ *We could see him striding across the field to take shelter from the rain.* (NOTE: **strides – striding – strode** /strəʊd/)

strike /straɪk/ *noun* the stopping of work by workers because of lack of agreement with management or because of orders from a trade union ○ *They all voted in favour of a strike.* ○ *A strike was avoided at the last minute.* ■ *verb* **1.** to stop working because of disagreement with management ○ *The workers are striking in protest against bad working conditions.* **2.** to hit something hard ○ *He struck her with a bottle.* ○ *She struck her head on the low door.* ○ *He struck a match and lit the fire.* **3.** (*of a clock*) to ring to mark an hour ○ *The clock had just struck one when she heard a noise in the corridor.* **4.** to come to someone's mind ○ *A thought just struck me.* ○ *It suddenly struck me that I had seen him somewhere before.* (NOTE: **strikes – striking – struck** /strʌk/)

string /strɪŋ/ *noun* **1.** a strong thin fibre used for tying up things such as parcels ○ *This string isn't strong enough to tie up that big parcel.* ○ *She bought a ball of string.* ○ *We've run out of string.* (NOTE: no plural in this sense: *some string; a piece of string*) **2.** one of the long pieces of fibre or wire on a musical instrument which makes a note when you hit it ○ *a guitar has six strings* ○ *He was playing the violin when one of the strings broke.* **3.** one of the strong pieces of fibre which form the flat part of a tennis racket ○ *One of the strings has snapped.*

strip /strɪp/ *noun* a long narrow piece of something ○ *He tore the paper into strips.* ○ *Houses are to be built along the strip of land near the church.* ■ *verb* to take off your clothes ○ *Strip to the waist for your chest X-ray.* ○ *He stripped down to his underpants.* (NOTE: **strips – stripping – stripped**)

stripe /straɪp/ *noun* a long line of colour ○ *He has an umbrella with red, white and blue stripes.*

strive /straɪv/ *verb* to try very hard to do something, especially over a long period of time ○ *He always strove to do as well as his brother.* ○ *Everyone is striving for a solution to the dispute.* (NOTE: **striving – strove** /strəʊv/ – **has striven** /ˈstrɪv(ə)n/)

strode /strəʊd/ past tense of **stride**

stroke /strəʊk/ *noun* **1.** a serious medical condition in which someone suddenly becomes unconscious because blood has stopped flowing normally to the brain ○ *He was paralysed after his stroke.* ○ *She had a stroke and died.* **2.** the act of hitting something such as a ball ○ *It took him three strokes to get the ball onto the green.* **3.** a style of swimming ○ *She won the 200m breast stroke.* ■ *verb* to run your hands gently over something or someone ○ *She was stroking the cat as it sat in her lap.*

strong /strɒŋ/ *adjective* **1.** who has a lot of strength ○ *I'm not strong enough to carry that box.* **2.** which has a lot of force or strength ○ *The string broke – we need something stronger.* ○ *The wind was so strong that it blew some tiles off the roof.* **3.** having a powerful smell, taste or effect ○ *I don't like strong cheese.* ○ *You need a cup of strong black coffee to wake you up.* ○ *There was a strong smell of gas in the kitchen.* ◊ **strength**

strongly /ˈstrɒŋli/ *adverb* in a strong way

strove /strəʊv/ past tense of **strive**

struck /strʌk/ past tense and past participle of **strike**

structure /ˈstrʌktʃə/ *noun* a building or something else that is built

struggle /'strʌg(ə)l/ *noun* a fight ○ *After a short struggle the burglar was arrested.* ■ *verb* to try hard to do something difficult ○ *She's struggling with her maths homework.* ○ *She struggled to carry all the shopping to the car.*

stubborn /'stʌbən/ *adjective* determined not to change your mind ○ *He's so stubborn – he only does what he wants to do.*

stuck /stʌk/ past tense and past participle of **stick**

student /'stju:d(ə)nt/ *noun* a person who is studying at a college, university or school ○ *All the science students came to my lecture.* ○ *She's a brilliant student.* ○ *Two students had to sit the exam again.*

studio /'stju:diəʊ/ *noun* **1.** a room where an artist paints ○ *She uses this room as a studio because of the good light.* **2.** a place where things such as films or broadcasts are made ○ *And now, back to the studio for the latest news and weather report.* ○ *They spent the whole day recording the piece in the studio.* **3.** a very small flat for one person, usually one room with a small kitchen and bathroom ○ *You can rent a studio overlooking the sea for £300 a week in high season.* (NOTE: The plural is **studios**.)

study /'stʌdi/ *noun* the work of examining something carefully to learn more about it ○ *The company asked the consultant to prepare a study into new production techniques.* ○ *The review has published studies on the new drug.* (NOTE: The plural is **studies**.) ■ *verb* **1.** to learn about a subject at college or university ○ *He is studying medicine because he wants to be a doctor.* ○ *She's studying French and Spanish in the modern languages department.* **2.** to look at something carefully ○ *She was studying the guidebook.* (NOTE: **studies – studying – studied**)

stuff /stʌf/ *noun* **1.** a substance, especially something unpleasant ○ *You've got some black stuff stuck to your shoe.* **2.** equipment or possessions ○ *Dump all your stuff in the living room.* ○ *Take all that stuff and put it in the dustbin.* ○ *All your photographic stuff is still in the back of my car.* ■ *verb* **1.** to push something into something to fill it ○ *He stuffed his pockets full of peppermints.* ○ *The £20 notes were stuffed into a small plastic wallet.* **2.** to put small pieces of food such as bread, meat or herbs inside meat or vegetables before cooking them ○ *We had roast veal stuffed with mushrooms.*

stuffy /'stʌfi/ *adjective* without any fresh air ○ *Can't you open a window, it's so stuffy in here?* (NOTE: **stuffier – stuffiest**)

stumble /'stʌmbəl/ *verb* **1.** to almost fall by hitting your foot against something ○ *He stumbled as he tried to get down the stairs in the dark.* **2.** to make mistakes when reading aloud or speaking ○ *She stumbled a little when had to read the foreign words.*

stump /stʌmp/ *noun* **1.** a short piece of something left sticking up, such as the main stem of a tree that has been cut down ○ *After cutting down the trees, we need to get rid of the stumps.* **2.** one of the three sticks placed in the ground in cricket ○ *The ball hit the stumps and the last man was out.*

stun /stʌn/ *verb* **1.** to make someone become unconscious with a blow to the head ○ *The blow on the head stunned him.* **2.** to shock someone completely ○ *She was stunned when he told her that he was already married.* (NOTE: **stuns – stunning – stunned**)

stupid /'stju:pɪd/ *adjective* **1.** not very intelligent ○ *What a stupid man!* **2.** behaving in a way that is not sensible ○ *It was stupid of her not to wear a helmet when riding on her scooter.* ○ *He made several stupid mistakes.*

sturdy /'stɜ:di/ *adjective* well made and not easily damaged (NOTE: **sturdier – sturdiest**)

stutter /'stʌtə/ *noun* a speech problem where you repeat the sound at the beginning of a word several times ○ *He is taking therapy to try to cure his stutter.* ■ *verb* to repeat the same sounds when speaking ○ *He stuttered badly when making his speech.*

style /staɪl/ *noun* **1.** a way of doing something, especially a way of designing, drawing or writing ○ *The room is decorated in Chinese style.* ○ *The painting is in his usual style.* ○ *That style was fashionable in the 1940s.* **2.** a fashionable way of doing things ○ *She always dresses with style.* ○ *They live in grand style.* ◊ **hairstyle**

subject /'sʌbdʒɪkt/ *noun* **1.** the thing which you are talking about or writing about ○ *He suddenly changed the subject of the conversation.* ○ *The newspaper has devoted a special issue to the subject of pollution.* **2.** an area of knowledge which you are studying ○ *Maths is his weakest subject.* ○ *You can take up to five subjects at 'A' Level.* **3.** □ **to be the subject of** to be the person or thing talked about or studied ○ *The painter Chagall will be the subject of our lecture today.* ○ *Advertising costs are the subject of close examination by the auditors.* **4.** (*in grammar*) a noun or pronoun which comes before a verb and shows the person or thing that does the action expressed by the verb ○ *In the sentence 'the cat sat on the mat' the word 'cat' is the subject of the verb 'sat'.*

subject matter /'sʌbdʒɪkt ˌmætə/ *noun* the subject dealt with in something such as a book or TV programme

submarine /'sʌbməriːn/ *noun* a special type of ship which can travel under water ○ *The submarine dived before she was spotted by enemy aircraft.* ■ *adjective* under the water ○ *a submarine pipeline*

submit /səb'mɪt/ *verb* to give something for someone to examine ○ *You are requested to submit your proposal to the planning committee.* ○ *He submitted a claim to the insurers.* ○ *Reps are asked to submit their expenses claims once a month.* (NOTE: **submits – submitting – submitted**) ■ to accept that someone has the power to make you do something you don't want to do

subsequent /'sʌbsɪkwənt/ *adjective* which comes later (*formal*) ○ *The rain and the subsequent flooding disrupted the match.* ○ *All subsequent reports must be sent to me immediately they arrive.*

subsequently /'sʌbsɪkwəntli/ *adverb* happening later or following something which has already happened ○ *I subsequently discovered that there had been a mistake.*

substance /'sʌbstəns/ *noun* a solid or liquid material, especially one used in chemistry ○ *A secret substance is added to the product to give it its yellow colour.* ○ *Toxic substances got into the drinking water.*

substantial /səb'stænʃəl/ *adjective* **1.** large or important ○ *She was awarded substantial damages.* ○ *He received a substantial sum when he left the company.* ○ *A substantial amount of work remains to be done.* **2.** large enough to satisfy someone ○ *We had a substantial meal at the local pub.* **3.** solid or strong ○ *This wall is too flimsy, we need something much more substantial.*

subtract /səb'trækt/ *verb* to take one number away from another (NOTE: **Subtracting** is usually shown by the minus sign – : **10 − 4 = 6:** say 'ten subtract four equals six'.)

subtraction /səb'trækʃən/ *noun* the act of subtracting one number from another

suburb /'sʌbɜːb/ *noun* an area on the edge of a town where there are houses and shops but not usually factories or other large industries

subway /'sʌbweɪ/ *noun* **1.** an underground passage along which people can walk, e.g. so that they do not have to cross a busy road ○ *There's a subway from the bus station to the shopping centre.* **2.** *US* an underground railway system ○ *the New York subway* ○ *It will be quicker to take the subway to Grand Central Station.* (NOTE: The London equivalent is the **tube** *or* **Underground**.)

succeed /sək'siːd/ *verb* to do well or to make a lot of profit ○ *His business has succeeded more than he had expected.*

success /sək'ses/ *noun* **1.** the fact of achieving what you have been trying to do ○ *She's been looking for a job in a li-*

brary, but without any success so far. **2.** the fact that someone does something well ○ *Her photo was in the newspapers after her Olympic success.* ○ *The new car has not had much success in the Japanese market.* (NOTE: The plural is **successes**.)

successful /sək'sesf(ə)l/ *adjective* who or which does well ○ *He's a successful business man.* ○ *She's very successful at hiding her real age.* ○ *Their trip to German proved successful.*

successfully /sək'sesf(ə)li/ *adverb* achieving what was intended

such /sʌtʃ/ *adjective* **1.** of this type ○ *The police are looking for such things as drugs or stolen goods.* □ **no such (person or thing)** a person or thing like that is not in existence ○ *There is no such day as April 31st.* ○ *Someone was asking for a Mr Simpson but there is no such person working here.* **2.** very; so much ○ *There was such a crowd at the party that there weren't enough chairs to go round.* ○ *It's such a shame that she's ill and has to miss her sister's wedding.* ◇ **such as** used for giving an example ○ *Some shops such as food stores are open on Sundays.*

suck /sʌk/ *verb* **1.** to hold something with your mouth and pull at it with your tongue ○ *The baby didn't stop sucking his thumb until he was six.* **2.** to have something in your mouth which makes your mouth produce water ○ *He bought a bag of sweets to suck in the car.*

sudden /'sʌd(ə)n/ *adjective* which happens very quickly or unexpectedly ○ *The sudden change in the weather caught us unprepared.* ○ *The bus came to a sudden stop.* ○ *His decision to go to Canada was very sudden.* ◇ **all of a sudden** suddenly ○ *All of a sudden the room went dark.*

suddenly /'sʌd(ə)nli/ *adverb* quickly and giving you a shock ○ *The car in front stopped suddenly and I ran into the back of it.* ○ *Suddenly the room went dark.* ○ *She suddenly realised it was already five o'clock.*

suffer /'sʌfə/ *verb* **1.** to receive an injury ○ *He suffered multiple injuries in the accident.* **2.** □ **to suffer from some-**

thing to have an illness or a fault ○ *She suffers from arthritis.* ○ *The company's products suffer from bad design.* ○ *Our car suffers from a tendency to overheat.*

sufficient /sə'fɪʃ(ə)nt/ *adjective* as much as is needed ○ *Does she have sufficient funds to pay for her trip?* ○ *There isn't sufficient room to put the big sofa in here.* ○ *Allow yourself sufficient time to get to the airport.*

suffix /'sʌfɪks/ *noun* letters added to the end of a word to make another word. Compare **prefix** (NOTE: The plural is **suffixes**.)

sugar /'ʃʊgə/ *noun* a substance that you use to make food sweet ○ *How much sugar do you take in your tea?* ○ *Can you pass me the sugar, please?*

suggest /sə'dʒest/ *verb* to mention an idea to see what other people think of it ○ *The chairman suggested that the next meeting should be held in October.* ○ *What does he suggest we do in this case?*

suggestion /sə'dʒestʃən/ *noun* an idea that you mention for people to think about ○ *We have asked for suggestions from passengers.* ○ *The company acted upon your suggestion.* ○ *Whose suggestion was it that we should go out in a boat?* ○ *I bought those shares at the stockbroker's suggestion.*

suit /suːt/ *noun* **1.** a set of pieces of clothing made of the same cloth and worn together, e.g. a jacket and trousers or skirt ○ *A dark grey suit will be just right for the interview.* ○ *The pale blue suit she was wearing was very chic.* **2.** one of the four sets of cards with the same symbol in a pack of cards ○ *Clubs and spades are the two black suits and hearts and diamonds are the two red suits.* ■ *verb* **1.** to look good when worn by someone ○ *Green usually suits people with red hair.* ○ *That hat doesn't suit her.* **2.** to be convenient for someone ○ *He'll only do it when it suits him to do it.* ○ *Thursday at 11 o'clock will suit me fine.*

suitable /'suːtəb(ə)l/ *adjective* which fits or which is convenient ○ *I'm looking for a suitable present* ○ *We advertised the job again because there were* *no suitable candidates.* ○ *A blue dress would be more suitable for an interview.*

suitcase /'suːtkeɪs/ *noun* a box with a handle which you carry your clothes in when you are travelling

sulk /sʌlk/ *verb* to show you are annoyed by not saying anything ○ *They're sulking because we didn't invite them.*

sum /sʌm/ *noun* **1.** a quantity of money ○ *He only paid a small sum for the car.* ○ *A large sum of money was stolen from his safe.* ○ *We are owed the sum of £500.* **2.** a simple problem in mathematics ○ *She tried to do the sum in her head.* **3.** the total of two or more numbers added together ○ *The sum of all four sides will give you the perimeter of the field.*

summary /'sʌməri/ *noun* a short description of what has been said or written, or of what happened, without giving all the details ○ *She gave a summary of what happened at the meeting.* ○ *Here's a summary of the book in case you don't have time to read it.* (NOTE: The plural is **summaries**.)

summer /'sʌmə/ *noun* the hottest season of the year, between spring and autumn ○ *Next summer we are going to Greece.* ○ *The summer in Australia coincides with our winter here in England.* ○ *I haven't any summer clothes – it's never hot enough here.*

summit /'sʌmɪt/ *noun* the top of a mountain ○ *It took us three hour's hard climbing to reach the summit.*

sun /sʌn/ *noun* **1.** a very bright star round which the earth travels and which gives light and heat ○ *The sun was just rising when I got up.* ○ *I'll try taking a photograph now that the sun's come out.* **2.** the light from the sun ○ *I'd prefer a table out of the sun.* ○ *She spent her whole holiday just sitting in the sun.*

sunburnt /'sʌnbɜːnt/ *adjective* (*of the skin*) damaged or made red by the sun

Sunday /'sʌndeɪ/ *noun* the seventh day of the week, the day between Saturday and Monday ○ *Last Sunday we went on a picnic.* ○ *Most shops are now open on Sundays.* ○ *Can we fix a lunch for next Sunday?* ○ *The 15th is a Saturday, so*

the 16th must be a Sunday. ○ *Today is Sunday, November 19th.*

sunk /sʌŋk/ past participle of **sink**

sunlight /'sʌnlaɪt/ *noun* the light which comes from the sun (NOTE: no plural)

sunny /'sʌni/ *adjective* **1.** with the sun shining ○ *Another sunny day!* ○ *They forecast that it will be sunny this afternoon.* **2.** where the sun often shines ○ *We live on the sunny side of the street.* ○ *Their sitting room is bright and sunny, but the dining room is dark.* (NOTE: **sunnier – sunniest**)

sunrise /'sʌnraɪz/ *noun* the time when the sun comes up in the morning

sunset /'sʌnset/ *noun* the time when the sun goes down in the evening

sunshine /'sʌnʃaɪn/ *noun* a pleasant light from the sun (NOTE: no plural)

super /'suːpə/ *adjective* very good (*dated*)

superlative /suˈpɜːlətɪv/ *adjective* extremely good ○ *He's a superlative goalkeeper.* ■ *noun* the form of an adjective or adverb showing the highest level when compared with another ○ *'Biggest' is the superlative of 'big.'*

supermarket /'suːpəmɑːkɪt/ *noun* a large store selling mainly food and goods for the house, where customers serve themselves and pay at a checkout

supervisor /'suːpəvaɪzə/ *noun* a person whose job is making sure that other people are working well

supper /'sʌpə/ *noun* the meal which you eat in the evening

supply /səˈplaɪ/ *noun* a store of something which is needed ○ *We have two weeks' supply of coal.* (NOTE: The plural is **supplies**.) ■ *verb* to provide something which is needed ○ *Details of addresses and phone numbers can be supplied by the store staff.* ○ *He was asked to supply a blood sample.* (NOTE: **supplies – supplying – supplied**) ◇ **in short supply** not available in large enough quantities to meet people's needs ○ *Fresh vegetables are in short supply during the winter.*

support /səˈpɔːt/ *noun* **1.** an object or structure which stops something from falling ○ *They had to build wooden supports to hold up the wall.* **2.** help or encouragement ○ *We have had no financial support from the bank.* **3.** an act of encouraging and helping someone, or of agreeing with their plans ○ *The chairman has the support of the committee.* ○ *She spoke in support of our plan.* ■ *verb* **1.** to hold something up to stop it falling down ○ *The roof is supported on ten huge pillars.* **2.** to provide money to help someone or something ○ *We hope the banks will support us during the development period.* **3.** to encourage someone or something ○ *Which football team do you support?* ○ *She hopes the other members of the committee will support her.*

supporter /sə'pɔːtə/ *noun* a person who encourages someone or something ○ *It sounds a good idea to me – I'm surprised it hasn't attracted more supporters.*

suppose /sə'pəuz/ *verb* **1.** to think something is likely to be true or to happen ○ *Where is the secretary? – I suppose she's going to be late as usual.* ○ *I suppose you've heard the news?* ○ *What do you suppose they're talking about?* ○ *Will you be coming to the meeting this evening? – I suppose I'll have to.* ○ *I don't suppose many people will come.* **2.** (*showing doubt*) what happens if? ○ *Suppose it rains tomorrow, do you still want to go for a walk?* ○ *He's very late – suppose he's had an accident?* ○ *Suppose I win the lottery!*

sure /ʃuə/ *adjective* without any doubt ○ *Is he sure he can borrow his mother's car?* ○ *I'm sure I left my wallet in my coat pocket.* ○ *It's sure to be cold in Russia in December.* ○ *Make sure or be sure that your computer is switched off before you leave.* ■ *adverb mainly US* meaning yes ○ *Can I borrow your car? – sure, go ahead!* ○ *I need someone to help with this computer program – sure, I can do it.*

surely /'ʃuəli/ *adverb* of course, certainly (*used mostly in questions where a certain answer is expected*) ○ *Surely they can't expect us to work on Sundays?* ○ *But surely their office is in Lon-*

don, not Oxford? ○ *They'll surely complain about the amount of work they have to do.*

surf /sɜːf/ *noun* **1.** a mass of white foam coming onto a beach on large waves ○ *The surf is too rough for children to bathe.* **2.** waves breaking along a shore ■ *verb* to ride on large waves coming onto a beach on a surf board ○ *I'd like to be able to surf.* ○ *It's too dangerous to go surfing today.*

surface /'sɜːfɪs/ *noun* the top part of something ○ *When it rains, water collects on the surface of the road.* ○ *The surface of the water was completely still.* ○ *He stayed a long time under water before coming back to the surface.* ○ *Dinosaurs disappeared from the surface of the earth millions of years ago.* ■ *verb* to come up to the surface ○ *The captain gave orders for the submarine to surface.* ○ *His fear of failure has surfaced again.*

surgeon /'sɜːdʒən/ *noun* a doctor who performs medical operations

surgery /'sɜːdʒəri/ *noun* **1.** treatment of disease in which doctors cut into or remove part of the body ○ *She had surgery to straighten her nose.* ○ *The patient will need surgery to remove the scars left by the accident.* (NOTE: no plural in this sense) **2.** a room where a doctor or dentist sees and examines patients ○ *I phoned the doctor's surgery to make an appointment.* (NOTE: The plural is **surgeries**.)

surname /'sɜːneɪm/ *noun* the name of someone's family, shared by all people in the family

surprise /sə'praɪz/ *noun* **1.** the feeling you get when something happens which you did not expect to happen ○ *He expressed surprise when I told him I'd lost my job.* ○ *To his great surprise, a lot of people bought his book.* ○ *What a surprise to find that we were at school together!* **2.** an unexpected event ○ *They baked a cake for her birthday as a surprise.* ○ *What a surprise to see you again after so long!* ■ *verb* to make someone surprised ○ *It wouldn't surprise me if it rained.* ○ *What surprises* *me is that she left without saying good-bye.*

surprised /sə'praɪzd/ *adjective* feeling or showing surprise ○ *She was surprised to see her former boyfriend at the party.* ○ *We were surprised to hear that he's got a good job.*

surprising /sə'praɪzɪŋ/ *adjective* which you do not expect ○ *There was a surprising end to the story.* ○ *Wasn't it surprising to see the two sisters together again?* ○ *It's hardly surprising she doesn't want to meet you again after what you said.*

surrender /sə'rendə/ *noun* giving in to an enemy because you have lost ○ *the surrender of the enemy generals* ■ *verb* to accept that you have been defeated by someone else ○ *Our troops were surrounded by the enemy and were forced to surrender.*

surround /sə'raʊnd/ *verb* to be all round something or someone ○ *The house is surrounded by beautiful countryside.* ○ *The President has surrounded himself with experts.*

survey¹ /'sɜːveɪ/ *noun* **1.** a way of finding out about something by asking people questions **2.** the careful examination of a building to see if it is in good enough condition

survey² /sə'veɪ/ *verb* **1.** to ask people questions to get information about something ○ *Roughly half the people we surveyed were in favour of the scheme.* ○ *They're surveying the site.* **2.** to measure land in order to produce a plan or map ○ *They're surveying the area where the new runway will be built.*

survival /sə'vaɪv(ə)l/ *noun* the state of continuing to exist ○ *The survival of the crew depended on the supplies carried in the boat.* ○ *The survival rate of babies has started to fall.*

survive /sə'vaɪv/ *verb* to continue to be alive after an experience such as accident, attack or serious illness ○ *It was such a terrible crash, it was miracle that anyone survived.* ○ *He survived a massive heart attack.*

survivor /sə'vaɪvə/ *noun* a person who is still alive after an experience such as an accident, attack or serious illness

suspect¹ /sə'spekt/ *verb* **1.** □ **to suspect someone of doing something** to think that someone may have done something wrong ○ *I suspect him of being involved in the robbery.* ○ *They were wrongly suspected of taking bribes.* **2.** to think that something is likely ○ *I suspect it's going to be more difficult than we thought at first.* ○ *We suspected all along that something was wrong.*

suspect² /'sʌspekt/ *noun* a person who is thought to have committed a crime ○ *The police arrested several suspects for questioning.* ■ *adjective* **1.** which is not reliable ○ *Such high figures for exports look a bit suspect to me.* **2.** which might be dangerous or illegal ○ *a suspect package*

suspense /sə'spens/ *noun* nervous excitement experienced while waiting for something to happen or for someone to do something

suspicious /sə'spɪʃəs/ *adjective* which seems to be wrong, dangerous or connected with a crime ○ *The police found a suspicious package on the station platform.* ○ *We became suspicious when we realised we hadn't seen him for three days.*

swallow /'swɒləʊ/ *verb* to make food or liquid pass down your throat from your mouth to the stomach ○ *He swallowed his beer and ran back to the office.* ○ *She swallowed hard and knocked on the door to the interview room.*

swam /swæm/ past tense of **swim**

swan /swɒn/ *noun* a large white water bird with a long curved neck

swap /swɒp/ *verb* to exchange something for something else ○ *Can I swap my tickets for next Friday's show?* ○ *Let's swap places, so that I can talk to Susan.* ○ *After every game the players swapped jerseys with the other team.* (NOTE: **swaps** – **swapping** – **swapped**)

swarm /swɔːm/ *noun* a large group of insects flying around together ○ *A swarm of flies buzzed around the meat.*

sway /sweɪ/ *verb* **1.** to move slowly and smoothly from side to side ○ *The crowd swayed in time to the music.* ○ *The palm trees swayed in the breeze.* **2.** to have an influence on someone ○ *The committee was swayed by a letter from the president.*

swear /sweə/ *verb* **1.** to make a serious public promise ○ *He swore he wouldn't touch alcohol again.* ○ *The witnesses swore to tell the truth.* **2.** to shout offensive or rude words ○ *They were shouting and swearing at the police.* ○ *Don't let me catch you swearing again!* (NOTE: **swears – swearing – swore – sworn**) ◇ **I could have sworn** I was completely sure ○ *I could have sworn I put my keys in my coat pocket.*

sweat /swet/ *noun* drops of salt liquid which come through your skin when you are hot or when you are afraid ○ *After working in the vineyard he was drenched with sweat.* ○ *He broke out into a cold sweat when they called his name.* ■ *verb* to produce sweat ○ *He ran up the hill, sweating and red in the face.*

sweater /ˈswetə/ *noun* a thick piece of clothing with sleeves that covers your upper body

sweatshirt /ˈswetʃɜːt/ *noun* a thick cotton shirt with long sleeves

sweep /swiːp/ *verb* **1.** to clear up dust and dirt from the floor with a brush ○ *Have you swept the kitchen floor yet?* **2.** to move quickly ○ *She swept into the room with a glass of wine in her hand.* ○ *The party swept to power in the general election.* ○ *A feeling of anger swept through the crowd.* (NOTE: **sweeps – sweeping – swept** /swept/)

sweet /swiːt/ *adjective* **1.** tasting like sugar, and neither sour nor bitter ○ *These apples are sweeter than those green ones.* **2.** very kind or pleasant ○ *He sent me such a sweet birthday card.* ○ *It was sweet of her to send me flowers.* ○ *What a sweet little girl!* ○ *How sweet of you to help me with my luggage!* ■ *noun* **1.** a small piece of sweet food, made with sugar ○ *She bought some sweets to eat in the cinema.* ○ *He likes to suck sweets when he is driving.* **2.** sweet food eaten at the end of a meal ○

What's on the menu for sweet? ○ *I'm afraid I haven't made a sweet.* ○ *I won't have any sweet, thank you, just some coffee.* ◇ **to have a sweet tooth** to like sweet food ○ *He's very fond of puddings – he's got a real sweet tooth!*

sweetness /ˈswiːtnəs/ *noun* a state of being sweet

swell /swel/ *verb* to become larger, usually because of an illness or injury ○ *Her feet started to swell.* (NOTE: **swells – swelling – swollen** /ˈswəʊlən/ – **swelled**) □ **to swell (up)** to become larger or to increase in size ○ *She was bitten by an insect and her hand swelled (up).*

swelling /ˈswelɪŋ/ *noun* a condition where liquid forms in part of the body, making that part swell up

swept /swept/ past tense and past participle of **sweep**

swerve /swɜːv/ *verb* to move suddenly to one side ○ *They think the car swerved to the left and hit a wall.* ○ *She had to swerve to avoid the bicycle.*

swift /swɪft/ *adjective* very fast ○ *Their phone call brought a swift response from the police.*

swim /swɪm/ *verb* to move in the water using your arms and legs to push you along ○ *She can't swim, but she's taking swimming lessons.* ○ *She swam across the English Channel.* (NOTE: **swims – swimming – swam** /swæm/ – **swum** /swʌm/) ■ *noun* an occasion when you swim ○ *What about a swim before breakfast?* ○ *It's too cold for a swim.*

swimmer /ˈswɪmə/ *noun* a person who is swimming

swimming /ˈswɪmɪŋ/ *noun* the activity or sport of moving through water using your arms and legs

swing /swɪŋ/ *verb* to move, or move something, from side to side or forwards and backwards, while hanging from a central point ○ *She picked up the baby and swung him round and round.* ○ *He swung up and down on the garden swing.* ○ *A window swung open and a man looked out.* (NOTE: **swings – swinging – swung** /swʌŋ/) ■ *noun* a seat held by two ropes or chains, to sit on and move backwards and forwards, usually outdoors ○ *She sat on the swing and ate an apple.*

switch /swɪtʃ/ *noun* a small object which you push up or down to stop or start a piece of electrical equipment ○ *The switch to turn off the electricity is in the cupboard.* ○ *There is a light switch by the bed.* ■ *verb* **1.** to do something different suddenly ○ *We decided to switch from gas to electricity.* **2.** to change or exchange something ○ *Let's switch places.* ○ *He switched flights in Montreal and went on to Calgary.* ○ *The job was switched from our British factory to the States.*

switch off *phrasal verb* to make an piece of electrical equipment stop ○ *Don't forget to switch off the TV before you go to bed.* ○ *She forgot to switch her car lights off* or *switch off her car lights.* ○ *The kettle switches itself off automatically when it boils.*

switch on *phrasal verb* to make a piece of electrical equipment start ○ *Can you switch the radio on – it's time for the evening news.* ○ *When you put the light on in the bathroom, the fan switches itself on automatically.*

swollen /'swəʊlən/ past participle of **swell** ■ *adjective* much bigger than usual

swoop /swuːp/ *verb* to come down quickly ○ *The planes swooped (down) low over the enemy camp.*

swop /swɒp/ *noun, verb* same as **swap**

sword /sɔːd/ *noun* a weapon with a handle and a long sharp blade

swore /swɔː/ past tense of **swear**

swum /swʌm/ past participle of **swim**

swung /swʌŋ/ past tense and past participle of **swing**

syllable /'sɪləb(ə)l/ *noun* a whole word or part of a word which has one single sound

symbol /'sɪmbəl/ *noun* a sign, letter, picture or shape which means something or shows something ○ *The crown was the symbol of the empire.* ○ *The olive branch is a symbol of peace.* ○ *Pb is the chemical symbol for lead.*

sympathetic /ˌsɪmpə'θetɪk/ *adjective* showing that you understand someone's problems

sympathise /'sɪmpəθaɪz/, **sympathize** *verb* to show that you understand someone's problems ○ *I sympathise with you, my husband snores too.* ○ *I get back pains, and I sympathise with all fellow sufferers.*

sympathy /'sɪmpəθi/ *noun* a feeling of understanding for someone else's problems, or after someone's death ○ *We received many messages of sympathy when my wife died.* ○ *He had no sympathy for his secretary who complained of being overworked.*

symptom /'sɪmptəm/ *noun* **1.** a change in the body, showing that a disease is present ○ *He has all the symptoms of flu.* **2.** a visible sign which shows that something is happening ○ *Rubbish everywhere on the pavements is a symptom of the economic crisis facing the borough.*

synonym /'sɪnənɪm/ *noun* a word which means almost the same as another word

syrup /'sɪrəp/ *noun* a sweet liquid ○ *To make syrup, dissolve sugar in a cup of boiling water.*

system /'sɪstəm/ *noun* **1.** a group of things which work together ○ *the system of motorways* or *the motorway system* ○ *the London underground railway system* **2.** a way in which things are organised ○ *I've got my own system for dealing with invoices.*

T

t /tiː/, **T** *noun* the twentieth letter of the alphabet, between S and U

table /'teɪb(ə)l/ *noun* **1.** a piece of furniture with a flat top and legs, used to eat or work at ○ *We had breakfast sitting round the kitchen table.* ○ *He asked for a table by the window.* ○ *She says she booked a table for six people for 12.30.* **2.** a list of numbers, facts, or information set out in an organised way

tablecloth /'teɪb(ə)l,klɒθ/ *noun* a cloth which covers a table during a meal

tablet /'tæblət/ *noun* a small round pill taken as medicine ○ *Take two tablets before meals.*

table tennis /'teɪb(ə)l ,tenɪs/ *noun* a game similar to tennis, but played on a large table with a net across the centre, with small round bats and a very light white ball

tackle /'tæk(ə)l/ *verb* **1.** to try to deal with a problem or job ○ *You can't tackle a job like changing the central heating system on your own.* ○ *You start cleaning the dining room and I'll tackle the washing up.* **2.** (*in football, etc.*) to try to get the ball from an opposing player ○ *He was tackled before he could score.* ■ *noun* equipment ○ *He brought his fishing tackle with him.*

tail /teɪl/ *noun* **1.** a long thin part at the end of the body of an animal or bird, which can move ○ *All you could see was a slight movement of the cat's tail.* ○ *The dog rushed up to him, wagging its tail.* **2.** an end or back part of something ○ *The tail of the queue stretched round the corner and into the next street.* ○ *I prefer to sit near the tail of the aircraft.*

take /teɪk/ *verb* **1.** to lift and move something ○ *She took the pot of jam down from the shelf.* ○ *The waiter took the tablecloth off the table.* **2.** to carry something to another place ○ *Can you take this cheque to the bank for me, please?*

3. to go with someone or something to another place ○ *He's taking the children to school.* ○ *They took the car to the garage.* ○ *We took a taxi to the hotel.* **4.** to steal something ○ *Someone's taken my watch.* **5.** to go away with something which someone else was using ○ *Someone has taken the newspaper I was reading.* ○ *Who's taken my cup of coffee?* **6.** to use or occupy something ○ *Sorry, all these seats are taken.* **7.** to do a test ○ *You must go to bed early because you'll be taking your exams tomorrow morning.* ○ *She had to take her driving test three times before she finally passed.* **8.** to accept something ○ *If they offer you the job, take it immediately.* **9.** to do certain actions ○ *We took our holiday in September this year.* ○ *She's taking a shower after going to the beach.* ○ *She took a photograph* or *took a picture of the Tower of London.* ○ *She needs to take a rest.* **10.** to need a certain amount of time or number of people ○ *It took three strong men to move the piano.* ○ *They took two days* or *it took them two days to get to London.* ○ *When he wants to watch a TV programme it never seems to take him long to finish his homework.* (NOTE: **takes – taking – took** /tʊk/ **– taken** /'teɪk(ə)n/)

take away *phrasal verb* **1.** to remove something or someone ○ *Take those scissors away from little Nicky – he could cut himself.* ○ *The ambulance came and took her away.* ○ *The police took away piles of documents from the office.* **2.** to subtract one number from another (NOTE: **Take away** is usually shown by the sign – : $10 - 4 = 6$: say 'ten take away four equals six'.)

take off *phrasal verb* **1.** to remove something, especially your clothes ○ *He took off all his clothes* or *he took all his clothes off.* ○ *Take your dirty boots off before you come into the kitchen.* ◊ **hat**

2. to make an amount smaller ○ *He took £25 off the price.* **3.** (*of a plane*) to leave the ground ○ *The plane took off at 4.30.*

take over *phrasal verb* **1.** to start to do something in place of someone else ○ *Miss Black took over from Mr Jones on May 1st.* ○ *When our history teacher was ill, the English teacher had to take over his classes.* ○ *The Socialists took over from the Conservatives.* **2.** to buy a business by buying most of its shares ○ *The company was taken over by a big group last month.*

take up *phrasal verb* **1.** to fill a space or time ○ *This settee takes up too much room.* ○ *Being in charge of the staff sports club takes up too much of my time.* **2.** to remove something which was on a floor or other low surface ○ *You will need to take up the rugs if you want to polish the floor.*

takeaway /'teɪkəweɪ/ *noun* a shop where you can buy cooked food to eat somewhere else ○ *There's an Indian takeaway round the corner.* ○ *We had a Chinese takeaway.* ■ *noun, adjective* a hot meal that you buy in a shop and eat somewhere else ○ *We had a takeaway Chinese meal.*

taken /'teɪkən/ past participle of **take**

tale /teɪl/ *noun* a story (*literary*) ○ *A tale of princesses and wicked fairies.*

talent /'tælənt/ *noun* an ability or skill ○ *Her many talents include singing and playing the piano.*

talented /'tæləntɪd/ *adjective* with a lot of talent

talk /tɔːk/ *verb* to say things ○ *I didn't understand what he was talking about.* ○ *We must talk to the neighbours about their noisy dog – it kept me awake again last night.* ■ *noun* **1.** a conversation or a discussion ○ *We had a little talk, and she agreed with what the committee had decided.* ○ *I had a long talk with my father about what I should study at university.* **2.** a lecture about a subject ○ *He gave a short talk about the history of the town.*

talk over *phrasal verb* to discuss something

talkative /'tɔːkətɪv/ *adjective* liking to talk a lot, or sometimes too much

tall /tɔːl/ *adjective* high, usually higher than normal ○ *the tallest building in London* ○ *Can you see those tall trees over there?* ○ *He's the tallest boy in his class.* ○ *How tall are you? – I'm 1 metre 68 centimetres.* ○ *His brother is over six feet tall.* (NOTE: **taller – tallest**. **Tall** is used with people and thin things like trees or skyscrapers; for things which are a long way above the ground use **high**: *high clouds, a high mountain.*)

tame /teɪm/ *adjective* a tame animal can live with people because it is no longer wild ○ *Don't be afraid of that fox – he's perfectly tame.*

tan /tæn/ *noun* a brownish-yellow colour of the skin after being in the sun ○ *She got a tan from spending each day on the beach.* ■ *verb* to get brown from being in the sun ○ *She tans easily – just half an hour in the sun and she's quite brown.* (NOTE: **tans – tanning – tanned**)

tank /tæŋk/ *noun* **1.** a large container for liquids ○ *How much oil is left in the tank?* **2.** an army vehicle which is covered in strong metal, has tracks instead of wheels and has powerful guns ○ *Tanks rolled along the main streets of the town.*

tap /tæp/ *noun* an object which you turn in order to let liquid or gas come out of a pipe ○ *He washed his hands under the tap in the kitchen.* ■ *verb* to hit something gently ○ *She tapped him on the knee with her finger.* ○ *A policeman tapped him on the shoulder and arrested him.* (NOTE: **taps – tapping – tapped**)

tape /teɪp/ *noun* **1.** a long narrow piece of cloth or plastic ○ *She stitched tape along the bottom of the sleeves to stop it fraying.* **2.** □ **magnetic tape** special plastic tape on which sounds and pictures can be recorded, also used for recording computer data ■ *verb* **1.** to record something on tape or on video ○ *The whole conversation was taped by the police.* ○ *I didn't see the programme because I was at work, but I've taped it.* **2.** to attach something with sticky tape ○ *She taped up the box before taking it to the post office.*

target /'tɑːgɪt/ noun **1.** an object which you aim at, e.g. with a gun ○ *His last shot missed the target altogether.* ○ *She hit the target three times in all.* **2.** something which you intend to achieve

task /tɑːsk/ noun something, especially a piece of work, that has to be done ○ *He had the unpleasant task of telling his mother about it.*

taste /teɪst/ noun **1.** the sense on your tongue that allows you to be aware of the flavour of something when you put it in your mouth ○ *I've got a cold, so I've lost all sense of taste.* **2.** a flavour of something that you eat or drink ○ *The pudding has a funny* or *strange taste.* ○ *Do you like the taste of garlic?* ○ *This milk shake has no taste at all.* ■ verb **1.** to notice the taste of something with your tongue ○ *Can you taste the onions in this soup?* ○ *She's got a cold so she can't taste anything.* **2.** to have a certain flavour ○ *This cake tastes of soap.* ○ *What is this green stuff? – It tastes like cabbage.* ○ *The pudding tastes very good.* **3.** to try food or drink to see if you like it ○ *Would you like to taste the wine?* ○ *She asked if she could taste the cheese before buying it.*

tasty /'teɪsti/ adjective with a pleasant taste (NOTE: **tastier – tastiest**)

taught /tɔːt/ past tense and past participle of **teach**

tax /tæks/ noun money taken by the government to pay for government services ○ *The government is planning to introduce a tax on food.* ○ *You must pay your tax on the correct date.* ○ *The newspaper headline says 'TAXES TO GO UP'.*

taxi /'tæksi/ noun a car which you can hire with a driver ○ *Can you call a taxi to take me to the airport?* ○ *Why aren't there any taxis at the station today?* ○ *There are no buses on Sunday afternoons, so we had to take a taxi to the party.* (NOTE: also often called a **cab** and sometimes **taxicab**)

tea /tiː/ noun **1.** a drink made from hot water which has been poured onto the dried leaves of a tropical plant ○ *Can I have another cup of tea* or *some more tea?* ○ *I don't like tea – can I have coffee instead?* **2.** a cup of tea ○ *Can we have two teas and two cakes, please?* **3.** the dried leaves of a tropical plant used to make a warm drink ○ *We've run out of tea, can you put it on your shopping list?* **4.** a meal eaten in the late afternoon or early evening ○ *The children have had their tea.*

teach /tiːtʃ/ verb to show someone how to do something ○ *She taught me how to dance.* ○ *He teaches maths in the local school.* (NOTE: **teaches – teaching – taught** /tɔːt/)

teacher /'tiːtʃə/ noun a person who teaches, especially in a school ○ *Mr Jones is our maths teacher.* ○ *The French teacher is ill today.* ○ *He trained as a primary school teacher.* ◊ **pet**

teaching /'tiːtʃɪŋ/ noun the work of being a teacher or of giving lessons ○ *The report praised the high standard of teaching at the college.* ○ *He was working in a bank, but has decided to go into teaching instead.*

team /tiːm/ noun **1.** a group of people who play a game together ○ *There are eleven people in a football team and fifteen in a rugby team.* ○ *He's a fan of the local football team.* ○ *Our college team played badly last Saturday.* **2.** a group of people who work together ○ *They make a very effective team.* ○ *In this job you have to be able to work as a member of a team.*

teapot /'tiːpɒt/ noun a container which is used for making tea in

tear¹ /tɪə/ noun a drop of salt water which forms in your eye when you cry ○ *Tears were running down her cheeks.* □ **in tears** crying ○ *All the family were in tears.* □ **to burst into tears** to suddenly start crying

tear² /teə/ verb **1.** to make a hole in something by pulling ○ *He tore his trousers climbing over the fence.* ○ *My coat is torn – can it be mended?* **2.** to pull something into small pieces ○ *He tore the letter in half.* ○ *She tore up old newspapers to pack the cups and saucers.* (NOTE: **tears – tearing – tore** /tɔː/ – **torn** /tɔːn/) ■ noun a place where something has a hole in it from being torn ○ *Can you mend the tear in my jeans?*

tease /tiːz/ *verb* to say or do something to annoy someone on purpose ○ *He teased her about her new haircut.* ○ *Stop teasing that poor cat.*

teaspoon /'tiːspuːn/ *noun* a small spoon for stirring tea or other liquid ○ *Can you bring me a teaspoon, please?*

technical /'teknɪk(ə)l/ *adjective* relating to industrial processes or practical work ○ *Don't bother with the technical details of how the machine works, just tell me what it does.* ○ *The instructions are too technical for the ordinary person to understand.*

technique /tek'niːk/ *noun* a way of doing something ○ *He developed a new technique for processing steel.* ○ *She has a specially effective technique for dealing with complaints from customers.*

technology /tek'nɒlədʒi/ *noun* the use or study of industrial or scientific skills ○ *We already have the technology to produce such a machine.* ○ *The government has promised increased support for science and technology.*

teenager /'tiːneɪdʒə/ *noun* a young person aged between 13 and 19 ○ *She writes stories for teenagers.*

teeshirt /'tiːʃɜːt/, **T-shirt** *noun* a light shirt with a round neck and no buttons or collar, usually with short sleeves

teeth /tiːθ/ plural of **tooth**

telephone /'telɪfəʊn/ *noun* a machine which you use to speak to someone who is some distance away ○ *I was in the garden when you called, but by the time I got to the house the telephone had stopped ringing.* ○ *She lifted the telephone and called the ambulance.* ■ *verb* to call someone using a telephone ○ *Your wife telephoned when you were out.* ○ *Can you telephone me at ten o'clock tomorrow evening?* ○ *I need to telephone our office in New York.* (NOTE: **Telephone** is often shortened to **phone**: *phone call, phone book.*)

telescope /'telɪskəʊp/ *noun* a piece of equipment for looking at objects which are very far away, consisting of a long tube with a series of lenses in it ○ *With a telescope you can see the ships very*

clearly. ○ *He watched the stars using a telescope in his back garden.*

television /ˌtelɪ'vɪʒ(ə)n/ *noun* **1.** sound and pictures which are sent through the air or along cables and appear on a special machine ○ *television programmes* ○ *We don't watch television every night.* ○ *Is there any football on television tonight?* **2.** a piece of electrical equipment which shows television pictures ○ *I switched off the television before going to bed.* (NOTE: **Television** is often written or spoken as **TV** /ˌtiː 'viː/.)

tell /tel/ *verb* **1.** to communicate something to someone, e.g. a story or a joke ○ *She told me a long story about how she got lost in London.* ○ *I don't think they are telling the truth.* **2.** to give information to someone ○ *The policeman told them how to get to the post office.* ○ *He told the police that he had seen the accident take place.* ○ *Don't tell my mother you saw me at the pub.* ○ *Nobody told us about the picnic.* **3.** □ **to tell someone what to do** to give someone instructions ○ *The teacher told the children to stand in a line.* ○ *Give a shout to tell us when to start.* **4.** to notice something ○ *He can't tell the difference between butter and margarine.* ○ *You can tell he is embarrassed when his face goes red.* (NOTE: **tells – telling – told** /təʊld/)

temper /'tempə/ *noun* the state of becoming angry ○ *You have to learn to control your temper.* ○ *He has a violent temper.* ○ *She got into a temper.*

temperature /'temprɪtʃə/ *noun* **1.** heat measured in degrees ○ *The temperature of water in the swimming pool is 25°.* ○ *Temperatures in the Arctic can be very low.* ○ *I can't start the car when the temperature is below zero.* ○ *Put the thermometer in the patient's mouth – I want to take her temperature.* **2.** an illness where your body is hotter than normal ○ *She's off work with a temperature.* ○ *The doctor says he's got a temperature and has to stay in bed.*

temple /'tempəl/ *noun* a building for worship, usually Hindu or Buddhist, or ancient Greek or Roman ○ *We visited the Greek temples on the islands.*

temporarily /ˌtemp(ə)'rerəli/ *adverb* for a short time only

temporary /'temp(ə)rəri/ *adjective* existing or lasting only for a limited time ○ *She has a temporary job with a construction company.* ○ *This arrangement is only temporary.*

tempt /tempt/ *verb* to try to persuade someone to do something, especially something pleasant or wrong ○ *Can I tempt you to have another cream cake?* ○ *They tried to tempt him to leave his job and work for them.*

ten /ten/ *noun* the number 10 ○ *In the market they're selling ten oranges for two dollars.* ○ *She's ten (years old) next week.* ○ *The next plane for Paris leaves at 10 (o'clock) in the evening.*

tend /tend/ *verb* **1.** to look after something ○ *His job is to tend the flower beds in front of the town hall.* **2.** □ **to tend to do something** to be likely to do something ○ *She tends to lose her temper very easily.*

tendency /'tendənsi/ *noun* the way in which someone or something is likely to act ○ *The photocopier has a tendency to break down if you try to do too many copies at the same time.* ○ *He has an unfortunate tendency to sit in a corner and go to sleep at parties.*

tender /'tendə/ *adjective* **1.** (*of food*) easy to cut or chew ○ *a plate of tender young beans* ○ *The meat was so tender, you hardly needed a knife to cut it.* **2.** showing love ○ *The plants need a lot of tender loving care.* **3.** painful when touched

tennis /'tenɪs/ *noun* a game for two or four players who use rackets to hit a ball over a net ○ *He's joined the local tennis club.* ○ *Would you like a game of tennis?*

tenor /'tenə/ *adjective* with a high pitch, similar to that of a tenor ○ *He plays the tenor saxophone.* ○ *He has a pleasant tenor voice.* Compare **bass** ■ *noun* a man who sings with the highest male voice ○ *The tenors start the song, followed by the sopranos.*

tense /tens/ *adjective* nervous and worried ○ *I always get tense before going to an interview.* ○ *The atmosphere in the hall was tense as everyone waited for the result of the vote.* ■ *noun* the form of a verb which shows the time when the action takes place

tension /'tenʃən/ *noun* **1.** nervous or worried feelings ○ *Tension built up as we waited for the result.* **2.** feelings of anger or hate between countries or races ○ *There is tension in the area caused by fighting between tribes.* **3.** the state of being tight ○ *You need to adjust the tension in your tennis racket.*

tent /tent/ *noun* a shelter made of cloth, held up by poles and attached to the ground with ropes

tenth /tenθ/ *adjective* number 10 in a series ○ *That's the tenth phone call I've had this morning.* ○ *She came tenth in a national competition.* ■ *noun* the thing that is number 10 in a series ○ *the tenth of April* or *April the tenth (April 10th)*

term /tɜːm/ *noun* **1.** one of the parts of a school or university year ○ *The autumn term ends on December 15th.* ○ *Next term I'll be starting to learn the piano.* **2.** a word or phrase which has a particular meaning ○ *He used several technical terms which I didn't understand.* ○ *Some people use 'darling' as a term of affection.*

terminal /'tɜːmɪn(ə)l/ *noun* a building at an airport where planes arrive or leave ○ *The flight leaves from Terminal 4.* ■ *adjective* referring to the last period of a serious illness that will lead to death ○ *The condition is terminal.*

terrace /'terəs/ *noun* **1.** a flat outdoor area which is raised above another area ○ *The guests had drinks on the terrace before going in to dinner.* **2.** a row of similar houses connected together

terrible /'terɪb(ə)l/ *adjective* very bad ○ *We shouldn't have come to this party – the music's terrible.* ○ *There was a terrible storm last night.*

terribly /'terɪbli/ *adverb* **1.** very ○ *I'm terribly sorry to have kept you waiting.* ○ *The situation is terribly serious.* **2.** in a very bad way ○ *The farmers suffered terribly from drought.*

terrific /tə'rɪfɪk/ *adjective* **1.** extremely good ○ *We had a terrific time at the par-*

ty. **2.** very big or loud ○ *There was a terrific bang and the whole building collapsed.*

terrify /'terɪfaɪ/ *verb* to make someone very frightened ○ *The sound of thunder terrifies me.* (NOTE: **terrifies – terrifying – terrified**)

territory /'terɪt(ə)ri/ *noun* **1.** a large area of land ○ *They occupied all the territory on the east bank of the river.* **2.** land which belongs to a country ○ *A group of soldiers had wandered into enemy territory.* **3.** an area which an animal or bird thinks belongs only to it ○ *Animals often fight to defend their territories.* (NOTE: The plural is **territories**.)

terror /'terə/ *noun* great fear ○ *They live in constant terror of terrorist attacks.*

terrorist /'terərɪst/ *noun* a person who practises terrorism ○ *Terrorists hijacked a plane and told the pilot to fly to Rome.* ■ *adjective* referring to terrorism ○ *Terrorist attacks have increased over the last few weeks.*

test /test/ *noun* **1.** an examination to see if you know something ○ *We had an English test yesterday.* ○ *She passed her driving test.* **2.** an examination to see if something is working well ○ *The doctor will have to do a blood test.* ○ *It is a good test of the car's ability to brake fast.* ■ *verb* **1.** to find out how well someone can do something or how well someone knows something ○ *The teacher tested my spoken German.* **2.** to examine someone or something to see if everything is working well ○ *We need to test your reactions to noise and bright lights.* ○ *He has to have his eyes tested.* ○ *She tested her new car in the snow.*

text /tekst/ *noun* the written parts of a document or book, not the pictures ○ *It's a book for little children, with lots of pictures and very little text.*

textbook /'tekstbʊk/ *noun* a book which students use to learn about the subject they are studying

text message /'tekst ˌmesɪdʒ/ *noun* a message sent by telephone, using short forms of words, which appear on the screen of a mobile phone

than /ðən, ðæn/ *conjunction* used to show a comparison ○ *It's hotter this week than it was last week.* ■ *preposition* used to link two parts of a comparison ○ *His car is bigger than mine.* ○ *She was born in London, so she knows it better than any other town.* ○ *You can't get more than four people into this lift.* ○ *It's less than five kilometres to the nearest station.*

thank /θæŋk/ *verb* to say or do something that shows you are grateful to someone for doing something for you ○ *She thanked the policeman for helping her to cross the street.* ○ *Don't forget to thank Aunt Ann for her present.*

thanks /θæŋks/ *noun* a word showing that you are grateful ○ *We sent our thanks for the gift.* ○ *We did our best to help but got no thanks for it.* ○ *The committee passed a vote of thanks to the school for having organised the meeting.* ○ *Many thanks for your letter of the 15th.* ■ *interjection* used to show you are grateful ○ *Do you want some more tea? – No thanks. I've had two cups already.* ○ *Anyone want a lift to the station? – Thanks, it's a long walk from here.*

thanks to /'θæŋks tuː/ *preposition* used for saying that someone or something is responsible for something or to blame for something

thank you /'θæŋk juː/ *interjection* showing that you are grateful ○ *Thank you very much for your letter of the 15th.* ○ *Did you remember to say thank you to your grandmother for the present?* ○ *Would you like another piece of cake? – No thank you, I've had enough.* ■ *noun* something that you do or say to show you are grateful ○ *Let's say a big thank you to the people who organised the show.*

that /ðæt/ *adjective* used to show something or someone that is further away or in the past ○ *Can you see that white house on the corner over there?* ○ *Do you remember the name of that awful hotel in Brighton?* Compare **this** (NOTE: The plural is **those**.) ■ *pronoun* something or someone that is further away ○ *That's the book I was talking about.* ○

Do you know who that is sitting at the next table? ○ *Is that the one? – Yes, that's it.* Compare **this** ■ *relative pronoun* used to give more information about someone or something just mentioned ○ *Where is the parcel that she sent you yesterday?* ○ *Can you see the man that sold you the ticket?* ○ *There's the suitcase that you left on the train!* (NOTE: When it is the object of a relative clause, **that** can sometimes be left out: *Where's the letter he sent you? Here's the box you left in the bedroom.* When it is the subject, **that** can be replaced by **which** *or* **who**: *a house that has red windows or a house which has red windows; the man that stole the car or the man who stole the car.*) ■ *conjunction* used after verbs like 'say' or 'think' and adjectives like 'glad' or 'disappointed', and after 'so' or 'such' ○ *The restaurant was so expensive that we could only afford one dish.* ○ *It rained so hard that the street was like a river.* ○ *We had such a lot of work that we didn't have any lunch.* ○ *There was such a long queue that we didn't bother waiting.* ○ *They told me that the manager was out.* ○ *I don't think they knew that we were coming.* ○ *I'm glad that the weather turned out fine.* (NOTE: **That** is often left out: *He didn't know we were coming; It's so hot in here we all want a drink of water.*) ■ *adverb* to such a degree ○ *You must remember him, it's not all that long ago that we had a drink with him.* ○ *His new car is not really that big.*

thaw /θɔː/ *noun* a time of warm weather which makes snow and ice melt ○ *The thaw came early this year.* ■ *verb* to melt ○ *The ice is thawing on the village pond.*

the /ðə/; *before a vowel* /ðiː/ *article* **1.** meaning something in particular, as opposed to 'a' ○ *Where's the book you brought back from the library?* ○ *That's the cat from next door.* ○ *The town centre has been made into a pedestrian zone.* **2.** used with something of which only one exists, e.g. in the names of places ○ *an expedition to the Antarctic* ○ *A spacecraft landed on the moon.* ○ *The sun came up over the hills.* **3.** used

for referring to a thing in general ○ *There's nothing interesting on the television tonight.* ○ *She refuses to use the telephone.* ○ *The streets are crowded at lunchtime.* ○ *Both sisters play the flute.* **4.** meaning something special ○ *It's the shop for men's clothes.* ○ *She's the doctor for children's diseases.* ○ *That's not the Charlie Chaplin, is it?* **5.** used to compare ○ *The more he eats the thinner he seems to get.* ○ *The sooner you do it the better.* ○ *This is by far the shortest way to London.* ○ *She's the tallest person in the office.*

theater /ˈθɪətə/ *noun* US spelling of **theatre**

theatre /ˈθɪətə/ *noun* a building in which plays are shown ○ *I'm trying to get tickets for the theatre tonight.* ○ *What is the play at the local theatre this week?* ○ *We'll have dinner early and then go to the theatre.*

their /ðeə/ *adjective* belonging to them ○ *After the film, we went to their house for supper.* (NOTE: Do not confuse with **there, they're.**)

theirs /ðeəz/ *pronoun* the one that belongs to them ○ *Which car is theirs – the Ford?* ○ *She's a friend of theirs.* ○ *The girls wanted to borrow my car – theirs wouldn't start.*

them /ðəm, ðem/ *pronoun* **1.** referring to people or things that have been mentioned before ○ *Do you like cream cakes? – No, I don't like them very much.* ○ *There's a group of people waiting outside. – Tell them to come in.* ○ *She saw her friends and asked them to help her.* **2.** referring to a single person, used instead of **him** or **her** ○ *If someone phones, ask them to call back later.*

theme /θiːm/ *noun* the main subject of a book or article ○ *The theme of the book is how to deal with illness in the family.*

themselves /ðəmˈselvz/ *pronoun* referring to the same people or things that are the subject of the verb ○ *Cats always spend a lot of time cleaning themselves.* ○ *It's no use going to the surgery – the doctors are all ill themselves.*

then /ðen/ *adverb* **1.** at that time in the past or future ○ *He had been very busy* *up till then.* ○ *Ever since then I've refused to eat oysters.* ○ *We're having a party next week. – What a pity! I'll be in Scotland then.* **2.** after that ○ *We all sat down, and then after a few minutes the waiter brought us the menu.* ○ *It was a busy trip – he went to Greece, then to Italy and finally to Spain.*

theory /'θɪəri/ *noun* **1.** an explanation of something which has not been proved but which you believe is true ○ *I have a theory which explains why the police never found the murder weapon.* **2.** a careful scientific explanation of why something happens ○ *Galileo put forward the theory that the earth turns round the sun.* **3.** a statement of general principles which may not apply in practice ○ *In theory the treatment should work, but no one has ever tried it.* (NOTE: The plural is **theories**.)

there /ðeə/ *adverb* **1.** in that place ○ *Is that black van still there parked outside the house?* ○ *Where have you put the tea? – There, on the kitchen counter.* **2.** to that place ○ *We haven't been to the British Museum yet. – Let's go there tomorrow.* ○ *Have you ever been to China? – Yes, I went there last month.* **3.** used when giving something to someone ○ *There you are: two fish and chips and a pot of tea.* (NOTE: Do not confuse with **their, they're**.) ■ *pronoun* used usually before the verb when the real subject follows the verb ○ *There's a little door leading onto the patio.* ○ *There's someone at the door asking for you.* ○ *There are some pages missing in my newspaper.* ○ *Were there a lot of people at the cinema?* ○ *There seems to have been a lot of rain during the night.*

therefore /'ðeəfɔː/ *adverb* for this reason ○ *I therefore have decided not to grant his request.* ○ *They have reduced their prices, therefore we should reduce ours if we want to stay competitive.*

thermometer /θə'mɒmɪtə/ *noun* an instrument for measuring temperature

these /ðiːz/ plural of **this**

they /ðeɪ/ *pronoun* **1.** referring to people or things ○ *Where do you keep the spoons? – They're in the right-hand drawer.* ○ *Who are those people in uni-*

form? – They're traffic wardens. ○ *The children played in the sun and they all got sunburnt.* **2.** referring to people in general ○ *They say it's going to be fine this weekend.* (NOTE: When it is the object, **them** is used instead of **they**: *We gave it to them*; *The police beat them with sticks*; also when it follows the verb **to be**: *Who's that? – It's them!*)

they're /ðeə/ *short form* they are (NOTE: Do not confuse with **their, there**.)

thick /θɪk/ *adjective* **1.** bigger than usual when measured from side to side ○ *He cut a slice of bread which was so thick it wouldn't go into the toaster.* ○ *The walls of the castle are three metres thick.* ○ *Some oranges have very thick skins.* ○ *He took a piece of thick rope.* **2.** growing close together ○ *They tried to make their way through thick jungle.* ○ *The field was covered with thick grass.* **3.** (*of a liquid*) which cannot flow easily ○ *If the paint is too thick add some water.* ○ *A bowl of thick soup is just what we need on a cold day like this.*

thief /θiːf/ *noun* a person who steals (NOTE: The plural is **thieves** /θiːvz/.)

thigh /θaɪ/ *noun* the part at the top of the leg between your knee and your hip

thin /θɪn/ *adjective* **1.** not fat ○ *The table has very thin legs.* ○ *He looks too thin – he should eat more.* **2.** not thick ○ *a plate of thin sandwiches* ○ *The book is printed on very thin paper.* ○ *The parcel was sent in a thin cardboard box.* **3.** (*of a liquid*) which flows easily, often because of containing too much water ○ *All we had for lunch was a bowl of thin soup.* ○ *Add water to make the paint thinner.*

thing /θɪŋ/ *noun* **1.** an object ○ *Can you see that black thing in the pan of soup?* ○ *What do you use that big blue thing for?* **2.** something in general ○ *They all just sat there and didn't say a thing.* ○ *The first thing to do is to call an ambulance.* ○ *That was a stupid thing to do!*

think /θɪŋk/ *verb* **1.** to consider something ○ *We never think about what people might say, we always do what we think is right.* **2.** to have an opinion ○ *I think London is a nicer town to live in than Frankfurt.* ○ *Everyone thinks we're* *mad to go on holiday in December.* ○ *The weather forecasters think it's going to rain.* ○ *The gang is thought to be based in Spain.* **3.** to make a plan to do something ○ *We're thinking we might open an office in New York.* (NOTE: **thinks – thinking – thought** /θɔːt/) ◇ **to think twice** to consider very carefully ○ *Think twice before you sign that contract.* ○ *I'd think twice about spending all the money you've saved.*

think about *phrasal verb* **1.** to have someone or something in your mind ○ *I was just thinking about you when you phoned.* ○ *All she thinks about is food.* **2.** to have an opinion about something ○ *What do you think about the government's plans to increase taxes?*

think of *phrasal verb* **1.** to consider a plan in your mind ○ *We are thinking of going to Greece on holiday.* **2.** to have an opinion about something ○ *What do you think of the government's plans to increase taxes?* ○ *I didn't think much of the play.* ○ *She asked him what he thought of her idea.* ◇ **to think better of something** to change your mind about something ○ *He was going to pay the whole cost himself, and then thought better of it.*

think up *phrasal verb* to invent a plan or new idea

third /θɜːd/ *adjective* **1.** number 3 in a series ○ *She came third in the race.* ○ *The cake shop is the third shop on the right.* ○ *It will be her third birthday next Friday.* **2.** next after the longest, best, tallest etc. (*followed by a superlative*) ○ *This is the third tallest building in the world.* ○ *He's the third most senior member of staff.* ■ *noun* **1.** the thing that is number three in a series ○ *Her birthday is on the third of March* or *March the third (March 3rd).* **2.** one of three equal parts of something ○ *A third of the airline's planes are jumbos.* ○ *Two-thirds of the staff are part-timers.*

thirsty /ˈθɜːsti/ *adjective* feeling that you want to drink ○ *It's so hot here that it makes me thirsty.*

thirteen /ˌθɜːˈtiːn/ *noun* the number 13 ○ *He's only thirteen (years old), but he*

can drive a car. ○ *She'll be thirteen next Monday.*

thirteenth /ˌθɜːˈtiːnθ/ *adjective* number 13 in a series ○ *It's her thirteenth birthday on Monday.* ■ *noun* the thing that is number 13 in a series ○ *The thirteenth of September* or *September the thirteenth (September 13th).*

thirtieth /ˈθɜːtiəθ/ *adjective* number 30 in a series ○ *her thirtieth birthday* (NOTE: With dates **thirtieth** is usually written **30th**: *May 30th, 1921*; *June 30th, 1896* (American style is *June 30, 1896*): say 'the thirtieth of June' or 'June the thirtieth' (American style is 'June thirtieth').) ■ *noun* the thing that is number 30 in a series

thirty /ˈθɜːti/ *noun* the number 30 ○ *He's thirty (years old).* ○ *Over thirty people complained.* □ **they are both in their thirties** they are both aged between 30 and 39 years old □ **the (nineteen-) thirties (1930s)** the period from 1930 to 1939

this /ðɪs/ *adjective, pronoun* used to show something which is nearer or in the present, in contrast to something else ○ *This is the shop I was telling you about.* ○ *I prefer these earrings to those ones.* ○ *I saw him on the train this morning.* ○ *My mother is coming for tea this afternoon.* ○ *I expect to hear from him this week.* (NOTE: The plural is **these**.) ■ *adverb* so much ○ *I knew you were going to be late, but I didn't expect you to be this late.*

thorn /θɔːn/ *noun* a thin pointed part on some plants ○ *Most roses have thorns.*

thorough /ˈθʌrə/ *adjective* **1.** dealing with everything very carefully ○ *The police have carried out a thorough search of the woods.* **2.** used for emphasis ○ *They made a thorough mess of it.* ○ *It was a thorough waste of time.*

thoroughly /ˈθʌrəli/ *adverb* **1.** in a complete and careful way ○ *We searched the garden thoroughly but couldn't find his red ball.* **2.** used for emphasis ○ *I'm thoroughly fed up with the whole business.*

those /ðəʊz/ plural of **that**

though /ðəʊ/ *adverb, conjunction* **1.** used for mentioning something that makes something else seem surprising ○ *Though tired, she still kept on running.* ○ *We don't employ a computer programmer, though many companies do.* **2.** but ○ *It is unlikely though possible.* ◇ **as though** as if ○ *His voice sounded strange over the telephone, as though he was standing in a cave.* ○ *That shirt doesn't look as though it has been ironed.* ○ *It looks as though there is no one in.*

thought /θɔːt/ past tense and past participle of **think** ■ *noun* an idea which you have when thinking ○ *He had an awful thought – suppose they had left the bathroom taps running?*

thoughtful /'θɔːtf(ə)l/ *adjective* **1.** thinking about something a lot ○ *He looked thoughtful, and I wondered if there was something wrong.* **2.** being sensitive to what other people want ○ *It was very thoughtful of you to come to see me in hospital.*

thousand /'θaʊz(ə)nd/ *noun* the number 1,000 ○ *We paid two hundred thousand pounds for the house (£200,000).* ○ *Thousands of people had their holidays spoilt by the storm.*

thousandth /'θaʊzənθ/ *adjective* number 1,000 in a series ○ *The tourist office gave a prize to their thousandth visitor.*

thrash /θræʃ/ *verb* to defeat another person or team easily (*informal*) ○ *She expects to be thrashed by the champion.*

thread /θred/ *noun* a long piece of cotton, silk, or other fibre ○ *A spider spins a thread to make its web.* ○ *Wait a moment, there's a white thread showing on your coat.*

threat /θret/ *noun* a warning to someone that you are going to do something unpleasant, especially if he or she does not do what you want ○ *Her former husband had been making threats against her and the children.* ○ *The police took the threat to the Prime Minister very seriously.* ○ *Do you think they will carry out their threat to bomb the capital if we don't surrender?*

threaten /'θret(ə)n/ *verb* to warn that you are going to do something unpleasant, especially if someone does not do what you want ○ *She threatened to go to the police.* ○ *The teacher threatened her with punishment.*

threatening /'θret(ə)nɪŋ/ *adjective* suggesting that something unpleasant will happen

three /θriː/ *noun* the number 3 ○ *She's only three (years old), so she can't read yet.* ○ *Come and see me at three (o'clock).* ○ *Three men walked into the bank and pulled out guns.* (NOTE: **three** (3) but **third** (3rd))

threw /θruː/ past tense of **throw** (NOTE: Do not confuse with **through**.)

thrill /θrɪl/ *noun* a feeling of great excitement ○ *It gave me a thrill to see you all again after so many years.* ○ *I experienced the thrill of sailing near to a waterfall.* ■ *verb* to make someone very excited ○ *We were thrilled to get your letter.*

thrilling /'θrɪlɪŋ/ *adjective* which makes you very excited

throat /θrəʊt/ *noun* **1.** the tube which goes from the back of your mouth down the inside of your neck ○ *I've got a sore throat.* ○ *She got a fish bone stuck in her throat.* **2.** your neck, especially the front part ○ *He put his hands round her throat and pressed hard.*

through /θruː/ *preposition* **1.** across to the inside of something ○ *The bullet went straight through the door.* ○ *She looked through the open door.* ○ *Cold air is coming in through the hole in the wall.* ○ *The street goes straight through the centre of the town.* ○ *She pushed the needle through the ball of wool.* **2.** during a period of time ○ *They insisted on talking all through the film.* ○ *Snow accumulated through the winter.* ■ *adverb* going in at one side and coming out of the other side ○ *Someone left the gate open and all the sheep got through.*

throughout /θruː'aʊt/ *preposition, adverb* in all or several parts of ○ *Throughout the country floods are causing problems on the roads.* ○ *Heavy snow fell throughout the night.*

throw /θrəʊ/ *verb* to send something through the air ○ *How far can he throw a cricket ball?* ○ *They were throwing stones through car windows.* ○ *She threw the letter into the wastepaper basket.* ○ *He was thrown into the air by the blast from the bomb.* (NOTE: **throws – throwing – threw** /θruː/ **– thrown** /θrəʊn/)

throw away *phrasal verb* to get rid of something which you do not need any more

throw out *phrasal verb* **1.** to push someone outside ○ *When they started to fight, they were thrown out of the restaurant.* **2.** to get rid of something which you do not need ○ *I'm throwing out this old office desk.*

throw up *phrasal verb* to let food come up from your stomach and out through your mouth (*informal*) ○ *The cat threw up all over the sofa.*

thrust /θrʌst/ *verb* to push something somewhere suddenly and hard ○ *He thrust the newspaper into his pocket.* ○ *She thrust the documents into her briefcase.* (NOTE: **thrusts – thrusting – thrust**) ■ *noun* the act of suddenly pushing something strongly ○ *He was killed with a thrust of his opponent's sword.*

thud /θʌd/ *noun* a dull, heavy noise ○ *His head hit the ground with a sickening thud.* ○ *They could hear the thud of the guns in the distance.* ■ *verb* to make a dull noise ○ *A stone thudded into the wall behind him.* (NOTE: **thuds – thudding – thudded**)

thumb /θʌm/ *noun* a part on the side of your hand that looks like a short thick finger ○ *The baby was sucking its thumb.* ○ *How she cried when she hit her thumb with the hammer!*

thump /θʌmp/ *noun* a dull noise ○ *There was a thump from upstairs as if someone had fallen out of bed.* ■ *verb* to hit someone hard with your fist ○ *He rushed up to the policeman and started thumping him on the chest.* ○ *She thumped him on the back when he choked.*

thunder /ˈθʌndə/ *noun* a loud noise in the air following a flash of lightning ○ *a tropical storm accompanied by thunder and lightning* ○ *He was woken by the sound of thunder.* ■ *verb* to make a loud noise in the air following lightning ○ *It thundered during the night.*

thunderstorm /ˈθʌndəstɔːm/ *noun* a storm with rain, thunder and lightning

Thursday /ˈθɜːzdeɪ/ *noun* the day between Wednesday and Friday, the fourth day of the week ○ *Last Thursday was Christmas Day.* ○ *Shall we arrange to meet next Thursday?* ○ *Today is Thursday, April 14th.* ○ *The club meets on Thursdays* or *every Thursday.* ○ *The 15th is a Wednesday, so the 16th must be a Thursday.*

thus /ðʌs/ *adverb* **1.** in this way ○ *The two pieces fit together thus.* ○ *She is only fifteen, and thus cannot vote.* **2.** as a result ○ *She is only fifteen, and thus is not able to take part in the over-sixteens competition.*

tick /tɪk/ *noun* **1.** a sound made every second by a clock ○ *The only sound we could hear in the room was the tick of the grandfather clock.* **2.** a mark written to show that something is correct ○ *Put a tick in the box marked 'R'.* ■ *verb* **1.** to mark something with a tick to show that you approve ○ *Tick the box marked 'R' if you require a receipt.* **2.** to make a quiet regular sound noise like a clock ○ *All you could hear was the clock ticking in the corner of the library.* ○ *Watch out! That parcel's ticking!*

ticket /ˈtɪkɪt/ *noun* **1.** a piece of paper or card which allows you to travel ○ *They won't let you get onto the train without a ticket.* ○ *We've lost our plane tickets – how can we get to Chicago?* **2.** a piece of paper which allows you to go into a place, e.g. a cinema or an exhibition ○ *Can I have three tickets for the 8.30 show please?* ○ *We tried several theatres but there were no tickets left anywhere.*

tickle /ˈtɪk(ə)l/ *verb* **1.** to touch someone in a sensitive part of the body in order to make him or her laugh ○ *She tickled his toes and made him laugh.* **2.** to cause a slight uncomfortable feeling on the skin of part of the body, or to have that feeling

tide /taɪd/ *noun* the regular rising and falling movement of the sea ○ *The tide came in and cut off the children on the rocks.* ○ *The tide is out – we can walk across the sand.*

tidily /'taɪdɪli/ *adverb* in a tidy way

tidy /'taɪdi/ *adjective* with everything arranged in the correct way or in an organised way ○ *I want your room to be completely tidy before you go out.* ○ *She put her clothes in a tidy pile.*

tie /taɪ/ *noun* **1.** a long piece of coloured cloth which men wear round their necks under the collar of their shirts ○ *He's wearing a blue tie with red stripes.* ○ *They won't let you into the restaurant if you haven't got a tie on.* **2.** a result in a competition or election where both sides have the same score ○ *The result was a tie and the vote had to be taken again.* ■ *verb* **1.** to attach something with string, rope or twine ○ *The parcel was tied with a little piece of string.* ○ *He tied his horse to the post.* ○ *The burglars tied his hands behind his back.* **2.** to have the same score as another team in a competition ○ *They tied for second place.* (NOTE: **ties – tying – tied**)

tiger /'taɪgə/ *noun* a large wild animal of the cat family which is yellow with black stripes and lives mainly in India and China (NOTE: The female is a **tigress**.)

tight /taɪt/ *adjective* **1.** fitting too closely ○ *These shoes hurt – they're too tight.* **2.** holding firmly ○ *Keep a tight hold of the bag, we don't want it stolen.*

tighten /'taɪt(ə)n/ *verb* to make something tight, or to become tight

tightly /'taɪtli/ *adverb* in a tight way

till /tɪl/ *preposition, conjunction* up to the time when ○ *I don't expect him to be home till after nine o'clock.* ○ *They worked from morning till night to finish the job.* ○ *We worked till the sun went down.* ■ *noun* a drawer for keeping cash in a shop ○ *There was not much money in the till at the end of the day.*

tilt /tɪlt/ *verb* **1.** to slope ○ *The shelf is tilting to the right.* ○ *You'll have to change places – the boat is tilting.* **2.** to put something in a sloping position ○ *He*

tilted the barrel over to get the last drops of beer out.

timber /'tɪmbə/ *noun* wood cut ready for building ○ *These trees are being grown to provide timber for houses.* (NOTE: no plural: for one item say *a piece of timber*)

time /taɪm/ *noun* **1.** a particular point in the day shown in hours and minutes ○ *What time is it* or *what's the time?* ○ *Can you tell me the time please?* ○ *The time is exactly four thirty.* ○ *Departure times are delayed by up to fifteen minutes because of the volume of traffic.* □ **to tell the time** to read the time on a clock or watch ○ *She's only three so she can't tell the time yet.* **2.** the hour at which something usually happens ○ *The closing time for the office is 5.30.* ○ *It's must be nearly time for dinner – I'm hungry.* ○ *Is it time for the children to go to bed?* **3.** an amount of hours, days, weeks, months or years ○ *There's no need to hurry – we've got plenty of time.* ○ *Do you have time for a cup of coffee?* ○ *He spent all that time watching the TV.* ○ *If the fire alarm rings, don't waste time putting clothes on – run out of the hotel fast.* **4.** a certain period ○ *We haven't been to France for a long time.* ○ *We had a letter from my mother a short time ago.* **5.** a particular moment when something happens ○ *They didn't hear anything as they were asleep at the time.* ○ *By the time the ambulance arrived the man had died.* ○ *You can't do two things at the same time.* **6.** a period when things are pleasant or bad ○ *Everyone had a good time at the party.* ○ *We had an awful time on holiday – the hotel was dreadful, and it rained solidly for ten days.* **7.** one of several moments or periods when something happens ○ *I've seen that film on TV four times already.* ○ *That's the last time I'll ask them to play cards.* ○ *Next time you come, bring your swimming things.* **8.** the rhythm of a piece of music ○ *It's difficult keeping time in a modern piece like this.* ○ *He tapped his foot in time to the music.* ■ *verb* to count something in hours, minutes and seconds ○ *I timed him as he ran round the track.* ○ *Don't forget to time the eggs – they have to cook for only* *three minutes.* ◇ **find time** /'faɪnd taɪm/ to do something even though you are busy ○ *In the middle of the meeting he still found time to phone his girlfriend.* ○ *We must find time to visit the new staff sports club.* ◇ **for the time being** temporarily ○ *We will leave the furniture as it is for the time being.* ◇ **in … time** after a particular period from now ○ *We're going on holiday in four weeks' time.* ◇ **to take time** to need a certain amount of time ○ *It didn't take you much time to get dressed.* ○ *Don't hurry me, I like to take my time.*

timetable /'taɪmteɪb(ə)l/ *noun* a printed list which shows the times at which something such as classes in school or trains leaving will happen ○ *We have two English lessons on the timetable today.* ○ *According to the timetable, there should be a train to London at 10.22.* ■ *verb* to arrange the times for something to happen ○ *You are timetabled to speak at 4.30.*

tin /tɪn/ *noun* 1. a silver-coloured soft metal ○ *Bronze is a mixture of copper and tin.* ○ *There have been tin mines in Cornwall since Roman times.* 2. a metal container in which food or another substance is sold and can be kept for a long time ○ *I'll just open a tin of soup.* ○ *She bought three tins of cat food.* ○ *We'll need three tins of white paint for the ceiling.* 3. any metal box ○ *Keep the biscuits in a tin or they'll go soft.* ○ *She puts her spare coins into a tin by the telephone.*

tingle /'tɪŋgəl/ *noun* a feeling like a lot of small sharp things sticking into your skin ○ *It didn't hurt, I just felt a tingle in my leg.* ○ *We felt a tingle of excitement as we queued for the roller coaster.* ■ *verb* to have a sharp prickling feeling ○ *'Are your fingers tingling?' asked the doctor.* ○ *It will tingle when I put the antiseptic on your cut.*

tinkle /'tɪŋkəl/ *noun* a noise like the ringing of a little bell ○ *the gentle tinkle of cow bells in the distance* ■ *verb* to make a little ringing noise ○ *The little bell tinkled as she went into the shop.*

tinned /tɪnd/ *adjective* preserved and sold in a tin

tin opener /'tɪn ˌəʊp(ə)nə/ *noun* an object used for opening tins of food

tiny /'taɪni/ *adjective* very small ○ *Can I have just a tiny bit more pudding?* ○ *The spot is so tiny you can hardly see it.* ○ *She lives in a tiny village in the Welsh mountains.* (NOTE: **tinier – tiniest**)

tip /tɪp/ *noun* 1. the end of something long ○ *She touched the page with the tips of her fingers.* ○ *He poked the dog with the tip of his walking stick.* 2. money given to someone who has provided a service ○ *The service hasn't been very good – should we leave a tip for the waiter?* ○ *The staff are not allowed to accept tips.* 3. advice on something which could bring you a benefit ○ *He gave me a tip about a horse which was likely to win.* ○ *She gave me a tip about a cheap restaurant just round the corner from the hotel.* 4. a place where rubbish from houses is taken to be thrown away ○ *I must take these bags of rubbish to the tip.* ■ *verb* 1. to pour something out ○ *He picked up the box and tipped the contents out onto the floor.* ○ *She tipped all the food out of the bag.* 2. to give money to someone who has helped you ○ *I tipped the waiter £1.* ○ *Should we tip the driver?* (NOTE: **tips – tipping – tipped**)

tiptoe /'tɪptəʊ/ *verb* to walk quietly on the tips of your toes ○ *She tiptoed into the room and looked at the baby.* (NOTE: **tiptoes – tiptoeing – tiptoed**)

tired /'taɪəd/ *adjective* 1. feeling that you want to sleep ○ *I'm tired – I think I'll go to bed.* ○ *If you feel tired, lie down on my bed.* 2. feeling that you need rest ○ *We're all tired after a long day at the office.* ◇ **tired out** feeling very tired or needing a rest

tiring /'taɪərɪŋ/ *adjective* which makes you tired

tissue /'tɪʃuː/ *noun* a soft paper handkerchief ○ *There is a box of tissues beside the bed.*

title /'taɪt(ə)l/ *noun* 1. the name of something, e.g. a book, play, painting or film ○ *He's almost finished the play but hasn't found a title for it yet.* 2. a word such as Dr, Mr, Professor, Lord, Sir or

Lady put in front of a name to show an honour or a qualification

to /tə, tʊ, tuː/ *preposition* **1.** showing direction or place ○ *They went to the police station.* ○ *Do you know the way to the beach?* ○ *The river is to the north of the town.* ○ *Everyone take one step to the right, please.* **2.** showing a period of time ○ *The office is open from 9.30 to 5.30, Monday to Friday.* ○ *She slept from 11.30 to 8.30 the following morning.* **3.** showing time in minutes before an hour ○ *Get up – it's five to seven (6.55).* ○ *The train leaves at a quarter to eight (7.45).* (NOTE: **To** is used for times between the half hour and o'clock: *3.35* = twenty-five to four; *3.45* = a quarter to four; *3.55* = five minutes to four. For times after the hour see **past**.) **4.** showing a person or animal that receives something ○ *Take the book to the librarian.* ○ *Pass the salt to your grandfather.* ○ *You must be kind to cats.* **5.** showing a connection or relationship ○ *They lost by twelve to nine.* ○ *There are four keys to the office.* ○ *In this class there are 28 children to one teacher.*

toast /təʊst/ *noun* pieces of bread which have been heated at a high temperature until they are brown ○ *Can you make some more toast?* ○ *She asked for scrambled eggs on toast.*

tobacco /tə'bækəʊ/ *noun* the dried leaves of a plant used to make cigarettes and cigars, and for smoking in pipes (NOTE: no plural)

today /tə'deɪ/ *noun* this day ○ *Today's her sixth birthday.* ○ *What's the date today?* ○ *There's a story in today's newspaper about a burglary in our road.* ■ *adverb* on this day ○ *He said he wanted to see me today, but he hasn't come yet.*

toddler /'tɒdlə/ *noun* a child who has just learnt to walk

toe /təʊ/ *noun* one of the five parts like fingers at the end of the foot ○ *She trod on my toe and didn't say she was sorry.*

together /tə'geðə/ *adverb* **1.** doing something with someone else or in a group ○ *Tell the children to stay together or they'll get lost.* ○ *Why don't we all go to the cinema?* **2.** joined with something else or with each other ○ *Tie the* sticks together with string. ○ *Do you think you can stick the pieces of the cup together again?* ○ *If you add all the figures together, you'll get the total sales.* ○ *We've had three sandwiches and three beers – how much does that come to all together?*

toilet /'tɔɪlət/ *noun* **1.** a bowl with a seat on which you sit to get rid of waste from your body ○ *There is a shower and toilet in the bathroom.* **2.** a room with a toilet bowl in it ○ *The ladies' toilet is at the end of the corridor.* ○ *The gents' toilets are downstairs and to the right.* ○ *There's a public toilet at the railway station.*

told /təʊld/ past tense and past participle of **tell**

tomato /tə'mɑːtəʊ/ *noun* a small round red fruit used in salads and cooking ○ *Tomatoes cost 30p per kilo.* ○ *We had a salad of raw cabbage and tomatoes.* ○ *Someone in the crowd threw a tomato at the speaker on the platform.* (NOTE: The plural is **tomatoes**.)

tomorrow /tə'mɒrəʊ/ *adverb* on to the day after today ○ *Are you free for lunch tomorrow?* ○ *I mustn't forget I have a dentist's appointment tomorrow morning.* ○ *We are going to an Italian restaurant tomorrow evening.* ■ *noun* the day after today ○ *Today's Monday, so tomorrow must be Tuesday.* ○ *Tomorrow is our tenth wedding anniversary.*

ton /tʌn/ *noun* a measure of weight equal to 2240 pounds ○ *a ship carrying 1000 tons of coal*

tone /təʊn/ *noun* a way of saying something, or of writing something, which shows a particular feeling ○ *His tone of voice showed he was angry.* ○ *She said hello in a friendly tone of voice.* ○ *You could tell from the tone of his letter that he was annoyed.*

tongue /tʌŋ/ *noun* **1.** the long organ in your mouth which can move and is used for tasting, swallowing and speaking ○ *The soup was so hot it burnt my tongue.* **2.** a language (*literary*) ○ *They spoke to each other in a strange foreign tongue.* ○ *It was clear that English was not his native tongue.* □ **mother tongue** *or* **native tongue** the language which you spoke when you were a little child ○ *She speaks English very well, but German is her mother tongue.*

tonight /tə'naɪt/ *adverb, noun* the night or the evening of today ○ *I can't stop – we're getting ready for tonight's party.* ○ *I'll be at home from eight o'clock tonight.* ○ *I don't suppose there's anything interesting on TV tonight.*

tonne /tʌn/ *noun* a measure of weight equal to 1,000 kilograms

too /tuː/ *adverb* **1.** more than necessary ○ *There are too many people to fit into the lift.* ○ *I think we bought too much bread.* ○ *It's too hot for us to sit in the sun.* **2.** (*often at the end of a clause*) also ○ *She had some coffee and I had some too.* ○ *She comes from Scotland too.*

took /tʊk/ past tense of **take**

tool /tuːl/ *noun* an object which you hold in your hand to do specific work, e.g. a hammer or a spade ○ *a set of tools for mending the car*

tooth /tuːθ/ *noun* one of a set of hard white objects in the mouth which you use to bite or chew food ○ *Children must learn to clean their teeth twice a day.* ○ *The dentist took one of her teeth out.* (NOTE: The plural is **teeth** /tiːθ/.)

toothbrush /'tuːθbrʌʃ/ *noun* a small brush which you use to clean your teeth (NOTE: The plural is **toothbrushes**.)

toothpaste /'tuːθpeɪst/ *noun* a soft substance which you spread on a toothbrush and then use to clean your teeth (NOTE: no plural: *some toothpaste, a tube of toothpaste*)

top /tɒp/ *noun* **1.** the highest place or highest point of something ○ *He climbed to the top of the stairs and sat down.* ○ *The bird is sitting on the top of the apple tree.* ○ *There is a roof garden on top of the hotel.* ○ *Look at the photograph at the top of page four.* ○ *Manchester United are still at the top of the league table.* □ **to feel on top of the world** to feel very healthy or very happy **2.** the flat upper surface of something ○ *a birthday cake with sugar and fruit on top* ○ *Do not put coffee cups on top of the computer.* ○ *The desk has a black top.* **3.** a cover for a container ○ *Take the*

top off the jar, and see what's inside. ○ *She forgot to screw the top back on the bottle.* **4.** a piece of clothing covering the upper part of the body ○ *She wore jeans and a yellow top.* ■ *adjective* **1.** in the highest place ○ *The restaurant is on the top floor of the building.* ○ *Jams and marmalades are on the top shelf.* **2.** best ○ *She's one of the world's top tennis players.* ◇ **on top of** /ɒn 'tɒp ɒv/ **1.** on the top surface of ○ *He put the book down on top of the others he had bought.* **2.** in addition to ○ *On top of all my office work, I have to clean the house and look after the baby.*

topic /'tɒpɪk/ *noun* the subject of a discussion or conversation ○ *Can we move on to another topic?*

topple /'tɒp(ə)l/ *verb* ○ *He lost his balance and toppled forwards.*

topple over *phrasal verb* to fall down

torch /tɔːtʃ/ *noun* a small electric light that you can carry ○ *Take a torch if you're going into the cave.* ○ *I always carry a small torch in the car.*

tore /tɔː/ past tense of **tear**

torn /tɔːn/ past participle of **tear**

tortoise /'tɔːtəs/ *noun* a reptile covered with a hard shell which moves very slowly on land and can live to be very old

toss /tɒs/ *verb* **1.** to throw something up into the air ○ *He tried to toss the pancake and it fell on the kitchen floor.* ○ *She tossed me her car keys.* **2.** to move something about ○ *The waves tossed the little boat up and down.* ○ *The horse tossed its head.* ■ *noun* **1.** the act of throwing something into the air **2.** a sharp movement of the head up and down ○ *With a toss of its head, the horse galloped off.*

total /'təʊt(ə)l/ *adjective* complete or whole ○ *The expedition was a total failure.* ○ *Their total losses come to over £400,000.* ■ *noun* the whole amount ○ *The total comes to more than £1,000.*

totally /'təʊt(ə)li/ *adverb* used for emphasis ○ *The house was totally destroyed in the fire.* ○ *I had totally forgotten that I had promised to be there.* ○ *He* disagrees totally with what the first speaker said.

touch /tʌtʃ/ *noun* **1.** the sense that allows you to be aware of something with the fingers ○ *The sense of touch becomes very strong in the dark.* **2.** the act of passing of news and information □ **to get in touch with someone** to contact someone ○ *I'll try to get in touch with you next week.* **3.** a gentle physical contact ○ *I felt a light touch on my hand.* **4.** a very small amount ○ *He added a few touches of paint to the picture.* ○ *There's a touch of frost in the air this morning.* ■ *verb* **1.** to feel something with your fingers ○ *The policeman touched him on the shoulder.* ○ *Don't touch that cake – it's for your mother.* **2.** to be so close to something that you press against it ○ *His feet don't touch the floor when he sits on a big chair.* ○ *There is a mark on the wall where the sofa touches it.*

touching /'tʌtʃɪŋ/ *adjective* making you feel emotion, especially affection or sympathy ○ *I had a touching letter from my sister, thanking me for my help when she was ill.*

tough /tʌf/ *adjective* **1.** (*of meat*) difficult to chew or to cut ○ *My steak's a bit tough – how's yours?* **2.** requiring a lot of physical effort, or a lot of bravery or confidence ○ *She's very good at taking tough decisions.* ○ *You have to be tough to succeed in business.*

tour /tʊə/ *noun* a holiday or journey in which you visit various places ○ *There are so many tours to choose from – I can't decide which one to go on.* ○ *She gave us a tour round the old castle.* ■ *verb* to go on holiday, visiting various places ○ *They toured the south of France.*

tourist /'tʊərɪst/ *noun* a person who goes on holiday to visit places away from their home ○ *The tourists were talking German.* ○ *There were parties of tourists visiting all the churches.* ○ *Trafalgar Square is always full of tourists.*

tow /təʊ/ *verb* to pull something behind a vehicle ○ *The motorways were crowded with cars towing caravans.* ○ *They towed the ship into port.* ■ *noun* the action of pulling something ○ *We got a* tractor to give us a tow to the nearest garage. (NOTE: Do not confuse with **toe**.)

towards /tə'wɔːdz/ *preposition* **1.** in the direction of ○ *The crowd ran towards the police station.* ○ *The bus was travelling south, towards London.* ○ *The ship sailed straight towards the rocks.* **2.** near in time ○ *Do you have any free time towards the end of the month?* ○ *The exhibition will be held towards the middle of October.* **3.** as part of the money to pay for something ○ *He gave me £100 towards the cost of the hotel.* **4.** in relation to ○ *She always behaved very kindly towards her father.*

towel /'taʊəl/ *noun* a large piece of soft cloth for drying something, especially your body ○ *There's only one towel in the bathroom.* ○ *After washing her hair, she wound the towel round her head.* ○ *I'll get some fresh towels.*

tower /'taʊə/ *noun* a tall structure ○ *The castle has thick walls and four square towers.*

town /taʊn/ *noun* a place, larger than a village, where people live and work, with houses, shops, offices, factories and other buildings ○ *There's no shop in our village, so we do our shopping in the nearest town.* ○ *They moved their office to the centre of town.*

toy /tɔɪ/ *noun* a thing for children to play with ○ *We gave him a box of toy soldiers for Christmas.* ○ *The children's toys are all over the sitting room floor.*

trace /treɪs/ *noun* something which shows that something existed ○ *The police found traces of blood in the kitchen.* ■ *verb* to find where someone or something is ○ *They couldn't trace the letter.* ○ *The police traced him to Dover.*

track /træk/ *noun* a rough path ○ *We followed a track through the forest.* ■ *verb* to follow someone or an animal ○ *The hunters tracked the bear through the forest.* ○ *The police tracked the gang to a flat in south London.*

trade /treɪd/ *noun* the business of buying and selling goods ○ *Britain's trade with the rest of Europe is up by 10%.* ■ *verb* to buy and sell goods, to carry on a business ○ *The company has stopped trading.* ○ *They trade in furs.*

trademark /ˈtreɪdmɑːk/, **trade name** /ˈtreɪd neɪm/ *noun* a particular name, design, etc., which has been registered by the manufacturer and which cannot be used by other manufacturers ○ *Acme is a registered trademark.* ○ *Their trademark is stamped on every item they produce.*

tradition /trəˈdɪʃ(ə)n/ *noun* beliefs, stories and ways of doing things which are passed from one generation to the next ○ *It's a family tradition for the eldest son to take over the business.* ○ *According to local tradition, the queen died in this bed.*

traditional /trəˈdɪʃ(ə)n(ə)l/ *adjective* done in a way that has been used for a long time ○ *On Easter Day it is traditional to give chocolate eggs to the children.* ○ *Villagers still wear their traditional costumes on Sundays.*

traditionally /trəˈdɪʃ(ə)nəli/ *adverb* according to tradition

traffic /ˈtræfɪk/ *noun* cars, buses and other vehicles which are travelling on a street or road ○ *I leave the office early on Fridays because there is so much traffic leaving London.* ○ *The lights turned green and the traffic moved forward.* ○ *Rush-hour traffic is worse on Fridays.*

traffic jam /ˈtræfɪk dʒæm/ *noun* a situation where cars, buses and other vehicles cannot move forward on a road because there is too much traffic, because there has been an accident or because of roadworks

tragedy /ˈtrædʒədi/ *noun* **1.** a serious play, film, or novel which ends sadly ○ *Shakespeare's tragedy 'King Lear' is playing at the National Theatre.* **2.** a very unhappy event ○ *Tragedy struck the family when their mother was killed in a car crash.* (NOTE: The plural is **tragedies**.)

tragic /ˈtrædʒɪk/ *adjective* very sad ○ *a tragic accident on the motorway*

trail /treɪl/ *noun* **1.** tracks left by an animal or by a criminal ○ *We followed the trail of the bear through the forest.* ○

The burglars left in a red sports car, and a police car was soon on their trail. **2.** a path or track ○ *Keep to the trail otherwise you will get lost.* ■ *verb* □ **to trail behind someone** to follow slowly after someone ○ *She came third, trailing a long way behind the first two runners.* ○ *The little children trailed behind the older ones.*

trailer /ˈtreɪlə/ *noun* **1.** a small goods vehicle pulled behind a car ○ *We carried all our camping gear in the trailer.* **2.** *US* a van with beds, a table, and washing facilities, which can be towed by a car **3.** parts of a full-length film shown as an advertisement for it ○ *We saw the trailer last week, and it put me off the film.*

train /treɪn/ *noun* a railway vehicle consisting of an engine and the coaches it pulls ○ *The train to Paris leaves from platform 1.* ○ *Hundreds of people go to work every day by train.* ○ *The next train to London will be in two minutes.* ○ *To get to Glasgow, you have to change trains at Crewe.* ■ *verb* **1.** to teach someone or an animal how to do a particular activity ○ *She's being trained to be a bus driver.* ○ *The dogs are trained to smell and find illegal substances.* **2.** to become fit by practising for a sport ○ *He's training for the 100 metres.* ○ *She's training for the Olympics.*

trained /treɪnd/ *adjective* who has been through a course of training

trainer /ˈtreɪnə/ *noun* a person who trains an athlete ○ *His trainer says he's in peak condition for the fight.* ■ *plural noun* **trainers** light sports shoes

training /ˈtreɪnɪŋ/ *noun* **1.** the activity of learning a skill ○ *The shop is closed on Tuesday mornings for staff training.* ○ *There is a short training period for new staff.* **2.** the activity of practising for a sport

transfer *verb* **1.** to move something or someone to another place ○ *The money will be transferred directly to your bank account.* ○ *She transferred her passport from her handbag to her jacket pocket.* ○ *He's been transferred to our New York office.* **2.** to change from one type of travel to another ○ *When you get to*

London airport, you have to transfer onto an internal flight. (NOTE: **transfers – transferring – transferred**)

transform /træns'fɔːm/ *verb* to change the appearance or character of someone or something completely ○ *The outside of the building has been transformed by cleaning.* ○ *The book has transformed my views on medical care.*

translate /træns'leɪt/ *verb* to put written or spoken words into another language ○ *Can you translate what he said?* ○ *He asked his secretary to translate the letter from the German agent.* ○ *She translates mainly from Spanish into English, not from English into Spanish.*

translation /træns'leɪʃ(ə)n/ *noun* writing or speech which has been translated ○ *I read Tolstoy's 'War and Peace' in translation.* ○ *She passed the translation of the letter to the accounts department.*

transparent /træns'pærənt/ *adjective* which you can see through ○ *The meat is wrapped in transparent plastic film.*

transplant[1] /'trænsplɑːnt/ *noun* **1.** the act of replacing a damaged organ or part of the body with a part from another body, or with a part from somewhere else on the same body ○ *He had a heart transplant.* **2.** an organ or piece of tissue which is transplanted ○ *The kidney transplant was rejected.*

transplant[2] /træns'plɑːnt/ *verb* **1.** to move a plant from one place to another ○ *You should not transplant trees in the summer.* **2.** to replace a damaged organ or other body part with a healthy part ○ *They transplanted a kidney from his brother.*

transport[1] /'trænspɔːt/ *noun* the movement of goods or people in vehicles ○ *Air transport is the quickest way to travel from one country to another.* ○ *Rail transport costs are getting lower.* ○ *What means of transport will you use to get to the hotel?*

transport[2] /træns'pɔːt/ *verb* to move goods or people from one place to another in a vehicle ○ *The company transports millions of tons of goods by rail*

each year. ○ *The visitors will be transported to the factory by helicopter.*

trap /træp/ *noun* an object used for catching an animal ○ *We have a mouse in the kitchen so we will put down a trap.* ■ *verb* to catch or hold someone or something ○ *Several people were trapped in the wreckage of the plane.* ○ *He was trapped on video as he entered the bank.* (NOTE: **traps – trapping – trapped**)

travel /'træv(ə)l/ *noun* the action of moving from one country or place to another ○ *Air travel is the only really fast method of going from one country to another.* ■ *verb* to move from one country or place to another ○ *He travels fifty miles by car to go to work every day.* ○ *He has travelled across the United States several times on his motorbike.* ○ *The bullet must have travelled several metres before it hit the wall.* (NOTE: **travels – travelling – travelled**. The US spelling is **traveling – traveled**.)

traveller /'træv(ə)lə/ *noun* **1.** a person who travels ○ *travellers on the 9 o'clock train to London* ○ *Travellers to France are experiencing delays because of the dock strike.* **2.** a person who has no fixed home and who travels around the country ○ *The fields were full of hippies and travellers.*

tray /treɪ/ *noun* a flat board for carrying food, and things like glasses, cups and saucers ○ *He had his lunch on a tray in his bedroom.* ○ *She bumped into a waitress who was carrying a tray of glasses.*

treacherous /'tretʃərəs/ *adverb* **1.** dangerous ○ *There are treacherous reefs just offshore.* ○ *Black ice is making the roads very treacherous.* **2.** not to be trusted ○ *His treacherous behaviour led to the loss of the town to the enemy.*

tread /tred/ *verb* to step or to walk ○ *She trod on my toe and didn't say she was sorry.* ○ *Watch where you're treading – there's broken glass on the floor.* (NOTE: **treads – treading – trod** /trɒd/ – **trodden** /'trɒd(ə)n/) ■ *noun* the top part of a stair or step which you stand on ○ *The carpet on the bottom tread is loose.* ○ *Metal treads are noisy.*

treasure /'treʒə/ *noun* jewels, gold, or other valuable things ○ *the treasures in* *the British Museum* ○ *They are diving in the Caribbean looking for pirates' treasure.*

treat /triːt/ *noun* a special thing which gives pleasure ○ *It's always a treat to sit down quietly at home after a hard day in the shop.* ■ *verb* **1.** to deal with someone or something ○ *She was badly treated by her uncle.* ○ *It you treat the staff well they will work well.* ○ *He didn't treat my suggestion seriously.* **2.** to give medical help to a sick or injured person ○ *After the accident some of the passengers had to be treated in hospital for cuts and bruises.* ○ *She is being treated for rheumatism.*

treatment /'triːtmənt/ *noun* **1.** a way of behaving towards something or someone ○ *The report criticised the treatment of prisoners in the jail.* ○ *What sort of treatment did you get at school?* **2.** a way of looking after a sick or injured person ○ *He is having a course of heat treatment.* ○ *The treatment for skin cancer is very painful.*

tree /triː/ *noun* a very large plant, with a thick trunk, branches and leaves ○ *The cat climbed up an apple tree and couldn't get down.* ○ *In autumn, the leaves on the trees in the park turn brown and red.* ○ *He was sheltering under a tree and was struck by lightning.*

tremble /'trembəl/ *verb* to shake because you are cold or afraid, or worried by something ○ *She was trembling with cold.* ○ *I tremble at the thought of how much the meal will cost.*

tremendous /trɪ'mendəs/ *adjective* very big ○ *There was a tremendous explosion and all the lights went out.* ○ *There's tremendous excitement as we wait for the election result.*

trend /trend/ *noun* a general tendency ○ *There is a trend away from small local food stores.* ○ *The government studies economic trends to decide whether to raise taxes or not.*

trial /'traɪəl/ *noun* **1.** a court case held before a judge ○ *The trial will be heard next week.* **2.** the act of testing something ○ *The new model is undergoing its final trials.*

triangle /'traɪæŋgəl/ *noun* a shape with three straight sides and three angles ○ *The end of the roof is shaped like a triangle.*

tribe /traɪb/ *noun* a group of people with the same race, language and customs ○ *She went into the jungle to study the jungle tribes.*

trick /trɪk/ *noun* a clever act to deceive or confuse someone ○ *The recorded sound of barking is just a trick to make burglars think there is a dog in the house.* ■ *verb* to deceive someone ○ *We've been tricked, there's nothing in the box.*

trickle /'trɪk(ə)l/ *verb* to flow slowly or gently ○ *Water trickled out of the cave.*

tricky /'trɪki/ *adjective* requiring a lot of skill, patience or intelligence ○ *Getting the wire through the little hole is quite tricky.*

tried /(ˈ ˌ ˑ)/ past tense and past participle of **try**

tries /traɪz/ 3rd person singular present of **try**

trigger /'trɪgə/ *noun* the part of a gun that you pull to fire it ○ *He pointed the gun at her and pulled the trigger.*

trim /trɪm/ *verb* to cut something to make it tidy ○ *Ask the hairdresser to trim your beard.* (NOTE: **trims – trimming – trimmed**) ■ *adjective* **1.** cut short to give a tidy appearance ○ *She always keeps her hedges trim.* **2.** slim and fit ○ *He keeps himself trim by going for a long walk every day.* (NOTE: **trimmer – trimmest**)

trip /trɪp/ *noun* a short journey ○ *Our trip to Paris was cancelled.* ○ *We're going on a trip to the seaside.* ■ *verb* to catch your foot in something so that you almost fall down ○ *She tripped as she was coming out of the kitchen with a tray of food.* (NOTE: **trips – tripping – tripped**)

trip over *phrasal verb* to catch your foot in something so that you fall ○ *She was running away from him when she tripped over.*

triumph /'traɪʌmf/ *noun* a great victory or great achievement ○ *They scored a triumph in their game against the*

French. ○ *The bridge is a triumph of modern engineering.*

triumphant /traɪˈʌmfənt/ *adjective* happy or proud because you have won

trod /trɒd/ past tense of **tread**

trodden /ˈtrɒd(ə)n/ past participle of **tread**

trolley /ˈtrɒli/ *noun* a small vehicle on wheels which is designed to be pushed ○ *They put the piano onto a trolley to move it out of the house.*

troop /truːp/ *noun* a large group of people ○ *She took a troop of schoolchildren to visit the museum.* ■ *plural noun* **troops** soldiers ○ *Enemy troops occupied the town.*

tropical /ˈtrɒpɪk(ə)l/ *adjective* relating to hot countries ○ *In tropical countries it is always hot.*

trot /trɒt/ *noun* the action of running with short regular steps, like a horse does ○ *Let's start today's exercises with a short trot round the football field.* ■ *verb* to run with short regular steps ○ *We've got no butter left, so I'll trot off to the shop to buy some.* ○ *She trotted down the path to meet us.* (NOTE: **trots – trotting – trotted**)

trouble /ˈtrʌb(ə)l/ *noun* problems or worries ○ *The trouble with old cars is that sometimes they don't start.* ○ *The children were no trouble at all.* ○ *We are having some computer trouble* or *some trouble with the computer.* ■ *verb* to make someone feel worried ○ *I can see that there's something troubling him.*

trousers /ˈtraʊzəz/ *plural noun* clothes which cover your body from the waist down, each leg separately ○ *He tore his trousers climbing over the fence.* ○ *She was wearing a red jumper and grey trousers.* ○ *He bought two pairs of trousers in the sale.*

truck /trʌk/ *noun* a goods vehicle used for carrying heavy loads (*informal*) ○ *Trucks thundered past the house all night.* ○ *They loaded the truck with bricks.*

true /truː/ *adjective* **1.** correct according to facts or reality ○ *What he says is simply not true.* ○ *It's quite true that she comes from Scotland.* ○ *Is it true that* he's been married twice? ◊ **truth 2.** faithful or loyal ○ *an expression of true love* ○ *She's a true friend.* ◊ **to come true** to happen as was predicted ○ *Her forecast of bad storms came true.* ◊ **true to life** like things really are

truly /ˈtruːli/ *adverb* used for emphasis ○ *He truly believes that was what happened.* ○ *I'm truly grateful for all your help.* ○ *Do you love me, really and truly?*

trumpet /ˈtrʌmpɪt/ *noun* a brass musical instrument which is played by blowing, with three parts which you press with your fingers ○ *He plays the trumpet in the school orchestra.* ○ *She practises the trumpet in the evenings.*

trunk /trʌŋk/ *noun* **1.** the thick stem of a tree ○ *Ivy was climbing up the trunk of the oak tree.* **2.** an elephant's long nose **3.** a large box for storing or sending clothes ○ *They sent a trunk of clothes in advance to the new house.*

trust /trʌst/ *verb* to be confident that someone is reliable ○ *You can trust his instructions – he knows a lot about computers.* ○ *I wouldn't trust him farther than I could kick him.* ■ *noun* a belief that something will work well or that someone will do something ○ *Don't put too much trust in his navigating skills.*

truth /truːθ/ *noun* things which are true ○ *Do you think he is telling the truth?* ○ *The police are trying to work out the truth about what happened.* ○ *I don't think there is any truth in his story.*

truthful /ˈtruːθf(ə)l/ *adjective* **1.** who always tells the truth ○ *She's a very truthful child.* **2.** giving true facts ○ *To be truthful, I'm not quite sure where we are.* ○ *The young man gave a truthful account of what happened.*

try /traɪ/ *verb* to make an effort to do something ○ *You have to try hard if you want to succeed.* (NOTE: **tries – trying – tried**) ■ *noun* an attempt to do something ○ *She's going to have a try at water skiing.* ○ *He had two tries before he passed his driving test.* (NOTE: The plural is **tries.**)

T-shirt /ˈtiː ʃɜːt/ *noun* another spelling of **teeshirt** ○ *She was wearing jeans and a*

T-shirt. ○ *No wonder you're cold if you went out in just a T-shirt.*

tube /tjuːb/ *noun* **1.** a long pipe for carrying liquids or gas ○ *He was lying in a hospital bed with tubes coming out of his nose and mouth.* ○ *Air flows down this tube to the face mask.* **2.** a soft container for a soft substance like toothpaste, which you squeeze to get the substance out ○ *I forgot to pack a tube of toothpaste.* ○ *I need a tube of glue to mend the cup.* ○ *She bought a tube of mustard.* **3.** (*in London*) the underground railway system ○ *It's quicker to take the tube to Oxford Circus than to go by bus.* ○ *You'll have to go by bus because there's a tube strike.*

tuck /tʌk/ *verb* to put something carefully into a narrow or small place ○ *She tucked the blanket around the baby.* ○ *He tucked the note into his shirt pocket.*

tuck in *phrasal verb* **1.** to fold something carefully around someone or something and push the ends in ○ *She tucked the baby in* or *She tucked the blanket in (around the baby).* **2.** to start eating enthusiastically ○ *The food's ready, everyone can tuck in.* ○ *We all tucked in to a huge lunch.*

tuck up /ˌtʌk ˈʌp/ to push the edge of the bedclothes around someone to keep them warm ○ *By eight o'clock the children were all tucked up in bed.*

Tuesday /'tjuːzdeɪ/ *noun* the second day of the week, the day between Monday and Wednesday ○ *I saw him in the office last Tuesday.* ○ *The club always meets on Tuesdays.* ○ *Shall we meet next Tuesday evening?* ○ *Today is Tuesday, April 30th.* ○ *The 15th is a Monday, so the 16th must be a Tuesday.* ○ *We went to the cinema last Tuesday.*

tug /tʌg/ *verb* to give something a sudden hard pull ○ *He tugged on the rope and a bell rang.* (NOTE: **tugs – tugging – tugged**) ■ *noun* a sudden pull ○ *He felt a tug on the line – he had caught a fish!*

tumble /'tʌmbəl/ *verb* to fall ○ *He tumbled down the stairs head first.* ○ *She arrived home late after the party and just tumbled into bed.*

tune /tjuːn/ *noun* a series of musical notes which have a pattern ○ *He wrote some of the tunes for the musical.* ○ *She walked away whistling a little tune.*

tunnel /'tʌn(ə)l/ *noun* a long passage under the ground ○ *The Channel Tunnel links Britain to France.* ○ *The road round Lake Lucerne goes through six tunnels.* ○ *They are digging a new tunnel for the underground railway.*

turkey /'tɜːki/ *noun* a large farm bird, similar to a chicken but much bigger, often eaten at Christmas ○ *We had roast turkey and potatoes.* ○ *Who's going to carve the turkey?*

Turkey /'tɜːki/ *noun* a country in the eastern Mediterranean, south of the Black Sea (NOTE: capital: **Ankara**; people: **the Turks**; language: **Turkish**; currency: **Turkish lira**)

turn /tɜːn/ *noun* **1.** a change of direction, especially of a vehicle ○ *The bus made a sudden turn to the left.* **2.** a road which leaves another road ○ *Take the next turn on the right.* ■ *verb* **1.** to go round in a circle ○ *The wheels of the train started to turn slowly.* ○ *Be careful – the machine goes on turning for a few seconds after it has been switched off.* **2.** to make something go round ○ *Turn the handle to the right to open the safe.* **3.** to change direction ○ *Turn left at the next traffic lights.* ○ *The car turned the corner too fast and hit a lamppost.* ○ *The path turns to the right after the pub.* **4.** to move your head or body so that you face in another direction ○ *Can everyone turn to look at the camera, please.* **5.** to change into something different ○ *Leaves turn red or brown in the autumn.* ○ *When he was fifty, his hair turned grey.*

turn into *phrasal verb* **1.** to change to become something different ○ *The witch turned the prince into a frog.* ○ *We are planning to turn this room into a museum.* **2.** to change direction and go into something ○ *We went down the main road for a short way and then turned into a little lane on the left.*

turn round *phrasal verb* to move your head or body so that you face in another direction

turn back *phrasal verb* to turn round and go back in the opposite direction

turn down *phrasal verb* to refuse something which is offered ○ *She has turned down a job* or *turned a job down in the town hall.*

turn off *phrasal verb* **1.** to make a piece of electrical equipment stop working ○ *Don't forget to turn the TV off when you go to bed.* ○ *Turn off the lights* or *turn the lights off – father's going to show his holiday films.* **2.** to leave a road you are travelling on ○ *Here's where we turn off.*

turn on *phrasal verb* to make a piece of electrical equipment start working ○ *Can you turn the light on* or *turn on the light – it's too dark to read.*

turn over *phrasal verb* to roll over ○ *The lorry went round the corner too fast and turned over.* ○ *Their boat turned over in the storm.*

turn up *phrasal verb* **1.** to arrive ○ *The food was spoiled because half the guests didn't turn up until nine o'clock.* ○ *He turned up unexpectedly just as I was leaving the office.* **2.** to be found in a particular place ○ *The police searched everywhere, and the little girl finally turned up in Edinburgh.* ○ *The keys turned up in my trouser pocket.* **3.** to make something louder or stronger ○ *Can you turn up the radio* or *turn the radio up – I can't hear it.* ○ *Turn up the gas* or *turn the gas up, the potatoes aren't cooked yet.*

turning /'tɜːnɪŋ/ *noun* a road which goes away from another road

tutor /'tjuːtə/ *noun* a teacher, especially a person who teaches only one student or a small group of students ○ *His first job was as private tutor to some German children.* ■ *verb* to teach a small group of students (*formal*) ○ *She earns extra money by tutoring foreign students in English.*

TV /ˌtiː 'viː/ *noun* a television ○ *They watch TV every night.* ○ *The TV news is usually at nine o'clock.* ○ *Some children's TV programmes are very dull.* ○ *The daughter of a friend of mine was on TV last night.*

twelfth /twelfθ/ *adjective* number 12 in a series ○ *It's her twelfth birthday next*

week. ○ *He came twelfth out of two hundred in the competition.* ■ *noun* the thing that is number 12 in a series ○ *Today is September the twelfth* or *the twelfth of September (September 6th).*

twelve /twelv/ *noun* the number 12 ○ *She's twelve (years old) tomorrow.* ○ *Come round for a cup of coffee at twelve o'clock.* ○ *There are twelve months in a year.*

twentieth /'twentiəθ/ *adjective* number 20 in a series ○ *She was twentieth out of twenty in the race.* ○ *It's her twentieth birthday on Wednesday.* ■ *noun* the thing that is number 20 in a series ○ *Today is December the twentieth* or *the twentieth of December (December 20th).*

twenty /'twenti/ *noun* the number 20 ○ *She's twenty (years old) next week.* ○ *They have over twenty pets.* (NOTE: **twenty-one (21), twenty-two (22)** etc., but **twenty-first (21st), twenty-second (22nd),** etc.) □ **he's in his twenties** he is between 20 and 29 years old □ **the (nineteen) twenties (1920s)** the years from 1920 to 1929

twice /twaɪs/ *adverb* two times ○ *Turn it off – I've seen that programme twice already.* ○ *Twice two is four, twice four is eight.* ○ *I'm fifteen, she's thirty, so she's twice as old as I am.*

twig /twɪg/ *noun* a little branch of a tree or bush ○ *There is a bud at the end of each twig.* ○ *The bird made its nest of twigs and leaves.*

twilight /'twaɪlaɪt/ *noun* a time when the light is weak, between sunset and night

twin /twɪn/ *adjective, noun* one of two babies born at the same time to the same mother ○ *he and his twin brother* ○ *She's expecting twins.*

twinkle /'twɪŋkəl/ *verb* (*of stars or eyes*) to shine with a little moving light ○ *His eyes twinkled as he showed the children the sweets he had bought.* ○ *We could see the lights of the harbour twinkling in the distance.*

twirl /twɜːl/ *verb* **1.** to twist something round in your hand ○ *I wish I could twirl a baton like those girls in the proces-*

sion. **2.** to spin round ○ *Models twirled round on the catwalk.*

twist /twɪst/ *verb* **1.** to wind something round something ○ *She twisted the string round a piece of stick.* **2.** to turn in different directions ○ *The path twisted between the fields.*

two /tuː/ *noun* the number 2 ○ *There are only two peppermints left in the box.* ○ *His son's only two (years old), so he can't read yet.* ○ *She didn't come home until after two (o'clock).*

tying /'taɪɪŋ/ present participle of **tie**

type /taɪp/ *noun* a group of people, animals or things that are similar to each other ○ *This type of bank account pays 10% interest.* ○ *What type of accommodation are you looking for?* ■ *verb* to

write with a computer or typewriter ○ *Please type your letters – your writing's so bad I can't read it.* ○ *She only typed two lines and made six mistakes.*

typewriter /'taɪpraɪtə/ *noun* a machine which prints letters or numbers on a piece of paper when keys are pressed

typical /'tɪpɪk(ə)l/ *adjective* having the usual qualities of a particular group or occasion ○ *Describe a typical day at school.* ○ *He's definitely not a typical bank manager.*

tyre /'taɪə/ *noun* a ring made of rubber which is put round a wheel ○ *Check the pressure in the car tyres before starting a journey.* ○ *They used an old tyre to make a seat for the garden swing.*

U

u /juː/, **U** *noun* the twenty-first letter of the alphabet, between T and V

ugly /ˈʌgli/ *adjective* unpleasant to look at ○ *What an ugly pattern!* ○ *The part of the town round the railway station is even uglier than the rest.* (NOTE: **uglier – ugliest**)

UK *abbr* United Kingdom ○ *Exports from the UK* or *UK exports rose last year.*

umbrella /ʌmˈbrelə/ *noun* a round frame covered with cloth which you hold over your head to keep off the rain ○ *Can I borrow your umbrella?* ○ *As it was starting to rain, he opened his umbrella.* ○ *The wind blew my umbrella inside out.*

unable /ʌnˈeɪb(ə)l/ *adjective* not able to do something ○ *I regret that I am unable to accept your suggestion.* ○ *She was unable to come to the meeting.* (NOTE: **be unable to** is a rather formal way of saying **can't**.)

unattractive /ˌʌnəˈtræktɪv/ *adjective* not attractive ○ *Her husband is a rather unattractive man.* ○ *The house is unattractive from the outside.*

unbearable /ʌnˈbeərəb(ə)l/ *adjective* so bad that you cannot accept it or deal with it

unbelievable /ˌʌnbɪˈliːvəb(ə)l/ *adjective* which is difficult to believe

unbreakable /ʌnˈbreɪkəb(ə)l/ *adjective* which cannot be broken

uncertain /ʌnˈsɜːt(ə)n/ *adjective* not sure, or not decided ○ *She is uncertain whether to accept the job.* ○ *He's uncertain about what to do next.* ○ *Their plans are still uncertain.*

uncle /ˈʌŋk(ə)l/ *noun* a brother of your father or mother ○ *He was brought up by his uncle in Scotland.* ○ *We had a surprise visitor last night – old Uncle Charles.*

uncomfortable /ʌnˈkʌmftəb(ə)l/ *adjective* not comfortable ○ *What a very uncomfortable bed!* ○ *Plastic seats are very uncomfortable in hot weather.*

uncommon /ʌnˈkɒmən/ *adjective* strange or unusual

uncommunicative /ˌʌnkəˈmjuːnɪkətɪv/ *adjective* not saying much, or not answering people

uncomplicated /ʌnˈkɒmplɪkeɪtɪd/ *adjective* easy to deal with or understand ○ *In children's books, the writing should be clear and uncomplicated.* ○ *The procedure is relatively quick and uncomplicated.*

unconscious /ʌnˈkɒnʃəs/ *adjective* in a physical condition in which you are not aware of what is happening ○ *He was found unconscious in the street.* ○ *She was unconscious for two days after the accident.*

uncontrolled /ˌʌnkənˈtrəʊld/ *adjective* which has not been controlled

under /ˈʌndə/ *preposition* **1.** in or to a place where something else is on top or above ○ *We all hid under the table.* ○ *My pen rolled under the sofa.* **2.** less than a number ○ *It took under two weeks to sell the house.* ○ *The train goes to Paris in under three hours.* ○ *Under half of the members turned up for the meeting.* ○ *The old table sold for under £10.*

underground¹ /ˌʌndəˈgraʊnd/ *adverb* under the ground ○ *The ordinary railway line goes underground for a short distance.* ○ *Worms live all their life underground.* ■ *adjective* built under the ground ○ *There's an underground passage to the tower.* ○ *The hotel has an underground car park.*

underground² /ˈʌndəgraʊnd/ *noun* a railway in a town, which runs under the ground ○ *Thousands of people use the underground to go to work.* ○ *Take the* *underground to go to Oxford Circus.* ○ *It's usually quicker to get across town by underground.* (NOTE: The London Underground is often called the **Tube**. In the United States, an underground railway is called a **subway**.)

underline *verb* to write a line under a word or figure ○ *He wrote the title and then underlined it in red.*

underneath /ˌʌndə'niːθ/ *preposition* under ○ *She wore a long green jumper underneath her coat.* ○ *Can you see if my pen is underneath the sofa?* ■ *adverb* under ○ *He put the box of books down on the kitchen table and my sandwiches were underneath!*

understand /ˌʌndə'stænd/ *verb* **1.** to know what something means ○ *Don't try to talk English to Mr Yoshida – he doesn't understand it.* **2.** to have sympathy for someone ○ *She's a good teacher – she really understands children.* **3.** to know why something happens or how something works ○ *I can easily understand why his wife left him.* ○ *I still don't understand how to operate the new laser printer.* (NOTE: **understands – understanding – understood** /ˌʌndə'stʊd/)

understanding /ˌʌndə'stændɪŋ/ *noun* **1.** the ability to understand something ○ *My understanding of how the Internet works is severely limited.* **2.** sympathy for someone else and their problems ○ *The boss showed no understanding when she told him about her financial difficulties.* ○ *The aim is to promote understanding between the two countries.* **3.** a private agreement ○ *We reached an understanding with the lawyers.* ○ *The understanding was that we would all go to the office after lunch.* ■ *adjective* sympathetic ○ *His understanding attitude was much appreciated.*

underwater /ˌʌndə'wɔːtə/ *adjective* below the surface of the water ○ *How long can you stay underwater?* ○ *He dived and swam underwater for several seconds.* ○ *She goes on holiday to the Red Sea to do underwater photography.*

underwear /'ʌndəweə/ *noun* clothes worn next to your skin under other clothes (NOTE: no plural)

undo /ʌn'duː/ *verb* to open something which is tied or fastened ○ *The first thing he did on getting home was to undo his tie.* ○ *Undo your top button if your collar is too tight.* (NOTE: **undoes** /ʌn'dʌz/ – **undid** /ʌn'dɪd/ – **undone** /ʌn'dʌn/)

undress /ʌn'dres/ *verb* to take your clothes off

undressed /ʌn'drest/ *adjective* having just taken off your clothes ○ *The children are getting undressed ready for bed.* ○ *Are you undressed yet?*

uneasy /ʌn'iːzi/ *adjective* nervous and worried (NOTE: **uneasier – uneasiest**)

unemployed /ˌʌnɪm'plɔɪd/ *adjective* without a job ○ *The government is encouraging unemployed teenagers to apply for training grants.*

unemployment /ˌʌnɪm'plɔɪmənt/ *noun* a lack of work ○ *The unemployment figures or the figures for unemployment are rising.*

uneven /ʌn'iːv(ə)n/ *adjective* not smooth or flat

unexpected /ˌʌnɪk'spektɪd/ *adjective* which is surprising and not what was expected ○ *We had an unexpected visit from the police.* ○ *His failure was quite unexpected.*

unexpectedly /ˌʌnɪk'spektɪdli/ *adverb* in an unexpected way

unfair /ʌn'feə/ *adjective* not fair ○ *It's unfair to expect her to do all the housework while her sisters don't lift a finger to help.*

unfairly /ʌn'feəli/ *adverb* in an unfair way

unfairness /ʌn'feənəs/ *noun* lack of justice or fairness

unfortunate /ʌn'fɔːtʃ(ə)nət/ *adjective* which makes you sad ○ *It was very unfortunate that she couldn't come to see us.*

unfortunately /ʌn'fɔːtʃ(ə)nətli/ *adverb* which you wish was not true ○ *Unfortunately the train arrived so late that she missed the meeting.*

unfriendly /ʌn'frendli/ *adjective* not acting like a friend (NOTE: **unfriendlier – unfriendliest**)

ungrateful /ʌnˈgreɪtf(ə)l/ *adjective* not grateful

unhappily /ʌnˈhæpɪli/ *adverb* in a sad way

unhappy /ʌnˈhæpi/ *adjective* sad, not happy ○ *He's unhappy in his job because his boss is always criticising him.* ○ *She looked very unhappy when she came out of the hospital.* ○ *The children had an unhappy childhood.* (NOTE: **unhappier – unhappiest**)

unhealthy /ʌnˈhelθi/ *adjective* not healthy, especially often ill ○ *I thought her face was an unhealthy colour.* (NOTE: **unhealthier – unhealthiest**)

uniform /ˈjuːnɪfɔːm/ *noun* special clothes worn by all members of an organisation or group ○ *He went to the fancy dress party dressed in a policeman's uniform.* ○ *Who are those people in French army uniform?* ○ *What colour is her school uniform?* ○ *The holiday camp staff all wear yellow uniforms.*

unimportant /ˌʌnɪmˈpɔːt(ə)nt/ *adjective* not important

union /ˈjuːnjən/ *noun* the state of being joined together, or the process of joining together ○ *We support the union of these various groups under one umbrella organisation.*

unique /juːˈniːk/ *adjective* different to anything else and therefore the only on of its type ○ *The stamp is unique, and so is worth a great deal.* ○ *He's studying the unique vegetation of the island.*

unit /ˈjuːnɪt/ *noun* **1.** one part of something larger ○ *If you pass three units of the course you can move to the next level.* **2.** one piece of furniture which can be matched with others ○ *The kitchen is designed as a basic set of units with more units which can be added later.* **3.** the amount used to measure something ○ *Kilos and pounds are units of weight.* **4.** a single number less than ten ○ *63 has six tens and three units.*

unite /juːˈnaɪt/ *verb* to join together into a single body

united /juːˈnaɪtɪd/ *adjective* joined together as a whole ○ *Relief workers from various countries worked as a united*

team. ○ *They were united in their desire to improve their working conditions.*

universal /ˌjuːnɪˈvɜːs(ə)l/ *adjective* which is understood or experienced by everyone in the world ○ *There is a universal hope for peace in the region.*

universe /ˈjuːnɪvɜːs/ *noun* all space and everything that exists in it, including the earth, the planets and the stars

university /ˌjuːnɪˈvɜːsɪti/ *noun* an educational institution where students study for degrees and where students and teachers do research ○ *You need to do well at school to be able to go to university.* ○ *My sister is at university.* (NOTE: The plural is **universities**.)

unkind /ʌnˈkaɪnd/ *adjective* acting in an unpleasant way to someone ○ *It was unkind of him to keep talking about her weight.* (NOTE: **unkinder – unkindest**)

unkindness /ʌnˈkaɪndnəs/ *noun* the action of treating someone unpleasantly

unless /ənˈles/ *conjunction* except if ○ *Unless we hear from you within ten days, we will start legal action.* ○ *I think they don't want to see us, unless of course they're ill.*

unlike /ʌnˈlaɪk/ *adjective, preposition* **1.** totally different from ○ *He's quite unlike his brother.* **2.** not normal or typical

unlikely /ʌnˈlaɪkli/ *adjective* **1.** not likely ○ *It's unlikely that many people will come to the show.* **2.** which is probably not true ○ *He trotted out some unlikely excuse about how his train ticket had been eaten by the dog.*

unlimited /ʌnˈlɪmɪtɪd/ *adjective* with no limits

unload /ʌnˈləʊd/ *verb* to remove a load from a vehicle

unlock /ʌnˈlɒk/ *verb* to open something which was locked

unluckily /ʌnˈlʌkili/ *adverb* with bad luck

unlucky /ʌnˈlʌki/ *adjective* not lucky, or bringing bad luck (NOTE: **unluckier – unluckiest**)

unnecessary /ʌnˈnesəs(ə)ri/ *adjective* which is not needed, or which does not have to be done ○ *It is unnecessary for* *you to wear a suit to the party.* ○ *She makes a lot of unnecessary phone calls.*

unoccupied /ʌnˈɒkjʊpaɪd/ *adjective* not being used by anyone

unpack /ʌnˈpæk/ *verb* to take things out of cases in which they were sent or carried

unpleasant /ʌnˈplez(ə)nt/ *adjective* not pleasant ○ *There's a very unpleasant smell in the kitchen.* ○ *Try not to be unpleasant to the waitress.*

unreasonable /ʌnˈriːz(ə)nəb(ə)l/ *adjective* not reasonable or fair

unselfish /ʌnˈselfɪʃ/ *adjective* thinking only of other people

unsightly /ʌnˈsaɪtli/ *adjective* very unpleasant to look at ○ *She has an unsightly scar on her face.*

unsuccessful /ˌʌnsəkˈsesf(ə)l/ *adjective* which does not succeed

unsuitable /ʌnˈsuːtəb(ə)l/ *adjective* not suitable

unsure /ʌnˈʃʊə/ *adjective* not sure ○ *She was unsure whether to go to work or to stay at home.* ○ *I'm unsure as to which route is the quickest.*

untidy /ʌnˈtaɪdi/ *adjective* not tidy (NOTE: **untidier – untidiest**)

untie /ʌnˈtaɪ/ *verb* to open something which is tied with a knot (NOTE: **unties – untying – untied**)

until /ʌnˈtɪl/ *conjunction* up to the time when ○ *She was perfectly well until she ate the strawberries.* ○ *He blew his whistle until the police came.* ■ *preposition, conjunction* up to the time when ○ *I don't expect to be back until after ten o'clock.* ○ *Until yesterday, I felt very well.*

untrue /ʌnˈtruː/ *adjective* not true

unusual /ʌnˈjuːʒʊəl/ *adjective* not normal or expected ○ *It is unusual to have rain at this time of year.* ○ *She chose a very unusual colour scheme for her sitting room.*

unwell /ʌnˈwel/ *adjective* in a bad state of health (NOTE: not used before a noun: *the baby was unwell* but *a sick baby*)

unwilling /ʌnˈwɪlɪŋ/ *adjective* not wanting to do something

up /ʌp/ *adverb* **1.** in or to a high place ○ *Put your hands up above your head.* ○ *What's the cat doing up there on the cupboard?* (NOTE: **up** is often used after verbs: *to keep up, to turn up*.) **2.** to a higher position ○ *His temperature went up suddenly.* ○ *The price of petrol seems to go up every week.* **3.** not in bed ○ *The children were still up when they should have been in bed.* ○ *They stayed up all night watching films on TV.* ○ *He got up at six because he had an early train to catch.* ○ *It's past eight o'clock – you should be up by now.* **4.** completely, entirely ○ *The puddles dried up quickly in the sun.* **5.** happening in an unpleasant or dangerous way ○ *Something's up – the engine has stopped!* ■ *preposition* **1.** in or to a high place ○ *They ran up the stairs.* ○ *She doesn't like going up ladders.* **2.** along ○ *Go up the street to the traffic lights and then turn right.* ○ *The house is about two hundred metres up the road.* ◇ **what's up?** what's the matter?

upon /ʌˈpɒn/ *preposition* **1.** on ○ *The church was built upon a grassy hill.* **2.** likely to happen soon ○ *The summer holidays will soon be upon us again.*

upper /ˈʌpə/ *adjective* higher or further up ○ *The upper slopes of the mountain are covered in snow.* ○ *He had a rash on his right upper arm.*

upright /ˈʌpraɪt/ *adjective* straight up ○ *He got dizzy as soon as he stood upright.* ○ *Put the backs of your seats into the upright position for landing.* ○ *She picked up the vase and placed it upright on the table.*

upset¹ /ʌpˈset/ *adjective* very worried or unhappy ○ *His parents get upset if he comes home late.* ■ *verb* **1.** to make someone worried or unhappy ○ *Don't upset your mother by telling her.* **2.** to knock something over ○ *He upset all the coffee cups.* (NOTE: **upsets – upsetting – upset**)

upset² /ˈʌpset/ *noun* **1.** an unexpected defeat ○ *There was a major upset in the tennis tournament when the number three seed was beaten in the first round.* **2.** a slight illness because of something you have eaten or drunk ○ *a stomach upset*

upside down /ˌʌpsaɪd 'daʊn/ *adverb* with the top underneath ○ *Don't turn the box upside down – all the papers will fall out.* ○ *The car shot off the road and ended up upside down in a ditch.* ○ *Bats were hanging upside down from the branches.*

upstairs /ˌʌp'steəz/ *adverb* on or to the upper part of something, e.g. a building or bus ○ *She ran upstairs with the letter.* ○ *I left my glasses upstairs.* ○ *Let's go upstairs onto the top deck – you can see London much better.* ■ *adjective* on the upper floors of a building ○ *We have an upstairs kitchen.* ○ *We let the one of the upstairs offices to an accountant.*

up to date /ˌʌp tə 'deɪt/, **up-to-date** *adverb* with the latest information ○ *I keep myself up to date on the political situation by reading the newspaper every day.*

upwards /'ʌpwədz/ *adverb* towards the top ○ *The path went upwards for a mile then levelled off.*

urban /'ɜːbən/ *adjective* **1.** relating to towns ○ *They enjoy an urban lifestyle.* **2.** living in towns ○ *The urban fox has become a menace in parts of London.*

urge /ɜːdʒ/ *noun* a strong wish to do something ○ *She felt an urge to punch him on the nose.* ■ *verb* to advise someone strongly to do something ○ *He urged her to do what her father said.* ○ *I would urge you to vote for the proposal.* ○ *Our lawyer urged us to be careful and avoid breaking the law.*

urgent /'ɜːdʒənt/ *adjective* which is important and needs to be done quickly ○ *He had an urgent message to go to the police station.* ○ *She had an urgent operation.* ○ *The leader of the council called an urgent meeting.* ○ *This parcel is urgent and needs to get there tomorrow.*

us /əs, ʌs/ *object pronoun* meaning me and other people ○ *Mother gave us each 50p to buy ice cream.* ○ *Who's there? – It's us!* ○ *The company did well last year – the management have given us a bonus.*

use¹ /juːz/ *verb* **1.** to take something such as a tool and do something with it ○ *Did you use a sewing machine to make your curtains?* ○ *The car's worth quite a lot of money – it's hardly been used.* ○ *Do you know how to use a computer?* ○ *Can I use this knife for cutting meat?* **2.** to take a substance and do something with it ○ *Don't use the tap water for drinking.* ○ *Does this car use much petrol?* ○ *Turn down the heating – we're using too much gas.*

use² /juːs/ *noun* **1.** a purpose ○ *Can you find any use for this piece of cloth?* **2.** the fact of being used ○ *The coffee machine has been in daily use for years.* **3.** □ **to make use of something** to use something ○ *You should make more use of your bicycle.*

used /juːzd/ *adjective* which is not new ○ *a shop selling used clothes*

used to /'juːzt tuː/ showing that something happened often or regularly in the past ○ *There used to be lots of small shops in the village until the supermarket was built.* ○ *When we were children, we used to go to France every year for our holidays.* ○ *The police think he used to live in London.* ○ *He used not to smoke a pipe.* (NOTE: The forms used in the negative and questions: *He used to work in London, He didn't use to work in London* or *He used not to work in London, Didn't he use to work in London?*)

useful /'juːsf(ə)l/ *adjective* who or which can help you do something ○ *I find these scissors very useful for opening letters.* ○ *She's a very useful person to have in the office.*

useless /'juːsləs/ *adjective* which is not useful

user /'juːzə/ *noun* a person who uses a tool or a service ○ *We have mailed the users of our equipment about the possible design fault.*

usual /'juːʒuəl/ *adjective* done or used on most occasions ○ *She took her usual bus to the office.* ○ *Is it usual for him to arrive so late?*

usually /'juːʒuəli/ *adverb* in most cases or on most occasions

utensil /juːˈtens(ə)l/ *noun* a tool or object used when cooking ○ *knives, bowls and other kitchen utensils*

utilise /ˈjuːtɪlaɪz/, **utilize** *verb* to use something (*formal*) ○ *He's keen to utilise his programming skills.*

V

v /viː/, **V** *noun* the twenty-second letter of the alphabet, between U and W

V /viː/ *noun* the Roman numeral for five or fifth ○ *King George V*

vacant /'veɪkənt/ *adjective* empty and available for you to use ○ *There are six rooms vacant in the new wing of the hotel.* ○ *Is the toilet vacant yet?*

vacation /və'keɪʃ(ə)n/ *noun* **1.** especially US a holiday ○ *The family went on vacation in Canada.* **2.** a period when the universities and law courts are closed ○ *I'm spending my vacation working on a vineyard in Italy.*

vague /veɪg/ *adjective* with no details

vain /veɪn/ *adjective* very proud of your appearance or achievements ○ *He's always combing his hair – he's very vain.* (NOTE: Do not confuse with **vein**.)

valid /'vælɪd/ *adjective* **1.** which can be lawfully used for a particular time ○ *Travellers must have a valid ticket before boarding the train.* ○ *I have a season ticket which is valid for one year.* ○ *He was carrying a valid passport.* **2.** which is acceptable because it is true ○ *That is not a valid argument or excuse.* ○ *She made several valid points in her speech.*

valley /'væli/ *noun* a long piece of low land through which a river runs ○ *Fog forms in the valleys at night.* ○ *A lot of computer companies are based in the Thames Valley.*

valuable /'væljuəb(ə)l/ *adjective* **1.** worth a lot of money ○ *Be careful, that glass is valuable!* ○ *The burglars stole everything that was valuable.* **2.** useful or helpful ○ *She gave me some very valuable advice.*

value /'væljuː/ *noun* an amount of money which something is worth ○ *the fall in the value of the yen* ○ *He imported goods to the value of £500.* ○ *Items of value can be deposited in the hotel safe*

overnight. ■ *verb* to consider something as being valuable ○ *She values her friendship with him.*

van /væn/ *noun* a covered goods vehicle ○ *A delivery van ran into the back of my car.* ○ *Our van will call this afternoon to pick up the goods.*

vanish /'vænɪʃ/ *verb* to disappear suddenly ○ *The magician made the rabbit vanish.*

variation /ˌveəri'eɪʃ(ə)n/ *noun* a change from one state or level to another ○ *The variation in colour* or *the colour variation is because the cloth has been dyed by hand.* ○ *The diagram shows the variations in price over a period of six months.*

variety /və'raɪəti/ *noun* **1.** differences ○ *Her new job, unlike the old one, doesn't lack variety.* **2.** a different type of plant or animal in the same species ○ *Do you have this new variety of rose?* ○ *Is this a new variety of potato?*

various /'veəriəs/ *adjective* several different ○ *The shop sells goods from various countries.* ○ *I'll be out of the office today – I have to see various suppliers.*

vary /'veəri/ *verb* **1.** to be different in different situations, or change within certain limits ○ *The temperature varies from 8 degrees C at night to 18 degrees C during the day.* **2.** to be different ○ *Prices of flats vary from a few thousand pounds to millions.* (NOTE: **varies – varying – varied**)

vase /vɑːz/ *noun* a container used for cut flowers, or simply for decoration

vast /vɑːst/ *adjective* extremely big, often extremely wide ○ *vast differences in price* ○ *A vast ship suddenly appeared out of the fog.*

vegetable /'vedʒtəb(ə)l/ *noun* a plant which is grown to be eaten but which is not usually sweet ○ *We grow potatoes, carrots and other sorts of vegetables in* the garden. ○ *The soup of the day is vegetable soup.* ○ *Green vegetables are a good source of dietary fibre.*

vegetarian /ˌvedʒɪˈteəriən/ *noun* a person who eats only fruit, vegetables, bread, eggs, etc., but does not eat meat, and sometimes not fish ○ *a range of vegetarian dishes* ○ *Our children are all vegetarians.*

vehicle /ˈviːɪk(ə)l/ *noun* a machine which carries passengers or goods, e.g. a car or bus ○ *a three-wheeled vehicle* ○ *Goods vehicles can park at the back of the building.*

vein /veɪn/ *noun* a small tube in the body which takes blood back to the heart ○ *The veins in her legs are swollen.* (NOTE: Do not confuse with **vain**.)

verb /vɜːb/ *noun* a word which shows an action, being or feeling, such as 'to hit' or 'to thank'

verbal /ˈvɜːb(ə)l/ *adjective* spoken and not written down ○ *She gave me a verbal account of what had happened.* ○ *It was a verbal agreement between the two of us.*

verdict /ˈvɜːdɪkt/ *noun* a decision made in a court

verse /vɜːs/ *noun* **1.** a group of lines which form a part of a song or poem ○ *We sang all the verses of the National Anthem.* ○ *She read the first verse to the class.* **2.** poetry ○ *He published a small book of verse.* (NOTE: no plural in this sense)

version /ˈvɜːʃ(ə)n/ *noun* **1.** a description of what happened as seen by one person ○ *The victim told her version of events to the jury.* **2.** a type of something, e.g. a work of art or model of car ○ *This is the film version of the novel.* ○ *He bought the cheapest version available.*

vertical /ˈvɜːtɪk(ə)l/ *adjective* standing or rising straight up ○ *He drew a few vertical lines to represent trees.* ○ *We looked at the vertical cliff and wondered how to climb it.*

very /ˈveri/ *adverb* used to make an adjective or adverb stronger ○ *It's very hot in the car – why don't you open a window?* ○ *Can you see that very tall pine tree over there?* ○ *The time seemed to* go very quickly when we were on holiday. ■ *adjective* used to make a noun stronger ○ *He did his very best to get tickets.* ○ *The scene takes place at the very beginning of the book.*

vessel /ˈves(ə)l/ *noun* a ship ○ *Vessels from all countries crowded into the harbour.*

via /ˈvaɪə/ *preposition* through ○ *We drove to London via Windsor.* ○ *We are sending the payment via our office in London.* ○ *The shipment is going via the Suez Canal.*

vibration /vaɪˈbreɪʃ(ə)n/ *noun* a fast and continuous shaking movement

vicious /ˈvɪʃəs/ *adjective* cruel and violent ○ *a vicious attack on an elderly lady*

victim /ˈvɪktɪm/ *noun* a person who is attacked or who is in an accident ○ *The victims of the train crash were taken to the local hospital.* ○ *She was the victim of a violent attack outside her front door.* ○ *Earthquake victims were housed in tents.*

victory /ˈvɪkt(ə)ri/ *noun* the fact of winning something, e.g. a battle, a fight or a game ○ *the American victory in the Olympics* ○ *They won a clear victory in the general election.* ○ *The guerrillas won a victory over the government troops.* (NOTE: The plural is **victories**.)

video /ˈvɪdiəʊ/ *noun* **1.** a machine which records TV programmes ○ *Don't forget to set the video for 8 p.m. before you go out.* **2.** a magnetic tape on which you can record TV programmes or films for playing back on a television set ○ *She bought a box of blank videos.* (NOTE: The plural is **videos**.)

view /vjuː/ *noun* **1.** what you can see from a certain place ○ *You can get a good view of the sea from the church tower.* ○ *We asked for a room with a sea view and were given one looking out over the bus depot.* **2.** a way of thinking about something ○ *In his view, the government ought to act now.*

vigilant /ˈvɪdʒɪlənt/ *adjective* staying very aware of possible danger ○ *The disease particularly affects young children, so parents must remain vigilant.*

village /'vɪlɪdʒ/ *noun* a small group of houses in the country, like a little town, often with a church, and usually some shops ○ *They live in a little village in the Swiss Alps.* ○ *The village shop sells just about everything we need.*

vine /vaɪn/ *noun* a climbing plant which produces grapes

vinegar /'vɪnɪgə/ *noun* a liquid with a sour taste, usually made from wine, used in cooking and for pickling

violence /'vaɪələns/ *noun* action which is intended to hurt someone ○ *Acts of violence must be punished.*

violent /'vaɪələnt/ *adjective* **1.** very strong ○ *The discussion led to a violent argument.* ○ *A violent storm blew all night.* **2.** using force to hurt people ○ *Her husband was a very violent man.*

violently /'vaɪələntli/ *adverb* **1.** with physical force, often with the intention of hurting ○ *This horse threw him violently onto the ground.* ○ *She hurled the bottle violently across the table.* **2.** with great feeling ○ *She violently rejected the accusations made against her.* ○ *He reacted violently to the injection.* ○ *The oysters made her violently sick.*

violin /vaɪə'lɪn/ *noun* a musical instrument with strings that hold under your chin and play with a bow

virtual /'vɜːtʃuəl/ *adjective* almost ○ *The company has a virtual monopoly of French wine imports.* ○ *His grandfather has become a virtual recluse.*

virtually /'vɜːtʃuəli/ *adverb* almost ○ *These shirts have been reduced so much that we're virtually giving them away.* ○ *It's virtually impossible to get tickets for the concert.*

virtual reality /ˌvɜːtʃuəl ri'ælɪti/ *noun* the simulation of a real-life scene or real events on a computer

virus /'vaɪrəs/ *noun* **1.** a very small living thing that causes disease by living in the bodies of people or animals ○ *Scientists have isolated a new flu virus.* ○ *Shingles is caused by the same virus as chickenpox.* **2.** a part of a computer program which is designed to destroy files on someone else's computer ○ *You must check the program for viruses.* (NOTE: The plural is **viruses**.)

visible /'vɪzɪb(ə)l/ *adjective* which can be seen

visibly /'vɪzɪbli/ *adverb* in a way which everyone can see

vision /'vɪʒ(ə)n/ *noun* **1.** your ability to see ○ *After the age of 50, the vision of many people begins to fail.* **2.** a thing which you imagine ○ *He had visions of himself stuck in London with no passport and no money.* ○ *She had visions of him being arrested for drug smuggling.*

visit /'vɪzɪt/ *noun* a short stay with someone or in a town or a country ○ *They had a visit from the police.* ○ *We will be making a short visit to London next week.* ○ *The manager is on a business visit to China.* ■ *verb* to stay a short time with someone or in a town or country ○ *I am on my way to visit my sister in hospital.* ○ *They are away visiting friends in the north of the country.* ○ *The group of tourists are going to visit the glass factory.* ○ *He spent a week in Scotland, visiting museums in Edinburgh and Glasgow.*

visitor /'vɪzɪtə/ *noun* a person who comes to visit ○ *How many visitors come to the museum each year?* ○ *We had a surprise visitor yesterday – the bank manager!*

vital /'vaɪt(ə)l/ *adjective* extremely important ○ *It is vital that we act quickly.* ○ *Oxygen is vital to human life.*

vitamin /'vɪtəmɪn/ *noun* an essential substance which is found in food and is needed for growth and health

vivid /'vɪvɪd/ *adjective* **1.** very bright ○ *vivid yellow sunflowers* ○ *the vivid colours of the Mediterranean beach* **2.** representing real events clearly ○ *She has a vivid imagination.* ○ *I had a really vivid dream last night.* ○ *She gave a vivid account of her experiences at the hands of the kidnappers.*

vocabulary /və'kæbjʊləri/ *noun* **1.** all the words used by a person or group of persons ○ *specialist legal vocabulary* ○ *She reads French newspapers to improve her French vocabulary.* **2.** a printed list of words ○ *There is a German-*

English vocabulary at the back of the book. (NOTE: The plural is **vocabularies**.)

voice /vɔɪs/ noun a sound made when you speak or sing ○ *I didn't recognise his voice over the telephone.* ○ *The chairman spoke for a few minutes in a low voice.*

volcano /vɒl'keɪnəʊ/ noun a mountain which lava, ash and gas may flow out of from time to time (NOTE: The plural is **volcanoes**.)

volume /'vɒljuːm/ noun **1.** the amount of sound ○ *She turned down the volume on the radio.* ○ *He drives with the car radio on at full volume.* **2.** the amount which is contained inside something ○ *What is the volume of this barrel?* **3.** one book, especially one in a series ○ *Have you read the third volume of his history of medieval Europe?*

voluntary /'vɒlənt(ə)ri/ adjective **1.** done because you want to do it, and done without being paid ○ *Many retired people do voluntary work.* **2.** done willingly, without being forced ○ *He made a voluntary contribution to the fund.*

volunteer /ˌvɒlən'tɪə/ noun a person who offers to do something without being paid or being forced to do it ○ *The*

school relies on volunteers to help with the sports day. ○ *The information desk is manned by volunteers.* ■ verb to offer to do something without being paid or being forced to do it ○ *He volunteered to collect the entrance tickets.* ○ *Will anyone volunteer for the job of washing up?*

vote /vəʊt/ noun the act of marking a paper, holding up your hand, etc., to show your opinion or to show who you want to be elected ○ *How many votes did you get?* ○ *There were only ten votes against the plan.* ■ verb to mark a paper, to hold up your hand, etc., to show your opinion or to show who you want to be elected ○ *Fifty per cent of the people voted in the election.* ○ *We all voted to go on strike.*

voter /'vəʊtə/ noun a person who votes or who has the right to vote

vowel /'vaʊəl/ noun one of the five letters, a, e, i, o and u, which represent sounds made without using the teeth, tongue or lips (NOTE: The letters representing sounds which are not vowels are **consonants**. Note also that in some languages 'y' is a vowel.)

voyage /'vɔɪɪdʒ/ noun a long journey, especially by ship or spacecraft ○ *the voyages of Sir Francis Drake*

W

w /'dʌb(ə)ljuː/, **W** *noun* the twenty-third letter of the alphabet, between V and X

wade /weɪd/ *verb* to walk through water ○ *They waded into the sea.*

wag /wæg/ *verb* to move something from side to side or up and down ○ *The dog ran up to him, wagging its tail.* ○ *The grandmother wagged her finger at the little boy who was picking the flowers.* (NOTE: **wags – wagging – wagged**)

wage /weɪdʒ/, **wages** /'weɪdʒɪz/ *noun* money paid, usually in cash each week, to a worker for work done ○ *The company pays quite good wages.* ○ *She is earning a good wage* or *good wages in the pizza restaurant.*

wagon /'wægən/ *noun* a railway truck used for carrying heavy loads

waist /weɪst/ *noun* **1.** the narrow part of the body between the bottom of the chest and the hips ○ *She measures 32 inches round the waist* or *has a 32-inch waist.* **2.** the part of a piece of clothing, e.g. a skirt, trousers or dress, that goes round the middle of your body ○ *The waist of these trousers is too small for me.* (NOTE: Do not confuse with **waste.**)

wait /weɪt/ *verb* to stay where you are, and not do anything until something happens or someone comes ○ *Wait here while I call an ambulance.* ○ *They had been waiting for half an hour in the rain before the bus finally arrived.* ○ *Wait a minute, my shoelace is undone.* ○ *Don't wait for me, I'll be late.*

waiter /'weɪtə/ *noun* a man who brings food and drink to customers in a restaurant

waitress /'weɪtrəs/ *noun* a woman who brings food and drink to customers in a restaurant (NOTE: The plural is **waitresses.**)

wake /weɪk/ *verb* **1.** to stop someone's sleep ○ *The telephone woke her* or *she was woken by the telephone.* ○ *I banged on her door, but I can't wake her.* ○ *He asked to be woken at 7.00.* **2.** to stop sleeping ○ *He woke suddenly, feeling drops of water falling on his head.* (NOTE: **wakes – waking – woke** /wəʊk/ **– woken**)

wake up *phrasal verb* **1.** to stop someone's sleep ○ *He was woken up by the sound of the dog barking.* **2.** to stop sleeping ○ *She woke up in the middle of the night, thinking she had heard a noise.* ○ *Come on, wake up! It's past ten o'clock.* ○ *He woke up to find water coming through the roof of the tent.*

Wales /weɪlz/ *noun* a country to the west of England, forming part of the United Kingdom ○ *There are some high mountains in North Wales.* ◊ **Welsh** (NOTE: capital: **Cardiff;** people: **the Welsh;** languages: **Welsh, English**)

walk /wɔːk/ *verb* **1.** to go somewhere on foot ○ *The baby is ten months old, and is just starting to walk.* ○ *She was walking along the high street on her way to the bank.* ○ *We walked slowly across the bridge.* ○ *The visitors walked round the factory.* □ **to walk someone home** to go with someone who is walking home ○ *It was getting late, so I walked her home.* **2.** to take an animal for a walk ○ *He's gone to walk the dog in the fields.* ○ *She walks her dog every morning.* ■ *noun* **1.** a usually pleasant journey on foot ○ *Let's all go for a walk in the park.* **2.** a distance which you cover on foot ○ *It's only a short walk to the beach.* ○ *It's only five minutes' walk from the office to the bank* or *the bank is only a five minutes' walk from the office.*

wall /wɔːl/ *noun* a structure made from things such as bricks or stones, built up to make one of the sides of a building, of a room or to surround a space ○ *The walls of the restaurant are decorated with pictures of film stars.* ○ *There's a* *clock on the wall behind my desk.* ○ *He got into the house by climbing over the garden wall.*

wallet /'wɒlɪt/ *noun* a small flat leather case for carrying things such as credit cards and banknotes in your pocket

wallpaper /'wɔːlpeɪpə/ *noun* paper with different patterns on it, covering the walls of a room ○ *The wallpaper was light green to match the carpet.*

wander /'wɒndə/ *verb* to walk around without any particular aim ○ *They wandered round the town in the rain.*

want /wɒnt/ *verb* **1.** to hope that you will do something, that something will happen, or that you will get something ○ *She wants a new car for her birthday.* ○ *Where do you want to go for your holidays?* ○ *He wants to be a teacher.* **2.** to ask someone to do something ○ *The manager wants me to go and see him.* ○ *I want those windows painted.* **3.** to need something ○ *With five children, what they want is a bigger house.* ○ *You want to take some rest.*

war /wɔː/ *noun* a period of fighting between countries ○ *Millions of soldiers and civilians were killed during the war.* ○ *In 1914 Britain was at war with Germany* or *Britain and Germany were at war.*

ward /wɔːd/ *noun* a room or set of rooms in a hospital, with beds for patients ○ *The children's ward is at the end of the corridor.* ○ *She was taken into the accident and emergency ward.*

wardrobe /'wɔːdrəub/ *noun* a tall cupboard in which you hang your clothes ○ *He moved the wardrobe from the landing into the bedroom.*

warehouse /'weəhaus/ *noun* a large building where goods are stored ○ *Our goods are dispatched from the central warehouse to shops all over the country.*

warm /wɔːm/ *adjective* **1.** fairly hot ○ *The temperature is below freezing outside but it's nice and warm in the office.* ○ *The children tried to keep warm by playing football.* ○ *Are you warm enough, or do you want another blanket?* ○ *This coat is not very warm.* ○ *The winter sun can be quite warm in Febru-*

ary. **2.** pleasant and friendly ○ *We had a warm welcome from our friends.* ○ *She has a really warm personality.* ■ *verb* to make something hotter ○ *Come and warm your hands by the fire.* ○ *I'll warm some soup.*

warmth /wɔːmθ/ *noun* the fact of being warm or feeling warm ○ *It was cold and rainy outside, and he looked forward to the warmth of his home.*

warn /wɔːn/ *verb* **1.** to inform someone of a possible danger ○ *Children are warned not to play on the frozen lake.* ○ *The group was warned to look out for pickpockets.* ○ *The guide warned us that there might be snakes in the grass.* **2.** to inform someone that something is likely to happen ○ *The railway has warned that there will be a strike tomorrow.* ○ *The weather forecast warned of storms in the English Channel.* (NOTE: You warn someone **of** something, or warn someone **that** something may happen.)

warning /'wɔːnɪŋ/ *noun* news about a possible danger ○ *He shouted a warning to the children.* ○ *The government issued a warning about travelling in some countries in the area.* ○ *Each packet of cigarettes has a government health warning printed on it.* ■ *adjective* which informs about a danger ○ *Red warning flags are raised if the sea is dangerous.* ○ *Warning notices were put up round the building site.*

wary /'weəri/ *adjective* aware of a possible problem with someone or something ○ *I am very wary of any of his ideas for making money.* (NOTE: **warier – wariest**)

was /wəz, wɒz/ past tense of **be**

wash /wɒʃ/ *verb* to clean something using water ○ *Cooks should always wash their hands before touching food!* ○ *I must wash the car before we go to the wedding.* ○ *The moment I had washed the windows it started to rain.* ○ *His football shirt needs washing.* ■ *noun* the action of cleaning, using water ○ *The car needs a wash.* ○ *He's in the bathroom, having a quick wash.*

wash up *phrasal verb* to clean objects

such as dirty cups, plates, knives and forks with water ○ *It took us hours to wash up after the party.* ○ *My brother's washing up, while I'm sitting watching the TV.*

washbasin /ˈwɒʃbeɪs(ə)n/ *noun* a container for holding water for washing the hands and face, which has taps and is usually attached to the wall of a bathroom

washing /ˈwɒʃɪŋ/ *noun* clothes which have been washed, or which are ready to be washed ○ *Put the washing in the washing machine.* ○ *She hung out the washing to dry.*

washing machine /ˈwɒʃɪŋ məˌʃiːn/ *noun* a machine for washing clothes (NOTE: A machine for washing plates and cutlery is a **dishwasher**.)

wasp /wɒsp/ *noun* an insect which has black and yellow bands of colour round its body and which can sting

waste /weɪst/ *noun* **1.** an unnecessary use of time or money ○ *It is a waste of time asking the boss for a rise.* ○ *That computer is a waste of money – there are plenty of cheaper models.* **2.** things which are no use and are thrown away ○ *Put all your waste in the rubbish bin.* ■ *verb* to use more of something than you need ○ *Don't waste time putting your shoes on – jump out of the window now.* ○ *We turned off all the heating so as not to waste energy.* (NOTE: **wastes – wasting – wasted**) ■ *adjective* useless and ready to be thrown away ○ *Waste products should not be dumped in the sea.* ○ *Recycle all your waste paper.*

watch /wɒtʃ/ *verb* **1.** to look at and notice something ○ *Did you watch the TV news last night?* ○ *We went to the sports ground to watch the football match.* ○ *Everyone was watching the children dancing.* **2.** to look at something carefully to make sure that nothing happens ○ *Watch the saucepan – I don't want the potatoes to burn.* ○ *Can you watch the baby while I'm at the hairdresser's?* ■ *noun* **1.** an object like a little clock which you wear on your wrist ○ *She looked at her watch impatiently.* ○ *What time is it? – my watch has stopped.* (NOTE: The plural in this sense is

watches) **2.** the activity of watching something carefully ○ *Visitors should be on the watch for pickpockets.* ○ *Keep a watch on the potatoes to make sure they don't burn.* (NOTE: no plural)

watch out *phrasal verb* to be careful ○ *Watch out! there's a car coming!*

water /ˈwɔːtə/ *noun* the liquid which falls as rain and forms rivers, lakes and seas. It makes up a large part of the bodies of living creatures, and is used for drinking and in cooking; also in industrial processes. ○ *Can we have three glasses of water please?* ○ *Cook the vegetables in boiling water.* ○ *Is the tap water safe to drink?* ○ *The water temperature is 60°.* (NOTE: no plural: *some water, a drop of water*) ■ *verb* to pour water on the soil round a plant to make it grow ○ *Because it is hot we need to water the garden every day.* ○ *She was watering her pots of flowers.*

waterfall /ˈwɔːtəfɔːl/ *noun* a place where a stream falls down a steep drop

waterlogged /ˈwɔːtəlɒgd/ *adjective* waterlogged ground is full of water, so the surface stays wet for a long time ○ *After so much rain, the waterlogged golf course had to be closed.* ○ *Most plants cannot grow in waterlogged soil.*

waterproof /ˈwɔːtəpruːf/ *adjective* which does not let water go through ○ *waterproof clothing* ○ *These boots aren't waterproof – my socks are soaking wet.*

wave /weɪv/ *noun* **1.** a raised mass of water on the surface of the sea, a lake or a river ○ *Waves were breaking on the rocks.* ○ *Watch out for big waves on the beach.* ○ *The sea was calm, with hardly any waves.* **2.** an up and down movement of your hand **3.** a regular curve on the surface of hair ○ *His hair has a natural wave.* **4.** a sudden increase in something ○ *A wave of anger surged through the crowd.* ■ *verb* **1.** to move up and down in the wind ○ *The flags were waving outside the town hall.* **2.** to make an up and down movement of the hand when saying 'hello', 'goodbye' or for attracting attention ○ *They waved until the car was out of sight.* ○ *They waved goodbye as the boat left the harbour.* □

to wave to someone to signal to someone by moving your hand up and down ○ *When I saw him I waved to him to cross the road.*

waver /'weɪvə/ *verb* to be unable to decide what to do ○ *He is still wavering about whether or not to leave the company.*

wax /wæks/ *noun* a solid substance made from fat or oil, used for making things such as candles and polish ○ *She brought a tin of wax polish and started to polish the furniture.*

way /weɪ/ *noun* **1.** the direction in which something can be found or in which someone or something is going ○ *Do you know the way to the post office?* ○ *The bus is going the wrong way for the station.* ○ *She showed us the way to the railway station.* ○ *They lost their way and had to ask for directions.* ○ *I'll lead the way – just follow me.* **2.** the means of doing something ○ *My mother showed me the way to make marmalade.* ○ *Isn't there any other way of making it?* ○ *He thought of a way of making money quickly.* ○ *The way she said it implied it was my fault.* **3.** □ **to make your way** to go to a place with some difficulty ○ *Can you make your way to passport control?* ○ *He made his way to the tourist information office.* **4.** the distance between one place and another ○ *The nearest bank is quite a long way away.* ○ *He's got a long way to go before he qualifies as a doctor.* **5.** a path or road which goes somewhere ○ *Our neighbours across the way.* ○ *I'll walk the first part of the way home with you.* **6.** a particular direction from here ○ *a one-way street* ○ *Can you tell which way the wind is blowing?* ○ *This way please, everybody!* **7.** a space where someone wants to be or which someone wants to use ○ *Get out of my way – I'm in a hurry.* ○ *It's best to keep out of the way of the police for a moment.* ○ *I wanted to take a short cut, but there was a lorry in the way.*

way in /ˌweɪ 'ɪn/ *noun* an entrance

way out /ˌweɪ 'aʊt/ *noun* an exit ○ *This is the way out of the car park.* ○ *He couldn't find the way out in the dark.*

way up /ˌweɪ 'ʌp/ *noun* a way in which something stands

we /wiː/ *pronoun* used by someone speaking or writing to refer to himself or herself and others ○ *He said we could go into the exhibition.* ○ *We were not allowed into the restaurant in jeans.* ○ *We had a wonderful holiday – we all enjoyed ourselves enormously.* (NOTE: When it is the object **we** becomes **us**: *We gave it to him*; *He gave it to us.* When it follows the verb **to be**, **we** usually becomes **us**: *Who is it? – It's us!*)

weak /wiːk/ *adjective* **1.** not strong ○ *After his illness he is still very weak.* ○ *I don't like weak tea.* **2.** not effective ○ *a weak leader* ○ *a weak argument* **3.** not having knowledge or skill ○ *She's weaker at science than at maths.* ○ *French is his weakest subject.* (NOTE: **weaker – weakest**. Do not confuse with **week**.)

wealth /welθ/ *noun* a large amount of money and property which someone owns ○ *His wealth was acquired in business.* (NOTE: no plural)

wealthy /'welθi/ *adjective* (*of a person*) very rich (NOTE: **wealthier – wealthiest**)

weapon /'wepən/ *noun* an object such as a gun or sword, which you fight with ○ *nuclear weapons* ○ *The crowd used iron bars as weapons.*

wear /weə/ *verb* **1.** to have something such as clothes or jewellery on your body ○ *What dress are you wearing to the party?* ○ *When last seen, he was wearing a blue raincoat.* ○ *She's wearing her mother's earrings.* ○ *She wears her hair very short.* **2.** to damage something or make it thin through using it ○ *I've worn a hole in the heel of my sock.* (NOTE: **wears – wearing – wore** /wɔː/ **– worn** /wɔːn/)

wear out *phrasal verb* **1.** to use something so much that it becomes broken and useless ○ *Walking across the USA, he wore out three pairs of boots.* **2.** □ **to wear yourself out** to become very tired through doing something ○ *She wore herself out looking after the old lady.*

weather /'weðə/ *noun* conditions outside, e.g. if it is raining, hot, cold or sunny ○ *What's the weather going to be like today?* ○ *If the weather gets any better, then we can go out in the boat.*

weave /wiːv/ *verb* **1.** to make cloth by twisting fibres over and under each other ○ *The cloth is woven from the wool of local sheep.* ○ *The new weaving machines were installed last week.* **2.** to make something by a similar method, but using things such as very thin pieces of wood or the dried stems of plants ○ *She learnt how to weave baskets.* (NOTE: **weaves – weaving – wove** /wəʊv/ – **woven** /'wəʊvən/)

web /web/ *noun* **1.** a net spun by spiders ○ *The garden is full of spiders' webs in autumn.* **2.** □ **the web** the thousands of websites and webpages within the Internet, which users can visit

webpage /'webpeɪdʒ/ *noun* a single file of text and graphics, forming part of a website

website /'websaɪt/ *noun* a collection of pages on the Web which have been produced by one person or organisation and are linked together

wedding /'wedɪŋ/ *noun* a marriage ceremony, when two people are officially made husband and wife ○ *This Saturday I'm going to John and Mary's wedding.*

wedge /wedʒ/ *noun* a solid piece of something such as wood, metal or rubber in the shape of a V ○ *Put a wedge under the door to hold it open.*

Wednesday /'wenzdeɪ/ *noun* the day between Tuesday and Thursday, the third day of the week ○ *She came for tea last Wednesday.* ○ *Wednesdays are always busy days for us.* ○ *Can we meet next Wednesday afternoon?* ○ *Wednesday the 24th would be a good date for a meeting.* ○ *The 15th is a Tuesday, so the 16th must be a Wednesday.*

weed /wiːd/ *noun* a wild plant that you do not want in a garden or crop

week /wiːk/ *noun* a period of seven days, usually from Monday to Sunday ○ *There are 52 weeks in the year.* ○ *The firm gives us two weeks' holiday at Easter.* ○ *It's my aunt's 80th birthday*

next week. ○ *I go to the cinema at least once a week.* (NOTE: Do not confuse with **weak**.)

weekend /wiːk'end/ *noun* Saturday and Sunday, or the period from Friday evening to Sunday evening ○ *We're going to the coast for the weekend.* ○ *Why don't you come to spend next weekend with us in the country?* ○ *At weekends, we try to spend time in the garden.*

weekly /'wiːkli/ *adjective, adverb* which happens or is published once a week ○ *We have a weekly paper which tells us all the local news.* ○ *The weekly rate for the job is £250.* ○ *Are you paid weekly or monthly?*

weigh /weɪ/ *verb* **1.** to measure how heavy something or someone is ○ *Can you weigh this parcel for me?* ○ *They weighed his suitcase at the check-in desk.* ○ *I weighed myself this morning.* **2.** to have a particular weight ○ *This piece of meat weighs 100 grams.* ○ *How much do you weigh?* ○ *She only weighs 40 kilos.*

weight /weɪt/ *noun* **1.** how heavy something is ○ *What's the maximum weight of parcel the post office will accept?* **2.** how heavy a person is ○ *His weight is less than it was a year ago.* **3.** something which is heavy ○ *If you lift heavy weights like paving stones, you may hurt your back.* (NOTE: Do not confuse with **wait**.)

weird /wɪəd/ *adjective* strange in a way that makes you feel nervous or frightened

welcome /'welkəm/ *verb* **1.** to greet someone in a friendly way ○ *The staff welcomed the new assistant to the office.* ○ *When we arrived at the hotel we were welcomed by a couple of barking guard dogs.* **2.** to be pleased to hear news ○ *I warmly welcome the result of the election.* ○ *I would welcome any suggestions as to how to stop the water seeping into the basement.* (NOTE: **welcomes – welcoming – welcomed**) ■ *noun* the action of greeting someone ○ *There was not much of a welcome from the staff when we arrived at the hotel.* ■ *adjective* met or greeted with pleasure ○ *They made me very welcome.* ◇ **you're wel-**

come! a reply to 'thank you' ○ *Thanks for carrying the bags for me – you're welcome!*

welfare /'welfeə/ *noun* the act or practice of providing the things which people need and which help them to be healthy ○ *The club looks after the welfare of the old people in the town.* ○ *The government has taken measures to reform the welfare system.*

well /wel/ *adverb* **1.** in a way that is satisfactory ○ *He doesn't speak Russian very well.* ○ *Our business is small, but it's doing well.* ○ *Is the new computer working well?* **2.** very much ○ *He got back from the office late – well after eight o'clock.* ○ *You should go to the Tower of London – it's well worth a visit.* ○ *There were well over sixty people at the meeting.* ○ *She's well over eighty.* ■ *adjective* healthy ○ *She's looking well after her holiday!* ○ *The secretary's not very well today – she's had to stay off work.* ○ *It took him some weeks to get well after his flu.* ■ *interjection* used for starting a sentence ○ *Well, I'll show you round the house first.* ○ *Well now, we've done the washing up so we can sit and watch TV.* ■ *noun* a very deep hole dug in the ground with water or oil at the bottom ◇ **as well** also ○ *When my aunt comes to stay she brings her two cats and the dog as well.* ○ *You can't eat fish and chips and a meat pie as well!* ◇ **as well as** in addition to ○ *Some newsagents sell groceries as well as newspapers.* ○ *She ate a slice of cheesecake as well as two scoops of ice cream.* ◇ **well done** used for praising someone for their success ○ *Well done, the England team!* ○ *Well done to all of you who passed the exam!*

well-known /,wel 'nəʊn/ *adjective* known by a lot of people

well-paid /,wel 'peɪd/ *adjective* earning a good salary

Welsh /welʃ/ *adjective* relating to Wales ○ *We will be going climbing in the Welsh mountains at Easter.* ■ *noun* **1.** □ **the Welsh** the people of Wales ○ *The Welsh are proud of their heritage.* ○ *The Welsh are magnificent singers.* **2.** the

language spoken in Wales ○ *Welsh is used in schools in many parts of Wales.*

went /went/ past tense of **go**

were /wə, wɜː/ 1st person plural past of **be**. 2nd person plural past of **be**. 3rd person plural past of **be**

west /west/ *noun* the direction in which the sun sets ○ *The sun sets in the west and rises in the east.* ○ *We live in a village to the west of the town.* ○ *Their house has a garden that faces west* or *a west-facing garden.* ■ *adjective* in or to the west ○ *She lives on the west coast of the United States.* ○ *The west part of the town is near the river.* ■ *adverb* towards the west ○ *Go west for about ten kilometres, and then you'll come to the national park.* ○ *The river flows west into the ocean.*

western /'westən/ *adjective* from or in the west ○ *Great Britain is part of Western Europe.* ○ *The Western part of Canada has wonderful scenery.*

wet /wet/ *adjective* **1.** covered in water or other liquid ○ *She forgot her umbrella and got wet walking back from the shops.* ○ *The chair's all wet where he knocked over his beer.* ○ *The baby is wet – can you change her nappy?* **2.** raining ○ *The summer months are the wettest part of the year.* ○ *There's nothing I like better than a wet Sunday in London.* **3.** not yet dry ○ *Watch out! – the paint's still wet.* (NOTE: **wetter – wettest**)

whale /weɪl/ *noun* a very large creature that lives in the sea ○ *You can take a boat into the mouth of the river to see the whales.*

what /wɒt/ *adjective* asking a question ○ *What kind of music do you like?* ○ *What type of food does he like best?* ■ *pronoun* **1.** the thing which ○ *Did you see what was in the box?* ○ *What we like to do most on holiday is just to visit old churches.* **2.** asking a question ○ *What's the correct time?* ○ *What did he give you for your birthday?* ○ *What happened to his car?* (NOTE: When **what** used to ask a direct question, the verb is put before the subject: *What's the time?* but not when it is used in a statement: *They don't know what the time is.*) ■ *adverb* showing surprise ○ *What* *a huge meal! ○ What beautiful weather!* ■ *interjection* showing surprise ○ *What! did you hear what he said? ○ I won the lottery! – What!*

whatever /wɒt'evə/ *pronoun* **1.** it does not matter what (*form of 'what' used for emphasis; in questions*) ○ *You can have whatever you like for Christmas.* ○ *She always does whatever she feels like doing.* ○ *I want that car whatever the price.* **2.** used instead of 'what' for emphasis in questions ○ *'I've sold the car.' 'Whatever for?' ○ Whatever made him do that? ○ Whatever does that red light mean?*

wheat /wiːt/ *noun* a plant of which the grain is used to make flour (NOTE: no plural)

wheel /wiːl/ *noun* **1.** a round object on which a vehicle such as a bicycle, a car or a train runs ○ *The front wheel and the back wheel of the motorbike were both damaged in the accident.* ○ *We got a flat tyre so I had to get out to change the wheel.* **2.** any similar round object which turns ○ *a steering wheel* ○ *gear wheels* ■ *verb* to push something along which has wheels ○ *He wheeled his motorbike into the garage.* ○ *She was wheeling her bike along the pavement.* ○ *The waiter wheeled in a sweet trolley.*

wheelbarrow /'wiːlbærəʊ/ *noun* a large container with one wheel at the front and two handles, used by people such as builders and gardeners for pushing heavy loads around

wheelchair /'wiːltʃeə/ *noun* a chair on wheels which people who cannot walk use to move around ○ *a special entrance for wheelchair users*

when /wen/ *adverb* at what time (*asking a question*) ○ *When is the last train for Paris? ○ When did you last go to the dentist? ○ When are we going to get paid? ○ Since when has he been wearing glasses? ○ I asked her when her friend was leaving.* (NOTE: After **when** used to ask a direct question, the verb is put before the subject: *When does the film start?; When is he coming?* but not when it is used in a statement: *He doesn't know when the film starts.; They can't tell me when he is coming.*)

■ *conjunction* **1.** at the time that ○ *When he was young, the family was living in London. ○ When you go on holiday, leave your key with the neighbours so they can feed the cat. ○ Do you remember the day when we all went for a picnic in the park? ○ Let me know when you're ready to go.* **2.** after ○ *When the speaker had finished, he sat down. ○ Wash up the plates when you've finished your breakfast.* **3.** even if ○ *The salesman said the car was worth £5,000 when he really knew it was worth only half that.*

whenever /wen'evə/ *adverb* at any time that ○ *Come for tea whenever you like.* ○ *We try to see my mother whenever we can* or *whenever possible.*

where /weə/ *adverb* **1.** (*asking a question*) in what place, to what place ○ *Where did I put my glasses? ○ Do you know where the restaurant is? ○ Where are the knives and forks? ○ Where are you going for your holiday?* **2.** in a place in which ○ *Stay where you are and don't move. ○ They still live in the same house where they were living twenty years ago.* ○ *Here's where the wire has been cut.* (NOTE: After **where** used to ask a direct question, the verb is put before the subject: *Where is the bottle?* but not when it is used in a statement: *He doesn't know where the bottle is.*)

whereas /weər'æz/ *conjunction* if you compare this with the fact that ○ *He likes tea whereas she prefers coffee.*

wherever /weər'evə/ *adverb* **1.** to or in any place ○ *You can sit wherever you want. ○ Wherever we go on holiday, we never make hotel reservations. ○ The police want to ask her questions, wherever she may be.* **2.** used instead of 'where' for emphasis ○ *Wherever did you get that hat?*

whether /'weðə/ *conjunction* **1.** used to mean 'if' for showing doubt, or for showing that you have not decided something ○ *Do you know whether they're coming? ○ I can't make up my mind whether to go on holiday now or later.* **2.** used for referring to either of two things or people ○ *All employees, whether managers or ordinary staff,* *must take a medical test.* (NOTE: Do not confuse with **weather**.)

which /wɪtʃ/ *adjective, pronoun* **1.** (*asking a question*) what person or thing ○ *Which dress are you wearing to the wedding?* ○ *Which boy threw that stone?* **2.** (*only used with things, not people*) that ○ *The French restaurant which is next door to the office.* ○ *They've eaten all the bread which you bought yesterday.*

while /waɪl/ *conjunction* **1.** at the time that ○ *He tried to cut my hair while he was watching TV.* ○ *While we were on holiday someone broke into our house.* ○ *Shall I clean the kitchen while you're having a bath?* **2.** showing difference ○ *He likes meat, while hi. sister is a vegetarian.* ○ *Everyone is watching TV, while I'm in the kitchen making the dinner.* **3.** although (*formal*) ○ *While there may still be delays, the service is much better than it used to be.* ■ *noun* a short time ○ *It's a while since I've seen him.* ◇ **in a while** in a short time, soon ○ *I'll be ready in a while.*

whine /waɪn/ *verb* **1.** to make a loud high noise ○ *You can hear the engines of the racing cars whining in the background.* ○ *The dogs whined when we locked them up in the kitchen.* **2.** to complain in a loud high voice that annoys other people ○ *She's always whining about how little money she has.* (NOTE: Do not confuse with **wine**. Note also: **whines – whining – whined**.)

whip /wɪp/ *noun* a long, thin piece of leather with a handle, used to hit animals to make them do what you want ○ *The rider used her whip to make the horse run faster.* ■ *verb* to hit someone or an animal with a whip ○ *He whipped the horse to make it go faster.* (NOTE: **whips – whipping – whipped**)

whirl /wɜːl/ *verb* to turn round quickly ○ *She put on her new skirt and whirled around for every one to see.* ○ *The children's paper windmills whirled in the wind.*

whiskey /ˈwɪski/ *noun* Irish or American whisky

whisky /ˈwɪski/ *noun* an alcoholic drink, made in Scotland from barley ○ *The company produces thousands of bottles of whisky every year.* (NOTE: The plural is **whiskies**.)

whisper /ˈwɪspə/ *verb* to speak very quietly, so that only the person you are talking to can hear ○ *He whispered instructions to the other members of the gang.* ○ *She whispered to the nurse that she wanted something to drink.* ■ *noun* a quiet voice, or words spoken very quietly ○ *She spoke in a whisper.*

whistle /ˈwɪs(ə)l/ *noun* **1.** a high sound made by blowing through your lips when they are almost closed ○ *She gave a whistle of surprise.* ○ *We heard a whistle and saw a dog running across the field.* **2.** a simple instrument which makes a high sound, played by blowing ○ *He blew on his whistle to stop the match.* ■ *verb* **1.** to blow through your lips to make a high sound ○ *They marched along, whistling an Irish song.* ○ *He whistled for a taxi.* **2.** to make a high sound using a small metal instrument ○ *The referee whistled to stop the match.*

white /waɪt/ *adjective* of a colour like snow or milk ○ *A white shirt is part of the uniform.* ○ *A white car will always look dirty.* ○ *Her hair is now completely white.* ○ *Do you take your coffee black or white?* ■ *noun* **1.** a person whose skin is pale ○ *Whites are in the minority in African countries.* **2.** a white part of something ○ *the white of an egg* ○ *The whites of his eyes were slightly red.* **3.** white wine ○ *A glass of house white, please.*

white lie /ˌwaɪt ˈlaɪ/ *noun* a lie about something unimportant, especially a lie told in order not to upset someone (*informal*)

who /huː/ *pronoun* **1.** (*asking a question*) which person or persons ○ *Who phoned?* ○ *Who are you talking to?* ○ *Who spoke at the meeting?* **2.** the person or the people that ○ *The men who came yesterday morning work for the electricity company.* ○ *Anyone who didn't get tickets early won't be able to get in.* ○ *There's the taxi driver who took us home last night.* (NOTE: After an object, **who** can be left out: *There's the man I* *saw at the pub.* When **who** is used to ask a direct question, the verb is put after 'who' and before the subject: *Who is that man over there?*, but not when it is used in a statement: *I don't know who that man is over there.* When **who** is used as an object, it is sometimes written **whom** /huːm/ but this is formal and not common: *the man whom I met in the office*; *Whom do you want to see?*)

whoever /huːˈevə/ *pronoun* (*emphatic form of 'who'*) no matter who, anyone who ○ *Whoever finds the umbrella can keep it.* ○ *Go home with whoever you like.*

whole /həʊl/ *adjective* all of something ○ *She must have been hungry – she ate a whole apple pie.* ○ *We spent the whole winter in the south.* ○ *A whole lot of people went down with flu.* ■ *noun* all of something ○ *She stayed in bed the whole of Sunday morning and read the newspapers.* ○ *The whole of the north of the country was covered with snow.* ○ *Did you watch the whole of the programme?* (NOTE: Do not confuse with **hole**.) ■ *adverb* in one piece ○ *The birds catch small fish and swallow them whole.*

whom /huːm/ ♦ **who**

whose /huːz/ *pronoun* **1.** (*asking a question*) which belongs to which person ○ *Whose is that car?* ○ *Whose book is this?* ○ *Whose money was stolen?* **2.** of whom ○ *the family whose house was burgled* ○ *the man whose hat you borrowed* ○ *the girl whose foot you trod on* (NOTE: Do not confuse with **who's**.)

why /waɪ/ *adverb* **1.** for what reason ○ *Why did he have to phone me in the middle of the TV film?* ○ *I asked the ticket collector why the train was late.* **2.** giving a reason ○ *She told me why she couldn't go to the party.* **3.** agreeing with a suggestion ○ *'Would you like some lunch?' 'Why not?'*

wicked /ˈwɪkɪd/ *adjective* very bad ○ *What a wicked thing to say!* ○ *It was wicked of them to steal the birds' eggs.*

wide /waɪd/ *adjective* **1.** which measures from side to side ○ *The table is three foot* or *three feet wide.* ○ *The river is not*

very wide at this point. **2.** including many things ○ *The shop carries a wide range of imported goods.* ○ *She has a wide knowledge of French painting.* ◊ **width** ■ *adverb* as far as possible, as much as possible ○ *She opened her eyes wide.* ○ *The door was wide open so we just walked in.*

widely /ˈwaɪdli/ *adverb* **1.** by a wide range of people ○ *It is widely expected that he will resign.* **2.** over a wide area ○ *Contamination spread widely over the area round the factory.* ○ *She has travelled widely in Greece.*

widow /ˈwɪdəʊ/ *noun* a woman whose husband has died and who has not married again

width /wɪdθ/ *noun* **1.** a measurement of something from one side to another ○ *I need to know the width of the sofa.* ○ *The width of the garden is at least forty feet* or *the garden is at least forty feet in width.* **2.** the distance from one side to another of a swimming pool ○ *She swam three widths easily.*

wife /waɪf/ *noun* a woman who is married to a man ○ *I know Mr Jones quite well but I've never met his wife.* ○ *They both came with their wives.* (NOTE: The plural is **wives** /waɪvz/.)

wig /wɪg/ *noun* false hair worn on the head

wild /waɪld/ *adjective* **1.** living naturally, not with people as a pet **2.** very angry or very excited ○ *He will be wild when he sees what I have done to the car.* ○ *The fans went wild at the end of the match.* **3.** not thinking carefully ○ *She made a few wild guesses, but didn't find the right answer.* ○ *They had the wild idea of walking across the Sahara.* ■ *adverb* without any control ○ *The crowds were running wild through the centre of the town.*

wildlife /ˈwaɪldlaɪf/ *noun* birds, plants and animals in their natural conditions

will /wɪl/ *modal verb* **1.** used to form the future tense ○ *The party will start soon.* ○ *Will they be staying a long time?* ○ *We won't be able to come to tea.* ○ *If you ask her to play the piano, she'll say 'no'.* **2.** used as a polite way of asking someone to do something ○ *Will everyone please sit down?* ○ *Will someone close the curtains?* ○ (formal) *Won't you sit down?* **3.** used for showing that you are keen to do something ○ *Don't call a taxi – I'll take you home.* ○ *The car will never start when we want it to.* ○ *Don't worry – I will do it.* (NOTE: the negative: **will not** is usually written **won't** /wəʊnt/. The past is: **would**, negative: **would not,** usually written **wouldn't.** Note also that **will** is often shortened to **'ll: he'll** = he will) ■ *noun* **1.** someone's desire that something will happen □ **against your will** without your agreement ○ *He was forced to pay the money against his will.* **2.** a legal document by which a person gives instructions about what should happen to his or her property after he or she dies ○ *He wrote his will in 1984.* ○ *According to her will, all her property is left to her children.* ○ *Has she made a will yet?* ◇ **at will** whenever someone wants to ○ *Visitors can wander around the gardens at will.*

willing /'wɪlɪŋ/ *adjective* keen to help ○ *Is there anyone who is willing to drive the jeep?* ○ *I need two willing helpers to wash the car.*

win /wɪn/ *verb* **1.** to beat someone in a game, or be first in a race or competition ○ *I expect our team will win tomorrow.* ○ *The local team won their match yesterday.* ○ *She won the race easily.* **2.** to get something as a prize ○ *She won first prize in the art competition.* ○ *He won two million pounds on the lottery.* ○ *She's hoping to win a new car in a competition in the paper.* (NOTE: **wins – winning – won** /wʌn/) ■ *noun* the act of winning a game, race or competition ○ *The local team has only had two wins so far this year.* ○ *We're disappointed, we expected a win.*

wind[1] /wɪnd/ *noun* air moving outdoors ○ *The wind blew two trees down in the park.* ○ *There's no point trying to use an umbrella in this wind.* ○ *There's not a breath of wind – the sailing boats aren't moving at all.*

wind[2] /waɪnd/ *verb* to twist round and round ○ *He wound the towel round his*

waist. ○ *She wound the string into a ball.* (NOTE: **winds – winding – wound** /waʊnd/)

wind up *phrasal verb* **1.** to turn a key to make a machine work ○ *When did you wind up the clock* or *wind the clock up?* **2.** to turn a key to make something go up ○ *Wind up your window if it starts to rain.* **3.** to be in a situation at the end of a period (*informal*) ○ *They wound up owing the bank thousands of pounds.*

window /'wɪndəʊ/ *noun* **1.** an opening in a surface such as a wall or door, which is filled with glass ○ *a seat by the window* ○ *I looked out of the kitchen window and saw a fox.* ○ *It's dangerous to lean out of car windows.* ○ *The burglar must have got in through the bathroom window.* **2.** any of several sections of a computer screen on which information is shown ○ *Open the command window to see the range of possible commands.*

windy /'wɪndi/ *adjective* when a strong wind is blowing (*informal*) (NOTE: **windier – windiest**)

wine /waɪn/ *noun* an alcoholic drink made from grapes ○ *We had a glass of French red wine.* ○ *Two glasses of white wine, please.* ○ *Should we have some white wine with the fish?*

wing /wɪŋ/ *noun* **1.** one of the two parts of the body, which a bird or butterfly etc. uses to fly ○ *The little birds were flapping their wings, trying to fly.* ○ *Which part of the chicken do you prefer: a leg or a wing?* **2.** one of the two flat parts sticking from the side of an aircraft, which hold the aircraft in the air ○ *He had a seat by the wing, so could not see much out of the window.*

wink /wɪŋk/ *verb* to shut and open one eye quickly, as a signal ○ *She winked at him to try to tell him that everything was going well.*

winner /'wɪnə/ *noun* **1.** a person who wins something ○ *The winner of the race gets a silver cup.* **2.** something which is successful ○ *His latest book is a winner.*

winter /'wɪntə/ *noun* the coldest season of the year, the season between autumn and spring ○ *It's too cold to do any gardening in the winter.* ○ *We're taking a winter holiday in Mexico.*

wipe /waɪp/ *verb* to clean or dry something with a cloth ○ *Wipe your shoes with a cloth before you polish them.* ○ *Use the blue towel to wipe your hands.*

wire /'waɪə/ *noun* **1.** a thin piece of metal or metal thread ○ *He used bits of wire to attach the apple tree to the wall.* ○ *The chip basket is made of woven wire.* **2.** □ **(electric) wire** thin metal thread along which electricity flows, usually covered with coloured plastic ○ *The wires seem to be all right, so there must be a problem with the computer itself.*

wisdom /'wɪzdəm/ *noun* general common sense and the ability to make good decisions

wise /waɪz/ *adjective* having intelligence and being sensible ○ *It was a wise decision to cancel the trip.* ○ *I don't think it's wise to keep all that money in the house.*

wish /wɪʃ/ *noun* **1.** what you want to happen **2.** a greeting ○ *Best wishes for the New Year!* ○ *Please give my good wishes to your family.* (NOTE: The plural is **wishes**.) ■ *verb* **1.** to want something to happen ○ *She sometimes wished she could live in the country.* ○ *I wish you wouldn't be so unkind!* **2.** to hope something good will happen ○ *She wished him good luck in his interview.* ○ *He wished me a Happy New Year.* ○ *Wish me luck – it's my exam tomorrow.*

witch /wɪtʃ/ *noun* a woman believed to have magic powers (NOTE: The plural is **witches**.)

with /wɪð, wɪθ/ *preposition* **1.** showing that things or people are together ○ *She came here with her mother.* ○ *My sister is staying with us for a few days.* (NOTE: **with** is used with many adjectives and verbs: *to agree with, to be pleased with*.) **2.** something which you have ○ *The girl with fair hair.* ○ *They live in the house with the pink door.* **3.** showing something which is used ○ *He was chopping up wood with an axe.* ○ *Since his accident he walks with a stick.* ○ *The crowd attacked the police with stones and bottles.* **4.** because of ○ *Her little*

hands were blue with cold. ○ *Half the people in the office are ill with flu.*

within /wɪ'ðɪn/ *preposition* inside an area or period of time ○ *The house is within easy reach of the station.* ○ *We are within walking distance of the shop.* ○ *I must go back for a another check within three months.* ○ *They promised to deliver the sofa within a week.*

without /wɪ'ðaʊt/ *preposition* **1.** not with ○ *They came on a walking holiday without any boots.* ○ *She managed to live for a few days without any food.* ○ *He was stuck in Germany without any money.* ○ *They were fined for travelling without tickets.* **2.** not doing something ○ *She sang for an hour without stopping.* ○ *They lived in the hut in the forest without seeing anybody for weeks.*

witness /'wɪtnəs/ *noun* **1.** a person who sees something happen or who is present when something happens ○ *The witness happened to be outside the house when it was burgled.* **2.** a person who is present when someone signs a document ○ *The contract has to be signed in front of two witnesses.* ○ *His sister signed as a witness.* ■ *verb* to be present when something happens, and see it happening ○ *Did anyone witness the accident?*

witty /'wɪti/ *adjective* clever and funny ○ *She gave a witty and entertaining speech.* (NOTE: **wittier – wittiest**)

wives /waɪvz/ plural of **wife**

wobble /'wɒb(ə)l/ *verb* to move from side to side in a way that is not smooth or steady ○ *The children made the jelly wobble in their bowls.* ○ *Don't wobble the table when I'm pouring coffee.*

woke /wəʊk/ past tense of **wake**

woken /'wəʊk(ə)n/ past participle of **wake**

wolf /wʊlf/ *noun* a wild animal like a large dog, which usually lives in groups in the forest ○ *At night the wolves came and howled outside the hut.* (NOTE: The plural is **wolves**.)

woman /'wʊmən/ *noun* an adult female person ○ *The manager is an extremely experienced woman.* ○ *There are very few women in government.* ○ *There are*

more and more women bus drivers.
(NOTE: The plural is **women** /'wɪmɪn/.)

won /wʌn/ past tense and past participle of **win**

wonder /'wʌndə/ *verb* **1.** to want to know something ○ *I wonder why the room has gone quiet.* ○ *If you don't ring home, your parents will start wondering what has happened.* **2.** to think about something ○ *I wonder how I can earn more money.* ○ *He's wondering what to do next.* **3.** asking a question politely ○ *We were wondering if you would like to come for dinner on Saturday.*

wonderful /'wʌndəf(ə)l/ *adjective* extremely good or enjoyable ○ *They had a wonderful holiday by a lake in Sweden.* ○ *The weather was wonderful for the whole holiday.* ○ *You passed your driving test first time? – Wonderful!*

wood /wʊd/ *noun* **1.** a hard material which comes from a tree ○ *The kitchen table is made of wood.* ○ *She picked up a piece of wood and put it on the fire.* ○ *A wood floor would be just right for this room.* (NOTE: no plural: *some wood, a piece of wood*) **2.** an area in which many trees are growing together ○ *The path goes straight through the wood.* ○ *Their house is on the edge of a wood.* (NOTE: The plural is **woods**. Do not confuse with **would**.)

wooden /'wʊd(ə)n/ *adjective* made out of wood ○ *In the market we bought little wooden dolls for the children.*

wool /wʊl/ *noun* **1.** long threads of twisted animal hair, used to make clothes or carpets etc. ○ *The carpet is made of wool.* ○ *I need an extra ball of wool to finish this pullover.* **2.** the hair growing on a sheep ○ *The sheep are sheared and the wool sent to market in early summer.*

woolly /'wʊli/ *adjective* made out of wool ○ *She wore a woolly hat.*

word /wɜːd/ *noun* **1.** a separate piece of language, either written or spoken ○ *This sentence has five words.* ○ *He always spells some words wrongly, such as 'though'.* **2.** something spoken ○ *She passed me in the street but didn't say a word.* ○ *I'd like to say a few words about Mr Smith who is retiring today.* **3.** a

promise which you have made □ **to give your word** to promise ○ *He gave his word that the matter would remain confidential.* □ **to keep your word** to do what you promised to do ○ *He kept his word, and the cheque arrived the next day.* □ **to take someone's word for it** to accept what someone says as being true ○ *OK, I'll take your word for it.* ◇ **to have a word with someone** to speak to someone ○ *I must have a word with the manager about the service.* ○ *The salesgirl had made so many mistakes, I had to have a word with her.* ◇ **without a word** without saying anything ○ *She went out of the room without a word.* ◇ **word for word** exactly as it is said or written ○ *Tell me what he said word for word.* ○ *A word-for-word translation often doesn't make any sense.*

word processing /ˌwɜːd 'prəʊsesɪŋ/ *noun* using a computer to produce, check and change texts, reports and letters etc.

word processor /ˌwɜːd 'prəʊsesə/ *noun* **1.** a small computer which is used to produce texts, reports and letters etc. ○ *She offered to write the letter for me on her word processor.* ○ *You can use my word processor to type your letter if you like.* **2.** a word-processing program which allows you to create texts, edit them and print them

wore /wɔː/ past tense of **wear**

work /wɜːk/ *noun* **1.** things that you do using your strength or your brain ○ *There's a great deal of work still to be done on the project.* ○ *There's too much work for one person.* ○ *If you've finished that piece of work, there's plenty more to be done.* ○ *Cooking for two hundred people every day is hard work.* **2.** a job done regularly to earn money ○ *He goes to work every day on his bicycle.* ○ *Work starts at 9 a.m. and finishes at 5 p.m.* ○ *Her work involves a lot of travelling.* ○ *He is still looking for work.* **3.** something which has been made, painted or written by someone ○ *the complete works of Shakespeare* ○ *An exhibition of the work of local artists.* ■ *verb* **1.** to use your strength or brain to do something ○ *I can't work in the gar-*

den if it's raining. ○ *He's working well at school, we're very pleased with his progress.* ○ *Work hard and you'll soon get a better job.* **2.** to have a job ○ *She works in an office in London.* ○ *He used to work in his father's shop.* ○ *She had to stop working when her mother was ill.* **3.** (*of a machine*) to run ○ *The computers aren't working.* ○ *The machine works by electricity.* **4.** to make a machine run ○ *She works the biggest printing machine in the factory.* ○ *Do you know how to work the microwave?* **5.** to be successful ○ *His plan worked well.* ○ *Will the plan work?* ○ *If the cough medicine doesn't work, you'll have to see a doctor.*

work out *phrasal verb* **1.** to solve a problem by looking at information or calculating figures ○ *I'm trying to work out if we've sold more this year than last.* □ **to work out at something** to amount to an amount ○ *The total works out at £10.50 per person.* **2.** to succeed ○ *Everything worked out quite well in the end.* □ **to work something out** to find a successful way of solving a problem **3.** to do exercises ○ *He works out every morning in the gym.*

worker /ˈwɜːkə/ *noun* **1.** a person who works ○ *She's a good worker.* ○ *He's a fast worker.* **2.** a person who works in a particular job ○ *The factory closed when the workers went on strike.* ○ *Office workers usually work from 9.30 to 5.30.*

working /ˈwɜːkɪŋ/ *adjective* relating to a job or to work ○ *the working population of a country* ○ *The unions have complained about working conditions in the factory.* ○ *He came to the party in his working clothes.* ■ *noun* a way or ways in which something works ○ *The workings of a car engine are a complete mystery to him.* ○ *I wish I could understand the workings of local government!*

working class /ˌwɜːkɪŋ ˈklɑːs/ *noun* a group in society consisting of people who work with their hands, usually earning wages not salaries

workman /ˈwɜːkmən/ *noun* a man who works with his hands (NOTE: The plural is **workmen**.)

works *plural noun* **1.** the moving parts of a machine ○ *I looked inside the clock and there seems to be dust in the works.* **2.** a factory ○ *The steel works will be closed next week for the Christmas holidays.* ■ **the works** everything (*informal*) ○ *They built a conservatory with a fountain, automatic lighting, a barbecue – the works!*

workshop /ˈwɜːkʃɒp/ *noun* a very small factory where things are made or repaired

world /wɜːld/ *noun* the earth on which we live ○ *Here is a map of the world.* ○ *She flew round the world twice last year.* ○ *He has to travel all over the world on business.* ○ *A round-the-world ticket allows several stopovers.*

worm /wɜːm/ *noun* a small thin animal which has no arms or legs and lives in the soil ○ *Birds were pecking at the soil for worms.*

worn /wɔːn/ past participle of **wear**

worn out /ˌwɔːn ˈaʊt/ *adjective* very tired ○ *He was worn out after the game of rugby.* ○ *She comes home every evening, worn out after a busy day at the office.*

worried /ˈwʌrid/ *adjective* unhappy because you think something bad will happen or because something bad has happened ○ *He had a worried look on his face.* ○ *She's looking worried.* ○ *I'm worried that we may run out of petrol.*

worry /ˈwʌri/ *verb* to make someone feel anxious ○ *She's always looks so tired, and that worries me.* (NOTE: **worries – worrying – worried**) ■ *noun* **1.** something that makes you anxious ○ *Go on holiday and try to forget your worries.* (NOTE: The plural is **worries**.) **2.** the state of being anxious ○ *She is a great source of worry for her family.* (NOTE: no plural)

worse /wɜːs/ *adjective* **1.** less good than something else ○ *It rained for the first week of our holidays, and the second week was even worse.* ○ *I think this film is worse than the one I saw last week.* ○ *Both children are naughty – but the little girl is worse than her brother.* **2.** more ill ○ *He's much worse since he started tak-*

ing his medicine. ■ *adverb* not as well ○ *He drives badly enough but his sister drives even worse.*

worship /'wɜːʃɪp/ *verb* **1.** to praise and respect God ○ *The ancient peoples worshipped stone statues of their gods.* **2.** to take part in a church service ○ *They worship regularly in the local church.* (NOTE: **worships – worshipping – worshipped**)

worst /wɜːst/ *adjective* worse than anything else ○ *I think this is the worst film he's ever made.* ■ *adverb* less well than anything or anyone else or than at any other time ○ *It's difficult to say which team played worst.* ○ *She works worst when she's tired.* ■ *noun* a very bad thing ○ *This summer is the worst for fifty years.*

worth /wɜːθ/ *adjective* **1.** □ **to be worth** to have a certain value or price ○ *This ring's worth a lot of money.* ○ *Gold is worth more than silver.* ○ *The house is worth more than £250,000.* **2.** □ **to be worth doing something** to find something good or helpful to do ○ *It's worth taking a map with you, as you may get lost in the little streets.* ○ *His latest film is well worth seeing.* ○ *The old castle is well worth visiting* or *is well worth a visit.* ■ *noun* a value ○ *Its worth will increase each year.* ○ *She lost jewellery of great worth in the fire.* ○ *Can you give me twenty pounds' worth of petrol?*

would /wʊd/ *modal verb* **1.** used as a polite way of asking someone to do something ○ *Would you please stop talking?* ○ *Would someone please tell me where the library is?* ○ *Would you like some more tea?* **2.** used as the past of 'will' ○ *He said he would be here for lunch.* ○ *She hoped she would be well enough to come.* ○ *He wouldn't go even if I paid him.* **3.** used as the past of 'will', showing something which often happens ○ *He would bring his dog with him, even though we asked him not to.* ○ *My husband forgot my birthday again this year – he would!* **4.** used for showing something which often happened in the past ○ *Every morning she would go and feed the chickens.* ○ *He would always be there waiting outside the station.* ○ *They*

would often bring us flowers. **5.** used following a condition ○ *I'm sure that if they could come, they would.* ○ *I would've done it if you had asked me to.* ○ *If she were alive, she would* or *she'd be a hundred years old today.* ○ *If it snowed we would* or *we'd go skiing.* (NOTE: The negative **would not** is usually written **wouldn't**. Note also that **would** is often shortened to **'d** *she'd be a hundred, he'd stay at home.* Note also that **would** is only used with other verbs and is not followed by **to**)

would rather *phrasal verb* to prefer

wound[1] /wuːnd/ *noun* a cut made on someone's body, usually in fighting ■ *verb* **1.** to hurt someone badly by cutting into their flesh ○ *Two of the gang were wounded in the bank robbery.* **2.** to hurt someone's feelings ○ *She was deeply wounded by what he said.*

wound[2] /waʊnd/ past tense and past participle of **wind**

wove /wəʊv/ past tense of **weave**

woven /'wəʊv(ə)n/ past participle of **weave**

wrap /ræp/ *verb* to cover something by putting something over it ○ *She wrapped the parcel in paper.* (NOTE: **wraps -wrapping – wrapped**) ■ *noun* **1.** a type of shawl that is put round the shoulders or the top part of the body ○ *She pulled her wrap closer around her.* **2.** a piece of material used to cover something ○ *Remove the wrap before putting the dish in the microwave.*

wrapping /'ræpɪŋ/ *noun* the paper or plastic used to wrap something up

wreck /rek/ *noun* **1.** a ship which has been sunk or badly damaged ○ *Divers have discovered the wreck on the seabed.* ○ *The wreck of the 'Mary Rose' was found in the sea near Southampton.* **2.** anything which has been damaged and cannot be used ○ *The police towed away the wreck of the car.* ○ *Their house is now a total wreck.* ■ *verb* to damage something very badly ○ *The ship was wrecked on the rocks in the storm.* ○ *The bank was wrecked by the explosion.*

wrestle /'res(ə)l/ *verb* to fight with someone to try to throw him to the ground ○ *The President's guards wrestled with the demonstrators.*

wriggle /'rɪg(ə)l/ *verb* to twist from side to side ○ *The baby wriggled in her father's arms.* ○ *The worm wriggled back into the soil.*

wring /rɪŋ/ *verb* to twist something, especially to get water out of it ○ *Wring the face cloth (dry) after you have used it.* ○ *He wrung out his shirt before putting it to dry.* (NOTE: **wrings – wringing – wrung** /rʌŋ/)

wrinkle /'rɪŋkəl/ *noun* a fold in the skin ○ *She had an operation to remove wrinkles round her eyes.*

wrinkled /'rɪŋkəld/ *adjective* full of lines or creases

wrist /rɪst/ *noun* the joint between the arm and the hand

write /raɪt/ *verb* **1.** to put words or numbers on paper etc. using a pen, pencil, computer etc. ○ *She wrote the address on the back of an envelope.* ○ *Write the reference number at the top of the letter.* **2.** to write a letter and send it to someone ○ *She writes to me twice a week.* ○ *Don't forget to write as soon as you get to your hotel.* **3.** to be the author of a book or music etc. ○ *He wrote a book on keeping tropical fish.* ○ *Didn't you know she used to write for the 'Sunday Times'?* (NOTE: **writes – writing – wrote** /rəʊt/ – **written** /'rɪt(ə)n/)

write down *phrasal verb* to write something

writer /'raɪtə/ *noun* a person who writes books or articles

writing /'raɪtɪŋ/ *noun* something which is written ○ *Please don't phone, reply in writing.* ○ *Put everything in writing, then you have a record of what has been done.*

written[1] /'rɪt(ə)n/ *adjective* which has been put in writing·

written[2] /'rɪt(ə)n/ past participle of **write**

wrong /rɒŋ/ *adjective* **1.** not correct ○ *He gave three wrong answers and failed the test.* ○ *That's not the right time, is it? – No, the clock is wrong.* ○ *You've come to the wrong house – there's no one called Jones living here.* ○ *I must have pressed the wrong button.* **2.** not suitable ○ *You came just at the wrong time, when we were bathing the children.* ○ *She was wearing the wrong sort of dress for a wedding.* **3.** not working properly ○ *There is something wrong with the television.* **4.** morally bad ○ *It's wrong to talk like that about her.* ○ *Cheating in exams is wrong.* **5.** making someone worried ■ *adverb* badly ○ *Everything went wrong yesterday.* ○ *She spelt my name wrong.*

wrongly /'rɒŋli/ *adverb* not correctly

wrote /rəʊt/ past tense of **write**

wrung /rʌŋ/ past tense and past participle of **wring**

XYZ

x /eks/, **X** *noun* the twenty-fourth letter of the alphabet, between W and Y ■ *symbol* **1.** a multiplication sign ○ *3 x 3 = 9.* (NOTE: say 'three times three equals nine') **2.** showing size ○ *The table top is 24 x 36cm.* (NOTE: say 'twenty-four by thirty-six centimetres')

X /eks/ *noun* the Roman numeral for ten or tenth

X-ray /'eks reɪ/ *noun* **1.** a type of radiation that doctors use for taking photographs of the inside of your body ○ *The X-ray examination showed the key was inside the baby's stomach.* ○ *The X-ray department is closed for lunch.* **2.** a photograph taken with X-rays ○ *The X-ray showed that the bone was broken in two places.* ○ *They will take an X-ray of his leg.* ○ *She was sent to hospital for an X-ray.* ■ *verb* to take an X-ray photograph of someone ○ *There are six patients waiting to be X-rayed.* ○ *They X-rayed my leg to see if it was broken.*

y /waɪ/, **Y** *noun* the twenty-fifth letter of the alphabet, between X and Z

yacht /jɒt/ *noun* **1.** a sailing boat used for pleasure and sport **2.** a large comfortable boat with a motor ○ *She spent her holiday on a yacht in the Mediterranean.*

yard /jɑːd/ *noun* **1.** a measurement of length, equal to 0.914 metres ○ *The police station is only yards away from where the fight took place.* ○ *Can you move your car a couple of yards as it is blocking the entrance to our garage?* **2.** an area of concrete at the back or side of a house ○ *We keep our bikes in the yard.*

yarn /jɑːn/ *noun* a long piece of wool used in knitting or weaving ○ *She sells yarn from the wool of her sheep.*

yawn /jɔːn/ *verb* to open your mouth wide and breathe in and out deeply when you are tired or bored ○ *He went on speaking for so long that half the people at the meeting started yawning or started to yawn.*

yeah /jeə/ *interjection* yes

year /jɪə/ *noun* **1.** a period of time lasting twelve months, from January 1st to December 31st ○ *Columbus discovered America in the year 1492.* ○ *Great celebrations which took place in the year 2000.* ○ *Last year we did not have any holiday.* ○ *Next year she's going on holiday in Australia.* ○ *The weather was very bad for most of the year.* □ **all year round** working or open for the whole year ○ *The museum is open all year round.* **2.** a period of twelve months from a particular time ○ *We spent five years in Hong Kong.* ○ *He died two hundred years ago today.* ○ *She'll be eleven years old tomorrow.* ○ *How many years have you been working for the company?*

yell /jel/ *verb* to shout very loudly ○ *The policeman yelled to her to get out of the way.*

yellow /'jeləʊ/ *adjective* of a colour like that of the sun or of gold ○ *His new car is bright yellow.* ○ *She's wearing yellow sandals.* ○ *At this time of year the fields are full of yellow flowers.* ■ *noun* the colour of the sun or gold ○ *Do you have any hats of a lighter yellow than this one?*

yes /jes/ *adverb* a word showing that you agree with someone, accept something, or give permission for something ○ *They asked her if she wanted to come and she said 'yes'.* ○ *Anyone want more coffee? – Yes, please.* ○ *You don't like living in London? – Yes I do!* ○ *Didn't you work in Scotland at one time? – Yes,*

I did. ○ *I need a clear answer – is it 'yes' or 'no'?*

yesterday /ˈjestədeɪ/ *adverb, noun* the day before today ○ *Yesterday was March 1st so today must be the 2nd.* ○ *She came to see us yesterday evening.*

yet /jet/ *adverb* now, before now, or until now ○ *Has the manager arrived yet?* ○ *I haven't seen her yet this morning.* ○ *Don't throw the newspaper away – I haven't read it yet.* ■ *conjunction* however ○ *He's very small and yet he can kick a ball a long way.* ○ *It was starting to snow, and yet he went out without a coat.*

yield /jiːld/ *noun* the quantity of a crop or a product produced from a plant or from an area of land ○ *What is the normal yield per hectare?* ■ *verb* **1.** to produce a result ○ *Their researches finally yielded the information they were looking for.* **2.** to produce a crop or a product ○ *This variety of rice can yield up to 2 tonnes per hectare.* ○ *The North Sea oil deposits yield 100,000 barrels a month.* **3.** to do or agree to do something that you have been trying not to do

yolk /jəʊk/ *noun* the yellow part inside an egg

you /jʊ, juː/ *pronoun* **1.** referring to someone being spoken to ○ *Are you ready?* ○ *You look tired, you should rest a bit.* ○ *If I give you my address will you give me yours?* ○ *Hello, how are you?* ○ *Are you both keeping well?* **2.** referring to anyone ○ *You never know when you might need a penknife.* ○ *You have to be very tall to be a policeman.* (NOTE: **You** is both singular and plural.)

young /jʌŋ/ *adjective* not old ○ *She's very young, she's only six.* ○ *He became Prime Minister when he was still a young man.* ○ *My little brother's much younger than me* or *than I am.* ○ *In the afternoon there are TV programmes for very young children.* ○ *This is where your Daddy lived when he was young.* ■ *noun* young animals or birds ○ *Animals fight to protect their young.*

youngster /ˈjʌŋstə/ *noun* a young person ○ *My grandparents don't understand today's youngsters.*

your /jɔː/ *adjective* belonging to you ○ *I hope you didn't forget to bring your toothbrush.* ○ *This letter is for your brother.*

yours /jɔːz/ *pronoun* belonging to you ○ *This is my car – where's yours?* ○ *My car's in the garage, can I borrow yours?*

yourself /jəˈself/ *pronoun* relating to 'you' as a subject ○ *Why do you wash the car yourself, when you could easily take it to the car wash?* ○ *Watch out for the broken glass – you might hurt yourself.* ○ *I hope you are all going to enjoy yourselves.* (NOTE: The plural is **yourselves**.)

youth /juːθ/ *noun* **1.** a young man ○ *Gangs of youths were causing trouble in the village.* ○ *A youth, aged 16, was arrested for possessing drugs.* **2.** a period when you are young, especially the time between being a child and being an adult ○ *In his youth he was a great traveller.* ○ *I haven't done that since the days of my youth!*

z /zed/, **Z** *noun US* the last and twenty-sixth letter of the alphabet

zap /zæp/ *verb* (*informal*) **1.** to hit or kill someone **2.** to shut down the television using the remote control (NOTE: **zaps – zapping – zapped**)

zero /ˈzɪərəʊ/ *noun* **1.** the number 0 ○ *To make an international call you dial zero zero (00), followed by the number of the country.* **2.** the temperature at which water freezes ○ *The temperature stayed below zero for days.* **3.** nothing at all ○ *They lost ten – zero.* (NOTE: The plural is **zeros**.)

zigzag /ˈzɪgzæg/ *adjective* used to describe a line which turns one way, then the opposite way ○ *There are zigzag lines painted at pedestrian crossings to show that cars must not stop there.*

zone /zəʊn/ *noun* an area ○ *Police cars are patrolling the inner city zones.*

zoo /zuː/ *noun* a place where wild animals are kept, and where people can go to see them

zoom /zuːm/ *verb* to go very fast ○ *Cars were zooming past me on the motorway.*

SUPPLEMENT

Irregular Verbs

Verb	Past tense	Past participle
arise	arose	arisen
awake	awoke	awoken
be	was, were	been
bear	bore	borne
beat	beat	beaten
become	became	become
begin	began	begun
bend	bent	bent
bet	bet	bet
bid	bid	bid
bind	bound	bound
bite	bit	bitten
bleed	bled	bled
blow	blew	blown
break	broke	broken
breed	bred	bred
bring	brought	brought
broadcast	broadcast	broadcast
build	built	built
burn	burnt, burned	burnt, burned
burst	burst	burst
buy	bought	bought
cast	cast	cast
catch	caught	caught
choose	chose	chosen
come	came	come
cost	cost	cost
creep	crept	crept
cut	cut	cut
deal	dealt	dealt
dig	dug	dug
do	did	done
draw	drew	drawn
dream	dreamed, dreamt	dreamed, dreamt
drink	drank	drunk
drive	drove	driven
eat	ate	eaten
fall	fell	fallen
feed	fed	fed
feel	felt	felt
fight	fought	fought
find	found	found
flee	fled	fled
fling	flung	flung
fly	flew	flown
forbid	forbade	forbidden
forecast	forecast	forecast
forget	forgot	forgotten
forgive	forgave	forgiven
freeze	froze	frozen
get	got	got, *(US)* gotten
give	gave	given
go	went	gone
grind	ground	ground
grow	grew	grown
hang	hung	hung
have	had	had
hear	heard	heard

Irregular Verbs

Verb	*Past tense*	*Past participle*
hide	hid	hidden
hit	hit	hit
hold	held	held
hurt	hurt	hurt
keep	kept	kept
kneel	knelt, kneeled	knelt, kneeled
knit	knit, knitted	knit, knitted
know	knew	known
lay	laid	laid
lead	led	led
lean	leant, leaned	leant, leaned
leap	leapt, leaped	leapt, leaped
learn	learnt, learned	learnt, learned
leave	left	left
lend	lent	lent
let	let	let
lie	lay	lain
light	lit	lit
lose	lost	lost
make	made	made
mean	meant	meant
meet	met	met
mistake	mistook	mistaken
overcome	overcame	overcome
overhear	overheard	overheard
overtake	overtook	overtaken
pay	paid	paid
put	put	put
quit	quit	quit
read	read	read
ride	rode	ridden
ring	rang	rung
rise	rose	risen
run	ran	run
saw	sawed	sawn
say	said	said
see	saw	seen
seek	sought	sought
sell	sold	sold
send	sent	sent
set	set	set
sew	sewed	sewed, sewn
shake	shook	shaken
shed	shed	shed
shine	shone	shone
shoot	shot	shot
show	showed	shown
shrink	shrank	shrunk
shut	shut	shut
sing	sang	sung
sink	sank	sunk
sit	sat	sat
sleep	slept	slept
slide	slid	slid
smell	smelt, smelled	smelt, smelled
sow	sowed	sown
speak	spoke	spoken
speed	sped	sped

Irregular Verbs

Verb	Past tense	Past participle
spell	spelt, spelled	spelt, spelled
spend	spent	spent
spill	spilt, spilled	spilt, spilled
spin	span	spun
split	split	split
spoil	spoilt, spoiled	spoilt, spoiled
spread	spread	spread
spring	sprang	sprung
stand	stood	stood
steal	stole	stolen
stick	stuck	stuck
sting	stung	stung
stink	stank	stunk
stride	strode	strode
strike	struck	struck
strive	strove	striven
swear	swore	sworn
sweep	swept	swept
swell	swelled	swelled, swollen
swim	swam	swum
swing	swung	swung
take	took	taken
teach	taught	taught
tear	tore	torn
tell	told	told
think	thought	thought
throw	threw	thrown
thrust	thrust	thrust
tread	trod	trodden
understand	understood	understood
undo	undid	undone
upset	upset	upset
wake	woke	woken
wear	wore	worn
weave	wove	woven
win	won	won
wind	wound	wound
wring	wrung	wrung
write	wrote	written